Visions Across the Americas

Short Essays for Composition

Eighth Edition

J. Sterling Warner
Evergreen Valley College

Judith Hilliard
San Jose State University

WADSWORTH
CENGAGE Learning

Australia • Brazil • Japan • Korea • Mexico • Singapore • Spain • United Kingdom • United States

Visions Across the Americas: Short Essays for Composition, Eighth Edition
Warner/Hilliard

Senior Publisher: Lyn Uhl

Director of Developmental Studies: Annie Todd

Development Editor: Cheri Dellelo

Assistant Editor: Beth Rice

Editorial Assistant: Matt Conte

Media Editor: Amy Gibbons

Marketing Manager: Elinor Gregory

Marketing Coordinator: Brittany Blais

Marketing Communications Manager: Linda Yip

Design and Production Services: PreMedia Global

Rights Acquisition Specialist: Amber Hosea

Cover Image: Maggie Sulayao

Library of Congress Control Number: 2011938978

Student Edition:

ISBN-13: 978-1-111-35026-0

ISBN-10: 1-111-35026-4

Wadsworth
20 Channel Center Street
Boston, MA 02210
USA

Cengage Learning is a leading provider of customized learning solutions with office locations around the globe, including Singapore, the United Kingdom, Australia, Mexico, Brazil, and Japan. Locate your local office at: **international.cengage.com/region**

Cengage Learning products are represented in Canada by Nelson Education, Ltd.

For your course and learning solutions, visit **www.cengage.com**

Purchase any of our products at your local college store or at our preferred online store **www.cengagebrain.com.**

Instructors: Please visit **login.cengage.com** and log in to access instructor-specific resources.

Printed in the United States of America
1 2 3 4 5 6 7 15 14 13 12

Preface to the Eighth Edition

A Cross-Cultural Emphasis: *Visions Across the Americas* takes an intensive look at cross-cultural issues and themes affecting the lives of Americans today as well as those in the past. Overall, these essays offer a broad perspective of selected topics, providing students with a chance to evaluate and reevaluate their biases, prejudices, or "programmed notions" about familiar subjects and controversial issues. Most importantly, our selections present good writings that are valuable tools for generating material, for writing logs and journals, for collaborative work activities, and for individual writing assignments, all of which encourage creativity and help the student to think and write clearly and critically.

Writers on Writing: We feature some professional writers discussing their craft at the beginning of the book to get students off to a good start. For instance, in *Chapter I: Communicating Is Language at Work,* Deborah De La Rosa's "Wild Ways with Words" illustrates the practice of active reading; Peter Elbow's "Freewriting" presents a method for generating ideas *freely,* avoiding writer's block; and Joanne Jaime's student essay, "Marriage: The Changing Institution," demonstrates how writers develop a controlling idea or thesis in stages. Meanwhile, Pat Mora's "Why I Am a Writer" and Ray Bradbury's "The Joy of Writing" explain the art and satisfaction that can come from writing, while Amy Tan's "My Mother's English" examines the power of words.

At a Glance—The Rhetorical and Thematic Table of Contents: In *Visions Across the Americas*' main table of contents, brief annotations provide readers with a bird's-eye-view of each rhetorically organized essay. However, we offer a thematic table of contents in which we have organized essays into categories (e.g., *Language and Culture, Americans and Immigrants, Lifestyles, American Society*) as well. That way, teachers can structure class readings pursuant to writing assignments according to what works best for them.

New Essays—Current Issues: Twelve new essays—eleven in the textbook and one in the Instructors' Resource Manual—appear in the eighth edition of this text, and they—along with other current, updated articles—offer a range of topics and issues for reading, discussion, critical thinking, and writing. From essays related to popular culture in American society such as "Let's Face It" (Sara Blake), "Why Talk? Interviews Matter!" (Kathleen Hudson), "Turning the Page: The Future of Reading is Backlit and Bright" (Anna Quindlen), "OMG: Tweeting, Trending, and Texting" (Mandana Mohsenzadegan), "Unmasking the Graphic Novel: Learning Summary and Close Reading Through Comics" (Adam Bessie), and "Wild Ways with Words" (Deborah De La Rosa) to articles on social, political, and scientific issues such as "Armchair Pharmacologists and the Media" (Roohi Vora), "The 21st Century Ragnarok: Is Profit Civilization's Only Motive?" (Ann Scheid), "Lera's Story" (Dan Archer and Olga Trusova), "Teaching for Social Justice: Academic Rigor with Love," (Carmen Carrasquillo Jay), "Honoring Sgt. Stewart: Wiccans Are Americans Too" (Charles Haynes), and "Why We Went to Iraq" (Bruce Henderson), the newest essays in *Visions Across the Americas* create additional opportunities for modern language study.

A Progressive Level of Difficulty: Generally arranged from the easiest to the most challenging essay, each chapter in *Visions Across the Americas* contains six readings. As in the seventh edition of *Visions Across the Americas,* with rare exception, we have complemented our brief biographies with photographs for each of the selection authors.

Pedagogy: A short discussion of a specific writing strategy appears at the beginning of each chapter in order to reinforce an understanding of rhetorical modes and their purposes in context. Following chapter introductions are brief lists of tips on how to develop a particular type of essay effectively—using a dominant rhetorical method (i.e., comparison and contrast, division and classification, or cause and effect).

An Emphasis on the Reading and Writing Connection: In order to emphasize the connection between reading and writing, we have designed specific questions and activities to engage students in reading. Each reading is accompanied by apparatus designed to help students organize their thinking about what they have read and prepare to write. Pre-reading Questions precede each essay, and all essays are followed by Post-reading Questions divided into the categories of: *Content, Strategies and Structures, Language and Vocabulary, Group Activities,* and *Writing Activities.*

Whereas instructors may modify our basic guidelines a bit, generally we suggest that students *first,* thoroughly consider Pre-reading Questions and do what they suggest prior to reading the selection. *Second,* scan the composition, underline, list, and then write the definition of each unfamiliar word. *Third,* carefully read the composition and jot down any notes or questions that come to mind in the margins of the text. *Fourth,* reread the selection after looking over the Post-reading Questions and then write the answers to the questions found in the other Post-reading apparatus.

Other Student Aids: For greater accessibility, we include additional writing topics at the end of each rhetorical chapter, and to increase *Visions'* usefulness as a reference, we feature a glossary of common literary and rhetorical terms at the back of the text. This reader primarily is designed to consider short essay development through rhetorical mode but does more than merely acquaint students with cause and effect, argumentation, narration, and so on. The selections also enrich students' vocabulary because clear, written expression often is a matter of good reasoning coupled with a broad command of words in the English language. Thus, many of the reading selections challenge and test the readers' growing abilities.

An Overview of the Writing Process: We are aware that many students may be unfamiliar with the reading-writing process. Therefore, apart from a discussion of reading strategies, we have included an overview of the writing process in Chapter 1 that (1) serves as a resource for students, and (2) allows instructors flexibility in teaching what we offer, disregarding it and/or combining our information with information from a standard rhetoric. We have narrowed our discussion of the writing process to:

- generating writing topics,
- organizing material for paragraphs and essays,
- sharpening, strengthening and developing one's thesis or controlling ideas,
- revising rough drafts, and
- editing compositions.

Once students have made the connection between reading and writing and realize how the two go hand-in-hand, they will not only read more clearly with greater retention but also be able to respond to material critically and confidently, which will be important to their growth as writers.

Revised Special Features: Several special features made their debut in the past two editions of *Visions Across the Americas,* including a section called "Point of View: Position of Authority," as well as "Transitions" in *Chapter 1: Communication Is Language At Work,* and a detailed discussion of "Irony and Voice" in *Chapter 7: Comparison and Contrast.* These, in addition to the *Documentation Appendix* and the *Internet Connection* assignments (requiring the use of online search engines and databases) sections discussed below—along with many other revised features—provide a multitude of fresh, compelling teaching opportunities for instructors and learning strategies for students.

Introduction to Documentation: *Visions Across the Americas* features a special Appendix, "MLA Documentation," at the end of the text explaining how, when, where, and why one should use the MLA (Modern Language Association) format for constructing parenthetical references within a text and writing a list of works cited at the end of it. To illustrate the effective use of documentation in context, we offer three essays, "Anima of Animé Revisited" (Grace Sumabat Estrada), "Online Learning and Student Success" (Mark Charles Fissel), "OMG: Tweeting, Trending, and Texting" (Mandana Mohsenzadegan) in *Chapter 11: Argumentation*. A fourth documented essay, "Why We Went to Iraq" (Bruce Henderson) at the end of *Chapter 12: Persuasion* further demonstrates how to insert parenthetical references in your text and construct a list of works cited.

The Internet Connection: To provide students with practice researching material on the Internet and documenting sources accordingly, we offer 29 optional assignments (at least two per chapter) requiring them to use the Internet and another online databases. A sampling of assignments which we call "Internet Connections" include topics such as: Modern Marriages; Sexism, Racism, and Prejudgement; Pilgrimages; Crisis in Faith/Science; Role-playing; Testimonies/Beliefs; Colloquialisms/Jargon/Slang; Model Minorities; Ecology; Poverty in America; Consumer Products; Interviews; Purpose and Process; Flirting; Irony; Passive Resistance; Urban Myths and Legends; Alternate Lifestyles and Parents; Guild and American Culture; Cosmetics and Makeovers; Holistic/Folk Medicine; Manzanar and Euphemisms; Animé versus Cartoons; Constitutional Rights; Evaluating Sources; HIV/AIDs; and Conspiracy Theories. Some assignments conclude with an essay while others focus on exercises that reinforce a research technique or a documentation skill. Even if a class does not require a term paper, research and references to readings usually can add depth and scope to an essay because they move a composition beyond the personal narrative by documenting the opinions of others.

Instructor's Resource Manual: Once again, the *Instructor's Resource Manual* for the eighth edition of *Visions Across the Americas: Short Essays for Composition* features suggested approaches to rhetorical sections, suggested responses to content and strategies and structures questions, a section about poetry and word use, and an expanded multicultural bibliography of great literature from the Americas and beyond. Additionally, the eighth edition of the *Instructor's Resource Manual* continues to offer brief professional essays describing writing techniques and tools, as well as approaches to writing assignments. Also, to complement "Lera's Story," a graphic novel excerpt on Human Trafficking, we offer "Unmasking the Graphic Novel: Learning Summary and Close Reading Through Comics" by Adam Bessie.

Meanwhile, we continue to present "Distance Learning and American Society" as a counterpoint to Mark Charles Fissel's "Online Learning and Student Success," as well as other essays that may serve as counterpoints to articles read in the main text such as Barbara Mikulski's "A Young Polish American Speaks Up: The Myth of the Melting Pot," Jane and Michael Stern's "Valley Girl," and Bruce Henderson's "Beyond the Spin: Sixties Assassinations and the Vietnam War." Whereas all "counterpoint" essays feature a complete Pre-reading and Post-reading apparatus, "Valley Girl" also outlines an extensive slang project.

Rounding off the *Instructor's Resource Manual* are reading comprehension quizzes/study guides for each essay in *Visions Across the Americas.* Finally, in addition to the hard copy *Instructor's Resource Manual* for the eighth edition of *Visions Across the Americas,* Wadsworth/Cengage Learning has prepared an instructor's website for the text.

Acknowledgments: Getting from one edition of a text to the next is a long process, and so we want to acknowledge our appreciation to all the instructors whose careful, critical comments helped us to shape the eight editions of *Visions Across the Americas:* Louis Agregan, Moorpark College; Shirley Brozzo, Northern Michigan University; Lawrence Carlson, Orange Coast College; Susan Dalton, Alamance Community College; Lynn M. Lowery Darby, Kentucky State University; Sarah Dye, Elgin Community College; Jeannie Edwards,

Memphis State University; Lloyd A. Flanigan, Piedmont Virginia Community College; Mary J. Flores, Lewis-Clark State College; Nancy Forrest, Alamance Community College; Gail J. Gerlach, Indiana University of Pennsylvania; Margie Glazier, Merced College; Stefanie Georgelos, College of Lake County; Carolyn Hartnett, College of the Mainland; Shirley Kahlert, Evergreen Valley College; William L. Knox, Northern Michigan University; Regina Lebowitz, New York City Technical College; Reginald F. Lockett, San Jose City College; Maryann McCall, Atlantic Cape Community College; Robert Mehaffy, American River College; Margaret Murray, Temple University; Lori Nelson, Chaffey College; Tamara O'Hearn, Ball State University; Jay Peterson, Atlantic Cape Community College; Joanne Pinkston, Daytona Beach Community College; Harry Rubinstein, Hudson Community College; Nancy Sessano, American River College; John Sklute, San Jose City College; Barbara Smith-Cunningham, Olivet College; Sherry Sullivan, South Puget Sound Community College; Sandra Trammell, Kentucky State University; Agapi Theodorou, Middle Tennessee State University; George T. Vaughn, Maysville Community College; Regina Van Epps, Atlantic Cape Community College; Elizabeth Williams, Alamance Community College; Jessica Stephens, Eastern Kentucky University; Linda Sloan, King's College; Brenda Dillard, Brazosport Community College; Jane Davis, Heald Business College; Kay Wade, Northeastern Illinois University, Chicago; Heidi Ramirez, Hartnell College; Melissa Rankin, Richland College; Marian Teachcy, South Piedmont Community College; Dani McLean, Fullerton College; Terri Cook, Santa Barbara City College; and Louis Agregan, Moorpark College.

Finally, our indebtedness to Stephanie Surface deserves special mention; her enthusiasm, support, and critical advice never wavered as she followed the first edition of our text from its inception to its completion.

We also want to thank the authors who have contributed to the eighth edition of *Visions Across the Americas;* Kevin Warner for his technical support; and our family, friends, and colleagues for their encouragement and patience. Furthermore, we would like to express our sincere gratitude to those at Wadsworth/Cengage Learning, particularly: Annie Todd, Wadsworth/Cengage Director of Developmental Studies; Erin Frost, Cengage Learning Humanities Sales Representative; Matt Christopherson, Wadsworth/Cengage/Houghton Mifflin Western Region Sales Specialist, Developmental English and Composition; Cheri Dellelo, Freelance Editor; Elizabeth Rice,

Assistant Editor, Developmental English; and Joseph Malcolm, Project Manager, for their time, enthusiasm, and support in preparing and promoting the eighth edition of our text.

Sterling Warner
Judith Hilliard

Rhetorical Contents

Internet Connections

Thematic Contents

Words, Information, and Communication

Language and Culture

*These essays appear in the *Instructor's Resource Manual* for *Visions Across the Americas,* Eighth Edition.

The Family

*These essays appear in the *Instructor's Resource Manual* for *Visions Across the Americas,* Eighth Edition.

Americans and Immigrants

Education and Intelligence

Places

*These essays appear in the *Instructor's Resource Manual* for *Visions Across the Americas,* Eighth Edition.

People

*These essays appear in the *Instructor's Resource Manual* for *Visions Across the Americas*, Eighth Edition.

Lifestyles

*These essays appear in the *Instructor's Resource Manual* for *Visions Across the Americas*, Eighth Edition.

Aging/Old Age

Racism, Sexism, Theism, and Ageism

*These essays appear in the *Instructor's Resource Manual* for *Visions Across the Americas,* Eighth Edition.

American Society

*These essays appear in the *Instructor's Resource Manual* for *Visions Across the Americas,* Eighth Edition.

Prejudices and Stereotypes

*These essays appear in the *Instructor's Resource Manual* for *Visions Across the Americas,* Eighth Edition.

Working in America

Tradition and Ritual

*These essays appear in the *Instructor's Resource Manual* for *Visions Across the Americas,* Eighth Edition.

Popular Culture

Science and Faith

*These essays appear in the *Instructor's Resource Manual* for *Visions Across the Americas,* Eighth Edition.

Technology, Cyberspace, and the Cosmos

Politics and Ecology

*These essays appear in the *Instructor's Resource Manual* for *Visions Across the Americas,* Eighth Edition.

Visual, Written, and Verbal Arts

Irony and Humor

*These essays appear in the *Instructor's Resource Manual* for *Visions Across the Americas,* Eighth Edition.

CHAPTER 1 Communicating Is Language at Work

Listening, speaking, reading, and writing all deal with communication. If you write a word, you create meaning by simply arranging letters in some sort of recognizable pattern. Words, whether spoken or written, assist people in expressing themselves, for instance, in relating a story, presenting an argument, or explaining a misunderstanding. The ability to communicate in one way or another enables you to explore ideas and issues outside of your realm of personal experience.

In the following essays, the authors explore many different issues about language use. Amy Tan looks at her mother's English and how it influences the way others perceive her. Peter Elbow is interested in the writing process, particularly in how one can generate topics and ideas by "freewriting." Examining her own motivations for writing, Pat Mora says she writes because she enjoys expressing herself and, more importantly, because she is Hispanic and feels a need to correct images of self-worth that have been hurt by the society around her. She believes *"that Hispanics need to take their rightful place in American literature."* In each instance, the author illustrates the power of language.

Before you start reading, it would be helpful to review the reading *process*—how to read carefully and correctly and how to become actively involved in the reading process. The following tips will help you to become an active reader.

Tips on Becoming an Active Reader

1. **Preview Your Reading.** Before you begin to read, preview the selection and get an idea of what to expect from the piece. Previewing means that you:

   - Read the title. Does it hint what the article or story will be about?
   - Scan the subheadings. What do they suggest about the order of this piece?
   - Read the opening and concluding paragraphs because main ideas are often presented and summarized in these sections. Is there a thesis or controlling idea presented in the first paragraph? Is there a concluding statement in the final paragraph?
   - Read any bibliographical or biographical prefaces. Who wrote the piece? When and where was the piece written? How might this information suggest something about the essay or story?

2. **Read closely.** After previewing material, pay attention to each word you read. Note details.
3. **Ask Questions.** Remain active while reading by making predictions about the piece. You can start with the title; turn it into a question by using one of the journalist's six queries *(who? what? where? when? why?* and *how?)*. As you read, question a character's motives, the validity of an argument, or the "meaning" of the piece. Ask yourself what the author attempts to accomplish, how the main point focuses his or her argument, and what makes this an effective or ineffective composition. (You should jot these questions down in the margins.)
4. **Make Connections.** To make connections between what you have read and your own life, constantly ask yourself what in your life is similar to this author's experiences or ideas. Begin by looking into your (1) *past* to find connections between the reading and yourself, (2) *the world* around you to see what relates to your reading, (3) *history* to see what in the past connects to what you are reading now, and (4) *former readings* to see what you already have experienced that affirms or challenges an author's ideas.
5. **Learn to Recognize Patterns That Lead to Coherence.** Try to discover a pattern of development: Is the author comparing and contrasting, moving from general to specific, showing cause and effect, or exploring a

problem and solution? How do patterns of development help to establish relationships between words, clauses, and phrases leading to an understanding of the writer's ultimate purpose?

6. **Underline and Jot Down Notes.** If you are an active reader, you will write a great deal in conjunction to reading, underlining points you think are essential to an understanding of the piece: the thesis, the main ideas, important examples and images, key words, and new vocabulary. Terms that cause confusion—unknown words, confusing passages that need rereading, and unfamiliar names—also should be underlined or noted in some way.
7. **Write in the Margins Quite a Bit.** Sometimes, your comments will be as simple as noting "thesis!" or "key term." Other times, they help with rereading: "What does all this mean?" "Confusing." At times, notes in the margins make judgments, such as "good point—we do all need love" or "this example does not prove the point."
8. **Reread and Reevaluate.** Since reading is a process similar to writing, there is a rereading stage. It is necessary to go back over particularly illustrative examples or what you feel are the main points of the essay; you might want to reread confusing sections, and search the passage for a key phrase that will clarify an idea. It is particularly helpful to read a confusing passage aloud, paying careful attention to the punctuation.
9. **Write.** After reading and rereading, you might begin to write by summarizing the ideas found in the essay, writing an evaluation of the piece, or establishing connections between different readings.
10. **Share with Others.** Sharing your thoughts with others can often produce a new line of thinking and better ideas for writing. How? You can discuss what you enjoyed or disliked about a piece, what you thought the author hoped to accomplish, what connections you made between the reading and your own experiences and observations, what passages you found confusing, what ideas you have on the subject matter, and how they either validate or reject the author's ideas. The following excerpt from Deborah De La Rosa's article "Wild Ways with Words" has been annotated in the same fashion that you will use to mark your own reading assignments. It further illustrates steps a writer might take to become actively involved in reading an article or story.

Deborah De La Rosa

Wild Ways with Words

Deborah De La Rosa, a Reading Specialist, has been on the cutting edge of both reading and composition pedagogies for years. She functioned as a driving force in the Evergreen Valley College Learning Communities program, as well as for online reading labs. She serves on the Faculty Association, including the negotiating team and as the grievance officer. Her articles frequently appear in *Faculty Matters*. The following instructor-oriented essay offers some tips on experimentation with and the use of vocabulary words.

---

attribution of human characteristics to nonhumans

prevention

boredom from lack of interest

Anthropomorphism? Deterrent? Ennui? What do these words have in common? Not much, but they do represent words that most underprepared college students have never seen in print nor heard spoken. We can come up with countless reasons why these words remain elusive to students, and why they might not be that important, but overall, they do help put a face on the lack of vocabulary "smarts" in many of the students we teach.

vague...

solutions, cures

Countless remedies for poor vocabulary development with college level students continue to exist and make up a good portion of reading instruction in college reading classes, yet most strategies do not really get at the root of the matter. Traditionally, students receive vocabulary instruction in the areas of dictionary skills, word parts and contextual clues.

Often times these activities fail to provide students with real experiences and instead become lessons in the form of drills and practice unrelated to real text. Perhaps examining traditional vocabulary practices in terms of realistic learning needs will shed some light on how to best serve future students.

what does real text mean?

figurative language example!

To begin, while a solid understanding of the many uses of a dictionary does matter and can be taught, the many aspects of a dictionary can appear confusing to students with limited vocabulary. Imagine finding out for the first time that the word "mean" does not simply refer to a disagreeable person, but is also a measure of numbers in statistics! And trying to unravel the fact that the word "mean" can be a noun, a verb and an adjective further complicates understanding the vocabulary challenged student. Consider the following examples of the use of the word for "mean." *I don't understand what you mean. She plays a mean game of poker. The realtor looked carefully at the mean figures for houses in the region.* A simple lesson focusing on a single word and its variations can open up new ways of understanding for the vocabulary-challenged student.

interesting possibilities for one word

Interestingly enough, many of us with well-developed vocabularies rarely relied on the dictionary for the true ownership of words and meanings. With a constantly shifting student population, the language needs of these students often require further consideration and new ideas and more innovative methods to make vocabulary improvement a reality.

new, ground-breaking

!! Word parts, while equally valuable in building vocabulary skills, can be memorized, but like most memorization, have little meaning if the student cannot deconstruct unfamiliar words.

take apart

before

As a strategy for untangling meaning, it seems to have limited use when students are faced again with real text rather than individual words. Add on the fact that word parts such as "pre" do not always function as a word part at the beginning of a word. The word *pregnant* is a good example. Another instance is the word *uncle. Pretty, press, reach* and *irony* all fall into this category as well. Again, the vocabulary-challenged student faces the reality of the difficulties involved in making up language limitations.

hints authors give to help define difficult or unusual words

word meaning same as another

strange term—why did the author choose this?

Contextual clues, while unquestionably the most efficient way to build vocabulary skills with real text, also come with a set of problems. Most instructional activities in this area burden students with the task of labeling types of context clues as definitions, synonyms, examples and explanation, to name a few. While in practice this may appear to make sense, to the students this activity only serves to confuse them more. Cognitively, this only creates additional frustration as they struggle with meaning and become burden with the task of also figuring out how the author conveys meaning.

So, where do this all leave the reading and/or composition instructor hoping to shed some light on vocabulary improvement in the hopes that students do experience some growth in their personal language? The following tips, while not complete, hopefully will help.

Tips for Vocabulary Instruction:

what is ownership?

1. **Students need to take ownership of new words.**

   Try to make students understand that owning their personal vocabulary takes time and effort Interacting in a variety of ways with new and unfamiliar words helps to ensure they become and remain part of their personal vocabulary. Words need to be read, written, heard and spoken to belong to us. One or two interactions with unfamiliar words won't make it happen. Real attention to improving one's personal vocabulary requires continual exposure to new and unfamiliar words. The college environment should help as students attend classes in different areas and become exposed to a wide variety of words. Most importantly, these newly experienced words need to be seen and understood in real and authentic texts, *not in isolation or on a flash card* with the dictionary definition.

contacts or associations

how do I do this?

one possible answer

2. **What about those vocabulary flash cards and vocabulary lists?**

I can't honestly say that flash cards or vocabulary lists never serve a useful purpose for students, but the notion that the memorization of words and their definitions imparts true meaning just doesn't succeed. At the most, remind students that college exposes us to a variety of disciplines and in some courses, flash cards for vocabulary development may be of some value. The key component in this approach is to encourage students to define new words using their own words, and not a dictionary or textbook definition. Relying on dictionary and textbook definitions only encourages memorization, a technique that does not necessarily result in true understanding or ownership of new words.

fields of study or work

part

3. **Understand the difference between the words you speak, the words you hear and the words you read and write.**

Students need to understand that the words they speak and hear and the words they write are quite different.

Everyday spoken language does not mirror the style of language required for college writing and in college textbooks. The need to develop reading and writing vocabulary relies heavily on the acts of reading and writing. Students must understand that it is the daily influence of listening to lectures, interacting with text, both by reading and writing, which over time unconsciously develops good language. Building vocabulary does not happen overnight; it happens from exposure to new and different reading and writing experiences. !!

4. **Don't throw away that dictionary.**

   A college student's environment should always include good reference material and a dictionary should be at the top of the list. The best way to fully understand what the dictionary provides in terms of words is for students to keep it close by and realize that it is more than just a place to check spelling and definitions. Students might engage the dictionary for other forms of understanding such as word origin, capitalization, slang and grammar usage. At such times, the dictionary acts as a tool to expand vocabulary in new and different ways—ways that foster greater understanding and usage of recently acquired words. Hopefully, deeper meaning will occur.

   I never thought of a dictionary as a tool

   good advice (remember this)

5. **Don't stop when reading when you come across a new and unfamiliar word.**

   Students need to keep moving forward when they read to avoid breaking down understanding. At best, students should always read with a pencil in hand to circle or underline new words. After completing the reading, checking the meaning with a dictionary is the first step. Next, go back and reread the selection to add new meaning back into the selection as an aid to understanding.

6. **Silly works.**

   In graduate school I had a professor who believed that difficult and unfamiliar words could be learned by creating silly sentences that highlighted meaning. Some believe that visual images help aid meaning. *pictures* It all comes down to creativity on the part of the student. Thinking of ways "outside the box" *to think differently, unconventionally* to improve vocabulary may help to unlock meaning. *I like this!* Consider the following "silly" examples: *Danny Detritus didn't know what to do with all the junk sitting in his room. Melanie Mellifluous made sweet flowing sounds as she marched to the menagerie.* Remember, the sillier the example, the better. Encourage students to use their creative juices *great image!* to design sentences that not only impart meaning, but also add some humor to their vocabulary development.

7. **The best cure for vocabulary development?**

   Read and write, read and write, read and write.

Responding to Readings: Constructing Paragraphs and Essays

Whether you are writing paragraphs or essays, all compositions have at least one principle in common: a need to develop a unified thought. A unified composition makes a point and does not wander as the writer develops the paragraph.

The facts, examples, reasoning, and evidence used to support a topic sentence—the idea controlling the focus of a paragraph—specifically back up what you initially say. For instance, to ensure unity in a paragraph with a topic sentence such as *"The physicians at Elizabeth Scott Memorial Hospital give the medical profession a bad name,"* a writer must show how and why *the physicians* give the medical profession a bad name. Discussing the nursing staff or hospital rooms is wandering from the controlling idea—the focus—of the paragraph, confusing the reader in the process.

Another topic sentence might be *"Graffiti remained the artistic expression of street youth during the second decade of the twenty-first century."* Here again, evidence will be required to prove the point or to justify your opinion. Your essay must include examples and reasons to illustrate how and why graffiti is more than just defacing and vandalizing public property. In other words, you will be *showing* your reader how graffiti is an art form.

Whether writing a paragraph or an essay, on paper or a computer, authors must first generate ideas to determine which direction they wish to take in the development of their topic. Thus, generating ideas is the first step in achieving an overall focus.

Generating Ideas and Establishing a Focus

One of the more difficult tasks a writer faces is coming up with original ideas about a topic. Original ideas don't just pop out of our heads every time we would like them to, so we must learn how to generate fresh perspectives about a topic by brainstorming in a variety of written ways such as clustering, freewriting, and listing. After generating several ideas on a topic, the author will want to focus on a specific controlling idea, either a topic sentence or a thesis statement.

Clustering words creates a visual picture of the relationships between ideas associated with a topic. To cluster thoughts, begin with a topic or stimulus word, freely associating words and ideas around the topic and drawing connections between your responses. For example, the cluster (see illustration) helped a student generate ideas and arrive at a focus on the general topic of war.

After analyzing her cluster, this student decided that, out of all the associations she had made with the word "war," there were four ideas that dominated her cluster—the major causes of war: hatred, power, self-defense, and religion. While her other information dealt with warfare, she decided to write on only the causes of war to give her paper focus. By eliminating information that did not fall into one of these four categories, the author narrowed her focus and prevented herself from wandering off the topic. Initially, the free association of thoughts allowed her to reach her controlling idea and major discussion points.

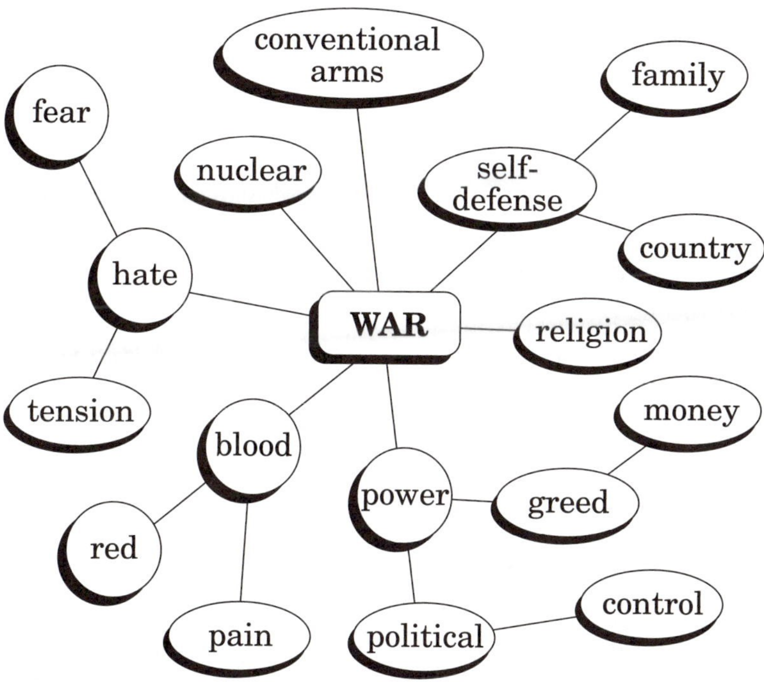

Listing offers yet another way to examine thoughts on a subject. Though no specific format for listing exists, most writers who make use of this technique simply write down one word or phrase and then another. Like other prewriting strategies used to generate ideas—especially clustering—listing is based on the concept that *one thought generates another;* therefore, all items on a list may be important. When freely associating words, it is hard to determine which word will lead the writer to a specific focus—the ultimate objective of the activity.

Freewriting is another popular way to brainstorm a general topic in order to arrive at a specific focus. When you freewrite, you should compose as quickly as you can, never stopping to edit. Since your goal is to associate ideas freely, you need not worry about formal essay structure, mechanics, or grammatical correctness. You are exploring your ideas by getting them into writing.

Peter Elbow

Freewriting

A graduate of Williams College, Peter Elbow has published numerous articles and books about the writing process, including *Writing Without Teachers* (1973); *Writing with Power* (1981); *Embracing Contraries: Explorations in Learning and Teaching: Sharing and Responding* (1999); and *Being a Writer: A Community of Writers Revisited* (2002). Now an Emeritus Professor from the University of Massachusetts' Department of English, he remains a very popular, compelling figure in writing theory and practice. In the following essay, Elbow offers some suggestions on how to begin the writing process: freewrite!

Pre-reading Questions

1. Have you ever used a pre-writing exercise to generate ideas for essay topics? Do you ever freewrite?
2. Write nonstop for five minutes expressing everything that comes to mind when you hear the word *freewriting.* Don't be concerned about grammatical or mechanical correctness at this time.

---

1 The most effective way I know to improve your writing is to do freewriting exercises regularly. At least three times a week. They are sometimes called "automatic writing," "babbling," or "jabbering" exercises. The idea is simply to write for ten minutes (later on, perhaps fifteen or twenty). Don't stop for anything. Go quickly without rushing. Never stop to look back, to cross something out, to wonder how to spell something, to wonder what word or thought to use, or to think about what you are doing. If you can't think of a word or a spelling, just use a squiggle or else write, "I can't think of it." Just put down something. The easiest thing is just to put down whatever is in your mind. If you get stuck it's fine to write "I can't think what to say, I can't think what

to say" as many times as you want; or repeat the last word you wrote over and over again; or anything else. The only requirement is that you *never* stop.

2 What happens to a freewriting exercise is important. It must be a piece of writing that, even if someone reads it, doesn't send any ripples back to you. It is like writing something and putting it in a bottle in the sea. The teacherless class helps your writing by providing maximum feedback. Freewritings help you by providing no feedback at all. When I assign one, I invite the writer to let me read it. But also tell him to keep it if he prefers. I read it quickly and make no comments at all and I do not speak with him about it. The main thing is that a freewriting must never be evaluated in any way; in fact there must be no discussion or comment at all.

3 Here is an example of a fairly coherent exercise (sometimes they are very incoherent, which is fine):

> I think I'll write what's on my mind, but the only thing on my mind right now is what to write for ten minutes. I've never done this before and I'm not prepared in any way—the sky is cloudy today, how's that? Now I'm afraid I won't be able to think of what to write when I get to the end of the sentence—well, here I am at the end of the sentence—here I am again, again, again, again, at least I'm still writing—Now I ask is there some reason to be happy that I'm still writing—ah yes! Here comes the question again—What am I getting out of this? What point is there in it? It's almost obscene to always ask it but I seem to question everything that way and I was gonna say something else pertaining to that but I got so busy writing down the first part that I forgot what I was leading into. This is kind of fun oh don't stop writing—cars and trucks speeding by somewhere out the window, pens clittering across peoples' papers. The sky is still cloudy—is it symbolic that I should be mentioning it? Huh? I dunno. Maybe I should try colors, blue, red, dirty words—wait a minute—no can't do that, orange, yellow, arm tired, green pink violet magenta lavender red brown black green—now that I can't think of any more colors—just about done—relief? Maybe.

Freewriting may seem crazy, but actually it makes simple sense. Think of the difference between speaking and writing. Writing has the advantage of permitting more editing. But that's its downfall too. Almost everybody interposes a massive and complicated series of editings between the time words start to be born into consciousness and when they finally come off the end of the pencil or typewriter onto the page. This is partly because schooling makes us obsessed with the "mistakes" we make in writing. Many people are constantly thinking about spelling and grammar as they try to write. I am always thinking about the awkwardness, wordiness, and general mushiness of my natural verbal product as I try to write down words.

4 But it's not just "mistakes" or "bad writing" we edit as we write. We also edit unacceptable thoughts and feelings, as we do in speaking. In writing there is more time to do it so the editing is heavier: when speaking, there's someone right there waiting for a reply and he'll get bored or think we're crazy if we don't come out with *something*. Most of the time in speaking, we settle for the catch-as-catch-can way in which the words tumble out. In writing, however, there's a chance to try to get them right. But the opportunity to get them right is a terrible burden: you can work for two hours trying to get a paragraph "right" and discover it's not right at all. And then give up.

5 Editing, *in itself*, is not the problem. Editing is usually necessary if we want to end up with something satisfactory. The problem is that editing goes on *at the same time* as producing. The editor is, as it were, constantly looking over the shoulder of the producer and constantly fiddling with what he's doing while he's in the middle of trying to do it. No wonder the producer gets nervous, jumpy, inhibited, and finally can't be coherent. It's an unnecessary burden to try to think of words and also worry at the same time whether they're the right words.

6 The main thing about freewriting is that it is *nonediting*. It is an exercise in bringing together the process of producing words and putting them down on the page. Practiced regularly, it undoes the ingrained habit of editing at the same time you are trying to produce. It will make writing less blocked because words will come more easily. You will use up more paper, but chew up fewer pencils.

7 Next time you write, notice how often you stop yourself from writing down something you were going to write down. Or else cross it out after it's written. "Naturally," you say, "it wasn't any good." But think for a moment about the occasions when you spoke well. Seldom was it because you first got the beginning just right. Usually it was a matter of a halting or even garbled beginning, but you kept going and your speech finally became coherent and even powerful. There is a lesson here for writing: trying to get the beginning just right is a formula for failure—and probably a secret tactic to make yourself give up writing. Make some words, whatever they are, and then grab hold of that line and reel in as hard as you can. Afterwards you can throw away lousy beginnings and make new ones. This is the quickest way to get into good writing.

8 The habit of compulsive, premature editing doesn't just make writing hard. It also makes writing dead. Your voice is damped out by all the interruptions, changes, and hesitations between the consciousness and the page. In your natural way of producing words there is a sound, a texture, a rhythm—a voice—which is the main source of power in

your writing. I don't know how it works, but this voice is the force that will make a reader listen to you, the energy that drives the meanings through his thick skull. Maybe you don't *like* your voice; maybe people have made fun of it. But it's the only voice you've got. It's your only source of power. You better get back into it, no matter what you think of it. If you keep writing in it, it may change into something you like better. But if you abandon it, you'll likely never have a voice and never be heard.

9 Freewritings are vacuums. Gradually you will begin to carry over into your regular writing some of the voice, force, and connectedness that creep into those vacuums.

Post-reading Questions

Content

1. What is freewriting? How do you begin to do it?
2. According to Elbow, what is one of the biggest obstacles in the writing process? To what extent do you agree with him? Why?
3. How can freewriting overcome "writer's block"?
4. According to Elbow, what is the result of "compulsive, premature editing"?

Strategies and Structures

1. Why does Elbow offer such an extensive example of freewriting? What questions does it tend to answer?
2. How does the author address his reader in this essay? Does he seem to be lecturing and/or "talking down" to his audience? Explain your answer by specifically referring to Elbow's word use and its effect on his overall delivery of information.
3. Why does Elbow devote so much time to the issue of editing? What point is he trying to make? How does he succeed or fail in his effort?
4. After reading Elbow's essay, are you convinced about the merits of freewriting? Explain.

Language and Vocabulary

1. When Elbow wrote this essay, he carefully avoided words that would have distracted the reader—words the reader would need to look up in the dictionary. How does his simple word choice help establish a reader/writer relationship? How is Elbow's own use of language and vocabulary "free" from the narrow confines of academic writing?

2. Elbow uses a simile to explain that freewriting "is like writing something and putting it in a bottle in the sea." After reading his entire essay, what do you think he meant by that comparison?

Group Activities

1. To explore the possibilities that freewriting can offer you in the way of generating ideas or focusing in on essay topics/issues, get together with two other students in class, select an initial topic (it will serve as a starting point), and all three of you write without stopping for five minutes. Then pick a second topic and write for another five minutes, this time editing your work as you write (precisely what Elbow warns against doing). At the end of ten minutes, have other group members evaluate both pieces of writing. Which was more natural?
2. Share other methods of pre-writing that you have found useful with the rest of your group. Show group members how you use a particular strategy to overcome writing blocks and to generate specific, meaningful paragraph/essay topics.

Writing Activities

1. Write for ten minutes without stopping, putting down every word or thought that creeps into your mind. Do not worry about grammar, mechanics, or even making sense. Next, write down a specific topic of your choice at the top of a clean page, underline it, and then freewrite for ten more minutes. What sorts of things did you end up saying about the topic or issue you wrote on? Pick one of them to function as the controlling idea in your thesis statement. How would you develop it?
2. Beginning today, freewrite for five minutes daily. Keep your freewritings in a bound notebook or portfolio of your choice. Like any pre-writing technique, freewriting is bound to be a bit disorganized and at times confusing, but don't worry about it. The objective of freewriting is not to produce a finished copy of an essay. As Elbow himself said, freewriting "is an exercise in bringing together the process of producing words and putting them down on the page."

Structuring Essays

Your essay is structured to support a thesis or controlling idea. Once you have arrived at a specific focus, the next step in the writing process is to organize your supporting points (topic sentences). Based on the purpose of your essay, you may want to arrange material in chronological or emphatic order. Leaving out steps in a process paper, for instance, will only confuse the reader. However you choose to organize your material, it should always develop your thesis logically and coherently.

Traditionally, essays have three different types of paragraphs. *Introductory paragraphs* expose the reader to an idea, concept, or argument and lead to a specific thesis. *Body paragraphs* contain specific topic sentences or discussion points—followed by evidence and analysis—that support a writer's thesis. *Concluding paragraphs* draw the discussion to a close, either summarizing major points and relating them to the thesis or providing a definite sense of closure. In essence, you have a beginning, middle, and end.

Introductory paragraphs acquaint your reader with a specific topic and ultimately focus on the controlling idea or thesis you plan to develop. Though a one-sentence introduction might inform your reader of your thesis, it seldom captures the reader's imagination or engages his or her intellect. Some of the more effective ways of leading a reader to a thesis or controlling idea include telling an illustrative story, providing startling or revealing facts or statistics, asking some provocative questions (often rhetorical questions—questions you plan to answer), or using a relevant quote. All of these introductory strategies lead quite naturally to a thesis statement.

A thesis statement introduces your subject, what you have to say about a subject, and how you plan to defend your point of view. Your plan of development breaks a broad topic into manageable units—paragraphs—and suggests the structure of your composition. How many paragraphs should you include in an essay? Although most people are familiar with a five-paragraph format—one introductory paragraph, three supporting paragraphs, and one concluding paragraph—in reality, an essay should contain as many paragraphs as necessary to justify or develop your thesis or controlling idea.

Introductory paragraph: Leading to a thesis statement of a controlling idea

Topic sentence #1: Supporting examples, details, and reasoning

Topic sentence #2: Supporting examples, details, and reasoning

Topic sentence #3: Supporting examples, details, and reasoning

Body Paragraphs
Note: The complexity of your thesis, **not an arbitrary formula** (e.g., an essay consists of five paragraphs) will determine the number of paragraphs needed to develop your essay. (See the sample essay by Joanne Jaime later in this chapter for an illustration of this.)

Concluding paragraph: Relating discussion points back to the thesis

In "Creatures That Haunt the Americas," for instance, in order to fully develop her controlling idea that *"When Africans reached the New World, the creatures [of African folktales] stepped ashore with them,"* Constance García-Barrio presents the reader with several illustrative paragraphs containing examples that support her thesis. Because her controlling idea is broad, García-Barrio must explore, explain, and support her thesis in several paragraphs in order to develop it adequately.

Body paragraphs support or develop a thesis through argument and examples. Like miniature essays, paragraphs tend to have a beginning, a middle, and an end. For example, a topic sentence is usually the starting point of a paragraph. Here the author alerts the reader to the controlling idea. Supporting examples and details, often referred to as primary and secondary support, comprise the bulk of the paragraph. Such information illustrates what an author has claimed. At the end of a paragraph, an author may offer a closing or transitional statement, which either summarizes the paragraph or leads to the next discussion point.

In "Distance Learning and American Society," Mark Fissel focuses paragraph 2 with the topic sentence: *"Distance learning via interactive video instruction makes teaching student-oriented and decentralized as opposed to instructor-oriented, centralized instruction in the traditional classroom."* The rest of Fissel's paragraph supports this claim by supplying examples and interviews. His paragraph is unified because he sticks to supporting his main point (topic sentence).

Concluding paragraphs draw the discussion to a close. In concluding paragraphs, the author strives to come up with a solution to a problem, refers to the information presented in the introductory paragraph, and makes predictions based upon the evidence presented. Just as he or she does not want to begin to develop an essay in an introductory paragraph, a writer will not want to develop new ideas in a conclusion. Keep in mind that the final sentence ideally should leave a lasting impression upon your reader. Once again, you may draw upon an anecdote or refer to information presented in your introduction to frame your essay as a whole.

Point of View: Position of Authority

To maintain unity and promote coherence in an essay, writers strive to maintain a consistent "point of view." Point of view in its simplest sense can be considered a position of authority. A personal experience, for instance, can best be expressed in first person (I, me, my; we, us, our). The particular point of view one selects to use in a composition indicates who is controlling the essay.

Point of View	Subject	Object	Possessive
First Person Singular	I	me	my, mine
Second Person Singular	you	you	your, yours
Third Person Singular	he, she, it	him, her, it	his, his, her, hers, its, its
First Person Plural	we	us	our, ours
Second Person Plural	you	you	your, yours
Third Person Plural	they	them	their, theirs

First person point of view: The author speaks through his or her personal experience (I, me, my; we, us, our). *I* and *we* are subject pronouns, *me* and *us* are object pronouns, and *my* and *our* indicate possession.
Second person point of view: The author speaks to another person (you, your). In the case of *you,* it is both subject and object, and *your* is possessive.
Third person point of view: The authors speaks about other people, places, and things (he, him, his; she, her, hers; it, its; they, them, their), where *he, she, it,* and *they* are subject pronouns, *him, her, it,* and *them* are object pronouns, and *his, her, its,* and *their* denote possession.

Appropriate Use of Point of View

First Person: When writing an expository essay where you provide details and examples based on your own experience, use the first person point of view. Why? You, the author, are the authority of the situation. When writing in first person, be careful not to mention what other people are thinking. The way to reveal this is by using dialogue and quotation marks, since you are not able to read a person's mind, as in the omniscient (all-knowing) point of view. (See Third Person.)

Example: When the truck hit me, I knew that the impact broke my arms and legs and my recovery would take months.

Second Person: The second person point of view has an author or speaker addressing at least one other person. Second person point of view is effective in process essays (those that tell the reader how to construct an object or complete a task).

Example: Once you have combined all the ingredients, pour the batter into the baking pan, place in the oven, and bake for 35 minutes at 375 degrees.

Unless you are writing a process-oriented paper (how to do something or how something was done), avoid the use of second person, for it too often can sound preachy and might alienate readers by seemingly talking down to them.

Third Person: The third person point of view features an anonymous narrator who has virtually free license to talk or write about people, objects, and locations. The narrator, above all, is allowed to go into people's minds and reveal what they are thinking. This is known as the omniscient or all-knowing point of view, and only the third person point of view lends itself to this.

Example: When Mary encountered the rapist, fear ran rampant through her body, and she could not imagine how she would survive.

Above all, writers must be careful to avoid shifting their points of view. Begin with one (i.e., first, second, or third person), and stay with that point of view. The following is an example of *shifting points of view,* which *must be avoided*:

Example: *One* must always change *their* clothes when *you* are going to a formal dinner, or *I* could be refused entry. (Very confusing!)

Rewritten correctly in *third person plural*, the sentence would read:

People *must always change* their *clothes when* they *are going to a formal dinner, or* they *could be refused entry.*

Lead-Ins and Concluding Sentences

Both *lead-in* and *concluding* sentences can play a crucial role in an effective essay. Lead-in sentences are those that expose readers to a topic or an issue, grabbing their interest and actively engaging them with the text. The following lead-in sentences taken from various essays presented in *Visions Across the Americas* all invite people to read on or intrigue them in some way.

- "My family believes itself to be camera-ready in spite of being Chinese."—*Leslie Bow*
- "The last inch of space was filled, yet people continue to wedge themselves along the walls of the Store."—*Maya Angelou*
- "Young women use it to reveal alluringly flattering self portraits; parents use it to spy on their kids; grandmothers use it to share cutesy pictures of their grandchildren."—Sara Blake
- "What is intelligence, anyway?"—*Isaac Asimov*
- "From the neck up, I am a nudist."—*Karen Ray*
- "Shakespeare was right. Thin people need watching."—*Susan Britt*
- "It is possible to stop most drug addiction in the United States within a very short time."—*Gore Vidal*
- "You ask me what is poverty? Listen to me. Here I am, dirty, smelly, and with no 'proper' underwear on and with the stench of my rotting teeth near you."—*Jo Goodwin Parker*
- "Do you know the difference between shame and guilt?"—*Philip Persky*
- "The beguiling presence of animé in North American culture cannot be ignored."—*Grace Sumabat-Estrada*
- "No matter which Bay Area Starbucks we walk into, the familiar text message ringtone of an iPhone (currently, the "glass" sound is the most popular) will be heard intermittently, as we wait in line for our double macchiato or white mocha."— *Mandana Mohsenzadegan*

Drawing an essay to an effective, satisfying conclusion can also be a difficult task. It is no secret that even professional writers often wait until they revise an essay before they construct a clincher sentence. Regardless of when the concluding sentence or sentences are written—in your first draft or revised draft—they should complement your work by drawing your discussion to a definite close. Concluding sentences are usually one of the following: (1) a call to action, (2) a prediction, (3) a quotation, (4) a final anecdote, or (5) a statement about the broader implications of your topic or issue. Note how the following conclusions exemplify these methods of bringing closure to an essay.

- ". . . Would Dickens have recognized a paperback of *A Christmas Carol* or, for that matter, a Braille version? Even on a cellphone screen, Tiny Tim can God-bless us, every one."—*Anna Quindlen*

- ". . . Between Mr. Muhammad's teachings, my correspondence, my visitors—usually Ella and Reginald—and my reading of books, months passed without my even thinking about being imprisoned. In fact, up to then, I had never been so truly free in my life."—*Malcolm X*
- ". . . Apart from what any critic had to say about my writing, I knew I had succeeded where it counted when my mother finished reading my first book and gave me her verdict. 'So easy to read.'"—*Amy Tan*
- ". . . Nonviolent resistance is not aimed against oppressors but against oppression. Under its banner consciences, not racial groups, are enlisted."—*Dr. Martin Luther King, Jr.*
- ". . . And if the strength of our democracy rests upon the participation of its people, then social justice in education feeds the collective in responsible and positive ways. As the late hip-hop artist Tupac Shakur insisted 'the power is in the people.'"—*Carmen Jay*
- ". . . Eye candy—films full of spectacular special effects and saccharine happy endings—cannot generate much growth in viewers. The best films make for a cinematic diet that enhances the psychological sinews and synapses that are life sustaining."—*Bill Swanson*
- ". . . A country song I once heard said it all for me: 'You've got to stand for something or you'll fall for anything.'"—*Stephanie Ericsson*
- ". . . The scenario reviewed here, involving the murders of three great American leaders, John F. Kennedy, Martin Luther King, Jr., and Robert F. Kennedy, in order to conduct a seemingly senseless war, may be dismissed by those who find it too painful to contemplate. Indeed, embracing this alternative view of recent history involves for many a radical revision of their views about the country they live in and the integrity of its leadership."—*Bruce Henderson*

Transitions

A transition is a word, phrase, or passage that links one topic or idea to another in writing. Overall, transitional expressions signal intended relationships between information, allowing you to smoothly present material as you move from one point to the next. (Some transitional expressions may signal more than one kind of relationship to a reader, depending on their context.) A good first step to use when revising an essay might be to read through it and add transitional expressions that improve understanding. Moreover, since they indicate relationships in time, space, direction, and so on, transitions improve coherence and eliminate choppiness in your writing. The following is but a partial list of transitional expressions and linking words:

Time Transitions: before, while, during, after, first, second, third, then, next, now, finally, meanwhile, subsequently
Addition Transitions: first of all, secondly, third, finally, last of all, in addition, moreover, furthermore
Illustration Transitions: for instance, for example, specifically, such as, as an illustration
Emphasis Transitions: furthermore, moreover, most of all, principally, especially, most importantly, especially significant
Spatial Transitions: above, below, inside, outside, here, there, beyond, behind, between, over, under
Change of Direction Transitions: but, consequently, however, yet, in contrast, otherwise, still, on the contrary, on the other hand, nevertheless, nonetheless
Conclusion Transitions: therefore, consequently, thus, as a result, then, in summary, in short, in conclusion, last of all, finally

Adverbial conjunctions, a popular group of joining words, also make excellent transitions (many are listed above). Functioning partly as adverbs and partly as linking words, the most common adverbial conjunctions (sometimes referred to as conjunctive adverbs) include:

additionally	*frequently*	*moreover*	*regardless*
consequently	*furthermore*	*nevertheless*	*subsequently*
eventually	*however*	*nonetheless*	*therefore*

Adverbial conjunctions, by their very nature, are extremely strong joining words and frequently are used to "lead-off" constructions. This way, they connect ideas between separate sentences, as well as the second clause in a compound sentence punctuated with a semicolon. As a good rule of thumb, always follow adverbial conjunctions with a comma.

Example: Catherine enjoys traveling; **nevertheless,** since she developed a fear of flying, she now spends most of her vacations at home.

Example: **Eventually,** after a long deep sleep, Andrea bathed, dressed, made breakfast, and went to work at the Boulder Creek Percolation Pond.

Revising and Editing

One draft of a paper, of course, will not usually result in a polished essay. Polished writing requires a great deal of work and is more than just a neatly rewritten or a grammatically or mechanically correct paper (a paper without a comma splice or subject–verb agreement error can still be thoroughly disunified and disorganized). Therefore, you will probably write several drafts before arriving at a finished product. After you get your basic material down on paper, you will be ready for the next step in the writing process: revision. A good rule of thumb is to remember that "good writing is a matter of *rewriting*."

When you revise, you'll want to consider your work from the viewpoint of the receptor (reader), rather than the creator (writer). In doing so, you will critique *what has been written* as opposed to *what you intended.* One way to approach the second draft—and all subsequent drafts—of an essay is to ask yourself questions like "How could I have said this better?" or "What seems to be missing here?" Jot down your answers to such questions in your margins because they will come in handy later on. The following are some other questions you may wish to bear in mind:

- Are there awkward, imprecise sentences? Where? Which sentences could be condensed and combined with other sentences?
- Do transitions and linking words establish clear relationships and promote coherence between words, clauses, sentences, and paragraphs?
- Is there a clearly defined thesis? Do all paragraphs support the thesis? How?
- Where might sentence variety improve the flow of information?
- Have major points been thoroughly justified or illustrated? How?
- Where might concrete nouns and active verbs replace vague nouns and passive verbs?
- Are the supporting paragraphs logically organized and thoroughly developed?

- Does the essay contain a satisfying and appropriate concluding paragraph?
- Are paragraphs unified?
- Is reasoning sound? Are conclusions logically drawn? How?

As you move from one draft to the next, organizing material, developing weak points, eliminating awkward constructions, and rewriting confusing sentences, you will want to remember the distinction between revision and editing skills. They represent two different steps in the composition process—not one and the same. You revise your material in order to present it in a logical, coherent, effective manner; you edit your writing so that it adheres to recognizable conventions of style, grammar, and usage. Each time you *finish revising a paper,* edit and correct grammatical and mechanical errors which interfere with clear written communication. The following student, Joanne Jaime, wrote three drafts of her essay, *discussing* the full range of her observations and feelings toward marriage and divorce in the first draft; *revising* awkward constructions, *adding* transitional words, and *addressing* unity, organization, coherence, and paragraph structure in the second draft; and *refining* syntax, *varying* sentence patterns, and *editing* careless grammatical or mechanical errors that could interfere with or impair a clear understanding of her subject in the third and final draft.

Joanne Jaime

Marriage: The Changing Institution

Joanne Jaime, a graduate of Santa Clara University, currently holds a management position in the medical device and diagnostics industry where she leads content development for product labeling and related process improvement projects. She continues to work privately as a freelance copywriter for small businesses and nonprofit organizations, as well as on her own short stories and poetry.

Over the past thirty years, the institution of marriage has fallen victim to the changes in our social and moral values. Infidelity, physical abuse, substance abuse, financial instability, job-related stress, conflicting goals, and lack of communication are problems often associated with the breakup of marriages. The current high divorce rate in the United States is directly related to our views about marriage, our motives for marriage, and our expectations of marriage.

Lead-in to thesis

Thesis statement

The vows "... in sickness and in health, 'til death do us part" were once taken literally. Marriage was viewed as a lifelong commitment. People married their first loves, settled down, and started a family. They didn't question whether their lives were fulfilling; they simply accepted the wisdom of tradition and their parents. In the end, the security of it all was comforting and they thanked God for their children and grandchildren. Divorce, on the other hand, was practically unheard of. It carried a social stigma and was synonymous with failure; something must have been wrong with people if they couldn't hold their marriages together. Divorced women, especially, were considered no good and sinful.

Discussion point #1 (views on marriage) with examples & reasoning

Today, all this does not necessarily hold true. Because of numerous social revolutions and movements in the 1960s—the sexual revolution, the civil rights movement, and the women's movement, among others—divorce is no longer considered an unacceptable practice. In fact, marriage conforms almost to the

Paragraph #3 takes discussion point #1 a step further, contrasting past & present social values same rules as a business deal. If we are not getting our money's worth, or if promises are broken, we have every right to dissolve our agreement. We are considered smart for cutting our losses and moving on with our lives. Besides, the beauty of marriage is what it symbolizes, not its true rewards and sacrifices. Although some of us like the idea of growing old with that one special person, the pursuit of individual happiness is what we truly cherish.

Discussion point #2 (motives for marrying). Note the effective use of rhetorical questions to establish the controlling idea about "motives"

Why bother getting married? Why don't people just live together and see what happens? Nowadays, many people do choose to live together indefinitely. However, before the sexual revolution, marriage was the only acceptable predecessor to having sex and children. Afterwards, the number of unmarried women who became pregnant increased. Pregnancy is still a strong reason that many people get married. The pressure to get married under this circumstance could easily account for many unhappy marriages. Going from a one-night stand to a marriage, baby included, is a long distance to travel in a short period of time. The absence of quality time can weaken the foundation of a marriage. Divorce is the most likely outcome.

Paragraph #5 is an extension of discussion point #2 on motives

People everywhere tend to get married for the wrong reasons, reasons other than love. Some people marry for financial gain, others for status or citizenship, and still others marry just because they are afraid of being alone. An acquaintance of mine, for instance, accepted $10,000 to marry her husband, François, and stay with him until he gained American citizenship. Another person I know married her husband so they could file a joint income tax return; they neither lived nor spent time with each other. If a person's motive for getting married is primarily self-serving, then the decision needs to be reconsidered. We should not get married to get divorced.

with some examples drawn from personal experiences.

A final reason for the increase in divorce rates is that marriage expectations have changed considerably over the years. Due to the increase of women in the work force, they are no longer dependent on men to be sole supporters. There is no longer any financial incentive for women to remain in bad marriages. On the contrary, divorce settlements sometimes offer considerable financial gain! Also, education has not only improved, it has become more accessible. There is a wealth of knowledge spewing forth from books, magazines, and TV talk shows: information about laws, domestic violence, support groups, and other social and moral issues. Education enables us to make better decisions in our lives, but we also learn to expect more from others and ourselves.

Discussion point #3 (the change in expectations of a marriage)

People constantly get married hoping to change their partners so they fit their ideals of the perfect husband or wife. Even worse, some people like my former math instructor marry a dysfunctional person with any number of problems and decide their mission in life is to become a "miracle worker,"

Paragraph #7 expands upon discussion point #3

reforming or saving that individual from himself or herself. Such relationships inevitably end in violence, despair, or disillusionment—such relationships should be avoided. Nowadays we do not have to stay in a rotten marriage or accept abuse from anyone. At the same time, in order to avoid these situations to begin with, we should take a good look at whom we are marrying before saying, "I do." Today we are ready to file for divorce at the least provocation. If we are not happy, we must ask ourselves whose responsibility it is to make us happy. Marriage is give-and-take. Divorce is giving up.

Conclusion reiterates main discussion points

There are several forces inside of marriage that can lead to discord and divorce. Some, such as the changing views about, the motivation for, and the expectations of a marriage, are more obvious than others. Still, the relationship between the husband and wife figures prominently in the success or failure of a marriage. More than ever before, love and respect are essential ingredients in a good marriage, for the future of marriage commitments is no longer tied to the dictates of the past. As the institution of marriage continues to evolve in the twenty-first century, we may go through even more changes and eventually come full circle. This ultimate decision, however, will be made by individuals—couples—not morality imposed by society at large.

Concludes essay with a prediction

***Internet Connection:* Joanne Jaime**

Modern Marriages

Select an online database of your own choice, enter the search term "marriage," and read a few essays that discuss some aspect of marriage in America today. Print out the full text of at least one of the articles, and then annotate it in the same manner as Jaime's essay (e.g., thesis statement, different discussion points, representative examples/facts, and the conclusion). Be sure to document your source correctly, using the MLA format. (See *Visions* 8th edition Appendix.)

Special Writing Activities: The Individual and Group Response

There are many ways an individual becomes an active writer and a creative thinker. Individually, a person might write notes and impressions in a journal, record responses to a reading in a reading/writing log, or create, analyze, and solve a problem in a thesis notebook. Other times, writers work together as a group, examine issues, exchange ideas, and ultimately write a composition. Whether you write alone or with others, the ultimate goals are usually the same: to generate ideas, to analyze a problem, and to structure a meaningful response to the issue or reading. The following section offers a few writing strategies to use individually or as a group that will assist you in completing some of the pre-reading and post-reading activities in this text.

Journals, Reading/Writing Logs, and Thesis Notebooks

A journal is one of the most popular resources used by writers. In a journal, the writer freely records observations (sometimes in a diary format), notes events and daily activities, and jots down plans and goals. Journal entries are usually informal, and the writer's concern is to record ideas and observations with little regard for grammatical or mechanical perfection. A journal should be a place to examine new ideas and reevaluate old ones; it is a place to explore feelings and attitudes without the fear of censorship or any type of judgment or evaluation. Many techniques such as freewriting and brainstorming offer ideal strategies for writing journal entries.

Both readers and writers alike record their responses to an analysis of a book, story, poem, essay, or play in reading/writing logs. What do they write about? After reading, they jot down their emotional responses to the issues or topics discussed. They may also create a dialogue with the text, asking questions and stating opinions such as "This is seldom true!" or "Why doesn't the author support her claim?" Under "Tips on Becoming an Active Reader" earlier in this chapter, you will find useful hints for keeping a reading/writing log.

Much like a journal or a reading/writing log, a thesis notebook records information. However, whereas the reading/writing log focuses on reactions and perceptions about readings, a thesis notebook deals mostly with expository writings. In particular, the writer probes ideas to determine whether they can function as a controlling idea and be developed into an essay. During this process, the writer attempts to narrow a topic, construct a thesis, and support it. As a result, a thesis notebook often contains several drafts of writing assignments. In addition to its usefulness when structuring essays, a thesis notebook provides a place to rough out creative writings such as poems, short stories, and even plays. Finally, since many of the pre-reading and post-reading questions in this text invite both informal and formal reader response, they are ideally suited for journal and reading/writing log assignments.

Many times, authors will combine characteristics of journals, logs, and notebooks under one cover because they all deal with the same thing: exploring and recording ideas and perceptions. A journal or notebook is seldom an end in itself but is more often a means of working out ideas that will lead to a formal written response.

Response and Summary

A summary takes a longer work and briefly condenses it for a reader. Oftentimes, practice in writing summaries can be a valuable exercise for a reader/writer. A summary, which is about one-fourth as long as the original material in length, requires the reader to reflect upon what he or she has read. Then, the *reader* will have to consider the main points (though often details are omitted) and as a *writer* will place them in some orderly sequence. As an ongoing journal activity, frequently summarize the essays you read in *Visions Across the Americas* to get a clear sense of other writers' ideas, and to practice critical thinking and writing. You might follow each summary you write with a personal response about the topic, issue, or essay in question. For instance, J. J., a student, wrote the following journal entry:

Summary	"Euphemisms" by Neil Postman explores the practice of calling things by a different name in order to attract more positive reactions and sentiment towards those things. He often uses the examples of changing "garbage man" to "sanitation engineer." In his essay, Postman doesn't criticize the practice of using euphemisms without reservation or qualification; he does, however, stress that it is mostly an art of disguising the true meaning of something. (Then again, even Postman states that there is no *true meaning of something.*)
Personal response	What Postman says is interesting. Even though all of his examples don't completely fit the points he tries to make, the general idea seems on target to me. We often have to fool ourselves in order to feel good—or to fool others to wake them up and get them focused. Of course, it is only our acceptance of a name or word that makes its definition concrete. If we squabble over what to call things, we'd be nowhere fast. On the other hand, I suppose people will always think what they want, and they'll be sure to make up new names to fit their way of thinking. Priorities and values don't necessarily change because of a name.

Writing a summary requires you to read material carefully in order to extract the part that represents the whole (the major discussion points that support a thesis). If a work is inaccurately represented, then the summary is of no use to anyone. You might also follow your close analytical reading, summary, and personal response with a comparative evaluation of viewpoints: an author's and your own.

A summary is not a paraphrase. When you paraphrase a written work, you place someone else's words into your own. Whereas a summary provides your reader with a brief gist of a longer work, a paraphrase offers a more detailed rewording of a piece of writing—usually to clarify meaning—and is approximately as long as the original work. (There is nothing brief about a paraphrase!)

Group Activities and Collaborative Writing

Although writers often work out concepts individually, they also collaborate (work together) to generate and evaluate ideas. In the "Group Activities" sections of this textbook, for instance, you will often be asked to brainstorm a topic or issue as a group, meaning you will initially share information or opinions without evaluating or judging them. Ideally, your group will have a wide range of responses to any given subject; that way, you will be able to consider a topic from as many points of view as possible before analyzing or writing about it. Group activities generate dialogue; each group member both listens and contributes to group discussion without the anxiety of being judged.

One outcome of group activities might be a collaborative composition. Here, authors work together to generate and compose an essay. To begin with, writers examine an issue in order to arrive at a specific focus and formulate a thesis. Next, after thorough discussion, they break the thesis down into sections that will serve as major points or topic sentences to structure their composition. Collaborative writers then use an essay map or outline in order to guide them as they write. Then, with one person acting as recorder/secretary, group members develop each major point (topic sentence); every individual offers his or her experiences or examples to support the group's thesis, thereby developing the rough draft. Once a draft is complete, all group members go over their collaborative effort, correcting careless errors and noting parts of the composition that need revision or more development.

There are many variations to a collaborative writing project. Sometimes, for instance, every group member may write a rough draft of an agreed-upon thesis, and then the group may combine them into one essay. Other times, group members may be responsible for individual sections of the collaborative essay. Regardless of how you approach a collaborative writing assignment, its strength rests on cooperation with, and participation by, each group member.

Summation

From reading and marking textbooks to generating ideas, structuring compositions, and engaging in group (collaborative) activities, the connection between reading and writing is ever-present. As you read through the remaining essays on language in this chapter—and the essays in this book as a whole—we suggest that you review this brief section on reading and writing frequently. Doing so will enable you to keep a clear perspective on how to read and write *actively*.

Pat Mora

Why I Am a Writer

Pat Mora was born and educated in Texas, first at Texas Western College, where she earned her bachelor's degree in 1963, and later at the University of El Paso, where she received her master's degree in 1967. Since then, she has been actively involved in cross-cultural studies, both as an instructor and an administrator. In her own work, Mora frequently draws from her Hispanic heritage. Her poetry and prose frequently appear in literary journals, popular magazines, and anthologies. She has published five award-winning poetry collections, *Chants* (1984), *Borders* (1986), *Communion* (1991), and *Adobe Roads* (2006), *Dizzy in Your Eyes: Poems about Love* (2010)—as well as a memoir, *House of Houses* (2008). She also wrote *Agua Santa: Holy Water* (1997), and *A Library for Juana: The World of Sor Juana Ines* (2002), and *ZING! Seven Creativity Practices for Educators and Students* (2010). The following essay explaining why Mora is a writer first appeared in the July/August 1990 issue of *The Horn Book Magazine.*

Pre-reading Questions

1. The title of Mora's essay, "Why I Am a Writer," seems to promise some sort of explanation or answer. Why do you imagine Mora or any other person would want to be a writer?
2. Do a freewriting in which you explain why and when you write.

---

1 I like people. I like long, slow lunches with my friends. I like to dance. I'm no hermit, and I'm not shy. So why do I sit with my tablet and pen and mutter to myself?

2 There are many answers. I write because I am a reader. I want to give to others what writers have given me, a chance to hear the voices of people I will never meet. Even if I met these authors, I wouldn't hear what I hear alone with the page—words carefully chosen, woven into a piece unlike any other, enjoyed by me in a way no other person will enjoy them. I love the privateness of writing and reading.

3 I write because I am curious. I am curious about me. Writing is a way of finding out how I feel about anything and everything. Now that I've left the desert where I grew up, for example, I'm discovering how it feels to walk on spongy autumn leaves and to watch snow drifting up on a strong wind. I notice what's around me in a special way because I am a writer. I notice my world more, and then I talk to myself about it on paper. Writing is my way of saving my feelings.

4 I write because I believe that Hispanics need to take their rightful place in American literature. We need to be published and to be studied in schools and colleges so that the stories and ideas of our people won't quietly disappear. Although I am happy when I finish the draft of a poem or story, I always wish that I wrote better, that I could bring more honor and attention to the *abuelitas*—grandmothers—I write about. That mix of sadness and pleasure frequently occurs in a writer's life.

5 Although we don't discuss it often because it is depressing, my people have been and sometimes still are viewed as inferior. We have all been hurt by someone who said, "You're not like us; you are not one of us. Speaking Spanish is odd; your family looks funny." Some of us decide we don't want to be different; we don't want to be part of a

group that is often described as poor and uneducated. I spoke Spanish at home to my grandmother and aunt, but I didn't always want my friends at school to know that I spoke Spanish. And I didn't like myself for feeling that way. I sensed it was wrong, but I didn't know why. Now I know.

6 I know that the society we live in affects us. It is not easy to learn to disregard the unimportant things about people—the car they drive, the house they live in, the color of their skin, the language they speak at home. It takes courage to face the fact that we all have ten toes, get sleepy at night, get scared in the dark. Some families, some cities, some states, and even some countries foolishly convince themselves that they are better than others. Then they teach their children this ugly lie. It's like a weed with burrs and stickers that prick people.

7 How are young people who are Hispanic or members of any ethnic group supposed to feel about themselves? Some are proud of their cultural roots. But television commercials are busy trying to convince us that our cars, clothes, and even our families aren't good enough. It is so hard to be yourself, your many interesting selves, because billboards and magazine ads tell you that being beautiful is being thin, blond, and rich, rich, rich. No wonder we don't always like ourselves when we look in the mirror.

8 So I write to try to correct these images of worth. I take pride in being a Hispanic writer. I will continue to write and to struggle to say what no other writer can say in quite the same way.

Post-reading Questions

Content

1. State some of the reasons Mora gives for writing.
2. Why does she say that "a mix of sadness and pleasure frequently occurs in a writer's life"?
3. Why didn't Mora speak Spanish in school? How did she feel about this decision?
4. In what ways does Mora attempt to "correct images of worth" through her writings?

Strategies and Structures

1. What personal example does Mora give to show that some people don't want to be different? How does Mora illustrate the "unimportant things about people"?
2. How do specific topic sentences help to lead the reader through each paragraph and organize the essay?

3. What is the effect of the repetition of lead-in phrases like "I write because"? What do you imagine the author is attempting to achieve?
4. In what way do the first and last paragraphs function as a framing device for the whole essay?

Language and Vocabulary

1. A simile is a comparison with the use of *like* or *as*. At the end of paragraph 6, Mora uses a simile to illustrate the effects of the ugly lies we tell about others. What is this simile? Is it an accurate image of cultural lies? Why? Why not?
2. Mora uses one Spanish word in her essay, *abuelitas*. How does she define this word for the non-Spanish speakers? When do you feel this would be an effective strategy in your own writing?

Group Activities

1. Mora claims that Hispanic authors need "to be studied in schools and colleges." Divide into small groups, go to the library, and find stories, essays, poems, and/or articles written by Hispanic authors. Choose the one you like best and write a summary of it to present to the class. Why do you imagine your particular author likes to write?
2. Mora tells us that "billboards and magazine ads tell you that being beautiful is being thin, blond, and rich, rich, rich." In small groups, look through several magazines and determine whether Mora's claim is true or not. Then, compare your findings with those of other groups.

Writing Activities

1. In a short composition, briefly explain why you are or are not "a writer." You might begin your paper much like Mora, using topic sentences with lead-ins such as *I write because* . . . or *I don't write because* . . .
2. Using ideas generated from Group Activity 2, write a brief essay in which you support or disprove Mora's claim that "magazine ads tell you that being beautiful is being thin, blond, and rich, rich, rich" with specific examples from your observations.

Ray Bradbury

The Joy of Writing

Ray Bradbury, an esteemed author of many science fiction classics, is also well-known for his nonfiction works, screenplays, television scripts, theatrical plays, and futuristic novels. Among his many works are: *The Martian Chronicles* (1950), *Fahrenheit 451* (1953), *Dandelion Wine* (1956), *Something Wicked This Way Comes* (1962), *Death Is a Lonely Business* (1985), *Yestermorrow: Obvious Answers to an Impossible Future* (1991), *Green Shadow, White Whale* (1992), *Quicker Than the Eye* (1996), *Driving Blind* (1997), *From The Dust Returned* (2001), *One More For the Road: A New Short Story Collection* (2002), *Bradbury Stories: 100 of His Most Celebrated Tales* (2003), *Bradbury Speaks: Too Soon from the Cave, Too Far from the Stars* (2005), *Farewell Summer* (2006)—*a sequel to Dandelion Wine,* and *We'll Always Have Paris: Stories* (2009). In addition to all of these, Bradbury has written plays such as *Wisdom 2016* (2010), and he frequently authors articles like "The Joy of Writing," which offers insights into the composition process. In the preface to *Zen and the Art of Writing* (1996), for instance, Bradbury invites his readers to approach writing the same way he does: "Every morning I jump out of bed and step on a landmine. The landmine is me. After the explosion, I spend the rest of the day putting the pieces together. Now, it's your turn. Jump!"

Pre-reading Questions

1. Who are some of your favorite authors, poets, musicians, artists, actors/actresses? Make a brief list of them.
2. How would you define "zest" and "gusto"? In what sort of situation might you use these words?

---

1 Zest. Gusto. How rarely one hears these words used. How rarely do we see people living, or for that matter, creating by them. Yet if I were asked to name the most important items in a writer's make-up, the things that shape his material and rush him along the road to where he wants to go, I could only warn him to look to his zest, see to his gusto.

2 You have your list of favorite writers; I have mine. Dickens, Twain, Wolfe, Peacock, Shaw, Molière, Jonson, Wycherly, Sam Johnson. Poets: Gerard Manley Hopkins, Dylan Thomas, Pope. Painters: El Greco, Tintoretto. Musicians: Mozart, Haydn, Ravel, Johann Strauss (!). Think of all these names and you think of big or little, but nonetheless important, zests, appetites, hungers. Think of Shakespeare and Melville and you think of thunder, lightning, wind. They all knew the joy of creating in large or small forms, on unlimited or restricted canvasses. These are the children of the gods. They knew fun in their work. No matter if creation came hard here and there along the way, or what illnesses and tragedies touched their most private lives. The important things are those passed down to us from their hands and minds and these are full to bursting with animal vigor and intellectual vitality. Their hatreds and despairs were reported with a kind of love.

3 Look at El Greco's elongation and tell me, if you can, that he had no joy in his work? Can you really pretend that Tintoretto's *God Creating the Animals of the Universe* is a work founded on anything less than "fun" in its widest and most completely involved sense? The best jazz says, "Gonna live forever; don't believe in death." The best sculpture, like the head of Nefertiti, says again and again, "The Beautiful One was here, is here, and will be here, forever." Each of the men I have listed seized a bit of the quicksilver of life, froze it for all time and turned, in the blaze of their creativity, to point at it and cry, "Isn't this good!" And it was good.

4 What has all this to do with writing the short story in our times?

5 Only this: If you are writing without zest, without gusto, without love, without fun, you are only half a writer. It means you are so busy keeping one eye on the commercial market, or one ear peeled for the avant-garde coterie, that you are not being yourself. You don't even know yourself. For the first thing a writer should be is—excited. He should be a thing of fevers and enthusiasms. Without such vigor, he might as well be out picking peaches or digging ditches; God knows it'd be better for his health.

6 How long has it been since you wrote a story where your real love or your real hatred somehow got onto the paper? When was the last time you dared release a cherished prejudice so it slammed the page like a lightning bolt? What are the best things and the worst things in your life, and when are you going to get around to whispering or shouting them?

7 Wouldn't it be wonderful, for instance, to throw down a copy of *Harper's Bazaar* you happened to be leafing through at the dentist's, and leap to your typewriter and ride off with hilarious anger, attacking their silly and sometimes shocking snobbishness? Years ago I did just that. I

came across an issue where the *Bazaar* photographers, with their perverted sense of equality, once again utilized natives in a Puerto Rican back-street as props in front of which their starved-looking mannikins postured for the benefit of yet more emaciated half-women in the best salons in the country. The photographs so enraged me I ran, did not walk, to my machine and wrote "Sun and Shadow," the story of an old Puerto Rican who ruins the *Bazaar* photographer's afternoon by sneaking into each picture and dropping his pants.

8 I dare say there are a few of you who would like to have done this job. I had the fun of doing it; the cleansing after effects of the hoot, the holler, and the great horselaugh. Probably the editors at the *Bazaar* never heard. But a lot of readers did and cried, "Go it, *Bazaar*, go it, Bradbury!" I claim no victory. But there was blood on my gloves when I hung them up.

9 When was the last time you did a story like that, out of pure indignation?

10 When was the last time you were stopped by the police in your neighborhood because you like to walk, and perhaps think, at night? It happened to me just often enough that, irritated, I wrote "The Pedestrian," a story of a time, fifty years from now, when a man is arrested and taken off for clinical study because he insists on looking at un-televised reality, and breathing un-air-conditioned air.

11 Irritations and angers aside, what about loves? What do you love most in the world? The big and little things, I mean. A trolley car, a pair of tennis shoes? These, at one time when we were children, were invested with magic for us. During the past year I've published one story about a boy's last ride in a trolley that smells of all the thunderstorms in time, full of cool–green moss-velvet seats and blue electricity, but doomed to be replaced by the more prosaic, more practical-smelling bus. Another story concerned a boy who wanted to own a pair of new tennis shoes for the power they gave him to leap rivers and houses and streets, and even bushes, sidewalks, and dogs. The shoes were to him, the surge of antelope and gazelle on African summer veldt. The energy of unleashed rivers and summer storms lay in the shoes; he had to have them more than anything else in the world.

12 So, simply then, here is my formula.

13 What do you want more than anything else in the world? What do you love, or what do you hate?

14 Find a character, like yourself, who will want something or not want something, with all his heart. Give him running orders. Shoot him off. Then follow as fast as you can go. The character, in his great love, or hate, will rush you through to the end of the story. The zest and gusto of his need, and there *is* zest in hate as well as in love, will fire the landscape and raise the temperature of your typewriter thirty degrees.

15 All of this is primarily directed to the writer who has already learned his trade; that is, has put into himself enough grammatical tools and literary knowledge so he won't trip himself up when he wants to run. The advice holds good for the beginner, too, however, even though his steps may falter for purely technical reasons. Even here, passion often saves the day.

16 The history of each story, then, should read almost like a weather report: Hot today, cool tomorrow. This afternoon, burn down the house. Tomorrow, pour cold critical water upon the simmering coals. Time enough to think and cut and rewrite tomorrow. But today—explode—fly apart—disintegrate! The other six or seven drafts are going to be pure torture. So why not enjoy the first draft, in the hope that your joy will seek and find others in the world who, reading your story, will catch fire, too?

17 It doesn't have to be a big fire. A small blaze, candlelight perhaps; a longing for a mechanical wonder like a trolley or an animal wonder like a pair of sneakers rabbiting the lawns of early morning. Look for the little loves, find and shape the little bitternesses. Savor them in your mouth, try them on your typewriter. When did you last read a book of poetry or take time, of an afternoon, for an essay or two? Have you ever read a single issue of *Geriatrics,* the Official Journal of the American Geriatrics Society, a magazine devoted to "research and clinical study of the diseases and processes of the aged and aging"? Or read, or even seen, a copy of *What's New,* a magazine published by the Abbott Laboratories in North Chicago, containing articles such as "Tubocurarene for Cesarean Section" or "Phenurone in Epilepsy," but also utilizing poems by William Carlos Williams, Archibald MacLeish, stories by Clifton Fadiman and Leo Rosten; covers and interior illustrations by John Groth, Aaron Bohrod, William Sharp, Russell Cowles? Absurd? Perhaps. But ideas lie everywhere, like apples fallen and melting in the grass for lack of wayfaring strangers with an eye and a tongue for beauty, whether absurd, horrific, or genteel.

18 Gerard Manley Hopkins put it this way:

Glory be to God for dappled things—
For skies of couple-color as a brinded cow;
For rose-moles all in stipple upon trout that swim;
Fresh-firecoal chestnut-falls; finches' wings;
Landscape plotted and pieced—fold, fallow, and plow;
And all trades, their gear and tackle and trim.
All things counter, original, spare, strange;
Whatever is fickle, freckled (who knows how?)
With swift, slow; sweet, sour; adazzle, dim;
He fathers-forth whose beauty is past change:
Praise Him.

19 Thomas Wolfe ate the world and vomited lava. Dickens dined at a different table every hour of his life. Molière, tasting society, turned to pick up his scalpel, as did Pope and Shaw. Everywhere you look in the literary cosmos, the great ones are busy loving and hating. Have you given up this primary business as obsolete in your own writing? What fun you are missing, then. The fun of anger and disillusion, the fun of loving and being loved, of moving and being moved by this masked ball which dances us from cradle to churchyard. Life is short, misery sure, mortality certain. But on the way, in your work, why not carry those two inflated pig-bladders labeled Zest and Gusto. With them, traveling to the grave, I intend to slap some dummox's behind, pat a pretty girl's coiffure, wave to a tad up a persimmon tree.

20 Anyone wants to join me, there's plenty of room in Coxie's Army.

Post-reading Questions

Content

1. What is the basic message in Bradbury's essay? Explain.
2. How does Bradbury's list of favorite authors, poets, musicians, artists, actors/actresses, and so on, compare with your own list of favorite people?
3. What does Bradbury imply about the power of the written word?
4. Explain what you imagine Bradbury means when he says, "Look for the little loves, find and shape the little bitternesses. Savor them in your mouth, [and] try them on your typewriter."

Strategies and Structures

1. What basic human instincts does Bradbury appeal to in order to engage his readers and connect with their lives and experiences?
2. How is Bradbury's insight that writing is "... almost like a weather report: Hot today, cool tomorrow," useful information for any writer? Why?
3. What does Bradbury imply about his own mind and his approach to writing? How might his approach to diverse topics and issues be beneficial to you as a writer?
4. In what way does Bradbury's use of the words "zest" and "gusto" in the beginning and conclusion of his essay provide a framing device for the entire composition? Explain how this strategy unifies the essay and brings it full circle.

Language and Vocabulary

1. Vocabulary: *zest, gusto, mannikins, emaciated, prosaic, Cesarean section, epilepsy, wayfaring, cosmos, dummox, persimmon.* After looking up the definitions for these words and phrases, write each in an original sentence using a variety of sentence patterns.
2. To what extent might some of Bradbury's references seem dated in "The Joy of Writing" (written in 1973)? Write a journal entry citing specific words, phrases, or references that might distinguish his prose from contemporary authors writing at the beginning of the twenty-first century.

Group Activities

1. After gathering in groups of four to five people, compare your responses to Language and Vocabulary question 2. What was the most common criticism among members of your group? To what extent was your criticism a heartfelt response to the question? If your group had an opportunity to discuss Bradbury's essay with him, what would you suggest that he revise or change and why?
2. Divide the list of authors, painters, and musicians in paragraphs 2 and 17 among members in your group. Then, go to your campus library (or online) and investigate the lives of these people. Do you find any evidence of their approaching their respective craft with "zest" and "gusto"? Share your findings and conclusions with the rest of the class. (Each group should research all the individuals Bradbury mentions in order to prepare for the class forum.)

Writing Activities

1. Write to a magazine, business, social agency, or restaurant and either attack or praise its policies, its snobbish, elitist attitudes, preferential treatment of topics, issues, or employees, and so on. A letter of praise, of course, would highlight positive rather than negative attributes of the magazine, business, social agency, or restaurant.
2. Following Bradbury's instructions, select a topic you either love or hate. Then write an essay, using "zest" and "gusto" to explain and defend your position on the topic. You might want to begin by making two lists—one for topics you love and one for topics you hate. Narrow each list by asking yourself, "What do I feel most passionate about?" Then, as Bradbury suggests, "Jump [right into the essay]!"

Amy Tan

My Mother's English

A freelance writer and author of the prize-winning book *The Joy Luck Club* (1989), Amy Tan currently lives in San Francisco with her family and is a popular lecturer. Her second novel, *The Kitchen God's Wife*, was released in 1991. In 1992, she published *The Moon Lady*, a children's book based on one of the chapters in *The Joy Luck Club*. Her other children's books include *The Siamese Cat* (1994). Tan's other novels include: *The Hundred Secret Senses* (1995), *The Bonesetter's Daughter* (2001), and *Saving Fish from Drowning* (2005). In addition to her novels and children's books, Tan's work includes a collection of essays, *Opposite of Fate: Memories of a Writing Life* (2003), and she sings sporadically for The Rock Bottom Remainders, a rock group that includes popular writers such as Dave Barry and Stephen King (their motto is "We play music as well as Metallica writes novels"). A humanitarian, Amy Tan has avidly sought to bring better awareness of Lyme disease to the public, as well as supported efforts for more research, and helped found *LymeAid 4 Kids*. The following excerpt about her "mother's English" is from a speech Tan delivered at the 1990 CATE (California Association of Teachers of English) Conference in San Francisco.

Pre-reading Questions

1. Who influenced the way you speak the most—your parents, your peers, or your teachers?
2. How do you use language when speaking with relatives, friends, teachers, and strangers? How does your language change depending on to whom you are speaking? When do you feel your verbal English accurately represents the "real you"? (Do you ever feel as if another person is doing the talking when you are speaking to others? When?)
3. When have you felt limited or particularly effective due to your inability or ability to read and write? (For example, have you ever had writer's block on an essay test?)

1 As you know, I am a writer and by that definition I am someone who has always loved language. I think that is first and foremost with almost every writer I know. I'm fascinated by language in daily life. I spend a great deal of time thinking about the power of language—the way it can evoke an emotion, a visual image, a complex idea or a simple truth. As a writer, language is the tool of my trade and I use them all, all the Englishes I grew up with.

2 A few months back, I was made keenly aware of the Englishes I do use. I was giving a talk to a large group of people, the same talk I had given many times before and also with notes. And the nature of the talk was about my writing, my life, and my book, *The Joy Luck Club*. The talk was going along well enough until I remembered one major difference that made the whole thing seem wrong. My mother was in the room, and it was perhaps the first time she had heard me give a lengthy speech, using a kind of English I had never used with her. I was saying things like "the intersection of memory and imagination," and "there is an aspect of my fiction that relates to this and thus." A speech filled with carefully wrought grammatical sentences, burdened to me it seemed with nominalized forms, past perfect tenses, conditional phrases, all the forms of standard English that I had learned in school and through books, a form of English I did not use at home or with my mother.

3 Shortly after that I was walking down the street with my mother and my husband and I became self-conscious of the English I was using, the English that I do use with her. We were talking about the price of new and used furniture and I heard myself saying to her, "Not waste money that way." My husband was with me as well, and he didn't notice any switch in my English. And then I realized why: because over the twenty years that we've been together he's often used that English with me and I've used that with him. It is sort of the English that is our language of intimacy, the English that relates to family talk, the English that I grew up with.

4 I'd like to give you some idea what my family talk sounds like and I'll do that by quoting what my mother said during a recent conversation which I videotaped and then transcribed. During this conversation, my mother was talking about a political gangster who had the same last name as her family, Du, and how the gangster in his early years wanted to be adopted by her family which was by comparison very rich. Later the gangster became more rich, more powerful than my mother's family and one day showed up at my mother's wedding to pay his respects. And here's what she said about that, in part, "Du You Sung having business like food stand, like off the street kind; he's Du like Du Zong but not Tsung-ming Island people. The local people call him Du, from the river east side. He belong that side, local people. That man want to ask Du Zong father take him in become like own family. Du Zong father look down on him but don't take seriously until that man becoming big like,

become a Mafia. Now important person, very hard inviting him. Chinese way: come only to show respect, don't stay for dinner. Respect for making big celebration; he shows up. Means gives lots of respect, Chinese custom. Chinese social life that way—if too important, won't have to stay too long. He come to my wedding; I didn't see it I heard it. I gone to boy's side. They have YMCA dinner; Chinese age I was nineteen."

5 You should know that my mother's expressive command of English belies how much she actually understands. She reads the *Forbes Report,* listens to *Wall Street Week,* converses daily with her stockbroker, reads all of Shirley MacLaine's books with ease, all kinds of things I can't begin to understand. Yet some of my friends tell me that they understand 50 percent of what my mother says. Some say maybe they understand 80 percent. Some say they understand almost nothing at all. As a case in point, a television station recently interviewed my mother and I didn't see this program when it was first aired, but my mother did. She was telling me what happened. She said that everything she said, which was in English, was subtitled in English, as if she had been speaking in pure Chinese. She was understandably puzzled and upset. Recently a friend gave me that tape and I saw that same interview and I watched. And sure enough—subtitles—and I was puzzled because listening to that tape it seemed to me that my mother's English sounded perfectly clear and perfectly natural. Of course, I realize that my mother's English is what I grew up with. It is literally my mother tongue, not Chinese, not standard English, but my mother's English which I later found out is almost a direct translation of Chinese.

6 Her language as I hear it is vivid and direct, full of observation and imagery. That was the language that helped shape the way that I saw things, expressed things, made sense of the world. Lately I've been giving more thought to the kind of English that my mother speaks. Like others I have described it to people as broken or fractured English, but I wince when I say that. It has always bothered me that I can think of no other way to describe it than broken, as if it were damaged or needed to be fixed, that it lacked a certain wholeness or soundness to it. I've heard other terms used, "Limited English" for example. But they seem just as bad, as if everything is limited, including people's perceptions of the Limited English speaker.

7 I know this for a fact, because when I was growing up my mother's limited English limited my perception of her. I was ashamed of her English. I believed that her English reflected the quality of what she had to say. That is, because she expressed it imperfectly, her thoughts were imperfect as well. And I had plenty of empirical evidence to support me: The fact that people in department stores, at banks, at supermarkets, at restaurants did not take her as seriously, did not give her good service, pretended not to understand her, or even acted as if they did not hear her.

8 My mother has long realized the limitations of her English as well. When I was fifteen she used to have me call people on the phone to pretend

I was she. In this guise, I was forced to ask for information or oftentimes to complain and yell at people that had been rude to her. One time it was a call to her stockbroker in New York. She had cashed out her small portfolio and it just so happened that we were going to New York the next week, our very first trip outside of California. I had to get on the phone and say in my adolescent voice, which was not very convincing, "This is Mrs. Tan." And my mother was in the back whispering loudly, "Why don't he send me check already? Two weeks late. So mad he lie to me, losing me money." Then I said in perfect English, "Yes, I'm getting rather concerned. You had agreed to send the check two weeks ago, but it hasn't arrived." And she began to talk more loudly, "What you want—I come to New York, tell him front of his boss you cheating me?" And I was trying to calm her down, making her be quiet, while telling this stockbroker, "I can't tolerate any more excuses. If I don't receive the check immediately I'm going to have to speak to your manager when I arrive in New York." And sure enough the following week, there we were in front of this astonished stockbroker. And there I was, red-faced and quiet, and my mother the real Mrs. Tan was shouting at his boss in her impeccable broken English.

9 We used a similar routine a few months ago for a situation that was actually far less humorous. My mother had gone to the hospital for an appointment to find out about a benign brain tumor a CAT scan had revealed a month ago. And she had spoken very good English she said—her best English, no mistakes. Still she said the hospital had not apologized when they said they had lost the CAT scan and she had come for nothing. She said that they did not seem to have any sympathy when she told them she was anxious to know the exact diagnosis since her husband and son had both died of brain tumors. She said they would not give her any more information until the next time; she would have to make another appointment for that, so she said she would not leave until the doctor called her daughter. She wouldn't budge, and when the doctor finally called her daughter, me, who spoke in perfect English, lo-and-behold, we had assurances the CAT scan would be found, they promised a conference call on Monday, and apologies were given for any suffering my mother had gone through for a most regrettable mistake. By the way, apart from the distress of that episode, my mother is fine.

10 But it has continued to disturb me how much my mother's English still limits people's perceptions of her. I think my mother's English almost had an effect on limiting my possibilities as well. Sociologists and linguists will probably tell you that a person's developing language skills are more influenced by peers. But I do think the language spoken by the family, especially immigrant families, which are more insular, plays a large role in shaping the language of the child . . . . [While this may be true, I always wanted, however,] to capture what language ability tests can never reveal—her intent, her passion, her imagery, the rhythms of her speech,

and the nature of her thoughts. Apart from what any critic had to say about my writing, I knew I had succeeded where it counted when my mother finished reading my first book and gave me her verdict. "So easy to read."

Post-reading Questions

Content

1. What is the focus of Tan's essay? Who and what does she talk about?
2. Tan speaks of many different "Englishes." What are they?
3. How do others characterize her mother's English? How does Tan feel about her mother's English?
4. What steps does Tan's mother take to hide her "broken English"? Why does she feel it is necessary to conceal the "limitations of her English"?

Strategies and Structures

1. Explain the purpose of Tan's opening paragraph. What does it establish? How does it prepare you for her discussion of her mother's English?
2. Tan says her mother's language is "full of observation and imagery." How does she support this claim throughout her essay?
3. How does the author demonstrate the difficulties others have with her mother's English?
4. How does Tan illustrate the effectiveness of her mother's direct, "broken English" in comparison to the author's use of the English language?

Language and Vocabulary

1. Vocabulary: *intersection, wrought, nominalized, transcribed, belies, empirical, portfolio, CAT scan, linguists.* To increase your vocabulary, look up the definitions of the above words in a dictionary. Even if you think you know the meanings, look them up to confirm what you know and expand your vocabulary with additional meanings. Then write synonyms (words or word groups with similar meanings) for each word in your writing log or journal.
2. For the most part, Tan keeps her language straightforward and simple in her essay, an excerpt from a speech. Why is her word choice particularly appropriate for listeners as opposed to readers? What limitations does a speaker face that a writer does not?

Group Activities

1. In the twenty-first century, many minorities face language discrimination. There have been several attempts by states

to recognize English as the official language of American citizens. As a group, research articles debating both sides of such initiatives and then discuss the following questions: Why are some people in favor of a national language and others against it? Do you feel Tan would feel such initiatives are necessary or fair?

2. Review "My Mother's English," and note all passages where Tan's mother expresses herself. In the incident with the stockbroker, Tan claims her mother's English was more effective than Tan's own "proper" English. Compare the two Englishes, and discuss why Tan would make such a claim.

Writing Activities

1. Write a paragraph or so in which you explain the differences in the language you use with your family and friends. Which is more formal? Which includes more slang? If you feel you speak to family and friends exactly alike, write a topic sentence expressing as much and then support your controlling idea with some specific, representative examples.
2. In a brief paragraph or so, describe a situation where your use of the English language—whether it was "standard" or "broken"—played an important part in the way others perceived you.

Internet Connection: Amy Tan

Sexism, Racism, and Prejudgment

In "My Mother's English," Amy Tan examines and illustrates how, in many instances, society prejudged her mother due to her limited English speaking skills and her gender. Where else does sexism limit equal opportunity and respect in society? Pre-write on the topic of sexism to determine your point of view on this issue; then consult an online database and research "sexism in society" in particular. You might want to consider sexism in politics, sexism in the workplace, sexism in the movies, and so on. Next, write an essay wherein you support a thesis about sexism in American society by comparing and contrasting how men and women are or are not treated differently by virtue of their gender. Use specific examples drawn from personal experience, obstervations of others, and readings. (Cite specific sources using the MLA Stylesheet explained in the Appendix.)

CHAPTER 2

Narration

Long before written languages appeared, people told stories. The only way many cultures preserved their history was through stories passed down from generation to generation. In many cultures, the storyteller's position in society was second only to that of royalty. Chants, a form of storytelling, were so important to the Hawaiians that a chanter was put to death for missing even one word of a story. Today, we still enjoy hearing and telling stories but need not fear the fate of Hawaiian chanters. Whether we are sitting around a roaring fire telling jokes or ghost stories, recalling memorable moments (good or bad), or narrating a humorous happening, we are engaged in the process of narration. We tell stories for many reasons: to inform, to entertain, or to persuade. Regardless of purpose, narration has many common elements.

Common Elements of Narration

Creating Chronological Order

Most narratives have a chronological order; that is, the events are told in the sequence in which they occurred. To unify their essays and to help readers through them, authors frequently use *time transitions,* words such as *initially, next, in addition, once, finally,* and so on. These transitional devices, often called linking words, appear in strategic places in the essay, indicating the relationship between phrases, clauses, and entire paragraphs. In "Saigon, April 1975," Nguyen Ngoc Ngan uses transitional expressions such as "later," "after waiting," "the very next day," "first," and "then" in order to lead his reader through the things he did to survive when the Viet Cong took over South Vietnam.

Alma Luz Villanueva uses similar transitional expressions in her narrative, "Leaps of Faith," with phrases such as "during the time," "when I began," "about two weeks later," and "as I sit," in order to clearly indicate time order crucial to understanding and appreciating how fictional characters evolved out of her personal experiences.

Developing Character

In order to develop a character, you will want to use concrete nouns and active verbs whenever possible. Doing so will *show* your reader what the person is like through his or her actions. For example, in "The Offering of the Pipe," rather than telling readers that the Buffalo Woman is supernatural, Black Elk shows us by writing, "*And as she sang, there came from her mouth a white cloud that was good to smell.*" Similarly, Maxine Hong Kingston uses vividly descriptive words and phrases such as "*Wei saw his arrow sticking in a ball of flesh entirely covered with eyes, some rolled back to show the dulling whites*" to describe a ghost. Such passages may horrify, amuse, or inform the reader, but one thing is certain: They rarely will put the reader to sleep!

Establishing Mood and Tone

Often times, authors draw on sensory imagery and use concrete details to engage the reader's imagination, establishing mood and tone. In "Journey to Nine Miles," when Alice Walker writes, "*By five o'clock, we were awake, listening to the soothing slapping of the surf and watching the sky redden over the ocean,*" she appeals to the reader's senses of sight and sound to establish a colorful, sensual tone that pervades the essay. Similarly, Arthur C. Clarke's narrator creates tension—establishing mood and tone—in the first few sentences of "The Star," while providing readers with a clear sense of time and place: "*It is three thousand light-years to the Vatican. Once I believed that space could have no power over Faith.*

Just as I believed that the heavens declared the glory of God's handiwork. Now I have seen that handiwork, and my faith is sorely troubled."

Regardless of whether narratives are intended to inform, entertain, or persuade, they have been used by storytellers and writers for ages—and continue to be used—to engage their readers' imaginations. In the process, writers have manipulated the elements of character, imagery, and plot to achieve their goals.

Tips on Writing Narrative Essays

1. Determine the purpose of your narrative. Do you plan to inform, argue an issue, define something, or simply write an amusing account for your reader?
2. Ask yourself for whom you are writing this narrative. (Your audience will determine how you will approach your topic and what sort of language you will use.)
3. Freewrite, brainstorm, or cluster your topic using the five *W*s (who, what, where, when, and why) and *H* (how). Once you have decided upon a particular focus or controlling idea for your composition, write the idea in the form of a thesis statement and construct your introductory paragraph.
4. Use time transitions (first, second, third, then, also) to highlight chronological order and write out your entire narrative, referring to your thesis statement to ensure continuity.
5. Create mood and tone in your narrative by using concrete nouns and active verbs. During the revision stage of writing, add small descriptive details to appeal to your reader's five senses. Attempt to enable your reader to visualize everything you are recounting.
6. Before writing your final copy, have someone read your paper and tell you whether he or she felt like a participant—or an observer—at the event you described. An impartial reader can often point out areas in your paper where you have assumed too much reader knowledge or sections that require additional attention.

Maxine Hong Kingston

Ghosts

The daughter of Chinese immigrants, Maxine Hong Kingston was born in Stockton, California. Her articles and stories have appeared in publications such as *Ms.*, *The New York Times*, and *New West*. Kingston's books include *The Woman Warrior: Memoirs of a Girlhood among Ghosts* (1976), which won the National Book Critics Circle award; *China Men* (1981), winner of the American Book Award; *Tripmaster Monkey* (1990); *Hawaii One Summer* (1998); *To Be a Poet* (2002); and *The Fifth Book of Peace* (2003). More recently, Kingston edited *Veterans of War, Veterans of Peace* (2006), which has been described as "a harvest of creative, redemptive storytelling—nonfiction, fiction, and poetry—spanning five wars and written by those most profoundly affected by it." The following narrative was taken from *The Woman Warrior.*

Pre-reading Questions

1. What does the title, "Ghosts," lead you to expect in Kingston's story?
2. Brainstorm the word *ghosts* in small groups or as a class. Use the *W* and *H* questions (*who, what, when, where, why,* and *how*) to generate ideas.

---

1 When the thermometer in our laundry reached one hundred and eleven degrees on summer afternoons, either my mother or my father would say that it was time to tell another ghost story so that we could get some good chills up our backs. My parents, my brothers, sisters, great-uncle, and "Third Aunt," who wasn't really our aunt but a fellow villager, someone else's third aunt, kept the presses crashing and hissing and shouted out the stories. Those were our successful days, when so much laundry came in, my mother did not have to pick tomatoes. For breaks we changed from pressing to sorting.

2 "One twilight," my mother began, and already the chills travelled my back and crossed my shoulders; the hair rose at the nape and the back of the legs. "I was walking home after doctoring a sick family. To get home I had to cross a footbridge. In China the bridges are nothing like the ones in Brooklyn and San Francisco. This one was made from rope, laced and knotted as if by magpies. Actually it had been built by men who had returned after harvesting sea swallow nests in Malaya. They had had to swing over the faces of the Malayan cliffs in baskets they had woven themselves. Though this bridge pitched and swayed in the updraft, no one had ever fallen into the river, which looked like a bright scratch at the bottom of the canyon, as if the Queen of Heaven had swept her great silver hairpin across the earth as well as the sky."

3 One twilight, just as my mother stepped on the bridge, two smoky columns spiraled up taller than she. Their swaying tops hovered over her head like white cobras, one at either handrail. From stillness came a wind rushing between the smoke spindles. A high sound entered her temple bones. Through the twin whirlwinds she could see the sun and the river, the river twisting in circles, the trees upside down. The bridge moved like a ship, sickening. The earth dipped. She collapsed to the wooden slats, a ladder up the sky, her fingers so weak she could not grip the rungs. The wind dragged her hair behind her, then whipped it forward across her face. Suddenly the smoke spindles disappeared. The world righted itself, and she crossed to the other side. She looked back, but there was nothing there. She used the bridge often, but she did not encounter those ghosts again.

4 "They were Sit Dom Kuei," said Great-Uncle. "Sit Dom Kuei."

5 "Yes, of course," said my mother. "Sit Dom Kuei."

6 I keep looking in dictionaries under those syllables. "Kuei" means "ghost," but I don't find any other words that make sense. I only hear my great-uncle's river-pirate voice, the voice of a big man who had killed someone in New York or Cuba, make the sounds—"Sit Dom Kuei." How do they translate?

7 When the Communists issued their papers on techniques for combating ghosts, I looked for "Sit Dom Kuei." I have not found them described anywhere, although now I see that my mother won in ghost battle because she can eat anything—quick, pluck out the carp's eyes, one for Mother and one for Father. All heroes are bold toward food. In the research against ghost fear published by the Chinese Academy of Science is the story of a magistrate's servant, Kao Chung, a capable eater who in 1683 ate five cooked chickens and drank ten bottles of wine that belonged to the sea monster with branching teeth. The monster had arranged its food around a fire on the beach and started to feed when Kao Chung attacked. The swan-feather sword he wrested from this monster can be seen in the Wentung County Armory in Shantung today.

8 Another big eater was Chou Yi-han of Changchow, who fried a ghost. It was a meaty stick when he cut it up and cooked it. But before that it had been a woman out at night.

9 Chen Luan-feng, during the Yuan Ho era of the T'ang dynasty (A.D. 806–820), ate yellow croaker and pork together, which the thunder god had forbidden. But Chen wanted to incur thunderbolts during drought. The first time he ate, the thunder god jumped out of the sky, its legs like old trees. Chen chopped off the left one. The thunder god fell to the earth, and the villagers could see that it was a blue pig or bear with horns and fleshy wings. Chen leapt on it, prepared to chop its neck and bite its throat, but the villagers stopped him. After that, Chen lived apart as a rainmaker, neither relatives nor the monks willing to bring lightning upon themselves. He lived in a cave, and for years whenever there was drought the villagers asked him to eat yellow croaker and pork together, and he did.

10 The most fantastic eater of them all was Wei Pang, a scholar-hunter of the Ta Li era of the T'ang dynasty (A.D. 766–779). He shot and cooked rabbits and birds, but he could also eat scorpions, snakes, cockroaches, worms, slugs, beetles, and crickets. Once he spent the night in a house that had been abandoned because its inhabitants feared contamination from the dead man next door. A shining, twinkling sphere came flying through the darkness at Wei. He felled it with three true arrows—the first making the thing crackle and flame; the second dimming it; and the third putting out its lights, sputter. When his servant came running in with a lamp, Wei saw his arrows sticking in a ball of flesh entirely covered with eyes, some rolled back to show the dulling whites. He and the servant pulled out the arrows and cut up the ball into little pieces. The servant cooked the morsels in sesame oil, and the wonderful aroma made Wei laugh. They ate half, saving half to show the household, which would return now.

11 Big eaters win. When the other passers-by stepped around the bundle wrapped in white silk, the anonymous scholar of Hanchow took it home. Inside were three silver ingots and a froglike evil, which sat on the ingots. The scholar laughed at it and chased it off. That night two frogs the size of year-old babies appeared in his room. He clubbed them to death, cooked them, and ate them with white wine. The next night a dozen frogs, together the size of a pair of year-old babies, jumped from the ceiling. He ate all twelve for dinner. The third night thirty small frogs were sitting on his mat and staring at him with their frog eyes. He ate them too. Every night for a month smaller but more numerous frogs came so that he always had the same amount to eat. Soon his floor was like the healthy banks of a pond in spring when the tadpoles, having just turned, sprang in the wet grass. "Get a hedgehog to help eat," cried his family. "I'm as good as a hedgehog," the scholar said, laughing. And at the end of

the month the frogs stopped coming, leaving the scholar with the white silk and silver ingots.

Post-reading Questions

Content

1. Which image(s) do you find powerful or interesting in Kingston's essay? Why?
2. What does it mean to be heroic from Kingston's cultural perspective? How does this compare or contrast with America's perspective on heroism?
3. How and why did her mother defeat the ghost? How and why did other ghost warriors conquer ghosts?
4. Why does the author bring Chinese words into the story?

Strategies and Structures

1. Where do you imagine Kingston could have obtained the information on the different ghost warriors?
2. How does Kingston demonstrate what it takes to defeat a ghost?
3. How does Kingston arrange the examples of the ghost warriors?
4. Identify linking words Kingston uses to unify and lead the reader through the essay.
5. How does she illustrate what is required to be a ghost warrior?

Language and Vocabulary

1. Vocabulary: *spindle, whirlwind, croaker, pluck, sputter, anonymous, ingots.* Look up these words in your dictionary and write a ten-sentence paragraph about one of the words.
2. Kingston's language is descriptive. What "mental pictures" did or can you draw from this story? What words make her descriptions vivid?

Group Activities

1. Write a collaborative ghost story. As a group, decide what the plot of your story will be. Next, have each member of the group write consecutive paragraphs. Then link your paragraphs together carefully, using transitions. Finally, proofread your essays, eliminating mechanical and grammatical errors, and as a group, read the essay, making final corrections.
2. As a group, discuss the peculiar habits of ghosts or heroes in your culture just as Kingston narrates the peculiar eating habits of ghosts in her culture.

Writing Activities

1. Using specific examples, write a narrative essay in which you illustrate your definition of a fiercely independent person at odds with the world around him or her.
2. Narrate a ghost story that you remember hearing as a child.

Black Elk

The Offering of the Pipe

Born in 1863, Black Elk was a holy man (*wichash wakon*) of the Oglala Sioux. As a boy, he witnessed the Battle of the Little Big Horn in 1876 and the near-demise of his people. In *Black Elk Speaks* (1931), the source of the following narrative, he tells his life story—which he was instructed to do in a vision—to John G. Niehardt. Niehardt himself is the author of several books on the American West and Native Americans.

Pre-reading Questions

1. Black Elk, a holy man, makes offerings to nature. In your cultural tradition, who are the holy men or women who make similar offerings to *unseen* powers?
2. Freewrite in your journal about ceremonies and sacred offerings. Then read Black Elk's narrative.

---

1 *Black Elk Speaks:*

My friend, I am going to tell you the story of my life, as you wish; and if it were only the story of my life I think I would not tell it; for what is one man that he should make much of his winters, even when they bend him like a heavy snow? So many other men have lived and shall live that story, to be grass upon the hills.

2 It is the story of all life that is holy and is good to tell, and of us two-leggeds sharing in it with the four-leggeds and the wings of the air and all green things; for these are children of one mother and their father is one Spirit.

3 This, then, is not the tale of a great hunter or of a great warrior, or of a great traveler, although I have made much meat in my time and fought for my people both as boy and man, and have gone far and seen strange lands and men. So also have many others done, and better than I. These things I shall remember by the way, and often they may seem to be the very tale itself, as when I was living them in happiness and sorrow. But now that I can see it all as from a lonely hilltop, I know it was the story of a mighty vision given to a man too weak to use it; of a holy tree that should have flourished in a people's heart with flowers and singing birds, and now is withered; and of a people's dream that died in bloody snow.

4 But if the vision was true and mighty, as I know, it is true and mighty yet; for such things are of the spirit, and it is in the darkness of their eyes that men get lost.

5 So I know that it is a good thing I am going to do; and because no good thing can be done by any man alone, I will first make an offering and send a voice to the Spirit of the World, that it may help me to be true. See, I fill this sacred pipe with the bark of the red willow; but before we smoke it, you must see how it is made and what it means. These four ribbons hanging here on the stem are the four quarters of the universe. The black one is for the west where the thunder beings live to send us rain; the white one for the north, whence comes the great white cleansing wind; the red one for the east, whence springs the light and where the morning star lives to give men wisdom; the yellow for the south, whence come the summer and the power to grow.

6 But these four spirits are only one Spirit after all, and this eagle feather here is for that One, which is like a father, and also it is for the thoughts of men that should rise high as eagles do. Is not the sky a father and earth a mother, and are not all living things with feet or wings or roots their children? And this hide upon the mouthpiece here, which should be bison hide, is for the earth, from whence we came and at whose breast we suck as babies all our lives, along with all the animals and birds and trees and grasses. And because it means all this, and more than any man can understand, the pipe is holy.

7 There is a story about the way the pipe first came to us. A very long time ago, they say, two scouts were out looking for bison; and when they came to the top of a high hill and looked north, they saw something coming a long way off, and when it came closer they cried out, "It is a woman!," and it was. Then one of the scouts, being foolish, had bad thoughts and spoke them; but the other said: "That is a sacred woman; throw all bad thoughts away." When she came still closer, they saw that

she wore a fine white buckskin dress, that her hair was very long and that she was young and very beautiful. And she knew their thoughts and said in a voice that was like singing: "You do not know me, but if you want to do as you think, you may come." And the foolish one went; but just as he stood before her, there was a white cloud that came and covered them. And the beautiful young woman came out of the cloud, and when it blew away the foolish man was a skeleton covered with worms.

8 Then the woman spoke to the one who was not foolish: "You shall go home and tell your people that I am coming and that a big tepee shall be built for me in the center of the nation." And the man, who was very much afraid, went quickly and told the people, who did at once as they were told; and there around the big tepee they waited for the sacred woman. And after a while she came, very beautiful and singing, and as she went into the tepee this is what she sang:

With visible breath I am walking
A voice I am sending as I walk.
In a sacred manner I am walking.
With visible tracks I am walking.
In a sacred manner I walk.

And as she sang, there came from her mouth a white cloud that was good to smell. Then she gave something to the chief, and it was a pipe with a bison calf carved on one side to mean the earth that bears and feeds us, and with twelve eagle feathers hanging from the stem to mean the sky and the twelve moons, and these were tied with a grass that never breaks. "Behold!" she said. "With this you shall multiply and be a good nation. Nothing but good shall come from it. Only the hands of the good shall take care of it and the bad shall not even see it." Then she sang again and went out of the tepee; and as the people watched her going, suddenly it was a white bison galloping away and snorting, and soon it was gone.

9 This they tell, and whether it happened so or not I do not know; but if you think about it, you can see that it is true.

10 Now I light the pipe, and after I have offered it to the powers that are one Power, and sent forth a voice to them, we shall smoke together. Offering the mouthpiece first of all to the One above—so—I send a voice:

11 Hey hey! hey hey! hey hey! hey hey!

12 Grandfather, Great Spirit, you have been always, and before you no one has been. There is no other one to pray to but you. You yourself, everything that you see, everything has been made by you. The star nations all over the universe you have finished. The four quarters of the earth you have finished. The day, and in that day, everything you have finished. Grandfather, Great Spirit, lean close to the earth that you may hear the voice I send. You towards where the sun goes down, behold me; Thunder Beings, behold me! You where the White Giant lives in power, behold me!

You where the sun shines continually, whence come the day-break star and the day, behold me! You where the summer lives, behold me! You in the depth of the heavens, an eagle of power, behold! And you, Mother Earth, the only Mother, you who have shown mercy to your children!

13 Hear me, four quarters of the world—a relative I am! Give me the strength to walk the soft earth, a relative to all that is! Give me the eyes to see and the strength to understand, that I may be like you. With your power only can I face the winds.

14 Great Spirit, Great Spirit, my Grandfather, all over the earth the faces of living things are all alike. With tenderness have these come up out of the ground. Look upon these faces of children without number and with children in their arms, that they may face the winds and walk the good road to the day of quiet.

15 This is my prayer; hear me! The voice I have sent is weak, yet with earnestness I have sent it. Hear me!

16 It is finished. *Hetchetu aloh!*

17 Now, my friend, let us smoke together so that there may be only good between us.

Post-reading Questions

Content

1. In this essay, what is the purpose of smoking the sacred pipe?
2. What is the significance of the four ribbons on Black Elk's pipe?
3. Who is the young woman in the white buckskin dress? Why does she come to Black Elk's people?
4. To whom does Black Elk pray and why? What other spirits does he mention and why?

Strategies and Structures

1. In paragraph 7, why does Black Elk digress from his main narrative? What purpose does the story of the Buffalo Woman serve?
2. How does Black Elk explain the origins of the sacred pipe?
3. Why does Black Elk begin and conclude this narrative with the same ceremony? What effect does this have on the reader?

Language and Vocabulary

1. Vocabulary: *withered, cleansing, bison, skeleton, tepee, earnestness.* Check your dictionary for the meanings of these words; write two or three paragraphs wherein you first make up and then narrate an event in the life of a Native American using each of the following words from the list above—*withered, bison,* and *tepee*—at least twice.
2. What context clues suggest the meaning of *hetchetu aloh?*

Group Activities

1. In groups of four, pair off and take turns interviewing each other. Then write a brief profile of each member in your group.
2. Compare your freewritings on ceremonies and sacred offerings with others in your group. What did your freewritings have in common? How did they differ? Overall, how does your group assess the importance of ritual in modern life in America?

Writing Activities

1. Write a story explaining your origins. Who were your ancestors? What significant events can you recall during different stages of growing up?
2. Write a narrative essay wherein you start with some sort of ceremony, digress, and then conclude with the initial ceremony.

Alice Walker

Journey to Nine Miles

In 1944, Alice Walker was born in Eatonton, Georgia—the eighth child of African-American sharecroppers. Her works include *The Third Life of Grange Copeland* (1970), *Revolutionary Petunias* (1973), *Meridian* (1976), *You Can't Keep a Good Woman Down* (1981), *The Color Purple* (1983) for which she won the Pulitzer Prize for fiction, *Temple of My Familiar* (1989), *Her Blue Body Everything We Know: Earthling Poems*, 1965–1990 (1991), *Possessing the Secret of Joy* (1992), *The Same River Twice: Honoring the Difficult* (1996), *Anything We Love Can Be Saved* (1997), *Sent by Earth* (2001), *The Way Forward Is With a Broken Heart* (2001), *Absolute Trust in the Goodness of the Earth: New Poems* (2003), *Now Is the Time to Open Your Heart: A*

Novel (2004), and *We Are the Ones We Have Been Waiting for: Inner Light in a Time of Darkness* (2007). Walker's recent nonfiction includes *Overcoming Speechlessness: A Poet Encounters the Horror in Rwanda, Eastern Congo, and Palestine/Israel* (2010). In addition to her own work, Walker writes and lectures on African-American authors such as Zora Neal Hurston, Jean Toomer, and Langston Hughes—individuals who provided some of the models and inspiration for her own writing. Walker, who has always considered herself a "womanist," became a spokesperson for problems in African-American families (especially those dealing with gender inequities), began one of the first women's studies courses in the United States, and served as an editor for *Ms.* magazine. In the following essay, excerpted from her second collection of essays, *Living by the Word* (1989), Walker relates a journey to the Jamaican gravesite of reggae legend Bob Marley, a journey of cultural and spiritual significance.

Pre-reading Questions

1. In your culture, is there a tradition of visiting the gravesites of ancestors or respected persons? Why do you go? What purpose(s) does it serve?
2. What sorts of preparations do you make for such visitations?

---

1 By five o'clock we were awake, listening to the soothing slapping of the surf and watching the sky redden over the ocean. By six we were dressed and knocking on my daughter's door. She and her friend Kevin were going with us (Robert and me) to visit Nine Miles, the birthplace of someone we all loved, Bob Marley. It was Christmas Day, bright, sunny, and very warm, and the traditional day of thanksgiving for the birth of someone sacred.

2 I missed Bob Marley when his body was alive, and I have often wondered how that could possibly be. It happened, though, because when he was singing all over the world, I was living in Mississippi being political, digging into my own his/her story, writing books, having a baby—and listening to local music, B. B. King, and the Beatles. I liked dreadlocks, but only because I am an Aquarian; I was unwilling to look beyond the sexism of Rastafarianism. The music stayed outside my consciousness. It didn't help either that the most political and spiritual of reggae music was suppressed in the United States, so that "Stir It Up" and not "Natty Dread" or "Lively Up Yourself" or "Exodus" was what one heard. And then, of course, there *was* disco, a music so blatantly soulless as to be frightening, and impossible to do anything to but exercise.

3 I first really *heard* Bob Marley when I was writing a draft of the screenplay for *The Color Purple.* Each Monday I drove up to my studio in the country, a taxing three-hour drive, worked steadily until Friday, drove

back to the city, and tried to be two parents to my daughter on weekends. We kept in touch by phone during the week, and I had the impression that she was late for school every day and living on chocolates.

4 My friends Jan and Chris, a white couple nearby, seeing my stress, offered their help, which I accepted in the form of dinner at their house every night after a day's work on the script. One night, after yet another sumptuous meal, we pushed back the table and, in our frustration at the pain that rides on the seat next to joy in life (cancer, pollution, invasions, the bomb, etc.), began dancing to reggae records: UB-40, Black Uhuru . . . Bob Marley. I was transfixed. It was hard to believe the beauty of the soul I heard in "No Woman No Cry," "Coming In from the Cold," "Could You Be Loved," "Three Little Birds," and "Redemption Song." Here was a man who loved his roots (even after he'd been nearly assassinated in his own country) and knew they extended to the ends of the earth. Here was a soul who loved Jamaica and loved Jamaicans and loved *being* a Jamaican (nobody got more pleasure out of the history, myths, traditions, and language of Jamaica than Bob Marley), but who knew it was not meant to limit itself (or even could) to an island of any sort. Here was the radical peasant-class, working-class consciousness that fearlessly denounced the *wasichu* (the greedy and destructive) and did it with such grace you could dance to it. Here was a man of extraordinary sensitivity, political acumen, spiritual power, and sexual wildness; a free spirit if ever there was one. Here, I felt, was my brother. It was as if there had been a great and gorgeous light on all over the world, and somehow I'd missed it. Every night for the next two months I listened to Bob Marley. I danced with his spirit—so much more alive still than many people walking around. I felt my own dreadlocks begin to grow.

5 Over time, the draft of the script I was writing was finished. My evenings with my friends came to an end. My love of Marley spread easily over my family, and it was as neophyte Rastas (having decided that *Rasta* for us meant a commitment to a religion of attentiveness and joy) that we appeared when we visited Jamaica in 1984.

6 What we saw was a ravaged land, a place where people, often Rastas, eat out of garbage cans and where, one afternoon in a beach cafe during a rainstorm, I overheard a 13-year-old boy offer his 11-year-old sister (whose grown-up earrings looked larger, almost, than her face) to a large hirsute American white man (who blushingly declined) along with some Jamaican pot.

7 The car we rented (from a harried, hostile dealer who didn't even seem to want to tell us where to buy gas) had already had two flats. On the way to Nine Miles it had three more. Eventually, however, after an agonizing seven hours from Negril, where we were staying, blessing the car at every bump in the road to encourage it to live through the trip, we arrived.

8 Nine Miles (because it is nine miles from the nearest village of any size) is one of the most still and isolated spots on the face of the earth. It is only several houses, spread out around the top of a hill. There are small, poor farms, with bananas appearing to be the predominant crop.

9 Several men and many children come down the hill to meet our car. They know we've come to visit Bob. They walk with us up the hill where Bob Marley's body is entombed in a small mausoleum with stained-glass windows: the nicest building in Nine Miles. Next to it is a small one-room house where Bob and his wife, Rita, lived briefly during their marriage. I think of how much energy Bob Marley had to generate to project himself into the world beyond this materially impoverished place; and of how exhausted, in so many of his later photographs, he looked. On the other hand, it is easy to understand—listening to the deep stillness that makes a jet soaring overhead sound like the buzzing of a fly—why he wanted to be brought back to his home village, back to Nine Miles, to rest. We see the tomb from a distance of about 50 feet, because we cannot pass through (or climb over) an immense chain link fence that has recently been erected to keep the too eager (and apparently destructive and kleptomaniacal) tourists at bay. One thing that I like very much: built into the hill facing Bob's tomb is a permanent stage. On his birthday, February 6, someone tells us, people from all over the world come to Nine Miles to sing to him.

10 The villagers around us are obviously sorry about the fence. (Perhaps we were not the ones intended to be kept out?) Their faces seem to say as much. They are all men and boys. No women or girls among them. On a front porch below the hill I see some women and girls, studiously avoiding us.

11 One young man, the caretaker, tells us that though we can't come in, there is a way we can get closer to Bob. (I almost tell him I could hardly be any closer to Bob and still be alive, but I don't want to try to explain.) He points out a path that climbs the side of the hill and we—assisted by half a dozen of the more agile villagers—take it. It passes through bananas and weeds, flowers, past goats tethered out of the sun, past chickens. Past the home, one says, of Bob Marley's cousin, a broken but gallant-looking man in his 50s, nearly toothless, with a gentle and generous smile. He sits in his tiny, nearly bare house and watches us, his face radiant with the pride of relationship.

12 From within the compound now we hear singing. Bob's songs come from the lips of the caretaker, who says he and Bob were friends. That he loved Bob. Loved his music. He sings terribly. But perhaps this is only because he is, though about the age Bob would have been now, early 40s, lacking his front teeth. He is very dark and quite handsome, teeth or no. And it is his humble, terrible singing—as he moves proprietarily about

the yard where his friend is enshrined—that makes him so. It is as if he sings Bob's songs *for* Bob, in an attempt to animate the tomb. The little children are all about us, nearly underfoot. Beautiful children. One little boy is right beside me. He is about six, of browner skin than the rest—who are nearer to black—with curlier hair. He looks like Bob.

13 I ask his name. He tells me. I have since forgotten it. As we linger by the fence, our fingers touch. For a while we hold hands. I notice that over the door to the tomb someone has plastered a bumper sticker with the name of Rita Marley's latest album. It reads: "Good Girl's Culture." I am offended by it; there are so many possible meanings. For a moment I try to imagine the sticker plastered across Bob's forehead. It drops off immediately, washed away by his sweat (as he sings and dances in the shamanistic trance I so love) and his spirit's inability to be possessed by anyone other than itself (and Jah). The caretaker says Rita erected the fence. I understand the necessity.

14 Soon it is time to go. We clamber back down the hill to the car. On the way down the little boy who looks like Bob asks for money. Thinking of our hands together and how he is so like Bob must have been at his age, I don't want to give him money. But what else can I give him, I wonder.

15 I consult "the elders," the little band of adults who've gathered about us.

16 "The children are asking for money," I say. "What should we do?"

17 "You should give it," is the prompt reply. So swift and unstudied is the answer, in fact, that suddenly the question seems absurd.

18 "They ask because they have none. There is nothing here."

19 "Would Bob approve?" I ask. Then I think, "Probably. The man has had himself planted here to feed the village."

20 "Yes," is the reply. "Because he would understand."

21 Starting with the children, but by no means stopping there (because the grown-ups look as expectant as they), we part with some of our "tourist" dollars, realizing that tourism is a dead thing, a thing of the past; that no one can be a tourist anymore, and that, like Bob, all of us can find our deepest rest and most meaningful service at home.

22 It is a long hot anxious drive that we have ahead of us. We make our usual supplications to our little tin car and its four shiny tires. But even when we have another flat, bringing us to our fourth for the trip, it hardly touches us. Jamaica is a poor country reduced to selling its living and its dead while much of the world thinks of it as "real estate" and a great place to lie in the sun; but Jamaicans as a people have been seen in all their imperfections and beauty by one of their own, and fiercely sung, even from the grave, and loved. There is no poverty, only richness in this. We sing "Redemption Song" as we change the tire; feeling very Jamaica, very Bob, very Rasta, very *no woman no cry.*

Post-reading Questions

Content

1. Why did Walker "miss" Marley's music at first? What event put her in touch with it?
2. Where does her appreciation of Marley lead her and her family? What does she find at the end of her journey?
3. What does Walker learn about the Jamaican people and "Rasta" culture?
4. Walker claims that "Jamaica is a poor country reduced to selling its living and its dead. . . ." Is this much different than America or any other country? How? Why? Explain.

Strategies and Structures

1. Walker uses a "journey motif" to structure her essay. Why does she choose to use this motif? What does this symbolize?
2. What sorts of linking devices does Walker use? How do they allow the reader to follow her on the journey to Marley's grave?
3. What images or descriptions create a definite mood in this essay?
4. How does the tone at the end of Walker's essay (when she is changing her tire for the *fourth* time) compare with the beginning? What might her return from her journey suggest?

Language and Vocabularies

1. Vocabulary: *Aquarian, acumen, sumptuous, neophyte, hirsute, kleptomaniacal, shamanistic, expectant.* Find the definitions of these words and be prepared to discuss how Walker uses them as she moves through her essay. Since you may not have encountered many of these words before reading this selection, choose three or four of them and write at least three sentences for each.
2. How is the title of this essay, "Journey to Nine Miles," significant?

Group Activities

1. Go to the library and find the lyrics to a Bob Marley song. How does he use words? (Pay particular attention to syntax.) Then, as a group, rewrite (paraphrase) his song lyrics using a complete paragraph for each word group. What do his lyrics lose in translation?
2. As a group, visit a rest home for elderly people, and after your visit, write a collaborative narrative detailing your group's reaction to what you see. Did the visit depress you, or did you leave with a renewed outlook on life?

Writing Activities

1. Narrate a journey that you took to fulfill some significant purpose. How did it begin? What obstacle(s) did you have to overcome before reaching your ultimate destination?
2. Write about a nonphysical journey—mental or spiritual—that has greatly changed your way of thinking. Consider what you were like prior to your journey as well as after it.

***Internet Connection:* Alice Walker**

Pilgrimages

Pilgrimages have been made to honor people, places, and events for centuries. Reflect on some of the pilgrimages or journeys you generated in the pre-reading activity for Walker's essay. Then, research the people, places, and things related to pilgrimages and journeys that you brainstormed by entering key terms into any online database. Next, browse through three or four articles describing a pilgrimage, and write a detailed description or summary of each pilgrimage experience. How do those who go on pilgrimages compare with each other? Are expectations fulfilled? In what way were the pilgrimages you studied different than, yet similar to, Walker's? Is a person who returns home after a pilgrimage ever the same? Use the answers to these questions to generate a thesis on pilgrimages or journeys, and use several narrative anecdotes (a short personal account of an incident or event) to illustrate it.

Nguyen Ngoc Ngan

Saigon, April 1975

Nguyen Ngoc Ngan, a refugee from South Vietnam who now lives in Toronto, Canada, has written 25 novels and short stories—all of which are considered best sellers in the Vietnamese literary market. The following excerpt from the prologue to his first published book, the *Will of Heaven* (1979), details some of his experiences after the fall of South Vietnam to his escape to the free world.

Pre-reading Questions

1. What unavoidable conflict have you ever faced? Have you ever been powerless to do what you wanted or thought was best for others? How did you react?
2. What do you know about Saigon or Vietnam? Read the first two paragraphs and then, based upon your own knowledge of Vietnam and what you read, make a list in which you guess (speculate) what will happen next.

---

1 Early in the morning of April 29, 1975, I sat bolt upright in bed, awakened by the sudden explosions shaking predawn Saigon. I glanced with concern at my wife, Tuyet Lan, asleep beside me, and my one-year-old son, Tran, lying peacefully in his crib by the window. Then I raced to the roof.

2 Reddish glows pulsated in the darkness to the west, accompanied by the deep rumbling of artillery. The glows seemed to be coming from the general direction of Tan Son Nhut airport. I shuddered, for there I knew that thousands of Vietnamese had assembled for the American airlift. That throbbing brilliance seemed the final incinerating flash of an almost endless war. From it could come only the blackened cinder of my country's defeat.

3 I stared at the scene with an aching heart. Who would have thought that all our agonizing years of death and sacrifice would finally be reduced to simply a reddish glow in the darkened western sky? I turned, and with leaden steps descended the stairs.

4 When I returned to the bedroom, my wife was sitting on the edge of our bed.

5 "Where have you been? When I woke up from the noise and found you gone, I was frightened." She stared up at me, her dark eyes large and fearful.

6 "I've just been up on the roof, checking. Those shells are falling miles away," I tried to reassure her. "You might as well try to get some more rest. It's only twenty past four."

7 "No, Ngan," she said, shaking her head. "Let's talk, be honest with me now, don't treat me like a child. I have to know! It's almost over, isn't it? They're not going to negotiate, are they? The Viet Cong are going to come right in with their tanks and soldiers. There'll be fighting in the streets." Then there was stark fear in her voice. "They'll do the same thing here that they did at Hue."

8 Tuyet Lan was referring to the Hue horror of Tet, 1968. She had had relatives among the more than two thousand civilians in the Northern city of Hue who were forced to dig shallow trenches, then were lined up in front of them and shot in cold blood. That grisly recollection now filled her with terror. She clung to me, her body trembling with sobs.

9 I brushed the tears from Tuyet Lan's eyes and tried to comfort her. She stared up at me, her gentle eyes full of fear.

10 "Isn't it possible," she finally asked tremulously, "that we could get on one of the flights out of Tan Son Nhut? I know there are many leaving who don't have proper credentials."

11 "There are no more flights out of Tan Son Nhut, Tuyet Lan," I said gently. "That's where they're shelling now."

12 Tuyet Lan paled. "But there must be boats," she persisted. "Yes, we must try to get on a boat down at the harbor. There'll be some American ships out there somewhere. They'll pick us up."

13 I was surprised to hear these words. Only two days before when I had asked her whether we should leave the country she had had entirely different views. But at that time there had been much talk about a negotiated peace and that General Duong Van ("Big") Minh, appointed president only the day before, was the one person who could achieve it. Then Tuyet Lan had said, "The war has kept you away from me so much, Ngan! Now that peace is coming, why not stay here and enjoy our life together for a change? Certainly, there's no better place to be than in our own homeland."

14 I recalled those words now as my wife stood before me, pale and tense.

15 "There'll be plenty of American ships out there, Ngan," she repeated, looking up at me imploringly.

16 I gathered her again in a gentle embrace. "We can try, Tuyet Lan," I said softly. "We can try."

17 So later that morning Tuyet Lan and I said good-bye to our parents and soon, with Tran, became part of the seething mass of humanity we found milling around the waterfront. It seemed hopeless. Thousands and thousands of people were there ahead of us, trying to get aboard the few boats. After waiting for two hours and still finding ourselves on only the periphery of the crowd, we edged our way out of the growing throng and set out again on the motor scooter for the American Embassy. We had heard that helicopter flights were beginning to leave from there.

18 As we approached the embassy, we saw its fortress-like walls surrounded by a boundless sea of people. Coming closer, we could see no evidence of any helicopters, and, upon inquiring, learned that the flights had not yet begun. Reluctantly I admitted to myself that it would require

a miracle for the three of us ever to get past the huge, grim-faced Marines at the gates, and finally we headed back home.

19 As we passed now-deserted American installations, we saw Vietnamese leaving the buildings, bending under the heavy burdens of boxes of food and cases of beer and soft drinks. At long last, it seemed, American aid was finally reaching the people.

20 That night I lay sleepless, twisting the radio dial, trying to pick up the BBC or the Voice of America broadcasts. Lately I had begun to lose faith in the BBC because of their consistently premature announcements of the fall of cities to the north, which added to the general panic prevailing there. Now they were saying that the Viet Cong would occupy Saigon tomorrow. With the night alive with the stammering clatter of machinegun fire and the crash of distant shells, the BBC pronouncement was very believable indeed.

21 The very next day, April 30, 1975, the North Vietnamese Army, with disarming cries of *hoa binh* ("peace"), swept triumphantly into Saigon. The world as I had known it for twenty-eight years ended abruptly.

22 I rose apprehensively at six-fifteen and opened the side window of the living room. It was still a bit dark, but I was able to discern some figures lying in our small yard near the cassia shrub. I called out, "Who's there?"

23 "Please excuse us for trespassing," came a woman's polite voice out of the semidarkness, "but the grass looked so inviting. We're from Hoc Mon. The Viet Cong are already there. In fact, they are here in Saigon. We have been running from the fighting but there's no place now to run."

24 A few minutes later I heard a heavy rumble that seemed to be getting closer to the house. I ran out into the street and looked up and down in the hazy morning light. In the distance I could see a tank approaching, loaded with ARVN (our Army of the Republic of Vietnam) soldiers.

25 From the other direction I could hear the ominous roar of several approaching tanks and blasts from other guns. Russian T-54's! There was going to be a battle right on our street, I thought, running back inside. The refugees were right. The Viet Cong were here and in strength. I roused Tuyet Lan and Tran and a few minutes later we were on my motor scooter, fleeing the scene of probable confrontation.

26 Frantically hopeful, we once again approached the Saigon harbor, which had become a scene of chaos. Cars, motorcycles, and people were hopelessly snarled as thousands fought to get aboard the few boats. Ahead of us at the waterfront we could see a boat pulling out, loaded almost to sinking. The crowd surged forward, fighting to be first on the next boat, and there was a wild melee to get aboard. This scene repeated itself several times until there were no more boats.

27 A few people had begun to drift sadly away when the shelling began. There was screaming. Everyone panicked and ran wildly for cover, blindly trampling the fallen. I clutched Tuyet Lan tightly by the hand and fled with Tran in my arms, looking helplessly for a building that would afford some protection. We passed the Saigon market and the sprawled bodies of some shelling victims. Finally I came upon a school building, and, thrusting Tuyet Lan ahead of me, went inside. It was packed. We all huddled fearfully there, waiting for the roof to crash down on us. At least it would take a direct hit to kill us; we were safe from random shell fragments.

28 It was in that building, over a tiny radio, that we heard our president of three days, General Duong Van Minh, offer his unconditional surrender and order a cease-fire. Some people heaved sighs of relief; others wept. A few sat staring silently into space. Someone near me commented that, earlier that morning, Minh had appealed to his army to put an end to all hostilities, and had implored "our brothers of the provisional government" to do likewise.

29 "They're our 'brothers' now," said my neighbor, smiling bitterly. "They're no longer the 'murdering Viet Cong.'"

30 Tuyet Lan and I sat in stunned silence as the building began to empty. It had all happened so quickly, but still, I was filled with self-recrimination for having been so indecisive during the last few days. I should have been firmer with Tuyet Lan, I thought. We could probably have gotten on one of those flights out of Tan Son Nhut. And instead of giving up so easily yesterday and going home, we should have tried the port at Nha Be. Boats most surely were leaving from there. I had just not planned properly; I had waited too long. Even though I had anticipated this inevitable moment for the past few days, some small part of me had hoped right up to the end that somehow the United States would ultimately come to our rescue. How could they do otherwise? Who would have thought that after all these years they would let this happen?

31 With a start I suddenly realized that everyone had left the building. Tuyet Lan and I were sitting there alone. We got up and headed for home through streets now filled with a palpable sorrow. We passed gruesomely mutilated shell victims sprawled on the streets. People hurried by them with averted eyes.

32 "How terrible it is to die like that at the last moment of the war," I said. "Just as peace comes."

33 Tuyet Lan made no answer. She held tightly to my hand as we hurried along the saddened street. A soft, warm rain was falling. Once Tuyet Lan stumbled slightly, and as I reached out to steady her, I saw that her eyes were blinded by tears.

34 Discarded weapons—M-16 rifles, Colt .45 automatics, grenades, bayonets, cartridge clips—were scattered where our soldiers had dropped them in their rush to acquire the anonymity of civilian attire. More than the words I had just heard on the radio, they brought home to me the full realization that now the war was completely lost.

35 When we arrived at home about three-thirty that afternoon, my father anxiously met us at the door. "You didn't make it!" he exclaimed sadly. "You didn't get away."

36 There were tears in his eyes, and despite his words, I could tell that he was glad to see us back. Now he would not be lonely. His shoulders sagged and his deeply lined face was haggard. In just the past few days he'd grown much older than his sixty years. I asked him about the tank battle that had seemed imminent when we had fled early that morning. He said he thought that a small flurry of fighting had taken place a considerable distance down the street, but it had not amounted to much.

37 "*Troi oi* [Good heavens], Ngan!" he then said impatiently. "Everybody's burning things—you'd better get busy! Burn everything that might be incriminating. They'll be here soon with their questions, making their eternal lists."

38 I spent that evening collecting and burning anything that would connect me or my family with active support of the fallen regime. This may perhaps seem to be a less than courageous thing to do by some who have never had their own instincts for survival put to a severe test. But the vivid recollections of Hue in 1968, and entire families of military officers and civil servants being put to death, gave impetus to all our actions now.

39 First I burned all my uniforms. Then I searched through Tuyet Lan's photograph albums for pictures of me in uniform. What a flood of memories that brought forth. I stared in amused disbelief at the very first photograph I found. It was of me standing alone in front of the barracks at the Infantry Officer Training Academy in Thu Duc in 1970. How raw and youthful I looked in my ill-fitting uniform and short military-style haircut! And how naive I actually was, then, of the war and the political situation. Except for the Tet Offensive I had been virtually untouched by the war. There was another photograph of me with Tuyet Lan, snapped by one of my fellow cadets. I had to smile, seeing how skinny and solemn I looked. But how lovely and innocent was Tuyet Lan. I came to another that had been enlarged and put on display on the table in the living room. It showed me, looking very fierce and proud, receiving my officer's commission from the academy deputy commandant, a colonel who was later murdered by the Viet Cong when he answered his doorbell one evening in Thu Duc. I stared at these photographs of only a few years ago as though they belonged to another age, and then slowly dropped them into the flames.

Post-reading Questions

Content

1. What does Ngan describe in his narrative account? What unavoidable conflict is he forced to face? Why?
2. Why was the author angry at the BBC network? Explain why his anger was or was not justified, logical, and fair.
3. Why did the author say, "The world as I had known it for twenty-eight years ended abruptly"? What did he mean?

Strategies and Structures

1. How does the author's firsthand experience of the U.S. pullout of Vietnam strengthen this narrative?
2. What is the tone or mood in Nguyen's passage? What events foreshadow his sense of impending doom?
3. Go through the text and underline specific words and phrases you believe that the author uses to state a general point in a powerful, memorable manner. Include derogatory terms that force a reaction such as shock or indignation in a reader. How are such words effective in context?
4. What makes Nguyen's descriptions vivid and clear? What sort of details can you recall after reading this essay?

Language and Vocabulary

1. Vocabulary: *imminent, haggard, melee, palpable, incriminating, impetus, ominous, self-recrimination, triumphantly, disarming, provisional.* Most of these vocabulary words suggest power or powerlessness in one way or another. Which words indicate futility, and which words describe the impending military takeover, the source of panic among the South Vietnamese?
2. Go back through the essay and locate instances where the author uses images that suggest sadness. Using the author's images and your own, write a paragraph about a time in your life that was particularly sad.

Group Activities

1. War is usually not what one thinks it will be like. During a war, people are given license to kill other human beings, ideally clear of conscience because of their noble cause. However, once a war ends, the same people who were mortal enemies are expected to act humanely toward each other. As a group activity, discuss the problems that you would expect people to have when they are *ordered* to make friends with their enemies. What is the difference between being

told to become friends and having the right to choose one's own friends?

2. How does your image of Vietnam, possibly influenced by the news media and movies such as *Apocalypse Now, Full Metal Jacket, Platoon,* and *Good Morning, Vietnam,* differ from the picture Nguyen draws of Americans pulling out of Saigon and the Viet Cong moving into what would become Ho Chi Minh City? It might be a good idea to select a group leader for this exercise so that everyone has an opportunity to talk, question, and respond to each other in the time allotted for this activity.

Writing Activities

1. Write an essay wherein you rationalize or reason how the instinct to survive would allow you to do things you usually would consider cowardly, dishonest, degrading, or immoral.
2. Has there ever been a time in your life when you figuratively or literally destroyed symbols of your past hopes or beliefs in order to pursue a realistic future? Limit your focus, and write a narrative about the event.

Alma Luz Villanueva

Leaps of Faith

A multi-talented author, Alma Luz Villanueva has earned popular acclaim and numerous awards for her poetry, short stories, essays, and novels. Her poetry blends the personal and political, anchoring the abstract in the sensual world, revealing a belief in the power of language to connect us to the world, to each other, and to ourselves. Collections of her verse include *Blood Root* (1977), *Life Span* (1984), *La Chingada* (1985), *Planet, with Mother May I* (1994), *Desire* (1998), which was nominated for the Pulitzer Prize, *The VIDA* (2002), and *Soft Chaos* (2008). In 1994, the Latin American Writers Institute singled out *Planet*, a collection of her poetry, for its depth, sensitivity, and wit. Villanueva's fictional works include: *Weeping Woman: La Llorona and Other Stories* (1994), a collection of short stories; *The Ultraviolet Sky* (1988), a novel and American Book Award winner that is listed in *500 Great Books By Women*; *Naked Ladies* (1997), another novel, for which she received a PEN Oakland Award for Fiction; and *Luna's California Poppies* (2003), a novel in the form of a diary. Her next novel, *The Infrared Earth*, is currently in search of a publisher. In addition to writing, Ms. Villanueva does guest teaching and gives readings and presentations at colleges, universities, and literary events.

Pre-reading Questions

1. Brainstorm the word "faith," and then jot down your personal definition of it. How might "faith" be a source of power and creativity?
2. What do you associate with the phrase, "waking dream"? Describe a "waking dream" of your own or that of a friend or a relative.

---

1 Today, March 25, 1996, I'm back at the beach (a beautiful, clear day after high winds yesterday). The comet Hyakutake is passing overhead, only ten million miles away. They say the last time it passed this way was 18,400 years ago, during the time humans were crossing the then-glaciated Bering Strait into North America. Last night Jules (who's fifteen now) and I went outside to see it through the binoculars. As I stared at the comet, its wide splash of light tail, it seemed I could see it move. I imagine my (our) ancestors crossing the Bering Strait, the immense, most incredible leap of faith to push forward. I imagine they dreamt their destination. They *knew* this continent was here. I imagined myself, 18,400 years ago, standing on ice; ice behind me, ice in front of me. I shuddered. How amazing we are, we humans.

2 I handed the binoculars to Jules. We were silent. Later, his father, Wilfredo, would come home late from teaching his class. Jules and I moved to Santa Cruz, California, in the fall of 1984 to be with his father (my partner and husband). This took a comparatively tiny leap of faith, but here we are. We rediscovered each other, with new boundaries, new territory, with some familiar expectations we had to resist (possessiveness, male/female roles, old, but ingrained, patriarchal roles), or we'd lose the together, again. We still have to resist, of course, and create (dream) our paths separately, and trust they will continue to meet and converge.

3 Today I sit on the sand, facing a cliff with eucalyptus trees growing on the edge of it. The largest one has roots extending all the way down

the steep cliff: gnarled, twining, *exposed*. Its other roots extend into the ground behind it, *hidden*. This, I think, is the ongoing task of the writer, and as I look at this tree, I see it's not an awkward sight. Not at all. It affords me a view of its life. There's beauty and grace in that.

4 During the time I've lived here in Santa Cruz, I've written three novels, a short story collection, and two books of poetry. When I began my first novel, *The Ultraviolet Sky*, it was with blind panic and seizures of terror; another leap of faith. I'd told family and friends I was going to write a novel (I told myself I was going to write a novel), and so not to was to admit defeat. Failure. So, I wrote the first fifty pages blind (yet dreaming), my heart in my throat.

5 My main character, Rosa, was a painter, and I had plans for her (until page one hundred or so). One morning when I sat down to write I just couldn't. Not a thing. I had no link. To the novel, to the plot, to any of the characters, and especially not to Rosa. It was as though everything and everyone, in the novel's world, had died; they refused to speak to me, much less appear. Though Rosa's character had sprung from me, my life, I could already see what she looked like, and she didn't look like me or walk like me or talk like me. She looked, walked, talked like *herself*. That morning I couldn't even glimpse Rosa. She was dead, everything was dead. And I was absolutely devastated, to my surprise; this had never happened to me before. All I could do was mourn, though I told no one at this point. I assumed this was the end of novels for me.

6 About two weeks later I was in the shower listlessly washing my hair, feeling pretty damned depressed, as though my usual sense of purpose and will were absent. I was just washing my hair. Suddenly, large as life (more vividly than I'd ever seen her), Rosa strode, and I mean *strode*, right into me. It was electrifying, orgasmic.

7 Quickly, I towel-dried, found the notebook I'd hidden from view, a pen, and sat to write. Anything. I got a fix on Rosa; or rather she had a fix on me. There she was, looking right at me. Sternly. She had some things to say about *her life*, and she set me straight. About the number of children she had—one; I'd given her two. How she felt about her lover, her work, her friends, the painting *she* envisioned and had to create, the world, as she perceived it. On and on. I sat there and listened. To my character, Rosa.

8 And that's how the novel was written; that's how I was allowed to write the novel, by allowing Rosa, and all the other characters, to reveal themselves to me, bit by bit, in their own time, in their own voice. Yet the vision, the central theme, was mine, and that's what I had to stay true to while struggling with the truth of the characters. As I look back on it now (and forward to future novels), I see a kind of passion play of self and ego(s). Self (eternal, wise, knowing) and ego (temporary, innocent/guilty, learning).

9 I learned a lot. There was magic in the writing process for me, the usual terror and wonder. Many times I would dream an especially difficult sequence—an outline, a piece of dialogue, a character's presence—making it possible to continue with fluidity.

10 The next novel, *Naked Ladies*, wasn't quite as terrifying. The process was similar, but certainly not the same. Each novel, each short story, each poem takes that leap of faith—that I ask (from my deepest longing) and that I'll be answered (from an endless, mysterious source: creation).

11 When I teach I try to convey this process to my students. I attempt to teach writing (creation) as the waking dream, dreaming awake, transformation of energy into matter. Imagine: it's the faith of a woman who's just learned she's pregnant. She imagines the darkness of her womb, the size of her womb, so small. She imagines the tiniest creature, a seahorse-child, a spiral-shaped creature, nestled in her womb. Invaded. Penetrated. Chosen. Blessed. Cursed. Captured. She imagines her life, whether it's possible. To create (this child, this novel, this poem, this painting, this equation). She imagines its birth (form, words, color, song, the unknown face). And she leaps. She allows. She struggles. She dreams. Until it is complete. Unto itself.

12 And then she lets go. She will create again. She will love again. If her faith is intact. If she is willing to leap, again and again, into the unknown, the undiscovered, the uncreated source.

13 As I sit here in the sweet spring sun, I think of my daughter, Antoinette, now thirty-five and a critical care registered nurse, with two children of her own: Ashley, fourteen—born in the same year as Jules, and Cody, eleven. My grandchildren are intelligent, beautiful, and very humorous. My son Ed, now thirty-three, is a professional bike racer and also attends college. Marc, who's twenty-nine, teaches high school biology (and is track coach) in Boulder, Colorado, and is also a writer. And Jules (fifteen) is a handsome, sensitive, boy-man who also has a gift for writing, and he's a bodyboarder and a surfer. All of them continue to complete themselves, unto themselves. They are their own creations.

14 As I sit here, dolphins surface to breathe revealing their fins, their black, shiny bodies. I read that dolphins arrived in the Monterey Bay about ten years ago, about the time I did. Last summer when I was swimming I saw a flash of darkness in the water; I nearly screamed as I registered SHARK. Then, a silky, smooth body brushed alongside my own: a dolphin. It was like being brushed by a jolt of joy. At fifty-one, I can truly say that my joy outweighs my sorrow, and I'm *grateful* to know this.

15 As I sit here a group of teenagers with a small boy are building a fort with washed-up driftwood. I wonder if the boy is their son or brother (people often thought Antoinette was my sister). I can see the boy is

loved; the way they play with him, touch him, include him. And I think: Wherever there's love, there's innocence. There's a beautiful innocence about this group. I feast my eyes.

16 There's a juggler a few feet away. He's very good, juggling three, then four frisbees.

17 And then there's the world, beyond what I can see, but I can *feel* it: Bosnia, China, Africa, Tibet, Mexico, Nicaragua, Russia, Turkey, Korea, Cambodia, India . . . The Earth as we're faced with a new, uncreated century.

18 As I sit here I pray that innocence survives, that the Earth survives (us), that we survive (as compassionate human beings), that the juggler be truly skilled. And I pray (to the Goddess and the God) that I may write for the rest of this lifetime, and dream always.

19 I wrote this poem yesterday ("Dear World" is a series of poems I started two years ago):

March 24, 1996

Dear World,
18,400 years ago, this comet
we call (in 1996) Hyakutake,
came close to the Earth (10 million
miles away, 10 million), but we

can see it with the naked
eye, floating in the sky like
a tail of light. The last
time it came within 10 million

miles, humans were just crossing
the terrible, icy glaciers,
the Bering Strait, into this
land mass, North America, one

of the floating, enduring Turtles.
The Turtles whispered, "Leap of
faith, dream, leap of faith, dream,"
as the comet edged its way

10 million miles, so close. 18,400
years later, the Turtles whisper,
"Leap of faith, one planet, leap
of faith, one people." This planet

floating through the stars, comets
coming home to sing to the Turtles:
"Cross the terrible, icy glaciers,
the human heart, leap."

20 It's mid-April. I've completed typing this essay, the poems, into my word processor. On my desk are two photographs, close together, that catch my eye. I realize I've never looked at them together. One is a photo of my grandmother, Jesus, at eighteen or nineteen, sitting with a friend. They're sitting in chairs next to each other; a large, white, fur rug extends from the floor to the back of their chairs. My grandmother's friend strikes an intellectual pose, placing her left hand to the side of her face as though considering something important; the other's in her lap. My grandmother has her left hand in her lap, while her right hand caresses the soft, sensual fur. Her face is sensual, intuitive, beautiful, a little sad. She is my ancestor.

21 The other photo is of me at nineteen with four-year-old Antoinette. I can't see my hands, but I remember. They washed diapers and sheets by hand when the children (Antoinette and Ed) had measles one after the other for a month, and I couldn't go to the laundry. I imagine my right hand is curled around my daughter's soft, slightly chubby baby's leg, exposed because of her dress. My face is sensual, intuitive, beautiful, a little sad. I imagine my left hand rests nervously in my lap (with nothing to do). My daughter's head eclipses the right side of my face; the left side is just me at nineteen.

22 I had no idea I would ever really write (and publish). In fact, I often thought I might not even survive. But I did. And I realize, now, that to survive I had to be transformed (reborn). I had to die. I have to do this dying cyclically in order to be reborn (a small, green snake slithered in front of me on a trail yesterday, reminding me of this truth, my new skin). But first, one must learn to die.

23 I *am my ancestor*. Thanks to the nineteen-year-old (twenty, thirty, forty-year-old) woman I was, I am the fifty-one-year-old woman I am now. Thanks to the dead and the living I have known (and not known), I am able to write these words. I write to remember the dead, all that is no more. I write to remember to love, all that yearns to be. Created.

Post-reading Questions

Content

1. Explain the significance of Villanueva's essay title, "Leaps of Faith."
2. Villanueva describes many leaps of faith in the course of her essay, beginning with her reference to the last time the Hyakutake comet passed Earth 18,400 years ago when the first humans crossed the Bering Strait. What do her observations show readers about human nature?
3. What does Villanueva consider to be the "ongoing task of a writer"?

4. Why does Villanueva teach writing as a "waking dream"? What extended comparison does she use to illustrate the creative process in paragraphs 11 through 13?
5. Who was Rosa? How did Villanueva get a "fix" on her? Explain the significance of the "encounter" between the two women—one fictional, one flesh and blood.

Strategies and Structures

1. Describe the tone of this essay. How does it complement Villanueva's subject matter?
2. How does the author's use of concrete nouns and active verbs make her narrative discussion vivid and clear? In what way does she enable readers to picture what she speaks about through her word choice?
3. Villanueva mentions her children at different stages in their lives throughout her essay. What might be her strategic purpose for doing this?
4. In what way does Villanueva's poem, dated March 24, 1996 and titled "Dear World," capture the essence—the entire mood, spirit, and point—of her essay?
5. How does the final paragraph in the essay, beginning with "I am my ancestor," relate back to the opening paragraph? How was Villanueva reborn?

Language and Vocabulary

1. Vocabulary: *glaciated, binoculars, ingrained, patriarchal, converge, seizures, devastated, orgasmic, envisioned, transformation, eclipses.* After checking definitions for the words, write a paragraph using at least five of them to describe the cause and/or effect of some sort of change.
2. What words used by Villanueva indicate the "leaps of faith" and the magical experiences she talks of throughout the essay?

Group Activities

1. In a small group, revisit how and why "there was magic in the writing process" for Villanueva. Consider, for instance, how the character of Rosa from *The Ultraviolet Sky* became dead to her, figuratively speaking, only to be reborn.
2. Individually, highlight all transitional words and linking devices that enable Villanueva to move from sentence to sentence, from paragraph to paragraph, with clarity and cohesiveness. Then, divide into groups and make an exhaustive collaborative list of connecting words in "Leaps of Faith." Next, read her essay out loud *omitting*

all highlighted words. How did the relationship between words, clauses, sentences, and paragraphs change? Briefly jot down your group's insight into the function of transitions and linking words based on your collaborative observations.

Writing Activities

1. Write an essay wherein you reflect upon, describe, and analyze special moments or experiences you would label as "leaps of faith" in your lifetime.
2. Compose an essay that uses a spin-off of the phrase "There was magic in the writing process" as your thesis statement. For instance, your thesis might be "There is magic in the process of making music," "There is magic in the process of earning money," or "There is magic in the process of painting pictures."

Arthur C. Clarke

The Star

Sir Arthur C. Clarke, one of the master science fiction writers of the twentieth century, achieved immense popularity for his famous movie, *2001: A Space Odyssey,* in 1968. Not only are over 20 million books in print, but also he won every science fiction award imaginable, among them the Science Fiction Writers of America Grand Master Award for Life Achievement in 1986. In addition to recognition of his literary talents, Sir Arthur, a former radar officer in the Royal Air Force, was nominated for the Nobel Peace Prize for his invention of the communications satellite, and Queen Elizabeth knighted him in 1998 for Services to Literature. Following is a partial list of his works of fiction: *Prelude to Space* (1951), *The Sands of Mars* (1951), *Islands in the Sky* (1952), *Against the Fall of Night* (1953), *Childhood's End* (1953), *Expedition to*

Earth (1953), *Earthlight* (1955), *Reach for Tomorrow* (1956), *The City and the Stars* (1956), *Tales from the White Hart* (1957), *The Deep Range* (1957), *Across the Sea of Stars* (1959), *A Fall of Moondust* (1961), *From the Ocean, From the Stars* (1962), *A Tales of Ten Worlds* (1962), *Dolphin Island* (1963), *Glide Path* (1963), *An Arthur C. Clarke Omnibus* (1965), *Prelude to Mars* (1965), *The Nine Billion Names of God* (1967), *2001: A Space Odyssey* (1968), *An Arthur C. Clarke Second Omnibus* (1968), *The Lion of Comarre & Against the Fall of Night* (1968), *Of Time and Stars* (1972), *The Wind from the Sun* (1972), *Rendezvous with Rama* (1973), *The Best of Arthur C. Clarke* (1973), *Imperial Earth* (1975), *Four Great SF Novels* (1978), *The Fountains of Paradise* (1979), *2010: Odyssey Two* (1982), *The Sentinel* (1983), *The Songs of Distant Earth* (1986), *2061: Odyssey Three* (1988), *A Meeting With Medusa* (1988), *Tales From Planet Earth* (1990), *The Ghost from the Grand Banks* (1990), *More Than One Universe* (1991), *3001: The Final Odyssey* (1997), *The Collected Stories of Arthur C. Clarke* (2000), and *Sunstorm* (2005)—co-authored with Stephen Baxter. He lived on Sri Lanka for over 33 years, survived the 2004 tsunamis, but passed away at 90 years old on March 18, 2008, leaving specific instructions that, "Absolutely no religious rites of any kind, relating to any religious faith, should be associated with my funeral." Though gone, Clarke remains one of the most prolific science fiction writers ever. The following short story, "The Star," initially appeared in *Infinity Science Fiction* in 1955 and was reprinted in *The Other Side of the Sky*, a collection of his works, in 1958.

Pre-reading Questions

1. Before you read Clarke's story, research two names—Peter Paul Rubens and Ignatius Loyola—online or in your college library. Jot down some notes about Loyola in particular, and then write a one paragraph biographical sketch about him.
2. Have you or anyone you know ever held a belief in someone or something only to become disillusioned and question your faith due to a particular situation or event? Explain.
3. Freewrite about "outer space," jotting down whatever comes to mind on the topic. You might want to consider impressions of "outer space" gleaned from movies, television, and any science fiction you have read.

---

1 It is three thousand light-years to the Vatican. Once I believed that space could have no power over Faith. Just as I believed that the heavens declared the glory of God's handiwork. Now I have seen that handiwork, and my faith is sorely troubled.

2 I stare at the crucifix that hangs on the cabin wall above the Mark VI computer, and for the first time in my life I wonder if it is no more than an empty symbol.

3 I have told no one yet, but the truth cannot be concealed. The data are there for anyone to read, recorded on the countless miles of magnetic tape and the thousands of photographs we are carrying back to Earth. Other scientists can interpret them as easily as I can—more easily, in all probability. I am not one who would condone that tampering with the Truth which often gave my Order a bad name in the olden days.

4 The crew is already sufficiently depressed; I wonder how they will take this ultimate irony. Few of them have any religious faith, yet they will not relish using this final weapon in their campaign against me—that private, good-natured but fundamentally serious war which lasted all the way from Earth. It amused them to have a Jesuit as chief astrophysicist: Dr. Chandler, for instance, could never get over it (why are medical men such notorious atheists?). Sometimes he would meet me on the observation deck, where the lights are always low so that the stars shine with undiminished glory. He would come up to me in the gloom and stand staring out of the great oval port, while the heavens crawled slowly round us as the ship turned end over end with the residual spin we had never bothered to correct.

5 It was, I think, the apparent incongruity of my position which . . . yes, *amused* . . . the crew. In vain I would point to my three papers in the *Astrophysical Journal,* my five in the *Monthly Notices of the Royal Astronomical Society.* I would remind them that our Order has long been famous for its scientific works. We may be few now, but ever since the eighteenth century we have made contributions to astronomy and geophysics out of all proportion to our numbers.

6 Will my report on the Phoenix Nebula end our thousand years of history? It will end, I fear, much more than that.

7 I do not know who gave the Nebula its name, which seems to me a very bad one. If it contains a prophecy, it is one which cannot be verified for several thousand million years. Even the word nebula is misleading: this is a far smaller object than those stupendous clouds of mist—the stuff of unborn stars—which are scattered throughout the length of the Milky Way. On the cosmic scale, indeed, the Phoenix Nebula is a tiny thing—a tenuous shell of gas surrounding a single star.

8 Or what is left of a star . . .

9 The "Rubens engraving of Loyola" seems to mock me as it hangs there above the spectrophotometer tracings. What would *you,* Father, have made of this knowledge that has come into my keeping, so far from the little world that was all the universe you knew? Would your faith have risen to the challenge, as mine has failed to do?

10 You gaze into the distance, Father, but I have traveled a distance beyond any that you could have imagined when you founded our Order a thousand years ago. No other survey ship has been so far from Earth: we are at the very frontiers of the explored universe. We set out to reach

the Phoenix Nebula, we succeeded, and we are homeward bound with our burden of knowledge. I wish I could lift that burden from my shoulders, but I call to you in vain across the centuries and the light-years that lie between us.

11 On the book you are holding the words are plain to read. AD MAIOREM DEI GLORIAM the message runs, but it is a message I can no longer believe. Would you still believe it, if you could see what we have found?

12 We knew, of course, what the Phoenix Nebula was. Every year, in *our* galaxy alone, more than a hundred stars explode, blazing for a few hours or days with thousands of times their normal brilliance before they sink back into death and obscurity. Such are the ordinary novae—the commonplace disasters of the universe. I have recorded the spectrograms and light-curves of dozens, since I started working at the lunar observatory.

13 But three or four times in every thousand years occurs something beside which even a nova pales into total insignificance.

14 When a star becomes a *supernova,* it may for a little while outshine all the massed suns of the galaxy. The Chinese astronomers watched this happen in 1054 a.d., not knowing what it was they saw. Five centuries later, in 1572, a supernova blazed in Cassiopeia so brilliantly that it was visible in the daylight sky. There have been three more in the thousand years that have passed since then.

15 Our mission was to visit the remnants of such a catastrophe, to reconstruct the events that led up to it, and, if possible, to learn its cause. We came slowly in through the concentric shells of gas that had been blasted out six thousand years before, yet were expanding still. They were immensely hot, radiating still a fierce violet light, but far too tenuous to do us any damage. When the star had exploded, *its* outer layers had been driven upwards with such speed that they had escaped completely from *its* gravitational field. Now they formed a hollow shell large enough to engulf a thousand solar systems, and at *its* center burned the tiny, fantastic object which the star had now become—a white dwarf, smaller than the Earth yet weighing a million times as much.

16 The glowing gas shells were all around us, banishing the normal night of interstellar space. We were flying into the center of a cosmic bomb that had detonated millennia ago and whose incandescent fragments were still hurtling apart. The immense scale of the explosion, and the fact that the debris already covered a volume of space many billions of miles across, robbed the scene of any visible movement. It would take decades before the unaided eye could detect any motion in these tortured wisps and eddies of gas, yet the sense of turbulent expansion was overwhelming.

17 We had checked our primary drive hours before, and were drifting slowly towards the fierce little star ahead. Once it had been a sun like our

own, but it had squandered in a few hours the energy that should have kept it shining for a million years. Now it was a shrunken miser, hoarding its resources as if to make amends for its prodigal youth.

18 No one seriously expected to find planets. If there had been any before the explosion, they would have been boiled into puffs of vapor, and their substance lost in the greater wreckage of the star itself. But we made the automatic search, as always when approaching an unknown sun, and presently we found a single small world circling the star at an immense distance. It must have been the Pluto of this vanished solar system, orbiting on the frontiers of the night. Too far from the central sun ever to have known life, its remoteness had saved it from the fate of all its lost companions.

19 The passing fires had seared its rocks and burnt away the mantle of frozen gas that must have covered it in the days before the disaster. We landed, and we found the Vault.

20 Its builders had made sure that we should. The monolithic marker that stood above the entrance was now a fused stump, but even the first long-range photographs told us that here was the work of intelligence. A little later we detected the continent-wide pattern of radioactivity that had been buried in the rock. Even if the pylon above the Vault had been destroyed, this would have remained, an immovable and all but eternal beacon calling to the stars. Our ship fell towards this gigantic bull's-eye like an arrow into its target.

21 The pylon must have been a mile high when it was built, but now it looked like a candle that had melted down into a puddle of wax. It took us a week to drill through the fused rock, since we did not have the proper tools for a task like this. We were astronomers, not archaeologists, but we could improvise. Our original program was forgotten: this lonely monument, reared at such labor at the greatest possible distance from the doomed sun, could have only one meaning. A civilization which knew it was about to die had made its last bid for immortality.

22 It will take us generations to examine all the treasures that were placed in the Vault. *They* had plenty of time to prepare, for their sun must have given its first warnings many years before the final detonation. Everything that they wished to preserve, all the fruits of their genius, they brought here to this distant world in the days before the end, hoping that some other race would find them and that they would not be utterly forgotten.

23 If only they had had a little more time! They could travel freely enough between the planets of their own sun, but they had not yet learned to cross the interstellar gulfs, and the nearest solar system was a hundred light-years away.

24 Even if they had not been disturbingly human as their sculpture shows, we could not have helped admiring them and grieving for their fate. They

left thousands of visual records and the machines for projecting them, together with elaborate pictorial instructions from which it will not be difficult to learn their written language. We have examined many of these records, and brought to life for the first time in six thousand years the warmth and beauty of a civilization which in many ways must have been superior to our own. Perhaps they only showed us the best, and one can hardly blame them. But their worlds were very lovely, and their cities were built with a grace that matches anything of ours. We have watched them at work and play, and listened to their musical speech sounding across the centuries. One scene is still before my eyes—a group of children on a beach of strange blue sand, playing in the waves as children play on Earth.

25 And sinking into the sea, still warm and friendly and life-giving, is the sun that will soon turn traitor and obliterate all this innocent happiness.

26 Perhaps if we had not been so far from home and so vulnerable to loneliness, we should not have been so deeply moved. Many of us had seen the ruins of ancient civilizations on other worlds, but they had never affected us so profoundly.

27 This tragedy was unique. It was one thing for a race to fail and die, as nations and cultures have done on Earth. But to be destroyed so completely in the flower of its achievement, leaving no survivors—how could that be reconciled with the mercy of God?

28 My colleagues have asked me that, and I have given what answers I can. (Perhaps you could have done better, Father Loyola, but I have found nothing in the *Exercitia Spiritualia* that helps me here.) They were not an evil people: I do not know what gods they worshipped, if indeed they worshipped any. But I have looked back at them across the centuries, and have watched while the loveliness they used their last strength to preserve was brought forth again into the light of their shrunken sun.

29 I know the answers that my colleagues will give when they get back to Earth. They will say that the universe has no purpose and no plan, that since a hundred suns explode every year in our galaxy, at this very moment some race is dying in the depths of space. Whether that race has done good or evil during its lifetime will make no difference in the end: there is no divine justice, *for there is no God.*

30 Yet, of course, what we have seen proves nothing of the sort. Anyone who argues thus is being swayed by emotion, not logic. God has no need to justify His actions to man. He who built the universe can destroy it when He chooses. It is arrogance—it is perilously near blasphemy—for us to say what He may not do.

31 This I could have accepted, hard though it is to look upon whole worlds and peoples thrown into the furnace. But there comes a point when even the deepest faith must falter, and now, as I look at my calculations, I know I have reached that point at last.

32 We could not tell, before we reached the nebula, how long ago the explosion took place. Now, from the astronomical evidence and the record in the rocks of that one surviving planet, I have been able to date it very exactly. I know what year the light of this colossal conflagration reached Earth. I know how brilliantly the supernova whose corpse now dwindles behind our speeding once shone in terrestrial skies. I know how it must have blazed low in the East before sunrise, like a beacon in that Oriental dawn.

33 There can be no reasonable doubt: the ancient mystery is solved at last. Yet—O God, there were so many stars you *could* have used.

34 What was the need to give these people to the fire that the symbol of their passing might shine above Bethlehem?

Post-reading Questions

Content

1. Who is the central narrator of "The Star," and what is his mission?
2. What do the narrator and the rest of the starship's crew discover on the only planet orbiting the remains of a supernova?
3. Why is the Jesuit astrophysicist disturbed by the conclusions he draws about the Star of Bethlehem? Would others with a different worldview have the same reaction? What does the priest's reaction tell you (as the reader) about the sensitivity of humans to an indifferent universe?
4. Although the narrator has learned that the supernova that destroyed the alien civilization was the Star of Bethlehem, he does not communicate the information to others. Why?
5. When people point to the incongruity of the Jesuit narrator's position as an astrophysicist, where does he direct them? What concerns him about his forthcoming report on the Phoenix Nebula?

Strategies and Structures

1. Explain how the narrator's early comments in "The Star" foreshadow the discovery that he reveals throughout the rest of the story.
2. In what way might Clarke's story demonstrate the "Voyage of the Hero" (departure, initiation, and return)?
3. How does the narrator's reference to several Latin writings remind readers of his Jesuit roots?
4. Explain the strategic purpose for the narrator's dialogue with a Ruben's engraving of Father Loyola, founder of the Jesuit Order. Why might such a dialogue present the narrator with an ideal opportunity to evenhandedly assess his religious beliefs on one hand and scientific knowledge on the other?

5. How do explanations of some of the scientific terms such as "supernova" that Clarke mentions promote clarity, understanding, and appreciation of his scientific and religious dilemma—a situation where he feels compelled to choose from one of two unsatisfactory alternatives?

Language and Vocabulary

1. Vocabulary: *Vatican, crucifix, Jesuit, astrophysicist, notorious, atheist, astronomical, Phoenix, nebula, stupendous, galaxy, novae, supernova, Cassiopeia, tenuous, white dwarf, detonated, millennia, incandescent, turbulent, monolithic, pylon, gigantic, archaeologists, interstellar, pictorial, vulnerable, profoundly, reconciled, arrogance, perilously, blasphemy, colossal, conflagration.* Although Clarke provides many explanations of scientific terms in context, he does not always define them. Select all scientific words from the above list and provide (1) a definition, and (2) an example of the correct use of the word in an original sentence or a paraphrase of a sentence in "The Star."
2. Make a table with three columns and label the first column "Science," the second column "Religion," and the third column "Nouns, Adjectives, Adverbs." Go through all the words from the above list, and place each word under the appropriate heading. Add "Loyola," "Order" and "Truth" (note—both of the last two are capitalized, suggesting importance or truth as prescribed by religious doctrine), and the Latin titles, *Ad Maiorem Dei Gloriam* (*"To the Greater Glory of God"*) and *Exercitia Spiritualia* (*Spiritual Exercises*—Father Loyola's major work) to your "Religious" words list. How does your final list reflect the balance between faith and science in the narrator's mind prior to his discovery about the doomed civilization?

Group Assignments

1. Have small groups brainstorm various situations where people may find themselves confronting discomfort because what they choose to believe seems at odds with verifiable facts. Then, select two situations on your list and fully discuss the emotional appeal of a belief versus the logical appeal of a verifiable fact. Is a belief more satisfying than a fact or vice-versa? Arrive at some sort of conclusion for each situation your group discusses.
2. In groups of four students or so, examine each paragraph in Clarke's story, and search for lines revealing reasons for the narrator's crisis of faith. Pay particular attention to Clarke's historical references and consider why he uses so many of

them. Assign a recorder to keep track of group findings and finally, in an open class discussion, have each group share what the members located.

Writing Assignments

1. Write a narrative essay in the same manner as Arthur C. Clarke. That is, have your narrative voice address an object or absent person and discuss how something you have experienced socially, educationally, religiously, and so on created a crisis of faith (e.g., faith in the justice system, nonprofit organizations, political parties, religious cults, global charities).
2. As a creative assignment, write a narrative essay from the point of view of one of the crew members on the same starship as the Jesuit astrophysicist. Have him or her address the story's narrator in the same manner that he had addressed Father Loyola. Therein, you might address the crew member's loneliness, something that only increases upon finding a highly intelligent, advanced civilization unable to solve its problems—including the impending doom of the planet—through science and technology. Here you might have your narrator focus on his or her crisis of faith in science for answers.

Internet Connection: Arthur C. Clarke

Crisis of Faith/Science

Locate several creation myths and at least two scientific creation theories on the Internet and print them out. Begin by first entering the key words "creation myths" into a search engine. A great variety of free databases—such as the one in your college library—allow you to access and download full text files. After gathering and printing out materials, enter at least two other key words explaining creation from a scientific perspective (e.g., the big bang theory, or the string theory). Create a *list of works cited* for at least ten of the entries. Where might belief in a religious myth (a myth is a metaphor for the unknown) overlap with a scientific explanation for creation?

Additional Topics and Issues for Narrative Essays

1. Write a short narrative essay about the culture shock you encountered after moving from one neighborhood or country to another.
2. Compose an essay about a time in your life when you gave in to peer pressure rather than sticking to your personal convictions.
3. As closely as you can remember, narrate a story one of your parents used to tell you about his or her life. To frame your composition, provide your reader with the reasons or occasions when your mother or father would tell you the story. Then, relate the story and conclude with your present perceptions about such moments with your parent(s).
4. Write a narrative about a person you met on a bus, plane, train, elevator, etc., who began to talk to you like an intimate friend. Describe the person. How did you react to him or her? Did you try to ignore the person? What was his or her response to what you did or said? What conclusions can you draw about such people?
5. Discuss a situation or event that taught you a valuable lesson about life or survival in America.
6. Write a personal narrative recounting a typical holiday meal with your family. What takes place before, during, and after the meal? It may be helpful to narrow your focus to a specific holiday such as Thanksgiving, New Year's, Hanukkah, Eid Al-Fitr, or Christmas.
7. Compose a narrative essay based on a social function or a sporting event in which you participated during the past year. Make sure you mention what your expectations were before the event as well as your feelings after it.
8. Write a humorous account of a recent concert, play, nightclub act, or sporting event that you attended. Your humor should reflect your attitude toward your subject matter (the event).
9. Write a narrative essay about a trip you made outside of or coming to the United States. Begin your narrative from your point of departure, highlighting significant points of your trip. Conclude your essay with some reflective thoughts about the trip. What did you like about it? Would

you go again? Would you recommend that someone else make the trip?

10. Look through the photographs of the authors in the Narration chapter, read their bylines, and select one author in particular to investigate in greater detail. Next, go to the Internet and locate the author's website, read his or her biography, and digest the material. Finally, compose a brief biography of your own about the author, narrating significant events and publications in his or her life.

CHAPTER 3 Description

Although many college readers include description in their narration chapter, we feel that the rhetorical strategy of description is worthy of consideration in its own right. To be sure, there is frequently a narrative element in descriptive compositions. You need only read Maya Angelou's "Champion of the World" (about Joe Louis defending his heavyweight title) or John Steinbeck's "The Snake" (about the mysterious woman who buys a snake, asks that Dr. Phillips feed it, and yet disappears from his life) to realize how narration and description tend to overlap, producing a visual picture of an event.

Details: Appealing to the Five Senses

What makes an essay memorable? How do specific details engage one's imagination and enable writers to vividly convey a setting, a person, an object, or a situation in general? One of the most effective strategies authors employ to accomplish such ends is to appeal to the five senses: *sight, sound, taste, touch,* and *smell*. Using such an appeal to sight, sound, and touch, N. Scott Momaday describes Rainy Mountain in the following way:

> *Winter brings blizzards, hot tornadic winds arise in the spring, and in the summer the prairie is an anvil's edge. The grass turns brittle and brown and it cracks beneath your feet. There are green belts along the rivers and creeks, linear groves of hickory and pecan, willow and witch hazel. At a distance in July or August the steaming foliage seems almost to writhe in fire. Great green and yellow grasshoppers are everywhere in the tall grass, popping up with the corn to sting the flesh, and tortoises crawl about on the red earth, going nowhere in plenty of time.*

In "Salvation," to capture the mood of his Auntee Reed's church at a revival meeting, Langston Hughes depicts the sights and sounds around him as he steps forward to get saved from sin: *"A great many old people came and knelt around us and prayed, old women with jet-black faces and braided hair, old men with work-gnarled hands. And the church sang a song about the lower lights are burning, some poor sinners to be saved. And the whole building rocked with prayer and song."*

Likewise, John Steinbeck appeals to his readers' senses of sight and sound in "The Snake" with descriptive passages such as: *"He got up and walked to the case by the window. On the sand bottom the knot of rattlesnakes lay entwined, but their heads were clear. The tongues came out and flickered a moment and then waived up and down feeling the air for vibrations. Dr. Phillips nervously turned his head. The woman was standing beside him. He had not heard her get up from the chair. He heard only the splash of water among the piles and the scampering of the rats on the wire screen."*

Katherine Barrett combines sight, sound, and touch in "Old Before Her Time," when she writes, *"She saw only a blur of sneakers and blue jeans, heard the sounds of mocking laughter, felt the fists pummeling her—on her back, her legs, her breasts, her stomach."* Capitalizing on our natural ability to see, to smell, to hear, to feel, and to taste when we compose an essay allows us to write more creatively and make what we say easy to picture.

Figurative Language: Appealing to the Imagination

While literal language can convey specific information and facts, occasionally you'll find the figurative use of language quite effective because it stimulates the imagination. Since figurative language tends to use strong imagery, it can often make abstract concepts come to life. At the same time, it can make your material more accurate and precise. Of all the figurative devices, *similes* and *metaphors* are the most frequently used.

When you make a comparison between two unlike objects using the words *like* or *as,* you are using a simile. When Momaday writes, *"Her long, black hair, always drawn and braided in the day, lay upon her shoulders and against her breasts like a shawl,"* we get a vivid description of what her hair resembled through association (it was *like* a shawl)—a *simile.* A metaphor compares one thing to another by stating that one thing is another. It is a device many authors in this chapter use at least once. Mori compares a room to a depot. When Joe Louis falls in the boxing ring, Angelou compares it to "*our people falling . . . another lynching, . . . One more woman ambushed and raped.*" In Langston Hughes' description narrative, he metaphorically refers to young children as "*little lambs.*"

Dialogue: Revealing Characters through Speech

In addition to using details to describe their characters, authors often employ dialogue that refines them, giving us a glimpse of their characters' actual personalities. In "Champion of the World," for example, Angelou uses colloquial language (slang/everyday speech) when one of her characters says, "*I ain't worried 'bout this fight. Joe's gonna whip that cracker like it's open season.*" Also, an occasional use of dialogue adds variety and interest to a descriptive narrative. In the line, "*It's been a long time since anyone hugged me,*" for instance, Katherine Barrett reveals the loneliness of old age effectively *without* directly telling the reader that the woman is lonely.

Actions: Describing People by What They Do

Actions, just as dialogue, go a long way toward revealing the physical and mental make-up of a speaker or character in an essay. What motivates a person to do anything? In "Confessions of a Quit Addict," Barbara Graham explains the power of *quitting* school, severing relationships, and moving around in life: "*Suddenly it seemed possible to reinvent myself, to discard my old life like last year's outfit and step into a new one—free from the responsibilities and relationships that had dragged me down.*" As Graham reflects on her subject, she also states, "*Still, I don't consider myself a 'recovering' quitter. That would put too negative a spin on an act that is sometimes the best, most honest, and most creative response to a life situation, as well as a tremendous source of energy and power.*"

Tips on Writing Descriptive Essays

1. Ask yourself questions such as, "What is the purpose of my essay? How will description further advance my purpose?"

2. Write sentences that appeal to the five senses: sight, sound, touch, taste, and smell. Add dialogue to provide variety.
3. Use adjectives (descriptive words) to further modify an object. For instance, when the word *house* is mentioned, each of us, undoubtedly, has a different mental image. When we use adjectives, however, each of us will have similar mental images (e.g., the *little, red, ramshackle, two-story* house is surrounded by *knee-high, withered grass* and a *broken-down, unpainted wooden* fence).
4. Modify verbs, adverbs, and adjectives with adverbs. For example: The track star raced *half-heartedly* to the finish line. The word *half-heartedly* is an adverb modifying the verb *raced.* An example of an adverb modifying an adjective is thus: The *extremely* overdressed girl felt out of place at the barbecue. The adverb *extremely* modifies the adjective *overdressed.* In the sentence "The crippled train inched *very* slowly up the mountain," the adverb *very* is modifying the other adverb *slowly.* Try using more adverbs in your writing to aid in description.
5. Employ figurative language such as metaphors and similes in order to stimulate the imagination and leave a lasting impression on your reader.

Langston Hughes

Salvation

A prolific writer and key figure in the Harlem Renaissance, Langston Hughes wrote sixteen books of poems, two novels, three collections of short stories, four volumes of "editorial" and "documentary" fiction, twenty plays, children's poetry, musicals and operas, three autobiographies, a dozen radio and television scripts, and dozens of magazine articles. In addition, he edited seven anthologies. Hughes' long and distinguished list of works includes his autobiographies: *Not Without Laughter* (1930), *The Big Sea* (1940), *I Wonder As I Wander* (1956); his poetry collections: *The Weary Blues* (1926), The *Negro Mother and other Dramatic Recitations* (1931), *The Dream Keeper* (1932), *Shakespeare In Harlem* (1942), *Fields of Wonder* (1947), *One Way Ticket* (1947), *The First Book of Jazz* (1955), *Selected Poems* (1959), and *The Best of Simple* (1961); and his novels: *Laughing to Keep From Crying* (1952), and *Tambourines To Glory* (1958). Also, Hughes edited several anthologies in an attempt to popularize black authors and their works. His posthumous publications included: *Five Plays By Langston Hughes* (1968), *The Panther and The Lash: Poems of Our Times* (1969), *Good Morning Revolution: Uncollected Writings of Social Protest* (1973), and *The Sweet Flypaper of Life with Roy DeCarava* (1984). Hailed as the Negro poet laureate, Langston Hughes died of cancer in his beloved Harlem in 1967. The following story, "Salvation," from his autobiography, *The Big Sea,* describes Langston's crisis of faith when he "was saved from sin" and yet "not really saved."

Pre-reading Questions

1. Brainstorm the word "salvation." What people or things do you associate with the word?
2. What is the difference between obligation and necessity, if any? That is, what makes people feel obligated to follow others as opposed to what they need to survive?

---

1 I was saved from sin when I was going on thirteen. But not really saved. It happened like this. There was a big revival at my Auntie Reed's church. Every night for weeks there had been much preaching, singing, praying, and shouting, and some very hardened sinners had been brought to Christ, and the membership of the church had grown by leaps and bounds. Then just before the revival ended, they held a special meeting for children, "to bring the young lambs to the fold." My aunt spoke of it for days ahead. That night I was escorted to the front row and placed on the mourners' bench with all the other young sinners, who had not yet been brought to Jesus.

2 My aunt told me that when you were saved you saw a light, and something happened to you inside! And Jesus came into your life! And God was with you from then on! She said you could see and hear and feel Jesus in your soul. I believed her. I had heard a great many old people say the same thing and it seemed to me they ought to know. So I sat there calmly in the hot, crowded church, waiting for Jesus to come to me.

3 The preacher preached a wonderful rhythmical sermon, all moans and shouts and lonely cries and dire pictures of hell, and then he sang a song

about the ninety and nine safe in the fold, but one little lamb was left out in the cold. Then he said: "Won't you come? Won't you come to Jesus? Young lambs, won't you come?" And he held out his arms to all us young sinners there on the mourners' bench. And the little girls cried. And some of them jumped up and went to Jesus right away. But most of us just sat there.

4 A great many old people came and knelt around us and prayed, old women with jet-black faces and braided hair, old men with work-gnarled hands. And the church sang a song about the lower lights are burning, some poor sinners to be saved. And the whole building rocked with prayer and song.

5 Still I kept waiting to *see* Jesus.

6 Finally all the young people had gone to the altar and were saved, but one boy and me. He was a rounder's son named Westley. Westley and I were surrounded by sisters and deacons praying. It was very hot in the church, and getting late now. Finally Westley said to me in a whisper: "God damn! I'm tired o' sitting here. Let's get up and be saved." So he got up and was saved.

7 Then I was left all alone on the mourners' bench. My aunt came and knelt at my knees and cried, while prayers and song swirled all around me in the little church. The whole congregation prayed for me alone, in a mighty wail of moans and voices. And I kept waiting serenely for Jesus, waiting, waiting—but he didn't come. I wanted to see him, but nothing happened to me. Nothing! I wanted something to happen to me, but nothing happened.

8 I heard the songs and the minister saying: "Why don't you come? My dear child, why don't you come to Jesus? Jesus is waiting for you. He wants you. Why don't you come? Sister Reed, what is this child's name?"

9 "Langston," my aunt sobbed.

10 "Langston, why don't you come? Why don't you come and be saved? Oh, Lamb of God! Why don't you come?"

11 Now it was really getting late. I began to be ashamed of myself, holding everything up so long. I began to wonder what God thought about Westley, who certainly hadn't seen Jesus either, but who was now sitting proudly on the platform, swinging his knickerbockered legs and grinning down at me, surrounded by deacons and old women on their knees praying. God had not struck Westley dead for taking his name in vain or for lying in the temple. So I decided that maybe to save further trouble, I'd better lie, too, and say that Jesus had come, and get up and be saved.

12 So I got up.

13 Suddenly the whole room broke into a sea of shouting, as they saw me rise. Waves of rejoicing swept the place. Women leaped in the air. My aunt threw her arms around me. The minister took me by the hand and led me to the platform.

14 When things quieted down, in a hushed silence, punctuated by a few ecstatic "Amens," all the new young lambs were blessed in the name of God. Then joyous singing filled the room.

15 That night, for the first time in my life but one for I was a big boy twelve years old—I cried. I cried, in bed alone, and couldn't stop. I buried my head under the quilts, but my aunt heard me. She woke up and told my uncle I was crying because the Holy Ghost had come into my life, and because I had seen Jesus. But I was really crying because I couldn't bear to tell her that I had lied, that I had deceived everybody in the church, that I hadn't seen Jesus, and that now I didn't believe there was a Jesus anymore, since he didn't come to help me.

Post-reading Questions

Content

1. What is the mood or atmosphere of the revival meeting that Hughes attends?
2. Who or what does Hughes figuratively refer to as "young lambs"?
3. What did Hughes anticipate at the revival, and how did his Auntie Reed help shape his expectations?
4. Explain what goes through Hughes' mind when the revival minister asks, "Why don't you come and be saved?"
5. Why is Hughes' salvation ironic and ultimately a source of discomfort for him?

Strategies and Structures

1. In what way do the first two sentences in "Salvation" set the stage for the rest of the story? How and why do they capture a reader's attention?
2. Identify at least two instances where Hughes uses figurative language in "Salvation."
3. How does Hughes build tension in his story? Consider the progression of events.
4. In what way does "Salvation," the title of Hughes' story, contrast with his actual beliefs?
5. Hughes uses dialogue very sparingly in his story; what might be his strategic purpose for this?

Language and Vocabulary

1. Vocabulary: *revival, congregation, serene, knickerbockers, ecstatic.* After looking up each word in the dictionary, write a paragraph describing a situation where you or someone you know found salvation in an activity; you need not limit your description to religious revivals.
2. Why might using figurative language be appropriate for describing details of a religious experience?

Group Activities

1. In small groups, discuss how and why individuals often try to surround themselves with people who share their values and beliefs. Have a group recorder jot down several collaborative conclusions and prepare to share them with the rest of the class.
2. Individually or as a group, locate and watch a television evangelist show where people gather to offer testimonies of faith. Have each group member write a brief summary of it using descriptive words and phrases so readers can visualize the occasion. Then compare and contrast each other's summaries. How did they differ? In what way were they similar? Finally, combine the individual summaries into a single document.

Writing Activities

1. Using specific details and examples—as well as figurative language—write an essay describing a situation or event where you or someone you know reacted to peer pressure and then regretted it later.
2. Get a copy of the Wadsworth/Cengage DVD version of "Salvation" and compare it to the written text. Does the film capture the emotional intensity of the story? Explain how the two presentations of Hughes' story differ. (Note: The first ten minutes of the twenty-five minute film do not appear in the written text, so begin your comparison where Langston and his Auntie Reed enter the church.)

Internet Connection: Langston Hughes

Testimonies/Beliefs

Enter the search term "testimony" or "testimonies" on an Internet research engine, an online database, or both. Narrow your search to types of testimonies (prison testimonies, food or commercial product testimonies, religious testimonies, political testimonies, gender testimonies). Select three articles that touch upon different kinds of testimonies, and write a summary of each, concluding the piece with documentation as it would appear in a list of *works cited.* You might want to apply your research to "Salvation" Writing Activity 2.

Katherine Barrett

Old Before Her Time

Katherine Barrett, a contributing editor at *Financial World*, has received numerous awards, including the New York State Society of CPA's Award for Excellence in Financial Journalism. She is also a contributing editor at *The Ladies' Home Journal* and a monthly columnist for *Glamour*. Her articles and columns have appeared in *Newsweek, Readers' Digest, Harper's, Better Homes and Gardens, Self, Redbook*, and *Working Woman*. Barrett co-authored *The Man Behind the Magic* (1991), a biography of Walt Disney, with her husband Richard Green; *Powering Up: How Public Managers Can Take Control of Information Technology* (2000); and *Investigating Artifacts: Making Masks, Creating Myths, Exploring Middens* (2002) with Linda Lipner and Gigi Dornfest. Additionally, she also wrote *Inside the Dream: The Personal Story of Walt Disney* (2001). The following essay originally appeared in the August 1983 issue of *The Ladies' Home Journal.*

Pre-reading Questions

1. In your opinion, what exactly is an *old* person? Who or what helped to shape your attitude about age?
2. What do you think when you see old people on the street? Do you talk with them or ignore them? Why? Would the way elderly people dress (e.g., well, modestly) influence your willingness to talk to them?
3. When an old person is on the bus, do you offer him or her your seat? Do you open doors for elderly people? Do you make fun of them? Do you ever think about what it will be like when you grow old—or do you think you will never age?

---

1 This is the story of an extraordinary voyage in time, and of a young woman who devoted three years to a singular experiment. In 1979, Patty Moore—then aged twenty-six—transformed herself for the first of many times into an eighty-five-year-old woman. Her object was to discover

firsthand the problems, joys and frustrations of the elderly. She wanted to know for herself what it's like to live in a culture of youth and beauty when your hair is gray, your skin is wrinkled and no men turn their heads as you pass.

2 Her time machine was a makeup kit. Barbara Kelly, a friend and professional makeup artist, helped Patty pick out a wardrobe and showed her how to use latex to create wrinkles, and wrap Ace bandages to give the impression of stiff joints. "It was peculiar," Patty recalls, as she relaxes in her New York City apartment. "Even the first few times I went out I realized that I wouldn't have to *act* that much. The more I was perceived as elderly by others, the more 'elderly' I actually became . . . I imagine that's just what happens to people who really are old."

3 What motivated Patty to make her strange journey? Partly her career—as an industrial designer, Patty often focuses on the needs of the elderly. But the roots of her interest are also deeply personal. Extremely close to her own grandparents—particularly her maternal grandfather, now ninety—and raised in a part of Buffalo, New York, where there was a large elderly population, Patty always drew comfort and support from the older people around her. When her own marriage ended in 1979 and her life seemed to be falling apart, she dove into her "project" with all her soul. In all, she donned her costume more than two hundred times in fourteen different states. Here is the remarkable story of what she found.

4 **Columbus, Ohio, May 1979.** Leaning heavily on her cane, Pat Moore stood alone in the middle of a crowd of young professionals. They were all attending a gerontology conference, and the room was filled with animated chatter. But no one was talking to Pat. In a throng of men and women who devoted their working lives to the elderly, she began to feel like a total nonentity. "I'll get us all some coffee," a young man told a group of women next to her. "What about me?" thought Pat. "If I were young, they would be offering me coffee, too." It was a bitter thought at the end of a disappointing day—a day that marked Patty's first appearance as "the old woman." She had planned to attend the gerontology conference anyway, and almost as a lark decided to see how professionals would react to an old person in their midst.

5 Now, she was angry. All day she had been ignored . . . counted out in a way she had never experienced before. She didn't understand. Why didn't people help her when they saw her struggling to open a heavy door? Why didn't they include her in conversations? Why did the other participants seem almost embarrassed by her presence at the conference—as if it were somehow inappropriate that an old person should be professionally active?

6 And so, eighty-five-year-old Pat Moore learned her first lesson: The old are often ignored. "I discovered that people really do judge a book by its cover," Patty says today. "Just because I looked different, people

either condescended or they totally dismissed me. Later, in stores, I'd get the same reaction. A clerk would turn to someone younger and wait on her first. It was as if he assumed that I—the older woman—could wait because I didn't have anything better to do."

7 **New York City, October 1979.** Bent over her cane, Pat walked slowly toward the edge of the park. She had spent the day sitting on a bench with friends, but now dusk was falling and her friends had all gone home. She looked around nervously at the deserted area and tried to move faster, but her joints were stiff. It was then that she heard the barely audible sound of sneakered feet approaching and the kids' voices. "Grab her, man." "Get her purse." Suddenly an arm was around her throat and she was dragged back, knocked off her feet.

8 She saw only a blur of sneakers and blue jeans, heard the sounds of mocking laughter, felt fists pummeling her—on her back, her legs, her breasts, her stomach. "Oh, God," she thought, using her arms to protect her head and curling herself into a ball. "They're going to kill me. I'm going to die . . . ."

9 Then, as suddenly as the boys attacked, they were gone. And Patty was left alone, struggling to rise. The boys' punches had broken the latex makeup on her face, the fall had disarranged her wig, and her whole body ached. (Later she would learn that she had fractured her left wrist, an injury that took two years to heal completely.) Sobbing, she left the park and hailed a cab to return home. Again the thought struck her: What if I really lived in the gray ghetto . . . what if I couldn't escape to my nice safe home . . . ?

10 Lesson number two: The fear of crime is paralyzing. "I really understand now why the elderly become homebound," the young woman says as she recalls her ordeal today. "When something like this happens, the fear just doesn't go away. I guess it wasn't so bad for me. I could distance myself from what happened . . . and I was strong enough to get up and walk away. But what about someone who is really too weak to run or fight back or protect herself in any way? And the elderly often can't afford to move if the area in which they live deteriorates, becomes unsafe. I met people like this and they were imprisoned by their fear. That's when the bolts go on the door. That's when people starve themselves because they're afraid to go to the grocery store."

11 **New York City, February 1980.** It was a slushy, gray day and Pat had laboriously descended four flights of stairs from her apartment to go shopping. Once outside, she struggled to hold her threadbare coat closed with one hand and manipulate her cane with the other. Splotches of snow made the street difficult for anyone to navigate, but for someone hunched over, as she was, it was almost impossible. The curb was another obstacle. The slush looked ankle-deep—and what was she to do? Jump over it? Slowly, she worked her way around to a drier spot, but the crowds were

impatient to move. A woman with packages jostled her as she rushed past, causing Pat to nearly lose her balance. If I really were old, I would have fallen, she thought. Maybe broken something. On another day, a woman had practically knocked her over by letting go of a heavy door as Pat tried to enter a coffee shop. Then there were the revolving doors. How could you push them without strength? And how could you get up and down stairs, on and off a bus, without risking a terrible fall?

12 Lesson number three: If small, thoughtless deficiencies in design were corrected, life would be so much easier for older people. It was no surprise to Patty that the "built" environment is often inflexible. But even she didn't realize the extent of the problems, she admits. "It was a terrible feeling. I never realized how difficult it is to get off a curb if your knees don't bend easily. Or the helpless feeling you get if your upper arms aren't strong enough to open a door. You know, I just felt so vulnerable—as if I was at the mercy of every barrier or rude person I encountered."

13 **Ft. Lauderdale, Florida, May 1980.** Pat met a new friend while shopping, and they decided to continue their conversation over a sundae at a nearby coffee shop. The woman was in her late seventies, "younger" than Pat, but she was obviously reaching out for help. Slowly, her story unfolded. "My husband moved out of our bedroom," the woman said softly, fiddling with her coffee cup and fighting back tears. "He won't touch me anymore. And when he gets angry at me for being stupid, he'll even sometimes . . ." The woman looked down, embarrassed to go on. Pat took her hand. "He hits me . . . he gets so mean." "Can't you tell anyone?" Pat asked. "Can't you tell your son?" "Oh, no!" the woman almost gasped. "I would never tell the children; they absolutely adore him."

14 Lesson number four: Even a fifty-year-old marriage isn't necessarily a good one. While Pat met many loving and devoted elderly couples, she was stunned to find others who had stayed together unhappily—because divorce was still an anathema in their middle years. "I met women who secretly wished their husbands dead, because after so many years they just ended up full of hatred. One woman in Chicago even admitted that she deliberately angered her husband because she knew it would make his blood pressure rise. Of course, that was pretty extreme . . . . "

15 Patty pauses thoughtfully and continues. "I guess what really made an impression on me, the real eye-opener, was that so many of these older women had the same problems as women twenty, thirty or forty. Problems with men . . . problems with the different roles that are expected of them. As a 'young woman' I, too, had just been through a relationship where I spent a lot of time protecting someone by covering up his problems from family and friends. Then I heard this woman in Florida saying that she wouldn't tell her children their father beat her because she didn't want to disillusion them. These issues aren't age-related. They affect everyone."

16 **Clearwater, Florida, January 1981.** She heard the children laughing, but she didn't realize at first that they were laughing at her. On this day, as on several others, Pat had shed the clothes of a middle-income woman for the rags of a bag lady. She wanted to see the extremes of the human condition, what it was like to be old and poor, and outside traditional society as well. Now, tottering down the sidewalk, she was most concerned with the cold, since her layers of ragged clothing did little to ease the chill. She had spent the afternoon rummaging through garbage cans, loading her shopping bags with bits of debris, and she was stiff and tired. Suddenly, she saw that four little boys, five or six years old, were moving up on her. And then she felt the sting of the pebbles they were throwing. She quickened her pace to escape, but another handful of gravel hit her and the laughter continued. They're using me as a target, she thought, horror-stricken. They don't even think of me as a person.

17 Lesson number five: Social class affects every aspect of an older person's existence: "I found out that class is a very important factor when you're old," says Patty. "It was interesting. That same day, I went back to my hotel and got dressed as a wealthy woman, another role that I occasionally took. Outside the hotel, a little boy of about seven asked if I would go shelling with him. We walked along the beach, and he reached out to hold my hand. I knew he must have a grandmother who walked with a cane, because he was so concerned about me and my footing. 'Don't put your cane there, the sand's wet,' he'd say. He really took responsibility for my welfare. The contrast between him and those children was really incredible. The little ones who were throwing the pebbles at me because they didn't see me as human. And then the seven-year-old taking care of me. I think he would have responded to me the same way even if I had been dressed as the middle-income woman. There's no question that money does make life easier for older people, not only because it gives them a more comfortable life-style, but because it makes others treat them with greater respect."

18 **New York City, May 1981.** Pat always enjoyed the time she spent sitting on the benches in Central Park. She'd let the whole day pass by, watching young children play, feeding the pigeons and chatting. One spring day she found herself sitting with three women, all widows, and the conversation turned to the few available men around. "It's been a long time since anyone hugged me," one woman complained. Another agreed. "Isn't that the truth. I need a hug, too." It was a favorite topic, Pat found—the lack of touching left in these women's lives, the lack of hugging, the lack of men.

19 In the last two years, she had found out herself how it felt to walk down Fifth Avenue and know that no men were turning to look after her. Or how it felt to look at models in magazines or store mannequins and *know* that those gorgeous clothes were just not made for her. She hadn't

realized before just how much casual attention was paid to her because she was young and pretty. She hadn't realized it until it stopped.

20 Lesson number six: You never grow old emotionally. You always need to feel loved. "It's not surprising that everyone needs love and touching and holding," says Patty. "But I think some people feel that you reach a point in your life when you accept that those intimate feelings are in the past. That's wrong. These women were still interested in sex. But more than that, they—like everyone—needed to be hugged and touched. I'd watch two women greeting each other on the street and just holding onto each other's hands, neither wanting to let go. Yet, I also saw that there are people who are afraid to touch an old person . . . they were afraid to touch me. It's as if they think old age is a disease and it's catching. They think that something might rub off on them."

21 **New York City, September 1981.** He was a thin man, rather nattily dressed, with a hat that he graciously tipped at Pat as he approached the bench where she sat. "Might I join you?" he asked jauntily. Pat told him he would be welcome and he offered her one of the dietetic hard candies that he carried in a crumpled paper bag. As the afternoon passed, they got to talking . . . about the beautiful buds on the trees and the world around them and the past. "Life's for the living, my wife used to tell me," he said. "When she took sick she made me promise her that I wouldn't waste a moment. But the first year after she died, I just sat in the apartment. I didn't want to see anyone, talk to anyone, or go anywhere. I missed her so much." He took a handkerchief from his pocket and wiped his eyes, and they sat in silence. Then he slapped his leg to break the mood and change the subject. He asked Pat about herself, and described his life alone. He belonged to a "senior center" now, and went on trips and had lots of friends. Life did go on. They arranged to meet again the following week on the same park bench. He brought lunch—chicken salad sandwiches and decaffeinated peppermint tea in a thermos—and wore a carnation in his lapel. It was the first date Patty had had since her marriage ended.

22 Lesson number seven: Life does go on . . . as long as you're flexible and open to change. "That man really meant a lot to me, even though I never saw him again," says Patty, her eyes wandering toward the gray wig that now sits on a wig-stand on the top shelf of her bookcase. "He was a real old-fashioned gentleman, yet not afraid to show his feelings—as so many men my age are. It's funny, but at that point I had been through months of self-imposed seclusion. Even though I was in a different role, that encounter kind of broke the ice for getting my life together as a single woman."

23 In fact, while Patty was living her life as the old woman, some of her young friends had been worried about her. After several years, it seemed as if the lines of identity had begun to blur. Even when she wasn't in

makeup, she was wearing unusually conservative clothing, she spent most of her time with older people and she seemed almost to revel in her role—sometimes finding it easier to be in costume than to be a single New Yorker.

24 But as Patty continued her experiment, she was also learning a great deal from the older people she observed. Yes, society often did treat the elderly abysmally . . . they were sometimes ignored, sometimes victimized, sometimes poor and frightened, but so many of them were survivors. They had lived through two world wars, the Depression and into the computer age. "If there was one lesson to learn, one lesson that I'll take with me into *my* old age, it's that you've got to be flexible," Patty says. "I saw my friend in the park, managing after the loss of his wife, and I met countless other people who picked themselves up after something bad—or even something catastrophic—happened. I'm not worried about them. I'm worried about the others who shut themselves away. It's funny, but seeing these two extremes helped me recover from the trauma in my own life, to pull *my* life together."

25 Today, Patty is back to living the life of a single thirty-year old, and she rarely dons her costumes anymore. "I must admit, though, I do still think a lot about aging," she says. "I look in the mirror and I begin to see wrinkles, and then I realize that I won't be able to wash *those* wrinkles off." Is she afraid of growing older? "No. In a way, I'm kind of looking forward to it," she smiles. "I *know* it will be different from my experiment. I *know* I'll probably even look different. When they aged Orson Welles in *Citizen Kane* he didn't resemble at all the Orson Welles of today."

26 But Patty also knows that in one way she really did manage to capture the feeling of being old. With her bandages and her stooped posture, she turned her body into a kind of prison. Yet, inside she didn't change at all. "It's funny, but that's exactly how older people always say they feel," says Patty. "Their bodies age, but inside they are really no different than when they were young."

Post-reading Questions

Content

1. What is the controlling idea of this essay?
2. How many times did Patty Moore dress as an elderly woman? In how many different states did she conduct her *experiment*?
3. Why did Moore want to "transform herself" into an "eighty-five-year-old woman"?
4. How did Moore's relationships with elderly people help her to pull the pieces of her life together?

Strategies and Structures

1. What are the seven lessons about life Patty Moore learned, and how did Barrett use them to unify the content of her essay?
2. Why do the first few words in some lines appear in boldface type? What do they signal to the reader?
3. In your opinion, how well does Barrett's narrative of Patty Moore's experiences illustrate the broader theme of her essay?
4. What strategies does Barrett use to keep her readers interested in her rather long essay?

Language and Vocabulary

1. Vocabulary: *condescending, audible, deteriorate, disillusion, revel, abysmal.* Use the following suffixes to change the above words from one word form to another: *-ly, -ment, -tion.* (For example, one could change *friend,* a noun, to *friendly,* an adjective.) Use both word forms in a sentence.
2. A lot of the dialogue in this essay is not really addressed to a particular person; rather, it is like a person thinking out loud. Analyze how the author's use of dialogue is appropriate to the theme of her essay.

Group Activities

1. Role-playing: Assume a role that definitely is not you or any member of your group. For example, you could dress as a street person or a business executive. Make sure you notice how people judge and treat you. Then dress exactly the opposite and see if people react differently towards you. Afterward, meet with your group and discuss the different reactions.
2. Semester Project: Keep a running journal account of role-playing you have done for the duration of this class, making sure to record the lessons you've learned, much as Moore did in this essay. After condensing your material, construct a unified composition in which you use the lessons you've learned to guide you in proving your thesis. Gather in small groups at the conclusion of the semester or quarter and share your role-playing essays.

Writing Activities

1. Take one of the lessons in life (the issue or moral it offers) that Moore experienced and use it as an essay topic. Take a definite position on the issue and argue/describe why it is true or untrue, using specific details drawn from personal experience.

2. Describe a situation where you learned something by role-playing (acting like another person, talking like another person, thinking like another person). Lead your readers through a sequence of narrated events to help them understand how role-playing in itself taught you a lesson. You might draw on your role-playing experiences from the second group activity.

***Internet Connection:* Katherine Barrett**

Role-playing

Role-playing in videogames or on the Internet has been both praised for offering opportunities to build strong moral character and criticized as a source of declining ethics, sensitivity, and decency. Research both the positive and negative side of role-playing; use the Internet to collect the most recent information on the topic. Take notes, and determine the strongest arguments for each point of view. When and where did you determine that role-playing is nothing more than a harmless exercise in exchanging realities? At what point might role-playing actually become dangerous? Finally, after doing some prewriting on the topic of role-playing—bearing your findings in mind—construct a thesis, and write an essay supporting your point of view with personal experience, observations of others, and research. Please document your readings according to the MLA stylesheet. (Consult the Appendix on documentation at the end of *Visions Across the Americas*, 8th edition.)

N. Scott Momaday

From The Way to Rainy Mountain

A member of the Kiowa tribe, N. Scott Momaday has spent his life telling the history and the tales of his people. He has published books such as the Pulitzer Prize-winning *The House Made of Dawn* (1968), *The Way to Rainy Mountain* (1969),

The Gourd Dancer (1976), *The Names: A Memoir* (1976), *The Ancient Child* (1989), In the *Presence of the Sun: Stories and Poems, 1961–1991* (1992), *Circle of Wonder: A Native American Christmas* (1993), and *More Than Bows and Arrows: The Legacy of the American Indians* (1994), *The Man Made of Words* (1998), and *In the Bear's House* (2000). In addition to being a well-respected author, Momaday also is an accomplished artist and has won several awards for both his paintings and drawings. His artistic sensitivity seems to transfer quite naturally into his writings, and as shown in the following descriptive excerpt from the introduction to *The Way to Rainy Mountain*, he often uses symbols and images to paint pictures with words.

Pre-reading Questions

1. How does the title suggest the essay's topic? Make a list of some of the possible things you think the author will write about.
2. The name of the mountain—Rainy Mountain—has several connotations. What connotations (feelings and/or images) do you associate with the words *rainy* and *mountain*?

---

1 A single knoll rises out of the plain in Oklahoma, north and west of the Wichita Range. For my people, the Kiowas, it is an old landmark, and they gave it the name Rainy Mountain. The hardest weather in the world is there. Winter brings blizzards, hot tornadic winds arise in the spring, and in summer the prairie is an anvil's edge. The grass turns brittle and brown and it cracks beneath your feet. There are green belts along the rivers and creeks, linear groves of hickory and pecan, willow and witch hazel. At a distance in July or August the steaming foliage seems almost to writhe in fire. Great green and yellow grasshoppers are everywhere in the tall grass, popping up like corn to sting the flesh, and tortoises crawl about on the red earth, going nowhere in plenty of time. Loneliness is an aspect of the land. All things in the plain are isolate; there is no confusion of objects in the eye, but *one* hill or *one* tree or *one* man. To look upon the landscape in the early morning, with the sun at your back, is to lose the sense of proportion. Your imagination comes to life, and this, you think, is where Creation was begun.

2 I returned to Rainy Mountain in July. My grandmother had died in the spring, and I wanted to be at her grave. She had lived to be very old and at last infirm. Her only living daughter was with her when she died, and I was told that in death her face was that of a child.

3 I like to think of her as a child. When she was born, the Kiowas were living the last great moment of their history. For more than a hundred years they had controlled the open range from the Smoky Hill River to the Red, from the headwaters of the Canadian to the fork of

the Arkansas and Cimarron. In alliance with the Comanches, they had ruled the whole of the southern Plains. War was their sacred business, and they were among the finest horsemen the world has ever known. But warfare for the Kiowas was preeminently a matter of disposition rather than survival, and they never understood the grim, unrelenting advance of the U.S. Cavalry. When at last, divided and ill-provisioned, they were driven onto the Staked Plains in the cold rains of autumn, they fell into panic. In Palo Duro Canyon they abandoned their crucial stores to pillage and had nothing then but their lives. In order to save themselves, they surrendered to the soldiers at Fort Sill and were imprisoned in the old stone corral that now stands as a military museum. My grandmother was spared the humiliation of those high gray walls by eight or ten years, but she must have known from birth the affliction of defeat, the dark brooding of old warriors.

4 Her name was Aho, and she belonged to the last culture to evolve in North America. Her forebears came down from the high country in western Montana nearly three centuries ago. They were a mountain people, a mysterious tribe of hunters whose language has never been positively classified in any major group. In the late seventeenth century they began a long migration to the south and east. It was a journey toward the dawn, and it led to a golden age. Along the way the Kiowas were befriended by the Crows, who gave them the culture and religion of the Plains. They acquired horses, and their ancient nomadic spirit was suddenly free of the ground. They acquired Tai-me, the sacred Sun Dance doll, from that moment the object and symbol of their worship, and so shared in the divinity of the sun. Not least, they acquired the sense of destiny, therefore courage and pride. When they entered upon the southern Plains they had been transformed. No longer were they slaves to the simple necessity of survival; they were a lordly and dangerous society of fighters and thieves, hunters and priests of the sun. According to their origin myth, they entered the world through a hollow log. From one point of view, their migration was the fruit of an old prophecy, for indeed they emerged from a sunless world.

5 Although my grandmother lived out her long life in the shadow of Rainy Mountain, the immense landscape of the continental interior lay like memory in her blood. She could tell of the Crows, whom she had never seen, and of the Black Hills, where she had never been. I wanted to see in reality what she had seen more perfectly in the mind's eye, and traveled fifteen hundred miles to begin my pilgrimage.

6 Yellowstone, it seemed to me, was the top of the world, a region of deep lakes and dark timber, canyons and waterfalls. But, beautiful as it is, one might have the sense of confinement there. The skyline in all directions is close at hand, the high wall of the woods and deep cleavages of shade. There is a perfect freedom in the mountains, but it belongs to the

eagle and the elk, the badger and the bear. The Kiowas reckoned their stature by the distance they could see, and they were bent and blind in the wilderness.

7 Descending eastward, the highland meadows are a stairway to the plain. In July the inland slope of the Rockies is luxuriant with flax and buckwheat, stonecrop and larkspur. The earth unfolds and the limit of the land recedes. Clusters of trees, and animals grazing far in the distance, cause the vision to reach away and wonder to build upon the mind. The sun follows a longer course in the day, and the sky is immense beyond all comparison. The great billowing clouds that sail upon it are shadows that move upon the grain like water, dividing light. Farther down, in the land of the Crows and Blackfeet, the plain is yellow. Sweet clover takes hold of the hills and bends upon itself to cover and seal the soil. There the Kiowas paused on their way; they had come to the place where they must change their lives. The sun is at home on the plains. Precisely there does it have the certain character of a god. When the Kiowas came to the land of the Crows, they could see the dark lees of the hills at dawn across the Bighorn River, the profusion of light on the grain shelves, the oldest deity ranging after the solstices. Not yet would they veer southward to the caldron of the land that lay below; they must wean their blood from the northern winter and hold the mountains a while longer in their view. They bore Tai-me in procession to the east.

8 A dark mist lay over the Black Hills, and the land was like iron. At the top of a ridge I caught sight of Devil's Tower upthrust against the gray sky as if in the birth of time the core of the earth had broken through its crust and the motion of the world has begun. There are things in nature that engender an awful quiet in the heart of man; Devil's Tower is one of them. Two centuries ago, because they could not do otherwise, the Kiowas made a legend at the base of the rock. My grandmother said:

> Eight children were there at play, seven sisters and their brother. Suddenly the boy was struck dumb; he trembled and began to run upon his hands and feet. His fingers became claws, and his body was covered with fur. Directly there was a bear where the boy had been. The sisters were terrified; they ran, and the bear after them. They came to the stump of a great tree, and the tree spoke to them. It bade them climb upon it, and as they did so it began to rise into the air. The bear came to kill them, but they were just beyond its reach. It reared against the tree and scored the bark all around with its claws. The seven sisters were borne into the sky, and they became the stars of the Big Dipper.

From that moment, and so long as the legend lives, the Kiowas have kinsmen in the night sky. Whatever they were in the mountains, they could be no more. However tenuous their well-being, however much they had suffered and would suffer again, they had found a way out of the wilderness.

9 My grandmother had a reverence for the sun, a holy regard that now is all but gone out of mankind. There was a wariness in her, and an ancient awe. She was a Christian in her later years, but she had come a long way about, and she never forgot her birthright. As a child she had been to the Sun Dances; she had taken part in those annual rites, and by them she had learned the restoration of her people in the presence of Tai-me. She was about seven when the last Kiowa Sun Dance was held in 1887 on the Washita River above Rainy Mountain Creek. The buffalo were gone. In order to consummate the ancient sacrifice—to impale the head of a buffalo bull upon the medicine tree—a delegation of old men journeyed into Texas, there to beg and barter for an animal from the Goodnight herd. She was ten when the Kiowas came together for the last time as a living Sun Dance culture. They could find no buffalo; they had to hang an old hide from the sacred tree. Before the dance could begin, a company of soldiers rode out from Fort Sill under orders to disperse the tribe. Forbidden without cause the essential act of their faith, having seen the wild herds slaughtered and left to rot upon the ground, the Kiowas backed away forever from the medicine tree. That was July 20, 1890, at the great bend of the Washita. My grandmother was there. Without bitterness, and for as long as she lived, she bore a vision of deicide.

10 Now that I can have her only in memory, I see my grandmother in the several postures that were peculiar to her: standing at the wood stove on a winter morning and turning meat in a great iron skillet; sitting at the south window, bent above her beadwork, and afterwards, when her vision failed, looking down for a long time into the fold of her hands; going out upon a cane, very slowly as she did when the weight of age came upon her; praying. I remember her most often at prayer. She made long, rambling prayers out of suffering and hope, having seen many things. I was never sure that I had the right to hear, so exclusive were they of all mere custom and company. The last time I saw her she prayed standing by the side of her bed at night naked to the waist, the light of a kerosene lamp moving upon her dark skin. Her long, black hair, always drawn and braided in the day, lay upon her shoulders and against her breasts like a shawl. I do not speak Kiowa, and I never understood her prayers, but there was something inherently sad in the sound, some merest hesitation upon the syllables of sorrow. She began in a high and descending pitch, exhausting her breath to silence; then again and again—and always the same intensity of effort, of something that is, and is not, like urgency in the human voice. Transported so in the dancing light among the shadows of her room, she seemed beyond the reach of time. But that was illusion; I think I knew then that I should not see her again.

11 Houses are like sentinels in the plain, old keepers of the weather watch. There, in a very little while, wood takes on the appearance of great age. All colors wear soon away in the wind and rain, and then the wood is burned

gray and the grain appears and the nails turn red with rust. The windowpanes are black and opaque; you imagine there is nothing within, and indeed there are many ghosts, bones given up to the land. They stand here and there against the sky, and you approach them for a longer time than you expect. They belong in the distance; it is their domain.

12 Once there was a lot of sound in my grandmother's house, a lot of coming and going, feasting and talk. The summers there were full of excitement and reunion. The Kiowas are a summer people; they abide the cold and keep to themselves, but when the season turns and the land becomes warm and vital they cannot hold still; an old love of going returns upon them. The aged visitors who came to my grandmother's house when I was a child were made of lean and leather, and they bore themselves upright. They wore great black hats and bright ample shirts that shook in the wind. They rubbed fat upon their hair and wound their braids with strips of colored cloth. Some of them painted their faces and carried the scars of old and cherished enmities. They were an old council of warlords, come to remind and be reminded of who they were. Their wives and daughters served them well. The women might indulge themselves; gossip was at once the mark and compensation of their servitude. They made loud and elaborate talk among themselves, full of jest and gesture, fright and false alarm. They went abroad in fringed and flowered shawls, bright beadwork and German silver. They were at home in the kitchen, and they prepared meals that were banquets.

13 There were frequent prayer meetings, and great nocturnal feasts. When I was a child I played with my cousins outside, where the lamplight fell upon the ground and the singing of the old people rose up around us and carried away into the darkness. There were a lot of good things to eat, a lot of laughter and surprise. And afterwards, when the quiet returned, I lay down with my grandmother and could hear the frogs away by the river and feel the motion of the air.

14 Now there is funeral silence in the rooms, the endless wake of some final word. The walls have closed in upon my grandmother's house. When I returned to it in mourning, I saw for the first time in my life how small it was. It was late at night, and there was a white moon, nearly full. I sat for a long time on the stone steps by the kitchen door. From there I could see out across the land; I could see the long row of trees by the creek, the low light upon the rolling plains, and the stars of the Big Dipper. Once I looked at the moon and caught sight of a strange thing. A cricket had perched upon the handrail, only a few inches away from me. My line of vision was such that the creature filled the moon like a fossil. It had gone there, I thought, to live and die, for there, of all places, was its small definition made whole and eternal. A warm wind rose up and purled like the longing within me.

15 The next morning I awoke at dawn and went out on the dirt road to Rainy Mountain. It was already hot, and the grasshoppers began to

fill the air. Still, it was early in the morning, and the birds sang out of the shadows. The long yellow grass on the mountain shone in the bright light, and a scissortail hied above the land. There, where it ought to be, at the end of a long and legendary way, was my grandmother's grave. Here and there on the dark stones were ancestral names. Looking back once, I saw the mountain and came away.

Post-reading Questions

Content

1. Why does Momaday return to Rainy Mountain? What effect does this trip have on him?
2. Who is the central character in Momaday's essay? What traits make up her character?
3. What is the history of the Kiowas? How did they come to reside below Rainy Mountain?
4. What journey does Momaday make? Where does he begin his essay? Where does he say he is going? Where does he conclude the essay?

Strategies and Structures

1. Momaday opens his essay with a description. What is the primary "mood" (see Glossary) of this description? What images create this mood? What images are most vivid? How does this description set up the tone for the rest of the essay?
2. Why does Momaday tell the story of the Kiowas? How is their story similar to the story of his grandmother?
3. In paragraph 10, what senses—sight, sound, smell, taste, and touch—does he use to describe his grandmother?
4. Momaday writes two descriptions of his grandmother's house—paragraphs 12–13 and 14. What are the two distinct differences between the descriptions? What images does Momaday use to create the two distinct moods?
5. What is the mood of the final paragraph? Is it different from the opening paragraph? What images create the mood?

Language and Vocabulary

1. Vocabulary: *knoll, range, plain, fork, canyon, highland meadows, caldron.* All of these vocabulary words are used to specify or explain geographical areas or features. After you look up the dictionary definition of the words, go back and see where and how Momaday uses them to describe the area around Rainy Mountain. Then, write a paragraph or so describing a geographical area you are familiar with (or an imaginary place), using at least five of the eight vocabulary words.

2. Momaday enables the reader to "relive" his trip to Rainy Mountain because he connects the different parts of his journey. What sorts of transitions and linking devices help the reader follow Momaday?

Group Activities

1. As a group, take a walk around the campus. As you walk, write down all that you can see, smell, taste, touch, and hear. After you finish your walk, decide on a dominant impression the campus projects: old, friendly, traditional, modern, busy, and so on. After you determine the dominant impression of the campus, decide which details from your notes illustrate this impression best.
2. Write a collaborative essay describing the classroom you are sitting in. Make sure everyone in your group contributes information and impressions. In addition to details, which help a reader to visualize the room, your essay should create a dominant mood.

Writing Activities

1. Write a description of a close relative. Include the history of the relative's heritage, the relative's past, and the relative's present.
2. Write a description of your hometown or homeland. In the same manner as Momaday, try to create a mood by careful use of details and images.

Barbara Graham

Confessions of a Quit Addict

Barbara Graham is a journalist, playwright, and author of such works as *Jacob's Ladder* (1987) and *Women Who Run with the Poodles: Myths and Tips for Honoring*

Your Mood Swings (1994), a book whose title takes a lighthearted response to Clarissa Pinkola Etés's more serious book, *Women Who Run with the Wolves: Myths and Stories of the Wild Woman Archetype,* which examines the "historical woman of progress" in a male-dominated society. Recent works include *Eye of My Heart* (April 2009). Her great use of irony in the following essay not only highlights her human folly in moving from one fantasy world to another, but it also describes the pilgrimage of her chronic addiction—quitting—from the moment she decided to drop out of college to the time she decides it may be time to become a "recovering quitter."

Pre-reading Questions

1. How do you feel about quitting? What negative feelings (if any) come to your mind when you hear the word? How were you raised to think about this concept?
2. Have you—or anyone you know—ever quit a job or school and gone off to seek your (their) fortune or explore the world with little or no money? What happened to you or the other person? If you've never done this, how do you feel about a person who has? Do you consider him or her brave, crazy, or stupid?

---

1 By the time I heard Timothy Leary chant "Turn on, tune in, drop out" from the stage of New York's Fillmore East, I had already quit college. The year was 1967, and Leary's battle cry was for me more a confirmation of what I already believed than a call to action.

2 I had never been much good at doing things that didn't arouse my passion. Even when I was a young girl, it was obvious that I had been born without the stick-to-it, nose-to-the-grindstone gene. I was stubborn, tenacious in my devotion to the people and things I loved, disdainful of everything else. There was no in-between. In high school I got straight A's in English and flunked math. When it came time for college, I enrolled at NYU because it was the only way I could think of to live in Greenwich Village and get my parents to pick up the tab. But I rarely made it to classes and dropped out one month into my sophomore year.

3 That was the first time I felt the rush of quitting, the instant high of cutting loose, the biochemical buzz of burning my bridges. The charge had to do not with leaving college for something else, but with leaving, period—the pure act of making the break. Suddenly it seemed possible to reinvent myself, to discard my old life like last year's outfit and step into a new one—free from the responsibilities and relationships that had dragged me down. I got an unlisted telephone number and warned my parents to stay away. "When one jumps over the edge, one is bound

to land somewhere," wrote D. H. Lawrence, and for a long time this was my mantra.

4 It didn't take long for me to find a collaborator, a master of disappearing acts who made me look like a rookie. Brian was ready to morph one life into the next on the turn of a dime. I became his loyal apprentice, and during the summer of 1968, shortly after Bobby Kennedy and Martin Luther King Jr. were gunned down, we sold everything we owned and quit our jobs, our friends, our apartment, the urban jungle, America and blight of Vietnam, and fled to Europe. But our new life didn't quite match our dreams: As winter neared, we found ourselves living in a rusty old van on the outskirts of Rome, hungry and cold and hard up for cash. From there, we boarded a freighter for Puerto Rico—which turned out not to be the nirvana we'd imagined, either—especially after the little episode with customs officials over a speck of hashish. Still, a pattern had been set: living in one place, dreaming of another, working at odd jobs (mine included secretary, salesgirl, cocktail waitress, draft counselor, nude model, warehouse clerk, candle maker), earning just enough money to get us to the next destination. We crisscrossed the United States, went north to British Columbia, and lived in every conceivable sort of dwelling from tenements and tents to farmhouses and plywood shacks. Sometimes I'd grow attached to a place and plant a garden, thinking that *this* time things would work out and we'd stay forever—or at least long enough to see the flowers bloom. But something always went wrong: It rained too much (British Columbia), the cost of living was too high (Colorado), the air wasn't pure enough (Southern California), or we couldn't find work that was meaningful, not to mention lucrative enough for us (everywhere).

5 For a long time it didn't matter that we weren't happy anywhere, because the rush of heading off into the unknown and starting over was more potent and trippy than anything we smoked, and we just kept going—even after our son, Clay, was born. But one day, in the mountains of Northern California, when our latest scheme for finding True Happiness—living close to nature, in a house we built, near another family—fell apart, I just snapped. In that moment I knew that I no longer had it in me to continue feeding on fantasies of a future that inevitably turned to dust. That night I made this entry in my journal: "I'm so sick of listening to ourselves talk about what's going to be—plans, plans, plans. I want to live in the present for once, not in the future. I mean *live,* settle down, make a home for my son." I had understood finally that the problem wasn't in the places we went or the people we found there but in ourselves. We could shed our surroundings but not our own skin. No matter who or what we left behind, our private demons followed, and our differences with one another erupted like a sleeping volcano the minute we stopped running. In the end, there

was nowhere left to go, no place left to leave behind, no one left to say good-bye to except each other.

6 It had taken thousands of miles and one child for me to understand that the quitting I took for freedom was as much of a trap as the social conventions we were trying to escape. Together, Brian and I had been so busy saying no to everything that might limit our options that, except for Clay, we'd neglected to say yes to anything. We had no careers, few friends, and no place to call home. Moreover, what had begun as a journey to find our "true" selves, independent of other people's expectations, had turned into an addictive cycle of fantasy and failure, followed by another stab at redemption. After seven years, I felt sad, spent, and more alienated than ever—from Brian, from the rest of the world, and, most frighteningly, from myself. More than anything, I longed to land *somewhere.*

7 Still, I don't consider myself a "recovering" quitter. That would put too negative a spin on an act that is sometimes the best, most honest, and most creative response to a life situation, as well as a tremendous source of energy and power. What's more, in the years since Brian and I went our separate ways, I've walked away from a marriage and a number of significant relationships, bailed out of college a second time (just a few credits shy of getting my degree), and moved back and forth across the country twice. As for my relationship to the workforce, it officially ended 15 years ago when I left a long-term (for me—it lasted all of eight months) position as the publicist for a hospital specializing in unusual diseases. I simply could not deal with a life in which I was expected to show up at the same place at the same time five days a week and not take frequent naps. So I did what any self-respecting jobaphobic would do: I became a writer.

8 But, paradoxically, knowing that I'll always have it in me to be a quit artist has in recent years made me want to hunker down, dig deeper, stick around long enough to watch the garden bloom. (I've even gone so far as to plant perennials.) This change has come gradually, on tiptoes, without the fanfare or splash of the Big Quit. Looking back at my current marriage of 12 years, I see that the constancy my husband and I have maintained despite our share of hard times would have, in the past, sent me scrambling in search of higher drama. For me, the act of staying put has required far more courage and humility than it once took to let go. This is somewhat ironic, considering that I used to believe that my capacity to turn my back and walk away from almost anyone or anything was a sure sign of bravery.

9 Over the years, I've also come to understand that even if I don't go chasing after change, it will do a perfectly good job of finding me. Upheavals, startling turns, and unpredictable shifts have all come unbidden—especially when I've been at my most settled. Besides, I've watched enough people I love die to know that no matter how hard we

try to be the sole authors of our own stories, life itself will eventually have its way and quit *us.*

10 And though sometimes I miss the rush of cutting loose—and, God knows, the impulse still arises—I've learned that, for the most part, it's impossible to travel deep and wide at the same time. Now it's simply more interesting, more richly satisfying, to mine my life just as it is, with all of its wild imperfections and—superficially, at least—lack of conspicuous drama. My family, my home, close friendships, the natural world, and the worlds conjured in my work constantly surprise me with their nourishment—a thick and complex root system I might never have known if I hadn't stopped severing the ties that bind.

Post-reading Questions

Content

1. Why is it so easy for Graham to adopt Timothy Leary's 1967 chant, "Turn on, tune in, drop out"? What makes her a good candidate for taking his advice, and what emotions come into play when she does?
2. Who becomes her collaborator, and how do they spend their lives? What pattern is soon established in their day-to-day living?
3. What helps Graham realize that she no longer has it in her to live in a fantasy world? What discovery does she make about the future at the same time? More importantly, what does she finally come to realize that she needs?
4. Why, however, doesn't she consider herself a "recovering quitter"? What has she done in the fifteen years since she left the father of her son, Clay?
5. What has Graham learned from her family, her home, close friendships, and the natural world?

Strategies and Structures

1. What is the purpose of beginning this essay with Timothy Leary's statement in 1967? What does this tell the reader about the author? How does she further this opinion in the next three paragraphs?
2. There are essentially two parts to this essay. How is this division advantageous to the author's purpose and for the reader's perception? How does Graham's realization that the problem wasn't in the places they went or with people they met but in themselves contribute to this division?
3. Why does Graham tell the reader that in no way is she a "recovering" quitter? Why does she not want us to jump to conclusions about her?

4. Although the author begins the essay by telling us that she is a quitter, how does she end the essay? What has she learned over the years? Is there a purpose in this revelation? How does it enhance the process of writing an essay?

Language and Vocabulary

1. Vocabulary: *tenacious, disdainful, collaborator, morph, nirvana, lucrative, redemption, paradoxical, upheaval, superficial.* After looking up the words that you do not know, use them in a paragraph or two to establish a sequence describing how the author first felt about being a quitter and what she has learned from her experiences.
2. Compose your own vocabulary list and use the words in a few paragraphs to describe what it is like to be addicted to success rather than quitting.

Group Activities

1. Assemble into groups and discuss the effects of the lifestyle portrayed in Graham's essay on the children who were born to these people. Do some research on this in the library and save your information to use in a future essay.
2. Gather into two or three groups and research the "Hippie Revolution" of the late 1960s and early 1970s. Who was Timothy Leary, and how did he and this era contribute to the author's desire to "quit"? After completing your research, form into two groups and debate the advantages and/or disadvantages of *dropping out* or *quitting.*

Writing Activities

1. Write a composition wherein you describe what it would be like if you suddenly quit school and/or your job. You should include how your parents and friends would accept this, and how you would defend yourself and justify your decision.
2. Using the information you obtained in Group Activities 2, write an essay in which you describe what it would be like to be a child born to parents who have no roots. A topic you might deal with could be: Does this lifestyle in any way affect a child's self-esteem? You might decide whether this lifestyle would be harmful or helpful.

John Steinbeck

The Snake

Born in Salinas, California, John Steinbeck (1902–1968) came from a family of moderate means. A premier American novelist, storywriter, playwright, and essayist, he received his college education at Stanford University, but he never graduated. He moved to New York in 1925, and there he attempted to establish himself as a freelance writer. When he failed to do so, Steinbeck returned to California. Although he had published fiction and nonfiction such as *Cup of Gold* (1929), *Pastures of Heaven* (1932), and *To a God Unknown* (1933). Steinbeck did not become widely known until *Tortilla Flat* (1935), a series of humorous stories about Monterey *paisanos.* Steinbeck's novels can all be classified as social novels dealing with the economic problems of rural labor, but there is also a streak of worship of the soil in his books, which does not always agree with his matter-of-fact sociological approach. After the rough and earthy humor of *Tortilla Flat,* he moved on to more serious fiction, often aggressive in its social criticism, to *In Dubious Battle* (1936), which deals with the strikes of the migratory fruit pickers on California plantations. He followed this with *The Red Pony* (1937), *Of Mice and Men* (1937), and a series of short stories collected in *The Long Valley* (1938). In the following year, he published what many consider his best work, *The Grapes of Wrath* (1939), a story about Oklahoma tenant farmers who, unable to earn a living from the land, moved to California where they became migratory farm workers. Some of his later works include: *The Sea of Cortez* (1941), *Cannery Row* (1945), *The Pearl* (1947), *East of Eden* (1952), *The Winter of Our Discontent* (1961), and *Travels with Charley* (1962). In 1962, the same year he received the Nobel Prize for Literature, he wrote a series of articles that championed President Lyndon B. Johnson's Vietnam War policies for *Newsday.* Unfortunately, this act prompted the *New York Post* to sharply criticize him for betraying his liberal past, and it divided many of his readers. In 1968, Steinbeck died of a heart attack in New York City. The following descriptive story, based on an actual incident that occurred in Ed "Doc" Rickett's laboratory, first appeared in the *Long Valley.*

Pre-reading Questions

1. Describe some of the characteristics of a snake, as well as what you associate with it. Do you know anybody you would describe as "snakelike"? Why?

2. Do a five to ten minute "freewrite" or "quickwrite"—a character sketch of either a "snakelike" person you know or what you would do to seem "snakelike" in the company of others.

3. Use a series of questions to help anticipate or predict what "The Snake" will be about; you might want to make marginal notations (e.g., questions about the story, confusion, intrigue, surprise, etc.).

---

1 IT WAS almost dark when young Dr. Phillips swung his sack to his: shoulder and left the tide pool. He climbed up over the rocks and squashed along the street in his rubber boots. The street lights were on by the time he arrived at his little commercial laboratory on the cannery street of Monterey. It was a tight little building, standing partly on piers over the bay water and partly on the land. On both sides the big corrugated-iron sardine canneries crowded in on it.

2 Dr. Phillips climbed the wooden steps and opened the door. The white rats in their cages scampered up and down the wire, and the captive cats in their pens moved for milk. Dr. Phillips turned on the glaring light over the dissection table and dumped his clammy sack on the floor. He walked to the glass cages by the window where the rattlesnakes lived, leaned over and looked in.

3 The snakes were bunched and resting in the corner of the cage, but every head was clear; the dusty eyes seemed to look at nothing, but as the young man leaned over the cage the forked tongues, black on the ends and pink behind, twittered out and waved slowly up and down. Then the snakes recognized the man and pulled in their tongues.

4 Dr. Phillips threw off his leather coat and built a fire in the tin stove; he set a kettle of water on the stove and dropped a can of beans into the water. Then he stood staring down at the sack on the floor. He was a slight young man with the mild, preoccupied eyes of one who looks through a microscope a great deal. He wore a short blond beard.

5 The draft ran breathily up the chimney and a glow of warmth came from the stove. The little waves washed quietly about the piles under the building. Arranged on shelves about the room were tier above tier of museum jars containing the mounted marine specimens the laboratory dealt in.

6 Dr. Phillips opened a side door and went into his bedroom, a book-lined cell containing an army cot, a reading light and an uncomfortable wooden chair. He pulled off his rubber boots and put on a pair of sheepskin slippers. When he went back to the other room the water in the kettle was already beginning to hum.

7 He lifted his sack to the table under the white light and emptied out two dozen common starfish. These he laid out side by side on the table.

His preoccupied eyes turned to the busy rats in the wire cages. Taking grain from a paper sack he poured it into feeding troughs. Instantly the rats scrambled down from the wire and fell upon the food. A bottle of milk stood on a glass shelf between a small mounted octopus and a jellyfish. Dr. Phillips lifted down the milk and walked to the cat cage, but before he filled the containers he reached in the cage and gently picked out a big rangy alley tabby. He stroked her for a moment and then dropped her in a small black painted box, closed the lid and bolted it and then turned on a petcock which admitted gas into the killing chamber. While the short soft struggle went on in the black box he filled the saucers with milk. One of the cats arched against his hand and he smiled and petted her neck.

8 The box was quiet now. He turned off the petcock, for the airtight box would be full of gas.

9 On the stove the pan of water was bubbling furiously about the can of beans. Dr. Phillips lifted out the can with a big pair of forceps, opened it, and emptied the beans into a glass dish. While he ate he watched the starfish on the table. From between the rays little drops of milky fluid were exuding. He bolted his beans and when they were gone he put the dish in the sink and stepped to the equipment cupboard. From this he took a microscope and a pile of little glass dishes. He filled the dishes one by one with sea water from a tap and arranged them in a line beside the starfish. He took out his watch and laid it on the table under the pouring white light. The waves washed with little sighs against the piles under the floor. He took an eyedropper from a drawer and bent over the starfish.

10 At that moment there were quick soft steps on the wooden stairs and a strong knocking at the door. A slight grimace of annoyance crossed the young man's face as he went to open. A tall, lean woman stood in the doorway. She was dressed in a severe dark suit—her straight black hair, growing low on a flat forehead, was mussed as though the wind had been blowing it. Her black eyes glittered in the strong light.

11 She spoke in a soft throaty voice, "May I come in? I want to talk to you."

12 "I'm very busy just now," he said half-heartedly. "I have to do things at times." But he stood away from the door. The tall woman slipped in.

13 "I'll be quiet until you can talk to me."

14 He closed the door and brought the uncomfortable chair from the bedroom. "You see," he apologized, "the process is started and I must get to it." So many people wandered in and asked questions. He had little routines of explanations for the commoner processes. He could say them without thinking. "Sit here. In a few minutes I'll be able to listen to you."

15 The tall woman leaned over the table. With the eyedropper the young man gathered fluid from between the rays of the starfish and squirted it into a bowl of water, and then he drew some milky fluid and squirted

it in the same bowl and stirred the water gently with the eyedropper. He began his little patter of explanation.

16 "When starfish are sexually mature they release sperm and ova when they are exposed at low tide. By choosing mature specimens and taking them out of the water, I give them a condition of low tide. Now I've mixed the sperm and eggs. Now I put some of the mixture in each one of these ten watch glasses. In ten minutes I will kill those in the fast glass with menthol, twenty minutes later I will kill the second group and then a new group every twenty minutes. Then I will have arrested the process in stages, and I will mount the series on microscope slides for biologic study." He paused, "Would you like to look at this first group under the microscope?"

17 "No, thank you."

18 He turned quickly to her. People always wanted to look through the glass. She was not looking at the table at all, but at him. Her black eyes were on him, but they did not seem to see him. He realized why—the irises were as dark as the pupils, there was no color line between the two. Dr. Phillips was piqued at her answer. Although answering questions bored him, a lack of interest in what he was doing irritated him. A desire to arouse her grew in him.

19 "While I'm waiting the first ten minutes I have something to do. Some people don't like to see it. Maybe you'd better step into that room until I finish."

20 "No," she said in her soft flat tone. "Do what you wish. I will wait until you can talk to me." Her hands rested side by side on her lap. She was completely at rest. Her eyes were bright but the rest of her was almost in a state of suspended animation. He thought, "Low metabolic rate, almost as low as a frog's, from the looks." The desire to shock her out of her inanition possessed him again.

21 He brought a little wooden cradle to the table, laid out scalpels and scissors and rigged a big hollow needle to a pressure tube. Then from the killing chamber he brought the limp dead cat and laid it in the cradle and tied its legs to hooks in the sides. He glanced sidewise at the woman. She had not moved. She was still at rest.

22 The cat grinned up into the light, its pink tongue stuck out between its needle teeth. Dr. Phillips deftly snipped open the skin at the throat; with a scalpel he slit through and found an artery. With flawless technique he put the needle in the vessel and tied it in with gut. "Embalming fluid," he explained. "Later I'll inject yellow mass into the venous system and red mass into the arterial system—for bloodstream dissection—biology classes."

23 He looked around at her again. Her dark eyes seemed veiled with dust. She looked without expression at the cat's open throat. Not a drop of blood had escaped. The incision was clean. Dr. Phillips looked at his

watch. “Time for the first group.” He shook a few crystals of menthol into the first watch-glass.

24 The woman was making him nervous. The rats climbed about on the wire of their cage again and squeaked softly. The waves under the building beat with little shocks on the piles.

25 The young man shivered. He put a few lumps of coal in the stove and sat down. “Now,” he said, “I haven’t anything to do for twenty minutes.” He noticed how short her chin was between lower lip and point. She seemed to awaken slowly, to come up out of some deep pool of consciousness. Her head raised and her dark dusty eyes moved about his room and then came back to him.

26 “I was waiting,” she said. Her hands remained side by side on her lap “You have snakes?”

27 “Why, yes,” he said rather loudly. “I have about two dozen rattlesnakes. I milk out the venom and send it to the anti-venom laboratories.”

28 She continued to look at him but her eyes did not center on him, rather they covered him and seemed to see in a big circle all around him. “Have you a male snake, a male rattlesnake?”

29 “Well, it just happens I know I have, I came in one morning and found a big snake in—in coition with a smaller one. That’s very rare in captivity. You see, I do know I have a male snake.”

30 “Where is he?”

31 “Why, right in the glass cage by the window there.”

32 Her head swung slowly around but her two quiet hands did not move. She turned back toward him. “May I see?”

33 He got up and walked to the case by the window. On the sand bottom the knot of rattlesnakes lay entwined, but their heads were clear. The tongues came out and flickered a moment and then waved up and down feeling the air for vibrations. Dr. Phillips nervously turned his head. The woman was standing beside him. He had not heard her get up from the chair. He had heard only the splash of water among the piles and the scampering of the rats on the wire screen.

34 She said softly, “Which is the male you spoke of?”

35 He pointed to a thick, dusty gray snake lying by itself in one corner of the cage. “That one. He’s nearly five feet long. He comes from Texas. Our Pacific coast snakes are usually smaller. He’s been taking all the rats, too. When I want the others to eat I have to take him out.”

36 The woman stared down at the blunt dry head. The forked tongue slipped out and hung quivering for a long moment. “And you’re sure he’s a male.”

37 “Rattlesnakes are funny,” he said glibly. “Nearly every generalization proves wrong. I don’t like to say anything definite about rattlesnakes, but—yes—I can assure you he’s male.”

38 Her eyes did not move from the flat head. “Will you sell him to me?”

39 "Sell him?" he cried. "Sell him to you?"

40 "You do sell specimens, don't you?"

41 "Oh—yes. Of course I do. Of course I do."

42 "How much? Five dollars? Ten?"

43 "Oh! Not more than five. But—do you know anything about rattlesnakes? You might be bitten."

44 She looked at him for a moment. "I don't intend to take him. I want to leave him here, but—I want him to be mine. I want to come here and look at him and feed him and to know he's mine." She opened a little purse and took out a five-dollar bill. "Here! Now he is mine."

45 Dr. Phillips began to be afraid. "You could come to look at him without owning him."

46 "I want him to be mine."

47 "Oh, Lord!" he cried, "I've forgotten the time." He ran to the table. "Three minutes over. It won't matter much." He shook menthol crystals into the second watchglass. And then he was drawn back to the cage where the woman still stared at the snake.

48 She asked, "What does he eat?"

49 "I feed them white rats, rats from the cage over there."

50 "Will you put him in the other cage? I want to feed him."

51 "But he doesn't need food. He's had a rat already this week. Sometimes they don't eat for three or four months. I had one that didn't eat for over a year."

52 In her low monotone she asked, "Will you sell me a rat?"

53 He shrugged his shoulders. "I see. You want to watch how rattlesnakes eat. All right. I'll show you. The rat will cost twenty-five cents. It's better than a bullfight if you look at it one way, and it's simply a snake eating his dinner if you look at it another." His tone had become acid. He hated people who made sport of natural processes. He was not a sportsman but a biologist. He could kill a thousand animals for knowledge, but not an insect for pleasure. He'd been over this in his mind before.

54 She turned her head slowly toward him and the beginning of a smile formed on her thin lips. "I want to feed my snake," she said. "I'll put him in the other cage." She had opened the top of the cage and dipped her hand in before he knew what she was doing. He leaped forward and pulled her back. The lid banged shut.

55 "Haven't you any sense," he asked fiercely. "Maybe he wouldn't kill you, but he'd make you damned sick in spite of what I could do for you."

56 "You put him in the other cage then," she said quietly.

57 Dr. Phillips was shaken. He found that he was avoiding the dark eyes that didn't seem to look at anything. He felt that it was profoundly wrong to put a rat into the cage, deeply sinful, and he didn't know why. Often he had put rats in the cage when someone or other had wanted to see it, but this desire tonight sickened him. He tried to explain himself out of it.

58 "It's a good thing to see," he said. "It shows you how a snake can work. It makes you have a respect for a rattlesnake. Then, too, lots of people have dreams about the terror of snakes making the kill. I think because it is a subjective rat. The person is the rat. Once you see it the whole matter is objective. The rat is only a rat and the terror is removed."

59 He took a long stick equipped with a leather noose from the wall. Opening the trap he dropped the noose over the big snake's head and tightened the thong. A piercing dry rattle filled the room. The thick body writhed and slashed about the handle of the stick as he lifted the snake out and dropped it in the feeding cage. It stood ready to strike for a time, but the buzzing gradually ceased. The snake crawled into a corner, made a big figure eight with its body and lay still.

60 "You see," the young man explained, "these snakes are quite tame. I've had them a long time. I suppose I could handle them if I wanted to, but everyone who does handle rattlesnakes gets bitten sooner or later. I just don't want to take the chance." He glanced at the woman. He hated to put in the rat. She had moved over in front of the new cage; her black eyes were on the stony head of the snake again.

61 She said, "Put in a rat."

62 Reluctantly he went to the rat cage. For some reason he was sorry for the rat, and such a feeling had never come to him before. His eyes went over the mass of swarming white bodies climbing up the screen toward him. "Which one?" he thought. "Which one shall it be?" Suddenly he turned angrily to the woman. "Wouldn't you rather I put in a cat? Then you'd see a real fight. The cat might even win, but if it did it might kill the snake. I'll sell you a cat if you like."

63 She didn't look at him. "Put in a rat" she said. "I want him to eat."

64 He opened the rat cage and thrust his hand in. His fingers found a tail and he lifted a plump, red-eyed rat out of the cage. It struggled up to try to bite his fingers and, failing, hung spread out and motionless from its tail. He walked quickly across the room, opened the feeding cage and cropped the rat in on the sand floor. "Now, watch it" he cried.

65 The woman did not answer him. His eyes were on the snake where it lay still. Its tongue flicking in and out rapidly, tasted the air of the cage.

66 The rat landed on its feet, turned around and sniffed at its pink naked tail and then unconcernedly trotted across the sand, smelling as it went. The room was silent. Dr. Phillips did not know whether the water sighed among the piles or whether the woman sighed. Out of the corner of his eye he saw her body crouch and stiffen.

67 The snake moved out smoothly, slowly. The tongue flicked in and out. The motion was so gradual, so smooth that it didn't seem to be motion at all. In the other end of the cage the rat perked up in a sitting position and began to lick down the fine white hair on its chest. The snake moved on, keeping always a deep 8 curve in its neck.

68 The silence beat on the young man. He felt the blood drifting up in his body. He said loudly, “See! He keeps the striking curve ready. Rattlesnakes are cautious, almost cowardly animals. The mechanism is so delicate. The snake's dinner is to be got by an operation as deft as a surgeon's job. He takes no chances with his instruments.”

69 The snake had flowed to the middle of the cage by now. The rat looked up, saw the snake and then unconcernedly went back to licking its chest.

70 It's the most beautiful thing in the world,” the young man said. His veins were throbbing. “It's the most terrible thing in the world.”

71 The snake was close now. Its head lifted a few inches from the sand. The head weaved slowly beat and forth, aiming, getting distance, aiming. Dr. Phillips glanced again at the woman. He turned sick. She was weaving too, not much, just a suggestion.

72 The rat looked up and saw the snake. It dropped to four feet and back up, and then—the stroke. It was impossible to see, simply a flash. The rat jarred as though under an invisible blow. The snake backed hurriedly into the corner from which it had come, and settled down its tongue working constantly.

73 “Perfect!” Dr. Phillips cried. “Right between the shoulder blades. The fangs must almost have reached the heart.”

74 The rat stood still, breathing like a little white bellows. Suddenly it leaped in the air and landed on its side. Its legs kicked spasmodically for a second and it was dead.

75 The woman relaxed, relaxed sleepily.

76 “Well,” the young man demanded, “it was an emotional bath, wasn't it?”

77 She turned her misty eyes to him. “Will he eat it now?” she asked.

78 “Of course he'll eat it. He didn't kill it for a thrill. He killed it because he was hungry.”

79 The corners of the woman's mouth turned up a trifle again. She looked back at the snake. “I want to see him eat it.”

80 Now the snake came out of its corner again. There was no striking curve in its neck, but it approached the rat gingerly, ready to jump back in case it attacked. It nudged the body gently with its blunt nose, and drew away. Satisfied that it was dead, the snake touched the body all over with its chin, from head to tail. It seemed to measure the body and to kiss it. Finally it opened its mouth and unhinged its jaws at the comers.

81 Dr. Phillips put his will against his head to keep it from turning toward the woman. He thought, “If she's opening her mouth, I'll be sick. I'll be afraid.” He succeeded in keeping his eyes away.

82 The snake fitted its jaws over the rat's head and then with a slow peristaltic pulsing, began to engulf the rat. The jaws gripped and the whole throat crawled up, and the jaws gripped again.

83 Dr. Phillips turned away and went to his work table. “You’ve made me miss one of the series,” he said bitterly. “The set won’t be complete.” He put one of the watch glasses under a low-power microscope and looked at it, and then angrily he poured the contents of all the dishes into the sink. The waves had fallen so that only a wet whisper came up through the floor. The young man lifted a trapdoor at his feet and dropped the starfish down into the black water. He paused at the cat, crucified in the cradle and grinning comically into the light. Its body was puffed with embalming fluid. He shut off the pressure, withdrew the needle and tied the vein.

84 “Would you like some coffee?” he asked.

85 “No, thank you. I shall be going pretty soon.”

86 He walked to her where she stood in front of the snake cage. The rat was swallowed, all except an inch of pink tail that stuck out of the snake’s mouth like a sardonic tongue. The throat heaved again and the tail disappeared. The jaws snapped back into their sockets, and the big snake crawled heavily to the corner, made a big eight and dropped its head on the sand.

87 “He’s asleep now,” the woman said. “I’m going now. But I’ll come back and feed my snake every little while. I’ll pay for the rats. I want him to have plenty. And sometime—I’ll take him away with me.” Her eyes came out of their dusty dream for a moment. “Remember, he’s mine. Don’t take his poison. I want him to have it. Goodnight.” She walked swiftly to the door and went out. He heard her footsteps on the stairs, but he could not hear her walk away on the pavement.

88 Dr. Phillips turned a chair around and sat down in front of the snake cage. He tried to comb out his thought as he looked at the torpid snake. “I’ve read so much about psychological sex symbols,” he thought. “I doesn’t seem to explain. Maybe I’m too much alone. Maybe I should kill the snake. If I knew—no, I can’t pray to anything.”

89 For weeks he expected her to return. “I will go out and leave her alone here when she comes,” he decided, “I won’t see the damned thing again.”

90 She never came again. For months he looked for her when he walked about in the town. Several times he ran after some tall woman thinking it might be she. But he never saw her again—ever.

Post-reading Questions

Content

1. *Who* was the mysterious woman in “The Snake,” a thinly veiled fictionalized account of an event that Steinbeck actually witnessed in Ed “Doc” Ricketts’ (Dr. Phillips in the narrative) laboratory?

2. *What* does the woman want and why?
3. *When* does the woman appear in "The Snake"? *How* and *why* does this create tension in the story?
4. *What* are some of the denotative (dictionary) definitions for "life," "death," "snake"—as well as some of their connotative (associated or implied) meanings?
5. *Where* does Steinbeck set most of the action in "The Snake"? *Why* would or *why* wouldn't another location have been equally suitable? Justify your answer with specific reasoning and examples.

Strategies and Structures

1. Review the glossary of "Literary and Rhetorical Terms" at the back of *Visions Across the Americas*, and then analyze how Steinbeck applies irony, tone, mood, style, and "sound" of language to achieve specific rhetorical purposes.
2. In *what* way does the author's use of transitions and linking devices provide a sense of chronology and coherence in this story?
3. To *what* effect does Steinbeck use words, images, and repeated information in his story? How do they add to his narrative as a whole?
4. *Why* do you think Steinbeck decided to use relatively simple diction (word choice) throughout his tale with a sprinkling of scientific and biological terms? Explain.
5. *How* does the mysterious woman fulfill her desire and thereby achieve her objective for visiting Dr. Phillips?

Language and Vocabulary

1. Vocabulary: *corrugated, clammy, preoccupied, specimens, troughs, forceps, microscope, eyedropper, grim ace, annoyance, glittered, half-heartedly, piqued, suspended, animation, inanition, scalpels, embalming, venous, arterial, dissection, consciousness, coition, captivity, entwined, vibration, scampering, monotone, objective, writhed, slashed, reluctantly, sniffed, mechanism, trifle, gingerly, nudged, unhinged, peristaltic, engulf, crucified, sardonic, psychological.* Place this list of words in your vocabulary log, and consult your dictionary for their definitions; keep a record of them. Next, go back and note how many of the vocabulary words in "The Snake" were used to modify and describe people, places, things, and actions. What would have been lost if Steinbeck had omitted all modifying and descriptive words? What does this tell you about the significance of words in context?
2. Make a list of all the words you can find in "The Snake" that suggest mystery, uneasiness, anxiety, fear, disgust, dread, and possibly shock or revulsion. Then, write a paragraph describing someone where you use at least two thirds of the words on your vocabulary list at least once.

Group Activities

1. Allow students to place themselves in groups of four or five members, and then ask them to compare their notes on Steinbeck's, "The Snake." Request that they identify some common areas of interest as opposed to what they "liked" or "disliked" to give them some practice in objectively expressing themselves. Next, have them put together a multimodal presentation entitled *Steinbeck and "The Snake"* (or something to that effect). Students could gather photos of Ed "Doc" Ricketts' lab, for instance, and put together a JPEG slide show, MPEG presentation, or YouTube video, blending Steinbeck reading his story, film clips, photographs and so on.
2. In small groups, summarize Steinbeck's short story, "The Snake," and then look up a short article on the Internet entitled, "About Ed Ricketts." (If your classroom has access to the Internet and a projection system, your instructor might be able to locate and display it on the large classroom screen.) Summarize that non-fiction account of Steinbeck's friend as well, and then compare and contrast the portrayal of the eccentric marine biologist in Steinbeck's story (Dr. Phillips) to the actual person (Ed "Doc" Ricketts).

Writing Activities

1. Brainstorm or pre-write using any combination of methods that works for you. For instance, you may want to cluster the word "snake," and identify as many positive and negative associations with the reptile as possible. Do the same with at least two other topics or issues that emerge from "The Snake" such as life and death, right and wrong in the balance of nature, clinical science, and morbid curiosity. What can you say about your observations? Fully argue, illustrate, and explain your original thesis with examples drawn from personal experience, observations of others, and readings.
2. Use multiple pre-writing strategies to gather impressions and assess your understanding of gender issues as presented in "The Snake," a fictionalized account of the mysterious, tall, slender woman who came to visit Dr. Phillips' laboratory.

Maya Angelou

Champion of the World

Born Marguerita Johnson in 1928, Maya Angelou spent her youth encountering one personal tragedy after another. Angelou's talents are many; she has acted in the television miniseries *Roots*, produced a series about Africa for PBS-TV, and written several volumes of poetry. A recipient of several honorary doctorates, Angelou is best known for her autobiography, *I Know Why the Caged Bird Sings* (1970). Other works include *Just Give Me a Cool Drink of Water 'for I Die* (1971), *Gather Together in My Name* (1974), *Singin' and Swingin' & Gettin' Merry Like Christmas* (1976), *And Still I Rise* (1978), *Shaker, Why Don't You Sing?* (1983), *All God's Children Need Traveling Shoes* (1986), *I Shall Not Be Moved* (1990), *Wouldn't Take Nothing for My Journey Now* (1993), *Lessons in Living* (1993), *Kofi and His Magic* (1996), *Even the Stars Look Lonesome* (1997), A *Song Flung Up To Heaven* (2002), and *Hallelujah! The Welcome Table: A Lifetime of Memories with Recipes* (2004). Angelou's career as a dancer, singer, and writer continues to flourish. She is a popular speaker at literary gatherings and conferences worldwide. Long esteemed by our nation's leaders, former President Gerald Ford appointed Angelou to the American Revolution Bicentennial Council in 1975, and she wrote and read the poem, "On the Pulse of Morning" (1993), at the inauguration of William Jefferson Clinton, the forty-second president of the United States. Most recently, Angelou published *Good Food All Day Long* (2010).

Pre-reading Questions

1. The following piece is an excerpt from Angelou's *I Know Why the Caged Bird Sings.* Without worrying about accuracy, explain the meaning behind the title of her autobiography in your journal or writing log.
2. Think about the title of this descriptive narrative, *"Champion of the World,"* a title taken directly from a phrase in the book. Then turn to the person sitting next to you and brainstorm the word *champion.* What qualities do you associate with a champion?

1 The last inch of space was filled, yet people continued to wedge themselves along the walls of the Store. Uncle Willie had turned the radio up to its last notch so that youngsters on the porch wouldn't miss a word. Women sat on kitchen chairs, dining-room chairs, stools and upturned wooden boxes. Small children and babies perched on every lap available and men leaned on the shelves or on each other.

2 The apprehensive mood was shot through with shafts of gaiety, as a black sky is streaked with lightning.

3 "I ain't worried 'bout this fight. Joe's gonna whip that cracker like it's open season."

4 "He gone whip him till that white boy call him Momma."

5 At last the talking finished and the string-along songs about razor blades were over and the fight began.

6 "A quick jab to the head." In the Store the crowd grunted. "A left to the head and a right and another left." One of the listeners cackled like a hen and was quieted.

7 "They're in a clinch, Louis is trying to fight his way out."

8 Some bitter comedian on the porch said, "That white man don't mind hugging that niggah now, I betcha."

9 "The referee is moving in to break them up, but Louis finally pushed the contender away and it's an uppercut to the chin. The contender is hanging on, now he's backing away. Louis catches him with a short left to the jaw."

10 A tide of murmuring assent poured out the door and into the yard.

11 "Another left and another left. Louis is saving that mighty right . . ." The mutter in the Store had grown into a baby roar and it was pierced by the clang of a bell and the announcer's "That's the bell for round three, ladies and gentlemen."

12 As I pushed my way into the Store I wondered if the announcer gave any thought to the fact that he was addressing as "ladies and gentlemen" all the Negroes around the world who sat sweating and praying, glued to their "master's voice."

13 There were only a few calls for R. C. Colas, Dr. Peppers, and Hires root beer. The real festivities would begin after the fight. Then even the old Christian ladies who taught their children and tried themselves to practice turning the other cheek would buy soft drinks, and if the Brown Bomber's victory was a particularly bloody one they would order peanut patties and Baby Ruths also.

14 Bailey and I laid the coins on top of the cash register. Uncle Willie didn't allow us to ring up sales during a fight. It was too noisy and might shake up the atmosphere. When the gong rang for the next round we pushed through the near-sacred quiet to the herd of children outside.

15 "He's got Louis against the ropes and now it's a left to the body and a right to the ribs. Another right to the body, it looks like it was low . . .

Yes, ladies and gentlemen, the referee is signaling but the contender keeps raining the blows on Louis. It's another to the body, and it looks like Louis is going down."

16 My race groaned. It was our people falling. It was another lynching, yet another Black man hanging on a tree. One more woman ambushed and raped. A Black boy whipped and maimed. It was hounds on the trail of a man running through slimy swamps. It was a white woman slapping her maid for being forgetful.

17 The men in the Store stood away from the walls and at attention. Women greedily clutched the babes on their laps while on the porch the shufflings and smiles, flirtings and pinching of a few minutes before were gone. This might be the end of the world. If Joe lost we were back in slavery and beyond help. It would all be true, the accusations that we were lower types of human beings. Only a little higher than apes. True that we were stupid and ugly and lazy and dirty and, unlucky and worst of all, that God Himself hated us and ordained us to be hewers of wood and drawers of water, forever and ever, world without end.

18 We didn't breathe. We didn't hope. We waited.

19 "He's off the ropes, ladies and gentlemen. He's moving towards the center of the ring." There was no time to be relieved. The worst might still happen.

20 "And now it looks like Joe is mad. He's caught Carnera with a left hook to the head and a right to the head. It's a left jab to the body and another left to the head. There's a left cross and a right to the head. The contender's right eye is bleeding and he can't seem to keep his block up. Louis is penetrating every block. The referee is moving in, but Louis sends a left to the body and it's an uppercut to the chin and the contender is dropping. He's on the canvas, ladies and gentlemen."

21 Babies slid to the floor as women stood up and men leaned toward the radio.

22 "Here's the referee. He's young. One, two, three, four, five, six, seven . . . Is the contender trying to get up again?"

23 All the men in the store shouted, "NO."

24 "—eight, nine, ten." There were a few sounds from the audience, but they seemed to be holding themselves in against tremendous pressure.

25 "The fight is all over, ladies and gentlemen. Let's get the microphone over to the referee . . . Here he is. He's got the Brown Bomber's hand, he's holding it up . . . Here he is . . ."

26 Then the voice, husky and familiar, came to wash over us—"The winnah, and still heavyweight champeen of the world . . . Joe Louis."

27 Champion of the world. A Black boy. Some Black mother's son. He was the strongest man in the world. People drank Coca-Colas like ambrosia and ate candy bars like Christmas. Some of the men went behind the Store and poured white lightning in their soft-drink bottles, and a few

of the bigger boys followed them. Those who were not chased away came back blowing their breath in front of themselves like proud smokers.

28 It would take an hour or more before the people would leave the Store and head for home. Those who lived too far had made arrangements to stay in town. It wouldn't do for a Black man and his family to be caught on a lonely country road on a night when Joe Louis had proved that we were the strongest people in the world.

Post-reading Questions

Content

1. Why were so many people gathered at Uncle Willie's store at night? What did they all have in common, "even the old Christian ladies"?
2. Why did the people who lived far away from Uncle Willie's store make arrangements to stay "in town" for the night?
3. While we know he is literally defending his heavyweight boxing title, Joe Louis is figuratively defending something else. What is it? (See paragraphs 16 and 17.)
4. How did the radio announcer's description of the fight affect the people in Willie's store?
5. Discuss different ways people at Uncle Willie's store celebrate the outcome of the fight.

Strategies and Structures

1. When and where is dialogue used in this narrative? What is its purpose? What would this narrative account lose if no dialogue had been included? Why?
2. What type of sentence pattern helps Angelou build suspense in this narrative? In what way do observations of those around her echo the author's own feelings? How do we know for sure?
3. What sort of details does Angelou offer her readers so they can visualize the scene she describes? Without rereading the narrative, jot down as many details as you can remember.
4. What images in the opening paragraph create an atmosphere of suspense and anticipation?

Language and Vocabulary

1. Vocabulary: Go through this descriptive narrative and locate any unfamiliar words. Write them down on a piece of paper, along with their dictionary definitions. Continue to add to your personal vocabulary list throughout the semester.
2. What instances of nonstandard English did you notice in this essay? What purpose does such language serve?

Group Activities

1. Go back through the essay and select four or five descriptive phrases. When you assemble in groups, share three of the phrases you wrote down on a separate piece of paper, stating the descriptive phrase you liked best and why. Using a different subject with different modifying words, rewrite each group member's favorite descriptive phrase twice.
2. Spend five minutes or so discussing what you think Uncle Willie's store looks like based upon the concrete details provided by Angelou (refer to your response to question 3 under Strategies and Structures). Next, locate a video copy of *I Know Why the Caged Bird Sings,* a television movie, in your college's audiovisual center, and watch the film. Pay particular attention to the sequence where everybody gets together at Uncle Willie's store to listen to the Joe Louis fight on the radio. Finally, compare and contrast the way your group pictured the occasion based upon Angelou's written description to the way the film presented (1) the store, and (2) the gathering of people on the night of the Joe Louis fight. (*Note:* Though Angelou adapted *I Know Why the Caged Bird Sings* for television, she was not the set designer.)

Writing Activities

1. Describe an incident that gave you a feeling of pride in your family, culture, nation, religious group, political group, or gender.
2. Construct a thesis that says something about afterthoughts, the things we think about after saying or not saying something. Then, develop your thesis by describing a recent argument or two you've had with another person, noting what you did *not* say or think about until after the argument (perhaps you wish you had said something but neglected to do so). Include dialogue in your descriptive essay to show rather than just tell your reader what you said and did.

Internet Connection: Maya Angelou

Colloquialisms, Jargon, Slang

Type the key words "colloquialisms," "jargon," and "slang," into an online database. What sites do you initially find? Refine your search and locate at least one list of colloquialisms, one list of modern "jargon," and one list of "slang" words. Then, write a paragraph or so about a recent social, political, or cultural event, integrating three or four terms and expressions from each list. What effect might informal language such as colloquialisms, jargon, and slang have on clear communication? What may be its advantages?

Additional Topics and Issues for Descriptive Essays

1. Describe a person, a place, or a thing that you fear. What is it that you fear, and when do you fear it most? What sorts of steps do you take to try and overcome your fear?
2. Write a description of your favorite place. Use specific details to make your essay vivid. You may want to answer some of the following questions: Where is this place? What kinds of things are there? Why do you like this place? When do you go there? How did you find this place? Who else goes there?
3. Write a visual portrait of what you perceive to be the youth of America. What or who are they? How do they dress, eat, and think? What sort of music do they listen and dance to? Try to avoid stereotypes when dealing with this subject. Make certain that you illustrate your claims with several representative examples drawn from personal experience, observations of others, and readings.
4. Describe your favorite or ideal meal. Use adjectives and adverbs to help your reader smell, taste, and visualize the meal spread before him or her.
5. Compose an essay describing a place usually considered undesirable to visit; for example, you may want to write about a trip to the local garbage dump, slaughterhouse, or cannery. Make sure to include all the unpleasant sights, sounds, and smells. After all, the purpose for using description in this sort of essay is to enable the reader to share in your experience.

6. Describe a sporting, social, or other cultural event that you attended and felt was quite significant in one way or another. Be sure to include the sounds, the sights, and any other sensual imagery that impressed you.
7. Using figurative language, describe two unlike objects, showing how they can be compared with each other by using similes and/or metaphors. (You may wish to review the chapter introduction, particularly if you intend to use an extended metaphor.)
8. Describe a meeting that you have had with a particularly colorful character, integrating dialogue exchanged between the two of you to add variety and interest to your essay.
9. Describe an area considered hostile to life that you know well from personal experience and that you feel has been given an unfair reputation. What is it about this area that most people do not realize but you are aware?
10. Based on personal experiences, observations, and findings from interviews and readings, write an essay describing what you think it will be like growing old in America and why you think it will be that way.

CHAPTER 4

Illustration and Example

Supporting a statement through the use of specific examples is essential to good, clear expository and argumentative writing. We illustrate what we claim with personal experiences, observations, and readings. Citing statistics can also support our examples. When we omit information that will help our reader to visualize our observations, we reduce our arguments to generalizations or simply reinforce stereotypes. In essence, writers use illustrations and examples like artists use brushes and paint; authors paint pictures with words for their readers.

Developing Your Thesis

After writing the thesis paragraph, writers then offer the reader detailed evidence to explain and support material. Where do writers gather their examples? Many authors illustrate their points using personal experience. For example, in her essay, "Let's Face It," Sara Blake draws on her expertise as an English professor on one hand and a social networking fan on another to illustrate how *Facebook "has expanded our vocabulary, filling it with terms referred to collectively as 'facebookisms.' It's created verbs from nouns, like* friend *and* defriend*. It's given new meaning to established words like* poke*, which has morphed from being a physical nudge with one's finger to an electronic nudge with the same results of attracting someone's attention . . . Similarly, the noun* tag *has become a verb meaning to identify people in a posted photograph."*

Observations, like personal experiences, can also vividly explain a point in an essay or other form of literature. By watching and listening to what others do and say, we gather a valuable reserve of material, material we can use in everyday conversations as well as essays. (This is one reason many writers keep diaries or journals of what they see.) A fine example of supporting a point with observations is Philip K. Chiu's mention of Chinese stereotypes in "The Myth of the Model Minority." Chiu illustrates a Chinese stereotype by referring to a film character, *"the insidious"* Fu Manchu, followed by a positive—but nonetheless inaccurate—Chinese stereotype: Charlie Chan. His specific examples illustrate general points.

In a similar manner, Ann Scheid uses specific examples of pollution and destruction to animal and plant life to raise an important question: "Is Profit Civilization's Only Motive?" as it moves on into the second decade of the twenty-first century? Or will greed and neglect lead to Armageddon—(Ragnarok if you will)? Additionally, her specific reference to recent ecological disasters coupled with historical and biblical references provide timelines of human relationships toward nature—adding depth and dimension to her discussion points. Citing the recent Gulf Oil Spill, Scheid notes that the catastrophe was *"so large that it put 12,000 people out of work, and, yet, those same people begged the U. S. government not to stop drilling in the Gulf. Not only were their lives threatened, but many wildlife species, including whales, tuna, and shrimp, dozens of species of birds, and land animals, such as, grey fox and white-tailed deer, and also amphibians, such as the alligator and the snapping turtle came under duress."*

If you are writing an essay on contemporary popular culture in America, you might cite Leslie Bow's "Camera Ready"—a humorous article examining the behavior people will adopt and the things they will do in order to become a contestant on *Family Feud* (or any other game show for that matter). Moving beyond a personal narrative, of course, and referring to a broad sampling of books, articles, reports, and other individuals' experience on game shows can make your examples more convincing than if you rely solely on your own knowledge to illustrate a theory or point. Initially citing an authoritative study on *why* more Americans are involved in some sort of physical fitness program today than thirty years ago, for instance, supports what *you may believe* with verifiable evidence.

Creating Vivid Examples

Simply supplying examples to support your points will not be enough to actively engage your reader's imagination, however. To hook your reader's interest and spark his or her imagination, you should make your examples specific and detailed, using concrete nouns and active verbs. Nouns are concrete when they create unmistakable images. Nouns like *things* and *stuff* are vague, imprecise words and may mislead or confuse your reader. Therefore, rather than writing, "Place your *things* on the counter," you would replace the vague word *things* with a word like *clothes, tools,* or *books*—a concrete noun!

Stephanie Ericsson's selected examples in "The Ways We Lie" tend to be vivid, memorable, and concrete. She goes into depth illustrating the lie of *deflecting,* showing how Clarence Thomas, accused of sexual harassment, testified that the Senate Committee hearings for his Supreme Court nomination were a *high-tech lynching: "Rather than defending himself, he took the offensive and accused the country of racism."* She also makes use of personal experience to illustrate the *out-and-out* lie, relating how her nephew blamed *"the murderers"* when he broke her fence.

Active verbs will also keep your reader involved in your essay. Often overlooked by the inexperienced writer, verbs can be the most powerful tool an author has for showing us what is happening as opposed to telling us. One way of making your essay vivid is to replace verbs that merely link ideas with verbs that indicate action. *William is angry at us* would be more effective written as *William scowled at us.* Why? The linking verb *is* links the subject, *William,* with the adjective, *angry.* The verb *scowl* shows the reader *William*'s mood instead of just telling us what he is: angry.

Dialogue, however brief, might do a great job illustrating a person's attitude and/or character. For instance, in Leslie Bow's "Camera Ready," when the emcee announced that "Patriotic Songs" would be the first category to consider on *Family Feud,* and her sister cried out, *"America the Beautiful,"* Bow's family responded with a hearty, *"Good answer! Good answer!"* All was going well as her other family members mentioned, *"The Star Spangled Banner!" "My Country 'Ti's of Thee!'"* and *"Yankee Doodle!"* Then her father hollered, *"Dixie!"* with just as much enthusiasm. Though she says that, *"I guess 'Dixie' would be patriotic if you lived in the Confederacy in say, the*

19th century," she knew better. *"Still we gamely screamed, 'GOOD ANSWER! GOOD ANSWER!' as if to make up for his deficiency. And 'HOOray! HOOray!"*

Visual representations of exploitation and violence highlight a very serious subject—human trafficking—in "Lera's Story," a graphic novel excerpt by Dan Archer and Olga Trusova. Therein, the authors chronicle and literally illustrate Lera's mental, physical, and sexual abuse after being trafficked from the Ukraine to Russia for illegal work. Because the comic book (graphic novel) has been recognized as an art form ideal for conveying serious, non-fiction subjects, the use of images and text enable Archer and Trusova to present compelling, disturbing information to viewers/readers about human trafficking in a documentary format.

Tips on Writing Illustration and Example Essays

1. The best use of illustration and example occurs when a writer has a clear idea of *what* he or she is trying to explain to the reader. To arrive at this point, you may want to freewrite, cluster, or use any method you find effective in generating ideas and limiting your thesis.
2. After you select a topic to write on, determine what sort of illustrations or examples would help to clarify your points and support them. Draw your examples from personal experiences, observations, and readings.
3. Whenever possible, use specific, concrete nouns so your reader will be able to picture vividly what you intend.
4. Complement your use of concrete nouns with verbs expressing action and mood. Again, this will enable you to *show* rather than simply *tell* your reader about your topic.
5. In most compositions, transitional words and phrases that indicate relationships between words, clauses, and entire paragraphs will help to lead your reader from one idea to the next, unifying the sections of your essay. To introduce an example in an illustration essay, use transitions such as *for instance* or *for example.*

Leslie Bow

Camera Ready

Leslie Bow is Associate Professor of English and Asian American Studies. A third generation Chinese American, Professor Bow grew up in the San Francisco Bay Area and received a B.A. from the University of California at Berkeley in 1984 and a Ph.D. from the University of California at Santa Cruz in 1993. She was on the faculties of Brown University and the University of Miami prior to arriving at the University of Wisconsin where she specializes in Asian American literature, ethnic American literature, and literature by women of color. The author of *Betrayal and Other Acts of Subversion: Feminism, Sexual Politics, Asian American Women's Literature* (Princeton 2001), Bow edited *The Scent of the Gods* (2010), and she is currently writing a book on the position of Asians in the segregated South and the processes of racial categorization.

Pre-reading Questions

1. Explain how one of your parents or other family members experienced "15 minutes of fame" in his or her life thus far. If you could choose the time and place for your own "15 minutes of fame," when would that happen, and where would it occur? Be as descriptive as you can.
2. Have you or has anybody you know ever auditioned for a part in a play, a spot on a televised game show, a dance contest, a talent show, etc.? Describe your actual experience—or what you think it would have been like—using illustrations and examples to help readers visualize the people you encountered, the things you did, as well as what made your audition a success or failure.
3. What do you associate with reality TV shows? Access YouTube on the Internet, and browse through what people have filmed and placed on it for others to view. In what way might a YouTube project be like a reality TV episode? Illustrate your answer with specific examples.

1 My family believes itself to be camera-ready in spite of being Chinese. So much so that when we tried out for the game show *Family Feud*, we mistakenly believed that it didn't matter whether you won or lost, it was how you appeared on camera.

2 The 1970s had just ended. *Charlie's Angels* had not yet been integrated. There was no *Survivor* with a "Team Asian." No liberal multiculturalism (nor yet its cynical detractors). Growing up, I learned to keep a low profile; the Vietnam War was coming to a messy conclusion, and a Filipina in New York had been pushed in front of a subway train after being mistaken for a member of the Viet Cong. It seemed proof that we all looked alike, a fact that might have great consequence for the criminally insane. Nevertheless, it was reasonable to think that times had changed.

3 I had never harbored a fixation about being on television, even though lately it seems to have taken hold of the American imagination. My sister Nancy spotted an opportunity for tryouts while she was interning for *That's Incredible!*, a real-person talent show hosted by John Davidson, Fran Tarkenton, and a spunky Cathy Lee Crosby. (Nancy actually persuaded Tarkenton to sign a rude autograph for our little sister, Melissa, that read "To Melissa, President of the Sissy-Butt Club. Best Wishes, Fran Tarkenton." This club, invented by me, required you to wear an inverted bucket over your head; I'm not sure why.)

4 The day of our audition, my sisters and I wore sundresses and heels; we believed that approximating the feminine ideal would increase our chances of getting on the show. Hopes of meeting then-host Richard Dawson, serial kisser, were deflated; tryouts were held in a generic Marriott near our town, far from Hollywood, but crowded with hopefuls who, like us, wanted their 15 minutes of fame. We firmly believed in our collective cuteness and, intuitively, that the time was right for more Asians on TV—after all, *Sesame Street* was multicultural.

5 So strong was our faith, our subtle challenge to the concept of meritocracy, that we didn't realize that we would have to actually *play the game*. Ushered into an overly air-conditioned conference room, we were confronted with our opponents, a family still standing after roundly defeating a seemingly identical group of wannabes who lingered on the margins, apparently uncertain whether or not they had been dismissed. Our competitors were yellow-haired, corn-fed folks—frightful in their average Americanness—who had driven all the way up from Fresno to be there. They wore T-shirts shouting out various slogans, attire that we found somewhat incomprehensible but now seems entirely appropriate. They didn't bother to dress up; they had only to be themselves.

6 It goes without saying that the secret to *Family Feud*—and its beauty—is that you have to reach for the lowest common denominator. The highest scores accrue to the most common answers in a survey of a mythical 100 people. If you fail to come up with an answer that the majority of

middle Americans might come up with, your opponents get the chance to steal the board. Forget eccentricities, regionalisms, or human uniqueness; winning the game depends upon answers everyone else would say. The game started promisingly with Nancy, our most competitive and most spunky, acting as team captain. She faced off against a teenager wearing a lowest-common-denominator kind of outfit—his shirt ordered us to FALL INTO THE GAP! I suspected he might be an albino; blond eyelashes seem so, so wrong.

7 At the moment the stand-in emcee announced our first category—Patriotic Songs—we realized we were sunk. But my sister rammed the fake button so hard at this announcement that she almost toppled the makeshift lectern marked "Property of the Burlingame Marriott." "America the Beautiful!" she cried.

8 "Good answer! Good answer!" We supported her enthusiastically, thinking that it was spirit and good looks that counted most. Her competitiveness won us the right to guess America's top nationalist melodies first, and we did well going down the line: "The Star-Spangled Banner!" "My Country 'Tis of Thee!" "Yankee Doodle!" we shouted. We wanted to be on TV. We wanted to be the Hatfields or the McCoys, it didn't matter which.

9 Then the emcee reached my father. "Dixie!" he hollered. I don't think you could find another Chinese man in the continental United States who conceives of this song as patriotic, but my father is from an anomalous Chinese American enclave in the Deep South and old habits die hard. I guess "Dixie" would be patriotic if you lived in the Confederacy in, say, the 19th century. Still, we gamely screamed "GOOD ANSWER! GOOD ANSWER!" as if to make up for his deficiency. And then, "HOOray! HOOray!"

10 The eccentricity cost us. In desperation, my sisters and I began bouncing up and down, clapping loudly for added measure, our cotton dresses flapping around us in the frigid air of the hotel room. Be spunky; nobody hates spunk—that's what we're all about. We still believed that it was not accuracy—how best you could approximate the norm and parrot it back—but personality, charm, and good old-fashioned can-do spirit that ultimately mattered. We thought that post-1970s America was ready for the spectacle of racial competition. So what if Detroit was losing ground to Japanese automakers? So what if Chinese kids were destroying the curve in math classes around the nation? So what if the country was still smarting from having failed to heed the wisdom—never get involved in a land war in Asia—later offered by Vizzini in *The Princess Bride*? We were wearing sundresses, dammit. We were Chinese, yes, but we were cute.

11 We were not invited back. We would never lock lips with the esteemed host. Our ability to mimic national fealty was only adequate, not prize-winning. We were crushed, but it wasn't about the money. It was also not

difficult for me to suspect that our inflated opinion of our ethnic attractiveness might be inaccurate—as Joe Jackson sings, they say that looks don't count for much and so there goes your proof. Or maybe there was another reason; the thing about being a minority is that you never really know for sure.

12 My Chinese American family had lost fair and square to the real Americans, but I couldn't help but wonder if the temporary emcee had had it in for us and selected that category purposely, not sharing our collective belief in our ready-for-prime-time qualities, our trust that times had changed, our faith in television itself.

13 But to think this way would mean that you had developed the kind of consciousness that would cause you to steer clear of subway tracks, suspecting that at any moment someone was going to mistake you for a communist and push you into the path of an oncoming train, no matter how pretty you were.

Post-reading Questions

Content

1. What did Bow's family believe at the start of the essay? How did their expectations differ from reality?
2. Why did Bow learn to "keep a low profile" in the 1970s? How does paragraph 2 help to clarify American popular culture at the end of the decade?
3. Explain what Bow meant when she described her family's competitors on *Family Feud* as "yellow-haired, corn-fed folks—frightful in their average Americanness." What does she seem to be implying about her own family?
4. When did Bow's sister hear about an opportunity to audition for *The Family Feud*?
5. Who is Richard Dawson, and why does Bow refer to him as the "serial kisser"? (You might need to search online for this.)

Strategies and Structures

1. How does Bow organize her essay?
2. Discuss Bow's strategic use of concrete example throughout her essay. How do they bring her family's experience on *Family Feud* to life?
3. How did Bow and her sisters dress on the day they auditioned for *Family Feud*? Why? In what way did their clothing contrast to what their opponents wore? Use specific references and examples to illustrate your answer.
4. Bow's family obviously knew how to play *Family Feud*. What might this suggest about the role of popular culture on television in general and game shows in particular in American society?

5. In what way does Bow's conclusion look back to her initial paragraphs and still emphasize that she believes the time is right for multiculturalism and change?

Language and Vocabulary

1. *Vocabulary: integrated, multiculturalism, cynical, detractor, consequence, harbored, fixation, interning, inverted, generic, collective, intuitively, subtle, meritocracy, ushered, slogan, incomprehensible, denominator, accrue, eccentricities, regionalism, albino, nationalist, continental, anomalous, deficiency, esteemed, mimic, fealty, communist.* Go through the vocabulary for Bow's essay, check their dictionary definitions, and then place them in your vocabulary log. Next, write a paragraph about American popular culture. Use as many new vocabulary words in your paragraph as you can.
2. Reexamine today's vocabulary words. Which words have the richest connotations (associated meanings)? Briefly explain the connotations referring to at least ten words from the vocabulary list.

Group Activities

1. Divide the class into groups, and have each group select a different game show to research. Begin by having each group member observe the game show on his or her own time. What is the objective of each game show—to guess the price of an object, to answer a question, to win a dance contest? In order to win, what must contestants be willing to do? Next, get back together with other group members in class, and plan a presentation. Finally, each group should share its findings with other class members. To what extent did peers reach similar conclusions about game shows? Were they degrading or empowering? How? Why?
2. Get into small groups and discuss how each person imagines that he or she would react if given an opportunity to audition or appear on a game show? If anyone in your group has been on a game show, then allow him or her to coordinate the group activity—but not dominate it.

Writing Activities

1. Over the years, *Family Feud* has had many emcees, yet the contestants on the game show never seem to change—regardless of gender, ethnicity, or age. Watch a few episodes

of *Family Feud* on television; it really does not matter if you watch reruns with Richard Dawson or the most recent emcee. Jot down notes and impressions of the families on the show, especially their behavior, and then generate a thesis about them using any pre-writing technique you find useful. You might say something like, "It takes little to win on the *Family Feud*, just a willingness to act silly." Whatever you select as your thesis, support your claims with actual examples drawn from personal observations of contestants on the game show, as well as referring to Bow's family and their experience at the *Family Feud* audition.

2. Using a wide variety of examples to illustrate your discussion points, write an essay showing how most Americans will or will not go to great lengths to earn their "15 minutes of fame" as a game show contestant. To do this, you should watch a variety of game shows to witness and record how people dress, talk, and behave. Then, use your favorite form of pre-writing to generate a thesis regarding what people are willing to do to be on television. Support your thesis drawing specific examples from the game shows you observed. Finally, bring all topic sentences—your discussion points—back into focus with your thesis when you write your concluding paragraph.

Sara Blake

Let's Face It

Sara Blake received her B.A. and M.A. in English from San Diego State University. Since 1986, she has been a Professor of English at El Camino College in Torrance, California. She teaches composition and literature courses in both online and traditional formats and has co-authored three textbooks for college composition. Blake has been a significant voice and respected leader in college English for years. She currently serves as Humanities Basic Skills Coordinator at her college. Her interests in popular culture—from the iconic nature of the Barbie Doll to the social networking phenomenon (the focus of her following essay)—have led to her current fascination with *Facebook* and the way it's impacting personal interaction and expression.

Pre-reading Questions

1. How much time do you or others you know tend to spend on *Facebook* or another online social network such as MySpace?
2. List the benefits and detriments of *Facebook* or any other social network. (Save your list for a group activity later on.)
3. Explain the ironic—if not sarcastic—tone of the following quotation: "How on earth did we stalk our exes, remember our co-workers' birthdays, bug our friends, and play a rousing game of Scrabulous before *Facebook*?"

---

1 Young women use it to reveal alluringly flattering self-portraits; parents use it to spy on their kids; grandmothers use it to share cutesy pictures of their grandchildren. It's led to the start up of new relationships and the breakup of established ones. People reconnect and disconnect; they play games, and they espouse causes. Extended families and friends use it to maintain contact with one another across distances. Companies use it to create a social presence and advertise their services. Organizations use it as a space for like-minded individuals to share their ideas. Artists, writers, and musicians use it as a way to find an audience for their work. It's a place to share opinions, to explore ideas, to rant, to complain, to gossip. Let's face it: *Facebook* has become a feature of contemporary life.

2 The story of *Facebook* is an American success story filled with intrigue and drama. The origins of *Facebook* are even explored in the 2010 film *The Social Network*, which chronicles the early legal clashes of founder Mark Zuckerberg. As a Harvard student, Zuckerberg began his activities by hacking into the college's photo directory of students known as a "facebook"—hence the origin of the social network's name. From its official start up in 2004 as a site for college students only, *Facebook* has rapidly grown to include the global Internet public. Today, according to the company's own statistics posted on the official website *Facebook.com*, *Facebook* boasts over 500 million "active users," 50% of whom log on each day. And, the "average user has 130 friends."

3 Among its other influences, *Facebook* has expanded our vocabulary, filling it with terms referred to collectively as "facebookisms." It's created verbs from nouns, like *friend* and *defriend*. It's given new meaning to established words like *poke*, which has morphed from being a physical

nudge with one's finger to an electronic nudge with the same results of attracting someone's attention. The term *flair*, once an abstract noun describing a person's aptitude (as in "a *flair* for dressing in style") has become a concrete noun referring to a virtual corkboard on which users can affix buttons. Similarly, the noun *tag* has become a verb meaning to identify people in a posted photograph. The term *facebookism* itself has taken on multiple meanings, joining the pantheon of other *–isms*, like racism and narcissism. It can be used to describe the act of judging people based on how many *Facebook* friends they have. It can also mean "characterized by total self-absorption," as in "She is living in a world of *facebookism*, where everything revolves around her."

4 *Facebook* serves as a portal to alternative virtual lives in places like Frontierville or Farmville. It can provide newsfeeds and so become a source of knowledge about the real world. Applications (in the electronic sense of the word) include games like Word Challenge and UNO, as well as educational applications to increase one's vocabulary or learn English. Entrepreneurs can create an ad to showcase new products. And *Facebook* has replaced AIM and freestanding chat rooms as a vehicle for electronic socializing.

5 But, for all its thrills—or more accurately because of its thrills—*Facebook* can also be the ultimate "time suck" —something so engrossing that we immerse ourselves in it for hours, neglecting things that are really important like going to work, preparing meals, picking kids up from school, or attending classes. In short, *Facebook* can be addicting. According to *Facebook*'s published statistics, "People spend over 700 billion minutes per month on *Facebook*." Just think what these people could accomplish in that time if it were spent on other things, like building houses for the poor or studying ways to achieve world peace, or even getting some exercise.

6 Furthermore, *Facebook* creates its own strict social conventions with a mine trap of hidden rules of behavior. What, for example, is the etiquette in responding to an email announcing that "So and so wants to be your friend"? Can the message just be ignored without totally offending someone who is reaching out in a kindly gesture? Is it mandatory to add the person even though he may be the hated bully from ninth grade in Minnesota or possibly the psychotic cousin of an ex-sister-in-law? And then there are those unfortunate posts, such as the photo from the drunken graduation night party or the snide comment about a friend composed in a moment of petty anger.

7 Whether or not *Facebook* has enhanced our lives is debatable. Many early enthusiasts have found that *Facebook* requires a commitment they're not ready to give. Some of these users have merely abandoned their *Facebook* accounts to languish in cyberspace. Other users have more dramatically opted to commit *Facebook* "suicide," deleting their

Facebook accounts altogether—though many would argue that, once created, an account can never actually be deleted.

8 As tempting as it may be to give up on the whole *Facebook* experience, disenchanted users might want to think carefully first. What about those hilarious pictures of the belly flop contest from last summer's Mexican cruise that Aunt Trudy in Newark, New Jersey, would find hilarious. And with enough practice, a person could be really, really good at Word Counters. And, after all, even the President of the United States has a *Facebook* page, even if it is maintained by an organization rather the president personally. Ultimately, whatever the drawbacks might be, one thing is clear: the social network phenomenon is here to stay.

Post-reading Questions

Content

1. How is Blake's essay title, "Let's Face It," a play on words on one hand and yet a suitable, focused title on the other? At what point might a reader make the connection between the two (cleverness and appropriateness)?
2. Who is Mark Zukerberg? What did he do?
3. To what extent, according to Blake, has *Facebook* enhanced people's lives? How and why would you agree and/or disagree with her observations? Illustrate your reasons with specific, concrete examples.
4. How would you explain *Facebook* etiquette to another? When and where does *Facebook* create "its own strict social conventions with a mine trap of hidden rules of behavior"? Identify some of the examples Blake presents, and then offer a few of your own.
5. Define—then discuss the possible limitations of—*Facebook* suicide.

Strategies and Structures

1. In her opening paragraph, how does Blake strategically "lead in" to her thesis statement? Why?
2. Consider Blake's entire essay—not just a single paragraph—and then assess how her selection of words, allusions, and examples seem to indicate her attitude towards *Facebook*.
3. How do transition words, phrases, and expressions establish a clear relationship between the various parts of Blake's essay? Offer some examples.
4. Review and then demonstrate ways that Blake addresses the six journalist questions—*who, what, when, where, why,* and *how*—throughout her essay.

5. Explain how Blake's closing remarks in paragraph 8 "look back" to her thesis and how her thesis "looks forward" to her conclusion.

Language and Vocabulary

1. Vocabulary: *alluringly, disconnect, contemporary, intrigue, chronicles, facebookism, collectively, morphed, virtual, pantheon, narcissism, engrossing, conventions, gesture, psychotic, mandatory, enhanced, enthusiasts, abandoned, phenomenon.* Which of the preceding words would you expect to find in a standard dictionary, and which might better be found in an online dictionary? Why?
2. Go over the vocabulary list from Blake's essay; write a paragraph about any social network using at least five to seven vocabulary words from Blake's essay.
3. In paragraph 3, Blake contends that *Facebook* has "expanded our vocabulary." What exactly does she mean by this? How does she explain and support her observations?

Group Activities

1. Gather in small groups and, one at a time, share each other's lists for Pre-reading Question #2 regarding *Facebook's* beneficial and detrimental effects on individuals in general and society as a whole. To what extent do group members seem united in opinion and where and when do they differ? Overall, did your group discover that *Facebook's* merits outweighed its shortcomings—or vice versa?
2. In a small group, brainstorm and record a brief list of *facebookisms*. Start with the *facebookisms* that Blake mentions in her article; add to her list as extensively as possible. Compare and contrast your findings with those of other groups in class.

Writing Activities

1. Using a wide variety of representative examples and illustrations, write an essay that builds upon—or disproves—Blake's claim that *Facebook* can be an ultimate "time suck."
2. Write an essay entitled "Facebook: a Pen and a Poke." Therein, argue that genuine human communication has improved or diminished as a result of social networking. Back up your discussion points with a variety of concrete, verifiable examples.

Philip K. Chiu

The Myth of the Model Minority

Chinese-American freelance writer Philip K. Chiu's works have appeared in many publications in the United States, including *U.S. News & World Report*, where this essay originally appeared in the "Rostrum" column. Chiu presently lives and writes in Carlsbad, California. In the following essay, Chiu discusses how stereotyping Asians—the model minority—has been somewhat oppressive; however, times have changed and so has society's perception of "the model minority."

Pre-reading Questions

1. What Chinese-American stereotypes are you familiar with? Make a list of the qualities you associate with people of Chinese ancestry.
2. How does the word *myth* affect the meaning of the essay title? What does it suggest about Chinese Americans being *the model minority*?

---

1 For years, Chinese Americans have been labeled a model minority. We read in the newspapers how diligently they have worked and saved. We see on television how quietly they obey the laws and how conscientiously they stay clear of crime. We learn in magazines how they climb the economic ladder and how much better than the Caucasian kids their children do in school.

2 But of late, we have been reading about a different side of Chinese American life. In January, *U.S. News* reported on Chinese gangs and their criminal activities. Not long afterward, a gun battle in the quiet streets of Pasadena, Calif., left two federal drug agents and two Chinese drug dealers dead. Now, the press is reporting on rising Chinese organized crime on the West Coast and citing the Pasadena incident as the latest manifestation.

3 What has happened to that law-abiding, humble Chinese American we have heard so much about? Have the media been wrong all these years? The answer is a complex one.

4 About 60 years ago, the silver screen gave us the insidious Fu Manchu and the ever inscrutable Charlie Chan. We heard about the dim opium dens and the filthy gambling halls. We saw slant-eyed, ever obedient little men toiling about with their pigtails freshly cut off. And we wondered just what kind of expression was "long time no see."

5 Then came World War II, and the Chinese became our allies. The pictures of a smiling, beautiful Madame Chiang Kai-Shek appeared in every newspaper. And we read about clean, amiable, upright and industrious Chinese Americans who, nearly a century before, had contributed to winning the American West by working day and night in the mines, on the farms and on the railroads.

6 The Korean War brought a picture of ferocious Chinese hordes marching to conquer Asia. And we learned that the Chinese spoke with forked tongues. They felt no pain when you stuck a needle in their tummies. They ate from their rice bowls with disgusting noises and giggled with delight when they stabbed you in the back.

7 The 1972 Nixon visit to China ushered in an era of high praise for anything Chinese. The newly discovered extraordinary accomplishments of Chinese Americans in the face of prejudice sent social scholars scrambling for answers. And it was in the late '70s and the early '80s that the scholars told the world that the Chinese Americans were the model minority.

8 Is the wind changing its direction again in 1988? I don't know for sure, but I do know that as a Chinese American I am glad to see reporting on the underside of Chinese American life. In part, I am tired of hearing how miraculously the well-behaved Chinese Americans have been doing, and I'm sick of reading about those bespectacled teenage bookworms who have contributed to exceptionally low juvenile-delinquency rates among Chinese American kids. But mostly I am fed up with being stereotyped as either a subhuman or superhuman creature.

9 Certainly, I am proud of the academic and economic successes of Chinese Americans and proud that many of us have excelled in science, the arts, law, medicine, business, sports and other endeavors. But it's important for people to realize that there is another side.

10 A few Chinese Americans steal when they are desperate; a few rape when nature overwhelms them; a few sell drugs when they see an easy way to make a buck; a few embezzle when instant fortunes blind them; a few murder when passions overtake them; and a few commit crimes simply because they are wicked.

11 It is about time for the media to report on Chinese Americans the way they are. Some are superachievers, most are average citizens, and a few are criminals. They are only human—no more and no less.

Post-reading Questions

Content

1. Why were Chinese Americans labeled the *model minority* in the late 1970s and the early 1980s? Who or what was responsible for furthering this stereotype?
2. What are some of the stereotypes Chinese Americans have been labeled with over the past sixty years?
3. Why does Chiu feel it is important for people "to realize that there is another side" to Chinese Americans, a side not associated with a model human being?
4. What does Chiu request that the media do? Why?

Strategies and Structures

1. Chiu begins and concludes his essay with references to the media. How does this frame his essay as a whole?
2. How successfully does Chiu illustrate the "superhuman" and the "subhuman" character traits of the Chinese? Why is a discussion of the two extremes of strategic importance to his essay's concluding paragraph?
3. Chiu provides a brief history of the stereotypes—including the model minority—placed on Chinese people by other members of American society, prior to answering the rhetorical question, "Have the media been wrong all these years?" What is the purpose of the history? What does it show the reader?

Language and Vocabulary

1. Vocabulary: *diligently, conscientiously, Caucasian, manifestation, insidious, inscrutable, opium, amiable, bespectacled, embezzle, endeavors.* Once you have looked up the meanings of these words, decide which of them fit your definition of a model minority. What makes these words positive, in your opinion? The remaining words should be looked over carefully. Why didn't you choose them? Do they have a negative meaning to you, or are they merely part of each human's reality?
2. Does Chiu's word usage reflect what we would expect of a writer from the model minority? What effect does Chiu's casual reference to crimes such as rape, robbery, drug use/sales, embezzlement, and murder—and the motivation behind each crime—have on a reader? Thoroughly explain your position on Chiu's word use.

Group Activities

1. Write a collaborative essay showing how the dominant stereotypes attributed to an ethnic group may never have been more than myths. Begin by brainstorming to come up with specific ethnic or gender stereotypes. Next, have each group member research a stereotype from a specific time period (like the 1940s), share his or her findings, and assemble the group essay.
2. Briefly share your knowledge about people like Charlie Chan, Fu Manchu, Madame Chiang Kai-Shek, as well as events like the Chinese Cultural Revolution, the student uprising at Tiananmen Square, the Korean War, and the Vietnam War. After your initial discussion, list other Chinese people who personify stereotypes of a given era. Also, try to think of one or two events involving people of Chinese origin in the last century, events which have prejudiced or typecast our perception of them.

Writing Activities

1. This article was written several years ago. At the time, Chiu asked, "Is the wind changing its direction again in 1988?" Here he was referring to the numerous stereotypes placed on the Chinese during the past sixty years. Write an essay in which you devise a thesis that answers Chiu's question. Use illustrations and examples to support what you say.
2. Is there a model social, political, or religious minority in the United States today? What is it? Does it suffer or benefit from stereotypes imposed upon it from individuals in a majority group? Why or why not? Compose an original thesis on this issue and demonstrate the truth of it through the use of illustration and example.

Internet Connection: Philip Chiu

Model Minorities

Get access to an online database, and enter the search term "model minority." Select an article that discusses the concept of model minorities and write a brief summary. Be sure to document your source correctly, using the MLA format. (See the *Visions* 8th edition Appendix.)

Ann Scheid

The 21st Century Ragnarok: Is Profit Civilization's Only Motive?

Ann Scheid, a Pittsburgh native, grew up in a family dedicated to letters and was constantly distressed about the environment in that area. After moving to California, she received a B.A. and M.A. in English and taught writing at several local two- and four-year colleges. A social and environmental activist since the 1960s, Scheid often has written on social matters ranging from overpopulation to the destruction of the rainforest. In the following essay, Scheid paints an apocalyptic (doomsday) picture of life on earth for future generations as we move into the second decade of the twenty-first century.

Pre-reading Questions

1. What do you consider "pollution"? Jot down as many types of pollution as you can, and share your list with your classmates. How were your responses similar and yet different?
2. Do you believe that the human race is capable of preserving planet earth or destined to destroy it? Why?
3. List any images that come to mind when you read the word "Ragnarok." Then, look up the term online or in a dictionary of mythic terms.

---

1 Human beings are an irritant to Mother Nature, and in spite of the fact that it took their brains five million years to evolve, She can rid Herself of them in an instant. This, however, may not be necessary, since humans seem to be racing to see if they can save Her the trouble. They behave so arrogantly, contending they are superior to Nature. Rain forests are being cut down or burned—not only polluting the air but also causing a drop in oxygen levels. The love affair people have with their automobiles, especially "gas hog" SUVs, adds to the pollutants in the air and is, yet, another nail in their coffins. Since prehistoric times, humans

have been stalking and killing animals, causing many, beginning with the mastodon and saber-toothed tiger, to become extinct. Modern civilization is rushing headlong to slaughter animals in wholesale lots, all the while trying to prove its superiority to Mother Nature, usually with disastrous results.

2 For thousands of years, humans also have been defacing the earth, making scars upon the land. The Vikings overpopulated their own lands and thus depleted the natural resources, which caused them to look for new areas to take advantage of. They then moved on to Iceland, Greenland, and the New World. Also, the throngs of people who responded to the lure of gold in the Yukon totally stripped mountainsides of trees above the Yukon River to make rafts in order to sail 500 miles to Dawson. Forty percent never made it! In the populated areas of the Himalayas very few trees remain since the citizens have cut them down for cooking and heating fires. With most of the trees gone, erosion occurs on a large scale, washing away most of the topsoil, making food production difficult. Even more disturbing is the fact that, due to large-scale cutting, the famous cedars of Lebanon, mentioned in the Bible, no longer exist. Along the same lines, so much of the rain forest in Panama is being destroyed that scientists are predicting the Panama Canal could fill with silt, thus prohibiting ships from crossing the isthmus, due to the effects of deforestation.

3 Deforestation and erosion, along with changing weather patterns, have led to the fastest-growing regions on this planet—deserts. All the while, populations are exploding worldwide and the proliferation of deserts means there is less arable land to feed the increasing number of people. Starvation on a massive scale will run rampant, and whenever a noted ecologist or environmentalist sends out warnings about such dangers to human life, very few consider giving up any of their conveniences. For instance, the holes in the ozone layer are getting larger, allowing more ultraviolet rays to hit the Earth, which often leads to skin cancer. Knowing this fact, many people still do nothing about the emissions that cause this to happen. They insist on using aerosols and traveling one-to-a-car, thus adding to the emissions, which cause the ozone holes to expand, leading to more cases of skin cancer—a vicious cycle, indeed.

4 To make matters even more critical, global warming is becoming an ever-increasing threat to the existence of humans and animals. Polar icecaps are melting, and sections the size of the state of Rhode Island are breaking off. Traveling toward the Temperate Zones, they begin to melt, placing an inordinate amount of fresh water into the oceans and causing an imbalance. In the North Atlantic, this would affect the Gulf Stream, which warms the British Isles. The fresh water would force the salt water to greater depths and inhibit the flow of the Gulf Stream. Great Britain would be plunged into an ice age, killing many animals and, undoubtedly,

causing a mass exodus south. Sea levels also would rise; countries, such as The Netherlands and Bangla Desh would be flooded since both of them are at exactly sea level or below. The people who flee from these areas, along with those from the British Isles, would further crowd the remaining lands. It is predicted that sea level could rise 200 feet in the future, thus wiping out all coastal areas around the world, forcing more people to move inland.

5 Humans further complicate their lives by allowing businesses to release pollutants in urban areas, in the name of profit. "Accidents" often take place at refineries where toxic fumes are released into the air that people and animals breathe. Pesticides are so widely used and pose such a threat that it is amazing all of them haven't been banned. When DDT was sprayed on plants, many birds died as a result. It was taken out of circulation, but even more powerful ones have been developed. The farming industry uses great amounts of pesticides. The toxins leach into the soil and contaminate the ground water. In California's Central Valley farm workers and their families have a higher rate of birth defects and cancer than areas not using pesticides. Chemical companies beside rivers are allowed to release their toxins into the water. In Southwestern Pennsylvania, it was discovered that the temperature of the water below such a factory was 183 degrees—in January! Another time that same river was so polluted that the chemicals on the surface caught fire! Even more disastrous is the fact that the area uses water from that river for drinking.

6 Governments, anxious to appease money-hungry corporations and their stockholders, have allowed timber companies into national forests to cut virgin-growth trees. Most of these businesses clear cut vast areas and often wait an inordinate amount of time to replant. Clear cutting leaves another scar upon the land in their most treasured and scenic areas and also leads to erosion. At the same time, the government is also considering giving permission for oil companies to drill in those sacred lands. Their rigs are hideously ugly and will mar the views for every visitor. Clear cutting and oil drilling also will interfere with the habitats of animals which inhabit our national parks and forests.

7 One corporation that is particularly guilty of abusing the environment is British Petroleum (BP). Before the 2010 oil spill in the Gulf of Mexico, a gigantic explosion occurred at their Texas City refinery in 2005, killing 15 people and injuring 170 others. Also, two weeks prior to the Gulf spill, BP admitted that malfunctioning equipment released over 530,000 pounds of chemicals into the air over that city. In 1999, one of BP's subsidiaries, BP Exploration Alaska (BPXA), illegally dumped hazardous wastes on the Alaska North Slope and was fined 22 million dollars. From 1993-95, BPXA failed to report illegally dumping waste oil,

paint thinner, and other toxic and hazardous substances by releasing them down the outer rim of the oil wells.

8 Apparently, BP can get away with any infraction against the environment and the citizens who make a living from it. The Gulf spill was so large that it put 12,000 people out of work, and, yet, those same people begged the U. S. government not to stop drilling in the Gulf. Not only were their lives threatened, but many wildlife species, including whales, tuna, and shrimp, dozens of species of birds, and land animals, such as, grey fox and white-tailed deer, and also amphibians, such as the alligator and the snapping turtle came under duress. Not only was oil leaked into the ocean, but also millions of gallons of dispersant were sprayed on the spill to break it up.

9 It is obvious how little BP cares about the environment of the United States. This became even more evident by the CEO, Tony Hayward's, reaction to pressures being applied by the government when he said, "I want my life back." He even took some time off to sail his yacht in a race in England. Fortunately, he was relegated to Siberia to work on Russian pipeline problems, but, at the same time, since 30% of the nation's oil production is derived from the Gulf of Mexico, the government has approved a number of offshore gulf drilling operations since the spill, and BP has been awarded two of them.

10 Experts have estimated that 200 species of plants and animals become extinct each day. This, for instance, can be caused by over fishing, either by enormous processing ships that scoop up thousands of fish at a time and freeze them at sea, or by fishing fleets. The U.S. Navy has contributed to the deaths of whales and dolphins with its new sonar. Marine biologists have examined the dead animals, and their ears had hemorrhaged, making them deaf and killing most of them. In the past, ranchers and farmers have contributed to the demise of the wolf in the lower 48 states when they were offered money for each wolf carcass produced. One of the most shameful acts committed by humans was the killing of millions of buffalo in the mid-1800s—for sport. People would shoot them from trains, and the animals would rot by the tracks. No one used the animals for clothes or food.

11 One hundred fifty years later, there are only a few buffalo alive, and coral reefs, which are composed of skeletons secreted by certain marine polyps, are beginning to experience the same fate. Due to a change in temperature in the oceans, pollutants, and the looting of coral by "collectors," ten percent of the reefs are now dead. By 2020, fifty percent will have died if nothing is done, yet divers think only of the profit they will make from the coral jewelry, and polluters think only of the money they will save by not disposing of toxics properly, and factories think only of not having to spend money to purify the emissions.

12 Burning questions never cease: When will governments—local, state, and federal—corporations, and the rest of the human race realize what is happening to this planet? When will the race for profit cease to consume them? Perhaps it will come about when there is no land left to farm and feed the burgeoning population, or there is no clean water left to drink, or wildlife to balance the ecosystem, or, more importantly, when their children start dying. By that time, however, it probably will be too late.

Post-reading Questions

Content

1. Identify the thesis in Scheid's essay. How does it provide the guiding focus for her discussion?
2. How have humans defaced the earth and destroyed its life forms? How long has this been a pattern of human behavior toward Nature? What examples does Scheid use to illustrate her argument?
3. To whom does the author seem to be appealing?
4. What could happen as a result of global warming and melting polar icecaps?
5. According to Scheid, how many species of plant and animal life become extinct each day?

Strategies and Structures

1. Explain the strategic purpose and ultimate effect of capitalizing the "m" and "n" in Mother Nature, as well as Scheid's upper case pronoun references such as "She" and "Her."
2. Scheid cites several authorities, facts, and statistics as she presents her argument. Which supporting information do you find most and least convincing? Why?
3. Scheid writes her essay using third person point of view; why is this most appropriate to her subject matter and objective for writing her essay? What might have been lost if she had chosen to write the same essay from a first or second person point of view? Explain your reasoning.
4. How does the author create and reinforce the believability of her thesis through the extensive use of historical and current examples of the human race's interaction with the environment and its creatures?
5. Why do you imagine that Scheid decided to offer her readers two rhetorical questions in the final paragraph before the concluding remarks to her essay? What is she inviting the reader to do?

Language and Vocabulary

1. Vocabulary: *Ragnarok, apocalyptic, irritant, inordinate, ecosystem, arrogantly, depleted, erosion, isthmus, deforestation, arable, ultraviolet rays, exodus, pollutants, burgeoning, proliferation, rampant,*

ozone, aerosol, gigantic, malfunctioning, subsidiaries, infraction, dispersant, relegated, sonar, hemorrhaged, polyps, emissions. Most of the vocabulary words for this essay fall into one of two categories: general vocabulary words, and those words which specifically illustrate and explain the topic at hand: threats to the environment. After looking up the vocabulary words in your dictionary, separate them into the appropriate groups, and write one pro and one con (if possible) paragraph about the threat to the environment.

2. Write a one-page summary of Scheid's essay using the vocabulary words listed in the Language and Vocabulary exercise number one.

Group Activities

1. Visit your college or university's Department of Environmental Studies, Natural Sciences, or Anthropology in small groups and interview faculty members. Prior to your visit, however, prepare a list of scripted interview questions or follow the advice of Kathleen Hudson in her essay, "Why Talk? Interviews Matter!" (*Chapter 6: Process Analysis*). Present your findings to the rest of the class in an oral presentation.
2. Go to a computer-assisted classroom, pair off, and research one aspect of an environmental problem facing modern society. Before engaging in research, make sure that every pair in class explores a different issue. For example, one pair might research the issue of global warming; another pair might look into articles on the dwindling Amazon rainforests, and so on. Print your findings and write a collaborative essay with your partner, citing sources when appropriate. Finally, staple all your printed articles to your collaborative essay, and submit it to your instructor.

Writing Activities

1. Using illustration and example, develop an essay showing what readers can do to become environmentally conscientious.
2. Write a letter to a local or federal government official using illustration and example to argue how and why he/she is or is not doing a good job fighting for issues that affect the world around us (e.g., promoting bills encouraging practices to decrease the greenhouse effect, to safeguard wildlife habitats, to protect the planet from needless destruction, and so on), or to point out a clear need for immediate action.

***Internet Connection:* Ann Scheid**

Ecology

Enter the keyword "ecology" into an online database or search engine. Next, narrow your search to "ecological disasters," and make a list of the ten most recent articles you can find on the topic. Write a works cited entry for each piece using conventions outlined in the MLA Sheet. (Refer to the Appendix at the back of the text to review the format.) You may want to refer to your articles as supporting evidence if you do a writing assignment based on one of the topics at the conclusion of Scheid's essay.

Stephanie Ericsson

The Ways We Lie

A screenwriter and advertising copywriter, Stephanie Ericsson is the author of *Shame Faced* and *Recovering Together.* She began writing a journal of her experiences after the loss of her husband while she was pregnant with their only child. Excerpts from Stephanie Ericsson's works have frequently appeared in magazines such as the *Utne Reader*. Her books include *Companion Through the Darkness: Dialogues on Grief* (1993) and *Companion into Dawn: Inner Dialogues on Loving* (1997). The following essay was composed from notes of the latter text.

Pre-reading Questions

1. Before reading this essay, jot down what you consider to be a lie. How do you or someone you know justify lying? Is a lie ever preferable to the truth? When? Where? Explain.
2. Make a list of all the "little lies" people use throughout their daily lives—such as "I'm busy for lunch" or "I love your hair"—in order to avoid conflicts or confrontations.

1 The bank called today and I told them my deposit was in the mail, even though I hadn't written a check yet. It'd been a rough day. The baby I'm pregnant with decided to do aerobics on my lungs for two hours, our three-year-old daughter painted the living-room couch with lipstick, the IRS put me on hold for an hour, and I was late to a business meeting because I was tired.

2 I told my client the traffic had been bad. When my partner came home, his haggard face told me his day hadn't gone any better than mine, so when he asked, "How was your day?" I said, "Oh, fine," knowing that one more straw might break his back. A friend called and wanted to take me to lunch. I said I was busy. Four lies in the course of a day, none of which I felt the least bit guilty about.

3 We lie. We all do. We exaggerate, we minimize, we avoid confrontation, we spare people's feelings, we conveniently forget, we keep secrets, we justify lying to the big-guy institutions. Like most people, I indulge myself in small falsehoods and still think of myself as an honest person. Sure I lie, but it doesn't hurt anything. Or does it?

4 I once tried going a whole week without telling a lie, and it was paralyzing. I discovered that telling the truth all the time is nearly impossible. It means living with some serious consequences: The bank charges me $60 in overdraft fees, my partner keels over when I tell him about my travails, my client fires me for telling her I didn't feel like being on time, and my friend takes it personally when I say I am not hungry. There must be some merit to lying.

5 But if I justify lying, what makes me different from slick politicians or the corporate robbers who raided the S & L industry? Saying it's okay to lie one way and not the other is hedging. I cannot seem to escape the voice deep inside me that tells me: When someone lies, someone loses.

6 What far-reaching consequences will I, or others, pay as a result of my lie? Will someone's trust be destroyed? Will someone else pay *my* penance because I ducked out? We must consider the *meaning of our actions.* Deception, lies, capital crimes, and misdemeanors all carry meanings. *Webster's* definition of a *lie* is specific: *1: a false statement or action especially made with the intent to deceive; 2: anything that gives or is meant to give a false impression.*

7 A definition like this implies that there are many, many ways to tell a lie. Here are just a few.

8 **The White Lie:** The white lie assumes that the truth will cause more damage than a simple, harmless untruth. Telling a friend he looks great when he looks like hell can be based on a decision that the friend needs a compliment more than a frank opinion. But, in effect, it is the liar deciding what is best for the lied to. Ultimately, it is a vote of no confidence. It is an act of subtle arrogance for anyone to decide what is best for someone else.

9 Yet not all circumstances are quite so cut-and-dried. Take, for instance, the sergeant in Vietnam who knew one of his men was killed in action but listed him as missing so that the man's family would receive indefinite compensation instead of the lump-sum pittance the military gives widows and children. His intent was honorable. Yet for twenty years this family kept their hopes alive, unable to move on to a new life.

10 **Facades:** We all put up facades to one degree or another. When I put on a suit to go to see a client, I feel as though I am putting on another face, obeying the expectation that serious businesspeople wear suits rather than sweatpants. But I'm a writer. Normally, I get up, get the kid off to school, and sit at my computer in my pajamas until four in the afternoon. When I answer the phone, the caller thinks I'm wearing a suit (though the UPS man knows better).

11 But facades can be dangerous because they are used to seduce others into an illusion. For instance, I recently realized that a former friend was a liar. He presented himself with all the right looks and the right words and offered lots of new consciousness theories, fabulous books to read, and fascinating insights. Then I did some business with him, and the time came to pay me. He turned out to be all talk and no walk. I heard a plethora of reasonable excuses, including in-depth descriptions of the big break around the corner. In six months of work, I saw less than a hundred bucks. When I confronted him, he raised both eyebrows and tried to convince me that I'd heard him wrong, that he'd made no commitment to me. A simple investigation into his past revealed a crowded graveyard of disenchanted former friends.

12 **Ignoring the Plain Facts:** In the '60s, the Catholic Church in Massachusetts began hearing complaints that Father James Porter was sexually molesting children. Rather than relieving him of his duties, the ecclesiastical authorities simply moved him from one parish to another between 1960 and 1967, actually providing him with a fresh supply of unsuspecting families and innocent children to abuse. After treatment in 1967 for pedophilia, he went back to work, this time in Minnesota. The new diocese was aware of Father Porter's obsession with children, but they needed priests and recklessly believed treatment had cured him. More children were abused until he was relieved of his duties a year later. By his own admission, Porter may have abused as many as a hundred children.

13 Ignoring the facts may not in and of itself be a form of lying, but consider the context of the situation. If a lie is a false action done with the intent to deceive, then the Catholic Church's conscious covering for Porter created irreparable consequences. The church became a coperpetrator with Porter.

14 **Deflecting:** I've discovered that I can keep anyone from seeing the true me by being selectively blatant. I set a precedent of being up-front about intimate issues, but I never bring up the things I truly want to hide; I just let people assume I'm revealing everything. It's an effective way of hiding.

15 Any good liar knows that the way to perpetuate an untruth is to deflect attention from it. When Clarence Thomas exploded with accusations that the Senate hearings were a "high-tech lynching," he simply switched the focus from a highly charged subject to a radioactive subject. Rather than defending himself, he took the offensive and accused the country of racism. It was a brilliant maneuver. Racism is now politically incorrect in official circles—unlike sexual harassment, which still rewards those who can get away with it.

16 Some of the most skillful deflectors are passive-aggressive people who, when accused of inappropriate behavior, refuse to respond to the accusations. This you-don't-exist stance infuriates the accuser, who, understandably, screams something obscene out of frustration. The trap is sprung and the act of deflection successful, because now the passive-aggressive person can indignantly say, "Who can talk to someone as unreasonable as you?" The real issue is forgotten and the sins of the original victim become the focus. Feeling guilty of name-calling, the victim is fully tamed and crawls into a hole, ashamed. I have watched this fighting technique work thousands of times in disputes between men and women, and what I've learned is that the real culprit is not necessarily the one who swears the loudest.

17 **Omission:** Omission involves telling most of the truth minus one or two key facts whose absence changes the story completely. You break a pair of glasses that are guaranteed under normal use and get a new pair, without mentioning that the first pair broke during a rowdy game of basketball. Who hasn't tried something like that? But what about the omission of information that could make a difference in how a person lives his or her life?

18 For instance, one day I found out that rabbinical legends tell of another woman in the Garden of Eden before Eve. I was stunned. The omission of the Sumerian goddess Lilith from Genesis—as well as her demonization by ancient misogynists as an embodiment of female evil—felt like spiritual robbery. I felt like I'd just found out my mother was really my stepmother. To take seriously the tradition that Adam was created out of the same mud as his equal counterpart, Lilith, redefines all of Judeo-Christian history.

19 Some renegade Catholic feminists introduced me to a view of Lilith that had been suppressed during the many centuries when this strong goddess was seen only as a spirit of evil. Lilith was a proud goddess who defied Adam's need to control her, attempted negotiations, and when this failed, said adios and left the Garden of Eden.

20 This omission of Lilith from the Bible was a patriarchal strategy to keep women weak. Omitting the strong-women archetype of Lilith from Western religions and starting the story with Eve the Rib helped keep Christian and Jewish women believing they were the lesser sex for thousands of years.

21 **Stereotypes and Clichés:** Stereotype and cliché serve a purpose as a form of shorthand. Our need for vast amounts of information in nanoseconds has made the stereotype vital to modern communication. Unfortunately, it often shuts down original thinking, giving those hungry for the truth a candy bar of misinformation instead of a balanced meal. The stereotype explains a situation with just enough truth to seem unquestionable. All the "isms"—racism, sexism, ageism, et al.—are founded on and fueled by the stereotype and the cliché, which are lies of exaggeration, omission, and ignorance. They are always dangerous. They take a single tree and make it a landscape. They destroy curiosity. They close minds and separate people. The single mother on welfare is assumed to be cheating. Any black male could tell you how much of his identity is obliterated daily by stereotypes. Fat people, ugly people, beautiful people, old people, large-breasted women, short men, the mentally ill, and the homeless all could tell you how much more they are like us than we want to think. I once admitted to a group of people that I had a mouth like a truck driver. Much to my surprise, a man stood up and said, "I'm a truck driver, and I never cuss." Needless to say, I was humbled.

22 **Groupthink:** Irving Janis, in *Victims of Group Think*, defines this sort of lie as a psychological phenomenon within decision-making groups in which loyalty to the group has become more important than any other value, with the result that dissent and the appraisal of alternatives are suppressed. If you've ever worked on a committee or in a corporation, you've encountered groupthink. It requires a combination of other forms of lying—ignorance of facts, selective memory, omission, and denial, to name a few.

23 The textbook example of groupthink came on December 7, 1941. From as early as the fall of 1941, the warnings came in, one after another, that Japan was preparing for a massive military operation. The Navy command in Hawaii assumed Pearl Harbor was invulnerable—the Japanese weren't stupid enough to attack the United States' most important base. On the other hand, racist stereotypes said the Japanese weren't smart enough to invent a torpedo effective in less than 60 feet of water (the fleet was docked in 30 feet); after all, U.S. technology hadn't been able to do it.

24 On Friday, December 5, normal weekend leave was granted to all the commanders at Pearl Harbor, even though the Japanese consulate in Hawaii was busy burning papers. Within the tight, good-ole-boy cohesiveness of the U.S. command in Hawaii, the myth of invulnerability stayed well entrenched. No one in the group considered the alternatives. The rest is history.

25 **Out-and-Out Lies:** Of all the ways to lie, I like this one the best, probably because I get tired of trying to figure out the real meanings behind things. At least I can trust the bald-faced lie. I once asked my five-year-old nephew, "Who broke the fence?" (I had seen him do it.) He answered, "The murderers." Who could argue?

26 At least when this sort of lie is told it can be easily confronted. As the person who is lied to, I know where I stand. The bald-faced lie doesn't toy with my perceptions—it argues with them. It doesn't try to refashion reality, it tries to refute it. *Read my lips . . .* No sleight of hand. No guessing. If this were the only form of lying, there would be no such thing as floating anxiety or the adult-children of alcoholics movement.

27 **Dismissal:** Dismissal is perhaps the slipperiest of all lies. Dismissing feelings, perceptions, or even the raw facts of a situation ranks as a kind of lie that can do as much damage to a person as any other kind of lie.

28 The roots of many mental disorders can be traced back to the dismissal of reality. Imagine that a person is told from the time she is a tot that her perceptions are inaccurate: *"Mommie, I'm scared."* "No you're not, darling." *"I don't like that man next door, he makes me feel icky."* "Johnny, that's a terrible thing to say, of course you like him. You go over there right now and be nice to him."

29 I've often mused over the idea that madness is actually a sane reaction to an insane world. Psychologist R. D. Laing supports this hypothesis in *Sanity, Madness & The Family,* an account of his investigation into the families of schizophrenics. The common thread that ran through all of the families he studied was a deliberate, staunch dismissal of the patient's perceptions from a very early age. Each of the patients started out with an accurate grasp of reality, which, through meticulous and methodical dismissal, was demolished until the only reality the patient could trust was catatonia.

30 Dismissal runs the gamut. Mild dismissal can be quite handy for forgiving the foibles of others in our day-to-day lives. Toddlers who have just learned to manipulate their parents' attention sometimes are dismissed out of necessity. Absolute attention from the parents would require so much energy that no one would get to eat dinner. But we must be careful and attentive about how far we take our "necessary" dismissals. Dismissal is a dangerous tool, because it's nothing less than a lie.

31 **Delusion:** I could write a book on this one. Delusion, a cousin of dismissal, is the tendency to see excuses as facts. It's a powerful lying tool because it filters out information that contradicts what we want to believe. Alcoholics who believe the problems in their lives are legitimate reasons for drinking rather than results of the drinking offer the classic example of deluded thinking. Delusion uses the mind's ability to see things in myriad ways to support what it wants to be the truth.

32 But delusion is also a survival mechanism we all use. If we were to fully contemplate the consequences of our stockpiles of nuclear weapons or global warming, we could hardly function on a day-to-day level. We don't want to incorporate that much reality into our lives because to do so would be paralyzing.

33 Delusion works as an adhesive to keep the status quo intact. It shamelessly employs dismissal, omission, and amnesia, among other sorts of lies. Its most cunning defense is that it cannot see itself.

34 These are only a few of the ways we lie. Or are lied to. As I said earlier, it's not easy to entirely eliminate lies in our daily lives. No matter how pious we may try to be, we will still embellish, hedge, and omit to lubricate the daily machinery of living. But there is a world of difference between telling functional lies and living a lie. Martin Buber once said, "The lie is the spirit committing treason against itself." Our acceptance of lies becomes a cultural cancer that eventually shrouds and reorders reality until moral garbage becomes as invisible to us as water is to a fish.

35 How much do we tolerate before we become sick and tired of being sick and tired? When will we stand up and declare our *right* to trust? When do we stop accepting that the real truth is in the fine print? Whose lips do we read this year when we vote for president? When will we stop being so reticent about making judgments? When do we stop turning over our personal power and responsibility to liars?

36 Maybe if I don't tell the bank the check's in the mail I'll be less tolerant of the lies told me every day. A country song I once heard said it all for me: "You've got to stand for something or you'll fall for anything."

Post-reading Questions

Content

1. According to Ericsson, what are the kinds of lies we all tell?
2. What does Ericsson assume about the "white lie"?
3. Why are facades destructive?
4. Why does she say, "Of all the ways to lie I like this one [the out-and-out lie] the best . . . "?
5. What is the author's definition of delusion?

Strategies and Structures

1. What is the purpose of Ericsson's anecdote (personal account or story) at the beginning of the essay?
2. Ericsson divides lies into several categories. In what way do her topic sentences frame her discussion of each type of lie? How does she illustrate the different categories of lies that she has devised?
3. Identify the three major parts to this essay, and explain their strategic purposes.

4. An author often uses a rhetorical question when he or she wishes to present an idea for consideration with no intention of receiving an answer from the readers. What are some of the rhetorical questions Ericsson uses in this essay, and how does she answer them?

Language and Vocabulary

1. Vocabulary: *haggard, pittance, facade, plethora, dioceses, perpetuate, harassment, Sumerian, Genesis, renegade, negotiations, patriarchal, psychological phenomenon, adhesive, staunch, amnesia, embellish, gamut.* Oftentimes when we write, word choices can indicate or suggest meaning or meanings beyond their literal definition. Go through the list of words above and show how the words you selected go beyond the dictionary meaning. Explain how these words give additional insight that just a dictionary could not provide.
2. Write a definition of each of the lies that Ericsson presents in this essay without referring back to the essay or to a dictionary or thesaurus.

Group Activities

1. In small groups, brainstorm your own categories of lies and then provide original examples of each type of lie.
2. Divide into pairs and write a brief skit—a dialogue between two people dramatizing some "common lies" that people tell on a daily basis. Draw on personal experience and readings for additional material. Finally, after you present your skit to the rest of the class and get feedback from your classmates, write a collaborative paper with your partner analyzing the nature and effects of telling extemporaneous or premeditated lies. (You may have ended up using both in your skit!)

Writing Activities

1. Have you ever been a victim of a lie of "delusion" at school, at work, or at home? What occurred? How did you come to terms with the lie? Write a short essay in which you reflect back and examine your experience. Use specific examples to illustrate how and why lies of "delusion" have been harmful to you.

2. Write an essay in which you offer your own categories of lies, providing examples to support your thesis. Use Group Activity 1 to generate ideas. You may wish to construct your paper much like Ericsson's with a definite introduction, the body consisting of your lies and an analysis of the lies you have categorized, and a conclusion wherein you reach some insight into the entire nature of lying.

Dan Archer

Olga Trusova

Lera's Story

From *Borderland: Seven Lives, Seven Stories As told by Victims of Human Trafficking*

Dan Archer is a comics journalist from the United Kingdom, now in California. He is now a 2010 John S. Knight Journalism Fellow at Stanford University and the creator of **www.archcomix.com.** His work has appeared in *The Guardian* (UK), *Huffington Post, Afternet.org,* and *Religious Dispatches.* Archer's coauthor, Olga Trusova, is an educator, originally from the Ukraine and now living and teaching in California.

As a 2009 Fulbright Fellow, Trusova spent a year conducting research and interviews for *Borderland: Seven Lives, Seven Stories as Told by Victims of Human Trafficking*—a Graphic Novel. One can find Trusova in San Francisco tinkering with design, technology, and new media.

Pre-reading Questions

1. Freewrite with focus on the topic of human rights. What privileges and liberties do all people deserve and why?
2. Jot down the first few things that come to mind when you hear the words "human trafficking," "child exploitation," "mail-order bride," "forced labor," and "sweatshop labor." Then discuss the connotations (associated meanings) for each word group.

Human Trafficking is defined as "the recruitment, transportation, transfer, harboring or receipt of persons, by means of the threat or use of force or other forms of coercion, of abduction, of fraud, of deception, of the abuse of power or of a position of vulnerability or of the giving or receiving of payments or benefits to achieve the consent of a person having control over another person, for the purpose of exploitation."

—"The Protocol to Prevent, Suppress and Punish Trafficking in Persons, especially Women and Children." The United Nations Convention Against Transnational Organized Crime, Palermo, Italy, December 2000.

From the Authors' Background to "Lera's Story":

1 In *Lera's Story*, we wanted to provide a personal account of how victims deal with their experiences, and chronicle the path that leads to their exploitation. "Lera" is a real person who came to the rehabilitation center after being trafficked from Ukraine to Russia for illegal work. Her story leading up to that moment is as equally important for understanding how she ended up in such a situation. She is part Roma living in Ukraine. Romani people are an ethnic group with origins in South Asia or Eastern Europe. They are widely dispersed with their largest concentrated populations in Europe, especially Central and Eastern Europe, with more recent diaspora populations in the Americas and, to a lesser extent, in North Africa and the Middle East.

2 The rehabilitation center where Lera stayed is run by the International Organization for Migration (IOM) in Kyiv, the capital of Ukraine, and has treated over 1,600 victims of sexual and/or labor exploitation since its opening in 2002.

Lera's Story
BASED ON A TRUE STORY
AS TOLD TO DOCTOR IRINA PAVLOVNA, PSYCHOLOGIST AT THE KYIV IOM CENTER, BY A FORMER VICTIM OF TRAFFICKING IN 2007.
*HER NAME HAS BEEN CHANGED
WITHIN WEEKS OF GIVING BIRTH TO LERA*

HER MOTHER, WHO WAS ROMA, DECIDED TO GET RID OF HER.

LERA'S FATHER, A RUSSIAN, WANTED NOTHING TO DO WITH THEM.

SO HER MOTHER MADE A CUT ON LERA'S LEG

AND LEFT HER IN A GARBAGE CAN, HOPING SHE WOULD BLEED TO DEATH.

WAAAAAAAAA

BUT SOMEONE FOUND HER
ВЫХОДА НЕТ

AND BROUGHT HER TO AN ORPHANAGE.

WHEN LERA TURNED 13, SHE DECIDED TO FIND HER MOTHER

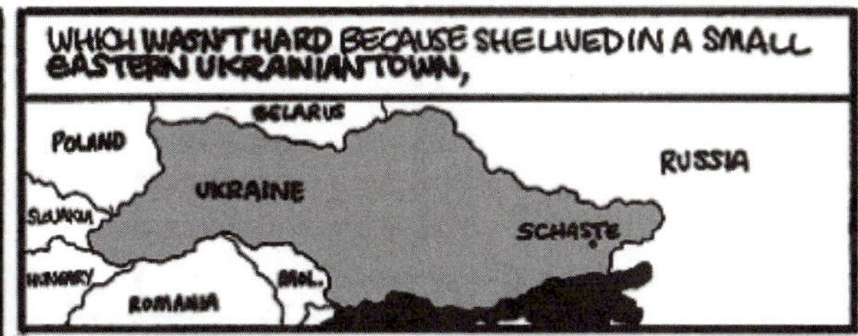
WHICH WASN'T HARD BECAUSE SHE LIVED IN A SMALL EASTERN UKRAINIAN TOWN,
BELARUS
POLAND
RUSSIA
UKRAINE
SCHASTE
ROMANIA

WHERE EVERYONE KNEW EACH OTHER'S STORIES.

AFTER RE-CONCILIATION, HER MOTHER DECIDED TO SELL LERA AS A BRIDE.
BUT ACCORDING TO SOME GYPSY LAWS, A BRIDE HAD TO BE A VIRGIN.

OF COURSE, LERA'S MOTHER DIDN'T KNOW HER DAUGHTER WAS NO LONGER A VIRGIN

AS CHILDREN IN THE ORPHANAGE HAD BEEN FREQUENTLY RAPED.
SO THE WEDDING SCHEME DIDN'T WORK AS PLANNED.

INSTEAD, SHE MADE LERA SELL POPPY STRAW.

SHE WAS ARRESTED AT 16 FOR DRUGS AND WENT TO JAIL FOR 4 YEARS.

IN PRISON, LERA TOOK SEWING CLASSES, BECAME A HEAD SEAMSTRESS—

AND MADE BEDDING AND TOWELS FOR THE INMATES.

BUT WHEN SHE GOT OUT, HER MISFORTUNE CONTINUED.

SOMEONE TOLD HER ABOUT A JOB IN MOSCOW:

LERA WENT, ONLY TO DISCOVER THAT IT WAS A SCAM.

SHE AND THE OTHER WOMEN WERE LOCKED IN A FACTORY AND MADE CLOTHES DAY AND NIGHT WITHOUT PAY.

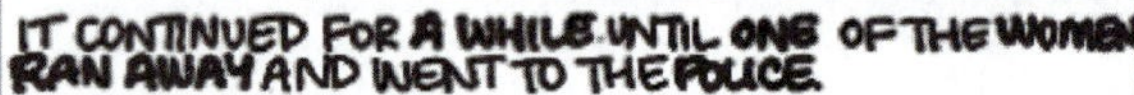
IT CONTINUED FOR A WHILE UNTIL ONE OF THE WOMEN RAN AWAY AND WENT TO THE POLICE.

EVERYONE WAS FREED DURING THE RAID

LERA NOW LIVES IN TERNOPIL AND HAS A SMALL BUSINESS

AS A WEDDING PHOTOGRAPHER.

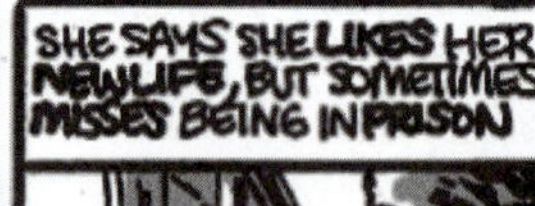
SHE SAYS SHE LIKES HER NEW LIFE, BUT SOMETIMES MISSES BEING IN PRISON

BECAUSE SHE WAS TAKEN CARE OF AND HAD FRIENDS THERE.

Post-reading Questions

Content

1. Who are the Romani people, and where do they have their origins (see Authors' Background Note to "Lera's Story").
2. Summarize the content of "Lera's Story," carefully considering how words and images work together and create meaning in a comic (graphic novel).
3. What kinds of exploitation, captivity, and abuse do the authors explore in "Lera's Story"? Be specific.
4. In your opinion, why should "a message" (in this case, serious, thought provoking content such as human trafficking) never be confused with the "messenger" (in this case, a graphic novel/comic)? What, for instance, may have been lost if Archer and Trusova had related "Lera's Story" in words alone? What was gained by the visual representation they used, and do you feel it was effective?
5. Why is human trafficking a global problem, and what role might consumers play in solving it?

Strategies and Structures

1. Paraphrase the quotation preceding "Lera's Story" about "the Palermo Protocol."
2. What visual techniques are used in the story to help the reader empathize with the characters? Consider what artistic details enable Archer to depict the brutal nature of some characters and sympathetic qualities of others.
3. Referring to at least three or four panels in the story, analyze the importance of lettering—the combination of art and writing in graphic novels and comics used to convey information and reinforce character.
4. "Image choice" plays an important role in a graphic novel—not unlike "word choice" in a poem. Why do you imagine Archer uses specific visuals in "Lera's Story"? What images are the most powerful or moving? How are the violent episodes of the story represented visually? How does one's "image choice" affect the message?
5. At the end of "Lera's Story," why does Lena say she sometimes misses prison? How and why is her remark rather ironic?

Language and Vocabulary

1. *chronicle, exploitation, diaspora, rehabilitation* (from the Author's Notes), and *reconciliation* (from the comic captions). Double-check the definitions for each of the five vocabulary words and note how they are used in context (e.g., the Author's Notes or the comic captions).

2. Overall, the simple vocabulary found in "Lera's Story" allows images to express the suffering and injustices involved in "human trafficking." Select two or three panels from the graphic novel excerpt, and explain the human emotions each image projects. How might a graphic novel/comic support the notion that "a picture's worth a thousand words"?

Group Activities

1. Collaboratively, research more information about Roma culture, laws, and traditions by contacting the European Roma Rights Center: www.errc.org. Then, reread "Lena's Story" out loud as a group. Discuss how background knowledge of Roma culture increased your group's appreciation of Lena's plight as well as how a combination of factors, including laws and traditions, contributed to her exploitation.
2. At the end of one class, divide into groups of four, elect a recorder for your group, and then have the other group members come to the next class with at least two comic books/ graphic novels. Compare and contrast the comics. How do illustrators differ? What do they have in common? Analyze how artists synthesize lines, medium, color, captions, etc., to convey a mood, emphasize a point, and express character. Time permitting, briefly present your group's insights.

Writing Activities

1. Using a variety of examples drawn from graphic novels, compare and contrast at least two treatments of serious subject matter in graphic novels such as *American Born Chinese, Burma Chronicles, Borderland, Safe Area Gorazde* / *Footnotes in Gaza,* and *Pyongyang.*
2. Carefully consider the advantages and disadvantages of tackling serious subject matter in the graphic novel format. Then, write an essay referring to literal and figurative (written) illustrations that demonstrate how non-fiction graphic novels such as *Barefoot Gen, Maus, and Persepolis* can be used effectively as a documentary form.
3. Discuss the notion of "seeing is believing" – comparing and contrasting the power and effect of a photo-essay, a graphic novel extract, and pure text representation of similar events. Which is more effective at connecting you with the story? Why? Are elements sacrificed in order to make that connection?

Additional Topics and Issues for Illustration and Example Essays

1. Painters or sketchers often are called illustrators. Find a painting or drawing, either in a museum or a book, and describe what the artist is attempting to illustrate in an essay.
2. Attend a meeting of the student government body on your campus or a city council meeting where you live and, through illustration and example, write a composition showing what issues were discussed and how they were resolved. Demonstrate how the interactions among the members of the council contributed to the resolutions.
3. Illustrate what it is like—or what you believe it would be like—to work in a fast-food restaurant. Remember your objective: You want to paint a vivid picture using words so your reader will be able to visualize what you are saying.
4. More and more frequently, people do not want to go out at night since they are afraid of being attacked. To what extent is this fear justified? Using examples and observations drawn from personal experience, develop a thesis supporting your point of view on this issue.
5. Illustrate the differences between what we refer to as "civilized" societies and those that are "underdeveloped" or "primitive." In order to avoid stereotyping, support every general point with at least two specific examples.
6. Construct an essay wherein you illustrate the benefits of using animals, instead of humans, to test the effects of new drugs, wonder cures, and cosmetics. If you believe such a practice is inhumane, illustrate the negative side of this issue. Make sure you illustrate what you believe using specific examples; do not just tell your reader what you think.
7. Construct a paper illustrating and exemplifying the reasons one should pursue higher education, a corporate management position, or a political office. Be sure to supply readers with plenty of representative examples that demonstrate and support each discussion point.
8. Providing illustrations and examples drawn from personal experiences, observations, and readings, write an essay demonstrating how human beings can be insensitive and

indifferent to the wants and needs of others. A variation of this same assignment might be to show how most people are compassionate and caring rather than cold and indifferent.

9. Illustrate what people can do to help stop the extinction of plants and animals by showing what will come about in the absence of them. If need be, do some research on the Internet, or at your college library. To add greater authority to your essay, be sure to cite reputable sources of information, using parenthetical footnotes, as well as a list of Works Cited. For more information, see the Appendix at the end of this text—as well as essays with documentation such as "Online Learning and Student Success" by Mark Charles Fissel.

10. Write an essay in which you illustrate the realities—both good and bad—of the mall culture, freeway culture, hip-hop culture, and so on. Provide a wide variety of examples, followed by an analysis to thoroughly explain each sub point of your thesis.

CHAPTER 5 Definition

Definition plays an important part in the development of most expository essays. Why? Without a clear definition of terms, a reader will have only a vague idea of what you are writing about. Specifically defining whom and what you are explaining will help you, the writer, focus on your goals, giving you less opportunity to digress and wander.

Frequently, writers define a problem, a group or subgroup, a concept, a place, another person, or themselves. By defining these things, writers may wish to call certain problems or concepts to the reader's attention or to dispel a currently popular definition and supply his or her own definition. For example, Jo Goodwin Parker defines "poverty" in order to call the reader's attention to the problems of the poor: hunger, dirt, and despair. On the other hand, Isaac Asimov writes his essay "What Is Intelligence, Anyway?" to dispel the myth that all intelligence can be measured and evaluated in an academic setting. To Asimov, a person's intelligence is based on the situation (e.g., the author is intelligent at the university but not at the auto repair shop).

Regardless of your reasons for defining something, you should be careful and concerned about how you define. For example, people often define themselves cautiously so as to be perceived in positive ways. In a recent United States presidential campaign, one candidate originally did not want to use the line "read my lips" because he had been advised that no U.S. president in modern memory had ever mentioned parts of the human body (with the possible exception of "heart") in a debate or speech. He hesitated—before he ultimately did use the line—concerned that people might define him as peculiar or immoral.

Writers have many techniques available to them when they create a definition; that is, they can arrange and develop their definitions in a variety of ways. However, all good writers realize that definition essays require them to do a considerable amount of research and pre-writing before they can even begin to organize their thoughts in a coherent fashion. Once the preliminary steps have been completed, the writer is ready to organize his or her major discussion points: supporting material that helps define the topic or issue. Some of the most common techniques writers use when they create definitions include the following.

Definition by Example

Often authors will offer a definition of a term, issue, or topic by giving examples and descriptions. For example, in her essay "What Is Poverty?" Parker explains poverty to us by offering examples of her own poverty-stricken life. *"Let me explain about housekeeping with no money. For breakfast I give my children grits with no oleo or cornbread without eggs and oleo. This does not use up many dishes. What dishes there are, I wash in cold water and with no soap. . . . Look at my hands, so cracked and red."* These examples solidify the definition of poverty in a graphic way for the reader. In another definition essay, "What Is This Thing Called Family," by Lee Herrick, the author announces, *"As a Korean adoptee raised by Caucasian parents, I have a unique perspective on the notion of family. It is not defined by physical similarity."* The bulk of his composition expands on this point, adding depth and scope, and appreciation to his definition of family. Sravani Banerjee's essay, "Pizza, Pakora and Pancit—The Importance of Global Education" defines a need, global education, and relates it not only to America but also to the world at large. Among other things, *"Global education challenges students to think in more complex ways about identity, society and history, as they discuss current world events and their interconnectedness with other parts of the world."*

Definition by History

Another technique that will aid in creating a definition is to offer the history of the term, issue, or topic being defined. By creating a historical context, the writer establishes where a term, issue, or topic has come from and how it has developed, what its uses have been throughout history, and how it has evolved. A good example of this might be the reference to a person as a Machiavellian. Historically, Nicollo Machiavelli wrote a book, *The Prince,* in the early 16th century. Therein he defined what it takes to be a successful leader, a Prince. Among other things, he claimed that "the practical maneuvers of the fox and the lion—the perfect combination of cunning and strength—are open to anyone who aspires to be a Prince," "the ends justifies the means," "it is better to be feared than to be loved," "perpetuating a clear and present danger can unify people," and "the activities of a ruthless man of action—a Prince—are explicitly beyond any label of good or evil that morality has to offer." Over the past five centuries, a Machiavellian has become synonymous with diabolical people and their actions—villains in literature, leaders in politics, and executives in the business world—who will stop at nothing to achieve their goals.

Definition by Comparison or Contrast

It is often useful to define an unknown term, issue, or concept by comparing or contrasting it with a known term, issue, or concept. The writer will take advantage of what the audience knows already to create a clear definition of what it may not know. Guillermo Gómez-Peña in his essay "Documented/Undocumented," contrasts his definition of himself and his culture with the definitions found in other cultures. *"I am Mexican but I am also Chicano and Latin American. At the border they call me* chilango *or* mexiquillo; *in Mexico City, it's* pocho *or* norteño; *and in Europe it's* sudaca. *The Anglos call me 'Hispanic' or 'Latino' . . . ."*

Definition by Negation

Though a bit more difficult, another way to write a definition paper is through negation, which is explaining what something is *not.* (This sometimes proves useful in developing an argumentative essay, too.) By clearly stating what qualities, characteristics, or concepts something lacks, a writer can create a clear picture of what something is. Often writers will disprove a popular definition, notion, or belief about something, as they set up a different definition of their own. For example, in "Does America Still Exist?" Richard Rodriguez argues that the "ideal" America is *not* what Americans believe it is. Still another example of definition by negation might be "What's in Your Toothpaste?" Therein, David Bodanis explains that an average tube of toothpaste is *not* a harmless consumer product that promotes healthy oral hygiene but a corrosive—even toxic—combination of chalk, water, paint, seaweed, antifreeze, paraffin oil, detergent, peppermint, formaldehyde, and fluoride.

In whatever way you decide to develop your definition, remember that definitions are a way to clarify your ideas, concepts, and issues. Writers often use a definition to call the reader's attention to a problem or to offer a counter-definition to a popular notion.

Tips on Writing Definition Essays

1. First, ask yourself questions to limit your topic. What do you want to define? Why do you want to define it?
2. Freewrite about your topic or issue in order to focus on what you want to define. Remember, an unfocused topic or issue will lead to a vague or unclear definition.
3. Gather information from a variety of sources that will aid in the development of your definition.
4. Organize your definition paper so that it has a clear pattern. If the reader must guess at what you are attempting to define and how you will define it, he or she may become confused or misinterpret your purpose.
5. Fully develop your definition with examples and specifics. You may find the strategies for development listed above useful.
6. As you proofread your essay prior to writing the final copy, ask yourself, "What is my purpose for writing this paper? Do my examples clearly illustrate the term, concept, or issue that I am defining? Where would additional examples strengthen my definition?"
7. Keep in mind that you are writing for a reader who may not be familiar with the term, topic, or issue you are defining. Your development with examples will create concrete meaning for the reader.

Isaac Asimov

What Is Intelligence, Anyway?

Born in the Soviet Union, Isaac Asimov immigrated with his parents to the United States in 1923 and earned a doctorate from Columbia University. A well-respected writer on general science, Asimov published numerous books and is one of the most prolific science-fiction writers of the twentieth century. His works of fiction and nonfiction include *I, Robot* (1950), *The Foundation Trilogy* (1951–53), *The Stars in Their Courses* (1976), *The Gods Themselves* (1977), *Isaac Asimov: The Complete Stories* (1990), *The Best Science Fiction of Isaac Asimov* (1991), and *The Exploding Suns: The Secrets of Supernovas* (1996) to name a few. Other nonfiction works include: *Asimov's Guide to the Bible: A Historical Look at the Old and New Testaments* (1988), *Isaac Asimov's Guide to Earth and Space* (1992), *Asimov Laughs Again: More Than 700 Favorite Jokes, Limericks, and Anecdotes* (1993), *I, Asimov* (1995), and *Asimov's Guide to Shakespeare: A Guide to Understanding and Enjoying the Works of Shakespeare* (2003). In the following essay, Asimov exams and questions the commonly accepted definition of intelligence.

Pre-reading Questions

1. What qualities do you associate with intelligence? If you have trouble thinking of specific things, freewrite or cluster the word.
2. Define a fair test of intelligence. Should people who work in different occupations take different tests to measure their knowledge? Explain.

---

1 What is intelligence, anyway? When I was in the army I received a kind of aptitude test that all soldiers took and, against a normal of 100, scored 160. No one at the base had ever seen a figure like that, and for two hours they made a big fuss over me. (It didn't mean anything. The next day I was still a buck private with KP as my highest duty.)

2 All my life I've been registering scores like that, so that I have the complacent feeling that I'm highly intelligent, and I expect other people

to think so, too. Actually, though, don't such scores simply mean that I am very good at answering the type of academic questions that are considered worthy of answers by the people who make up the intelligence tests—people with intellectual bents similar to mine?

3 For instance, I had an auto-repair man once, who, on these intelligence tests, could not possibly have scored more than 80, by my estimate. I always took it for granted that I was far more intelligent than he was. Yet, when anything went wrong with my car I hastened to him with it, watched him anxiously as he explored its vitals, and listened to his pronouncements as though they were divine oracles—and he always fixed my car.

4 Well, then, suppose my auto-repair man devised questions for an intelligence test. Or suppose a carpenter did, or a farmer, or, indeed, almost anyone but an academician. By every one of those tests, I'd prove myself a moron. And I'd *be* a moron, too. In a world where I could not use my academic training and my verbal talents but had to do something intricate or hard, working with my hands, I would do poorly. My intelligence, then, is not absolute but is a function of the society I live in and of the fact that a small subsection of that society has managed to foist itself on the rest as an arbiter of such matters.

5 Consider my auto-repair man, again. He had a habit of telling me jokes whenever he saw me. One time he raised his head from under the automobile hood to say: "Doc, a deaf-and-dumb guy went into a hardware store to ask for some nails. He put two fingers together on the counter and made hammering motions with the other hand. The clerk brought him a hammer. He shook his head and pointed to the two fingers he was hammering. The clerk brought him nails. He picked out the sizes he wanted, and left. Well, doc, the next guy who came in was a blind man. He wanted scissors. How do you suppose he asked for them?"

6 Indulgently, I lifted my right hand and made scissoring motions with my first two fingers. Whereupon my auto-repair man laughed raucously and said, "Why, you dumb jerk, he used his voice and asked for them." Then he said, smugly, "I've been trying that on all my customers today." "Did you catch many?" I asked. "Quite a few," he said, "but I knew for sure I'd catch you." "Why is that?" I asked. "Because you're so goddamned educated, doc, I *knew* you couldn't be very smart."

7 And I have an uneasy feeling he had something there.

Post-reading Questions

Content

1. According to Asimov, what is intelligence?
2. What sort of intelligence does Asimov, an academic, have? Is it any better than the intelligence of the auto mechanic or blue-collar worker? Why?

3. How did Asimov value IQ tests at the start of his essay, and what made him reconsider his position?

Strategies and Structures

1. Why does Asimov include several short episodes in this paper (e.g., time in the army, a trip to an automobile mechanic)? How do they assist him in defining *intelligence?*

2. What would happen if Asimov placed his trip to the automobile mechanic prior to his discussion of his performance on IQ tests? Why do you think he arranged his material as he did?

3. What might have been Asimov's strategic purpose for concluding his essay with a one-sentence paragraph?

Language and Vocabulary

1. Vocabulary: *KP, complacent, indulgently.* Outside of KP (*kitchen police*), the other two vocabulary words deal with qualities associated with someone who is lacking intelligence. What other characteristics do you associate with an unintelligent person? Write a list of them, and, through repeated usage for at least three days, make them a part of your everyday speech.

2. How many of Asimov's words *sound* intelligent? Make some sort of chart of important-sounding or scholastic words (be sure you know their definitions) and spend a day consciously using them whenever you have an opportunity. How did others react to your use of words? Did using *big* words make you feel more or less intelligent? Why?

Group Activities

1. In pairs, in much the same way as Asimov reported his conversations with his mechanic, visit a person who runs a business neither of you knows anything about. Interview him or her, and then write a collaborative summary of this person's intelligence. In what areas do you feel superior to this person, and in what ways is his or her intelligence superior to your own?

2. When the class has been divided into four or five groups, have each group member write down three things he or she knows little about as well as three things he or she knows much about. Compare notes and find a common element of expertise in your group (e.g., math, "street smarts," science, philosophy). Next, make up an intelligence quiz based on questions from your group's area of expertise (ten questions), and make copies of it for the rest of the class. Finally, with the exception of your own, take each group's intelligence quiz, correct them all as a class, and graph the results for each test. What do the results imply about intelligence tests? Did the outcome of the class exercise confirm Asimov's conclusions about IQ tests? How?

Writing Activities

1. Write an essay defining your own conception of intelligence. As Asimov has done, cite some specific instances that demonstrate how and why your definition is valid. Feel free to refer to Group Activity 2.
2. Make up a list of the qualities you associate with stupidity, lunacy, or another human characteristic. Focus on a recurring theme from your list and use it as the controlling idea in an essay defining your topic.

Guillermo Gómez-Peña

Documented/Undocumented

Besides writing, Guillermo Gómez-Peña works as a visual artist and frequently dramatizes the dilemma of the "border-crosser" in the theater, on the radio, and through the cinema. Often regarded as a pioneer in US Latino and Latin American performance art, Gómez-Peña's legendary pieces include, *Border Brujo* (1988), *The Couple in the Cage* (1992), *The Crucifixion Project* (1994), *The Temple of Confessions* (1995), *The Mexterminator Project* (1997–99), *The Living Museum of Fetishized Identities* (1999–2002), and the *Mapa/Corpo Series* (2004–2008). Besides being a founding member of the *Border Arts Workshop/Taller de Arte Fronterizo*, he is the editor of the experimental arts magazine *The Broken Line/La Lunea Quebrada*. Gómez-Peña edited *Made in Aztlan: Centro Cultural de la Raza* (1987), and his other works include *Warrior for Gringostroika* (1993), *The New World Border: Prophecies, Poems, & Loqueras for the End of the Century* (1996), *Dangerous Border Crossers: The Artist Talks Back* (2000), and—along with Enrique Chagoya—*Friendly Cannibal* (1996). *Temple of Confessions: Mexican Beasts and Living Santos*, written with Roberto

Sifuentes, was published in November 1996. Ruben Martínez translated the following Gómez-Peña essay that initially appeared in the *L.A. Weekly* in 1988.

Pre-reading Questions

1. What images of Mexican Americans do we find on television and in the newspapers? Who are they? Where are they from? What is their history? When did they become a part of American history? How does the rest of society perceive them? As a class, share your perceptions of this culture. Remember these are only perceptions and not hard-and-fast definitions.
2. Gómez-Peña defines himself as "a border-crosser" in the essay you are about to read. What do you think—without reading the essay—might be some typical characteristics of a border-crosser?

---

1 I live smack in the fissure between two worlds, in the infected wound: half a block from the end of Western Civilization and four miles from the start of the Mexican-American border, the northernmost point of Latin America. In my fractured reality, but a reality nonetheless, there cohabit two histories, languages, cosmologies, artistic traditions, and political systems which are drastically counterposed. Many "deterritorialized" Latin American artists in Europe and the U. S. have opted for "internationalism" (a cultural identity based upon the "most advanced" of the ideas originating out of New York or Paris). I, on the other hand, opt for "borderness" and assume my role: My generation, the *chilangos* [slang term for a Mexico City native], who came to "el norte" fleeing the imminent ecological and social catastrophe of Mexico City, gradually integrated itself into otherness, in search of that other Mexico grafted onto the entrails of the et cetera . . . became Chicano-ized. We de-Mexicanized ourselves to Mexi-understand ourselves, some without wanting to, others on purpose. And one day, the border became our house, laboratory, and ministry of culture (or counterculture).

2 Today, eight years after my departure (from Mexico), when they ask me for my nationality or ethnic identity, I can't respond with one word, since my "identity" now possesses multiple repertories: I am Mexican but I am also Chicano and Latin American. At the border they call me *chilango* or *mexiquillo;* in Mexico City it's *pocho* or *norteño;* and in Europe it's *sudaca.* The Anglos call me "Hispanic" or "Latino," and the Germans have, on more than one occasion, confused me with Turks or Italians. My wife Emilia is Anglo-Italian, but speaks Spanish with an Argentine accent, and together we walk amid the rubble of the Tower of Babel of our American post-modernity.

3 The recapitulation of my personal and collective topography has become my cultural obsession since I arrived in the United States. I look for the traces of my generation, whose distance stretches not only from Mexico City to California, but also from the past to the future, from pre-Columbian America to high technology and from Spanish to English, passing through "Spanglish."

4 As a result of this process I have become a cultural topographer, border-crosser, and hunter of myths. And it doesn't matter where I find myself, in Califas or Mexico City, in Barcelona or West Berlin; I always have the sensation that I belong to the same species; the migrant tribe of the fiery pupils.

Post-reading Questions

Content

1. What does Gómez-Peña mean when he begins his essay by writing, "I live smack in the fissure between two worlds, in the infected wound"? How might this explain his sense of "fractured reality"? What do the words "fractured reality" suggest?
2. What is the history of *chilangos?* Where are they originally from and where did they flee? Finally, why did they flee?
3. What names do others use when defining Gómez-Peña? What does he use when defining himself?
4. How does Gómez-Peña's definition of himself explain why he has "become a cultural topographer, border-crosser, and hunter of myths"?

Strategies and Structures

1. How does the opening sentence set the theme of the essay? What tension does it create? How does it limit the scope of the essay?
2. Gómez-Peña defines his "self" in two ways. What are they? How does he organize the essay around these two ways of defining one's self?
3. How does the title of Gómez-Peña's essay define his topic as a whole?

Language and Vocabulary

1. Vocabulary: *fissure, cohabit, cosmologies, counter-posed, deterritorialized, ecological, post-modernity, recapitulation, topography.* After looking up the definitions in the dictionary, reread the essay. Does the topic take on a new meaning for you? Explain.
2. Take the word *topography,* and make an essay map (see Glossary) of your own cultural background.

Group Activities

1. As a group, research one culture or social segment in the United States. What is its history? How have others used names to define this group? What names have members of this group used to define themselves? Be prepared to present your findings to the rest of the class.
2. Create a collage that defines your group. Use magazine photos, newspaper headlines, and so on. Finally, translate (define) your visual collage into the written language.

Writing Activities

1. Write a short essay in which you define yourself by providing the history of your family and by stating the perceptions others have of you. Here you might mention names and categories others use to label you.
2. Compose an essay in which you explain what you feel it means to grow up caught between two cultures, two realities.

Jo Goodwin Parker

What Is Poverty?

When Jo Goodwin Parker originally published this article, she preferred that the editor present no byline. Therefore, in keeping with the spirit of its initial publication, we continue to reprint Parker's article without any biographical data about its author. However, we sincerely would like to thank Parker for her generosity.

Pre-reading Questions

1. Write a three-sentence definition of *poverty*. Who are the poor? Why are they poor? Where do the poor usually live? What problems must poor people overcome?

2. What insights and experiences have shaped your attitude towards poor people? Do you feel superior to them? Do they make you angry? Do they cause you to feel despair? Do you try to help out "needy" or "poor" people? If so, why? If not, why not?

---

1 You ask me what is poverty? Listen to me. Here I am, dirty, smelly, and with no "proper" underwear on and with the stench of my rotting teeth near you. I will tell you. Listen to me. Listen without pity. I cannot use your pity. Listen with understanding. Put yourself in my dirty, worn out, ill-fitting shoes, and hear me.

2 Poverty is getting up every morning from a dirt- and illness-stained mattress. The sheets have long since been used for diapers. Poverty is living in a smell that never leaves. This is a smell of urine, sour milk, and spoiling food sometimes joined with the strong smell of long-cooked onions. Onions are cheap. If you have smelled this smell, you did not know how it came. It is the smell of the outdoor privy. It is the smell of young children who cannot walk the long dark way in the night. It is the smell of the mattress where years of "accidents" have happened. It is the smell of the milk which has gone sour because the refrigerator long has not worked, and it costs money to get it fixed. It is the smell of rotting garbage. I could bury it, but where is the shovel? Shovels cost money.

3 Poverty is being tired. I have always been tired. They told me at the hospital when the last baby came that I had chronic anemia caused from poor diet, a bad case of worms, and that I needed a corrective operation. I listened politely—the poor are always polite. The poor always listen. They don't say that there is no money for iron pills, or better food, or worm medicine. The idea of an operation is frightening and costs so much that, if I had dared, I would have laughed. Who takes care of my children? Recovery from an operation takes a long time. I have three children. When I left them with "Granny" the last time I had a job, I came home to find the baby covered with fly specks, and a diaper that had not been changed since I left. When the dried diaper came off, bits of my baby's flesh came with it. My other child was playing with a sharp bit of broken glass, and my oldest was playing alone at the edge of a lake. I made twenty-two dollars a week, and a good nursery school costs twenty dollars a week for three children. I quit my job.

4 Poverty is dirt. You can say in your clean clothes coming from your clean house, "Anybody can be clean." Let me explain about housekeeping with no money. For breakfast I give my children grits with no oleo or cornbread without eggs and oleo. This does not use up many dishes. What dishes there are, I wash in cold water and with no soap. Even the cheapest soap has to be saved for the baby's diapers. Look at my hands, so cracked and red. Once I saved for two months to buy a jar of Vaseline

for my hands and the baby's diaper rash. When I had saved enough, I went to buy it and the price had gone up two cents. The baby and I suffered on. I have to decide every day if I can bear to put my cracked sore hands into the cold water and strong soap. But you ask, why not hot water? Fuel costs money. If you have a wood fire it costs money. If you burn electricity, it costs money. Hot water is a luxury. I do not have luxuries. I know you will be surprised when I tell you how young I am. I look so much older. My back has been bent over the wash tubs every day for so long, I cannot remember when I ever did anything else. Every night I wash every stitch my school age child has on and just hope her clothes will be dry by morning.

5 Poverty is staying up all night on cold nights to watch the fire knowing one spark on the newspaper covering the walls means your sleeping child dies in flames. In summer poverty is watching gnats and flies devour your baby's tears when he cries. The screens are torn and you pay so little rent you know they will never be fixed. Poverty means insects in your food, in your nose, in your eyes, and crawling over you when you sleep. Poverty is hoping it never rains because diapers won't dry when it rains and soon you are using newspapers. Poverty is seeing your children forever with runny noses. Paper handkerchiefs cost money and all your rags you need for other things. Even more costly are antihistamines. Poverty is cooking without food and cleaning without soap.

6 Poverty is asking for help. Have you ever had to ask for help, knowing your children will suffer unless you get it? Think about asking for a loan from a relative, if this is the only way you can imagine asking for help. I will tell you how it feels. You find out where the office is that you are supposed to visit. You circle that block four or five times. Thinking of your children, you go in. Everyone is very busy. Finally, someone comes out and you tell her that you need help. That never is the person you need to see. You go see another person, and after spilling the whole shame of your poverty all over the desk between you, you find that this isn't the right office after all—you must repeat the whole process, and it never is any easier at the next place.

7 You have asked for help, and after all it has a cost. You are again told to wait. You are told why, but you don't really hear because of the red cloud of shame and the rising cloud of despair.

8 Poverty is remembering. It is remembering quitting school in junior high because "nice" children had been so cruel about my clothes and my smell. The attendance officer came. My mother told him I was pregnant. I wasn't, but she thought that I could get a job and help out. I had jobs off and on, but never long enough to learn anything. Mostly I remember being married. I was so young then. I am still young. For a time, we had all the things you have. There was a little house in another town, with hot water and everything. Then my husband lost his

job. There was unemployment insurance for a while and what few jobs I could get. Soon, all our nice things were repossessed and we moved back here. I was pregnant then. This house didn't look so bad when we first moved in. Every week it gets worse. Nothing is ever fixed. We now had no money. There were a few odd jobs for my husband, but everything went for food then, as it does now. I don't know how we lived through three years and three babies, but we did. I'll tell you something, after the last baby I destroyed my marriage. It had been a good one, but could you keep on bringing children in this dirt? Did you ever think how much it costs for any kind of birth control? I knew my husband was leaving the day he left, but there were no good-byes between us. I hope he has been able to climb out of this mess somewhere. He never could hope with us to drag him down.

9 That's when I asked for help. When I got it, you know how much it was? It was, and is, seventy-eight dollars a month for the four of us; that is all I ever can get. Now you know why there is no soap, no needles and thread, no hot water, no aspirin, no worm medicine, no hand cream, no shampoo. None of these things forever and ever and ever. So that you can see clearly, I pay twenty dollars a month rent, and most of the rest goes for food. For grits and cornmeal, and rice and milk and beans. I try my best to use only the minimum electricity. If I use more, there is that much less for food.

10 Poverty is looking into a black future. Your children won't play with my boys. They will turn to other boys who steal to get what they want. I can already see them behind the bars of their prison instead of behind the bars of my poverty. Or they will turn to the freedom of alcohol or drugs, and find themselves enslaved. And my daughter? At best, there is for her a life like mine.

11 But you say to me, there are schools. Yes, there are schools. My children have no extra books, no magazines, no extra pencils, or crayons, or paper and most important of all, they do not have health. They have worms, they have infections, they have pink-eye all summer. They do not sleep well on the floor, or with me in my one bed. They do not suffer from hunger, my seventy-eight dollars keep us alive, but they do suffer from malnutrition. Oh yes, I do remember what I was taught about health in school. It doesn't do much good. In some places there is a surplus commodities program. Not here. The country said it cost too much. There is a school lunch program. But I have two children who will already be damaged by the time they get to school.

12 But, you say to me, there are health clinics. Yes, there are health clinics and they are in the towns. I live out here eight miles from town. I can walk that far (even if it is sixteen miles both ways), but can my little children? My neighbor will take me when he goes; but he expects to get paid, *one way or another.* I bet you know my neighbor. He is that large

man who spends his time at the gas station, the barbershop, and the corner store complaining about the government spending money on the immoral mothers of illegitimate children.

13 Poverty is an acid that drips on pride until all pride is worn away. Poverty is a chisel that chips on honor until honor is worn away. Some of you say that you would do *something* in my situation, and maybe you would, for the first week or the first month, but for year after year after year?

14 Even the poor can dream. A dream of a time when there is money. Money for the right kinds of food, for worm medicine, for iron pills, for toothbrushes, for hand cream, for a hammer and nails and a bit of screening, for a shovel, for a bit of paint, for some sheeting, for needles and thread. Money to pay in *money* for a trip to town. And, oh, money for hot water and money for soap. A dream of when asking for help does not eat away the last bit of pride. When the office you visit is as nice as the offices of other governmental agencies, when there are enough workers to help you quickly, when workers do not quit in defeat and despair. When you have to tell your story to only one person, and that person can send you for other help and you don't have to prove your poverty over and over and over again.

15 I have come out of my despair to tell you this. Remember I did not come from another place or another time. Others like me are all around you. Look at us with an angry heart, anger that will help you help me. Anger that will let you tell of me. The poor are always silent. Can you be silent too?

Post-reading Questions

Content

1. What does Parker claim poverty is? Look at the beginning of each paragraph for some specific definitions. Next, jot down her definitions of poverty and compare them to the list you wrote as a pre-reading activity.
2. How is poverty difficult for Parker's children? List some specific examples.
3. In what ways does Parker try to obtain help, and what problems does she encounter?
4. Why are people's opinions and prejudices Parker's greatest obstacles?

Strategies and Structures

1. What writing strategy does the author use at the beginning of most paragraphs? Do you notice a recurring pattern? What is it?
2. How does Parker develop each paragraph? What details make each paragraph memorable?

3. How does Parker defend her inability to get help? How does she discount the usual solutions society has for poverty (e.g., welfare, education, and health clinics)?
4. In the final paragraph, how does the author use a question to involve the reader in the issue of poverty?

Language and Vocabulary

1. Vocabulary: *chronic, immoral, illegitimate, antihistamines, enslaved.* Which of these words tend to produce a negative feeling in you? Why? Pick one of the negative words and cluster the feelings the word evokes. Save your list.
2. Note the author's use of adjectives to describe the subhuman conditions in which her family lives. For instance, instead of writing "Poverty is looking into a future," she writes, "Poverty is looking into a black future." How many other such adjectives can you find?

Group Activities

1. Pair off for an extracurricular group activity. Go to one of the charity or social-welfare organizations in town and interview a social worker about the life of the poor. After this, determine whether Parker was exaggerating the problem.
2. Create a realistic list of possible solutions to Parker's problem: poverty in small groups. Consider the possible role of government programs, charity organizations, and individual participation in your solution.

Writing Activities

1. Define a social problem (homelessness, sexism, racism) imitating Parker's style, beginning several of your paragraphs with *"your topic is . . ."* to define your topic or issue.
2. Using adjectives to highlight the futility of the situation, write a short definition essay on *Growing Up in Poverty.*

***Internet Connection:* Jo Goodwin Parker**

Poverty in the United States

Enter the phrase "war on poverty" into your search engine or your college library's database. You might limit your search to articles written in the last ten years. Browse the articles matching your key words, and look for essays that either offer a definition of poverty or a solution to it in the United States. Generally speaking, how well did authors of the researched articles take Parker's definition of poverty into consideration before presenting a plan of action to eliminate national poverty? Is the "war on poverty" being addressed realistically? Keeping the definitions of and the solutions to poverty proposed by your articles in mind, write an essay either agreeing or disagreeing with the notion that eliminating poverty in the United States would be a relatively simple task and could be accomplished in a short period of time. Be sure to reference your source materials.

Richard Rodriguez

Does America Still Exist?

A San Francisco native, Richard Rodriguez is the son of Mexican immigrants. His articles frequently appear in *Change*, *The American Scholar*, and *The Saturday Review*. His works include *Hunger of Memory* (1982), which relates the conflict of ethnic identification and American cultural assimilation, *A Qualitative Study of Identity Development in Gay Chicano Males* (1991), *Days of Obligation: An Argument with My Mexican Father* (1992), *King's Highway* (2000), and *Brown: The Last Discovery of America* (2003). Additionally, he co-authored several other works such as *Making Independent Films: Advice from the Filmmakers*, with Liz Stubbs (2000). In the following essay, Rodriguez develops his definition of America by arguing what the country "is not."

Pre-reading Questions

1. What are some traditional symbols and words associated with America? What do they stand for?

2. Who are Americans? Is America a common culture or a diverse culture? Are all its citizens truly equal in the eyes of society?

3. Is there a common "American Dream"? If so, what is it?

---

1 For the children of immigrant parents the knowledge comes easier. America exists everywhere in the city—on billboards, frankly in the smell of French fries and popcorn. It exists in the pace: traffic lights, the assertions of neon, the mysterious bong-bong-bong through the atriums of department stores. America exists as the voice of the crowd, a menacing sound—the high nasal accent of American English.

2 When I was a boy in Sacramento (California, the fifties), people would ask me, "Where you from?" I was born in this country, but I knew the question meant to decipher my darkness, my looks.

3 My mother once instructed me to say, "I am an American of American descent." By the time I was nine or ten, I wanted to say, but dared not reply, "I am an American."

4 Immigrants come to America and, against hostility or mere loneliness, they recreate a homeland in the parlor, tacking up postcards or calendars of some impossible blue—lake or sea or sky. Children of immigrant parents are supposed to perch on a hyphen between two countries. Relatives assume the achievement as much as anyone. Relatives are, in any case, surprised when the child begins losing old ways. One day at the family picnic the boy wanders away from their spiced food and faceless stories to watch other boys play baseball in the distance.

5 There is sorrow in the American memory, guilty sorrow for having left something behind—Portugal, China, Norway. The American story is the story of immigrant children and of their children—children no longer able to speak to grandparents. The memory of exile becomes inarticulate as it passes from generation to generation, along with wedding rings and pocket watches—like some mute stone in a wad of old lace. Europe. Asia. Eden.

6 But, it needs to be said, if this is a country where one stops being Vietnamese or Italian, this is a country where one begins to be an American. America exists as a culture and a grin, a faith and a shrug. It is clasped in a handshake, called by a first name.

7 As much as the country is joined in a common culture, however, Americans are reluctant to celebrate the process of assimilation. We pledge allegiance to diversity. America was born Protestant and bred Puritan, and the notion of community we share is derived from a seventeenth-century faith. Presidents and the pages of ninth-grade civics

readers yet proclaim the orthodoxy: We are gathered together—but as individuals, with separate pasts, distinct destinies. Our society is as paradoxical as a Puritan congregation: We stand together, alone.

8 Americans have traditionally defined themselves by what they refused to include. As often, however, Americans have struggled, turned in good conscience at last to assert the great Protestant virtue of tolerance. Despite outbreaks of nativist frenzy, America has remained an immigrant country, open and true to itself.

9 Against pious emblems of rural America—soda fountain, Elks hall, Protestant church, and now shopping mall—stands the cold-hearted city, crowded with races and ambitions, curious laughter, much that is odd. Nevertheless, it is the city that has most truly represented America. In the city, however, the millions of singular lives have had no richer notion of wholeness to describe them than the idea of pluralism.

10 *"Where you from?" the American asks the immigrant child. "Mexico," the boy learns to say.*

11 Mexico, the country of my blood ancestors, offers formal contrast to the American achievement. If the United States was formed by Protestant individualism, Mexico was shaped by a medieval Catholic dream of one world. The Spanish journeyed to Mexico to plunder, and they may have gone, in God's name, with an arrogance peculiar to those who intend to convert. But through the conversion, the Indian converted the Spaniard. A new race was born, the *mestizo,* wedding European to Indian. José Vasconcelos, the Mexican philosopher, has celebrated this New World creation, proclaiming it the "cosmic race."

12 Centuries later, in a San Francisco restaurant, a Mexican-American lawyer of my acquaintance says, in English, over *salade niçoise,* that he does not intend to assimilate into gringo society. His claim is echoed by a chorus of others (Italian-Americans, Greeks, Asians) in this era of ethnic pride. The melting pot has been retired, clanking, into the museum of quaint disgrace, alongside Aunt Jemima and the Katzenjammer Kids. But resistance to assimilation is characteristically American. It only makes clear how inevitable the process of assimilation actually is.

13 For generations, this has been the pattern. Immigrant parents have sent their children to school (simply, they thought) to acquire the "skills" to survive in the city. The child returned home with a voice his parents barely recognized or understood, couldn't trust, and didn't like.

14 In Eastern cities—Philadelphia, New York, Boston, Baltimore—class after class gathered immigrant children to women (usually women) who stood in front of rooms full of children, changing children. So also for me in the 1950s. Irish-Catholic nuns. California. The old story. The hyphen tipped to the right, away from Mexico and toward a confusing but true American identity.

15 I speak now in the chromium American accent of my grammar school classmates—Billy Reckers, Mike Bradley, Carol Schmidt, Kathy O'Grady. . . . I believe I became like my classmates, became German, Polish, and (like my teachers) Irish. And because assimilation is always reciprocal, my classmates got something of me. (I mean sad eyes; belief in the Indian Virgin; a taste for sugar skulls on the Feast of the Dead.) In the blending, we became what our parents could never have been, and we carried America one revolution further.

16 "Does America still exist?" Americans have been asking the question for so long that to ask it again only proves our continuous link. But perhaps the question deserves to be asked with urgency—now. Since the black civil rights movement of the 1960s, our tenuous notion of a shared public life has deteriorated notably.

17 The struggle of black men and women did not eradicate racism, but it became the great moment in the life of America's conscience. Water hoses, bulldogs, blood—the images, rendered black, white, rectangular, passed into living rooms.

18 It is hard to look at a photograph of a crowd taken, say, in 1890 or in 1930 and not notice the absence of blacks. (It becomes an impertinence to wonder if America *still* exists.)

19 In the sixties, other groups of Americans learned to champion their rights by analogy to the black civil rights movement. But the heroic vision faded. Dr. Martin Luther King, Jr., had spoken with Pauline eloquence of a nation that would unite Christian and Jew, old and young, rich and poor. Within a decade, the struggles of the 1960s were reduced to a bureaucratic competition for little more than pieces of a representational pie. The quest for a portion of power became an end in itself. The metaphor for the American city of the 1970s was a committee: one black, one woman, one person under thirty . . . .

20 If the small town had sinned against America by too neatly defining who could be an American, the city's sin was a romantic secession. One noticed the romanticism in the antiwar movement—certain demonstrators who demonstrated a lack of tact or desire to persuade and seemed content to play secular protestants. One noticed the romanticism in the competition among members of "minority groups" to claim the status of Primary Victim. To Americans unconfident of their common identity, minority standing became a way of asserting individuality. Middle-class Americans—men and women clearly not the primary victims of social oppression—brandished their suffering with exuberance.

21 The dream of a single society probably died with *The Ed Sullivan Show*. The reality of America persists. Teenagers pass through big-city high schools banded in racial groups, their collars turned up to a uniform

shrug. But then they graduate to jobs at the phone company or in banks, where they end up working alongside people unlike themselves. Typists and tellers walk out together at lunchtime.

22 It is easier for us as Americans to believe the obvious fact of our separateness—easier to imagine the black and white Americas prophesied by the Kerner report (broken glass, street fires)—than to recognize the reality of a city street at lunchtime. Americans are wedded by proximity to a common culture. The panhandler at one corner is related to the pamphleteer at the next who is related to the banker who is kin to the Chinese old man wearing an MIT sweatshirt. In any true national history, Thomas Jefferson begets Martin Luther King, Jr., who begets the Gray Panthers. It is because we lack a vision of ourselves entire—the city street is crowded and we are each preoccupied with finding our own way home—that we lack an appropriate hymn.

23 Under my window now passes a little white girl softly rehearsing to herself a Motown obbligato.

Post-reading Questions

Content

1. Where does Rodriguez claim America exists? What does he feel symbolizes America?
2. What is more important in America, individuality or membership? According to Rodriguez, where do we stand in relationship to each other?
3. Why does Rodriguez feel the 1960s were so important to American history? What has happened since that era?
4. According to Rodriguez, did the dream of a single society probably die? What proof does he offer?

Strategies and Structures

1. Rodriguez develops his definition of America by stating what it is *not* (arguing through negation). How effective is this strategy? If the author had reversed his strategy and told us what America is, would this have inspired any creative or critical thinking on the part of the reader? Why or why not?
2. How does Rodriguez explain his definition of America? Through abstract discussion or concrete examples? Why does he choose one over the other?
3. In what other ways does the author develop his definition?

Language and Vocabulary

1. Vocabulary: *assimilation, reciprocal, inarticulate, congregation, gringo, chromium, bureaucratic, metaphor, exuberance.* Read the

sentences in which these words are found and try to determine their definitions. Then look up each one in the dictionary and see how accurate your determinations were. What does this exercise show you about reading words in context? What did you discover about dictionary use?

2. Without looking up their definitions, use the following words in a paragraph: *conscience, secession, secular, beget, pamphleteer, allegiance, plunder.* As you did in the previous exercise, check your usage in the dictionary after you draft your paragraph, noting how context assisted you in using words you were not too familiar with. Then, rewrite your paragraph, making changes to improve the sense and to eliminate faulty usage.

Group Activities

1. If possible, get into culturally diverse groups and discuss what you have in common. For instance, do you eat foods, listen to music, or enjoy the sports of another culture? What are the greatest differences among the members of your group? Have you ever wanted to attend social functions of a different culture but were afraid to? What questions have you always wanted to ask about another culture?
2. In a group forum analyze precisely what America is. Begin by asking yourselves what is and is not American? What historical facts can your group brainstorm supporting your position? Do people have a tendency to stereotype Americans? Why? You may want to save the information that you've collected for Writing Activity 2, below.

Writing Activities

1. Compose an original essay wherein you define a concept, a country, or a person through *negation.* That is, focus your attention on arguing what someone or something *is not* to define your topic. Make sure you use specific examples to illustrate what you claim.
2. Write an argument of fact, defining and defending your concept of America. Consider what you were taught when you were little about the United States (e.g., land of the free where everyone has an equal opportunity to achieve—where everything is fair). Does your personal experience support what you were told? How? Why?

Sravani Banerjee

Pizza, Pakora and Pancit—The Importance of Global Education

Sravani Banerjee has been teaching English Composition and Literature at Evergreen Valley College since 1997. She is also an instructor in the ASPIRE program which caters to the specific needs of Asian and South Pacific Islander students. Banerjee serves as an advisor for the ASPIRE program, the Honors program, and the Desi club on campus. She is actively involved in the Academic Senate and the Mentoring program. In addition to other campus responsibilities, she develops and teaches learning communities and incorporates Service Learning in her classes. Currently, Sravani Banerjee serves as ECCTYC Region III Director and presents at local and national conferences such as the English Council of California Two-Year Colleges (ECCTYC) and the national Young Rhetoricians' Conference (YRC) on college composition and rhetoric. Banerjee has a passion for traveling around the world and aspires to visit the Seven Wonders of the World. Formerly, she spent a week in Salzburg, Austria, at the Salzburg Global Seminar for educators. In the following essay she emphasizes the importance of global education in our colleges and universities.

Pre-reading Questions

1. What is the first thing that comes to your mind when you hear the two words, "global education"? Why? What experiences inform your opinions?
2. Why might learning about and gaining an appreciation of world cultures be important? Who would benefit from this? How might a "global education" enrich all of our lives?

---

1 As I look around my classroom and view the faces of my students from at least five different countries and a multitude of cultures, I become intensely aware of my role as a global educator. Our community colleges, especially in the Bay Area are mini global villages catering to students from several ethnicities/cultures. It is our responsibility as educators

to infuse a global perspective in our curricula with the hope that it will eventually lead to a globally-educated student population.

2 This summer I spent a week in Salzburg, Austria at the Salzburg Global Seminar, discussing the critical challenges confronting the global community, the role of educators in this community and innovative solutions to these global issues. Amidst the picturesque and pristine landscape of Salzburg we had "fierce conversations" and animated debates on controversial issues such as America's role in globalism, rapid economic growth in China and India and sustainability issues, manufacturing sweatshops, genocide in Darfur, the war in Iraq, global terrorism, global warming, immigration policies of the United States and other countries etc. We interacted and collaborated with colleagues from other institutions of higher education to get a fresh perspective on global issues, and discuss practical methodologies to implement in the classroom, thus enhancing our skills as global educators.

3 For as long as I can remember, global education in the form of cultural, social and religious diversity has been an integral part of my life. Growing up in India in the seventies, I experienced the last vestige of British colonialism. As a child I learned to balance my life between studying the Bible and singing hymns at my Catholic school while participating, with as much zeal, in all the customary *puja* rituals in a traditional Hindu home. Christmas was as much a part of my consciousness as was *Durga puja*. As an army officer's daughter, I traveled extensively moving from city to city, being exposed to yet another language, another religion and another culture. Consequently, I grew up learning three languages, Bengali, my mother tongue, Hindi, the national language in India, and English. In my early twenties, I moved to America as a new bride embracing yet another culture. Although I had grown up listening to the Beatles, and reading *Nancy Drew*, *Archie* comics, Hawthorne, James Joyce, Faulkner and Poe amongst others, moving nine thousand miles away from home and adjusting to the American lifestyle was quite a challenge. As an immigrant and a global citizen, I empathize with and am painfully aware of the anxieties, challenges and issues many of our students face every day.

4 Global education is imperative in educational institutions because it broadens our perspective and challenges stereotypes. For instance, in the aftermath of the September 11th devastation, many Sikhs all over the United States were physically assaulted and even fatally wounded. The victims were mistakenly identified as Muslims since the perpetrators were unable to distinguish between the Sikh *Pagri* and the Muslim turban—a heinous crime resulting from sheer ignorance. In some cultures getting a tattoo is taboo because it involves desecrating the body, while in others it is venerated. For instance, in order to be a chief in the Samoan culture, a person must endure the excruciating pain of intricately designed tattoos, thus proving his courage and fortitude as a future leader.

5 Global education enables students to have a better understanding about other cultures and religions. For instance, the veil or the *burqa* that some of us see as restrictive to women is considered by many Muslims as a form of protection from the evil eye, safeguarding the honor and respect of women. Another stereotype is regarding arranged marriages which are often labeled as constraining, abusive and unhappy. While most westerners are astounded and appalled at the thought of arranged marriages, many South Asians will expound the virtues and positive aspects of these marriages.

6 Global education challenges students to think in more complex ways about identity, society and history, as they discuss current world events and their interconnectedness with other parts of the world. For example, the fluctuating stock market in Hong Kong affects us adversely, or an oil crisis in the Middle East results in increasing our gas prices.

7 Furthermore, global education helps students recognize, understand and accept different cultural values and attitudes. For instance, professors in Asian cultures are highly revered and seldom questioned; however, in Western cultures, the relationship is rather informal and students in higher education often address their professors by first name, something unheard of and considered utterly disrespectful and reprehensible in Asian cultures.

8 Global education prepares students to successfully compete in a diverse and increasingly global marketplace by making them aware of cultural nuances. In many Asian cultures it is inappropriate to make eye contact with a superior; however, in America a person who does not make eye contact is considered untrustworthy. In the Japanese culture, exchanging gifts while conducting business is customary; however, in the American culture, this may be viewed as a form of bribery and completely unethical. Being unaware of such cultural differences can result in miscommunication and misunderstandings at the work place.

9 Thus, a global citizen is a person who is intensely aware of global issues, understands global interconnectedness, embraces and celebrates cultural diversity, and above all contributes in some form to perpetuate global citizenship.

10 Most educational institutions have several activities pertaining to global education primarily in the form of cultural celebrations, but there is a need for a more comprehensive and cohesive campus-wide global-education program. Universities and colleges could adopt various policies to encourage this. They could offer incentives to students to participate in study abroad programs and encourage faculty to organize and facilitate these study-abroad programs. The administrators and faculty could facilitate campus-wide discussions and activities on global issues such as global warming, depletion of natural resources, access to clean water, global terrorism etc. Furthermore, faculty members could incorporate discussion

of global issues in classroom assignments and introduce students to an array of international authors. Faculty, staff and administrators could organize multicultural activities and celebrations on campus and promote service learning activities pertaining to global issues. Finally, the colleges could develop a transferrable Global Education major.

11 As an English instructor, I try to make my students more globally aware. One of our classroom projects celebrates our diversity. Each student has to write a paper and do an oral presentation on one aspect of his/her culture. They are free to discuss religion, food habits, special ceremonies and/or customs. This project promotes greater cross-cultural understanding creating an atmosphere of collaboration and mutual respect that is conducive to learning. Most importantly, the project broadens perspectives, challenges stereotypes, and prepares students for an increasingly global work environment. The presentations include an array of topics ranging from the significance of the *Quinceanera* to bride burning and dowry deaths in India.

12 Last semester, at the end of a diversity presentation on the Five Pillars of Islam, a student approached me and said "So it looks like all these religions preach pretty much the same stuff, so. . . . what's all the fighting about?"

13 I know I have made a difference, and at least one student is acquiring a global perspective.

Post-reading Questions

Content

1. How does Banerjee define a "global citizen"?
2. According to Banerjee, why is global education so important? Give specific examples.
3. What can institutions (K-12 through college) do to support global education?
4. In Paragraph 2, what does Banerjee mean by "fierce conversations" and "animated debates"?
5. Referring to specific examples, show how Banerjee's life-long experiences help her to define aspects of a global education.

Strategies and Structures

1. Why do you imagine the author chose to use "definition" as the main method of development for her essay? At what point did other rhetorical strategies overlap and to what effect?
2. How does Banerjee establish herself as a credible authority on the subject of global education?
3. Why does Banerjee tell her readers that, "I had grown up listening to the Beatles, and reading Nancy Drew, *Archie* comics, Hawthorne, James Joyce, Faulkner and Poe amongst others"?

4. Banerjee opens many of her body paragraphs with two words, "global education," followed by a verb that defines some aspect of the concept (e.g., "Global education prepares . . . ."). Why do you imagine she does this? How might readers respond to her intentional repetition of key words?
5. How does the single sentence at the end of Banerjee's essay pull her discussion to a satisfying close? In what way does it demonstrate the merits of a global education?

Language and Vocabulary

1. *Vocabulary: picturesque, pristine, curricula, sweat shops, sustainability, genocide, interacted, methodologies, vestige, implement, colonialism, zeal, empathize, restraining, constraining, perpetrator, heinous, venerated, desecrating, interconnectedness, adversely, imperative, excruciating, fluctuating, utterly, reprehensible, diverse, taboo, astounded, appalled, expound, facilitate, depletion, nuances, dowry, perspectives.* After finding the definitions to the vocabulary words in your dictionary, add them to your vocabulary log and then review their use in context. How would you classify most of the vocabulary words? Do they have positive or negative connotations (see Glossary)? Explain.
2. Banerjee's essay contains several foreign words used mostly as nouns (e.g., *puja, Durga puja, Pagri, burqa, Quinceanera*) that were not included in the original vocabulary list. How well did she define such words in context so that readers would not get confused?

Group Activities

1. Refer to paragraph 11 in Banerjee's essay and modify her diversity project to your own liking. Ultimately, create a class forum in which each student takes five minutes to "do an oral presentation on one aspect of his/her culture."
2. Assemble in small groups and research and discuss the global implications of one the following topics:
   - human trafficking
   - rapid economic growth in China and India and sustainability issues
   - manufacturing sweatshops around the world
   - genocide in Darfur
   - the wars in the Middle East
   - global terrorism
   - global warming
   - immigration policies of the United States and other countries.

Have each group define its research topic, and prepare a five to ten minute class "global news brief." Integrate a variety of audio and visual aids into each presentation in order to help the class appreciate and comprehend the complex "global implications" of each topic/issue.

Writing Activities

1. What is your personal definition of a "global citizen"? Do you consider yourself "globally educated?" If so, how and why? Do you know others who fit your definition? After pre-writing on this topic and arriving at a focus—your thesis—write an essay defining the characteristics of a "global learner." Conclude your essay with a prediction or an insight—something that will round off your essay on one hand and possibly serve as a starting point for future conversations on the other.
2. Go back to Group Activity 2 and select one of the topics for additional research. Brainstorm the topics and issues once again, and write an essay defining a problem of global concern—an argument of fact, if you will. Towards the end of your essay, you will want to provide a logical, beneficial, realistic plan of action that could solve the problem.

Lee Herrick

What Is This Thing Called Family?

Lee Herrick was born in Daejeon, South Korea in 1970, adopted at ten months, and raised in California. He is the author of *Coping With Vertigo*, a poetry chapbook, and *This Many Miles from Desire* (2007), a volume of poetry. Additionally, Herrick is the founding editor of In the Grove. Herrick has also served as guest editor of *New Truths: Writing in the 21st Century by Korean Adoptees*, and he sits on the board of directors for the *Journal of Korean Adoption Studies*. His poems have been published in *ZYZZYVA*, *Berkeley Poetry Review*, *Hawaii Pacific Review*, and *The Bloomsbury Review*, among others, and in anthologies such *as Highway 99: A Literary Journey Through California's Great Central Valley*, 2nd Ed. and *The Place That Inhabits Us: Poems from the San Francisco Bay Watershed*. Presently, Herrick lives in Fresno, California, where he teaches at Fresno City College.

Pre-reading Questions

1. Have you or anyone you know been adopted by people other than biological parents or relatives?
2. What is your concept of family, and from where did it evolve (e.g., an ideal, your childhood experiences, television or movie role models)?

---

1 As a Korean adoptee raised by Caucasian parents, I have a unique perspective on the notion of family. It is not defined by physical similarity. I look nothing like them. I am Asian and they are Caucasian, as is my sister (adopted as well, from Alameda). But the subtle similarities one acquires through family are inevitable—the sighs, the way one lifts her eyebrows in curiosity or disdain. We joke about having each others' traits, but they are habits or quirks, not the same shape of nose or chin.

2 My sister and I were raised in California's East Bay Area and later in the Central Valley. In the 1970s, the towns weren't as diverse as they are now. But we had great childhoods. We had a sibling rivalry for the ages, but deep down there was a whole lot of love. I remember her defending me when racial slurs would come my way.

3 "He's Korean," Holly would say, when the other kids would tell me "Go back to where you came from, Chinaman." She would intervene and change the subject when I was asked irritating questions like "What *are* you?" and "How can *she* be your sister?" I think of my sister like a defender, a protector. I also now realize that as much as she was defending me, she was defending herself and her right as an adoptee to have a brother who looked like me.

4 I remember an incident when I came home from grade school one day, sniffling and trying to conceal my tears after a day of particularly aggressive taunting—the subject at hand was my "flat face." It was hurtful and brought me to tears on the long walk home after the bus dropped me off. But it was also very strange to me because I was raised in a Caucasian family, so the boy taunting me looked like my cousins . . . why was he so mean? It was also confusing because I didn't have an Asian accent, nor

did I speak Korean or any other Asian language. My favorite baseball team was the Oakland A's, my favorite player Reggie Jackson. I loved *Star Wars*, Batman, and eventually Atari—all things 70s. I felt normal (whatever that is). Many well-intentioned people also told me "you're so American!" or "you're not like other Asians I've met." To this day I am wary of all these suspect declarations.

5 I walked in the front door, Phil Donahue's inquisitive lisp coming from the television. My mother noticed I had been crying. She bent down like a baseball catcher and took my face into her open hands, wiping my tears with her thumbs. "Oh, honey, what's *wrong*?" she asked.

6 I sniffed and wiped my nose with the back of my hand. "Nothing," I said.

7 "Honey, I'm your mom. You can tell me," she said.

8 "My face isn't flat, is it?" I asked, feeling the small mound of my nose on my face, proving it wasn't flat. I was still sniffling.

9 I can still remember the hurt look on her face, the sadness. I can't remember exactly what she said, but it was something about how some people are just ignorant and to let it "roll right off" my back. I felt better that day, and time after time throughout my life as I encountered difficult times I would often repeat her mantra in my head. She gave me something to use. Years later, as I was defining the term *idiot* in high school, acting out some of my anger, she would often be the one to spell out the conditions of my grounding. Of course, years later I came to appreciate the support (and discipline) she and my father gave me. Some things just take a while.

10 My father is a quiet man. I think of him as the model for giving of yourself as much as you can. Once, when I was fifteen or sixteen, at the height of my selfish teen years, he asked me if I wanted to help him volunteer serving hot dogs at the local Peach Fair.

11 "Do I get paid?" I asked, clearly not hearing the word *volunteer*.

12 "No," he said. He left, no doubt wondering what kind of person I was becoming.

13 He is also the kindest, most soft-spoken, modest person I know. I have never heard him scream, not even when my sister and I were raising all kinds of hell as teenagers. Sure, he gets mad, but his calm demeanor is a trait I have always admired (and probably never successfully emulated).

14 Being a Korean adoptee has been wonderful but undoubtedly challenging. Anger, kindness, and forgiveness have all been a part of my life. To varying degrees I have to believe they are a part of all families. To say the least, being separated from one's birth mother is not easy to come to terms with, and it is complicated further by being in an interracial family. But that is what we are—a family.

15 I have come to believe that family goes far beyond a child's eyes looking like her mother and father's, or a child having the same mannerisms as her parents (which we do, in fact, have). It is more than a name or the number of bedrooms in a home. I have come to believe that family is about love and struggle and adapting. That there are many different types of family and that they evolve—2.5 kids and a white fence, single parent families, those involving incarceration, illness (or a combination of all of these)—family is a wide term with plenty of room for interpretation.

16 Yes, I think about my birth parents from time to time, although I have not met them. But several years ago I returned to Seoul, the capital city where I was born. It felt like going home—no one staring at me because I was the only Asian in a room, eating barbecued squid and kimchi from the street vendor, shopping in Lotte World and the Namdaemun Market, seeing the ancient temples and modern skyscrapers downtown.

17 But while it felt like home, it really wasn't. Home is about family, the people who will stand up for you and say "He's Korean." It is about people who comfort you and tell you that your face is *not* flat. It is not about perfection; it is about trying to be a good person (I realize this now when I am volunteering). It is about getting opportunities and support, discipline and the chance to fail and be responsible. No family member, no matter how present or absent, fills just one role. My sister is the protector but also an inspiration for kindness. My mother is a support system but also the creative force. My father is a role model but also a support system. They are all hilarious and have great work ethics. I can only hope just an ounce of this rubbed off on me. I hope I can honor their names and lives, as well as the names and lives of my birth parents. I hope to instill similar notions of unconditional love with my own family, however we look, wherever we go, whatever the shape of our faces and dreams.

Post-reading Questions

Content

1. Explain Herrick's perspective on "the notion of family."
2. Why does Herrick mention Reggie Jackson, *Star Wars*, Batman, Atari, and Phil Donahue in his essay?
3. Describe Herrick's father; why is he a special person?
4. What is Herrick's concept of "home" all about? What did his visit to Seoul seem to lack?
5. Ultimately, what has Herrick "come to believe"?

Strategies and Structures

1. How did Herrick's sister, mother, and father each contribute to developing his character?
2. Both Lee Herrick and his sisters were adoptees. How and why did this create a special bond between them?
3. In what way does Herrick's concluding paragraph look back to the opening paragraph, and how does his introductory paragraph look forward to the conclusion? Overall, how does Herrick unify his material clearly, coherently, and effectively as he writes?
4. Does Herrick's definition of family transcend social, economic, and ethnic barriers?
5. Describe the strategic purpose for Herrick's extended discussion of "a day of particularly aggressive taunting."

Language and Vocabulary

1. Vocabulary: *intervene, adoptee, taunting, incarceration, mannerisms.* Check the dictionary meaning for each vocabulary word in "What Is This Thing Called Family," and then write a list of at least three antonyms (words meaning the opposite of another word) and three synonyms (words carrying the same or almost the same meaning of a word) for each. Then briefly assess the connotations—associated meanings—for each antonym and synonym. Can you make any conclusions about Herrick's careful word choice in his essay? Could he have just as easily used the word "arbitrate" in place of "intervene," for instance? Why or why not?
2. Overall, how would you describe Herrick's diction—word choice—in his essay? Does it seem to suit his subject? Why or why not?

Group Activities

1. In small groups, research adoption agencies online. What tend to be the requirements for prospective parents/guardians who want to adopt a child? Ideally, have each group research different adoption agencies from a large city in your area. How long is the list of adopters? What is the waiting period to adopt a child, if any? Are there restrictions? Assemble your group's information and prepare a report to share with the rest of the class. Ultimately, all groups will want to compare and contrast their findings.
2. As a collaborative activity, select at least two other essays in *Visions Across the Americas* that deal with family issues. (See the Thematic Table of Contents for a list of these articles.) First, compare and contrast how each article defines the family unit. Next, identify the essay's tone and the author's

attitude towards his subject matter. Take notes. Finally, write a collaborative essay where members develop an agreed upon thesis. One of your goals in this assignment will be to practice using phrases introducing quotations or an author's ideas such as: "According to Timothy Leary . . . ," "Contrary to what Megan McGuire claims in 'Growing Up with Two Moms' . . . ," "As Lee Herrick states . . . ," "In the words of Dr. Martin Luther King, Jr . . . . ," "Anna Quindlen says it best in 'Playing God With No Sleep,'" and so on. These kinds of phrases announce what will follow and/or connect differing perspectives on a topic; furthermore, they help guide readers through your essay and eliminate choppy, unrelated sentence constructions.

Writing Activities

1. Write an essay where you literally and/or figuratively argue that people seek adoption by a country, a social organization, religious group, political party and so on. Some of your discussion points might include the need to belong and establishment of identity.
2. Write an essay comparing and contrasting the challenges Herrick faced as an international adoptee in "What Is This Thing Called Family?" to the obstacles Megan McGuire faced as a child growing up with lesbian parents in "Growing Up With Two Moms."

Internet Connection: Lee Herrick

Adoption/Family

Using an online research engine, locate the *Visions Across the Americas* 8th edition website at [___]. Find Jackie Durant's essay, "When Worlds Col-lied," read it, and ultimately contrast her attitude towards her biological mother to Herrick's relationship towards his adoptive mother. In what way is Durant's grandmother similar to Herrick's mom? Which seems healthier? Why? Write an essay wherein you define your own concept of family, citing Herrick's examples that show what family "is" and allude to Duant's essay to define families by "what they are not." Use at least three parenthetical references from each essay, and include a list of *works cited* at the conclusion of your essay. (See the Appendix for the MLA Stylesheet.)

Additional Topics and Issues for Definition Essays

1. In a well supported, thoroughly developed essay, compare and contrast Asimov's definition of human intelligence (earlier in this chapter) with your own definition of artificial intelligence.
2. Write an essay in which you define one of the following: love, hate, peace, loneliness, or happiness. Because such qualities are difficult to measure, you'll want to provide several representative examples to win your reader over to your viewpoint.
3. Define "elevator music." What is it? Where is it heard most? Need a person be in an elevator to experience such music? After your initial definition, illustrate the effects of this music on people who, unwillingly, are subjected to it.
4. Freewrite on what it means to be an independent or a dependent person. Then compose an essay in which you define yourself as one of the above, supporting your ideas with examples drawn from personal experience.
5. Define the concepts of liberalism and conservatism. Which is better? Do you consider yourself a liberal or a conservative? Why? Integrate information from recent news articles that justifies the concept you have chosen.
6. Write an essay defining "success." Is it being well paid for your work? Is it being happy or content with what you do? Is it joy in helping others? Use specific examples and references to illustrate your definition.
7. In a thoroughly developed essay, define the rights and privileges of a sovereign nation. In these times, why might respecting the rights of sovereign nations and their people be crucial in establishing and maintaining peaceful coexistence?
8. Define the steps a person might take to survive the trauma of being a victim of a mean practical joke, a violent crime (rape or battery), or a bad, though unearned, reputation?
9. Write a definition essay about positive parent-teenager relationships by illustrating what they should not be (definition by negation).

10. Go on the Internet and look up the key term "Farm Aid," reading as many articles as you can on the subject. Then freewrite until arriving at an original thesis. Compose a definition essay explaining the mission and objectives of Farm Aid. What is its history, and what are its prospects for the future? Support your essay using information gleaned from personal experience, interviews, and readings, such as those you did online.

CHAPTER 6

Process Analysis

What is process analysis? In contrast to narration, which relates *what* happens, or cause-and-effect, which explains *why* something occurs, process analysis addresses the question of *how.* Of crucial importance in explaining *how* would be to carefully organize materials and mark them with time transitions (e.g., first, second, third). Such linking devices help a reader follow a process from start to finish. When do we use process analysis? Usually, process analysis explains one of two things: *how* to do something (directive process analysis) or *how* something is or was done (informative process analysis).

Directive Process Papers: How to Do Something

Like most expository strategies, process analysis explains. We are all familiar with the process of explaining how to do something. If we aren't explaining to others how to do something, then others may be explaining to us how to do something. Think for a moment about the last time you gave another person directions on how to get somewhere. What did you do? Undoubtedly, you told the person which direction to go, and you explained where and when to make left or right turns. In doing so, you were actively involved with a process; you were analyzing the possibilities and determining what a person had to do in order to reach a desired destination.

The "how to" essay is deceptively simple. That is, while an author may have no trouble explaining how to read a book, how to mow a lawn, or how to ride a bike, he or she may find it difficult to "hook" the interest of the intended audience. Why? The topics sound rather dull and will be just as dull as their titles promise when fully written unless the writer creates a reason—real or contrived—why such a topic is relevant and therefore *meaningful* to its reader.

Using directive process analysis as her dominant method of essay development, for instance, Christine Ng explains both sides of effective flirtation: *"People need to realize that the skills and behavior they would expect to view on* Jackass, *a crude television show, are not necessary in order to become the center of attention. Flirting between couples should consist of lighthearted, civil interaction with one another that may give the impression of sexual interest, not a locker-room gross-out contest. Once you realize what is or isn't a flirtatious act, you will be ready to study and implement the rules of flirtation."*

Informational Process Essays: How Something Is/Was Done

Process analysis can also be an effective way of informing someone how a process occurs. Informative process analysis explains topics such as how a tree grows, how a gas engine runs, how solar batteries collect energy, or how a worm regenerates itself. Such information is usually expressed in some sort of logical sequence process. Joyce Jarrett, for example, informs readers of the sequential turn of events on her first day at school—events that propelled her to *"new liberty more out of curiosity than out of a sense of mission"* in her essay, "Freedom." Other times the division between directive and informative process analysis papers overlaps to some extent. A prime example would be Kathleen Hudson's "Why Talk? Interviews Matter!" Though her essay predominantly focuses on informative process analysis—how she interviews people—Hudson also provides readers with tips that they can use for the same purpose; in other words, she offers directive as well as informative information. She recommends that interviewers, *"Pay attention, and always be ready to throw down the script prepared questions. Let intuition fashion spontaneous questions. Go down new roads and explore. Every conversation between two people creates a new world, one which both inhabit for a short time. Johnny Winter and I were scheduled for a twenty-minute interview. We quit talking when it was time to get more tattoos (I got a Pegasus on my shoulder) about two hours later. My script did not cover this conversation.*" That is, after suggesting what any good interviewer should be prepared to do—depart from prepared questions—she illustrates how she followed her own advice.

Similar to Hudson, both informative and directive process analysis are at work in Heidi Ramirez's essay, "Community Re-discovered." On one hand, Ramirez discusses how *"Solutions to rekindle the spirit of community have been jumpstarted by national projects such as The Project for Public Spaces, which utilizes grassroots efforts to find third spaces—outside work and home that build community spirit"* (informative process analysis). On the other hand, she suggests ways people could re-build community (directive process analysis).

Informative process analysis is not limited to investigative reporting or to the natural sciences, of course. Rather than explaining a natural relationship, Malcolm X discusses the strategy (process) he used to increase his "word-base" in "A Homemade Education." Similar to Jarrett, Malcolm X uses process analysis to inform us rather than to direct us (tell us how to do something). Granted, it is possible to imitate what another person did in hopes of achieving the same results; we see this in the acting world and political arena daily. Nonetheless, there is an unmistakable difference between imitating to achieve an end (informative process analysis) and following directions to accomplish a task (directive process analysis).

One might say that Luis M. Valdez actually blends informative with directive process analysis in his essay called "Perspectives on 'Borders.'" Indeed, early in the essay, he uses informational process analysis to explain how something was done (the Mayan achievements). His essay could also be directive in that he specifically suggests what must be acknowledged for harmony and pluralism to be possible in the diverse societies of the Americas.

Tips on Writing Process Analysis Essays

1. Have a clear sense of the process you plan to explain, whether it is informative or directive. When in doubt, check a reliable source; don't try to bluff your way through an introduction and assume that your reader will perceive the controlling idea of your composition.

2. Use transitional words and linking devices indicating *time* in order to lead your reader from step to step, point to point.
3. Bear in mind that as with any expository essay, your goal in writing is to *explain how* to do something (directive process analysis) or how something is or was done (informative process analysis). Avoid getting sidetracked on issues that would only confuse your reader.
4. Make sure to use key words and specific references. These will help your reader to remain focused on the controlling idea or purpose of your essay.
5. Review your rough draft and carefully check your work for omitted steps in a process, adding them as necessary. Sometimes it is helpful to continuously ask yourself: Who? What? When? Where? Why? How?

Kathleen Hudson

Why Talk? Interviews Matter!

Kathleen Hudson, Ph.D., has taught in the English Department at Schreiner University in Kerrville, Texas, since 1985. She is also director of the Texas Heritage Music Foundation (www.texasheritagemusic.org) and vice president of Past Is Prologue (www.schreiner.edu/pip), two organizations that produce educational programs at Schreiner University through the Center for Innovative Learning. Her monthly articles on Texas music appear on a website for tourism, www.hill-country-visitor.com, and in two publications. Hudson is available for workshops, presentations, and lectures on many aspects of learning (Native American learning stories, stories and songs in the classroom, teaching by heart, and more). Her nonfiction books include *Telling Stories, Writing Songs* (2000) and *Women in Texas Music: Stories and Songs* (2007). In the following essay, Hudson explains how interviews provide a fertile basis for generating writing ideas.

Pre-reading Questions

1. What are some of the advantages or verbal communication—talking? What, if any, might be some of its disadvantages?
2. Have you ever interviewed a person? Who? For what? When? Where? How did (or would) you prepare to do so?
3. Speculate on how interviewing someone face to face might uncover ideas, facts, and details that you could use to illustrate, explain, and argue discussion points in writing.

---

1 People love to tell stories; stories hold people together. I began collecting the stories of Texas musicians in 1986 at the Memphis Blues Awards. Willie Nelson and B. B. King were co-hosting the event. Both men shared their stories with me, one during a press conference and one after the show at the party. With both men I talked about "Night Life," a classic hit written by Willie and transformed into a blues classic by B. B. I knew at that moment that I wanted to continue collecting the stories songwriters and musicians have to tell. In fact, I wanted to document the entire Texas music scene, in the field, gathering the stories on my little tape recorder. I really wanted to collect the stories all creative people have. Stop! That's the way my mind works; things just keep getting bigger. The vision keeps expanding. Regardless of who tells the story, an interview captures the moment.

2 Nonetheless, *captured moments* rarely become an end in themselves. Sooner or later, the judge, the editor in me, had to take over. The project called for discrimination, choosing. So I created the Texas Heritage Music Foundation in 1987, an organization to preserve and perpetuate the traditions in Texas music. My ever-growing collection of interviews became the heart of an organization committed to the possibility that telling stories and singing songs make a difference in the world.

3 Following years of collecting these stories, these "interviews," I began to reflect on the source of my success in each conversation. First, I broke a few rules. Since I didn't have a background in journalism, I hadn't read the part about keeping myself, the interviewer, out of the interview. I began each interview with a comment about myself, a way for the artist to see a connection with me. Then we were off and running. (In retrospect, I would not have done anything differently.)

4 Before an interview, I often generate a list of interesting questions, and then I throw the list away during the conversation. Why? A good interview is like a jazz performance; neither depends on scripted material. Instead, the saxophone player responds to the band even while leading the band. In a similar manner, I just listen to the response I receive, and then I respond to the person in front of me. The worst scene for

an interviewer is to just go down a list of questions, regardless of the response. For example, consider what is missing in the following:

Hudson: Tell me about your most profound experience that led to a song.

Interviewee: Oh, my dad died when I was a teenager, and I was devastated. I wrote about it in school, and one day I tried a song. It all just came out, in one piece. When I was about 30, my mom was in a wreck. She was left without her legs.

Hudson: Now tell me about your most successful moment on stage.

That's not a conversation! Instead of such predictable or canned questions and answers, I keep my attention on the other person and respond to the words I hear. True, I often feel like that trapeze artist flying without a net, but I trust my own years of experience, my own intuition, my own listening to generate the interview I'm seeking.

5 Allow people to tell their stories during an interview. I learned this lesson one time I interviewed Stevie Ray Vaughan, a blues musician. He had gotten out of rehab and did not want to talk about music. Vaughan told me how it felt to be whole and healthy. He told me how much he loved his life. He told me he wanted to warn other young musicians about the tragedies of drug addiction. As I put down the phone, I thought at first that I had missed the chance to really interview him. Then I realized that by allowing him to tell the story that mattered most to him, I did, indeed, have a great interview. Apart from allowing people to "tell their stories" rather than responding to packaged, dead-end questions, successful interviewers tend to follow a few basic guidelines.

6 Do some research before the interview to enrich the possibilities of a great conversation. I'd listen to the entire Leonard Cohen album, drawn over and over to "The Ballad of the Absent Mare." I raise and train horses, and I've often perceived of myself as one running free. Therefore, when I walked into the backstage area of the Austin Opry House, I began the interview saying, "I am the original absent mare. Where did you get that horse imagery?" I began the interview stating something about myself, something true for me. Leonard took over from that point, telling me all about watching his own horses at a place he once owned in Tennessee.

7 Trust your own vision, your own life when choosing the interview, whether you intend use it as a way to generate writing, a way to conduct research, or a way to collect important information. That is, trust what you bring to the interview, whether it's years of experience or an hour's worth of research. Once you have established trust with your interviewee, reinforce it with positive body language and genuine interest.

8 Set out to interview a person—like most journalists—with certain goals in mind, certain questions to answer. As a feature writer, I decide

to explore—something you will want to consider when conducting your own interviews. Once, for instance, when I was interviewing Townes Van Zandt, I heard myself coming up with questions I'd never asked before. Townes told me about the blues scene in Houston, about Lightnin' Hopkins, and about women with short hair. Lightnin' said, "I don't want no woman whose hair is shorter than mine." Townes told me about haircuts. He told me about the voices he often heard and had to drown out. He told me about his deep friendship with Choctaw writer Roxy Gordon. "We were born on the same day, March 7," Townes explained. "We're blood brothers."

9 Take notes. The interviewer works as a tool; the desired end results can shape the questions being asked. Personally, I always prefer to let language be the tool that carves out meaning, not just a bridge to convey ideas. For instance, an editor looking over my manuscript, *33 Interviews with Texas Songwriters*, commented, "The one with Townes is a bit disjointed." How could it be otherwise? I didn't need to shape the conversation to sound like all the other interviews I've done in my life. It needed to sound like Townes. Thus, I advise you to be true to yourself. Since you are not David Letterman, Oprah Winfrey, Jay Leno, Ricky Lake, or Jerry Springer, you don't need to act or talk like them.

10 Listen carefully and look deeply into the lives of those you interview. Only then will the true dimension of one's story surface. For instance, I looked deeply at the literary interests inherent in Texas songwriting and came upon information I would never have guessed. In our first interview, Joe Ely wanted to talk about reading Allen Ginsberg. I knew we might share other literary interests, so I went down that road. Cormac McCarthy and Clive Barker surfaced as other common interests. Robert Earl Keen also mentioned Cormac McCarthy. I discovered another blues artist, Steve Earl, is writing short stories and that Keen wants to write a novel. By delving deeply and listening carefully to the multiple interests expressed by musicians—or anyone you interview—the interview reveals the complexity and richness of stories that matter to them and, by extension, to us.

11 Pay attention, and always be ready to throw down the script. Let intuition fashion spontaneous questions. Go down new roads and explore. Every conversation between two people creates a new world, one which both inhabit for a short time. Johnny Winter and I were scheduled for a twenty-minute interview. We quit talking when it was time to get more tattoos (I got Pegasus on my shoulder) about two hours later. My script did not cover this conversation.

12 Like anyone who interviews others, I'm a collector. I collect rocks, Belle Starr stories, writers' stories, friends' stories, and the stories of many other cultures (to use in my mythology class at Schreiner College). As such, I believe Paula Underwood, founder of the Past is Prologue

and author of *The Walking People*, who said, "Story can create the space in which new and necessary thinking can occur. It can be the process through which we build increasing awareness of life and its many options, through which we show ourselves—in time—the many paths that lie open to us."

13 Stories capture moments; stories stimulate thinking; and stories open entire worlds with which many of us may connect. The interview process inspired me to continue collecting stories, spaces where new thinking can occur. I find myself inviting all I meet to "Tell me your story."

Post-reading Questions

Content

1. Identify what Hudson says should be the most important objective of an interview. Would you agree or disagree with her? Why?
2. Discuss the events that inspired Hudson to gather stories on "the entire Texas music scene."
3. Before interviewing a person, why does Hudson recommend doing some research on a him or her? How does she demonstrate this guideline in practice?
4. Explain the implications of Hudson's comment that she often feels like a "trapeze artist flying without a net" as she interviews people.
5. Hudson opens paragraph 11 with the statement, "Pay attention, and always be ready to throw down the script." In what way does her anecdote about a twenty minute interview with guitarist Johnny Winter graphically demonstrate a commitment to her own advice?

Strategies and Structures

1. How does Hudson use the first three and and final two paragraphs in her directive process anaylsis essay as a framing device for discussing interview techniques? Why do you imagine she stresses "the story" as the "big picture" and the interview as part of it?
2. Along with blues icon B.B. King, Hudson makes a lot of concrete references to legendary Texas songwriters. How do such references add authority to her exposition? What might have been lost without them and why? In your opinion, what is the difference between "name-dropping" and significant "allusions"?
3. Apart from general research, Hudson advises people to prepare a "list of interesting questions" before an interview and then throwing them away. Why? What is often the result of such a strategy?

4. In what way, according to Hudson, will talking directly, listening carefully, and responding deeply to a person being interviewed produce the best results?
5. Analyze the strategic purpose for—and the ultimate effect of—using "anaphora," (the repetition of the first word at the beginnings of successive clauses) in the topic sentence, "Stories capture moments; stories stimulate thinking; and stories open entire worlds with which many of us may connect," for the final paragraph in Hudson's essay.

Language and Vocabulary

1. Vocabulary: Straightforward and easily accessible, the vocabulary in Hudson's essay presents no particular challenge. Some of her comparisons, on the other hand, offer food for thought. To gain a full appreciation of her jazz/interview analogy (extended comparison), however, look up *jazz* in the dictionary or on the Internet. In your opinion, how might an interview be appropriately—or inappropriately—explained as jazz performance? Discuss its characteristics if eacg in a brief paragraph.
2. Frequently, an author's choice of language reflects his or her attitude toward a subject. What words or word groups seem to indicate Hudson's attitude toward *talking* in general and *interviewing* people in particular?

Group Activities

1. In recent years, "town hall meetings" where all people have an opportunity to ask questions and receive answers have grown in popularity. Assemble in groups and identify three or four major community problems. Next, collaboratively write a list of questions, a list that each member will then use to interview people in the community who can address these concerns. For example, if water pollution concerns your group, one or more of its members might talk to people who work at a water treatment plant.
2. Invite a member of your college community to attend your class and pretend (role play) that he or she is a candidate interviewing for the position that he or she currently holds (e.g., college president, humanities professor, grounds supervisor, district chancellor, and so on). Prior to the class visitation, generate a list of questions that the group's members in general, and the class as a whole, believe would be important to ask. Next, have each class member take a turn asking a question. Following the interview, break into smaller groups and share your feelings about the person who was

just interviewed. Finally, based on everyone's input, write a collaborative composition arguing why the person deserves to be an employee of your district. An alternative approach to this activity would be to explain how and why the formal interview procedure that was used in class was or was not an adequate process to assess the candidate's strengths and weaknesses.

Writing Activities

1. Write an "informational" process essay explaining how knowledge of past events or experiences in your life has served as "a prologue" for the present. How, for instance, did scientific, medical, sociological, and technological achievements in your lifetime shape the last part of the twentieth century and set the stage for changes—positive or negative—as you moved into the new millennium? In this essay, you will explain how something was done, concluding with a speculation on what may happen as a result of it.
2. Interview a local celebrity, comedian, actor, actress, or musician, and then use the responses to your questions (planned ahead of time or otherwise) as the basis for a process essay explaining how you ultimately "learned someone's story."

Internet Connection: Kathleen Hudson

Interviews

Place the key word "interview" in your favorite Internet search engine or another online database. How many articles match your search? You next might try to narrow your results by adding the name of a celebrity or public figure to your key search. Select one interview in particular, and write five sentences, starting with a lead-in sentence of a quotation taken from the interview (e.g., As Mark Twain said, "When I was a boy of fourteen, my father was so ignorant I could hardly stand to have the old man around. But, when I got to be twenty-one, I was astonished at how much he had learned in seven years.") Cite the source of your interview at the conclusion of this assignment.

Luis M. Valdez

Perspectives on "Borders"

Luis M. Valdez is well known for his work with the Chicano Theater and for founding El Teatro Campesino. A graduate in English at San Jose State University, Valdez writes his plays, called *actos*, in both English and Spanish. They deal with issues of social importance and are meant as much to inform as to entertain. His dramas include *The Shrunken Head of Pancho Villa* (1963), *The Sellouts* (1967), *Dark Root of a Scream* (1971), *Zoot Suit* (1978), *Luis Valdez's Early Works: Actos, Bernabe, and Pensamiento* (1990), *Taking It to the Streets: The Social Protest Theater of Luis Valdez and Amiri Baraka* (1997), and *Mummified Deer and Other Plays* (2005). Valdez's other credits include the movie *La Bamba* (1987), which he wrote and directed, and the Peabody Award-winning *Corridos: Tales of Passion and Revolution* (1982), which he produced for PBS (1987). The following essay was taken from a talk Valdez presented at a public humanities lecture in 1986. It appeared in its present form in *Columbus & After: Rethinking the Legacy* (A Touring Chautauqua Program of the California Council for the Humanities and the Oregon Council for the Humanities).

Pre-reading Questions

1. Are borders always visible to the naked eye? What purpose do borders serve?
2. What symbols (tokens of identity or something that stands for or represents something else) do you identify with and why?

---

1 It's curious that Amerigo Vespucci lent his name to the continent. There's a tremendous coincidence here because this place, this Western Hemisphere, this America, had another ancient name before the coming of the Europeans. The Mayans used to call it "Amaruca." "Amaruca" means the land of the feathered serpent. Mexico means feathered serpent. Boundaries, borders between the material and the spiritual. Mysteries of this gigantic part of the world, this place that was new and old at the same moment, this place that was a place of endless fascination

and endless mystery. And yet it had a map that was sketched in the *Popol Vuh,* which is the book of the ancient Quiché Maya, the Mayan Bible if you will. It survived as creation stories for the children so the priests didn't completely destroy it. It was an oral tradition anyway, and was finally transferred to print in the 18th century. So it has come down to us as a damaged fragment, but nevertheless enough is there for us to be able to see this map of ancient America and the promise. Because you see if there's anything that ancient America understood, it was time. The functioning of time. The Mayans were able to predict the future—360,000 years ahead. They predicted the conquest of America by men who came dressed in armor on these creatures that came to be known as horses. One of the South American pre-Columbian leaders had a dream, and he had one of his artists sketch and eventually sculpt a figure that he had dreamed, that he had seen in this vision. And it was the image of a Conquistador, in armor, 200 years before the coming of the Spanish.

2 The Mayans were mathematicians. I never tire of saying they invented zero along with other people, but they had zero a long time. The circle. That's what zero is, the circle, cero. They understood the workings of time, and there are books of prophecy—if you know how to read them—they predict our time. I'm not claiming that the Mayans knew everything. They made a few mistakes in their time. But it's a piece of human knowledge that whether we know it or not, we have been fusing together for 500 years. This hemisphere and that hemisphere, opposites that unite. Thirteen colonies. Thirteen colonies united. According to some kind of plan.

3 Did you know that the early Americans who arrived here from Europe studied the Indian tribes and what they saw were plans, methods of being together that they had never encountered before? Confederacies. The confederacy of the Iroquois led to a concept of United States, which was still a very new and fresh concept in Europe. The confederacy of Mayapan in the Yucatan Peninsula. There was stuff seeping up from the land. There was a spirit here, this fresh new world, and that seduction of America has been irresistible. There's more to America than just transplanted European culture. The destiny of America is greater than any of us can possibly imagine. I'm a cockeyed optimist, ok? Because I believe that the strength of our humanity lies in our infinite and spiritual potential. I believe that at the heart of all material being is energy, is spirit, is belief. And so that makes me very optimistic about America in spite of the whips and the lashes and the deaths and the killings. I believe that we will get by, that we will evolve, that America will complete her destiny, and it is going to take all of us to be able to do it.

4 Let's go back to the *Popol Vuh.* We're talking about borders now. There is a border that defines the human being as a material and spiritual being. We have all learned that we're *Homo sapiens,* wise monkeys. The monkey is a symbol of intelligence in the *Popol Vuh,* and in the classic Chinese

novel *Monkey.* The wise monkey is a symbol for humanity. Now let me offer you another symbol for our human being—the feathered serpent. You are a feathered serpent that is evolving and crawling out of the seeds of your being. And once in awhile you get caught up in the dead skins of your life. You know biologically we go through a complete cellular change every seven to nine years. We're totally renewed. So in one sense, biologically, you crawl out of a dead skin. You evolve out of yourself. The feathers are necessary because they represent our spiritual being.

5 Now the Spanish Conquistadors and the missionaries who came to the New World didn't understand that these pre-Columbian cultures were infatuated with the devil. They didn't understand Earth symbols. And yet it continues to be present in our American mentality. The symbol of the rattlesnake is an early North American symbol. "Don't tread on me." You don't step on a rattlesnake. Those little rattlers are symbols of time, and so like a snake, America continues to crawl out of itself and evolve. And the dead skins fall away as we emerge clean and fresh with a new skin, so new, so fresh, that at times it is painful. And these times that we are going through right now are precisely like that.

6 These are painful times, and yet they are very exciting times. Many people in this country are intimidated and frightened by the brown hordes pouring across the border, the non-border, this border that cannot hold. And so they want to declare English the official language of the United States. But I tell you that you cannot keep something natural from happening. The evolution of America has always involved north and south migration. It was the Europeans who gave it east and west. And we're happy to have it because what that did is to set up the four directions. Another ancient symbol, the Christian cross. The cross represents four directions, and in the *Popol Vuh* they speak of the upper world and the lower world and right at the point where the two worlds meet there is a crossroads that leads from one to the other. It's like the belly-button of the world. Right at that intersection, four roads meet—the white road, the black road, the yellow road, and the red road. What they represent to me is the promise of America—that four roads will meet and will bear new fruit in this ancient land. You can represent it any way that you like—racially, culturally.

7 The representations of what these people mean to each other ultimately represents a whole, that sphere, the power of the sun, the power of the planet that pulls from within to hold it together in space. And so we, our humanity, is a humanity that must pull from within and hold us together, but not without recognizing the four corners of the universe, certainly the four human corners of human civilization. It is important that Europe came to these shores. It is important that Asia came to these shores. It is important that there was a pre-Columbian America here waiting to blend and to create something greater than the parts. A whole vision of humanity.

Post-reading Questions

Content

1. What does the author mean when he talks about the "brown hordes pouring across the border, the nonborder, this border that cannot hold"?
2. What is the controlling idea or thesis of this essay? Where does it appear?
3. In your opinion, what is the most striking image that Valdez presents in this essay? Why do you find it particularly powerful?
4. Earlier in this text, Gómez-Peña dealt with the issue of "crossing borders" in his essay, "Documented/Undocumented." How do the tone and content of Valdez's essay compare with the tone and content of Gómez-Peña's essay?
5. What symbols of wholeness that come from different cultures does the author present?

Strategies and Structures

1. How does the author structure the material in this essay? (Does his composition consist of one or more parts?)
2. In what way is Valdez's essay an example of informational process analysis? What other rhetorical strategies are at work here?
3. Why do you think Valdez uses so many similes (see Glossary) in this essay? Do they serve a strategic purpose? Explain your answer.
4. How persuasive is Valdez's account of history? Why? Do you agree with his vision of the possibilities of the future? Why or why not?
5. "Perspectives on 'Borders'" was taken from a public humanities lecture presented in 1986. What characteristics of spoken English are evident in this transcription of his talk? How do or don't they interfere with clearly written communication?

Language and Vocabulary

1. Vocabulary: *hemisphere, serpent, confederacy, seduction, irresistible, Homo sapiens, intimidate.* Look up the definitions in the dictionary and write the words that you did not know in your permanent vocabulary list. Many of these words begin with prefixes (one or more sounds or letters placed before a word to indicate a derivative meaning). Carefully go over each of the words, checking your dictionary, to see which words begin with prefixes. Then list the meaning of the prefix and state how the prefix changes the meaning of the root word.
2. Valdez uses symbols from many cultures throughout this essay. For instance, he points out that monkeys are symbols of intelligence in the "Mayan Bible," *Popol Vuh.* Go through the essay and list the other symbols that Valdez uses. How do these contribute to Valdez's idea of "a whole vision of humanity"?

Group Activities

1. Break into small groups and create a list of as many cultures in the United States as you can think of. Then focus on the four or five cultures that you know best, listing and discussing the contributions each has made to American society.
2. Borders tend to confine and restrict people. Sometimes they are erected for positive purposes. Discuss the following with your group: What are some of the positive purposes of borders? What are the effects of borders? How do cultures create "borders" that keep others out and their own people in? As a society, how can we dismantle the negative borders and promote cultural pluralism?

Writing Activities

1. Beginning with historical background, write an essay persuading someone that his or her worldview—including the borders that define this worldview—does him or her more harm than good. Incorporate informational process analysis in this effort to persuade someone to change his or her worldview.
2. Valdez calls for a multicultural American society. What steps can we take to create such a society—one in which people are appreciative of individuals from diverse cultures? Write a process analysis essay explaining how this goal can be achieved realistically.

Joyce M. Jarrett

Freedom

Joyce M. Jarrett, associate professor of English at Hampton University, has authored many creative works, all of which she notes have grown out of her African-American experience. She has also coauthored *Pathways: A Text for Developing Writers* (1990) and *Heritage: African American Readings for Writing* (1996). Originally published in *Between Worlds* (1986), the following essay reflects on one of Jarrett's struggles during the civil rights movement.

Pre-reading Questions

1. Brainstorm and write a journal entry about personal freedom. What would you require to be free? What would make you feel restrained or imprisoned?
2. If you had been born without freedom (as you define it), how would it affect your daily interaction with others, your education, your employment, and possibly your future?

"Born free, as free as the wind blows, as free as the grass grows, born free to follow your heart."

—*(Don Black)*

1 My first illusion of freedom came in 1966, many years following the Supreme Court's decision on school desegregation. Of course to a fifteen-year-old girl, isolated, caged like a rodent in the poverty-stricken plains of the Magnolia State [Mississippi], Brown vs. the Board of Education had no meaning. Though many must have thought that my decision to attend the all-white city high school that fall, along with 49 other blacks, was made in protest or had evolved from a sense of commitment for the betterment of my people, nothing could have been further from the truth. Like a rat finding a new passageway, I was propelled to my new liberty more out of curiosity than out of a sense of mission.

2 On the first day of school, I was escorted by hordes of national guardsmen. Like a funeral procession, the steady stream of official-looking cars followed me to the campus. Some patrolmen were parked near campus gates, while others, with guns strapped to their sides, stood near building entrances. Though many of my escorts had given me smiles of support, still I was not prepared for what I encountered upon entering my new school.

3 There, I had to break through lines of irate white protestors, spraying obscenities at me while carrying their denigrating signs: "KKK Forever," read one; "Back to Africa," said another. And as I dashed toward the school door, blinded with fear, I nearly collided with another sign that screamed, "Nigger Go Home."

4 Once inside the fortress, I was ushered by school administrators and plain-clothes police to and from my respective classes. The anger and fear that I had felt outside of those walls were numbed by the surprisingly

uneventful classroom experiences—until I went to geometry, my last scheduled class for that day.

5 As I sauntered into the classroom and took a seat, there was a flurry of activity. When everyone had settled, I sat in the center of the class, surrounded by empty desks—on each side, and in front and back.

6 "We have a nigger in the class," someone shouted.

7 "Let's get quiet and make the best of it," Mr. Moore smugly replied. Then he proceeded with the course orientation.

8 Near the end of the class, I mustered up enough courage to ask a question, so, nervously, I raised my hand. Keeping silent, Mr. Moore stared, and stared, and stared at me until my arm grew heavy and began to tremble. My heart sank, and my picture of freedom shattered in infinite pieces as he said, "I see that there are no questions. Class dismissed."

9 I have always blamed myself for that crushing moment. Why did I allow myself to be overlooked? Why did I not feel free? That painful, dehumanizing incident within itself did not provide any answers, though it signaled the beginning of my search. And finally, through years of disappointments, I discovered the truth—the truth that had evaded me during those high school years.

10 Freedom is not a gift, but a right. Officials did not, could not, award "freedom." It had to be something that I wanted, craved, demanded. The Supreme Court had liberated me of many external restrictions, but I had failed to liberate myself. In some instances internal constraints can be more binding than the overt ones. It is impossible to enslave one who has liberated oneself and futile to pry off the external chains of an internally bound person. Only when there is emancipation of both body and soul are any of us truly *free* to follow our hearts.

Post-reading Questions

Content

1. What does the narrator mean when she writes about her "first illusion of freedom"? How does her curiosity contribute to that first illusion?
2. Outside of the school, the narrator encountered crowds of angry white people protesting against integration. Once within the school, why was she lulled into a false sense of security? In what way was her geometry class a "wake-up call"?
3. Describe how the geometry teacher demonstrates his racism. In what way does he make the author feel invisible?
4. Why does Jarrett blame herself for the "crushing moment" in the geometry classroom? Do you think she had an accurate conception of freedom?

Strategies and Structures

1. Explain how and why the scene in the geometry classroom provides the climatic moment in Jarrett's essay. Would it have been appropriate for her to have placed it earlier in the essay? Why or why not? How does this incident signal the beginning of her "search" for freedom?
2. Jarrett begins her essay mentioning her "first illusion of freedom." How does she conclude her piece? In what way does her introductory paragraph look forward to her concluding paragraph—and how does her concluding paragraph look back at her introductory paragraph?
3. In ten compact paragraphs, how does the author lead her readers from teenage innocence, believing that desegregation had no meaning for her, to the mature conclusion that "Only when there is emancipation of both body and soul are any of us truly *free* to follow our hearts"?
4. An important part of writing is maintaining a sensitivity to the reader. Bearing this in mind, how does Jarrett convey her experience with racism and prejudice without alienating her readers?

Language and Vocabulary

1. Vocabulary: *desegregation, horde, irate, denigrating, saunter, dehumanizing, crave, futile, emancipation.* After you look up the vocabulary words, write a paragraph explaining how the words help to capture the intensity of Jarrett's realizations as she moved from innocence to enlightenment.
2. Discuss the *denotation* and *connotation* (see the Glossary) of words in this essay. What connotations, for instance, does "fortress" carry? How might reference to a fortress reinforce the theme of false security?

Group Activities

1. In small groups, go to your college library and investigate the Supreme Court's decision in *Brown* v. *Board of Education*. How did it provide for the desegregation of schools? To what extent did this ruling succeed in its intentions? Share your findings in a class forum.
2. Why do people allow themselves to be overlooked in painful, dehumanizing situations? Form into groups, assign a recorder, and brainstorm as many answers to this question as you can. What do your answers suggest about human nature? State your group's major insights and analyze them both in context to Jarrett's essay and the world you live in today.

Writing Activities

1. Write an essay in which you defend the notion that "freedom is not a gift, but a right." Support your composition with facts, details, and examples drawn from observations, personal experiences, and readings.
2. Brainstorm the idea of freedom. (You might look back to your pre-reading responses for Jarrett's essay.) Then construct a paper detailing an incident where, like the narrator in "Freedom," you moved from an innocent sense of the world to the harsh realities provided by that experience.

Heidi Ramirez

Community Re-discovered

Heidi Ramirez all levels of composition at Hartnell College in Salinas. She revived The Art of John Steinbeck course at Hartnell College and has designed curriculum for three new learning communities on campus. Additionally, she also plays violin with the Hartnell College Symphony. Ramirez, has been actively involved in The English Council of California Two-Year Colleges for years as the ECCTYC Region III Co-director. Formerly the ECCTYC 2007 Conference Chair, Ramirez also served as ECCTYC President; she currently writes for *inside english* as well as other literary journals, and continues to be a community advocate. In the following essay, Ramirez uses process analysis to demonstrate how people are "Re-discovering Community."

Pre-reading Questions

1. What immediately comes to your mind when you hear the word, "community"? When and how do you use the word "community"?
2. Have you ever "discovered" anything? What? Why would a concept, a belief, an item, and so on need to be "re-discovered"?

1 I think of community as a living organism that engages its members in activity and mutual exchange of ideas. Simply put, starting a conversation with neighbors is social interchange, the building block of any community. Why is this basic step so difficult and yet so important? Knowing your neighbors and others in the community assures continuance of organization, communication, and problem solving, signs that your community is healthy and provides for the well being of its residents.

2 In any community, there are several and varying ways in which residents fulfill a sense of community: participating in intramural sports, attending farmers' markets, walking with neighbors, attending political meetings, helping the elderly, visiting the library, and volunteering for youth groups. It's knowing the people in these interchanges, not just being familiar with faces, that build strong community. Unfortunately, when this basic engagement is overlooked, communities can begin to disintegrate.

3 In some neighborhoods, tagging is becoming more prevalent. It defaces homes, fences, and even cars, and to me this symbolizes something unsettling. What would have normally been seen on abandoned businesses and alleys is now showing up on thriving business storefronts and individual homes. What has happened to our communities? Between work schedules and commute time, contact with neighbors has been lost and this weakens response time in community clean-up and in preventing burglaries. Therefore, we need to reconsider relationships with our neighbors and in a wider scope, community.

4 To curb the outbreak of burglaries and tagging in my neighborhood, the city recommended forming a Neighborhood Watch program. Following this recommendation, my neighbors and I set a meeting time to work with representatives from the program and then several of us partnered together to walk the area, distribute fliers, and inform others of the meeting. Reminder phone calls followed. As a result of these efforts, close to 75 people showed up at our first Neighborhood Watch meeting where neighbors felt unified in sharing their concerns about protecting the community. We realized there was work to be done in restoring and maintaining a healthy neighborhood.

5 Taking part in Neighborhood Watch meetings might be considered an unusual way of meeting others. This approach was different from the one I encountered growing up, where neighbors knew each other through the children, borrowed each other's tools, and planned potlucks around back-to-school time. But through this first exchange, there have been positive results: more neighborly visits, participation in community clean-up, and our connection to one another. Normally, this type of community building was an assumed part of a neighborhood. My discovery has been that city government is helping to rekindle and move the process of neighborliness along. The growing numbers of Neighborhood Watch signs in nearby and outer communities show this force at work.

6 However different the origins of community building, the impetus for civic mindedness is building social capital. Social capital is the forming of social networks and recognizing the value they have for the individual and the larger group. In the book, *Bowling Alone: The Collapse and Revival of American Community* (2000), Robert D. Putnam, Professor of Public Policy at Harvard, shares research concerned with the decline of community involvement. Citing several interviews with Americans in 1999, Putnam unveiled a major problem with weakened community bonds. Of those surveyed, over 80 percent believed that moral values and trust were stronger when they were growing up. Additional responses indicated that individuals should be more involved in communities even if it takes up more of their time.

7 Recognizing the need for better quality of life requires commitment. Individuals such as Martin Luther King, Jr., Cesar Chavez, and more recently Cindy Sheehan recognized this need and answered the call. In fact, their local community work turned into national movements. Moreover, their efforts and achievements demonstrate that *grassroots organizing* remains the backbone of American democracy.

8 Recently, community organization became a topic of discussion in the present election. At the 2008 Republican Convention, Sarah Palin, a vice-presidential candidate, had the following to say about community organizing in reference to Barack Obama's community service record: "I guess a small-town mayor is sort of like a community organizer, except that you have actual responsibilities." In response, presidential candidate Barack Obama's campaign stated: "Let's clarify something for them right now. Community organizing is how ordinary people respond to out-of-touch politicians and their failed policies."

9 Organizers like Curt Gabrielson do just this—respond to an unmet need in their community. By taking part in the Environmental Science Workshop, Curt Gabrielson—a Watsonville, California resident—supported the drive for more community youth activities. This project provides a place for youths to go after school to build science and art projects from recycled materials. The informal environment fosters self-discovery and sparks learning through conservation. Here, youths learn that making mistakes and analyzing them is part of rebuilding.

10 What has made this project so successful is the aspect of community space. The interaction that occurs in this environment demonstrates to the youths that they *can* build something, which carries an important individual benefit to the outer community. As Gabrielson clarifies, "It keeps youths off the street, out of harm's way, and offers instead a constructive, stimulating environment. Youths go back to the community with self-confidence and assurance of their contribution."

11 The concept of designing your own community project is certainly not new, but what the Environmental Science Workshop stresses is that

every community can have one. Gabrielson suggests the following steps for developing the project:

A) Find the space and create the atmosphere
B) Invite the youth
C) Encourage mixed age groups so youths can learn from one another
D) Use flexible methods to encourage everyone's participation
E) Create an open structure environment and sample idea for Project of the Day
F) Encourage drop-in hours scheduling
G) Maintain safety

Curt Gabrielson's process encourages others to take charge of similar projects in their own communities and neighborhoods.

12 Another project emerging in neighborhoods is the design of a walkable community, which encourages healthier lifestyles and positive social interactions through walking. Since walking is the most affordable mode of transportation, a walkable community enables this effort by having a centralized downtown sustained by planning public transits and mixed use store fronts along that route.

13 The process of creating a walkable community begins with ideas from the residents and city council regarding city planning and zoning, traffic calming, and bike and pedestrian facility design. Walkable Communities, Inc., a non-profit consulting firm formed in 1996, helps cities plan in their quest for achieving sustainable communities. Dan Burden, its founder, makes it his mission to visit and walk communities throughout the country to assess how changes made in city planning can make areas more livable, the end result being happy, healthier residents.

14 When I think of additional projects to help implement in my community, I consider more social and playful activities designed for children. Besides parks and playgrounds, why not a carousel designed by local artists depicting the diversity of the area? How about increasing bike lanes to encourage more teens and adults to ride throughout town? Working with our community allows us to see ourselves as agents of change and discover the pleasure of civic virtue. In this endeavor, we contribute to a more secure future.

Post-reading Questions

Content

1. Characterize the *tone* of "Community Re-discovered." What seems to be Ramirez's attitude toward her subject?

2. In what way do specific, concrete references and allusions throughout Ramirez's essay relate to aspects of popular culture, past and present?
3. According to Ramirez, what is a "walkable community"?
4. How can community redesign help to reinforce "positive community relationships"?
5. Describe the recent trend in crime prevention. How does it relate to community?

Strategies and Structures

1. Analyze the rhetorical function of the first paragraph in Ramirez's essay. How is it more than simply an introduction to a topic?
2. Why does the author cite, *Bowling Alone: The Collapse and Revival of American Community?* What evidence does it provide?
3. In what way might local artists "rediscover and celebrate community"?
4. Why does Ramirez refer to public figures and community involvement planners such as Dan Burden?
5. Explain how Ramirez draws her essay to a close. Where does she bring her readers? What opportunities await us all?

Language and Vocabulary

1. Vocabulary: *organism, mutual, assure, continuance, residents, intramural, volunteer, interchange, engagement, tagging, prevalent, symbolize, unsettling, abandoned, alley, thriving, storefront, schedules, commute, burglaries, scope, outbreak, partnered, unified, restoring, encountered, potluck, assumed, rekindle, impetus, "civic mindedness," capital, networks, revival, unveiled, bonds, commitment, grassroots, backbone, democracy, clarify, out-of-touch, recycled, self-discovery, conservation, aspect, interaction, constructive, stimulation, atmosphere, flexible, mode, walkable, centralized, enables, sustain, transit, route, council, pedestrian, carousel, depicting, diversity.* Write a paragraph in which you explain the benefits of building a "community" of some sort. Use a minimum of seven words from the vocabulary list for this assignment. Finally, keep all words in your vocabulary log for future reference.
2. Which of the vocabulary words lend themselves to a discussion of designing a community project? How? Why? What does the Environmental Science Workshop stress?

Group Activities

1. Divide into groups and analyze whether or not the author is correct in her assessment that community is like "a living organism that engages its members in activity"? Then, write a collaborative essay in which your group agrees or disagrees with Ramirez. Offer new examples that support

her claim if you agree with her. If your group disagrees with her beliefs, be certain to explain just what "does" hold society—or gathering of people with common interests (e.g., sports, fine arts, religion, politics)—together.

2. Get into small groups and discuss how each person imagines himself or herself in ten years. In what ways do members believe they will change, and to what extent will they remain the same? How many people in your group believe that they will be socially active, eager to maintain and/or re-build their immediate social community? How? Why? Have the recorder jot down the group's projections. If group members had written "Community Re-discovered" as a collaborative exercise, how might they revise the content and focus of Ramirez's essay?

Writing Activities

1. Write an *informative* process analysis paper explaining the origin or demise of a subculture or counterculture in America (e.g., motorcycle gangs, surfers, rednecks, rappers, punk rockers, Internet addicts) as well as how the counterculture community can—or never will be re-discovered.
2. Brainstorm the word "youth"; what patterns emerge from your responses? Compose an essay providing survival strategies for senior citizens in America—a society that worships youth and the importance of staying young. Support your essay with examples drawn from personal experience, observations, interviews, or readings.

Malcolm X

A Homemade Education

Born Malcolm Little in Omaha, Nebraska, in 1925, Malcolm X, the son of a black separatist preacher, spent his early childhood in middle America. When his father died, Malcolm X became involved with life on the streets, which ultimately led to his imprisonment for burglary. Denouncing his Christian name—his slave name—he took the name "X" and became devoted to the Black Muslim movement that was headed by the honorable Elijah Muhammad. Malcolm X began to correspond with Elijah Muhammad while still in prison, and Malcolm X's desire to further his writing skills was directly responsible for the "homemade education" discussed in the following essay, an excerpt from *The Autobiography of Malcolm X*. Malcolm X's relationship with Elijah led him to become a militant leader of the black revolution. Ironically, he was preaching the brotherhood of humanity when he was assassinated in 1965.

Pre-reading Questions

1. What are the denotations and connotations (see the Glossary) of the word *homemade?* How would you personally relate the word "homemade" to the educational process?
2. List the steps you would take if your education were left entirely up to you, without the aid of teachers or parents. What would you do to build your vocabulary, how would you empower yourself as a writer, and how would you develop a thorough knowledge of the world around you?

---

1 It was because of my letters that I happened to stumble upon starting to acquire some kind of homemade education.

2 I became increasingly frustrated at not being able to express what I wanted to convey in letters that I wrote, especially those to Mr. Elijah Muhammad. In the street, I had been the most articulate hustler out there—I had commanded attention when I said something. But now, trying to write simple English, I not only wasn't articulate, I wasn't even functional. How would I sound writing in slang, the way I would *say* it, something such as, "Look, daddy, let me pull your coat about a cat, Elijah Muhammad—"

3 Many who today hear me somewhere in person, or on television, or those who read something I've said, will think I went to school far beyond the eighth grade. This impression is due entirely to my prison studies.

4 It had really begun back in Charlestown Prison, when Bimbi first made me feel envy of his stock of knowledge. Bimbi had always taken charge of any conversation he was in, and I had tried to emulate him. But every book I picked up had few sentences which didn't contain anywhere from one to nearly all of the words that might as well have been in Chinese. When I just skipped those words, of course, I really ended up with little idea of what the book said. So I had come to the Norfolk Prison Colony still going through only book-reading motions. Pretty

soon, I would have quit even these motions unless I had received the motivation that I did.

5 I saw that the best thing I could do was get hold of a dictionary—to study to learn some words. I was lucky enough to reason also that I should try to improve my penmanship. It was sad. I couldn't even write in a straight line. It was both ideas together that moved me to request a dictionary along with some tablets and pencils from the Norfolk Prison Colony school.

6 I spent two days just riffling uncertainly through the dictionary's pages. I'd never realized so many words existed! I didn't know *which* words I needed to learn. Finally, just to start some kind of action, I began copying.

7 In my slow, painstaking, ragged handwriting, I copied into my tablet everything printed on that first page, down to the punctuation marks.

8 I believe it took me a day. Then, aloud, I read back, to myself, everything I'd written on the tablet. Over and over, aloud, to myself, I read my own handwriting.

9 I woke up the next morning, thinking about those words—immensely proud to realize that not only had I written so much at one time, but I'd written words that I never knew were in the world. Moreover, with a little effort, I also could remember what many of these words meant. I reviewed the words whose meanings I didn't remember. Funny thing, from the dictionary's first page right now, that "aardvark" springs to my mind. The dictionary had a picture of it, a long-tailed, long-eared, burrowing African mammal, which lives off termites caught by sticking out its tongue as an anteater does for ants.

10 I was so fascinated that I went on—I copied the dictionary's next page. And the same experience came when I studied that. With every succeeding page, I also learned of people and places and events from history. Actually the dictionary is like a miniature encyclopedia. Finally the dictionary's A section had filled a whole tablet—and I went on into the B's. That was the way I started copying what eventually became the entire dictionary. It went a lot faster after so much practice helped me to pick up handwriting speed. Between what I wrote in my tablet, and writing letters, during the rest of my time in prison I would guess I wrote a million words.

11 I suppose it was inevitable that as my word-base broadened, I could for the first time pick up a book and read and now begin to understand what the book was saying. Anyone who has read a great deal can imagine the new world that opened. Let me tell you something: from then until I left that prison, in every free moment I had, if I was not reading in the library, I was reading on my bunk. You couldn't have gotten me out of books with a wedge. Between Mr. Muhammad's teachings, my correspondence, my visitors—usually Ella and Reginald—and my

reading of books, months passed without my even thinking about being imprisoned. In fact, up to then, I had never been so truly free in my life.

Post-reading Questions

Content

1. What led Malcolm X to improve his vocabulary? That is, what were the initial problems that he had with reading, and how did these lead to his desire to build his vocabulary?
2. What steps did Malcolm X take to increase his vocabulary?
3. What were his emotional responses after he copied the first page of the dictionary?
4. How did reading affect Malcolm X's outlook on life?

Strategies and Structures

1. Malcolm X starts many of his paragraphs with the first-person pronoun "I." What effect does this have on the essay, and what does it suggest about the results of education?
2. Malcolm X concludes paragraph 11 by writing "In fact, up to then, I had never been so truly free in my life," referring to his ability to read. How does this concluding statement sum up the value of a homemade, personally tailored education as opposed to the rigid learning methods often used in schools?
3. What transitions lead the reader from one step in Malcolm X's educational process to the next?
4. What phrases does Malcolm X use to keep his writing conversational? Which phrases does he use to suggest that he is educated? What is the effect of balancing these two styles? What does it suggest about the author's personality?

Language and Vocabulary

1. Vocabulary: *articulate, hustler, emulate, riffling, inevitable, bunk.* As Malcolm X did, write down the entire dictionary definitions of the aforementioned words, and bring them with you to your group activity.
2. In paragraph 2, Malcolm X suggests that slang cannot be written. Brainstorm a list of your own slang. Why is slang more effective on the streets or among your peers than it is in an academic setting or with your grandparents?

Group Activities

1. Devise some homemade, as opposed to traditional, methods for learning the above vocabulary words. Also devise some

homemade study techniques that you can use in your other classes.

2. As we move further into the second decade of the twenty-first century, people frequently debate whether prisoners should be educated or simply be punished. How do you feel about this issue? Ideally, what takes place when a person *serves time* in a prison? How does punishment alone rehabilitate prisoners—or does it? In groups, prepare to debate both sides of this issue in a seminar situation.

Writing Activities

1. Research a current educational program in a local prison. Describe the program in detail, answering such questions as: who is involved, what are the benefits and problems, where does the program take place, when is a prisoner or instructor eligible for such a program, why is such a program in place, and how does the program work? Your job is to inform your readers about this program. (Your local research librarian can help you to find out where to get such information.)
2. Write a process essay wherein you explain how to acquire and use common sense to resolve the majority of the problems you encounter in daily life. Make sure that you present your material in clear, sequential steps.

Internet Connection: Malcolm X

Purpose and Process

In a search engine of your choice, type in any number of key words that will call up articles on how to do something (e.g., how to become rich, how to become popular, how to attract attention to yourself, how to win a sport, and so on) or how something was done (e.g., the process for building the Golden Gate Bridge or the process of questioning crime suspects). Read at least three of the articles you locate and then place the discussion points (steps to the process) for each essay you read in an outline format. Document the three articles that you selected using the MLA format for parenthetical references and a list of works cited. (See the Appendix.)

Christine Ng

Bringing Out the Flirt in You

Born in Singapore, Christine Ng was a student at Evergreen Valley College before graduating from the University of California at Berkeley with a degree in English and a minor in Religious Studies. A published poet, essayist, and freelance writer, she has been a communicator on many levels, including a technical writer for a high tech company in Mountain View, California as well as EBAY Incorporated. Her writings are based largely on her interactions with people, pop culture, biblical texts, the tastes and sounds of Southeast Asia, and the new cultural discoveries she makes every day living in the San Francisco Bay Area. Oscar Wilde, Milton, Shakespeare, Haruki, Murakami, and Michele Roberts remain favorites, and Ng aspires to write her greatest work one day. In the following essay, "Bringing Out the Flirt in You," Ng explores and discusses the essentiality of flirting and the ramifications of violating flirting taboos, as well as the intricacies of mastering such an age-old art.

Pre-reading Questions

1. What is the first thing that comes to your mind when you feel like flirting with someone? Explain where, when, and why a person might flirt.
2. Do you or someone you know like to flirt in any place in particular? Why?

"You know you don't have to act with me, Steve. You don't have to say anything, and you don't have to do anything . . . . not a thing. Oh, well maybe just whistle. You know how to whistle, don't you, Steve? You just put your lips together and blow."

—Lauren Bacall in TO HAVE AND HAVE NOT

1 Have you ever felt an overpowering urge to make yourself known to another individual? From women's fluttering coy eyelids to men's prowling advances, subtle cues have grown into sexual signals. Why does the desire to use small physical and verbal cues to attract the opposite sex

still persist? Simple. People enjoy flirting—the healthy, harmless, usually sexual banter between individuals—and it serves an important, if not necessary, role in socializing. As such, people strive to become experts at the art of flirtation, a process rooted in physical appearance and mannerisms.

2 Attracting attention and finding a mate in the animal kingdom entails the art of flirtation based largely on physical beauty and strength. The male lion bristles his proud mane, and the lionesses work tirelessly to do his bidding and attract his attention. Similarly, the confident male peacock struts about, with his beautiful tail of blue-green feathers spread out, hoping to attract the plain brown female. Unlike other animals, however, humans are much more discerning about their appearance prior to flirtatious acts. Though the animal mating ritual requires only one mate to preen excessively during a limited time period, humans—both male and female—often spend hundreds of dollars a year making sure they always look attractive. One of the best selling products on Sephora.com is *Lip Fusion*, a lip-gloss that contains marine collagen micro-spheres that are absorbed into lips and create a beautiful pout, all without the aid of surgery. At thirty-six dollars, this best-selling wonder product costs much more than conventional lip-gloss, yet stores can't seem to keep it in stock! Similarly, with their obsession for designer jeans and expensive hair treatments, men also find themselves drawn to artifice and activities that might help enhance their appearance. Unquestionably, the dawn of the metrosexual has arrived. As a male co-worker jokingly told me while discussing diets and his Lucky Brand jeans, "Hey, it takes a lot of work to look this good!" With all these men and women trying their best to look good, it is clear that in this society, starting to enhance one's finer physical qualities before attempting to flirt is vital.

3 In addition to physical appearance, physical mannerisms also become important, effective tools—or potential liabilities—during the flirting process. Snorting while laughing, burping the national anthem, and spewing beer out of noses are turn-offs, and few want their other halves (well, at least people who enjoy social etiquette) to practice these behaviors when eating dinner with their families. People need to realize that the skills and behavior they would expect to view on *Jackass,* a crude television show, are not necessary in order to become the center of attention. Flirting between couples should consist of lighthearted, civil interaction with one another that may give the impression of sexual interest, not a locker-room gross-out contest. Once you realize what is or isn't a flirtatious act, using physical appearance and mannerisms to your best advantage, you will be ready to study and implement the rules of flirtation.

4 First, when flirting, remember to establish eye contact rather than looking at the ground. However, do not overdo eye contact while talking.

I've seen people stare so intensely they look like crazed stalkers, so tone down if you know your eyes can blaze holes into concrete. Sometimes looking into another's eyes and then turning away will be enough! You have to make the person know you are interested—but certainly not desperate. Also, remember to listen to the object of your flirtation. If you allow your mind to wander, you may miss significant verbal cues requesting a response. Flirting involves a lot of friendly smiles, giggles, and gestures that a person does not share with just anyone. According to Catherine Yumul, a college student, "You can begin flirting by fluttering eyelids, flipping hair, laughing politely, and winking. The inattentive flirt may remain oblivious to the dynamic potential of a situation. That being said, if someone laughs out loud at your jokes, establishes eye contact, and comes within the three foot circle of personal space, success is probably close at hand."

5 Second, allow flirtation to flourish by knowing how to reciprocate flirting cues, whether at an intimate dinner for two, or in a large social setting. First impressions can make or break a successful flirt. This brings to mind a chat I had with my cousin. He asked me for my opinion about a girl he liked, and we began by analyzing her behavior and body language. Time after time, she had laughed at his jokes, established eye contact with him, hit him on the knee, and often told him he was funny. Based on her flirtatious overtures, and assuming he would respond mutually—given a chance—I told him to go ahead and ask her out to dinner, confident that the date would go well. I could not have been more wrong. The next day, he revealed to me that he had been a half an hour late, showed up dressed in disheveled athletic gear, and even let his female friend tag along! At this point, I slapped myself on the forehead, and called him stupid. It was bad enough to be late and look unconcerned about his appearance, but bringing a female friend was the worst thing he could have done on a date with another woman. Overnight, he seemed to have forgotten that flirting requires "give and take" to thrive. Instead, his looks and actions displayed apparent lack of interest in his date. Successful flirtation, therefore, requires the essential ability to interpret cues and act accordingly.

6 Third, besides avoiding inappropriate behavior, refrain from embracing advice gleaned from superficial flirtation guides. Though they might raise self-esteem or build self-confidence temporarily, magazines like *Cosmopolitan* often fall short of bringing out the true flirt in you, opting instead for sensational headlines that scream, "How to Get Your Man" and telling women that wearing a short skirt with a matching plunging neckline and heels will do the trick. Magazines for men are no better either. In *FHM*, famous for its "100 Sexiest Women" countdown, there is an abundance of articles about "beer, babes and fast facts" that teach men how to get a woman to do a variety of things. These sexist magazines

can't teach people anything they don't already know about flirting. An extremely unattractive trait, desperation, can be smelled a mile away. Desperate times do not call for desperate measures in this case, for such tactics will only make one feel cheap.

7 Fourth, since no best place to flirt exists, select a location that's right for you. Social situations may cause anxiety for many people, but technology has remedied that situation with the introduction of cyber flirting. With the inventions of friend-based *MySpace* and *Friendster*, you may even find a friend of a friend you find attractive and ask her or him out. My aforementioned cousin who "struck out" in a conventional flirting situation even has asked a girl out based on seeing her profile on *Facebook*, a college based database that allows a person to send messages to another at a university of interest. By testing the waters by looking at profiles and pictures, the Internet has given us various avenues and means to initiate flirting.

8 These days, many lonely, insecure people venture into an Internet chat room, flirt, and establish relationships without having ever seen the other person. This increasingly popular method of flirtation liberates people from the confines of conformity and a physical ideal—at least, until they exchange photos. Now, with all the upgrades on instant messenger software, dozens of ways to express flirtatious thoughts and actions exist through icons. A representative list includes:

;-) *represents* "a wink"
requests "don't tell anyone"
:) or :-) *symbolizes* "the smile"
:-$ *indicates* "embarrassed"
(YN) *reveals* "fingers crossed"
:-O *projects* "surprise"
:\ *conveys* "the worried face"

LOL *means* "laughing out loud"
XOXO *expresses* "love & kisses"
g *stands for* "giggle"
;-(*denotes* "sadness"
:P *suggests* "joking face"

Clearly, the Internet has answered dreams for want-to-be flirts afraid of social situations.

9 Fifth, whenever and wherever you flirt, remember to behave within social bounds. This applies to all occasions, although when you are in a bar or club, the loud music may never let you exchange eloquent banter. In that case, the combination of desperate intoxicated people and cheesy pick up lines (a very lousy attempt at flirting) might go unnoticed or actually work. Otherwise, remember to stick to being polite and engaging, and let your natural effervescence shine through. Whether face-to-face or online, focus on common interests during conversation, and be

enthusiastic when the other half begins to open up. Though some people are not conversationalists, focusing on the other individual and his/her interests is always helpful.

10 Finally, no matter what forum you chose for playful repartee, keep in mind that flirting is natural and should not be forced. When taken to extremes, "over the top" flirting undermines any healthy intent. Indeed, sometimes a fine line exists between innocent flirtation and aggressive behavior that could be considered pornographic. Paris Hilton's infamous Carl's Junior's Spicy BBQ Burger commercial offers a perfect example of this. Considered by many as "too hot for television," Hilton spent only *seven* seconds out of a *sixty* second commercial holding a Spicy BBQ Burger. The rest of the time she sensuously washed a car, taking time to suggestively soap down her own body, tracing her considerable assets with suds. Did she connect with her target audience? No doubt. Did her "over the top" mannerisms befitting a wet t-shirt contest tastefully promote Spicy BBQ Burgers? Probably not.

11 Thus, although the media attempt to turn flirting into women wearing garments that leave little to the imagination or ogling men with pickup lines penned by clueless minds, we need to ignore such superficial, demeaning stereotypes and trite—possibly offensive—behavior. Instead, focus on self-improvement. Makeover shows that don't rely on plastic surgery such as *Queer Eye for the Straight Guy* on Bravo, or *What Not to Wear* on TLC constantly demonstrate how a clean-shaven face or a bit of blush on the cheeks can transform one's appearance and improve self-confidence instantly. So go ahead and do the same. Improve your posture, shave your *Unabomber* beard, and let the transformation begin.

12 As concluded by novelist Victor Hugo, "God created the flirt, as soon as he made the fool." Though we are oftentimes fools, flirts or even both, we can try to avoid compromising situations where playful intentions send conflicting messages. Reject the desire to wear that smutty top so you can get a free drink, and resist wearisome pickup lines such as inquiring whether a person's tired because he or she has been running through your mind all night. Be yourself; enjoy the natural pleasures of flirting, and more than anything else, allow your natural confidence and personality to shine through. That way, flirting will make you nobody's fool.

Post-reading Questions

Content

1. On one hand, Ng claims that "eye contact" plays a key role in the flirtation process, and yet she carefully qualifies what she says.

Why? What should a couple bear in mind when gazing into each other's eyes?

2. Why does Ng spend so much time telling readers what not to do rather than directly informing them about the best way to perfect the flirtation process?
3. When does flirtation "flourish"? What must one be able to do and why?
4. Explain the difference between playful and "over the top" flirting according to Ng. Do you agree or disagree with her assessment? Why?
5. What final advice does Ng offer readers about the art of flirtation?

Strategies and Structures

1. How does Ng use process analysis as the dominant technique for developing her essay? Would any other rhetorical strategy have worked as well? Explain.
2. In her essay, Ng frequently refers to readings and television programs to illustrate her explanations. How and why do such references add depth to her claims?
3. How does Ng's discussion of cyber flirting, Internet chat rooms, and flirtatious icons help to modernize her examination of flirting—an age-old topic?
4. Why do you imagine Ng prefaced her essay with the famous Lauren Bacall quotation: "You know you don't have to act with me, Steve. You don't have to say anything, and you don't have to do anything. . . . not a thing. Oh, well maybe just whistle. You know how to whistle, don't you, Steve? You just put your lips together and blow." How do these lines from *To Have and Have Not* (a movie) set the tone for an essay about flirting?
5. In what way does Ng's quotation by novelist Victor Hugo, "God created the flirt, as soon as he made the fool," echo many of the discussion points presented throughout her essay? How does it assist her in bringing her essay to a satisfactory close?

Language and Vocabulary

1. Vocabulary: *prowling, persist, mannerisms, discerning, ritual, preen, collagen, micro-spheres, obsession, artifice, enhance, metrosexual, stalkers, inattentive, oblivious, flourish, reciprocate, inappropriate, abundance, tactics, remedied, aforementioned, conventional, initiate, icons, effervescence, conversationalists, forum, repartee, undermine, pornographic, infamous, superficial, demeaning, compromising, wearisome*. Many of the vocabulary words from this essay carry a negative connotation (see the Glossary). After looking up the meanings of all these

vocabulary words, construct a paragraph or two discussing the negative side of flirting; use at least seven of the vocabulary words in this assignment.

2. Look up the definition of "flirting" and "flirtatious," and then reexamine Ng's word choice in her essay. In what way do many of her references reinforce the ideal interplay in the flirtation process? Can you think of additional words that she might have used? Explain.

Group Activities

1. Divide the class into two groups, one representing the male perspective and the other the female perspective on flirting. Then, have each group assess the reliability of Christine Ng's information according to the group they represent. Finally, gather as a class and debate the "truth about flirting" according to Ng, adding your personal experience, observations of others, and readings on the subject to further support your position.
2. Gather in groups of three or four students and assess the first three paragraphs of Ng's essay. What do they attempt to establish? For instance, what is the rhetorical effect of her opening sentence? Why do you imagine Ng referred to flirtation rituals among other animals before focusing her attention on humans? Finally, write a brief collaborative critique of Ng's opening paragraphs, including their effect on the entire essay.

Writing Activities

1. Using process analysis as the major method of development, explain how to avoid the dangers of flirting on the Internet—as well as in Internet dating. Use specific examples like Ng—and possibly some readings—to illustrate your discussion points.
2. Do some research, including looking at the Internet for articles, browsing through your college library, and interviewing friends and relatives of all ages and from as many cultures as possible on the topic of flirting. Then, write a process analysis paper where you explain "how to flirt" most effectively in a particular place.

Internet Connection: Christine Ng
Flirting

What gossip headlines do you recall as we move further in the second decade of the twenty-first century? What role did mere flirtatious banter play in celebrity gossip headlines? Plenty. Justin Bieber Flirts With Tina Fey in 'SNL' Promo; R&B recording artist and songwriter Rianna and baseball star Marc Kemp have been christened "iPhone" flirts; in the same month, Lady Gaga's "Alejandro," a music video, figuratively flirts with blasphemy and controversy. What literal and figurative flirtations can we expect—or do we want to read about—in the coming years and decades? Research celebrity flirts, as well as directive process analysis essays, blogs, and websites on the Internet. How do different authors encourage and/or caution flirtation on the net? What lessons, if any, can we learn from celebrities? Write an essay where you present information drawn from readings as primary evidence to support your thesis. Be sure to use the correct MLA format for documenting online resources as well as a list of works cited. (Refer to the Appendix to review how to use parenthetical citations and prepare a "List of Works Cited.")

Additional Topics and Issues for Process Analysis Essays

1. Compose a process paper explaining how to make work easier. Begin by limiting your focus a bit so that your reader will have a pretty good idea of what you mean by "work" (e.g., physical labor or mental labor). Then explain your "how to" process, illustrating each step with specific examples.
2. Write an informative process analysis explaining how you would raise a child compared with how you were raised. What would be the advantages of your method of child rearing? Why do you think your parents raised you the way they did?
3. Making sure that you develop each discussion point, write an essay explaining one of the following topics:

   a. How to enjoy studying and still be popular
   b. How to earn A's without studying

   c. How to embarrass your friends in public and still maintain your dignity
   d. How to research your family roots or chart a family tree

4. Write a *directive* process analysis explaining how you would overhaul our present educational system (either high school or college). What can parents, teachers, and students do?

5. Make a list of things you have witnessed in your life that you consider meaningful and important. Select one particular incident, such as your graduation from high school or your wedding day, and trace the process you went through from start to finish.

6. Write an original directive process analysis paper explaining how to thoroughly relax after work or school, how to make other people miserable and remain happy yourself, or how to enjoy living with several people in a very small apartment or house. Your paper may have either a serious or humorous tone.

7. Compose a paper in which you explain how you learned to sing, dance, or play a musical instrument, or tell someone else how to do it.

8. Write a humorous or satirical paper in which you explain how to run a company into the ground and end up being a billionaire.

9. Select a topic or field of interest after watching one of the home improvement or cooking shows on television. At the end of the show, get the information that is usually provided on how to acquire a copy of the show's transcript, and send for it. In your own words, relate how to do something or how something was done, based on the transcript.

10. Write an informational process essay in which you describe the burial practices of a culture other than your own. (This may necessitate some research on your part.) What do these practices suggest about the culture's attitude toward life as well as toward death?

CHAPTER

7 Comparison and Contrast

Some rhetorical strategies used in developing essays are really second nature to us. We compare and contrast every day of our lives, so much so that some psychologists believe that it is our most elemental thinking strategy. When we compare, we look at the similarities between two or more things. When we contrast, we look at the differences between them. Think about a trip to the grocery store. What types of things do we compare and contrast as we shop? We may compare the usefulness of items. We may compare and contrast the quality of items. We may contrast the prices of two items. When we write, we also often compare and contrast. In school, we may compare and contrast two different points of view on a topic. At work, we may write a report comparing and contrasting two competitors. In Cobie Kwasi Harris's essay "River of Memory: The Ebb and Flow of Black Consciousness Across the Americas," he uses the rhetorical mode of comparing and contrasting to reveal information about customs, religions, belief systems, and individuals. Additionally, his comparative exposition highlights differences between slaves in the United States and those in the Caribbean and South America.

In "Teaching for Social Justice: Academic Rigor with Love," Carmen Carrasquillo Jay takes a comparative look at two-year college students and four-year university students, two-year college students as portrayed in "Good Will Hunting" to the real two-year college students in our classrooms, as well as *social justice* as it's frequently misrepresented by religious/political groups versus *social justice* in practice. Using comparison and contrast, Jay explains that, "As I facilitate critical inquiry in my classroom, I understand that my role is not to indoctrinate students into any particular ideology, but to empower them to reflect and make their own judgments about various ideological stances. To understand the difference between an opinion and an argument. . . .”

Successful writers know that when they compare and contrast, the most important step is gathering as much information as possible about the items or ideas being compared and contrasted. Many of the pre-writing strategies mentioned in the opening chapter on writing can help you to gather the necessary information. One way that is most effective is to make a similarities list and a differences list: First, list all the similarities between the items or ideas; next, list all the differences between them.

Once a writer has gathered enough information and begins to write, he or she will often clearly introduce the items or ideas to be analyzed in the opening paragraph. For example, Suzanne Britt, in “That Lean and Hungry Look,” introduces her topic in the first two sentences of her essay: *“Caesar was right. Thin people need watching.”*

Many writers choose to use thesis statements. For instance, in E. B. White’s essay, “Education,” he states his thesis at the beginning of his second paragraph: *“The shift from city school to country school was something we worried about quietly all last summer.”* He creates tension—although with ironic examples—between his son’s present way of life (and schooling) and what it will be like at a country school; White wonders if his son will be able to adapt to the new environment.

Developing Essays Using Comparison and Contrast

How you structure a comparison and contrast essay depends on the intended audience (the reader), the subject matter, and your purpose for writing. There are two basic methods for organizing comparison and contrast essays: the *point-by-point method* and the *block method*.

In the *point-by-point* method, the author considers one point of comparison or contrast at a time, analyzing the two subjects in alternate sentences or paragraphs. In “They Shut My Grandmother’s Room Door,” Andrew Lam frequently uses the point-by-point technique of development to compare and contrast American and Vietnamese cultural attitudes: *"But if agony and pain are part of Vietnamese culture, pleasure is at the center of America's culture. While Vietnamese holidays are based on death anniversaries, birthdays are celebrated here* [in the United States]."

In the *block* method (also called the summary approach), the author first analyzes one item or idea completely and then analyzes the second item or idea, being sure to compare and contrast the same points in the same order as the first. The block method of comparison guarantees that discussion points will offer unified development. However, widely separated discussion points also might be less clear or more difficult to remember. Thus, the block method works best for relatively simple topics that contain a limited number of comparative elements. White uses a modified block format to structure his composition; an outline of White's essay would look something like this:

I. The country school
II. The city school (paragraphs 2 & 3)
- Clothes
- Transportation
- The school
- Instructors/caregiver
- Actual education

III. The country school (paragraphs 4 & 5)
- Clothes
- Transportation
- The school
- Instructors/caregiver
- Actual education

IV. Conclusion: The better school

Many, if not most, essays do not strictly follow a single pattern. An author may mix and blend strategies as he or she feels necessary to give the reader a clear explanation of the topics. For example, notice how Andrew Lam mixes both methods in "They Shut My Grandmother's Room Door," where the first part of his composition is primarily *block*, and the second part tends to develop his material using the *point-by-point* method. Regardless of what strategy you use, remember that comparing and contrasting people, places, and things is a means to an end (proving or supporting a thesis), not an end in itself.

Irony and Voice

As human beings, we tend to try to mask our emotional reactions to situations and people. Sometimes, we mask them so thoroughly that we ourselves do not understand them. Classic examples include the idea that we project our fears of the "beasts within ourselves" onto any handy "other" that we encounter—such as when we choose enemies in a war situation. If we proclaim that we hate people who ignore deadlines, it is often because we fear our own tendencies to procrastinate. If we, as specialists in gerontology, ignore Patty Moore's "old" person at our conference, it is because we fear growing old. (See Katherine Barrett's essay, "Old Before Her Time," in *Chapter 3: Description.*) As individuals and as literary characters, we search for the *Bluebird of Happiness* (a universally accepted symbol of cheerfulness, happiness, prosperity, and so on), and then, *ironically*, find it in our own back yards, where we have been almost frantically ignoring it. We assume that the grass is very green "over there" and that what we have is inferior—including a spouse or significant other. Now that's *ironic*!

Irony suggests that some circumstance, incident, or a personal experience may be completely unlike or even the opposite of what is actually said or written. Thus, recognizing irony enables a person to understand "a reality different from a masking appearance." As such, when a writer praises or criticizes someone or something, he or she often intends just the opposite. Although irony tends to be more easily identified in speech than in writing, tools such as hyperbole (exaggeration for the point of emphasis) and understatement (mildly expressing a grave situation) can alert readers about the double significance of someone or something.

There are several kinds of irony including verbal irony, dramatic irony, and situational irony. Verbal irony appears in many forms of literature. In "The Cask of Amontillado," for instance, Edgar Allan Poe uses dialogue to impart verbal irony, particularly Montresor's concern for the health of his victim, Fortunado. The speaker in an essay also can communicate such irony.

Ironic remarks should not be confused with sarcasm because even though both may express the opposite of what they seem to say, sarcasm contemptuously mocks and ridicules; it is harsher, more cynical and bitter than irony. Additionally, sarcastic statements tend to be direct and often are calculated to hurt someone whereas ironic ones are implied. In the long run, the measured and restrained tone of verbal irony is more effective (possibly even more cutting) than a nasty, heavy, sarcastic statement like, "I'm *really* glad to see you."

Dramatic irony has been used since Greek drama began. In this plot device, the audience knows more than the protagonist. For instance, in *Oedipus Rex*, the supreme irony is stated when Oedipus condemns the individual who killed Laius, his father, and orders the immediate capture and punishment of the person; at the same time, the audience knows that Oedipus is responsible for the murder. Perhaps more modern examples of dramatic irony can be seen in films where viewers are aware of things the film's characters never seem to consider. In typical horror movies, for example, young lovers, oblivious to the people who recently have died or disappeared in a park, meet there for a night of bliss; meanwhile, the audience knows that a killer lurks in the shadows, waiting for his next victims.

Situational irony defies logical cause-and-effect relationships and justifiable expectations. A person stranded on an island, surrounded by water, who dies of dehydration would be one example of situational irony. A man who has waited all week to eat at an expensive restaurant with high-school friends, only to come down with the stomach flu, would be another.

Cultural situational ironies include the idea that we (United States residents) got our framework for democratic processes from the New England Iroquois Indians and then destroyed their society, conveniently hiding what we were doing from ourselves. The problems of prejudice and stereotypes are full of irony: We say that Asians are a "model majority" and then overlook them at promotion time (see Philip K. Chiu's essay, "The Myth of the Model Minority," in *Chapter 4: Illustration and Example*); advertisers highlight the amazing effects of prescription drugs, but too often gloss over (or place information in an unreadable font) dangerous facts such as these *wonder drugs* may lead to dependence or cause sudden death (see Roohi Vora's essay, "Armchair Pharmacologists and the Media" in *Chapter 8: Division and Classification*); and often, the rationale we hear for gender superiority disproves itself (see Dave Barry's essay, "A GPS Helps a Guy Always Know Where His Couch Is" in *Chapter 12: Persuasion*).

One of the pitfalls of irony is that readers will assume that what you state is what you actually believe. Remember, if you are setting out to write an ironic essay, be careful to let your reader know what you are trying to accomplish. Susan Britt does just this in her essay, "That Lean and Hungry Look" (*Chapter 7: Comparison and Contrast*). She begins by warning readers that *"Caesar was right. Thin people need watching."* Then she writes an absurd analysis by comparing and contrasting thin people and fat people in society, making thorough use of hyperbole and understatement. As in most comparison and contrast papers, she does not compare and contrast opposites just for the sake of doing so; she has a purpose for writing her essay: to expose the irrational, unreliable, foolish nature of stereotypes. In short, Britt does not really fear or dislike thin people nor does she champion fat people in the simplistic ways expressed in her essay. Instead, she wants to admonish people for their frequent acceptance of stereotypes, and possibly their own acts of stereotyping.

One of the most ironic pieces of writing in the English language is Jonathan Swift's famous satire, "A Modest Proposal." The title obviously is an understatement since Swift is suggesting that the Irish raise their children to sell as food—something hinted at by the subtitle of his essay: "For Preventing the Children of Poor People in Ireland from Being a Burden to Their Parents or Country, and for Making Them Beneficial to the Public." When people read this essay, they are often appalled by the proposition until they realize that Swift, a brilliant satirist, wanted to shame the English for their inhumane treatment the Irish, and to chastise the Irish for their lack of industry, which could eliminate their dependence on English landlords for work or food. Of course, Swift's "A Modest Proposal" is only a slight exaggeration of the excuses made by greedy governments pretending to do the "humane" thing while indulging in the worst forms of prejudice and selfishness. More current examples might include countries that are trying to "help" other countries by destroying them.

Barbara Ehrenreich's essay, "Liposuction: The Key to Energy Independence," offers readers a twenty-first century modest proposal where she identifies a problem—dependency on fossil fuel—and then reasons that since we [Americans] are such an obese society, we can try liposuction to produce liquid fat, which in turn can be used as an alternative fuel. For a more extensive exercise on developing awareness of and sensitivity to various forms of irony, see the *Internet Connection* exercise following "That Lean and Hungry Look" later on in this chapter.

Tips on Writing Comparison and Contrast Essays

1. Select topics that offer a clear basis for comparison and contrast. That is, make sure your items for comparison are closely enough related to make a meaningful analysis. (Avoid comparing apples with oranges.)
2. Use an effective pre-writing activity to gather as much information as possible, keeping in mind that you are looking for similarities and differences.
3. Write a thesis statement that clearly explains whether you will be analyzing differences and/or similarities and that introduces the two items or ideas of your essay.
4. Decide on a clear organizational pattern for your essay, either the point-by-point method, the block method, or a blend of the two patterns.
5. As you edit, be sure that you compared and contrasted the same points for each item or idea, preferably in the same order.

Barbara Ehrenreich

Liposuction: The Key to Energy Independence

An award-winning reporter and essayist, Barbara Ehrenreich has written articles for a very broad range of publications, including *The Atlantic Monthly, Esquire, The Nation, the New York Times Magazine, the New Republic, Vogue, the Wall Street Journal, the Washington Post Magazine, Harper's,* and *Time,* where she currently serves as the concluding essayist of the magazine. Among Ehrenreich's many books are *The Hearts of Men* (1983), *Fear of Falling* (1989), *The Worst Years of Our Lives* (1990), *The Snarling Citizen* (1995), *Blood Rites: Origins and History of the Passions of War* (1998), *Nickel and*

Dimed: On (Not) Getting By in America (2002), *Our Media, Not Theirs: The Democratic Struggle Against Corporate America* (2003), *For Her Own Good: Two Centuries of the Expert's Advice to Women* (2005), *Dancing in the Streets: A History of Collective Joy* (2007), *Global Woman: Nannies, Maids, and Sex Workers in the New Economy* (2005), *This Land Is Their Land: Reports from a Divided Nation* (2009), and *Bright-sided: How the Relentless Promotion of Positive Thinking is Undermining America* (2010). As the *Boston Globe* mentioned in its review of *The Worst Years of Our Lives*, "Ehrenreich's scorn withers, her humor stings and her radical light shines on." Ehrenreich's following essay appeared on Barabara's Blog (see http://www.barbaraehrenreich.com/) on June 23, 2008 and in *The Nation* on July 7, 2008.

Pre-reading Questions

1. Brainstorm a list of some alternative energy resources, including those that may seem odd or outrageous.
2. What are a few of the long-term limitations of fossil fuel? Pre-write/quick-write for five minutes on the topic of "oil dependency."

---

1 Everyone talks about our terrible dependency on oil—foreign and otherwise—but hardly anyone mentions what it *is*. Fossil fuel, all right, but whose fossils? Mostly tiny plants called diatoms, but quite possibly a few Barney-like creatures went into the mix, like Stegosaurus, Brontosaurus and other giant reptiles that shared the Jurassic period with all those diatoms. What we are burning in our cars and keeping our homes warm or cool with is, in other words, a highly processed version of corpse juice.

2 Think of this for a moment, if only out of respect for the dead. There you were, about 100 million years ago, maybe a contented little diatom or a great big Brontosaurus stumbling around the edge of a tar pit—a lord of the earth. And what are you now? A sludge of long-chain carbon molecules that will be burned so that some mammalian biped can make a CVS run for Mountain Dew and chips.

3 It's an old human habit—living off the road kill of the planet. There's evidence, for example, that early humans were engaged in scavenging before they figured out how to hunt for themselves. They'd scan the sky for circling vultures, dash off to the kill site—hoping that the leopard that did the actual hunting had sauntered off for a nap—and gobble up what remained of the prey. It was risky, but it beat doing your own antelope tracking.

4 We continue our career as scavengers today, attracted not by vultures but by signs saying "Safeway" or "Giant." Inside these sites, we find bits of dead animals wrapped neatly in plastic. The killing has already been done for us—usually by underpaid immigrant workers rather than leopards.

5 I say to my fellow humans: It's time to stop feeding off the dead and grow up! I don't know about food, but I have a plan for achieving fuel self-sufficiency in less time than it takes to say "Arctic National Wildlife Refuge." The idea came to me from reports of the growing crime of French fry oil theft: Certain desperate individuals are stealing restaurants' discarded cooking oil, which can then be used to fuel cars. So the idea is: Why not skip the French fry phase and harvest high-energy hydrocarbons right from ourselves?

6 I'm talking about liposuction, of course, and it's a mystery to me why it hasn't occurred to any of those geniuses who are constantly opining about fuel prices on MSNBC. The average liposuction removes about half a gallon of liquid fat, which may not seem like much. But think of the vast reserves our nation is literally sitting on! Thirty percent of Americans are obese, or about 90 million individuals or 45 million gallons of easily available fat—not from dead diatoms but from our very own bellies and butts.

7 This is the humane alternative to biofuels derived directly from erstwhile foodstuffs like corn. Biofuels, as you might have noticed, are exacerbating the global food crisis by turning edible plants into gasoline. But we could put humans back in the loop by first turning the corn into Doritos and hence into liposuctionable body fat. There would be a reason to live again, even a patriotic rationale for packing on the pounds.

8 True, liposuction is not risk-free, as the numerous doctors' websites on the subject inform us. And those of us who insist on driving gas guzzlers may soon start depleting their personal fat reserves, much as heroin addicts run out of useable veins. But the gaunt, punctured, look could become a fashion statement. Already, the combination of a tiny waist and a huge carbon footprint—generated by one's Hummer and private jet—is considered a sign of great wealth.

9 And think what it would do for our nation's self-esteem. We may not lead the world in scientific innovation, educational achievement, or low infant mortality, but we are the global champions of obesity. Go here and you'll find America well ahead of the pack when it comes to personal body fat, while those renowned oil-producers—Saudi Arabia, Venezuela and Iran—aren't even among the top 29. All we need is a healthy dose of fat pride and for CVS to start marketing home liposuction kits. That run for Mountain Dew and chips could soon be an energy-neutral proposition.

Post-reading Questions

Content

1. Ehrenreich uses humor to define fossil fuel. According to her, what do we burn in our cars? What keeps "our homes warm and cool"?

2. Why does the author send her readers back 100 million years to what we might have been and return them to the present by asking, "And what are you now?"
3. Ehrenreich compares humans to their ancestors exhibiting how the latter lived "off the road kill of the planet" by announcing, "We continue our career as scavengers today." What are we attracted to today, and how are our habits similar to those of our ancestors?
4. In the middle of her essay, Ehrenreich develops a way to lessen our dependency on fossil fuel. Summarize her plan.
5. How much liquid fat is removed during the liposuction process she describes? Who or what does she compare and contrast to persuade her readers that her scheme would work so well for Americans?

Strategies and Structures

1. Reread Ehrenreich's essay, making note of each humorous reference. Is the author serious about her suggestions, or does she have some other purpose? (Review the section "Irony and Voice" in the introduction to *Chapter 7: Comparison and Contrast*.)
2. How does Erdrich's use of irony help move the action along?
3. Although the author uses a great deal of humor in this essay, she also makes use of many facts (i.e., "thirty percent of Americans are obese") that should cause the reader to stop and think. Point out three or four of these facts, and indicate how they affect you.
4. What was the author's purpose in comparing "those of us who insist on driving gas guzzlers" that may soon deplete "their personal fat reserves" with "heroin by addicts [who] run out of useable veins?"
5. Ultimately, Ehrenreich humorously shows the readers how their self-esteem can be improved. Do you think Americans are proud of their "personal body fat?" Does she have some other purpose here?

Language and Vocabulary

1. Vocabulary: *liposuction, fossil, Stegosaurus, Brontosaurus, Jurassic, mammalian biped, scavenger, opining, hydrocarbons, erstwhile, innovation.* After finding and reviewing the definitions of these words, determine which ones pertain to the earth 100 million years ago. How did these words help Ehrenreich to get her point across when she was comparing modern humans with those who lived 100 million years ago?
2. Explain how many of the vocabulary words contribute to the author's use of humor and irony.

Group Activities

1. Go to your college's library or a computer center and investigate the procedure for liposuction. Is it considered a major or minor procedure? Even though Ehrenreich uses this procedure in a humorous way, are there any dangers associated with this surgery? How does this fact contribute to the irony in the essay even more?
2. The author, obviously, is attempting to get humans to consider other ways to achieve energy independence; therefore, go to the Environmental Studies Department at your school and investigate another way to reduce our dependency on fossil fuel. Save your information for a writing assignment.

Writing Activities

1. Return and review the energy alternatives you generated in Pre-reading Question 1 and collected in Group Activity 2. Next, compose an essay in which you compare and/or contrast the way fossil fuel is produced for use today and energy alternatives that can reduce our dependency on oil tomorrow.
2. Ehrenreich suggests that ancient humans are similar to today's inhabitants. Write an essay in which you compare and/or contrast our ancestors with us. How are we similar, and in what ways have we changed significantly?

Andrew Lam

They Shut My Grandmother's Room Door

Andrew Lam is a Vietnamese immigrant who currently resides in San Francisco, where he was the associate editor for the Pacific News Service, a regular commentator for National Public Radio's "All Things Considered," and current editor at New American Media. His real love, however, is writing fiction. His articles have appeared in *Nation, Mother Jones,* and the *Washington Post*—as well as many anthologies—and his work has been acknowledged by many prestigious organizations. Lam won the Thomas Stock Award for Excellence in International Journalism (1991), a Rockefeller Fellowship (1992/93), and the Asian American Journalism Award for Commentary. Along with De Tran and Hai Dai Nguyen, Lam edited *Once upon a Dream . . . : The Vietnamese-American Experience* (1995), and he wrote *Perfume Dreams: Reflections on the Vietnamese Diaspora* (2005), which won a PEN/Beyond Margins Award. Most recently, Lam published *Birds of Paradise* (2011), and he is presently working on a novel, another collection of short stories, and another book of essays.

Pre-reading Questions

1. What holidays, customs, or rituals do you associate with death?
2. Where do you imagine you will end up in your old age? Answer this question before reading Lam's essay. (Write your answer in a notebook.)

---

1 When someone dies in the convalescent home where my grandmother lives, the nurses rush to close all the patient's doors. Though as a policy death is not to be seen at the home, she can always tell when it visits. The series of doors being slammed shut remind her of the firecrackers during Tet.

2 The nurses' efforts to shield death are more comical to my grandmother than reassuring. "Those old ladies die so often," she quips in Vietnamese, "everyday's like new year."

3 Still, it is lonely to die in such a place. I imagine some wasted old body under a white sheet being carted silently through the empty corridor on its way to the morgue. While in America a person may be born surrounded by loved ones, in old age one is often left to take the last leg of life's journey alone.

4 Perhaps that is why my grandmother talks now mainly of her hometown, Bac-Lieu: its river and green rich rice fields. Having lost everything during the war, she can now offer me only her distant memories: Life was not disjointed back home; one lived in a gentle rhythm with the land; people died in their homes surrounded by neighbors and relatives. And no one shut your door.

5 So it goes. The once gentle, connected world of the past is but the language of dreams. In this fast-paced society of disjointed lives, we are swept along and have little time left for spiritual comfort. Instead of relying on neighbors and relatives, on the river and land, we deal with the

language of materialism: overtime, escrow, stress, down payment, credit cards, tax shelter. Instead of going to the temple to pray for good health we pay life and health insurance religiously.

6 My grandmother's children and grandchildren share a certain pang of guilt. After a stroke which paralyzed her, we could no longer keep her at home. And although we visit her regularly, we are not living up to the filial piety standard expected of us in the old country. My father silently grieves and my mother suffers from headaches. (Does she see herself in such a home in a decade or two?)

7 Once, a long time ago, living in Vietnam we used to stare death in the face. The war in many ways had heightened our sensibilities toward living and dying. I can still hear the wails of widows and grieving mothers. Though the fear of death and dying is a universal one, the Vietnamese did not hide from it. Instead we dwelt in its tragedy. Death pervaded our poems, novels, fairy tales and songs.

8 But if agony and pain are part of Vietnamese culture, pleasure is at the center of America's culture. While Vietnamese holidays are based on death anniversaries, birthdays are celebrated here. American popular culture translates death with something like nauseating humor. People laugh and scream at blood and guts movies. The wealthy freeze their dead relatives in liquid nitrogen. Cemeteries are places of big business, complete with colorful brochures. I hear there are even drive-by funerals where you don't have to get out of your own car to pay your respects to the deceased.

9 That America relies upon the pleasure principle and happy endings in its entertainments does not, however, assist us in evading suffering. The reality of the suffering of old age is apparent in the convalescent home. There is an old man, once an accomplished concert pianist, now rendered helpless by arthritis. Every morning he sits staring at the piano. One feeble woman who outlived her children keeps repeating, "My son will take me home." Then there are those mindless, bedridden bodies kept alive through a series of tubes and pulsating machines.

10 But despair is not newsworthy. Death itself must be embellished or satirized or deep-frozen in order to catch the public's attention.

11 Last week on her 82nd birthday I went to see my grandmother. She smiled her sweet sad smile.

12 "Where will you end up in your old age?" she asked me, her mind as sharp as ever.

13 The memories of monsoon rain and tropical sun and relatives and friends came to mind. Not here, not here, I wanted to tell her. But the soft moaning of a patient next door and the smell of alcohol wafting from the sterile corridor brought me back to reality.

14 "Anywhere is fine," I told her instead, trying to keep up with her courageous spirit. "All I am asking for is that they don't shut my door."

Post-reading Questions

Content

1. Explain what the door symbolizes in Lam's essay.
2. How is the grandmother's life in America different from life in Vietnam? Why?
3. What are the most striking differences between American and Vietnamese culture presented in this essay?
4. How do people deal with their fear of death?

Strategies and Structures

1. Discuss how Lam's first and last paragraphs "frame" the real point of this composition. What image appears in both paragraphs, and how does it function as a unifying device?
2. Where does Lam gather information to illustrate his essay? How is it effective?
3. Omitting the initial sentence in each paragraph, reread this article. How does the essay's clarity and meaning change? What might this suggest to us about the importance of opening (topic) sentences?
4. What specific examples illustrate Lam's ideas? How are the comparisons and contrasts strengthened by his use of specific examples? What is the overall effect?

Language and Vocabulary

1. Vocabulary: *convalescent, morgue, disjointed, pang, filial, pervaded, liquid nitrogen, arthritis, monsoon.* Many of the words in this list deal with suffering and death. Using the antonyms (see Glossary) to those words, write a short paragraph or two dealing with Lam's subject. Does the meaning change? What does this suggest about proper word selection for your essays?
2. Lam frequently makes use of alliteration (see the Glossary) in this composition. Why might a writer use alliteration? What is the effect of such phrases as "last leg of life's journey," "rich rice fields," and "wails of widows"? What other examples of alliteration can you find in Lam's essay?

Group Activities

1. Get into groups and compare and contrast your responses to Pre-reading Question 2: "Where do you imagine you will end up in your old age?" Has reading this essay changed your response? In what way did reading this essay sharpen your focus on where you want to be when you are old?

2. Brainstorm different ways that one can take care of an elderly relative. What are the advantages and disadvantages to each solution? Describe the benefits and new problems that accompany each solution?

Writing Activities

1. Compare and contrast how you plan to take care of your parents with Lam's description of American elderly care practices today. Comparison and contrast should be used here as the means of explaining your points as effectively as possible. Be sure to use specific examples.
2. Model an essay after Lam's composition, using the introductory and closing paragraphs as a framing device. Write a comparative paper explaining why you are for or against placing elderly people in rest homes. As you compare, you should make sure that your position on the issue is clear; however, be sure to carefully consider both sides of the issue prior to forming your conclusion.

Carmen Carrasquillo Jay

Teaching for Social Justice: Academic Rigor with Love

An English professor, community activist, student advocate, and literary scholar, Carmen Carrasquillo Jay teaches all levels of composition and literature at Miramar College in San Diego. Among her many responsibilities, she coordinates the Honors Program, works as editor-in-chief for *Community Voices*, Miramar College's literary magazine, has served as writer/editor of Miramar College's *Student Retention Strategies Handbook* and designer/editor of the *Cultural Diversity Newsletter*. The recipient of a National Endowment for the Humanities Study Grant, Jay's scholarship includes "Maria Luisa Bombal, Luisa Valenzuela, and Isabel Allende: A Modernist

Vision." Jay continues to be a frequent panelist and speaker at local, state, and national conferences. Her presentations include: "Deconstructing Media Images: Empowering Student Writers," "Problematic Gender Roles in Mary Shelley's *Frankenstein*," and "Activating the Senses—Harmonizing the Arts: Films, Music, Literature, and Thought." In the following essay, Jay exposes how colleges can transform education settings into places of true engagement and inclusion—an environment of *academic rigor with love*—by comparing and contrasting two-year college students to four-year college students, two-year college students as portrayed in *Good Will Hunting* to the real two-year college students, and social justice as often misrepresented by religious/political groups versus social justice in practice.

Pre-reading Questions

1. Before reading Carmen Jay's essay, define what the term "social justice" means to you.
2. In a short paragraph, predict what you imagine Jay will discuss in her essay based upon its title, "*Teaching for Social Justice: Academic Rigor with Love.*"

---

1 *Good Will Hunting* is arguably a film with many admirable qualities. Robin Williams, proving that he can excel in a dramatic role, is the grieving widower and college psychology professor. Matt Damon (Will Hunting) is the boy math genius whose abusive past is holding him back. Ben Affleck plays Will's devoted friend and confidant. When their worlds intersect, there is much to note about the bonds that sustain us and about the resilience of the human spirit. Yet, there is one scene in the film that I find unsettling. While much of the film's action takes place in and around MIT (Massachusetts Institute of Technology), the camera hovers briefly over one classroom at the local community college. There, distracted and disinterested students face a comic Williams, who has to tell jokes to get them focused on the lecture: "Next time, I'll tell you about Freud and why he did enough cocaine to kill a small horse." My ambivalence about this scene centers on the fact that while the MIT students are represented as a dedicated, academically motivated cohort, the community college students, students who are most likely unable to afford the prestigious university, are clearly not as concerned about their education. Approaching my twentieth year as a community college professor, I can say with all assurance that these are *not* my students.

2 Over my tenure, I have witnessed what bell hooks has called the transformative power of education. In a 1997 video documentary, when hooks recounts her teaching experiences and compares the students in Harlem to those she taught at an Ivy League university, she finds that the

difference between them was *not* ability or intellectual talent but a differing sense of *agency*. While the first group struggles against power structures that disenfranchise and disempower them, the latter believes they are marked for success. Bearing testimony to what is needed to transform education, hooks emphasizes a pedagogy of hope based on critical inquiry and literacy. Like hooks, I have observed students who perceive that their cultural backgrounds or lived experiences are devalued by the dominant discourse. This devaluation signifies less credibility, command or presence within the larger societal context. In short, many students have no voice. Unlike the fictional students of the film, my students are *indeed* motivated to enroll in college and pursue academic goals. However, many, if not most of them, must contend with the voicelessness borne out of their prior negative experiences. Voicelessness complicates students' ability to engage successfully with college level reading and writing assignments, assignments which often stress application of higher level reasoning skills. If compositionists agree that good writing contains a distinctive voice, an authoritative presence on the page, then imagine how difficult it is to articulate an authentic voice when one has not yet developed the agency to claim a voice.

3 Countering voicelessness involves my own positive beliefs in my students' academic potential and in the value of their *quehaceres de la vida*, the funds of knowledge (a term coined by Moll) that they bring to the classroom. I do my best to integrate into my curriculum my students' resource-rich cultural and social capital. When learning is more relevant to my students' lived experience, they themselves find ways to unclip their wings, to fly unfettered, to liberate their voices and sing. My sincere desire to assist in my students' voice liberation is a form of teaching for social justice.

4 What does it mean to teach for social justice? Expressing their opinions on this topic, some television personalities have decried social justice in education as a form of teaching with a liberal bias. On the contrary, what Banks has termed "equity pedagogy" is about empowerment, not indoctrination. I employ numerous strategies meant to empower students to think for themselves. First of all, seeking to value my students' voices, I demonstrate in as active a way as possible that their voices matter, that we are *all* (me included) learners participating in an inclusive, collaborative environment. Equally important, I also underscore the idea that I am not the giver of Truth; instead, I seek to facilitate their inquiry about many truths. Choosing topics, themes, media images, songs of protest and other items that weave students' backgrounds and home experiences into the fabric of our classroom is integral to social justice teaching. In addition to respecting students' home languages and cultures, I am explicit about discourse norms and ways of knowing. For many of my students, success often means

gaining knowledge about both academic content *and* college culture. I have also found it valuable to teach my students about specific, positive, nonviolent forms of communication and to emphasize principles of cooperation and respect.

5 As I facilitate critical inquiry in my classroom, I understand that my role is not to indoctrinate students into any particular ideology, but to empower them to reflect and make their own judgments about various ideological stances. To understand the difference between an opinion and an argument, to be able to decode popular cultural constructs for a variety of possible messages, to analyze an argument for its use of logic or credibility—all of these tools are useful in fostering agency and liberating students' voices. Those voices are not meant to imitate mine, but rather to express their rich diversity; hence, whether it be a paper defending conservative talk radio or advocating for gay marriage rights, multiple perspectives come to the foreground as students seek to claim their voices in coherent, persuasive, and authoritative ways. My students write personal narratives about injustices they have encountered; they select freely real world topics of interest to them; and they often share their epiphanies with me. Meaningful dialogue about social problems they care about can yield thoughtful, engaged citizens of the world, the ultimate purpose of social justice in education.

6 I remember my composition student, Monique.* Despite much anti-Muslim sentiment that she often contended with on an almost daily basis, she earned her Master's degree in Journalism and started her own newspaper column in Hawaii. Michael, who has four children and manages bi-polar disorder, secured a full scholarship to one of the University of California campuses. And most recently, there is Haylee, who overcame alcohol addiction, devoted herself to academically rigorous honors classes, and transferred to Berkeley. Earning a Certificate in Global Competencies, Haylee had opportunities in my classroom to consider the interconnectedness of global cultures and to contemplate the role she wished to play upon the world's stage. I believe she is poised to participate in democratic life and will use her distinctive voice to create social change. Overcoming prejudice, managing family responsibilities and disabilities, or countering outside pathologies while staying on the academic path is clearly not easy. Yet, my students do this every single day, and I am proud to walk beside them for a brief time through this journey.

7 I see the faces of my students, and they are missing in the community college classroom depicted in *Good Will Hunting*. The film fails to notice the students whom I serve. Committed to the principle of teaching for social change, my vision is one of academic rigor with love. I do love my students. It is a radical, Freirean kind of love. The commitment to revolutionary love means I seek to fortify my students' ability to, as Freire

argued, "read the world." Students can learn how to "read" or demystify voice (power) and voicelessness (powerlessness). Demystification of voice cultivates a re-positioning of the self as pro-active and agentic. Engaged with real world social problems, my students have used the power of their voices, both orally and through the written word, in persuasive and public ways. If voice is indeed about power, then students who claim and raise their voices can work to change the world as they deem necessary. And if the strength of our democracy rests upon the participation of its people, then social justice in education feeds the collective in responsible and positive ways. As the late hip-hop artist Tupac Shakur insisted, "the power is in the people."

*All names are pseudonyms.

Post-reading Questions

Content

1. How do Jay's community college students compare to those portrayed in the movie *Good Will Hunting*?
2. What did bell hooks, one of the people mentioned in Jay's essay, claim was the major difference between her students in Harlem and those she instructed at an Ivy League university
3. Why have some television personalities "decried [criticized] *social justice* in education"? What do they claim?
4. According to Jay, what is the "ultimate purpose of social justice in education"? What can it foster and development?
5. Why might what previous negative experiences *Voicelessness* complicate students' ability to engage successfully with college-level reading and writing assignments?

Strategies and Structures

1. How and why does Jay structure her essay on *social justice in education* by beginning and concluding it with references to the movie *Good Will Hunting*?
2. Look up an online biography for Paulo Freire. Who is he? Explain some of the possible reasons that Jay referred to Freire in her essay.
3. How and why does Jay "weave students' backgrounds and home experiences" into the classroom?
4. Why do you imagine that Jay spends so much time discussing the accomplishments of her former students? What purpose did they have in common and how were they different? What did they all ultimately achieve?
5. Why do you think that Jay decided to conclude her social justice essay with Tupac Shakur's quotation, "The power is in the people"?

Language and Vocabulary

1. Vocabulary: *confidant, interact, resilience, ambivalence, cohort, prestigious, transformative, agency, disenfranchise, disempower, pedagogy, devaluation, credibility, authoritative, unfettered, decried, equity, empowerment, indoctrination, norms, decode, constructs, epiphanies, sentiment, bi-polar, pathologies, fortify, demystify, cultivate, pseudonyms.* Consult your dictionary to reinforce or clarify your understanding of Jay's vocabulary words; are they or are they not appropriate to her subject matter? Explain your response.
2. Why do you think Jay selected so many challenging vocabulary words in her discussion of social justice? Identify at least five words you found particularly confusing or unclear, and then look up synonyms (words expressing the same or similar meaning) for them.

Group Activities

1. In small groups, do some online research on hip-hop songs (or songs from any other genre) that contain lyrics for social justice. Some examples are Tracy Chapman's *Why*?, Woody Guthrie's *This Land is Your Land*, or Tupac Shakur's *Me Against the World*. What inequity or injustice is the song about? Does the song offer a solution to the problem? First, identify the issue, concern, or theme of the song; then, select lyrics you think are key to understanding the song's main concerns. Next, plan a class presentation with your group members. The presentation can include sample lyrics, a sample YouTube clip, a PowerPoint, a poster, or a live performance.
2. In pairs, brainstorm social injustices facing your neighborhood, modern society, or the world at large. As you brainstorm, write down your ideas on a list. Choose one social injustice you would like to learn more about and clear the topic with your instructor. Each pair will explore a different social justice issue and write a collaborative essay. Some topics to consider include: sweatshops, religious discrimination, racial or ethnic discrimination, poverty, animal testing, environmental problems, gang violence, etc.

Writing Activities

1. Compare and contrast two movies, songs, television shows or poems that are concerned with a social justice issue. What do they have in common? How are they different? What does

each one say can be done about the injustice? Do you find them to be convincing? Use plenty of specific evidence.

2. According to Martin Luther King, Jr., "Injustice anywhere is a threat to justice everywhere." Think about a social injustice that you consider a threat in today's world. Consider more than one side of the issue before deciding on the solution you would like to propose; then, write a letter to the editor of a newspaper. The letter should summarize different opinions on the issue before stating your own position.
3. Write an essay where you argue for or against the notion that students who learn how to "read" or demystify voice (power) and voicelessness (powerlessness) become socially active, globally responsible citizens.

E. B. White

Education

Elwyn Brooks White (1899–1985) was a well-known essayist and contributing editor for *The New Yorker*. In collaboration with author James Thurber, White wrote the satire *Is Sex Necessary?* (1929). White's other works include *The Lady Is Cold* and various books for children, including *Stuart Little* (1945), *Charlotte's Web* (1952), and *The Trumpet of the Swan* (1970). White also revised William Strunk's *The Elements of Style*. His essays frequently appeared in magazines, including *The New Yorker* and *Harper's*. The following essay comparing and contrasting life in country and city schools first appeared in the March 1939 issue of *Education*.

Pre-reading Questions

1. Explain what it means to "get an education"? How can anyone tell if another has truly been educated?
2. Freewrite on the topic of *American* education. What meanings, ideas, and opinions do you associate with it?

1 I have an increasing admiration for the teacher in the country school where we have a third-grade scholar in attendance. She not only undertakes to instruct her charges in all the subjects of the first three grades, but she manages to function quietly and effectively as a guardian of their health, their clothes, their habits, their mothers, and their snowball engagements. She has been doing this sort of Augean task for twenty years, and is both kind and wise. She cooks for the children on the stove that heats the room, and she can cool their passions or warm their soup with equal competence. She conceives their costumes, cleans up their messes, and shares their confidences. My boy already regards his teacher as his great friend, and I think tells her a great deal more than he tells us.

2 The shift from city school to country school was something we worried about quietly all last summer. I have always rather favored public school over private school, if only because in public school you meet a greater variety of children. This bias of mine, I suspect, is partly an attempt to justify my own past (I never knew anything but public schools) and partly an involuntary defense against getting kicked in the shins by a young ceramist on his way to the kiln. My wife was unacquainted with public schools, never having been exposed (in her early life) to anything more public than the washroom of Miss Winsor's. Regardless of our backgrounds, we both knew that the change in schools was something that concerned not us but the scholar himself. We hoped it would work out all right. In New York our son went to a medium-priced private institution with semi-progressive ideas of education, and modern plumbing. He learned fast, kept well, and we were satisfied. It was an electric, colorful, regimented existence with moments of pleasurable pause and giddy incident. The day the Christmas angel fainted and had to be carried out by one of the Wise Men was education in the highest sense of the term. Our scholar gave imitations of it around the house for weeks afterward, and I doubt if it ever goes completely out of his mind.

3 His days were rich in formal experience. Wearing overalls and an old sweater (the accepted uniform of the private seminary), he sallied forth at morn accompanied by a nurse or a parent and walked (or was pulled) two blocks to a corner where the school bus made a flag stop. This flashy vehicle was as punctual as death: Seeing us waiting at the cold curb, it would sweep to a halt, open its mouth, suck the boy in, and spring away with an angry growl. It was a good deal like a train picking up a bag of mail. At school the scholar was worked on for six or seven hours by half a dozen teachers and a nurse, and was revived on orange juice in mid-morning. In a cinder court he played games supervised by an athletic instructor, and in a cafeteria he ate lunch worked out by a dietitian. He soon learned to read with gratifying facility and discernment and to make Indian weapons of a semi-deadly nature. Whenever one of his classmates fell low of a fever the news was put on the wires and there were breathless phone calls to physicians, discussing periods of incubation and allied magic.

4 In the country all one can say is that the situation is different, and somehow more casual. Dressed in corduroys, sweatshirt, and short rubber boots, and carrying a tin dinner-pail, our scholar departs at the crack of dawn for the village school, two and a half miles down the road, next to the cemetery.

5 When the road is open and the car will start, he makes the journey by motor, courtesy of his old man. When the snow is deep or the motor is dead or both, he makes it on the hoof. In the afternoons he walks or hitches all or part of the way home in fair weather, gets transported in foul. The schoolhouse is a two-room frame building, bungalow type, shingles stained a burnt brown with weather-resistant stain. It has a chemical toilet in the basement and two teachers above the stairs. One takes the first three grades, the other the fourth, fifth, and sixth. They have little or no time for individual instruction, and no time at all for the esoteric. They teach what they know themselves, just as fast and as hard as they can manage. The pupils sit still at their desks in class, and do their milling around outdoors during recess.

6 There is no supervised play. They play cops and robbers (only they call it "Jail") and throw things at one another—snowballs in winter, rose hips in fall. It seems to satisfy them. They also construct darts, pinwheels, and "pick-up sticks" (jackstraws), and the school itself does a brisk trade in penny candy, which is for sale right in the classroom and which contains "surprises." The most highly prized surprise is a fake cigarette, made of cardboard, fiendishly lifelike.

7 The memory of how apprehensive we were at the beginning is still strong. The boy was nervous about the change too. The tension, on that first fair morning in September when we drove him to school, almost blew the windows out of the sedan. And when later we picked him up on the road, wandering along with his little blue lunch-pail, and got his laconic report "All right" in answer to our inquiry about how the day had gone, our relief was vast. Now, after almost a year of it, the only difference we can discover in the two school experiences is that in the country he sleeps better at night—and *that* probably is more the air than the education. When grilled on the subject of school-in-country vs. school-in-city, he replied that the chief difference is that the day seems to go so much quicker in the country. "Just like lightning," he reported.

Post-reading Questions

Content

1. What is the controlling idea in this essay?
2. In paragraph 3, although White says that at the city school, his son's "days were rich in formal experiences," the images, examples, and diction he chooses to back up that statement

seem to indicate otherwise. What is the true nature of his son's experiences? Explain your answer using specific details from White's essay to illustrate what you say.

3. What does White's son wear when he goes to school in the city? How does his choice of clothing change when he attends school in the country? Is one mode of dress more appropriate than another? Explain.
4. Contrast White's depictions of city school teachers to his depictions of country school teachers. As human beings, how are they different and how are they alike?
5. What vivid details and examples in this essay help you to envision the distinct differences (at least, according to White's experience) between education at *city schools* and education at *country schools?*

Strategies and Structures

1. How does the tone of this essay reflect the author's attitude toward city (private) schools and country (public) schools?
2. Why do you think that White admits his bias toward public schools in the second paragraph? How might this lighthearted examination of the origins of his bias serve a larger purpose in his essay?
3. How does White use irony in this essay? How, for instance, do the things you relate to the word *scholar* contrast with the sort of learning White's son receives in the city school?
4. Which method of structuring comparative essays tends to be *predominant* in this essay? Why do you imagine White selected one method of organization over another?
5. In the final paragraph, White informs us that his son initially thinks that education at the country school is just "all right," but later states that days go by quickly—"just like lightning." How does the final sentence sum up White's general attitude toward country schools?

Language and Vocabulary

1. Vocabulary: *Augean, regimented, gratifying, discernment, bungalow, milling, laconic.* Write down each of these words on a sheet of paper and locate the dictionary definition for each. Next, determine what an antonym (word that carries an opposite meaning) for each word might be. You may use your own intuition and experience to predict an appropriate antonym for *"Augean."*
2. White frequently uses figurative language such as metaphors (direct comparison) and similes (comparisons with the use of *like* or *as*) in this essay—as well as hyperbole (exaggeration of a point for emphasis). Search through the essay and locate as many examples of each type of figurative language as you can. (Suggestion: Highlight the metaphors, similes, and so on, in

your textbook.) Then write a brief paragraph—possibly using figurative language yourself—explaining what effect the use of figurative language had on you as a reader.

Group Activities

1. Divide into groups and select a "group recorder" to write down the material other members generate. Brainstorm the terms, "natural education" versus "clinical education." Make a separate list for each. Attempt to match every *natural* method of education with its corresponding *clinical* or artificial counterpart. Make copies of the list for all group members, and then for homework, have each person draft a comparative essay on the topic. Finally, assemble once again with your group and blend your individual insights into one collaborative essay.
2. Many educational practices today differ from educational practices of the past. For a group assignment, explore the similarities and differences between the past and present. First, have each group member interview either his or her parents or grandparents about educational practices in their day. (Before your interview, you may want to brainstorm a series of appropriate questions as a group.) Next, do an individual freewriting on educational practices today; try to draw comparisons and contrasts with your parents' or grandparents' experiences. Finally, get together with your group, share your findings, and then draw some general conclusions about the similarities and differences between the two different generations. (It might be interesting to note whether the people you interview went to country schools or city schools.)

Writing Activities

1. Compose an essay in which you compare and contrast high school with college, a city school with a country school, or a private school with a public school. How are they similar yet different? What are the differences? What specific experiences have you had that illustrate these differences? Which do you prefer, and why do you prefer it?
2. Write an essay in which you compare and/or contrast the American educational system with an educational system

from another country. You may gather the needed information in several ways: Interview someone who has been educated in another country, interview a teacher who has taught in another system, research another system in the library, and/or watch a documentary on another educational system. As you gather your information, take notes on the similarities and differences between the other system and the American educational system.

***Internet Connection:* E. B. White**

Educational Practices

Briefly surf the web and search for information about teaching/learning practices in higher education from at least three different countries. What similarities did your discover? How do practices differ significantly from country to country and why? Finally, double check your conclusions by going back online and corroborating evidence gleaned from your intial Internet search. How might corroborating findings enable you to evaluate source material for future critical thinking and writing assignments?

Suzanne Britt

That Lean and Hungry Look

Suzanne Britt is a journalist and essayist whose articles have appeared in a wide range of news magazines, journals, and newspapers: the *Dickens Dispatch, Newsweek,* the *Des Moines Register and Tribune*, the *Baltimore Sun, Newsday,* and the *New York Times*. Her books include *Skinny People Are Dull and Crunchy Like Carrots* (1982) and *Show and Tell* (1983). Britt often develops her satirical essays by using irony and some form of comparison and contrast. She particularly enjoys exposing the follies of human behavior and the absurdity of stereotypes. As Britt said in the preface to

A Writer's Rhetoric (1988), "Competent writers are imitators; compelling writers are original." The following essay that originally appeared in the "My Turn" column of *Newsweek* magazine illustrates how one's natural voice, humor, and the use of irony can become "compelling" rhetorical tools.

Pre-reading Questions

1. What negative things do you associate with being *thin*? To what extent are your associations stereotypes?
2. What are some positive qualities you associate with being *fat*? Again, are your associations based on fact or fiction?

---

1 Caesar was right. Thin people need watching. I've been watching them for most of my adult life, and I don't like what I see. When these narrow fellows spring at me, I quiver to my toes. Thin people come in all personalities, most of them menacing. You've got your "together" thin person, your mechanical thin person, your condescending thin person, your tsk-tsk thin person, your efficiency-expert thin person. All of them are dangerous.

2 In the first place, thin people aren't fun. They don't know how to goof off, at least in the best, fat sense of the word. They've always got to be adoing. Give them a coffee break, and they'll jog around the block. Supply them with a quiet evening at home, and they'll fix the screen door and lick S&H green stamps. They say things like "there aren't enough hours in the day." Fat people never say that. Fat people think the day is too damn long already.

3 Thin people make me tired. They've got speedy little metabolisms that cause them to bustle briskly. They're forever rubbing their bony hands together and eyeing new problems to "tackle." I like to surround myself with sluggish, inert, easygoing fat people, the kind who believe that if you clean it up today, it'll just get dirty again tomorrow.

4 Some people say the business about the jolly fat person is a myth, that all of us chubbies are neurotic, sick, sad people. I disagree. Fat people may not be chortling all day long, but they're a hell of a lot nicer than the wizened and shriveled. Thin people turn surly, mean and hard at a young age because they never learn the value of a hot-fudge sundae for easing tension. Thin people don't like gooey soft things because they themselves are neither gooey nor soft. They are crunchy and dull, like carrots. They go straight to the heart of the matter while fat people let things stay all blurry and hazy and vague, the way things actually are. Thin people want to face the truth. Fat people know that there is no truth. One of my thin friends is always staring at complex, unsolvable problems and saying,

"The key thing is . . ." Fat people never say things like that. They know there isn't any such thing as the key thing about anything.

5 Thin people believe in logic. Fat people see all sides. The sides fat people see are rounded blobs, usually gray, always nebulous and truly not worth worrying about. But the thin person persists, "If you consume more calories than you burn," says one of my thin friends, "you will gain weight. It's that simple." Fat people always grin when they hear statements like that. They know better. Fat people realize that life is illogical and unfair. They know very well that God is not in his heaven and all is not right with the world. If God was up there, fat people could have two doughnuts and a big orange drink anytime they wanted it.

6 Thin people have a long list of logical things they are always spouting off to me. They hold up one finger at a time as they reel off these things, so I won't lose track. They speak slowly as if to a young child. The list is long and full of holes. It contains tidbits like "get a grip on yourself," "cigarettes kill," "cholesterol clogs," "fit as a fiddle," "ducks in a row," "organize," and "sound fiscal management." Phrases like that.

7 They think these 2000-point plans lead to happiness. Fat people know happiness is elusive at best and even if they could get the kind thin people talk about, they wouldn't want it. Wisely, fat people see that such programs are too dull, too hard, too off the mark. They are never better than a whole cheesecake.

8 Fat people know all about the mystery of life. They are the ones acquainted with the night, with luck, with fate, with playing it by the ear. One thin person I know once suggested that we arrange all the parts of a jigsaw puzzle into groups according to size, shape and color. He figured this would cut the time needed to complete the puzzle by at least 50 per cent. I said I wouldn't do it. One, I like to muddle through. Two, what good would it do to finish early? Three, the jigsaw puzzle isn't the important thing. The important thing is the fun of four people (one thin person included) sitting around a card table, working a jigsaw puzzle. My thin friend had no use for my list. Instead of joining us, he went outside and mulched the boxwoods. The three remaining fat people finished the puzzle and made chocolate double-fudged brownies to celebrate.

9 The main problem with thin people is they oppress. Their good intentions, bony torsos, tight ships, neat corners, cerebral machinations and pat solutions loom like dark clouds over the loose, comfortable, spread-out, soft world of the fat. Long after fat people have removed their coats and shoes and put their feet up on the coffee table, thin people are still sitting on the edge of the sofa, looking neat as a pin, discussing rutabagas. Fat people are heavily into fits of laughter, slapping their thighs and whooping it up, while thin people are still politely waiting for the punch line.

10 Thin people are downers. They like math and morality and reasoned evaluation of the limitations of human beings. They have their skinny little acts together. They expound, prognose, probe and prick.

11 Fat people are convivial. They will like you even if you're irregular and have acne. They will come up with a good reason why you never wrote the great American novel. They will cry in your beer with you. They will put your name in the pot. They will let you off the hook. Fat people will gab, giggle, guffaw, gallumph, gyrate and gossip. They are generous, giving and gallant. They are gluttonous and goodly and great. What you want when you're down is soft and jiggly, not muscled and stable. Fat people know this. Fat people have plenty of room. Fat people will take you in.

Post-reading Questions

Content

1. What is the point of this essay? Upon what do you base your conclusions?
2. Why does Britt compare thin people with fat people?
3. With what group of people does Britt identify? How do you know for sure?
4. Who offer better companionship, thin people or fat people? Why? Consider the characteristics of each—according to Britt—when answering this question.
5. According to Britt, fat people tend to be quite knowledgeable and philosophic. What representative examples does she use to illustrate these qualities?

Strategies and Structures

1. What is the tone or mood of Britt's essay, and what is the function of its humor?
2. Explain the effect of opening several consecutive paragraphs with the same phrase.
3. What impact do Britt's generalizations have on her essay as a whole? Why does she dwell on extreme notions of thin and fat? How do we know she is not being mean spirited?
4. How could such liberal use of generalizations be deadly in the hands of an inexperienced writer? Do generalizations undermine the quality of Britt's essay? Justify your opinion.
5. Why does Britt focus on contrasts—differences— rather than mention things that thin and fat people have in common?

Language and Vocabulary

1. Vocabulary: *metabolisms, wizened, nebulous, cerebral, rutabagas, prognose, gab, guffaw, galumph, gyrate.* Write down a synonym—a word that has the same (or nearly the same) meaning as

another word—for as many of the vocabulary words as you can. When you are finished or cannot think of any more words, find a synonym for the unknown words by asking your classmates; likewise, share your work with others.

2. When Britt writes about people, attitudes, or behavior patterns that are opposite in nature, she often reinforces this sense of opposition through her word choice. Go back over the essay and make a list of words she associates with thin and words she associates with fat.

Group Activities

1. In small groups, get a copy of Shakespeare's *Julius Caesar* and read Act I, Scene ii, where Caesar mentions the "lean and hungry look." To whom is he referring? Why? Next, assess why Britt would chose to allude to Shakespeare and the "lean and hungry look" in her essay title. What does her allusion add or announce to readers familiar with the reference? Write a short, collaborative explanation for your conclusions and share it with other groups. To what extent did everyone tend to reach similar insights and at what point—if any—did insights differ?
2. For a group project, locate a copy of one of Britt's best-known essays such as "Love and Hate" or "Neat People vs. Sloppy People." Compare the techniques she employs in that essay when contrasting oppositions (love and hate, neat and sloppy) with those used when she contrasts thin and fat people in "That Lean and Hungry Look." What patterns exist in her writing style? How are they identifiable?

Writing Activities

1. Using a mixture of humor and seriousness similar to Britt's, write an essay comparing and contrasting two people, places, or things to demonstrate the stupidity and/or reliability of stereotypes.
2. Write an essay in which you try to rigidly categorize two types of people (e.g., young/old, rich/poor, coordinated/awkward) and thereby illustrate a controlling idea or thesis on the nature of stereotypes. Again, your primary method of essay development will be comparison and contrast.

Internet Connection: **Suzanne Britt**

Irony

Consult a research engine to locate various definitions of irony. Make a list of different kinds of irony you find, including an example of each. Next return to Britt's essay and identify the numerous instances of irony throughout. Finally, write an essay analyzing the content of Britt's essay, considering how using irony enables her to subtlety project her attitude towards her subject—particularly the absurdity of stereotyping anyone or anything. Document your source materials for readers who may want to read more about types of irony. (Consult the Appendix for the MLA documentation format.)

Cobie Kwasi Harris

River of Memory: The Ebb and Flow of Black Consciousness Across the Americas

Cobie Kwasi Harris, Associate Professor of Political Science, San Jose State University, San Jose, California, is an editor and author of one of the essays for *Readings in Black Political Economy*, published in 1999. Formerly, he lived and taught in Africa for three years. Currently, Harris hosts several radio programs on station KPFA, Berkeley, California, as well as a weekly program for three years at the same station, sponsored by Pacific News Service. Additionally, Harris has written several articles on civil and military relations in Africa, and is a noted lecturer and speaker on democratization in Africa and race relations in the United States. Harris continues to teach, write, and speak on issues pertaining to "Black Consciousness Across the Americas."

Pre-reading Questions

1. What does it mean to be enslaved? What do you think dignity means to enslaved people?
2. Get into groups of two or three and discuss how hope can spring from terrible circumstances. Write your responses in a journal entry.

Defir a la Force
(Defiance to Violence)

You who stop, you who weep,
You who one day die without knowing why,
You who fight, who watch while Another sleeps,
You who no longer laugh with your eyes,
You, my brother, full of fear and anguish,
Raise yourself and cry No!

—*David Diop*

1 One of the most compelling stories of the modern period is the inability of slave masters to crush the Black spirit to be free. It is also how African peoples kept afire the embers of liberty and dignity while enduring the terrors of slavery. The indomitable spirit of Black people has led them to continue to struggle for freedom, despite enduring unspeakable crimes, such as the raping of their mothers, the selling of their children like potatoes, or the killing of their fathers in front of them, and endless other humiliations. It is the mystery of this spirit of resistance against all odds that makes the Black liberation struggle for honor and justice one of the defining activities of modern times.

2 The struggle began in Africa when Europeans tried to extract humanity from the indigenous people, in hope of creating a human animal devoid of reason and spirit. They then objectified Africans' status by calling them chattel. In so doing, Europeans were able to steal African lands by enslaving the people who lived on them. The struggle of African people in their quest for freedom is best represented by the metaphor of a river because rivers twist and turn, and when a river's path is blocked, it finds another way to flow. Religion, rebellion, and arts and culture, which slaves encoded as a way to keep the flames of independence and honor alive, will help relate the story.

3 Just as African people were regarded as inferiors, so too were their religions. Their slave masters insisted that they adopt Christianity instead of keeping their African beliefs. The main difference between the

African and European/Semitic idea of God is the role of Spirits in the world. In the African tradition, it is commonly believed that Spirits exist between God and human beings. There are essentially five Spirits: Nature and Human Spirits are the major ones. Nature Spirits are divided into two parts: sky and earth. Human Spirits also are divided into two parts: long-deceased (ancestors) and the recently deceased (living dead). These forces, which may be described as "Divinities" or "Deities," serve as a bridge connecting living and deceased members of a family and community. They also connect the living to the inanimate spheres, and animate spheres to humanity.

4 The preceding brief description illustrates how different African religious thought is from the stereotypes slave traders used to justify enslaving the Africans. What is important is that Africans, in turn, used European religious stereotypes as a cover to practice their own religions. The Europeans believed that Africans had no notion of a transcendental God and only prayed to rocks, trees, and rivers. This belief allowed the slaves to preserve their religious traditions and practices, which came to be known as Candomble in Brazil, Santeria in Cuba, and Voodoo in Haiti. Another tradition that facilitated the fusion of African religious practice was the use of ancestor worship. Catholics make pilgrimages to places where earlier Church leaders lived and died, they pray for their patron saint to intervene in their lives, and they ask saints to bless their animals and crops. They also have a ritualistic blood sacrifice every communion where they symbolically eat the body and drink the blood of Jesus as a way to obtain everlasting life. Of course, the role of the saints in the Catholic Church is the role that ancestors play in African religion. Hence, slaves were able to preserve their dignity in South and Central America and the Caribbean because they were able to fuse their belief structure with that of European Christianity.

5 The preservation and integrity of the African religious system directly led to revolt throughout the Americas. In short, there is a direct correlation between the retention of African religion and culture, and insurrection. Haiti, which developed Voodoo, the most overt and institutional system in the Americas, was the scene of the only slave revolt in recorded history that successfully overthrew slavery. As a result, in the eighteenth century Haiti became the first free republic in the world, but revolts by African people also occurred throughout the modern slave world. In the case of slaves in the U.S., although they revolted, they did not have any of the major results that occurred throughout the rest of the modern slave world. This was due to the fact that they retained the least amount of their African religion.

6 This tragedy occurred for several reasons: The U.S. was a latecomer to plantation agriculture, and the mining of gold and silver was not as

extensive as it was in Latin America. Perhaps the most important reason was that the U.S. did not have a constant influx of new Africans because Britain began prohibiting ships on the high seas, and laws were passed in the U.S. to stop the importing of slaves. Hence the U.S. slave owners were forced to breed slaves as they did horses and cows. This, in turn, meant that every succeeding generation of slaves bred in America would have less and less of the African material culture, such as rituals, cosmologies, secret societies, and naming ceremonies.

7 Even though the U.S.'s enslaved Africans did not retain as many memories as those in other parts of the Americas, they still retained enough to incorporate the African call-and-response tradition into their Christianity. Slaves in the U.S. immediately began to identify more with the Old Testament than the New because in the Old Testament is the story of the liberation of an enslaved people from Egypt and the wicked Pharaoh. For enslaved Blacks, the U.S. was Egypt, and the slave master was the contemporary Pharaoh. The greatest slave revolt in the U.S. was led by Nat Turner, a self-taught minister who stated that he had visions similar to those that Moses had. Both had visions that prophesized death as a just punishment against a land and its people that had held others in bondage. Whereas Moses served as God's messenger to inform the Pharaoh that his God would kill all Egyptian first-born sons, Nat Turner claimed that God told him to act as the Angel of Death himself and to kill each white man, woman, and child. Moses, of course, is considered a hero who liberated his people by warning them how to avoid being slaughtered. In contrast, people judged Turner insane, tortured, and lynched him. As a result of that incidence, the river of African consciousness was diverted and slowed in the U.S., but it never stopped.

8 One of the best examples of how Africans combined their beliefs with those of Western religions is seen in the name of one of the first Black churches in the U.S., the African Methodist Episcopalian Church. The Black church essentially was the only place that slaves could gather collectively without disturbing their masters and their families. This church space and places in wooded areas and swamps were named "hush spaces" where slaves could nurture the desire for freedom and justice. They also were places where slaves would meet to determine who could be trusted to travel on the Underground Railroad to gain their independence. The indomitable spirit that enslaved Africans had for liberty and equality would flow in those "hush spaces."

9 Another major dimension that nurtured and cultivated the spirit of Black resistance against becoming the imagined stereotype of the slave master was brought about through the arts, such as: sculpture/painting, textiles, dance, singing/dancing, drumming, and story telling.

Fortunately for the slaves, the slave masters were blinded by their belief that they were the superior race and that the Africans were devoid of the consciousness that would allow them to create art. Ironically, the masters' belief in their own supremacy provided a "hush space" right under their eyes, which allowed the slaves to maintain the embers of freedom and justice and keep them aglow in their souls.

10 The arts and religion took shape because they were fused together in traditional African beliefs and served as an incubator that prevented the slave master from destroying the cultural memory of Africa. In African religion and art, dance, music, and story telling are indispensable parts of ritual and practice. Masks and sculptures are designed in ways to show the elemental forces of good and evil. Other dimensions of life are evident in uses of the body. For example, white is the color of mourning in some African religions; therefore, if people cover their bodies with white chalk, it is a sign of grief. Music was also a powerful means of communication for the scattered villages within a region. The drum was especially effective since it was used like a telephone. In fact, in New Orleans, in an area of the city called "Conga Square," a traitor informed the masters to stop slaves from playing drums since they were using them to mobilize people for a slave revolt. The drums also kept the Black consciousness flowing.

11 The first recorded revolt of an enslaved African occurred in 1502 on the island of Hispaniola when an escaped slave joined the indigenous people's rebellion against the Spanish. It still continues today—five hundred years later. There also were revolts in Santa Domingo, Mexico, Puerto Rico, Cuba, Venezuela, Honduras, and Colombia. In Colombia and Cuba, the liberated villages were called Palenques, and in Venezuela they were known as Cumbes. In the U.S., a significant contribution of the slaves was to join the Underground Railroad and flee to Canada. Perhaps their greatest contribution to their liberation struggle, however, was when they stopped working and producing food to support the Confederate Army. Instead, they joined Sherman's march to the sea, seized territory and developed communities that were self-sustaining.

12 The failure of slavery to actually transform Black people into beasts of burden without souls or minds serves as a torchlight for all those who suffer. Further, the Europeans' unsuccessful attempt to crush Black's consciousness and their driving spirit for liberty and dignity demonstrates that anyone and everyone can say "no" to the oppressor. Any individual can choose to submit to domination or can resist by saying "no!" Black people never have accepted the ideal that the slave master has always hoped that they would—a docile and happy slave.

Post-reading Questions

Content

1. What metaphor does Harris use to express "the struggle of African people in their quest for freedom"? How and why does the metaphor capture the spirit of the paper?
2. According to Harris what is "one of the best examples of how Africans combined their beliefs with those of western religions"?
3. Explain what Harris describes as a "hush space." How did this "hush space" allow Africans to cultivate and nurture indigenous art forms?
4. What is the "main difference between the African and European/ Semitic idea of God . . ."? How did the African slaves devise a cover "to practice their own religions"?
5. Where did the first revolt of an enslaved African occur according to Harris? What followed and continues today?

Strategies and Structures

1. What does Harris achieve through his analogy between the visions of Nat Turner and Moses?
2. How does Harris' introductory paragraph lead to the thesis "It is the mystery of this spirit of resistance against all odds that makes the Black liberation struggle for honor and justice one of the defining activities of modern times"?
3. What was a drum comparable to? Why did some slave masters stop their slaves from playing drums?
4. Why is the rhetorical mode of comparison and contrast the most effective method that Harris could employ to develop his essay?
5. How does the quote at the beginning of Harris' essay anticipate or foreshadow the concluding paragraph?

Language and Vocabulary

1. Vocabulary: *dignity, indomitable, indigenous, devoid, objectify, chattel, Semitic, inanimate, transcendental, facilitated, fusion, patron, intervene, dimension, cultivated, liberation.* After reviewing the definitions of each vocabulary word, determine which words have negative or positive connotations. How did selection of words carrying connotative meanings add depth to Harris' discussion?
2. Look for any words that deal with enslavement in this essay. First write a paragraph using these words. Next look up the antonyms (opposite meanings) in a thesaurus and write a contrasting paragraph dealing with the opposite of enslavement.

Group Activities

1. Go to the library or an electronic classroom and look up the word slavery. Then locate three to five incidents in history where men have enslaved fellow human beings. What were the justifications? Did the slaves rebel or give in to oppression? As slaves, how were men and women treated differently? In the twenty-first century are we still in the business of slavery, perhaps skillfully cloaked by politicians as legal, ethical behavior? Share your findings and take notes for a subsequent writing assignment.
2. Divide the class into two diverse groups and prepare for a debate. One side will favor the use of slavery and the benefits derived from it, and the other, of course, will take the opposite point of view, being in favor of permanently abolishing slavery.

Writing Activities

1. Return to the information collected in Group Activity 1, and write an essay in which you compare and/or contrast the methods that two of the societies you investigated used to enslave people, stating the reasons each group used to justify the treatment of these people.
2. Again referring to the information collected in Group Activity 1, compare and/or contrast how separate enslaved peoples reacted to bondage. What happened when the slaves rebelled? Did they gain freedom or were they imprisoned? Also what happened to the slaves who gave into repression? How long were they enslaved, and how did they gain their freedom? Finally, how did each oppressor treat men and women?

Additional Topics and Issues for Comparison and Contrast Essays

1. Compare and contrast two very different magazines such as *Time* and *U.S. News & World Report,* the *New Republic* and *Mother Jones*, *People* and *US;* compare their similarities and discuss their different characteristics (e.g., the sort of ads, number of pictures, and choice of subjects).

How does the intended audience for each magazine determine its characteristics?

2. Using the strategy of comparison and contrast, develop an essay in which you argue that one car, sport, movie star, sports hero (or team) is better than another.
3. Compare and contrast the most popular social activities in your parents' or grandparents' day to the most popular social activities of today.
4. Compare two places that you have visited (e.g., countries, restaurants, parks).
5. Contrast two likely candidates for public office in an upcoming election. Consider their qualifications for the office they seek. A variation of this assignment would be to compare dirty campaign tactics (which often ignore issues of public concern) to dignified ones.
6. Compare two characters in a novel, short story, or play you have read, or two people in a television show or movie you have seen.
7. Compare and contrast stereotypes between two cultures or between males and females for an ultimate purpose, determined by your thesis statement.
8. Write an essay in which you contrast the portrayal of a particular ethnic group on television and/or movies with your knowledge of and experiences with that particular ethnic group's culture.
9. Compare and contrast two sides of a current social issue in your community (e.g., banning smoking in all public areas). Your strategy of comparison and contrast should ultimately lead your reader to a sound conclusion.
10. Compare and contrast countercultures or subcultures (hip-hop/rappers, goths, skin-heads, surfers, hippies, beatniks, bikers, nudists, yuppies, flappers, slackers) in America from different eras. This topic may require a little bit of research, but most of your information can be gathered by talking to people who lived during different time periods.

CHAPTER 8 Division and Classification

When we divide and classify, we take a large and complicated subject and break it into smaller parts more easily handled by the writer and more easily grasped by the reader. Sometimes the smaller parts, or categories, are readily apparent, but at other times, we must carefully analyze our larger subject in order to discover how it breaks apart. As with other strategies, division and classification can be seen and used in everyday life. For instance, your college is more than likely divided into schools, divisions, and/or departments. You probably have a school of humanities, which contains an art department, an English department, a philosophy department, and a speech and communications department.

When we write, we divide and classify in order to make a subject clear to the reader. We may hope that by clarifying an issue or subject like racism, as Martin Luther King, Jr., does in his essay, "The Ways of Meeting Oppression," our reader will be motivated to take some sort of action. Other times, a writer might choose to discuss a large, contestable issue by examining it in smaller parts, such Roohi Vora did in her essay, "Armchair Pharmacologists and the Media." By dividing and classifying the topic of pharmaceutical drugs, she subdivides them so she can take an in-depth look at what advertisers claim and show how they encourage people to "self-diagnose" themselves and then seek a doctor's prescription for them—downplaying any potential health hazards. Vora's background in medicine makes her *"appalled at the advertisers for adopting such callous behavior in presenting a drug to the viewers who can easily be labeled armchair pharmacologists."* Moreover, *"the average viewer cannot make a sound judgment about the efficacy of a drug/medicine based on the insufficient information provided, yet it is very common to find these ads displayed everywhere.*" For whatever reason we divide and classify a subject—as well as subdivide—we usually follow a few basic steps.

When we start to divide and classify a subject, we need to clearly divide it into recognizable parts. We should analyze our subject from several points of view until we feel that we have found the clearest and most appropriate categories in which to break it. Obviously, Robertson Davies in his essay "A Few Kind Words for Superstition" carefully considered the many forms of superstition found in his community before he divided it into four forms: Vain Observances, Divination, Idolatry, and Improper Worship of a True God. Still another example of division and classification would be David Bodanis' "What's in Your Toothpaste?" Therein, David Bodanis divides and classifies the ingredients of an average tube of toothpaste and discusses how it is *not* a harmless consumer product that promotes healthy oral hygiene but a corrosive—even toxic—combination of chalk, water, paint, seaweed, antifreeze, paraffin oil, detergent, peppermint, formaldehyde, and fluoride.

After you have carefully analyzed your subject and divided it into parts, it may help to create a rough outline or some other form of notes to help guide you as you write. A rough set of notes for Constance García-Barrio's essay "Creatures That Haunt the Americas" might look like this:

I. Creatures from Africa that stalk children
   - Hairy Man
   - Guije
   - Tunda
   - Deformed woman

II. Creatures from Africa that haunt adults
   - Ciguapa
   - Lobisón
   - The ghost of the slave owner

At any time during the writing process, you should feel free to revise or delete certain parts of your outline, but as a general rule, a scratch outline will help to keep you from wandering off the subject and into less important or irrelevant points.

As in most of your essays, use clear transitions to help guide your reader. Simple transitions such as *first, second,* and *third* can be very helpful. Often, by simply keeping your points clearly separated (divided), you can write an essay that is easy to follow. What is an excellent film, and when do movies amount to little more than *mind candy?* Bill Swanson examines this topic and reveals some interesting answers—including the fact that *"filmmaking is both an art form and a business"*—by dividing and classifying films as well as film viewers. Though he claims, *"the effect a film has, though, has as much to do with the film viewer as the film itself,"* he also illustrates that *"the best films make for a cinematic diet that enhances the psychological sinews and synapses that are life sustaining."*

Once you have written a rough draft, you should go back over your essay and ask yourself if you have achieved your purpose. How do your categories and sub-categories help to achieve your original goal—possibly to persuade your audience into a certain action or to reveal a hidden truth about your subject? If a category does not ultimately contribute to your goal, you should delete it from your essay.

Tips on Writing Division and Classification Essays

1. Decide why you are classifying and dividing this subject. Keep this purpose in mind as you analyze your subject and compose your essay.
2. Carefully analyze your subject from many different points of view, looking for clear dividing lines.
3. Make some rough notes or an outline to help guide you during your writing. (Feel free to make alterations to your outline as necessary; it may be necessary to revise your outline several times.)
4. Use clear transitions to guide your reader and unify the parts of your essay.
5. Use controlling ideas and/or topic sentences to make your divisions clear. Then use specifics and details to help illustrate your divisions.
6. Carefully reread your rough draft, looking for inappropriate and irrelevant points or categorizations and eliminating them.

Roohi Vora

Armchair Pharmacologists and the Media

Roohi Vora clearly represents global learning at its best. An English Major at Evergreen Valley College, Vora received her Masters in English and Comparative Literature at San Jose State University and holds a BSc. (Bachelor in Science) and an M.B.B.S. (Bachelor in Medicine and Surgery) from Pakistan. A vibrant, active instructor and student club advisor, Vora currently serves as a lecturer at San Jose State University and at Evergreen Valley College and teaches critical thinking and all levels of composition. Keeping in mind the diverse backgrounds and varied learning styles of the student population, she fashions her courses to accommodate all her students by incorporating a number of activities that engage the students in a safe and conducive educational environment. Vora has become a familiar face at state and national conferences, presenting papers at the Young Rhetoricians' Conference (YRC) 2009 in Monterey and the English Council of California Two-Year Colleges (ECCTYCC) 2009 conference in Pasadena, to name a few. Additionally, Vora participates in writing workshops, attends seminars, and remains an active member of a local book group and Shakespeare group. During the spring semester 2010, Vora became the recipient of both the San Jose State University *"Lecturer of the Year Award 2009-2010"* and the *"Evergreen Valley College 2010 Distinguished Adjunct Faculty Member of the Year Award."* Vora's articles have appeared in numerous textbooks and journals, while her poetry and short stories have appeared in *Nota Bene*, *Leaf by Leaf*, and *Reed Magazine*, among others.

Pre-reading Questions

1. Have you or anyone you know been persuaded to ask your physician to prescribe one of the pharmaceutical drugs advertised on the internet, radio, or television; in magazines, journals; and even on billboards?
2. Freewrite with focus about three wonder drugs that would appeal to people for any number of reasons: vanity, ego, pride, wants, desires, and so on. How might advertisers market such

drugs? In your opinion, what would people be willing to risk to achieve the drugs' promised effects?

---

1 "Cymbalta is indicated for the treatment of depression. Ask your doctor if Cymbalta is right for you. Try Cymbalta for free." Just as the Yahoo! page flickers to life, our eyes are drawn to a compelling statement in an advertisement for Cymbalta (duloxetine HCl), Delayed Release Capsules. Captivated, we continue reading, marveling at the miracles of the wonder drug, Cymbalta, as they promise to dramatically unfold before our eyes, but voila! Our eyes search in vain. All that can be discovered on further research is Important Safety Information about Cymbalta, and small print that is filled with a list of complications that leave us with feelings of frustration and betrayal by the advertiser of the product. However, websites such as Yahoo! are just one aspect of media that advertisers use to draw unsuspecting audiences in to buying drugs they know either very little or nothing about.

2 Having a medical background, I am often appalled at the advertisers for adopting such callous behavior in presenting a drug to the viewers who can easily be labeled armchair pharmacologists. With limited (layman level) knowledge of the subject, the average viewer cannot make a sound judgment about the efficacy of a drug/medicine based on the insufficient information provided, yet it is very common to find these ads displayed everywhere.

3 So, what then are the different media choices that advertisers use to relay inadequate drug/medicine information to prospective buyers (consumers) that can be more harmful than helpful in the treatment of a condition? Rather than providing a cure, or offering an effective solution, these drug ads create more long-term problems for the consumer. Drug advertisements most commonly observed/heard by viewers appear on websites online, YouTube, television, radio, magazines, newspapers, and even billboards.

4 Cymbalta is an example of an ad shown continuously on Yahoo!, a popular website. It not only treats depression but also pain caused by complications of Diabetes or pain caused by Fibromyalgia. This medication may, however, interact with other medications with drastic results; one also needs to watch out for worsening depression or suicidal thoughts, and for feelings of agitation, anxiousness and panic to name a few. Driving may be hazardous and so on and so forth. As one reads about Cymbalta, the ad for Pristiq, another drug for treating depression pops up on the screen. Pristiq is approved for the treatment of major depressive orders in adults. One can observe that this statement is the only positive bit about this drug. Everything else listed in the ad are disclaimers such as: Patients should be watched for becoming agitated, irritable, hostile, aggravated, impulsive or restless, and that these

symptoms should be reported to the patient's health care professional right away. The ad ends with this ambivalent piece of knowledge: Please see full Prescribing Information, including boxed warning, and Medication Guide for patients. One is overwhelmed by the advertiser's insensitivity.

5 An example of a deceptive drug ad on YouTube would be the new Lipitor commercial. It clearly states that "Lipitor is FDA approved to reduce the risk of heart attack and stroke." However, all the other information is in small print. According to Dr. Shamima Abbas, a family physician at Kaiser Permenante (an integrated managed care organization), patients self diagnose and pressure the doctors to prescribe drugs that are not always suitable for them. She adds that patients asking for Lipitor do not realize the high risk of taking this medicine. Lipitor is a newer statin (a group of medications that reduce cholesterol), and there are many other less expensive statins approved prior to Lipitor (no generic is available for Lipitor) to treat high cholesterol levels. Hence, the ad provides only half the information. It gives the impression that this is the top drug to treat the condition—the ultimate solution to all problems.

6 To the contrary, according to Dr. Abbas, generics are available for statins other than Lipitor, and the criteria for prescribing medication to a patient is the achievement of the goal—treating patient condition effectively and making it cost effective at the same time. Patient tolerance is also important to the doctor in making this decision. If there are no side effects to the other statins already in use, why change? However, since many patients have become aware that physicians are authorized to prescribe a new drug, they manipulate their doctors into writing them the prescription of their choice! These patients are the online doctors for you!

7 Advisers also attract people's attention through magazines that range from fashion to sports. When asked to write an ad analysis essay based on Aristotle's rhetoric, some students from my English composition 1-A class selected drug ads from popular magazines to analyze devices of persuasion which, according to Aristotle, can be divided into three parts: appeal to audience's reason or logic (logos), appeals to its values or ethics (ethos), and appeals to its emotions (pathos). These students considered their chosen advertisement as an argument that tried to persuade its target audience to buy products by appealing to its values and fantasies.

8 One student, Jennifer, chose the ad on Vyvanase which began: "My son Michael needs ADHD [attention deficit hyperactivity disorder] symptom control throughout the day. Even at 8 pm. Our doctor prescribed Vyvanase." The image of Michael, who is diagnosed with ADHD, is clear and focused in contrast to the blurred background. Michael gazes directly into the camera and straight at the viewer to demonstrate how focused an ADHD patient can be after taking Vyvanase to the extent that the young patient is capable of doing well in school as hinted by the sharpened pencil placed straight and orderly in front of Michael's hand. The side effects of Vyvanase and cautions to check before taking the

drug are mentioned but are written in a smaller font and more bunched together to make them harder to read. In contrast, the parent's narrative appears underlined in colored, bold font.

9 According to Jennifer, the ad presents a problem many parents could very likely relate to or sympathize with and follow up with a solution in the form of the product in the ad supported by certified professionals and clinical research. The advertisers behind the promotion of Vyvanase wisely chose elements according to what would not so much appeal as attempt to fulfill he consumers' need for reassurance on the actions they can take to preserve the well being of a loved one. Jennifer is correct in her assessment, but unfortunately, what the viewer misses is the small print in the form of Important Safety Information such as: Vyvanase is a stimulant medicine. Abuse of stimulants may lead to dependence. Misuse of stimulants may cause sudden death.

10 In a similar manner, in its May issue of 2010, *Health* magazine, primarily designed for women, advertised HydroxyCut Advanced, a calorie-burning supplement that comes in caplets and also in powder form one can mix with a bottle of water. HydroxyCut Advanced is intended to boost one's metabolism and increase energy, and thereby burn calories. In the ad, a slender Caucasian woman with sandy blonde hair and a perfect golden tan poses in a pearly white sports bra and ocean blue workout pants. She holds a white beach ball in her hands and in the background is the image of a baby blue sky, a calm ocean, and a warm clean beach. To the left of this image, the product is advertised.

11 The HydroxyCut ad does not consist of images alone. The text in the ad is very promising as well: "America's #1 selling THERMOGENIC," appears at the very top inside a gold medal like outline. Right below the medal winning statement appears another encouraging comment: "Get the Best for your Body." The product comes in a red, purple, and white box, and showcases its name in the center. A reminder that the product boosts metabolism, burns calories and increases energy appears to the left of the box. However, one fails to look at the warnings such as: *Consult a medical doctor before use if you have been treated for, diagnosed with, or have a family history of any medical condition, or if you are using any prescription or over the counter drug, since one serving (2 caplets) of this product contain about as much caffeine as 2 cups of coffee. Caffeine sensitive individuals may experience symptoms including restlessness, nervousness, tremors, headaches, anxiety, palpitations, increased heart rate or difficulty sleeping.* Would one still want to try HydroxyCutAdvanced after having read this list of tiresome side effects?

12 Online websites, YouTube, and magazine ads are not the only means of attracting viewers. Advertisers have the ultimate solution up their sleeve—television! Watch the CNN news one evening and a flurry of advertisements will appear on the screen every ten minutes. After dinner, the perfect time to snare middle-aged women who relaxing in front

of their TV sets, the screen comes alive with a set of questions and a pleasant female voice asks: *Do you have: Noticeable wrinkles and fine lines? Skin damaged from sun or smoking? Lost radiant, youthful appearance?* If you answer "Yes" to any of these questions (a vibrant blue bottle appears)," the advertiser claims you need Hydroxatone AM PM. A phone number then flashes on the screen along with the line: "Exclusive trial offer," showing a woman with glowing skin in the background. The trick is that one has to call in the next five minutes to receive a mystery gift, offered only on TV. The ad further emphasizes that the gift bags for this product have been given to celebrities at the Emmy Awards.

13 This sales pitch often works, even though the small print indicates that this is a dramatization, and although Hydroxatone is "Dermatologist Recommended," it has only undergone "Independent Clinical Study," and results may wary. As one can gauge, the urgency in the ad does not give the viewer time to research the product, and many often end up buying it—after all, it is only a phone call away! Ignorance, when voluntary, is criminal, notes Samuel Johnson. The advertiser has won, ending the sound byte by encouraging the viewer to take quick action!

14 Overall, Armchair Pharmacologists are akin to Armchair Quarterbacks who often sit in front of their television sets and criticize what quarter backs do as if they were experts, even though they do not know the first thing about effectively running a football team but have all the advice in the world. People who watch drug ads online, on TV, and on YouTube become online doctors diagnosing themselves and prescribing their own medication without having the knowledge and background. The advertisers will often create a need for a certain drug and then offer words of caution. It is hard to determine the ethos in these ads; however, as Samuel Johnson would say: "Knowledge is of two kinds. We know a subject ourselves, or we know where we can find information about it," thus the consumers or the viewers can take charge of the situation by becoming more aware of their options and making intelligent choices based on research—may it be in response to an online [article], YouTube, magazine, or television advertisement. In Nietzsche's words, it's "Better know nothing than half know many things."

Post-reading Questions

Content

1. Explain how the new Lipitor ad exemplifies a deceptive drug commercial.
2. According to Dr. Shamima Abbas, what do her patients request on a more frequent basis all the time?
3. Advertisers tend to be rather successful in convincing people that they will benefit from a product—whether they actually

need it or not. What typical information do people tend to overlook? Offer some specific examples drawn from Vora's essay.

4. In what ways are "armchair pharmacologists" and "armchair quarterbacks" very much alike? To what extent do they differ?
5. Why might it be "better to know nothing than half know many things" when it comes to the pharmaceutical drugs advertised through popular media?

Strategies and Structures

1. Analyze how Vora's essay title, "Armchair Pharmacologists and the Media," immediately attracts her readers' attention and alerts them to her discussion topic.
2. Why does Vora mention the fact that she has a background in medicine in her second paragraph? What does this establish?
3. How does Vora divide and classify media promoting popular use of pharmaceutical drugs?
4. In what way do transitions and linking devices create clear connections between words, clauses, phrases, and entire paragraphs in this essay?
5. Discuss some of the strategies and techniques advertisers use to lure middle-aged women into requesting a particular medication from their doctors.

Language and Vocabulary

1. Vocabulary: *pharmacologist, compelling, captivated, appalled, callous, layman, inadequate, prospective, diabetes, fibromyalgia, disclaimers, agitated, aggravated, impulsive, symptoms, ambivalent, overwhelmed, deceptive, Kaiser Permeante, diagnose, cholesterol, generic, tolerance, manipulate, rhetoric, deficit, hyperactivity, reassurance, assessment, calorie, supplement, caplets, metabolism, thermogenic, tremors, palpitations, akin.* Select five to ten words from the vocabulary list for Vora's essay and use them to write an original paragraph about positive and/or negative health issues.
2. Apart from modifying words, Vora uses several medical terms and biological references throughout her essay. Make a list of at least six of them and discuss the denotative (dictionary) and connotative (associated meanings) for each word. How does Vora's use of medical references add depth and substance to her claims?

Group Activities

1. In small groups, go to the library or use classroom (or personal) Internet connections to locate some ads for real pharmaceutical drugs as well as parodies of them on YouTube. How are details in actual commercials and parodies of them a lot alike? To what extent do they differ? Be prepared to

discuss your observations with and possibly make visual presentations of your findings to the rest of the class.

2. Review the section on *irony* in the introductory notes to Chapter 7: Comparison and Contrast; then, gather in small groups and invent an imaginary drug (smart medication, peace medication, personality medication, etc.) that would attract users, and write a sentence or so about it. Following your medication's description, write an ironic warning that explains potential side effects of your group's imaginary medication.

Writing Activities

1. After pre-writing about the benefits and dangers of pharmaceutical drugs, devise a controlling idea about them. Next, write an essay wherein you develop your thesis by dividing, classifying, subdividing, and analyzing your own list of three or four common pharmaceutical ads—excluding those already mentioned by Vora—as seen on TV, the Internet, and so on.
2. Compose an essay where you prove or disprove Samuel Johnson's idea that the consequences of voluntary ignorance is criminal—particularly when it comes to exposing oneself to the dangers of "self-diagnosis" and demand for "prescription drugs." Feel free to refer to the classification and division of information cited in Vora's essay; however, the primary evidence used to support your thesis should come from other sources such as personal experience, observations of others (including advertisers on television and the Internet), and readings.

Martin Luther King, Jr.

The Ways of Meeting Oppression

Martin Luther King, Jr., a Baptist minister and civil rights leader during the 1950s and 1960s, preached nonviolence when advocating civil disobedience and sought to end segregation. His writings include *Stride Toward Freedom* (1958) and the highly anthologized "Letter from the Birmingham Jail." On August 28, 1963, King led over 200,000 black and white people to the Lincoln Memorial in Washington, D.C. There he delivered his renowned speech, "I Have a Dream," during the centennial of Abraham Lincoln's Emancipation Proclamation, which freed the slaves in the United States. In 1964, at the age of 35, King became the youngest person ever to receive the Nobel Peace Prize. Four years later, on April 4, 1968, he was assassinated in Memphis, Tennessee.

Pre-reading Questions

1. What is oppression? What freedoms does an oppressor deny another person?
2. Have you ever been oppressed? What did you do to try and change the situation you were in? Was your method of overcoming oppression successful? If so, how?

---

1 Oppressed people deal with their oppression in three characteristic ways. One way is acquiescence: the oppressed resign themselves to their doom. They tacitly adjust themselves to oppression, and thereby become conditioned to it. In every movement toward freedom some of the oppressed prefer to remain oppressed. Almost 2800 years ago Moses set out to lead the children of Israel from the slavery of Egypt to the freedom of the Promised Land. He soon discovered that slaves do not always welcome their deliverers. They become accustomed to being slaves. They would rather bear those ills they have, as Shakespeare pointed out, than flee to others that they know not of. They prefer the "fleshpots of Egypt" to the ordeals of emancipation.

2 There is such a thing as the freedom of exhaustion. Some people are so worn down by the yoke of oppression that they give up. A few years ago in the slum areas of Atlanta, a Negro guitarist used to sing almost daily: "Been down so long that down don't bother me." This is the type of negative freedom and resignation that often engulfs the life of the oppressed.

3 But this is not the way out. To accept passively an unjust system is to cooperate with that system; thereby the oppressed become as evil as the oppressor. Noncooperation with evil is as much a moral obligation as is cooperation with good. The oppressed must never allow the conscience of the oppressor to slumber. Religion reminds every man that he is his brother's keeper. To accept injustice or segregation passively is to say to the oppressor that his actions are morally right. It is a way of allowing his conscience to fall asleep. At this moment the oppressed fails to be his brother's keeper. So acquiescence—while often the easier

way—is not the moral way. It is the way of the coward. The Negro cannot win the respect of his oppressor by acquiescing; he merely increases the oppressor's arrogance and contempt. Acquiescence is interpreted as proof of the Negro's inferiority. The Negro cannot win the respect of the white people of the South or the peoples of the world if he is willing to sell the future of his children for his personal and immediate comfort and safety.

4 A second way that oppressed people sometimes deal with oppression is to resort to physical violence and corroding hatred. Violence often brings about momentary results. Nations have frequently won their independence in battle. But in spite of temporary victories, violence never brings permanent peace. It solves no social problem; it merely creates new and more complicated ones.

5 Violence as a way of achieving racial justice is both impractical and immoral. It is impractical because it is a descending spiral ending in destruction for all. The old law of an eye for an eye leaves everybody blind. It is immoral because it seeks to humiliate the opponent rather than win his understanding; it seeks to annihilate rather than to convert. Violence is immoral because it thrives on hatred rather than love. It destroys community and makes brotherhood impossible. It leaves society in monologue rather than dialogue. Violence ends by defeating itself. It creates bitterness in the survivors and brutality in the destroyers. A voice echoes through time saying to every potential Peter, "Put up your sword." History is cluttered with the wreckage of nations that failed to follow this command.

6 If the American Negro and other victims of oppression succumb to the temptation of using violence in the struggle for freedom, future generations will be the recipients of a desolate night of bitterness, and our chief legacy to them will be an endless reign of meaningless chaos. Violence is not the way.

7 The third way open to oppressed people in their quest for freedom is the way of nonviolent resistance. Like the synthesis in Hegelian philosophy, the principle of nonviolent resistance seeks to reconcile the truths of two opposites—the acquiescence and violence—while avoiding the extremes and immoralities of both. The nonviolent resister agrees with the person who acquiesces that one should not be physically aggressive toward his opponent; but he balances the equation by agreeing with the person of violence that evil must be resisted. He avoids the nonresistance of the former and the violent resistance of the latter. With nonviolent resistance, no individual or group need submit to any wrong, nor need anyone resort to violence in order to right a wrong.

8 It seems to me that this is the method that must guide the actions of the Negro in the present crisis in race relations. Through nonviolent resistance the Negro will be able to rise to the noble height of opposing

the unjust system while loving the perpetrators of the system. The Negro must work passionately and unrelentingly for full stature as a citizen, but he must not use inferior methods to gain it. He must never come to terms with falsehood, malice, hate, or destruction.

9 Nonviolent resistance makes it possible for the Negro to remain in the South and struggle for his rights. The Negro's problem will not be solved by running away. He cannot listen to the glib suggestion of those who would urge him to migrate en masse to other sections of the country. By grasping his great opportunity in the South he can make a lasting contribution to the moral strength of the nation and set a sublime example of courage for generations yet unborn.

10 By nonviolent resistance, the Negro can also enlist all men of good will in his struggle for equality. The problem is not a purely racial one, with Negroes set against whites. In the end, it is not a struggle between people at all, but a tension between justice and injustice. Nonviolent resistance is not aimed against oppressors but against oppression. Under its banner consciences, not racial groups, are enlisted.

Post-reading Questions

Content

1. What are the three ways "oppressed people deal with their oppression"?
2. Why, according to King, do some people prefer to remain oppressed? How do such people undermine the quest for equality and reinforce injustice?
3. Explain why King says that "violence as a way of achieving racial justice is both impractical and immoral."
4. Discuss the advantages of nonviolent resistance over both acquiescence and violence to cause change. How does King argue this point?

Strategies and Structures

1. In what way does King strategically use historical instances of oppressed people to illustrate each of the three ways of dealing with oppression?
2. How does King's division/classification of material help a reader to read, comprehend, and evaluate the merit of each type of resistance to oppression?
3. King presents the three ways of dealing with oppression (acquiescence, violence, and nonviolence) in a particular order. What would have happened if he had reversed or mixed this present sequence of material? What does your conclusion point out about the importance of organizing the parts of an essay?

Language and Vocabulary

1. Vocabulary: *acquiescence, tacitly, corroding, annihilate, desolate, synthesis, sublime.* Denotation is the dictionary definition of a word; connotations are the associated meanings of the word (see the Glossary). Reread through the first two ways of dealing with oppression, acquiescence, and violence—noting King's choice of vocabulary. Make a list of the words you encounter that have negative connotations (e.g., acquiescence suggests giving in, laziness). Then read through the last part of King's essay where he discusses nonviolence (peaceful resistance), making a list of words that have positive connotations. Overall, how does King use "connotations" to win his readers over to his point of view?
2. Several times in his essay, King refers to African Americans as Negroes. How do such references and similar references in other compositions indicate the time period when the work was written? Why might knowledge of when something was written be of interest to a reader?

Group Activities

1. Divide into three groups, review all content and strategy questions, and then study one way King mentions of resisting oppression in greater detail. Each group will be responsible for a different strategy for overcoming oppression. Your group will ultimately *teach* the rest of the class the section of King's essay dealing with the type of resistance you studied.
2. Go to your learning resource center on campus and locate some recordings or videotapes of King. In particular, search for his famous "I Have a Dream" speech. (After listening to his speech, you may also want to get a copy of it from the library and read it.) Discuss the impact King's speech had on group members and then reevaluate each of the ways of fighting oppression in view of his ultimate goal.

Writing Activities

1. Write an essay wherein you classify and divide one of the following topics in order to explain it: ways of making friends, ways of reacting to aggressive people, ways of influencing people with the language that you use (e.g., big or dirty words), or ways of dealing with fame, racism, or sexism.

2. Leaving the method you agree with until last, write an essay explaining the ways people deal with *stress* or *depression*. (King structured his discussion of nonviolence this way when he wrote about ways to overcome oppression.)

***Internet Connection:* Martin Luther King, Jr.**

Passive Resistance

Enter the keywords "passive resistance" into an internet research engine of your choice. Select a couple of articles that discuss how passive resistance has been used historically—and/or recently—to bring social justice and unethical practices to the attention of mainstream society. Referring to King's essay and the materials your researched, write an expository essay explaining how and why "passive resistance" is still a great vehicle for social change. Cite your sources using parenthetical references explained in the Appendix of *Visions Across the Americas*, 8th edition. Also, place a list of *works cited* at the end of your composition.

Robertson Davies

A Few Kind Words for Superstition

A novelist, playwright, and scholar, Robertson Davies (1913–1995) remains one of Canada's best-known authors. Davis wrote more than two dozen books, including *Fifth Business* (1970), *The Manticore* (1972), *World of Wonders* (1975), *The Rebel Angels* (1983), *What's Bred in the Bone* (1985), *The Lyre of Orpheus* (1989), *Voice from the Attic: Essays on the Art of Reading* (1990), *Murther and Walking Spirits* (1991), *Reading and Writing* (1993), *The Cunning Man* (1996), *The Merry Heart: Reflections on Reading, Writing, and the World of Books* (1998), and *High Spirits: A Collection of Ghost Stories* (2002).

Pre-reading Questions

1. What is a superstitious person? Do you consider yourself superstitious? Why or why not?
2. If superstition is folly, why don't most business buildings have a 13th floor indicated on the elevator panel? Why don't airplanes have a row 13?
3. What part does superstition play in your daily life? What cultural roots lie behind your superstitions?

---

1 In grave discussions of "the renaissance of the irrational" in our time, superstition does not figure largely as a serious challenge to reason or science. Parapsychology, UFOs, miracle cures, transcendental meditation, and all the paths to instant enlightenment are condemned, but superstition is merely deplored. Is it because it has an unacknowledged hold on so many of us?

2 Few people will admit to being superstitious; it implies naiveté or ignorance. But I live in the middle of a large university, and I see superstition in its four manifestations, alive and flourishing among people who are indisputably rational and learned.

3 You did not know that superstition takes four forms? Theologians assure us that it does. First is what they call Vain Observances, such as not walking under a ladder, and that kind of thing. Yet I saw a deeply learned professor of anthropology, who had spilled some salt, throwing a pinch of it over his left shoulder; when I asked him why, he replied, with a wink, that it was "to hit the Devil in the eye." I did not question him further about his belief in the Devil: But I noticed that he did not smile until I asked him what he was doing.

4 The second form is Divination, or consulting oracles. Another learned professor I know, who would scorn to settle a problem by tossing a coin (which is a humble appeal to Fate to declare itself), told me quite seriously that he has resolved a matter related to university affairs by consulting the *I Ching*. And why not? There are thousands of people on this continent who appeal to the *I Ching*, and their general level of education seems to absolve them of superstition. Almost, but not quite. The *I Ching*, to the embarrassment of rationalists, often gives excellent advice.

5 The third form is Idolatry, and universities can show plenty of that. If you have ever supervised a large examination room, you know how many jujus, lucky coins, and other bringers of luck are placed on the desks of the candidates. Modest idolatry, but what else can you call it?

6 The fourth form is Improper Worship of the True God. A while ago, I learned that every day, for several days, a $2 bill (in Canada we have

$2 bills, regarded by some people as unlucky) had been tucked under a candlestick on the altar of a college chapel. Investigation revealed that an engineering student, worried about a girl, thought that bribery of the Deity might help. When I talked with him, he did not think he was pricing God cheap because he could afford no more. A reasonable argument, but perhaps God was proud that week, for the scientific oracle went against him.

7 Superstition seems to run, a submerged river of crude religion, below the surface of human consciousness. It has done so for as long as we have any chronicle of human behavior, and although I cannot prove it, I doubt if it is more prevalent today than it has always been. Superstition, the theologians tell us, comes from the Latin *supersisto,* meaning to stand in terror of the Deity. Most people keep their terror within bounds, but they cannot root it out, nor do they seem to want to do so.

8 The more the teaching of formal religion declines, or takes a sociological form, the less God appears to great numbers of people as a God of Love, resuming his older form of a watchful, minatory power, to be placated and cajoled. Superstition makes its appearance, apparently unbidden, very early in life, when children fear that stepping on cracks in the sidewalk will bring ill fortune. It may persist even among the greatly learned and devout, as in the case of Dr. Samuel Johnson, who felt it necessary to touch posts that he passed in the street. The psycho-analysts have their explanation, but calling a superstition a compulsion neurosis does not banish it.

9 Many superstitions are so widespread and so old that they must have risen from a depth of the human mind that is indifferent to race or creed. Orthodox Jews place a charm on their doorposts; so do (or did) the Chinese. Some peoples of Middle Europe believe that when a man sneezes, his soul, for that moment, is absent from his body, and they hasten to bless him, lest the soul be seized by the Devil. How did the Melanesians come by the same idea? Superstition seems to have a link with some body of belief that far antedates the religions we know—religions which have no place for such comforting little ceremonies and charities.

10 People who like disagreeable historical ceremonies recall that when Rome was in decline, superstition proliferated wildly, and that something of the same sort is happening in our Western world today. They point to the popularity of astrology, and it is true that sober newspapers that would scorn to deal in love philters carry astrology columns and the fashion magazines count them among their most popular features. But when has astrology not been popular? No use saying science discredits it. When has the heart of man given a damn for science?

11 Superstition in general is linked to man's yearning to know his fate, and to have some hand in deciding it. When my mother was a child,

she innocently joined her Roman Catholic friends in killing spiders on July 11, until she learned that this was done to ensure heavy rain the day following, the anniversary of the Battle of Boyne, when the Orangemen would hold their parade. I knew an Italian, a good scientist, who watched every morning before leaving his house, so that the first person he met would not be a priest or a nun, as this would certainly bring bad luck.

12 I am not one to stand aloof from the rest of humanity in this matter, for when I was a university student, a gypsy woman with a child in her arms used to appear every year at examination time, and ask a shilling of anyone who touched the Lucky Baby; that swarthy infant cost me four shillings altogether, and I never failed an examination. Of course, I did it merely for the joke—or so I thought then. Now, I am humbler.

Post-reading Questions

Content

1. Explain the ultimate point of Davies' essay. Where does he stand on the topic of superstition?
2. Why is "Vain Observances" an appropriate title for the author's first category of superstition? Name a few examples of "Vain Observances" that you can remember from your childhood.
3. In your experience, as well as according to Davies, why will few people admit it if they are superstitious? With what is superstition generally associated?
4. How might referring to the *I Ching* (a Chinese book offering general advice on how to act) be similar to consulting an oracle?

Strategies and Structures

1. What kind of superstition do you think is most common? In what order does Davies divide and classify superstition? What does he talk about first? Second? Third? Fourth?
2. According to Davies, what are the four divisions of superstition? Can you think of any other division he might have made?
3. In the final paragraph, Davies mentions how, during examination week as a student, he spent a shilling to touch a gypsy lady's "Lucky Baby." Why?
4. Davies refers to the reaction of distinguished professors to exemplify the first two kinds of superstitions. Why might an example of professors acting superstitiously be more effective and thought provoking than farmers acting superstitiously?

Language and Vocabulary

1. Vocabulary: *minatory, placated, cajoled, antedates, proliferated, philter.* One of the ways to understand words and their

meanings better is to learn the origin of the word. Your dictionary is the first tool you should employ for this task. For instance, the word "expand," which means "to spread out or unfold," is listed as coming from Middle English "expanden," which comes from the Latin word *expandere: ex-*(out) + *pandere* (to spread.) Trace the origins of each of the above words and use each in a sentence. If you cannot find such explanations in your dictionary, use an etymological dictionary (one that traces the origin and historical development of a word), which can be found in your school library.

2. Make a list the words in your present vocabulary that begin with the prefix "super-". What common meaning do all of these words share? How do the words on your list change meaning if you eliminate the prefix?

Group Activities

1. Write down two superstitions that came to your mind while you were reading this essay. Now write down two other superstitions that have their roots in your cultural origins. Next, break into groups and share your various superstitions. Which were most common? Did you find that many superstitions were universal? How? Finally, write a short collaborative essay whose thesis is based on your group's findings.
2. Interview several people one-on-one and as a group; your questions should focus on what the people say they believe and how they behave. You might also ask the people you interview for a sample of the kind of superstitions they grew up with. Have everyone who claims that he or she does not believe in superstition give you a definition of the word. What percentage of the people you interviewed admitted they believed or reacted to some superstitions? Did group interviews differ significantly from one-on-one interviews? How? Why?

Writing Activities

1. Using some of the material gathered in Group Activity 2, write a thoroughly developed essay in which you divide and classify superstitions or folk beliefs.
2. Write an essay in which you defend the importance of superstition in American society. Make sure you cite several

specific superstitions (other than the ones mentioned by Davies) and show how their existence often influences our actions. You may want to consult an online list of superstitions, but be sure that you specifically relate any of the superstitions that you mention in your essay to your theses.

Constance García-Barrio

Creatures That Haunt the Americas

Constance García-Barrio, a native Philadelphian, has roots that reach back to Fredericksburg, Virginia, home of her great-grandmother, Rose Wilson Ware, or Maw, born into slavery about 1851. A widely published author, García-Barrio's articles have appeared in magazines and newspapers such as *Pennsylvania Magazine*, *The Christian Science Monitor*, *Essence*, and the *Philadelphia Inquirer*. She speaks English, Spanish, and Chinese and earned her doctorate in Romance languages. Currently, García-Barrio teaches at West Chester University, West Chester, Pennsylvania, and she continues to write.

Pre-reading Questions

1. Brainstorm the word *haunt*. What do you associate with the word? What is its dictionary definition?
2. Describe some of the scary creatures, ghosts, and/or monsters that are common in the stories of your culture? When did you hear about these creatures? What do they do that makes them frightening?
3. What kinds of creatures do you think García-Barrio will be describing in her essay?

---

1 When Africans were forced into slaving ships, the creatures, invisible, slipped in with them. A witch's brew of supernatural beings, these were

creatures remembered from stories from the homeland. When Africans reached the New World, the creatures stepped ashore with them.

2 The supernatural beings made their homes in the mountains, rivers, and forests of the Americas, wherever the Africans went. The Hairy Man, for example, has the run of Georgia's woods, according to a story told by a former slave from that state. The Hairy Man is a fat, ugly little man with more hair all over than hell has devilment. Tricky as he is hairy, he can shrink or swell at will. He's afraid of dogs and is most at home near rivers. The Hairy Man spends his time capturing careless children.

3 The guije seems to be a Caribbean cousin of the Hairy Man, the way the late Cuban centenarian Esteban Montejo tells it in *The Autobiography of a Runaway Slave*. The guijes, or jigues, are mischievous little black men who wear no clothes and live near rivers. Their heads are like a frog's. Black people have a natural tendency to see them, according to Montejo. Guijes pop out of the river to admire a señorita as she bathes, especially during Holy Week. The guijes are also known to carry off children.

4 The Tunda looms large in the folklore of Esmeraldas, a predominantly black province on the northern coast of Ecuador, notes Afro-Ecuadorian writer Adalberto Ortiz. Local legend has it that in the 1530s a ship whose cargo included twenty-three enslaved blacks was traveling from Panama to Peru. As it skirted Ecuador's northern coast, the ship struck a reef. In the confusion that followed, the blacks scrambled from the vessel, swam ashore, and fought with Indians occupying the land.

5 After one especially fierce battle, dying blacks and Indians moaned so much that the noise reached hell and disturbed the devil. He decided he'd have to exterminate both sides if he wanted peace and quiet. So the devil went to Esmeraldas disguised as an African prince, Macumba. But before he could carry out his plan, a lively, buxom Esmeraldeña caught his fancy. He married her and settled down, as much as the Devil can ever settle.

6 One of the creatures born from their union is the Tunda, a deformed black woman with huge lips and clubfoot. As a child of the devil, the Tunda can't have children, so she's taken to carrying off those of black folk in Esmeraldas. The Tunda can make herself look like a member of the potential victim's family. She lures people into the forest, then stuns them by breaking wind in their faces. After this they lose their will power and are easily led to her lair, usually a place in or near water.

7 Adalberto Ortiz mentioned that there are similarities between the Tunda, a character in Afro-Colombian stories and the Quimbungo from Bantu folklore.

8 If some creatures pursue black children, others stalk adults. The Afro-Dominican Ciguapa is a gorgeous but strange being who lives in the island's forests. She comes out at night to steal food but is never

caught since she escapes by jumping from tree to tree. Her beauty has won many hearts, but she uses her magic to destroy men. Wise to her ways, they try to avoid her. But she can fool them. The Ciguapa's feet are on backward, so they think she's going when she's coming.

9 Tales of the Lobisón, or Wolfman, made many an Afro- Uruguayan peasant cringe. Legend has it that every Friday night at midnight the seventh consecutive son in a family turns into an animal. This animal has a wolf's body and a misshapen pig's head. It commits acts too horrible to tell. It has great supernatural powers, and only by wounding the Lobisón and drawing its blood can it be made to return to human form.

10 The old and new worlds blend in the Lobisón legend. The story shows the influence of Bantu, European, and certain South American Indian cultures.

11 Some tales of the supernatural arose from historic events in which blacks took part. Such was the case with Spanish America's struggle for independence from Spain from 1810 to 1822. One Afro-Uruguayan story tells of a rich but miserly man who treated his slaves cruelly. Emancipated before the wars of independence, the newly freed blacks demanded money with which to start a new life. They knew their former master had gold nuggets hidden in the house. When he refused to give them anything, they killed him.

12 The money remained hidden after the murder until a platoon of black soldiers camped near the old house during the wars of independence. The location of the treasure was revealed to them by the ghost of a black who had remained with the master even after emancipation. The soldiers divided the cache, each receiving a nice sum. The ghost had waited years but finally saw that his black countrymen got the money.

13 Like the ghost who showed the soldiers the treasure, black folktales bring to light sometimes forgotten cultural treasures Africans brought to the Americas.

Post-reading Questions

Content

1. Where do the creatures described by García-Barrio originate? How did they get here?
2. García-Barrio describes the actions of these creatures. What are some actions or deeds common to them all? What do these common elements suggest about the creatures?
3. According to legend, why did the devil decide to exterminate the "blacks and Indians"? What happened to him on his way to exterminate them? What creature evolved as the end result of the devil's actions?

4. García-Barrio claims, "As a child of the devil, the Tunda can't have children . . . . " What characteristics do you associate with the devil and his offspring? How might these characteristics prevent them from having children?

Strategies and Structures

1. Identify the thesis of this essay. Is it stated directly or implied? What is the strategic purpose of the opening paragraph?
2. García-Barrio writes vivid descriptions of the different creatures that "haunt the Americas." What are some of the images she uses to create vivid physical descriptions? What is the purpose of these vivid descriptions?
3. Discuss how García-Barrio organizes her essay. What general categories do the different creatures fit into? Why might García-Barrio divide the essay in such a way?
4. What is the purpose of the last paragraph? Aside from summarizing the essay, what might be some of its other purposes?

Language and Vocabulary

1. Vocabulary: García-Barrio uses many unfamiliar geographical names: *Georgia's woods, Caribbean, Esmeraldas, Ecuador, Panama, Peru, Colombia, Uruguay.* Where are these different places located? What are the unique geographical characteristics of these regions? What makes them particularly suitable to tales about frightening creatures?
2. García-Barrio uses the prefix "Afro-" before many words: "Afro-Colombian," "Afro-Dominican," "Afro-Uruguayan." (1) Write a definition for the prefix "Afro-." (2) Write a definition for each of the root words. (3) Write a definition for the word that is made when the prefix and roots are combined.

Group Activities

1. Once you have divided into groups, discuss who usually passes on the stories of creatures such as ghosts or monsters. To whom are these stories often told? When are they often told? What are the purposes of such frightening folktales about creatures? What is the function of such imaginative creatures in our culture? What specifics in the stories that García-Barrio retells illustrate your ideas?
2. Some people have suggested that stories about creatures and monsters are really imaginative representations of our individual and cultural fears. What do the creatures in García-Barrio's essay suggest about the fears of their creators? In other words, what might their fears be? Create a

list of some of the creatures and monsters in the different cultures your group represents and then, next to each creature's name, list the fears it represents. According to your analysis, what fears do most cultures have in common? Why do we have these common fears?

Writing Activities

1. García-Barrio divides and classifies the creatures of African Americans into: those that haunt children, those that haunt adults, those that came to America from Africa, and those that are a hybrid of African and European cultures. Write an essay in which you classify the creatures and monsters of your own culture. First, brainstorm a list of creatures. Second, divide these creatures into general categories (e.g., creatures associated with holidays, creatures associated with certain regions, creatures associated with certain historical events). Finally, write your essay to clearly illustrate your division, using transitions and vivid descriptions.
2. Write an essay in which you explain the origin of a specific folktale, ghost story, or myth from your culture. It may be useful to divide your topic into smaller units (paragraphs) as you develop your ideas.

***Internet Connection:* Constance García-Barrio**

Urban Myths and Legends

Research the keywords "urban myths" and "urban legends" on an online database and other media sources. Continue your research by going through numerous articles explaining verifiable or questionable evidence for representative "urban myths" and/or "urban legends." Based on Constance García-Barrio's article and your own research, what conclusions can your draw about "urban myths" and 'urban legends"? Express your ultimate conclusion in your thesis paragraph, and then write an essay examining "urban myths" in your city, state, or country, using the MLA format for listing *parenthetical references* and a list of *works cited* to document your material (see the Appendix).

Bill Swanson

How Films Feed the Mind *or* When I'm Hungry, I Don't Want to Eat Candy

Bill Swanson (1950–2007) taught humanities, writing, and film classes at South Puget Sound Community College in Olympia, Washington. He has co-edited two books with Michael Nagler: *Wives and Husbands: Twenty Stories about Marriage* and *Stolen Moments: Twenty Stories about Desire*. He is also the coauthor of a college reader, *Projections: Brief Readings on American Culture* with Sterling Warner. In the following essay, Swanson employs division and classification to distinguish different types of movies and the criteria we use to judge them. Although there have been many blockbusters since the original date this article was written, film critics and directors alike seem to still agree with Swanson's findings.

Pre-reading Questions

1. As a pre-writing exercise, cluster "films" and "movies." What do you associate with each reference and why? In what ways are the two words alike and yet different?
2. What types of movies do you attend most often at the theater or watch at home? Explain how each film type you mention "feeds" a personal interest or need.

Experience is never limited, and it is never complete; it is an immense sensibility, a kind of huge spider-web of the finest silken threads suspended in the chamber of consciousness, and catching every air-borne particle in its tissue. It is the very atmosphere of the mind; and when the mind is imaginative . . . it takes to itself the faintest hints of life, it converts the very pulses of the air into revelations.

—Henry James, "The Art of Fiction"

1 Novelist Henry James thought it important to be a person "on whom nothing is lost." He meant the world has a lot to offer if we have the eyes to see it. This applies to everything we perceive, including movies and the effects they have on us. Some help us develop psychologically, to become more complete human beings, and other films are just a way of distracting us from understanding ourselves. The effect a film has, though, has as much to do with the film viewer as the film itself.

2 The mind, Henry James says, is a spider-web that catches even the minutest particles. Nothing really escapes its attention. The bigger the web grows, the more intricate and complex the design, the more that gets caught in it. Web-making is a metaphor for maturity and psychological development. The mind spins out its fine fibers when stimulated to grow, when challenged to think in new ways, when asked to solve new kinds of problems. Any person who has ever seen a spider on a windy fall day, when the strands of web become detached from the stems of plants or the limbs of a tree, will have a picture for the way the mind scurries about and strives to maintain its mode of perception. As the world is constantly changing, our minds are constantly adapting to the changes by making small modifications in our "web" of understanding. We seek new experiences because they give us new knowledge; they help us to expand our sense of self and grow. This is one of the reasons we travel, read books, listen to music and go to movies. All this activity feeds our brain, which is a hungry and busy little spider.

3 When watching a film, twenty-four frames per second pass by our eyes, but they have a cumulative impact; they become part of consciousness, and the imagination goes to work on them trying to find out what they mean. This is how films add to our experience. Our minds take in little bits of information just as they do when we aren't watching a movie, but movies have a way of fooling the mind. We *believe* movies more than books because we literally see things happen before our eyes. This explains why people react so emotionally to violence in films. The violence is all simulated; no one really gets hurt. Still, we get so caught up in the action; we forget this and cringe when we see fights and bloody gunplay on the screen. Our consciousness feels the effect even more powerfully than when violence takes place in real life. Our hearts beat faster; our adrenaline rushes. We get excited. I have been struck by the incongruity of fistfights in real life. The fighters look like bad stuntmen: clumsy and flailing, with punches flying but rarely hitting their mark. The "real" life cannot live up to the choreography of "reel" life. By "real" I mean the actual experiences we have when we are not in a theatre; by "reel" I mean the simulated experiences that take place in movies that resemble actuality but are fabricated to create psychological effects on the audience. Movie events are constructed to produce calculated

effects, and they usually succeed. Movies give us a much broader range of experiences to respond to than we would encounter in the ordinary experience of our daily lives. We are broadened and deepened in our experience by vicarious participation in areas of life that are new and different to us.

4 Around the same time Henry James wrote his essay on fiction, his brother, William James, was working on his own book, *The Principles of Psychology*. This was also the era when cinema was invented. It seems unlikely that either William or Henry James saw many films, but their ideas about how the mind works help us understand why we watch movies and how they influence us.

5 William James observed in his textbook that the mind is a, "stream of consciousness," not simply a repository of perceptions, memories, and ideas. It's more like a river than a bank vault. As a flow of images constantly moving, the mind consists of *moving pictures*. This is why we enjoy movies so much. They mimic consciousness itself which also has the subjective capacity to make jump cuts, crane shots or close-ups. The mind's eye has a flexible lens and a mobile tripod. A movie doesn't just show us how the world looks; *it shows us how a mind works*. It jumps around quite a bit to create a coherent narrative out of sense impressions. We "edit" our memories the way a film editor does, creating mental montages used to communicate with ourselves and with others. We can't possibly remember everything we see, so we edit it down into memories we can re-play over and over like our own personal videos. Memories help us to make sense out of our own lives; they become *our* personal story. The movies we see also become part of our memories. Sometimes they have a life-changing impact upon us by giving us insight into our own experience. We carry them with us in memory, and we can compare them to our own experience and reflect on the differences. If movies weren't meaningful in this way, no one would want to spend time watching them. If we watch films closely, we can glean meaningful information from them, especially if they are constructed in ways that challenge us to pay close attention and to reflect upon what we have seen.

Everyone in a Theatre Watches the Same Film, But Not Everyone *Sees* the Same Film

I am not entertained by entertainment.

—Cynthia Ozick, author of The Shawl. *Her response to a request from the New York Times for her list of books for summer reading.*

6 Each film represents a style of perception, a way of looking at the world. For the time that you are watching a movie, the camera mimics the subjective point of view of a particular person who looks at specific things from a specific angle. The camera notices certain things and not others. As we watch, we come to identify with this way of seeing. There are certain conventions of cinematography that we all recognize without even thinking about them—the close-up, the pan, a shot/reverse shot. These methods allow the camera to break down the all-at-once world that surrounds us into a series of shots that create a fluid mosaic of images moving through time. The fragments of the world are edited together and the audience must use its imagination to put it all back together and make sense out of it.

7 If you think of a film as a purely imaginary experience, as a dream created by all the people listed in the credits, then the movie viewer is someone who pays money to inhabit someone else's dream in order to make sense out of it. When we watch a movie, we dream someone else's dream just for a little while. We accept the illusion that we are looking at the real world. We forget, as soon as the lights go down, that we are sitting in a theatre looking at lights and shadows projected on a screen. The real world—the actual world we live in—resides outside the theatre. Audiences experience the *reel* world of fabricated illusions dancing around on a screen accompanied by dialogue and music. Films thus become an interior, psychological experience. They resemble the real world, but they are only analogies for the real world that condense time and experience into a two-hour story. During this time anything can happen. It could be anything, from *Beauty and the Beast* to *A Beautiful Mind*. Whatever it is, we just accept it as real and participate in it by identifying with the characters and the actions they take.

8 Filmmakers have various motives for making films because filmmaking is both an art form and a business. Certain films like *Star Wars* or *Titanic* are blockbusters because they create an easily accessible world with fantasies that appeal to almost any audience. They make it easy to get involved with the story because they simplify human experience into familiar categories of good and evil, and love and death. Films that make it easy for audiences to participate are more immediately entertaining than films that ask audiences to stretch a bit and experience something new and unfamiliar. Every person has a Comfort Zone within which are contained their unquestioned assumptions about the world, their basic beliefs, their familiar ways of thinking about what is natural or normal or right. Films that reinforce the borders of the Comfort Zone are entertaining. They are "feel good" movies because they make viewers feel more comfortable about themselves and what they believe. Filmmakers who make Comfort Zone films are often rewarded by vast profits. For

examples of Comfort Zone films, here is a list of the Top Ten Grossing Films World Wide:

1.	*Titanic* (James Cameron, USA, 1997)	$1,835,300,000
2.	*The Lord of the Rings: The Return of the King* (Peter Jackson, USA/New Zealand, 2003)	$1,129,219,252
3.	*Harry Potter and the Sorcerer's Stone* (Chris Columbus, USA, 2001)	$968,600,000
4.	Star Wars: Episode 1: The Phantom Menace (George Lucas, USA, 1999)	$922,379,000
5.	*The Lord of the Rings: The Two Towers* (Peter Jackson, New Zealand/USA, 2002)	$921,600,000
6.	*Jurassic Park* (Steven Spielberg, USA, 1993)	$919,700,000
7.	*Shrek 2* (Andrew Adamson, USA, 2004)	$880,871,036
8.	Harry Potter and the Chamber of Secrets (Chris Columbus, 2002)	$866,300,000
9.	*Finding Nemo* (Andrew Stanton and Lee Unkrich, 2003)	$865,000,000
10.	*The Lord of the Rings: The Fellowship of the Ring* (Peter Jackson, New Zealand/USA, 2001)	$860,700,000

(Source: imdb.com)

9 What do these films have in common? The Comfort Zone movies are essentially children's movies in which human beings behave like cartoon characters. This doesn't apply to *Finding Nemo* or *Shrek* because they *are* cartoons. Adventure stories with melodramatic villains, elaborate quest journeys and plenty of action, they are spectacles that thrill the eyes and the imagination with threats to the main characters that are always external beings—dinosaurs, dragons, space aliens—or forces of nature—icebergs, predatory animals. The main characters are usually good and innocent. Their motives are transparent and child-like (though real children are never this simple). The special effects represent the latest in action film technology. The happy, triumphal endings provide both emotional closure and plot points that allow for continuation, that is, sequels. They are very expensive and successful serials. The earliest of these films, *Star Wars*, was made in 1977, but most are more recent. These films have benefited from young people who like to see a favorite film several times and from older people who want to return to their Comfort Zone when they see a film. Usually called "escapist" entertainment, they represent an escape from the actual conflicts, frustrations and disappointments of everyday life.

10 In these films the good guys and the bad guys are clearly defined and the good guys win—or at least their values are shown to be true and valid. Values like love, friendship, loyalty, and honesty are shown to be the greatest sources of human fulfillment. Messages like this easily gain universal approval. These values ***are*** the greatest sources of human fulfillment, but these films do not adequately represent the psychological struggle involved in making conflicting values a functional part of everyday life. It is not a mistake for films to champion these values, but it is a mistake to put them in the pure realm of fantasy, to remove them from the complexity of lived psychological experience. By creating such stark contrast between good and evil these films eliminate mixed motives, difficult choices, and moral ambiguity. The characters rarely have to choose between conflicting ethical values. Designed for maximum international distribution, simple mythic stories communicate to people everywhere because the conflicts are external and don't require conflicted, personal dialogue or particular cultural knowledge.

11 Though these films have dialogue, they might be described as preverbal. When I saw *Titanic* (number one on the list), I was struck by how much it resembled a silent film; I would have enjoyed it more if it was a silent film! The dialogue was so predictable and wooden most audiences could have imagined better lines if they'd been allowed to. *Titanic* uses a plot idea very popular in the silent era: the damsel in distress. In 1914, only two years after the real Titanic went down, Pearl White starred in a twenty-part serial called *The Perils of Pauline* in which a fair-haired girl must escape from her rich guardian in order to run off with her true love and in the process falls from an air-balloon, escapes a burning house and is nearly run over by a train, among other life-threatening events. Eighty-three years later James Cameron was able to recycle this movie fantasy, add computer graphics, and bring in close to two billion dollars. An old-fashioned tear-jerker, it succeeded so well because it adds so little to a formula for sentimental adventure that is based upon putting virtuous young girls in danger and pinning all their hopes on the redeeming power of love. This was a melodramatic cliché in 1914! Yet the film had unprecedented success because it was aimed directly at the center of the Comfort Zone, and it hit its target. The performances of Kate Winslett and Leonardo DiCaprio carried the whole thing off because audiences liked them and believed in their innocence. They were the very image of Young Love. Cooler heads, mostly film critics, snickered and sniffed their noses at the whole thing, but it made little difference.

12 Think of the differences between *Titanic* and *Memento*. Christopher Nolan's film literally reverses our expectations by having the story move backward in time. Also, he mixes black and white with color footage, and gives the story a narrator who can't retain short-term memories. *Memento* asks audiences to identify with a character who is not a

conventional hero, not even a conventional *film noir* hero. A difficult film, it gets better and better with multiple viewings as various bits of information begin to cohere in the mind. Its tightly constructed story raises questions about the nature of memory, the relation of memory to a sense of self, the necessity of memory in order to have conscience. It is not simple entertainment in which we sit back amused by special effects and daring actions. Films like *Memento* are more engaging than entertainment because they require us to put clues together, to perceive subtle details, and come up with our own coherent understanding of the film. Though few people will experience the unusual brain injury depicted in *Memento*, all of us struggle to remember things, and eventually realize that the things we remember define who we are. When we lose our memories, we lose a big part of our identity.

Conventional and Unconventional Films

13 Filmmaking ranges from the conventional to the unconventional. Conventional films have a comforting psychological effect, even if they are about violent or disturbing things. *Saving Private Ryan*, for example, is full of grisly and horrific violence, but in the end, it reinforces the beliefs that the Nazis were evil, the soldiers who died on D-Day made a heroic sacrifice and that dying for your country is a noble death. These are not new or controversial ideas, and were probably already held by most people in the audience before they came to see the movie. Watching *Saving Private Ryan* was like watching one of the propaganda films made during World War II like *Bataan* or *The Sands of Iwo Jima*, except that *Saving Private Ryan* was much more technologically sophisticated and explicit about combat and death. If you compare it to an unconventional war film like *Apocalypse Now*, you will see how films can work on a different level of communication. Francis Coppola's 1978 film, not a blockbuster when it was released, failed for several years to turn a profit and made it difficult for Coppola to get financial backing to do another film. With the passing of time (and the invention of the VCR), however, this film has been reconsidered and now appears on any list of the best films of the 1970s.

14 Gradually, the complexity and meaning of *Apocalypse Now* revealed itself to audiences. At first audiences found its dark vision of moral ambiguity, political confusion, military betrayal and drug-induced paranoia hard to accept. It is not a Comfort Zone film. We're not sure who the "good guys" are or what the main character should do—should an American officer assassinate another American officer? Coppola said in a press conference at the Cannes Film Festival when the film was released that he did not want it to be *about* the Vietnam War but to *be* the Vietnam War. This sounded pretentious to people at the time, but Coppola

meant he wanted audiences to come away from the film with the same confusion, dismay and dread that both Vietnam War protesters and veterans struggled to describe and understand. *Apocalypse Now* was no pleasant two hour diversion; it was a filmic descent into hell. And audiences did not enjoy the trip, but they were moved by it.

15 Such films raise questions that movie producers and financiers are inclined to ask: If you're not planning to give audiences what they want, why do you expect anyone to come and see your film? What audiences want, it turns out, is varied. On the one hand, they do want to have a predictable, familiar experience. This explains why sequels and remakes do quite well at the box office even when they don't get good reviews. Many people, for example, went to see *Men in Black II* to find out if they would have the same good time they had watching the first version. Film reviewers mostly mocked it as a not very clever attempt to cash in on reputation of the first film. Audiences went to see it anyway because it was something they knew they could relate to. It didn't become another blockbuster, but it still brought in more profit than the average independent film.

16 Popular taste, however, is not the only criterion for judging films. Since 1952, *Sight and Sound*, a magazine published by the British Film Institute, has been taking a poll of critics and directors every ten years that asks them to name the ten best films ever made. The list below is a sample of the Directors' Poll from 2002. None of the Top Ten Grossing Films was mentioned by any of the critics or directors. Here is the list (I have added annotations to explain why I think they were chosen).

Sight and Sound Directors' Top Ten Poll 2002—The Best Films (108 Directors)

(Actually eleven films because of ties in the voting.)

17 **1.** ***Citizen Kane*** (Orson Welles, USA, 1940)

This film is ranked first because of its technical innovations in lighting, framing, editing, sound, and narrative structure. The story of Charles Foster Kane, a power hungry newspaper owner, is narrated from **five different points of view,** and raises questions about how it is possible to know any person completely or to ever know for certain what is true about anything.

18 **2.** ***The Godfather*** **and** ***The Godfather Part II*** (Francis Coppola, USA, 1972/1974)

Like *Citizen Kane*, these films are about the American Dream and the effects of striving for power and wealth. In this case Michael

Corleone emerges as the godfather of a Mafia family whose interests he is dedicating to serving and in the process destroys the family. These films reveal **the deep ambivalences** built into the immigrant experience so deeply embedded in American culture. The values that are necessary for survival have a way of turning on those who adopt them. Both films also contain cinematic innovations in lighting, use of color, editing, narrative structure and acting styles.

19 **3.** ***8 1/2*** (Federico Fellini, Italy, 1963)

A film director half-finished with his ninth film experiences a psychological crisis in which his past life passes before his eyes in the form of memories, fantasies, and excerpts from his previous films. This displays **the ever-changing nature of the mind,** that turns around and around in the present like a merry-go-round. This film asks us to reflect upon the nature of the self. It shows how difficult it is to answer the question: Who am I?

20 **4.** ***Lawrence of Arabia*** (David Lean, Britain, 1962)

A wide screen epic shot in the Arabian Desert, *Lawrence of Arabia* used color photography with expressive and overpowering vividness. Also, it depicts the life of the real T.E. Lawrence who became a British war hero in World War I fighting for the empire and at the same time allied himself with the indigenous aspirations of the Arabs. As a man caught between his conscience and his loyalty to his country, he symbolizes the **confusion and ambivalence created by political change** in the twentieth century.

21 **5.** ***Dr. Strangelove, Or How I Stopped Worrying and Learned to Love the Bomb*** (Stanley Kubrick, USA, 1963)

A classic work of satire that rivals the best works of literature, *Dr. Strangelove* reveals the incipient madness built into the Cold War arms race with nuclear weapons. It shows the subversions of **rational policy making by paranoia, patriotism, bureaucracy, secrecy, and megalomania.** One of the most politically influential films ever made, it provokes both laughter and a chilling dread of accidental nuclear war.

22 **6.** ***Ladri di Biciclette/The Bicycle Thief*** (Vittorio De Sica, Italy, 1948)

A desperate man on the verge of unemployment and homelessness searches the crowded Roman streets for his stolen bicycle that he must have for work. Like a biblical parable, this film uses simplicity to plumb the depths of despair and conscience. It makes us ask ourselves: **What would you do to survive?**

23 **7.** ***Raging Bull*** (Martin Scorsese, USA, 1980)

The cinematography, camera movement and editing of this film show how technique can create meaning in a film. More than a boxing film, *Raging Bull* is an exploration of rage itself, **the irrational urge to define ourselves by violent acts of control and domination.** This film shows us that love and anger are both attached to passionate urges that are difficult to control. Though apparent opposites, these two emotions are shown to be inextricably linked.

24 **8.** ***Vertigo*** (Alfred Hitchcock, USA, 1954)

In *Vertigo* the power of a sexual and romantic obsession causes a police detective to **re-examine his whole life, his need for control over others and his own hidden guilt.** The elaborate plot, disguises and mistaken identities raise fundamental questions about how accurate our perceptions of other people can be. Do we see other people as they are or as we wish they were? How do we see ourselves?

25 **9.** ***Rashomon*** (Akira Kurosawa, Japan, 1950)

Set in medieval Japan, this story of a rape, murder and trial is told from multiple points of view and, like *Citizen Kane*, it **shows how subjective perceptions make it difficult to arrive at objective conclusions.** The testimony here doesn't quite add up to a coherent explanation of the events, and the film asks us to consider whether it is possible to get beyond self-interest and unconscious lying when expressing our personal perception of the world.

26 **10.** ***La Règle du jeu/Rules of the Game*** (Jean Renoir, France, 1939)

A shooting party at a French country house just before World War II provides the setting for a comedy about love, betrayal and reconciliation. Mistaken identities, whispered rumors, class distinctions, marital jealousy, and gunshots in the night bring the whole party to a confused conclusion. Renoir tells us that when it comes to making choices, **"everyone has their reasons."**

27 **11.** ***Seven Samurai*** (Akira Kurosawa, Japan, 1954)

Seven unemployed samurai are hired by farmers to defend their remote village from a marauding band of brigands. Samurai and villagers face the impending battle in several different ways. The film is **a study in the diverse ways individuals find courage in the face of adversity and death.** For the final battle scene, a blur of swords, horses, mud and rain, Kurosawa used ten cameras and put together a masterpiece of film editing.

(Source: www.bfi.org.uk)

28 Some observations:

- These films were made between 1939 and 1980; the blockbusters were made between 1977 and 2003.
- There are five American films; two Italian, two Japanese, one French, and one British; all the blockbusters are American or English-language films.
- Eight of the directors' choices are in black and white; all the blockbusters are in color.
- None of the directors' choices have children or teenagers as the central characters; all of the blockbusters have children or teenagers as central characters.
- Both lists contain films with many technical innovations though the blockbusters have more fantasy-related special effects.
- All of the blockbusters, except Titanic, contain supernatural phenomena; none of directors' choices contain supernatural phenomena.

The directors' choices represent a range of cultures and time periods. Complex works that utilize multiple narratives and intense interior conflicts and states of mind, they contain extraordinary acting performances that provide insight into ambivalent feelings and mixed motives. The highlighted phrases in the annotations above are meant to emphasize that these films are about *human dilemmas that stretch intelligence and feeling to the limits by placing the characters in complex situations where difficult decisions must be made*. The heroes (or anti-heroes) are not necessarily noble or courageous; they are flawed, confused, and torn in different directions, but they carry on with their lives. Their conflicts are not between themselves and impersonal aliens or villains or natural forces but arise from profound interior moments when they have to decide who they really are, what they really believe, and what it is really possible for them to accomplish. They learn to accept their own limitations and the limitations of others; they face disappointment, failure and death without illusions. This may sound on the surface like pretty depressing movies, but that is not the effect they have. That is not why they are on the list. These films, serious and moving, carry the emotional and intellectual weight that communicates a deeper understanding of what it is to be alive and aware of yourself as a thinking and feeling being. They contribute to psychological growth.

29 William James argued in *The Principles of Psychology*, that psychological development is related to having new perceptions, or seeing familiar situations in fresh ways. These films show us powerful hypothetical scenes that we mentally participate in and see how the consequences play out in the story. The films on the *Sight and Sound* list create a complex picture of reality that represents an analogy for our own psychological complexity. These films reflect a multi-faceted reality where several things are going

on simultaneously. They imitate the psychological phenomena that James described. The films display the restless, complicated consciousness that moves continuously from image to image, moment to moment.

30 Reflection upon powerful and complex films (or other great works of art) encourages the mental focus and tenacious self-examination that is related to personal growth. Eye candy—films full of spectacular special effects and saccharine happy endings—cannot generate much growth in viewers. The best films make for a cinematic diet that enhances the psychological sinews and synapses that are growth producing and life sustaining.

Post-reading Questions

Content

1. Explain the difference between conventional and unconventional films. Illustrate your response with specific examples drawn from Swanson's essay.
2. Why do people react so strongly to violence in films?
3. According to Swanson, what is one of the reasons why we probably "enjoy movies so much"? What relationship exists between the *mind* and *films*?
4. Why do two or more people who watch the same movie in a theater often see a different film?
5. Identify some "comfort zone" movie characteristics of "Comfort Zone" movies. Mention a few of the examples Swanson uses to illustrate this film category.

Strategies and Structures

1. In what way does Swanson divide and classify films? How many times does he do so in his essay and for what purpose?
2. Analyze the function of paragraph 2 in Swanson's essay. With what does it provide his readers?
3. Discuss Swanson's strategic rationale for including film lists in his article. To what extent do these lists strengthen and clarify his analysis?
4. Why does Swanson mention both Henry James and his brother, William? What does the allusion to them and their work add to this essay?
5. Exactly why do films like *Star Wars* and *Titanic* become blockbusters? How might this help to explain why "filmmaking is both an art form and a business"?

Language and Vocabulary

1. Vocabulary: *minutest, metaphor, detached, cinema, repository, mimic, subjective, conventions, cinema -tography, fabricated, stark, predictable, vir tuous, cliché, unprecedented, spectrum,*

propaganda, ambiguity, paranoia, filmic, indigenous, aspirations, incipient, bureaucracy, parable, megalomania, samurai, annotations, dilemmas, hypothetical, analogy. Review how Swanson used each vocabulary word on this list in context. If you are uncertain of a word's definition, look it up in a dictionary. Then, write a short paragraph about a recent film you saw, using at least seven of today's vocabulary words.

2. Go over today's vocabulary list, select ten words from it, and then use a dictionary or a thesaurus to locate one synonym (word carrying the same meaning) and one antonym (word carrying an opposite meaning) for at least five words on the list.

Group Activities

1. Before gathering in small groups, generate your own list of the ten best movies for the previous year (e.g., if you read this essay in 2012, then consider all films from 2011). Include specific reasons, examples, and other criteria you applied to determine how and why particular films belong on your list. Next, gather in groups, compare lists and justifications for "best films," and arrive at a single list reflecting the collaborative judgment of your group members. Finally, write an original annotation for each film on the list.

2. Gather in groups of four people, brainstorm together, and determine your own definition of (1) entertaining movies, and (2) excellent movies. Then generate a list of films, past and present, that might appear on either list. Finally, as a group, divide and classify each other's film choices based on the group's definition of entertaining and excellent movies. When and where did you locate films that fit appropriately on both lists? For subsequent writing assignments, have the group recorder make and copy a master list of films for each group member.

Writing Activities

1. Write an essay agreeing with or disputing Swanson's contention that "The effect a film has, though, has as much to do with the film viewer as the film itself." Divide your argument into three to five major discussion points that you plan to defend in the body of your essay. Gather examples of several films and film viewers to offer representative support for your claim.

2. Refer to the film list generated in Group Activity 1. Reflect on your personal definition of entertaining and excellent films—the definitions that you wrote prior to the group activity. Do some pre-writing on the issue of what constitutes an entertaining movie versus an excellent film, and arrive at a thesis. Finally, write an essay where you convince readers on the reliability of your entertaining and excellent film definitions. Feel free to directly disagree or agree with Swanson's definition. However, be certain that you offer some original justifications for dividing and classifying films in both categories.
3. Write a division and classification essay wherein you research the most recent data on "great movies" and "Comfort Zone" movies. You might take the basic premise of Swanson's essay and update his claims and adjust his conclusions based on recent evidence, including director polls.

David Bodanis

What's in Your Toothpaste?

David Bodanis earned a degree in mathematics from the University of Chicago and has done work in theoretical biology and population genetics. He traveled to Paris and started his journalism work as a copyboy for the *International Herald Tribune.* His books include: *The Body Book: A Fantastic Voyage to the World Within* (1984), *The Secret House* (1986), *The Secret Garden: Dawn to Dusk in the Astonishing Hidden World of the Garden* (1992), *The Secret Family: Twenty-Four Hours Inside the Mysterious World of Our Minds and Bodies* (1997), *E = Mc²* (2000), and *Passionate Minds: Emilie du Chatelet, Voltaire, and the Great Love Affair of the Enlightenment* (2007). This last essay is taken from *The Secret House.*

Pre-reading Questions

1. Exactly how careful are you about the foods and other products that you put into or onto your body? Do you read the labels or

ask restaurants what ingredients they use, or do you not care? Explain your answer in detail.

2. Why do you imagine that a warning printed on all toothpaste tubes advises users to contact a Poison Control Center right away if more than the usual amount of toothpaste required for brushing is swallowed?

---

1 Into the bathroom goes our male resident and after the most pressing need is satisfied it's time to brush the teeth. The tube of toothpaste is squeezed, its pinched metal seams are splayed, pressure waves are generated inside, and the paste begins to flow. But what's in this toothpaste so carefully being extruded out?

2 Water mostly, 30 to 45 percent in most brands: ordinary, everyday simple tap water. It's there because people like to have a big gob of toothpaste to spread on the brush, and water is the cheapest stuff there is when it comes to making big gobs. Dripping a bit from the tap onto your brush would cost virtually nothing; whipped in with the rest of the toothpaste the manufacturers can sell it at a neat and accountant-pleasing $2 per pound equivalent. Toothpaste manufacture is a very lucrative occupation.

3 Second to water in quantity is chalk: exactly the same material that schoolteachers use to write on blackboards. It is collected from the crushed remains of long-dead ocean creatures. In the Cretaceous seas chalk particles served as part of the wickedly sharp outer skeleton that these creatures had to wrap around themselves to keep from getting chomped by all the slightly larger other ocean creatures they met. Their massed graves are our present chalk deposits.

4 The individual chalk particles—the size of the smallest mud particles in your garden—have kept their toughness over the eons, and now on the toothbrush they'll need it. The enamel outer coating of the tooth they'll have to face is the hardest substance in the body—tougher than skull, or bone, or nail. Only the chalk particles in toothpaste can successfully grind into the teeth during brushing, ripping off the surface layers like an abrading wheel grinding down a boulder in a quarry.

5 The craters, slashes, and channels that the chalk tears into the teeth will also remove a certain amount of build-up yellow in the carnage, and it is for that polishing function that it's there. A certain amount of unduly enlarged extra-abrasive chalk fragments tear such cavernous pits into the teeth that future decay bacteria will be able to bunker down there and thrive; the quality control people find it almost impossible to screen out these errant super-chalk pieces, and government regulations allow them to stay in.

6 In case even the gouging doesn't get all the yellow off, another substance is worked into the toothpaste cream. This is titamum dioxide. It

comes in tiny spheres, and it's the stuff bobbing around in white wall paint to make it come out white. Splashed around onto your teeth during the brushing it coats much of the yellow that remains. Being water soluble it leaks off in the next few hours and is swallowed, but at least for the quick glance up in the mirror after finishing it will make the user think his teeth are truly white. Some manufacturers add OptiCal whitening dyes—the stuff more commonly found in washing machine bleach—to make extra sure that that glance in the mirror shows reassuring white.

7 These ingredients alone would not make a very attractive concoction. They would stick in the tube like a sloppy white plastic lump, hard to squeeze out as well as revolting to the touch. Few consumers would savor rubbing in a mixture of water, ground-up blackboard chalk, and the whitener from latex paint first thing in the morning. To get around that finicky distaste the manufacturers have mixed in a host of other goodies.

8 To keep the glop from drying out, a mixture including glycerine glycol—related to the most common car antifreeze ingredient—is whipped in with the chalk and water, and to give *that* concoction a bit of substance (all we really have so far is wet colored chalk) a large helping is added of gummy molecules from the seaweed *Chondrus Crispus.* This seaweed ooze spreads in among the chalk, paint, and antifreeze, then stretches itself in all directions to hold the whole mass together. A bit of paraffin oil (the fuel that flickers in camping lamps) is pumped in with it to help the moss ooze keep the whole substance smooth.

9 With the glycol, ooze, and paraffin we're almost there. Only two major chemicals are left to make the refreshing, cleansing substance we know as toothpaste. The ingredients so far are fine for cleaning, but they wouldn't make much of the satisfying foam we have come to expect in the morning brushing.

10 To remedy that, every toothpaste on the market has a big dollop of detergent added too. You've seen the suds detergent will make in a washing machine. The same substance added here will duplicate that inside the mouth. It's not particularly necessary, but it sells.

11 The only problem is that by itself this ingredient tastes, well, too like detergent. It's horribly bitter and harsh. The chalk put in toothpaste is pretty foul-tasting too for that matter. It's to get around that gustatory discomfort that the manufacturers put in the ingredient they tout perhaps the most of all. This is the flavoring, and it has to be strong. Double rectified peppermint oil is used—a flavorer so powerful that chemists know better than to sniff it in the raw state in the laboratory. Menthol crystals and saccharin or other sugar simulators are added to complete the camouflage operation.

12 Is that it? Chalk, water, paint, seaweed, antifreeze, paraffin, oil, detergent, and peppermint? Not quite. A mix like that would be irresistible to the hundreds of thousands of individual bacteria lying on the surface of even an immaculately cleaned bathroom sink. They would get in, float in the water bubbles, ingest the ooze and paraffin, maybe even spray out enzymes to break down the chalk. The result would be an uninviting mess. The way manufacturers avoid that final obstacle is by putting something in to kill the bacteria. Something good and strong is needed, something that will zap any accidentally intrudant bacteria into oblivion. And that something is formaldehyde—the disinfectant used in anatomy labs.

13 So it's chalk, water, paint, seaweed, antifreeze, paraffin oil, detergent, peppermint, formaldehyde, and fluoride (which can go some way towards preserving children's teeth)—that's the usual mixture raised to the mouth on the toothbrush for a fresh morning's clean. If it sounds too unfortunate, take heart. Studies show that thorough brushing with just plain water will often do as good a job.

Post-reading Questions

Content

1. The author begins by relating the experience of a man completing his grooming one morning. He echoes the title by asking "But what's in this toothpaste . . . ?" Does he successfully follow this thesis throughout the essay?
2. Why might some people find the ingredients in toothpaste harmless or frightening?
3. What are the manufacturers' reasons for putting all of the ingredients in toothpaste?
4. Why do manufacturers add detergent to toothpaste?
5. How do manufacturers avoid that final obstacle of bacteria invading the toothpaste and making an "uninviting mess"?

Strategies and Structures

1. Assess Bodanis' purpose for informing readers of the ingredients in their toothpaste.
2. Why does he begin the essay so matter-of-factly?
3. What ingredients does he list first? What is the effect of listing the most harmless to begin with?
4. Why does the author then cover the taste and smell of the ingredients?
5. What hope does Bodanis give the reader at the conclusion of his essay?

Language and Vocabulary

1. Vocabulary: *glycerine, glycol, Chondrus Crispus, paraffin oil, double rectified peppermint oil, menthol crystals, saccharin, formaldehyde, fluoride.* Bodanis uses many words that have chemical meanings. Research each of these words, and determine how harmful these chemicals are to the human body. (Do not use a regular dictionary; try one dealing with chemicals.)
2. Locate the following words that the author uses in his essay: *Cretaceous, cavernous, gouging, finicky, antifreeze, immaculately,* and use some of them, along with the chemicals, to write a letter to a manufacturer complaining about the effects on the human body, asking the company to desist or you will no longer purchase the product.

Group Activities

1. Go to a supermarket or an online resource and investigate the ingredients in foods we often assume are safe for consumption, such as cereal, baby food, and powdered milk. For example, how much sugar is there in items such as soda pop, frozen desserts, peanut butter, and salad dressing? Report your findings to the class. Take into consideration people with diseases like diabetes, high blood pressure, and heart disease.
2. Research the fast-food industry. For instance, how much salt is there in a typical milkshake? How much salt is there in French fries? Do the hamburgers contain low fat meat? What oil is used to fry the potatoes and burgers? Talk to people who work in your college cafeteria to ascertain if healthy ingredients are used to produce healthy meals. Also interview your fellow students to determine whether they are guided by health considerations when they choose what they eat. Report your findings to the class.

Writing Activities

1. Take the answers to your investigations of the foods we often eat and write an essay similar to Bodanis' warning the public about the ingredients in foods that most of us have assumed were safe for eating.
2. After investigating the fast-food industry and interviewing students, compose an essay wherein you advise these students what is the safe course to follow as far as maintaining their health. You might also investigate the health-food stores in your area.

Internet Connection: David Bodanis

Consumer Products

Consumer products tend to be very misleading in nature. Many times, manufacturers create a market where none existed by making people paranoid and convincing them that they need to spend money on unnecessary products. Using a research engine or online date base, enter the key words "unnecessary consumer products" or "dangerous consumer products." Find at least three articles that detail the dangers of using such things as prescription medication advertised on television. Ultimately, write an essay entitled "Dangerous Products Around and Within Us." Use the articles you located online to help support your original thesis regarding consumer products, and document your sources as explained in the Appendix of *Visions Across the Americas* 8th edition.

Additional Topics and Issues for Division and Classification Essays

1. After devising a thesis on the issue of racism, divide and classify the issue in order to develop each part of your topic thoroughly.
2. Divide and classify different kinds of relationships in order to gain a better insight into your own life.
3. Compose an essay in which you classify the different ways you have noticed that you and others deal with problems. (Some people, for instance, deal with problems by seeking solitude, others by confronting problems head-on, and still others by seeking advice from friends.)
4. Compose an essay discussing the different types of fears a child might have that might affect his or her behavior. How do these fears change as the child grows older—or do they?
5. Examine the different careers available to you, dividing them into distinct categories, and conclude your essay with the most likely profession you will pursue in your future.
6. Discuss the subject majors that are available from your college or university. What are the characteristics of each

major? What job opportunities can a student look forward to upon graduation?

7. We all speak and write in different ways, depending on the situation and audience. Write an essay examining a specific topic and discuss (1) how you would talk to your friends about your subject, (2) how you would inform a professor or government official about your topic, and (3) how you would compose a formal essay on it.

8. Write an essay wherein you classify and divide your concept of "sloppiness" or "untidiness." Begin your essay with a catchy title. How you divide and classify your topic will largely depend on what you have to say about it.

9. Construct an essay wherein you use the techniques of division and classification to explain gender initiation rites, religious initiation rites, children's initiation rites, academic/social initiation rites, business initiation rites, cultural initiation rites, and so on.

10. Many people feel art is only decorative, but after careful analysis it becomes apparent that art serves many functions in American society. Write an essay in which you classify and divide the different uses of art in America.

CHAPTER 9

Cause and Effect

When we explain the causes and/or the effects of something, we are busy explaining *why* something occurs (cause) and/or *the consequence of an action* (effect). There are immediate and secondary (contributing) causes that lead to an effect, as well as immediate and long-range effects from an action. When our stomachs begin to make noises after going without food for two days, we can identify an immediate cause: hunger. However, more often than not, a string of causes leads to an ultimate effect. By the same token, a number of causes can lead to numerous effects—not just one.

Structuring Cause-and-Effect Essays

Usually, a writer will begin to develop a topic using the strategy of cause and effect by stating the effect(s) of something in a thesis paragraph and then examining the cause or multiple causes. For instance, in "Labor and Capital: The Coming Catastrophe," Carlos Bulosan cites the fattening of industrialists by profits, their investing profits in idle luxury, their quarreling among themselves, and causing the depression as reasons for discontent among the workers.

In "Growing Up with Two Moms," Megan McGuire demonstrates the second method of organizing a cause-and-effect essay. She focuses her discussion on the *effects* of growing up with gay parents (mother and partner) rather than the *causes* of gay relationships. For instance, early in the essay she states, *"I was afraid everything I had gained socially would disappear if anyone ever found out that while they went home after volleyball practice to their Brady Bunch dinners with Mom and Dad, I went home to two moms."* Ironically, McGuire ultimately points out that her feelings of awkwardness in having two moms had nothing to do with the family unit—but with *"other people's ignorance."* Similarly, Karen Ray structures her essay, "The Naked Face," by initially stating reasons why she does not wear makeup (her *"nakedness is partly pragmatic and partly philosophical"*) and then explaining the effects of wearing or not wearing makeup in society from a historical as well as a personal perspective. While Rose Anna Higashi spends a good deal of time discussing the causes or reasons for her hobby of *"eating with immigrants,"* she spends a larger portion of her essay explaining its positive effects. All in all, *"food is more nourishing eaten in community."*

Because the result (effect) of something like falling in love or being attracted to somebody has its basis in chemistry (a cause or multiple causes), Anastasia Toufexis uses *cause* and *effect* strategies as her dominate method of development in "The Right Chemistry." Note how her following passage clearly illustrates cause-and-effect relationships: *"Lovers often claim that they feel as if they are being swept away* [an effect]. *They're not mistaken; they are literally flooded by chemicals, research suggests* [causes]. *A meeting of eyes, a touch of hands or a whiff of scent sets off a flood that starts in the brain and races along the nerves and through the blood. The results are familiar: flushed skin, sweaty palms, heavy breathing. If love looks suspiciously like stress, the reason is simple: the chemical pathways are identical."*

In yet other instances, an essay may focus as much on the reasons why something occurs (the cause[s]) as the result (effect[s]) of an action. Phillip Persky, for example, cites reasons why his confused sense of pride and shame in his parents (cause) led to feelings of guilt (effect). The fact that his parents were oblivious to his *"shame and, by extension, the resulting guilt,"* only intensified the situation, especially since, as he grew older, he *"became much more appreciative of [his] parents' accomplishments in the United States under such difficult conditions."*

Regardless of whether your essay moves from cause to effect(s), from effect to cause(s), or has a fairly balanced combination of the two, your explanations should answer the question "why" something has happened.

Cause-and-Effect Fallacies

Post hoc ergo propter hoc: The post hoc fallacy deals with faulty cause-and-effect relationships, something you that will definitely want to avoid when writing any composition. Literally, the Latin phrase translates as: "It happened *after* this; therefore, it happened *because* of this." A good example of the post hoc fallacy would be a sentence like "My sister won a million dollars last night because she found a lucky penny in the morning." In many instances, one event's following another does not produce a cause-and-effect relationship. Thus, in the case of the previous sentence, the person could very well have found a penny and won a million dollars on the same day, but one (finding a penny) did not cause the other (winning a million dollars) to occur.

Tips on Writing Cause-and-Effect Essays

1. While almost any essay may contain an element of causation, for the purpose of this essay select a topic that can be best explained by focusing on causes and/or effects. A discussion of two cars, for instance, would be a poor choice for a cause-and-effect topic; this lends itself to comparison and contrast.
2. After you have selected a topic or issue, pre-write (cluster, freewrite, brainstorm, list) to determine the focus of your composition. Will you initially mention causes and devote the majority of your composition to a discussion of the short-term and long-range effects of your topic? Or will you move from mentioning the results of an action to discussing its causes?
3. Will your cause and effect essay be written to inform somebody of something or persuade? Determine this early on—ideally before you draft your essay.
4. Check your work carefully for faulty cause-and-effect relationships. Never mistake coincidence as evidence of a valid cause-and-effect relationship.
5. Ask yourself questions like the following: What sort of evidence have I offered to prove what I say? Are my examples specific and compelling? Would my examples convince even the most doubtful reader? How much do I rely on my reader simply to agree with what I say? And, most importantly, have I thoroughly addressed the question *why?*

Megan McGuire

Growing Up with Two Moms

Megan McGuire, an 18-year-old student at Mills College at the time she wrote this essay for the November 4, 1996 issue of *Newsweek* magazine, examines her childhood embarrassment that her mother was a lesbian. She hid the truth from friends and lied about her mother, but in retrospect, she is proud of her family.

Pre-reading Questions

1. Do you think that gay parents can do as good a job at raising children as straight parents can? Why or why not?
2. Did you ever feel that you needed to hide the truth about your family from your immediate friends and acquaintances? Jot down your response to this question in your writing log or journal.

---

1 When I was growing up, the words "fag" and "queer" and "dyke" were everywhere, even though we lived in a relatively tolerant community, Cambridge, Mass. I even used them myself to put down someone I didn't like. If you were a fag or a dyke, you were an outcast. All that changed when I was 12. My mother had a friend, Barb, who started spending the night, though she lived minutes away. One night when Barb wasn't there, I asked my mother, "Are you gay?" I can only remember the "yes"—and the crying. All I could think was that she couldn't be gay. It wasn't fair. She was one of "those" people.

2 I always thought my family was normal. By the time I was 5, my mother and father no longer lived together. My brother and I split our time between our parents. My father remarried, and my mother dated men. We assumed our parents were straight. That's all you see on TV.

3 As it turned out, we didn't have a stereotypical family. The years after my mother came out to me were very difficult for me and my

brother. We had just moved from Washington, D.C. We had to start over, and at the same time we had to lie about our mom. In school I wanted to be liked, so I laughed at the jokes about gays. I had yet to figure out how to make a friend I could trust with my secret. I wasn't ready to talk about my family because I wasn't ready to deal with it myself.

4 High school was the hardest. I was into all kinds of clubs, but I was afraid everything I had gained socially would disappear if anyone ever found out that while they went home after volleyball practice to their Brady Bunch dinners with Mom and Dad, I went home to two moms. My brother and I would never allow Mom and Barb to walk together or sit next to each other in a restaurant. We wouldn't have people spend the night; if we did have friends over, we would hide the gay literature and family pictures. When a friend asked about the pink triangle on our car, my brother told him it was a used car and we hadn't had time to take the sticker off. We lived like this for three years, until we moved to a house with a basement apartment. We told our friends Barb lived there. It was really a guest room.

5 Ironically, our home life then was really the same as a straight family's. We had family meetings, fights, trips and dinners. My brother and I came to accept Barb as a parent. There were things she could never have with us the way our mother did. But she helped support us while my mother got her Ph.D. in public health. And she pushed my brother and me to succeed in school, just like a mom.

6 With the help of a really great counselor and a friend who had a "it's not a big deal and I knew anyway" attitude, I started to become more comfortable with my two-mom family. The spring of my junior year, a local newspaper interviewed me for an article on gay families. I was relieved, but also afraid. The day the article appeared was incredibly tense. I felt like everyone was looking at me and talking about me. One kid said to my brother, "I saw the article, you fag." My brother told him to get lost. Some people avoided me, but most kids were curious about my family. People asked if I was gay. I chose not to answer; as teenagers, most of us can't explain the feelings in our minds and bodies.

7 Last year, in my final year of high school, I decided to speak at our school's National Coming Out Day. Sitting up front were my best friend, my mother, my brother and my counselor, Al. That day was the best. I no longer had to laugh at the jokes or keep a secret. I hoped I was making a path for others like me: a kid with a gay parent, scared and feeling alone. After my speech, I lost some friends and people made remarks that hurt. But that only made me stronger. The hardest thing to deal with is other people's ignorance, not the family part. That's just like any other family.

Post-reading Questions

Content

1. What caused McGuire's discomfort and embarrassment as a child?
2. When was her mother's sexual preference hardest on her and why?
3. What was McGuire's home life like? Did it really differ that much from the home life of her friends? Explain.
4. At what point in her life did McGuire come to terms with her "two moms"?
5. Following the speech she gave at her school's National Coming Out Day, how did some of her friends treat her? What did McGuire realize about them?

Strategies and Structures

1. In addition to using cause and effect to describe her childhood with "two mothers," what other literary technique does McGuire use to develop her essay?
2. How does the tone reflect the author's attitude, and what purpose does this serve?
3. Why is the testimonial approach to McGuire's essay so appropriate to her subject matter? What might have been lost if she had opted to discuss *growing up with two moms* from a strictly scientific point of view?
4. Explain what you consider to be the most thought-provoking part of McGuire's essay.
5. To what extent do you believe that the length of McGuire's essay is sufficient to analyze her subject matter? Do you believe more detail or further exposition would have added to her discussion? Why or why not? How?

Language and Vocabulary

1. Vocabulary: *fag, queer, dyke, gay, stereotypical.* What is "pejorative language"? Look up the word "pejorative" in your dictionary, as well as in your thesaurus. What are the denotative and connotative meanings of a pejorative word? How are most of the vocabulary terms above pejorative?
2. How does the author's simple word choice lend clarity to the real focus of McGuire's essay (a girl growing up with two mothers)?

Group Activities

1. Break into groups and brainstorm as many pejorative terms for as many groups of individuals as you can. What pejorative terms, for instance, refer to straight people, to men, to women, to people of color, to politicians, and so on?

2. Have all groups go to the library and make a copy of the articles on gay families in the November 4, 1996, issue of *Newsweek* magazine (the source of Megan McGuire's article). After reading each article, do some additional research on (1) what growing up in a gay family can or might be like, and (2) the future probability of the social acceptance of gay families. Finally, divide the class into two groups: those who think that gay couples should "have the right to adopt children" and those who oppose granting gay couples such a right. Debate both sides of the issue, attempting to clearly distinguish between social prejudice, beliefs about traditional families, and the idea that gay people can be as good at parenting as straight people can.

Writing Activities

1. Construct an essay where you examine the cause(s) of discomfort for children who grow up in a single-parent, a two-mother, or two-father family, and the positive or negative effect(s) from such an upbringing. Providing plenty of representative examples that justify your claims will be an essential part of your essay.
2. Write a composition explaining the reasons (causes) and results (effects) of taking pride in your family, your career, your physical appearance, your moral character, your personal ethics, and so on. Did you always "take pride" in your topic?

Internet Connection: Megan McGuire

Alternative Lifestyles & Family

McGuire concludes that growing up with two loving mothers had more positive than negative effects on her, and that people who criticize gay unions as unnatural and harmful to children demonstrate ignorance. Look up "alternative lifestyles and parenting" and/or "gay marriages" on your favorite search engine or online database. What reasoning do some people use to limit "lifestyle choices" to gay couples that wish to raise a family and/or get married? Which recent articles confirm McGuire's conclusions? After jotting down responses to these questions, document specific source materials so that your readers can locate them. (See the Appendix on MLA documentation at the end of the text.)

Carlos Bulosan

Labor and Capital: The Coming Catastrophe

Carlos Bulosan was born in Luzon in the central Philippines and spent the first seventeen years of his life working in fields with his father or selling fish at the public market with his mother. Bulosan came to America in 1930 and worked as a migrant worker, a union activist, and a writer. Bulosan published several books, including *The Laughter of My Father* (1942), *America Is in the Heart* (1977), *The Philippines Is in the Heart: A Collection of Short Stories* (1979), and *If You Want to Know Who We Are: A Carlos Bulosan Reader* (1983). In the following essay, Bulosan expresses his views on the need for unions to protect the laborer from exploitation by an employer.

Pre-reading Questions

1. Cluster the word "capitalism." What positive and negative associations do you relate with the word?
2. Who controls most of the money in America? Who is responsible for producing our nation's wealth?

---

1 Labor is the issue of the day. It has always been the issue. It is high time we should understand why thousands of workers' lives are sacrificed; why millions of dollars' worth of property are destroyed in the name of labor.

2 As in all industrial countries, America's wealth is concentrated in the hands of the few. This wealth is socially produced and privately appropriated. This precisely means that the wealth of the United States is produced by the people, the workers as a whole, and distributed by the industrialists. The contradictions of the social production and the private distribution of wealth [brings about] all social problems.

3 Industrialists are fattened by profits. Profits are sucked from the very blood of the workers. This profiteering scheme is made possible by speed-ups, long hours and brutal methods. It is by driving workers into a most intolerable condition that the profiteers grow impregnable.

There is a better term for this condition: barbarism. But do not think they spend their profits in philanthropic ventures. They invest it in the forces of production, machines, etc. They spend it in idle luxury. Have you seen a banker's daughter throwing away thousands of dollars for a sick dog? They pay more attention to animals than to us. Have you seen a manufacturer's machinery housed and guarded by a cordon of armed men? We are nearly [destroyed] in their riot for profits.

4 But the industrialists have also a quarrel among themselves. The bigger ones pool together and drive out the smaller ones. This struggle goes on until only one or two are left to dictate in the market. The bigger the combines they have, the more enormous profits they acquire, which means more exploitation. This goes on until society constricts and workers are thrown into the streets to starve. Do not believe that economic depressions are natural phenomena. All depressions are made, and inevitable when the markets are overflowing with surplus: Crisis is bound to come. The only solution that capitalism could give is war. This is why the coming war is more threatening and dangerous than the previous ones. All wars are fought for profit. That is why we must sacrifice everything for the prevention of war. For war is not only the slaughter of humanity but also the destruction of culture, the barbarization of man. We must die for peace and not for profit.

5 Labor and capital are sharp enemies. There never was any amnesty between them and there shall never be. One or the other stay[s]. The most disastrous proposal is compromise between them. This will never do: it only means the demoralization of the workers, the betrayal of these advanced groups working among the exploited and oppressed.

6 Unionism is one way of fighting for a better living condition. We are lucky to have in this country a considerable strong group which is fighting for us workers. But this is only a stepping-stone available in democracies. Unionism is a way to economic freedom. But we must have political freedom also. We could have this through unionisms. We must have everything or nothing.

Post-reading Questions

Content

1. What does Bulosan state are the causes of "labor exploitation"? What are the implied effects of such exploitation?
2. According to Bulosan, what are the causes of economic depression?
3. Why does Bulosan say that we must avoid war at all costs? Do you agree with him? Why or why not?
4. Although the author wrote this essay in 1937, much of what he says is true today. What issues discussed in his essay are relevant to our modern workforce? How? Why?

Strategies and Structures

1. Why does Bulosan take a commonly accepted notion that wars are justified by noble ideals and claim that wars are fought for profit? Which idea about war do you believe? Why?
2. Reread the topic sentences in each of the body paragraphs of the essay; in what way does Bulosan break down his theme? How well does he build upon his previous points?
3. Bulosan concludes his essay talking about the need for unionism to achieve better living. Does his composition logically build up to his conclusion? How? Why?

Language and Vocabulary

1. Vocabulary: *profiteering, intolerable, impregnable, philanthropic, cordon, exploitation, phenomena, slaughter, amnesty.* What do the majority of these words suggest to you? Which do you find more closely associated with labor?
2. Although Bulosan is quite descriptive in this essay, most of his descriptions produce a negative feeling in the reader (e.g., "Profits are sucked from the very blood of the workers"). Write two or three paragraphs in which you present "profits" in a positive way.

Group Activities

1. Discuss capital or money. Is there anything positive that can be said about money other than it can "buy" people, places, and things? Would you change your present opinion about money or the capitalist system if you were a farm laborer picking fruits and vegetables for four dollars an hour?
2. Break the class up into two groups—one group representing the interests of laborers and the other group representing the interests of big business—and prepare a class debate arguing which is more essential to the well-being of a capitalist society. Write a summary of the debate, explaining which group presented the best argument. (You need not be faithful to your group.)

Writing Activities

1. If you were a top industrialist, how would you spend your profits? Would you go out of your way to improve working conditions for your laborers or invest your money in schemes to make you even greater profits? Focusing in on

either the causes or the ultimate effects of your actions, write a composition explaining the rationale for what you would do with your money.

2. Write an essay comparing and contrasting the unions mentioned by Bulosan in his article written in 1937 and unions of today. Have people's attitudes towards unions changed? Are the unions of today more, less, or equally as effective as those of 1937? Are unions necessary today? Why or why not? Make sure you support your statements with verifiable facts, not only personal opinions.

Karen Ray

The Naked Face

Karen Ray is a full-time writer whose articles, columns, and essays have appeared in many magazines and periodicals throughout the nation: *Glamour, Science Digest, Working Woman, Christian Science Monitor*, and the *New York Times*. Ray's novels include *The Proposal* (1981), *Family Portrait* (1983), *Come Home to Darkness* (1991), and *The T. F. Letters* (2000). She now lives and writes at home in Arlington, Texas.

Pre-reading Questions

1. When do you feel "naked" or incomplete in front of other people? Why?
2. Do you like "beauty aids" such as makeup? Who determines what is and what is not beautiful?
3. What is the relationship between fashion and beauty?

---

1 From the neck up, I am a nudist.

2 No mascara for me. No eyeliner, no lipstick, no blush, no powder, foundation, eye shadow, highlighter, lip pencil or concealing stick.

3 My nakedness is partly pragmatic and partly philosophical. Just getting my eyes open in the morning is a feat. I have neither the will nor the ability to apply makeup when I can hardly see straight. At night, the most I can manage is brushing my teeth. I'm afraid that removing makeup would go the same way as scrubbing the sink and cleaning the oven. Also I rub my eyes occasionally, which doesn't help the makeup. Neither does my baby daughter.

4 My philosophical reasons are less defined. I don't like the idea of having to put cosmetics on my face to appear in public. Many women who wear makeup every day don't look "themselves" without it. I remember running home one long ago Saturday morning to tell my mother that a strange lady had come out of the Johnsons' house and picked up their newspaper. Turned out Mrs. Johnson just hadn't gotten her "face" on yet that morning.

5 My college roommate wouldn't step out the door without her makeup. I've heard sad stories of women who didn't want their husbands to see them as they really are and a pathetic one about a husband who forbade his wife to be seen without makeup. (The latter marriage is no longer intact.)

6 Most people don't go this far. Women use cosmetics to hide imperfections, to accentuate good points, to add drama and to feel polished. Many women in fact look "better" with makeup though, of course, our idea of beauty is tremendously affected by fashion. There are probably millions of men who would look "better" wearing makeup, but I've never met a man who did.

7 Recently a major women's magazine placed various amounts of makeup on a hypothetical job applicant, then asked managers and personnel directors which face they would hire. It should come as no surprise that in a magazine whose major advertisers are cosmetics companies the woman with the naked face was not awarded the job.

8 It has not always been so. During the 19th century, unadorned innocence was the height of fashion. Intricate hairstyles and colors were out of fashion and lip coloring was thought to be downright vulgar. The Roman poet, Ovid, in his famous poem *Ars Amatoria* (*Art of Love*), criticized Roman women for their excessive use of artifice. At various times Christian leaders have taught that makeup was sinful. A ridiculous attitude, but the opposite stand is equally absurd. To say, in one's mind if not with one's mouth, that a woman is not fully dressed without a full facial complement is crazy.

9 My friend Mary is manager in a technical area at a Fortune 100 company. Not long ago, she was in a business meeting when—in the middle of arguing an especially sticky point—a male superior leaned over and asked, "Why don't you wear makeup?" When she recovered, Mary asked her questioner why he didn't wear makeup. The response, "Because I'm

not a girl." Focus on makeup, whether the right amount for the job, the profession or the company, often seems to be just one more excuse for not taking women seriously in the work world. Much of the worry about makeup is really a worry about being accepted.

10 According to Fenja Gunn's recent history of cosmetics, *The Artificial Face,* makeup has been used throughout history to help create an ever-changing ideal of beauty. Prehistoric body painting and tattooing began as pagan ritual, in part to camouflage defenseless man and to help conjure up the fiercer qualities of animals.

11 Later, Egyptian eye paint also helped guard against eye diseases of the region and so children and men, as well as women, were encouraged to use kohl. Fashions changed with the time and geography, reaching a peak of ridiculousness in 18th century England. During that time the fashionable woman (and man, too) wore false eyebrows made of mouseskin. Natural beauty was usually destroyed by about age 30 from the use of lead-based cosmetics. The scarlet or black patch, or *mouche,* originated as a cover for smallpox scars but became a fashion symbol. Lipstick and rouge were popular. Perfume was fashionable, in part, because bathing was not.

12 Modern women, who are glad we have grown past such things, may be surprised to learn that, as in Elizabethan or Egyptian days, talc and rice are still the base of face powders. Waxes, oils and fats are still used as binding agents and as the primary ingredients in lipstick and complexion creams. Red ochre, used as a cosmetic coloring since civilized antiquity, is still used for that purpose. Women who favor pearlized lipstick, however, may be relieved to discover that there is now an artificial substance responsible for the silvery glitter, a role historically filled by fish scales.

13 On a recent dreary afternoon, I decided that a little lipstick might cheer me up. There wasn't much time to be cheered, however, because my baby daughter soon smeared it all over my face, shirt and her clothes. My friend Debbie has two small boys and refuses to give it up: "The lady at the cosmetics counter gets positively gleeful whenever she sees me." Debbie's boys, two and four, have experimented generously with the use of cosmetics on themselves, the walls and furniture.

14 I wash my face with soap that costs $8.50 a bar, even though I am not convinced it's better than hand soap. Occasionally I use the cleansers, toners and scrubs that come along in the bonus package. But when it comes time for the colors and enhancers and concealers, I hesitate. In high-minded moments I like to think this is because my self-confidence comes from inside, not from a collection of products.

15 At the same time, I admit to being proud of my fingernails. They are naturally strong and hard. Even with housework and baby, it is easy to keep them long. I keep thinking it might be nice to show them off a little more. One of these days I'm going to have a manicure.

Post-reading Questions

Content

1. In what way is Ray's decision not to wear makeup—and thereby remain naked—"partly pragmatic and partly philosophical"?
2. Why does the author spend time discussing the history of cosmetic use? What were some of the historical reasons for wearing rouge and perfume?
3. When did human beings begin to use makeup? In what way did prehistoric humans try to enhance their natural beauty? How do we know?
4. Ray claims that "our idea of beauty is tremendously affected by fashion." What evidence does she offer to support what she says? Do you agree with her? Why?
5. What might modern women be surprised to learn about cosmetics? What might they be "relieved to discover"?

Strategies and Structures

1. What does Ray's one-sentence opening paragraph accomplish? What effect did it have on you, the reader?
2. How does the author's use of specific examples strengthen her essay?
3. Paragraph 2 consists of what we recognize as fragmented sentence structures—structures that we are generally told to avoid. However, in context, how do these fragments shed light on the essay's title and initial paragraph, clarifying the focus for the rest of the composition?
4. What is the tone or mood of this essay? Where does it become firmly established? How does the author feel about makeup use?
5. Explain the irony of Ray's final paragraph. Does it call the rest of Ray's attitudes toward makeup or artificial aids to beauty into question? Why or why not?

Language and Vocabulary

1. Vocabulary: *mascara, eyeliner, lipstick, blush, foundation, highlighter, lip pencil, concealing stick, cosmetics, artifice, kohl, mouche.* All of these vocabulary words deal with makeup or are some type of makeup. If you are not familiar with the different sorts of makeup discussed, look up their definitions in your dictionary or ask your friends what they are used for. Then write both the type of makeup and its definition on a sheet of paper. Next, make a list of cosmetics and their uses that were not mentioned by the author in this essay.
2. This essay contains a very *personal* voice. What pronouns, phrases, and specifics contribute to this *personal* voice?

Group Activities

1. Get into groups and brainstorm at least *ten* questions about wearing or not wearing makeup. Next, individually interview friends and strangers, jotting down their responses to your questions. Interview people of all ages, of both genders, and from a wide range of social, economic, and ethnic backgrounds; then write a brief essay on the topic of "beauty aids" in modern society. The next time your group assembles, pass out copies of each other's essays and read them. Then, as a group, categorize the common uses of cosmetics among men and women in America. Note which categories men do not fall into. Finally, from the viewpoint of advertising executives, how would your group increase the male market for cosmetics? Write a five-point plan.
2. Go to the library after class and have each group member select three different popular magazines (e.g., *People, GQ, Us.*). Then go through your magazines, noting the number of ads that deal with beauty aids, from eyeliner and lipstick to hair transplants and cologne. Next, get together with your group and make a master list of your findings. You may want to use statistics your group has gathered in one of the following writing assignments. Therefore, remember to write down the names and issue dates of the magazines you reviewed.
3. Over the weekend, participate in a small group activity that involves makeup. For instance, you might get together with three other people (male or female) who never wear makeup and go somewhere Saturday night outrageously painted like peacocks. Whatever you do, write a brief group summary of your activity, including your initial plans, and what you learned about yourself and others with regard to makeup.

Writing Activities

1. What is the relationship between cosmetic use and sexism in American society? Write an essay explaining how and why the media in America make women feel dependent upon "beauty aids" to be presentable or complete human beings.
2. Compose an essay entitled "The Masked Face," wherein you argue that you have a strong philosophical and logical basis for wearing makeup. Illustrate your material with examples drawn from personal experience, observations, and readings.

***Internet Connection:* Karen Ray**

Cosmetics and Makeovers

What sorts of "makeovers" are most popular among men and women in the United States today and why? To locate information on this subject, research the terms "makeover" and "cosmetics" by entering them on a search engine of your choice. According to the articles you find, to what extent does the media create "needs" where none may have existed? Construct a thesis on this topic and write an essay explaining the cause/effect relationship between what one believes is essential and what really is necessary for a healthy existence. Be sure to document your sources using the MLA Style sheet. (See the Appendix.)

Phillip Persky

Guilt

Phillip Persky, Professor emeritus of English at San Jose State University, San Jose, California, also was Foreign Student Advisor for nearly twenty-five years at the university. Among other things, he taught English in Rome under a Fulbright Award, in Nigeria under the auspices of Southern Illinois University and the Ford Foundation, and in Micronesia through the Pacific Islands Project of SJSU. In the following essay, Persky distinguishes between guilt and shame, drawing from his own personal experiences and observations of others.

Pre-reading Questions

1. When in your life have you experienced guilt, and what happened—if anything—as a result? Did your initial shame in someone or something later become a source of guilt?
2. What is your attitude toward your parents? When have you experienced pride and/or shame because of them? How did you deal with this?

1 Do you know the difference between shame and guilt? A generation ago the distinction was clearer: Shame was private and guilt was public. Today such distinctions are observed less often. The situation I'm writing about took place when I was 14–15 years old—that is over 60 years ago. Yet, I still think about it, occasionally, and I still feel ashamed when I do. It was the way in which my parents spoke English that bothered me so much then. They knew no English when they arrived in the United States as immigrants from Poland and learned English slowly by listening, repeating and just plain trying hard.

2 My parents were oblivious to my shame and, by extension, the resulting guilt. They had come from a small town in Poland, Harodok, bordering Russia. It was a time of poverty in the ghettos, and those who could tried to come to America: then, as now, a country of promise. They lived first in Canal Fulton, Ohio, and then moved to Southeast Kansas to Caney. In order to support his family—my mother and two brothers—Dad began driving an old horse and cart around town buying junk and old rope. Shortly thereafter, the family moved to Independence, a town a short distance away and somewhat larger by a couple of thousand. There Dad, still with horse and cart, began the Persky Iron and Metal Company. The year was 1914, the year the United States entered World War I.

3 Later, during World War II, I remember well when there was a solemn ceremony of taking a metal statue and an old cannon, which had commemorated World War I, from the front of Memorial Hall downtown and hauling them in a civic procession to the junk yard where they would eventually be used to make ammunition for the military. Three generations later, in 1999, my sister-in-law still lives in Independence, and the company still does business under its fourth ownership, and until recently, under the family name, something of which I am very proud.

4 I remember many things about my childhood and youth in Independence. Those were happy times. My parents worked hard and were devoted to their children. I belonged to the Sea Scouts, a branch of the Boy Scouts, where the emphasis was on water sports—swimming and canoeing. I also worked for a grocery store through the kindness of my father, who, unbeknownst to me, had paid the grocer for hiring me. It wasn't until a week later that the store owner decided that I was worth the quarter an hour and that my father didn't have to pay it. Family was everything; nonetheless, there still was an underlying shame of my parents, and I always felt guilty because of it.

5 At home they spoke Yiddish with each other, an amalgam of many Central and Eastern European languages and German; in the United States it includes a smattering of English. People referred to such languages as "Broken English"—the term used then. It was the language

used in business, with friends, and with me. Although I got the gist of what was being spoken in Yiddish, I never learned to speak it—never needed to. While many people confuse Yiddish with Hebrew, the official language of prayer and religious ceremonies, as well as that of modern Israel, I didn't embrace that language either because I had no need for it in my daily life.

6 My parents subscribed to the *Jewish Daily Forward*, a newspaper written in Yiddish and carrying most of the national news of the day. There were also radio and, later, TV. In short, my parents were reasonably well-aware of what was going on in the world. Dad could read English with difficulty and did so with pride; however, Mother could not. If anyone asked her if she had studied English in America, she replied that as a newly-arrived, young woman in this country, she had begun night school. One evening after class, she was sure she was being followed and fearing for her safety, she never returned. Perhaps.

7 Ironically, my guilt stemmed from a confused sense of shame fused with pride in my parents. I knew how hard they worked. I knew how much they loved my brothers and me. Nonetheless, I also knew that I was ashamed of the way they spoke "Broken English"—with its distinctive Yiddish accent. Granted, no one had difficulty understanding my parents' English, and they were well-respected by everyone in the community. However, to me that Yiddish accent seemed to mark them as immigrants—uneducated foreigners. Attempting to distance myself from such social trappings only intensified my feelings of guilt.

8 As I grew older and began teaching English classes for foreign students at the University of Kansas, I became much more appreciative of my parents' accomplishments in the United States under such difficult conditions. This teaching experience motivated me to teach abroad in Italy, Nigeria, Taiwan, and many islands of Micronesia, including Palau and Pohnpei. More and more I have realized that difference is a strength, rather than a liability, and that shame is the result of discomfort and not a viable social construct for guilt. Indeed, I was reminded of a quote from *The Prophet* by Gibran, "Much of your pain is self-chosen." Reflecting to that time, I now realize that perhaps I was more concerned with my own perceived pain and neglected to think of my parents' struggles, achievements, and strides toward dignity.

9 In Santa Clara County, California, where I now live, there are literally hundreds of thousands of immigrants from nearly every country of the world, and I wonder if their second and third generation children also share in my shame and guilt. I hope not. Instead, I would hope that they can appreciate the sacrifices and hardships their parents probably have endured to live here and to adjust to a different culture and a new life. It is a magnificent tribute to this country that so many can become such successful, devoted Americans. Diversity and culture are ideals which one

should be proud of, not ashamed. The United States has gone from being the "melting pot of the world" to a nourishing "mixed salad." For myself, I, too, have come a long way from my childhood, but I still experience feelings of guilt for being ashamed of my parents' "Broken English."

Post-reading Questions

Content

1. What bothered Persky about his parents?
2. Why is guilt a natural consequence of shame? What led the author from one to the other?
3. What does the author remember about his childhood and youth in Independence? Why might his positive memories trigger an occasional sense of guilt?
4. Why does Persky bother to distinguish Yiddish from Hebrew, and what made it unnecessary for him to learn either?
5. The author's teaching experience gave him insight and appreciation of individuals who strive to learn a language other than their native tongue. What did that ultimately motivate him to do?

Strategies and Structures

1. In the opening paragraph, how does Persky clearly establish the point and direction of his essay?
2. Explain the purpose for the author's detailed discussion of his parents' poverty, aspirations, and ultimate accomplishments. How does this information relate to the rest of the essay?
3. Persky concludes paragraph 6 with a rhetorical fragment. What is the effect of this single word following his discussion? What does this insinuate?
4. Toward the end of the essay, the author has moved from shame to appreciation of his parents. However, has this changed his feelings of guilt about the past? Please explain your answer.
5. The concluding paragraph of the essay places the theme into a different perspective of personal guilt. Explain the ethical and emotional strength of Persky's appeal to the new immigrants who might look at their parents the same way that he did.

Language and Vocabulary

1. Vocabulary: *distinction, oblivious, ghettos, commemorated, civic, perceived, liability, underlying, magnificent*. "Shame" and "guilt" have negative connotations, but many of the above words do not. What might this imply about the author?
2. Identify when and where Persky uses "emotionally charged words" in his essay. What does he accomplish by using them?

Group Activities

1. Get into groups and share experiences wherein you initially felt ashamed and then guilt. How were your experiences similar to, and in what way were they different from, the experiences of other members in your group? Share your general perceptions of guilt with the rest of the class.
2. Persky seems to indicate that hands-on experiences with teaching English to foreign students gave him a new appreciation of the difficulty in learning a new language. Break up into groups of four or five people and have each member describe his or her experience learning a second language. When did you begin to take pride in your new language, or did you? Ultimately, did your group's attitude toward learning a new language reinforce or weaken the author's argument?

Writing Activities

1. Brainstorm the word "guilt," making as many associations with the word as you can. Focus on a particular aspect of guilt to explore in detail; state it as the thesis. You might, for instance, analyze four or five motivating factors behind the concept of guilt, as well as people, situations, and institutions that reinforce one's sense of daily understanding of the word.
2. Take the line, "Much of your pain is self-chosen" by Gibran from paragraph 8, and paraphrase the statement to use as the thesis of an essay. Fully develop your essay with examples drawn from personal experiences, observations, and readings. Strive to move your argument beyond the personal narrative by varying the examples you use and analyze.

Internet Connection: **Phil Persky**

Guilt and American Culture

Review how Phil Persky explained the cause and effect of guilt in his life. Using InfoTrac, Google, Bing, or another reseach engine, enter two key words—the first being an ethnicity, culture, gender, lifestyle, religious group, political party, and so on—and the second being the word "guilt" (e.g., Catholic guilt, male guilt, Republican guilt, and so on). Take notes on your findings;

then, write a short composition in which you explain some of the causes and effects of guilt as it relates to American society. In modern society, what tends to be the relationship between guild and remorse? Reference your sources as you go along, (e.g., According *Miranda Baker's Blog* on January 3, 2011, . . .).

Rose Anna Higashi

Eating with Immigrants

A Professor of English, Rose Anna Higashi, specializes in Japanese, English, and Asian literature, as well as composition. Her poems frequently appear in numerous magazines, textbooks, and professional journals. After the publication of her personal journal and poetry collection, *Blue Wings* (1995), she wrote the scholarly text, *Finding the Poet* (1996), a book on writing poetry and about self-discovery. Additionally, she has written several novels such as *Waiting for Rain* (1995), *The Learning Wars* (2000), *Keeping Secrets* (2001), and *Catholic Girls* (2002). Over the years, many people, places, and things have helped shape Higashi's prose and piety: her hometown, Joplin, Missouri; authors Matsuo Basho, Gerard Manley Hopkins, and Robert Browning; and mysticism and spirituality. Currently, Higashi is assembling a collection of her dramatic monologues. In the following essay, she discusses her favorite pastime: eating with immigrants, people can give anyone "a refresher course in the positive effects that traditional cultures can have on life in America."

Pre-reading Questions

1. What sorts of food do you like to eat and why? Do you like to eat at restaurants?
2. How would you characterize the workers at your favorite restaurant or fast-food outlet? Describe them using concrete nouns and active verbs.

1 My husband and I share a hobby—eating. Clearly this is not an unusual activity, but we like to specialize. Our interest is in eating in immigrant restaurants, more particularly, places where the owners, cooks, serving staff and customers are all first generation Americans. Why do we like immigrant restaurants? First of all, the food is good. Real people who grew up eating the food they are cooking prepare it. This is not fast food or food based on chain restaurant formulas. Immigrant food has real ingredients, like fresh ginger, fresh vegetables that didn't come out of a plastic freezer bag, and nutritious elements like tofu, bean sprouts and yogurt. Secondly, immigrant restaurants are sensible. The prices are reasonable and there is no silly pretentiousness. Immigrants are busy people who don't have time to put on airs. Snobbishness is for people who have been in this country for at least two generations. And finally, immigrant restaurants are happy places. Immigrants have hope. They have come to America believing that their lives can be better, and they've brought their families along with them on the greatest, bravest and riskiest adventure of their lives. Along with a good meal, a person who eats in an immigrant restaurant can receive a refresher course in the positive effects that traditional cultures can have on life in America.

2 Last Saturday, while we were eating dim sum at a Chinese immigrant restaurant, my husband and I got a pleasant reminder of the importance of family values and intergenerational respect. As we were nibbling on our fresh broccoli and turnip cakes, a glance around the huge room revealed not a single person eating alone. We noticed large family groups seated together at round tables sharing food from the lazy Susan in the center. Elderly grandparents sat next to young children who refilled the old folks' teacups without being told to do so. Even teenagers seemed unembarrassed by being seen in public with their parents. Attentive family members assisted senior citizens into and out of the restaurant. And children were allowed to be themselves. Babies got to cry and toddlers got to run around under the tables, and no one got angry if the kids spilled their noodles. And there was no "children's menu" nonsense. Everybody ate the same food.

3 There was plenty of evidence of the good old-fashioned work ethic at the dim sum restaurant too. The large staff of hostesses, waiters and waitresses, busboys, women pushing the carts filled with food, cooks and cashiers worked together like bees in a hive. Although each had a specific task to perform, I noticed that they automatically helped each other out when the need arose. When the restaurant got busy, the host himself helped bus tables and set them up for the next customers. When she came to our table with our bill, the cashier noticed that we had leftover food and quickly brought us some boxes rather than waiting for our server to get them. Not one employee was goofing off or adopting a "that's not my job" attitude. What a painful contrast with some of America's fast food

restaurants where the poorly trained help are so busy talking to each other that they can hardly be bothered to wait on a customer.

4 Whether we're eating sushi and soybeans at a little Japanese place where no one speaks English, enjoying freshly made *larb* at our favorite Thai restaurant or snacking on *kim chee* and *bibim bap* at a Korean tofu house, we like to dine with immigrants because of the upbeat ambience. There is no room for boredom and cynicism among first generation Americans. The woman who cooks the fabulous meals at our favorite Indian restaurant always comes out of the kitchen and asks us if we are enjoying the food, and she is genuinely pleased that we are. The owner of our local taqueria calls us "amigos" and actually means it. Immigrants have come from difficult circumstances believing that life is still worth living. They have traveled long distances, suffered culture shock and financial deprivation, and they have observed some of the truths of life along the way. Immigrants know that disrespect and self-centered egotism will not help them succeed. The traditional emphasis on community, combined with excellence in individual effort, treasured historically by both the Native Americans and the founders of the U.S. Constitution, is brought back to us through our immigrants as reminders of what we once valued before selfishness, arrogance and greed became the norm.

5 I sigh with sadness when I read the predictable letters to the editor of my local newspaper blaming immigrants for such social ills as lack of affordable housing, the deterioration of our educational system and even terrorism. I wish that the people who write these letters would go down to the neighborhood Vietnamese *pho* shop for a simple bowl of noodles elegantly garnished with fresh basil and limes and served with courtesy and respect by a man who suffered horribly in his previous life yet loves his new country and hopes for a better life for his children. Somehow, tea tastes better among people who have left bitterness behind, and food is more nourishing eaten in community.

Post-reading Questions

Content

1. Why does Higashi like "eating in immigrant restaurants . . . where the owners, cooks, serving staff and customers are all first generation Americans"? Does she appear to be a first generation immigrant herself?
2. What evidence of the "good old-fashioned work ethic" did Higashi encounter at her local "dim sum" restaurant?
3. Why does the author "sigh with sadness" when she reads letters "to the editor" in her local newspaper?

4. Higashi says that she and her husband enjoy eating at immigrant restaurants "because of the upbeat ambiance." What does she imply are the immediate causes for such positive eating atmospheres?
5. Make a brief list of the representative immigrant restaurants mentioned by Higashi, as well as any outstanding details that she offers about each.

Strategies and Structures

1. What cause-and-effect relationship does Higashi specifically establish in her thesis sentence? How does it provide a guiding focus for the rest of her essay?
2. Describe the tone of "Eating With Immigrants." What does it lend to Higashi's discussion?
3. How do Higashi and her husband get a "pleasant reminder of the importance of family values" by eating at a Chinese restaurant? In what way does their "pleasant reminder" reinforce her essay's thesis?
4. Why do you imagine Higashi strategically selected cause and effect as the dominant rhetorical method of development in "Eating With Immigrants"? Cite at least two examples from the essay to help illustrate and explain your answer.
5. In what way does the last sentence in Higashi's essay tie together all of her discussion points?

Language and Vocabulary

1. Vocabulary: *cynicism, deprivation, deterioration.* Add these words to your vocabulary log. Then write an original sentence using each word.
2. Go through Higashi's essay and identify places where she introduces a word group followed or preceded by a definition of it. Then, using a similar technique, write a paragraph about foods you eat to an audience that may not be aware of them. (Example: "Jessica likes to eat *poi*, a tarot root dish with the consistency of pudding.")

Group Activities

1. Pair off in a computer-assisted classroom, and search the Internet for information on ethnic foods—particularly those you eat very seldom. Next, research restaurants that you and your partner would like to visit. Narrow your list to one restaurant, eat there, and then write a collaborative critique of the establishment, noting such things as food quality, service, atmosphere, and so on.

2. In small groups, go back through Higashi's essay sentence-by-sentence, paragraph-by-paragraph, and analyze it in terms of (1) organization, (2) coherence, (3) support, (4) sentence skills, and (5) overall effectiveness. Also, be sure to mention the numerous ways she denotes cause-and-effect relationships throughout her essay.

Writing Activities

1. Write an essay wherein you argue the American weakness for fast foods curtails or strengthens one's ongoing exploration of restaurants featuring international or immigrant foods. Consider the eating habits of your friends, yourself, and your family as you prewrite on this topic.
2. What hobby or pastime do you enjoy? Using the rhetorical mode of cause and effect, write an essay explaining why you enjoy your chosen hobby, how you were introduced to it, and the consequences of nurturing a hobby in your daily life.

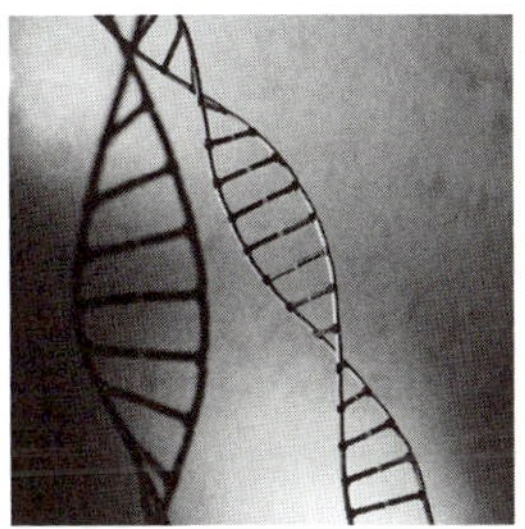

Anastasia Toufexis

The Right Chemistry

Anastasia Toufexis, a former editor at *Time* magazine, began her pre-med career at Smith College and insists that its basic science curriculum attracted her more than the prospect of becoming a doctor. Before joining *Time* magazine in 1978, she had been a staff writer for a physicians' newspaper. During the years Toufexis has been practicing medical journalism, she says that she often found herself "trying to elucidate medical matters that scientists themselves" were "hard pressed to explain." Toufexis' work continues to be printed in numerous journals and magazines, including *Psychology Today,* and she is currently finishing her first book. Toufexis published the following column, "The Right Chemistry," in *Time* Magazine on Monday, February 15, 1993. In it she develops her essay using cause-and-effect strategies to demonstrate the natural relationship between body chemistry on one hand, and personal attraction and human emotions on the other.

Pre-reading Questions

1. How do you feel about romantic love? Do you believe it should last "forever"?
2. What do you look for in a mate or partner?
3. What part do chemicals play in love? Do they contribute to the euphoria (joy or ecstasy) of falling in love?

---

1 O.K., let's cut out all this nonsense about romantic love. Let's bring some scientific precision to the party. Let's put love under a microscope.

2 When rigorous people with Ph.D.s after their names do that, what they see is not some silly, senseless thing. No, their probe reveals that love rests firmly on the foundations of evolution, biology and chemistry. What seems on the surface to be irrational, intoxicated behavior is in fact part of nature's master strategy—a vital force that has helped humans survive, thrive and multiply through thousands of years. Says Michael Mills, a psychology professor at Loyola Marymount University in Los Angeles: "Love is our ancestors whispering in our ears."

3 It was on the plains of Africa about 4 million years ago, in the early days of the human species, that the notion of romantic love probably first began to blossom—or at least that the first cascades of neurochemicals began flowing from the brain to the bloodstream to produce goofy grins and sweaty palms as men and women gazed deeply into each other's eyes. When mankind graduated from scuttling around on all fours to walking on two legs, this change made the whole person visible to fellow human beings for the first time. Sexual organs were in full display, as were other characteristics, from the color of eyes to the span of shoulders. As never before, each individual had a unique allure.

4 When the sparks flew, new ways of making love enabled sex to become a romantic encounter, not just a reproductive act. Although mounting mates from the rear was, and still is, the method favored among most animals, humans began to enjoy face-to-face couplings; both looks and personal attraction became a much greater part of the equation.

5 Romance served the evolutionary purpose of pulling males and females into long-term partnership, which was essential to child rearing. On open grasslands, one parent would have a hard—and dangerous—time handling a child while foraging for food. "If a woman was carrying the equivalent of a 20-lb. bowling ball in one arm and a pile of sticks in the other, it was ecologically critical to pair up with a mate to rear the young," explains anthropologist Helen Fisher, author of *Anatomy of Love*.

6 While Western culture holds fast to the idea that true love flames forever (the movie *Bram Stoker's Dracula* has the Count carrying the torch beyond the grave), nature apparently meant passions to sputter out in

something like four years. Primitive pairs stayed together just "long enough to rear one child through infancy," says Fisher. Then each would find a new partner and start all over again.

7 What Fisher calls the "four-year itch" shows up unmistakably in today's divorce statistics. In most of the 62 cultures she has studied, divorce rates peak around the fourth year of marriage. Additional youngsters help keep pairs together longer. If, say, a couple have another child three years after the first, as often occurs, then their union can be expected to last about four more years. That makes them ripe for the more familiar phenomenon portrayed in the Marilyn Monroe classic *The Seven-Year Itch*.

8 If, in nature's design, romantic love is not eternal, neither is it exclusive. Less than 5 percent of mammals form rigorously faithful pairs. From the earliest days, contends Fisher, the human pattern has been "monogamy with clandestine adultery." Occasional flings upped the chances that new combinations of genes would be passed on to the next generation. Men who sought new partners had more children. Contrary to common assumptions, women were just as likely to stray. "As long as prehistoric females were secretive about their extramarital affairs," argues Fisher, "they could garner extra resources, life insurance, better genes and more varied DNA for their biological futures. Hence those who sneaked into the bushes with secret lovers lived on—unconsciously passing on through the centuries whatever it is in the female spirit that motivates modern women to philander."

> *Love is a romantic designation for a most ordinary biological—or, shall we say, chemical?—process. A lot of nonsense is talked and written about it.*
>
> —*Greta Garbo to Melvyn Douglas in* Ninotchka

9 Lovers often claim that they feel as if they are being swept away. They're not mistaken; they are literally flooded by chemicals, research suggests. A meeting of eyes, a touch of hands or a whiff of scent sets off a flood that starts in the brain and races along the nerves and through the blood. The results are familiar: flushed skin, sweaty palms, heavy breathing. If love looks suspiciously like stress, the reason is simple: the chemical pathways are identical.

10 Above all, there is the sheer euphoria of falling in love—a not-so-surprising reaction, considering that many of the substances swamping the newly smitten are chemical cousins of amphetamines. They include dopamine, norepinephrine and especially phenylethylamine (PEA). Cole Porter knew what he was talking about when he wrote "I Get a Kick out of You." "Love is a natural high," observes Anthony Walsh, author of *The Science of Love: Understanding Love and Its Effects on Mind and Body*.

"PEA gives you that silly smile that you flash at strangers. When we meet someone who is attractive to us, the whistle blows at the PEA factory."

11 But phenylethylamine highs don't last forever, a fact that lends support to arguments that passionate romantic love is short-lived. As with any amphetamine, the body builds up a tolerance to PEA; thus it takes more and more of the substance to produce love's special kick. After two to three years, the body simply can't crank up the needed amount of PEA. And chewing on chocolate doesn't help, despite popular belief. The candy is high in PEA, but it fails to boost the body's supply.

12 Fizzling chemicals spell the end of delirious passion; for many people that marks the end of the liaison as well. It is particularly true for those whom Dr. Michael Liebowitz of the New York State Psychiatric Institute terms "attraction junkies." They crave the intoxication of falling in love so much that they move frantically from affair to affair just as soon as the first rush of infatuation fades.

13 Still, many romances clearly endure beyond the first years. What accounts for that? Another set of chemicals, of course. The continued presence of a partner gradually steps up production in the brain of endorphins. Unlike the fizzy amphetamines, these are soothing substances. Natural pain-killers, they give lovers a sense of security, peace and calm. "That is one reason why it feels so horrible when we're abandoned or a lover dies," notes Fisher. "We don't have our daily hit of narcotics."

14 Researchers see a contrast between the heated infatuation induced by PEA, along with other amphetamine-like chemicals, and the more intimate attachment fostered and prolonged by endorphins. "Early love is when you love the way the other person makes you feel," explains psychiatrist Mark Goulston of the University of California, Los Angeles. "Mature love is when you love the person as he or she is." It is the difference between passionate and compassionate love, observes Walsh, a psychobiologist at Boise State University in Idaho. "It's Bon Jovi vs. Beethoven."

15 Oxytocin is another chemical that has recently been implicated in love. Produced by the brain, it sensitizes nerves and stimulates muscle contraction. In women it helps uterine contractions during childbirth as well as production of breast milk, and seems to inspire mothers to nuzzle their infants. Scientists speculate that oxytocin might encourage similar cuddling between adult women and men. The versatile chemical may also enhance orgasms. In one study of men, oxytocin increased to three to five times its normal level during climax, and it may soar even higher in women.

16 One mystery is the prevalence of homosexual love. Although it would seem to have no evolutionary purpose, since no children are produced, there is no denying that gays and lesbians can be as romantic as anyone else. Some researchers speculate that homosexuality results from

a biochemical anomaly that occurs during fetal development. But that doesn't make romance among gays any less real. "That they direct this love toward their own sex," says Walsh, "does not diminish the value of that love one iota."

> *"A certain smile, a certain face"*
>
> —*Johnny Mathis*

17 Chemicals may help explain (at least to scientists) the feelings of passion and compassion, but why do people tend to fall in love with one partner rather than a myriad of others? Once again, it's partly a function of evolution and biology. "Men are looking for maximal fertility in a mate," says Loyola Marymount's Mills. "That is in large part why females in the prime childbearing ages of 17 to 28 are so desirable." Men can size up youth and vitality in a glance, and studies indeed show that men fall in love quite rapidly. Women tumble more slowly, to a large degree because their requirements are more complex; they need more time to check the guy out. "Age is not vital," notes Mills, "but the ability to provide security, father children, share resources and hold a high status in society are all key factors."

18 Still, that does not explain why the way Mary walks and laughs makes Bill dizzy with desire while Marcia's gait and giggle leave him cold. "Nature has wired us for one special person," suggests Walsh, romantically. He rejects the idea that a woman or a man can be in love with two people at the same time. Each person carries in his or her mind a unique subliminal guide to the ideal partner, a "love map," to borrow a term coined by sexologist John Money of Johns Hopkins University.

19 Drawn from the people and experiences of childhood, the map is a record of whatever we found enticing and exciting—or disturbing and disgusting. Small feet, curly hair. The way our mothers patted our head or how our fathers told a joke. A fireman's uniform, a doctor's stethoscope. All the information gathered while growing up is imprinted in the brain's circuitry by adolescence. Partners never meet each and every requirement, but a sufficient number of matches can light up the wires and signal, "It's love." Not every partner will be like the last one, since lovers may have different combinations of the characteristics favored by the map.

20 O.K., that's the scientific point of view. Satisfied? Probably not. To most people—with or without Ph.D.s—love will always be more than the sum of its natural parts. It's a commingling of body and soul, reality and imagination, poetry and phenylethylamine. In our deepest hearts, most of us harbor the hope that love will never fully yield up its secrets, that it will always elude our grasp.

Post-reading Questions

Content

1. According to the author, when and where did the notion of romantic love probably first begin to "blossom"?
2. How did physical appearance and personal attraction become a much greater part of the love equation?
3. Even though men are usually assumed to be unfaithful, what does Toufexis reveal about women?
4. Explain the difference between early love and mature love.
5. What, according to the author, causes heavy breathing, sweaty palms, and flushed skin in lovers?

Strategies and Structures

1. How does Toufexis grab her reader's attention in the first two sentences of the essay?
2. Explain how Toufexis enables her reader to understand—if not appreciate—the effects of chemicals connected with love.
3. Explain how the author tries to clearly describe our attraction towards different people.
4. What, according to Toufexis, is the mystery of homosexuality, and does this diminish the value of that love?
5. The author's conclusion draws us back to the introduction by telling us that we will probably not be satisfied with the scientific point of view. What will love always be to most of us?

Language and Vocabulary

1. Vocabulary: *anthropologist, phenomenon, clandestine, adultery, designation, euphoria, dopamine, norepinephrine, phenylethylamine, amphetamine, psychobiologist, oxytocin, myriad.* Look up the meanings of these words and enter them into your writing log or journal. Then reread the sentences where they appear in Toufexis' essay.
2. Even though this essay deals with love, very few of the words reveal this. Go through the essay and choose the words that convey this emotion. Could the author have avoided the use of all the chemicals to portray love?

Group Activities

1. Break up into groups of four or five people, and interview others regarding their views of love. You might ask the following questions (as well as a few original ones): Do they believe in true love and/or long-term relationships? Should people remain together for their children? Do they have any

idea how many chemicals are involved in the love process? Record their answers and save them for a future essay.

2. In a group, visit the Chemistry Department at your school and inquire about the chemicals mentioned in Toufexis' essay. Is anyone in the department aware of the capabilities of these chemicals? Record their answers and report to the class.

Writing Activities

1. Using the answers you collected from Group Activity 1, compose an essay similar to Toufexis' using answers recorded by those you interviewed as evidence in support of your claims. Did those you interviewed believe in the same causes and/or effects that Toufexis has written about, or do they believe that love is some kind of magical process that cannot be explained?
2. Write a cause/effect essay in which you explore the reasons for divorce, discussing the "four-year itch," the "seven-year itch," and Fisher's contention that the human pattern has been "monogamy with clandestine adultery." What role does chemistry play in this situation?

Additional Topics and Issues for Cause-and-Effect Essays

1. Compose an essay regarding the cause(s) and/or effect(s) of watching so much television in American society. You may want to limit your audience to adults, teenagers, or children.
2. Compose an essay explaining the effects of growing up in a one-parent family. In developing your essay, try to avoid clichés.
3. Since they often looked so much like real weapons, a few years ago toy guns began to appear in stores in a variety of colors to indicate their nature (a toy versus a threatening weapon). Based on personal observation and readings, compose an essay discussing the effects of this action by toy makers. Has America's interest in firearms decreased? Has it had any effect on crime (formerly people used toy guns to commit robberies and other acts of violence)?

4. Compose a paper explaining how aging affects an animal's temperament, agility, eating habits, and character in general. To begin this assignment, freewrite about the pets you or your family have owned or known over the years.
5. Write about the cause(s) and/or effect(s) of one of the following: role-playing, shoplifting, flirting, stereotyping.
6. What causes pollution and what are the effects of unchecked pollution? Who are the main culprits, and why do they pollute? You will want to incorporate authoritative sources in your essay. (A good source of information would be an environmental studies department. If your college has such a department, consult with professors or majors in that field.)
7. Describe a person who irritates or frustrates you abnormally. What does this person do that frustrates you so? Does this person clean too much, watch television excessively, expect favors, or complain too much? Write an essay in which you concentrate on the causes and/or the effects of your irritation. Use specific details to demonstrate your point.
8. Write an essay in which you examine either the cause(s) or the effect(s) of owning an exotic animal, bird, reptile, fish, and so on. (Why does one purchase exotic creatures to begin with, and what often becomes of them in the long run?)
9. Write an essay explaining the causes and/or effects of an *injustice*. You could write about social, economic, political, or ecological *injustices* as presented in the news.
10. Based on interviews, observations, experiences, and readings, write an essay describing what you believe it will be like to grow old in America. Make sure to "qualify" how and why multiple causes could lead to an ultimate effect or effects (or vice versa).

CHAPTER 10

Combined Strategies

We could have entitled this chapter "Additional Essays"; however, there is one point that we wanted to emphasize with the title: Essays rarely use only one rhetorical strategy for development—a point that is quite obvious from our selections here. In "American Horse," for instance, Louise Erdrich blends narration, description, and illustration to paint a visual picture of a special moment when she relates how Albert American Horse said, *"For grace"* as he took a dead butterfly from his car's grille, *"a black and yellow one, and rubbed it on Albertine's collarbone and chest and arms until the color and the powder of it were blended into her skin."* As he said, *"For grace,"* his daughter, Albertine, felt *"a strange lightening in her arms,* her chest." Moreover, *"The way he said it, grace meant everything the butterfly was. The sharp delicate wings. The way it floated over grass. The way its wings seem to breathe fanning in the sun. The wisdom of the way it blended into flowers or changed into a leaf."*

Charles Haynes blends characteristics of journalistic writing (short sentences and brief paragraphs) with exposition in "Honoring Sgt. Steward: Wiccans Are Americans Too." In the process, he employs several rhetorical methods of development, coupling illustration and example with cause-and-effect, when he argues that the United States has "no business asking soldiers to die for religious freedom abroad" if it cannot be guaranteed at home. In "Curanderismo: A Healing Art," Cynthia Lopez combines narration and description as she explains how Western medical practices have limitations that create barriers between would-be patients and medical practitioners, and that *curanderismo,* the Mexican art of healing, provides those alienated from "high tech" medicine a way to holistically address their needs and *"bring a sense of balance to all."*

Neil Young's guest editorial for *Guitar Magazine*, "The CD and the Damage Done," offers readers another glimpse of combined rhetorical strategies at work in writing. Using illustration and example, along with description and figurative language, Young takes issue with digital recordings because, in his opinion, they do not capture an ideal listening experience: *"Your brain is capable of taking in an incredible amount of information, and the beauty of music should be like water washing over you. But digitally recorded music is like ice cubes washing over you."*

Jeanne Wakatsuki Houston also uses more than one rhetorical strategy when she develops her recollection of her arrival at Manzanar, a Japanese internment camp, during World War II. On one hand, simple narration provides Wakatsuki Houston with a vehicle to chronologically tell her story. On the other hand, cause and effect strategies are also at work in the essay. While Houston clearly alludes to the reason or cause for her family's move to Terminal Island, Boyle Heights, and ultimately Manzanar (anti-Asian sentiment as a result of the war in the Pacific), her essay deals with the consequences or effects the moves had on her—as well as those around her—as a child.

It may be a good idea to determine the dominant rhetorical strategies at work in the following selections and review the introductory chapters dealing with each. For example, one would review narration, illustration and example, and process analysis after reading Reginald Lockett's "How I Started Writing Poetry." No single rhetorical strategy made this essay work; rather, a mixture of strategies created a coherent composition that (1) explains, in a sense, the rites of passage (narration); (2) uses details and references to make people, places, and things come alive (illustration and example); and (3) draws on informational process analysis to vividly describe how something was done—how, against the odds, he started to write poetry (process analysis). No new knowledge is required to blend two rhetorical techniques; in fact, it comes quite naturally. For instance, you may begin a process or illustrate something by first defining it or argue for a cause by narrating a story. Still other times in the act of classifying and dividing a subject, you may be using some other rhetorical strategy without being aware of it. Exposition means to expose or explain and is not limited to a single method of development.

Tips on Writing Expository Essays

After pre-writing to arrive at a specific focus, answer the following questions:

1. Have you sufficiently narrowed your thesis?
2. What is the point of this expository essay? What are you trying to explain and what rhetorical strategies lend themselves naturally to your objective?
3. Who is your audience? What tone or mood is most appropriate in addressing your audience and your occasion for writing?
4. Does your essay have an interesting introductory paragraph, a thoroughly supported thesis, and a satisfying conclusion?
5. What details make your essay memorable? When you revise your paper, what information could you add that would increase reader interest?
6. Did you vary your sentence patterns to add variety and interest?
7. How often did you use transitions and linking devices to establish relationships between words, phrases, clauses, and entire paragraphs?
8. Did you carefully proofread your work for careless spelling, verb tense agreement, pronoun agreement, and subject/verb agreement errors?
9. Did you punctuate all complete ideas with a period, question mark, or exclamation point in order to avoid run-on sentences or comma splices?
10. Were all partial ideas combined with other sentences to avoid fragments?
11. Did you revise awkward, misleading sentences—sentences that forced your audience to read and reread your essay in order to understand what you meant?
12. Did you defend your discussion points or merely make a list of them?

Charles Haynes

Honoring Sgt. Stewart: Wiccans Are Americans Too

Dr. Charles C. Haynes, director of the Religious Freedom Education Project at the Newseum, writes and speaks extensively on religious liberty and religion in American public life. Best known for his work on First Amendment issues in public schools, for over two decades Haynes has been the principal organizer and drafter of consensus guidelines on religious liberty in schools, endorsed by a broad range of religious and educational organizations. In January 2000, three of these guides were distributed by the U.S. Department of Education to every public school in the nation. Haynes is the author or co-author of six books, including *First Freedoms: A Documentary History of First Amendment Rights in America* (2006) and *Religion in American Public Life* (2001). His column, "Inside the First Amendment," appears in newspapers nationwide. Widely quoted in news magazines and major newspapers, Haynes is also a frequent guest on television and radio. He has been profiled in *The Wall Street Journal* and on ABC's "Evening News." In 2008, he received the Virginia First Freedom Award from the Council for America's First Freedom. Haynes, the senior scholar at the First Amendment Center, holds a master's degree from Harvard Divinity School and a doctorate from Emory University. The following article was initially published in "Inside the First Amendment" on June 25, 2006 and with the author's permission, updated in 2010. Therein, Haynes explains how Sgt. Patrick Stewart's widow fought an 18-month battle to enable her to engrave the Wiccan symbol (a five-pointed star inside a circle) on the standard plaque for military war heroes who died in action at the veterans' cemetery in Fernley, Nevada.

Pre-reading Questions

1. What is an "inalienable right"? To what extent do you believe that most Americans respect the fact that all U.S. citizens are guaranteed "inalienable rights" by the constitution, regardless of gender, ethnicity, religion, political party, or sexual orientation? Who or what comes to mind when you think about religious toleration? Why?
2. The First Amendment of the U.S. Constitution states, "Congress shall make no law respecting an establishment of religion, or

prohibiting the free exercise thereof." To the best of your memory, when has this guaranteed right been challenged?

---

1 The recent flap involving Wiccans in the military was a conflict that should never have happened. But years of foot-dragging by the Department of Veterans Affairs turned an easy case into a major controversy complete with charges of discrimination and threats of lawsuits.

2 All the VA needed to do was announce that the pentacle—a five-pointed star that symbolizes the Wiccan faith—had been added to the list of 38 "emblems of belief" approved for placement on government headstones and memorials. No big deal, end of story. Instead, the VA kept saying that it was "reviewing the process"—and would make a decision at some indeterminate time in the future.

3 Roberta Stewart heard this bureaucratic mumbo-jumbo for 18 months. She just wanted to honor her husband, Patrick, a member of the Nevada National Guard killed in combat during September 2005 in Afghanistan. Sgt. Stewart, who was posthumously awarded the Bronze Star and Purple Heart, among other honors, was a Wiccan.

4 But Stewart's request to have a pentacle engraved on her husband's memorial plaque was repeatedly denied pending review of the VA policy. His space on the Northern Nevada Veterans Wall remained blank.

5 Eventually, the VA had no choice but to allow the pentacle. Why? Start with the fact that Nevada politicians from both parties as well as advocacy groups from the left and right demanded the change.

6 Then there was the small matter of the First Amendment: It's clearly unconstitutional for the government to deny the Wiccan symbol while permitting symbols of many other religions. If approval of the pentacle was inevitable, why did the VA take so long to make a decision?

7 For Roberta Stewart it was a long and frustrating eighteen months. But other Wiccans had been pushing for VA recognition of the pentacle for more than nine years [before Roberta Stewart]. (According to the Department of Defense, some 1,900 active-duty service members identify themselves as Wiccans.)

8 At first blush, the years of VA stonewalling doesn't make sense. A glance at the 38 approved emblems suggests that any religion can make the list. In addition to all of the world's major faiths, a number of small, obscure sects are represented, such as Eckankar (a New Age group that espouses out-of-body travel). Even the atheists have a symbol. If the VA applied some kind of religious test to keep out the Wiccans, it's hard to fathom what it might have been.

9 Previously, the VA blamed the rules. Applicants had to provide documentation from a central authority certifying a symbol as representative

of that religion. Since Wiccans have no recognized head or hierarchy, their applications were rejected. Rules are rules.

10 Bipartisan outrage over Sgt. Stewart's case inspired a new set of rules. Now applicants are required to provide historic background and documentation of use to get a symbol approved. Roberta Stewart filled out all of the forms—but she still had to wait.

11 So what was the problem? The VA didn't talk. But the delay may have had to do with the fact that Roberta Stewart went public. Putting atheists on the list when no one paid attention was one thing, but announcing recognition of the Wiccan pentacle in the glare of the media spotlight was another.

12 Few people have even heard of Eckankar, but almost everyone has an opinion about Wiccans. Unfortunately, most of what people think they know about Wicca is false. Although Wiccans have nothing to do with black magic or satanic worship (Wicca is a nature-based religion centered on a belief that the divine permeates all life), try explaining that to a misinformed public.

13 The VA probably remembered the last time Wiccans in the military made headlines. About ten years ago, news reports of Wiccan ceremonies at Fort Hood and other bases provoked some conservative Christian groups to call on Christians not to enlist or re-enlist in the Army.

14 Under the First Amendment, the Army had no choice then, just as the VA has no choice now, but to accommodate Wiccans in the same way it accommodates other religious groups. But any "acceptance" of witches—who have long been demonized in Christian history—is certain to stir up trouble for the military.

15 It's also possible that VA lawyers began to realize that any guidelines for government-sanctioned "emblems of belief," however carefully crafted, were unworkable. In a nation where people are completely free to choose in matters of faith, the government should stop trying to figure out which symbols are "acceptable" and instead allow each family to choose whatever symbol best represents their convictions. In other words, cut through all of the bureaucratic red tape and jettison the "emblems of belief" list entirely.

16 Regardless, the VA should have acted immediately to honor Roberta Stewart's request and fill in the blank space reserved for Sgt. Stewart. After all, if we can't live up to religious freedom at home, we have no business asking soldiers to die for religious freedom abroad.

Post-reading Questions

Content

1. Who was Sgt. Patrick Stewart? What happened to him?
2. Summarize the major flap involving Wiccans in the U.S. military that Haynes discusses in his essay.

3. How many "emblems of belief" had been approved for "placement on government headstones and memorials" before adding the pentacle to the list?
4. In the end, why did the VA (Veteran's Affairs) have no other choice than to add the five-pointed star that symbolized the Wiccan faith to the "accepted" emblems of belief?
5. Historically speaking, how has Roberta Stewart led a crusade to defend "First Amendment Rights" as they pertain to religious worship?

Strategies and Structures

1. How does the author's credentials and expertise establish him as an authority on religious freedom and the First Amendment (review Haynes' byline)?
2. Why does Haynes spend a good deal of time—in two different paragraphs—discussing Eckankar? What does the "NEW AGE group" believe in and advocate?
3. How would you characterize the tone of Haynes' essay?
4. Why were Wiccan applications for a symbol on the accepted "emblems" list denied time and again by the VA?
5. In what way does Haynes refocus the controlling idea of his essay with his concluding sentence, "After all, if we can't live up to religious freedom at home, we have no business asking soldiers to die for religious freedom abroad." How does it relate to soldiers like Sgt. Stewart?

Language and Vocabulary

1. Vocabulary: *discrimination, emblems, indeterminate, mumbo-jumbo, posthumously, pentacle, inevitable, atheists, fathom, bipartisan, provoked, accommodate, convictions, jettison*. Which of the vocabulary words above refer to a person, place, or thing, and which words tend to function as modifying words? Why might writers want to be sure to incorporate concrete nouns, active verbs, and vivid modifying words in the final draft of an essay?
2. Write a personal response to Haynes' essay, using at least five new vocabulary words from it, in a journal or notebook. You might use these impressions in a future writing assignment.

Group Activities

1. Briefly investigate other instances where Wiccans and/or other minority religions have been persecuted or deprived of religious liberties guaranteed by the *U.S. Constitution* in small groups. After twenty minutes or so of research and group discussion, share your collaborative findings with the rest of the class. Your instructor might have you look up material about Wiccans in computer-assisted classrooms,

college libraries, or personal laptops, and/or cell phones with Internet access.

2. Pair off and compare and contrast each other's responses to Language and Vocabulary question 2. What impressed you most about Haynes' information and reasoning?

Writing Activities

1. Write an essay wherein you compare and contrast Haynes' essay, "Honoring Sgt. Stewart: Wiccans are Americans Too" to Laycock's essay, "Peyote, Wine, and the First Amendment" in Chapter 11. How do both defend the rights of minority religious groups to freedom of worship, a right guaranteed by the First Amendment.
2. In a well-supported essay with a title similar to Haynes' (e.g., "Honoring Choice: Vegans Are Human Too"), argue a minority religious, social, or economic group deserves the same privileges and respect of dominant groups.

Cynthia Lopez

Curanderismo: A Healing Art

A freelance writer from San Francisco, Cynthia Lopez wrote this essay while completing her master's degree in health administration at the University of Southern California. Lopez was formerly one of the managing editors for *Intercambios*, has worked for a civil rights law firm, and is currently active on the San Mateo County AIDS Advisory Committee. The following essay was printed in *Intercambios* in the winter of 1990.

Pre-reading Questions

1. What *healing arts* do you use for ailments and discomforts—*arts* that are not acknowledged modern medical practices?
2. Cluster the term "folk medicine." What do you associate with medicine?

1 "Western medicine alone limits people," says Elena Avila, R.N., M.S.N., and practitioner of curanderismo, the art of Mexican folk healing. With origins in pre-Columbian times and influenced by 16th century Spanish health care traditions, curanderismo uses herbs, ritual prayer, music, dance, and massage to cure people.

2 "It's a way of healing," explains Avila, "by seeking balance in all areas of life: social, physical, and spiritual."

3 One need only visit the mercado in almost any Mexican town to find the art of curanderismo in practice. Amid the stalls of modern-day commercial goods one can still find the local *yerbería,* or herb store, specializing in plants, ointments, and incense, designed to aid in the healing process. The dispensers of these cures often practice the medical knowledge handed down from generations. It's a form of traditional, holistic medicine, not well understood nor accepted in the United States, although some practitioners, like Elena Avila, believe that curanderismo can be practiced alongside modern medicine.

4 Avila began her study of Mexican folk medicine as a nursing student at the University of Texas. A first generation Chicana and native of El Paso, she was asked by an Anglo professor to speak about curanderismo. That request led her to a curandera in the El Paso–Juarez area, and hence initiated her journey into Mexican folk medicine. She was an apprentice for two years, visiting curanderos throughout Mexico and the southwestern United States. She studied Aztec dancing and participated in rituals in many of the "power places" in Mexico.

5 At the same time, she chalked up an impressive list of medical degrees and clinical experience. After earning her registered nurse degree, she was nurse manager of the Psychiatry Department of Thomason General Hospital in El Paso. She later became the hospital's director of maternal/child nursing. In 1981, she made a move to Los Angeles, as clinical coordinator of the UCLA Neuropsychiatric Institute. Two years later, she returned to her native Southwest to direct the Albuquerque Rape Crisis Center. It was a position she held for four years.

6 Avila now has her own private practice at home, where she specializes in resolving emotional problems of adult children of alcoholics, rape survivors, adult incest survivors, and addicts, among others. Business professionals as well as aging Native Americans from the surrounding reservations have sought her counsel. Curanderismo plays an integral part in her practice.

7 "I have altars in my treatment rooms, and I get a lot of my supplies from Mexico," she explains. She uses romero and ruda, both plants, when performing *limpias,* a kind of spiritual cleansing for returning balance to the life of a person. She also treats *susto pasado,* or chronic shock which causes the spirit to hide after a person suffers from trauma. Some patients have sought her help when suffering from *envidia,* a kind of negative energy created when one person is extremely jealous of another.

8 Nevertheless, Avila claims she had to redefine some ideas behind curanderismo to make it powerful for her patients. "When someone tells me '*alguien me hizo mal*' (someone harmed me) it affirms a belief that people outside of us have more power than ourselves. I work with the opposite idea that what I do empowers people to not become victims of others," she said.

9 While Avila incorporates the tenets of curanderismo into her practice, she won't hesitate to refer patients to a physician if she suspects a medical problem. The many years she spent as a nurse helped hone her ability to spot diseases requiring additional intervention. Perhaps this cooperative relationship between healers and physicians is what could enhance curanderismo's sometimes bad reputation with the medical establishment. Skeptical physicians often blame a misdiagnosed serious disease on curanderismo. The fact remains that for Hispanics, who have always comprised a large part of the uninsured, a visit to the curandero can provide an alternative to no health care at all.

10 An understanding of traditional Mexican medicine can help practitioners of Western medicine earn the confidence of their Mexican patients. Avila is a firm believer in sharing the knowledge she has gained and conducts workshops throughout the country on curanderismo to interested medical practitioners. Health care workers admitted to better cultural understanding once they learned that simply touching a child avoided the magical disease of *mal de ojo* or "evil eye," which makes a child susceptible to illness, or that egg or soap on the head of a baby is treatment for *mollera caido* or fallen fontanel attributed to dislocated internal organs.

11 A tradition of folk medicine is common in cultures throughout Latin America and elsewhere, with practices that may seem very alien to some. Avila acknowledges that some people still liken curanderismo to witchcraft. "The drive in society is to assimilate, to abandon the past, and although I don't deny that there are *brujos* or witches, I consider curanderismo a healing art," she said. And the holistic approach is what more and more people may be looking for as modern medicine becomes more specialized and to many people, alienating. Incorporating the new with the traditional may bring a sense of balance to all.

Post-reading Questions

Content

1. What does curanderismo use to cure people? What are its healing properties?
2. In your opinion, does the author have a solution for those alienated by modern medicine? Explain your answer.
3. Make a list of the medical degree and clinical experiences Avila acquired prior to directing the Albuquerque Rape Crisis Center.

4. What did Avila specialize in once she began her private practice at home?
5. Why might understanding "traditional Mexican medicine" help practitioners of Western medicine earn the confidence of their Mexican patients?

Strategies and Structures

1. How do the first and last sentences in this essay frame Lopez's discussion of curanderismo?
2. Why does the author discuss Avila's qualifications and experiences as a practitioner of Western medicine in such detail?
3. The events in this essay follow a chronological progression. Jot down a brief list of transitional words, phrases, and linking devices which move the reader coherently from point to point.
4. Explain the possible reason why the author expands her focus on folk medicine in Mexico to folk medicine throughout South America in paragraph 11.
5. Why do you think that Lopez frequently uses Spanish words throughout her essay? What does she accomplish by doing so?

Language and Vocabulary

1. Vocabulary: *practitioner, holistic, dispensers, susceptible, fontanel, assimilate.* Use each of these words in a sentence dealing with some aspect of medicine, healing, or illness.
2. What are the denotative meanings of "folk medicine" and "faith healing"? What connotative meaning does each term carry? How might the use of either term prejudice a person who believes in the power of Western medicine? Why?

Group Activities

1. Explore the breadth of folk medicine throughout the world. Begin by breaking the class down into groups of four or five people. Each group should select the folk medicine from a particular culture to research in detail. Visit the library and gather as much information about your group's cultural practices as possible; each group member should be responsible for material. Finally, in a class forum, present your group's findings.
2. Assemble into groups and discuss myths surrounding the medical profession. You might consider everyone from dentists and surgeons to general practitioners and chiropractors. Ultimately, write a collaborative paragraph explaining how and why your group feels "health attitudes" are shaped by the medical myths around us.

Writing Activities

1. Write an essay in which you present your own definition of *folk medicine,* using specific, concrete examples to illustrate what you say.
2. Using information drawn from class forums and personal research, compare and contrast the folk medicine practiced by two societies that do not fully embrace Western medicine.

***Internet connection:* Cynthia Lopez**

Holistic/Folk Medicine

Do some limited online research to gather information about "holistic medicine," "folk medicine," and "neuropathic medicine," to use in an original essay that you write on the topic *alternatives to Western medicine.* To what extent does your research confirm or dispute Lopez's conclusions in "Curanderismo: A Healing Art"? Write a thesis stating your conviction on this topic, and thoroughly argue and support what you claim with evidence drawn from your authoritative research; make certain to document your source material as explained in the Appendix to *Visions Across the Americas*, 8th edition.

Neil Young

The CD and the Damage Done

Born in Toronto, Ontario, Canada in 1945, Neil Young has become one of the more memorable, prolific, and influential folk-rock musicians in the United States. Legend has it that his love affair with music began after his father gave him a ukulele one Christmas, and in no time at all, he developed an affinity for the guitar and banjo. He began to play music with others before dropping out of high school so he could devote himself to his band. In addition to folk-rock, Young made significant contributions to rock and roll, country, and experimental music. His career as a recording artist spans over thirty years. He made his mark on music both as a soloist and as a member of various musical groups, including: Neil Young and the Squires; The Mynah Birds; Buffalo Springfield; Crazy Horse; and Crosby, Stills, Nash, and Young. Many critics have referred to Young as the Grandfather of Grunge—a musical style usually characterized by strong, "dirty" guitar riffs and distorted guitar solos. His albums (solo and with other bands) include: *Buffalo Springfield* (1967), *Buffalo Springfield Again* (1968), *Everybody Knows This Is Nowhere* (1969), *After the Gold Rush* (1970), *Dé ja Vu* (1970), *Journey Through The Past* (1972), *Harvest* (1972), *Time Fades Away* (1973), *On the Beach* (1974), *Zuma* (1975), *Long May You Run* (1976), *Stars 'N Stripes* (1977), *Decade* (1977), *Comes a Time* (1978), *Rust Never Sleeps* (1979), *Hawks & Doves* (1980), *Trans* (1982), *Everybody's Rockin'* (1983), *Old Ways* (1985), *Year of the Horse* (1987), *This Note's for You* (1988), *Freedom* (1989), *Ragged Glory* (1990), *Harvest Moon* (1992), *Unplugged* (1993), *Sleeps with Angels* (1994), *Mirror Ball* (1995), *Broken Arrow* (1996), *Silver & Gold* (2000), *Are You Passionate?* (2002), *Greatest Hits* (2004), *Prairie Winds* (2005), and *Chrome Dreams II* (2007). The following essay from "Digital Is a Huge Rip-off" is a guest editorial Neil Young wrote for the *Guitar Player.* Are digital recordings (CDs) as effective as vinyl albums? Neil Young believes not.

Pre-reading Questions

1. Do you own and/or listen to an ipod?
2. How would you describe what you "hear" in a digital recording? What are its characteristics? Why do you think Young claims, "We are living in the darkest age of musical sound. When they started capturing music on records a long time ago—on 78's—the sound was pretty shaky. Then it got a little better, and from that point on, right up to the beginning of digital recording, everything that was done was better than the digital recordings that are being made today. Digital is completely wrong. It's a farce"?

---

1 They've improved digital technology to the point where you can at least say, "Hey, that's music." But your brain and your heart are starved for a challenge, and there's no challenge, there are no possibilities, there's no imagination. You're hearing simulated music. Your brain is capable of taking in an incredible amount of information, and the beauty of music should be like water washing over you. But digitally recorded music is like ice cubes washing over you. It's not the same.

2 My album *Everyone Knows This Is Nowhere* is now available on CD, but it's not as good as the original, which came out in 1969. Listening to a CD is like looking through a screen window. If you get right up next to a screen window, you can see all kinds of different colors through each hole. Well, imagine if all that color had to be reduced to only one color per hole—that's what digital recording does to sound. All that gets

recorded is what's dominant at each moment. I would like to hear guitars again, with the warmth, the highs, the lows, the air, the electricity, the vibrancy of something that's real, instead of just a duplication of the dominant factors. It's an insult to the brain and heart and feelings to have to listen to this and think it's music.

3 There's a certain emptiness in the air these days. You think that it might be today's music, because it just isn't as heartfelt as yesterday's. Everybody says, "Well, business came in and took over, and they ruined music," but that's just an excuse. The real reason is technical. It's not that people don't have souls anymore. All these bands have got huge souls and can't wait to play; they just can't figure out why their albums don't sound as good as some of the things they used to hear.

4 I've been making records for twenty-six years, and I'm telling you: from the early 1980s up till now, and probably for another ten or fifteen years to come—this is the darkest time ever for recorded music. We'll come out the other end and it'll be okay, but we'll look back and go, "Wow, that was the digital age. I wonder what that music really sounded like. We got so carried away that we never even really recorded it. We just made digital records of it." That's what people will say—mark my words.

Post-reading Questions

Content

1. Neil Young wrote the song, "The Needle and the Damage Done," allegedly because one of his band members overdosed on heroin, and he wanted to expose it for what it was—"the worst drug ever." Why do you think Young alludes to that song title in his guest editorial, "CD and the Damage Done"?
2. What seems to be the controlling idea or thesis in this piece?
3. According to Young, what seems to be missing in digital recordings? Do you agree? (Think back to your description of digital recordings from Pre-reading Question 2.)
4. In Young's opinion, what should listening to music "be like"? How does this experience differ between analog and digital recordings?
5. To what extent does Young prove that "digital is a farce"—or does he? Explain.

Strategies and Structures

1. How does Young use his own recordings as evidence to support his claims? To what extent does such evidence influence your opinion about the analog and digital recording argument?

2. Explain Young's strategic analogy between *listening* to a CD and *looking* through a screen door. How might Young's comparison of a visual to an audio experience help to *picture* the concept of why you hear—or don't hear—on one hand, and yet possibly make you question the logic of Young's proof on the other hand?
3. Apparently, digitally recording music does something to sound—at least according to Young. What happens?
4. How do some explain "the emptiness in the air these days," and why would Young disagree with their assessment? How logical do you consider his counterargument? Why?
5. What prediction does Young make in his concluding paragraph, and how does it bring the somewhat gloomy editorial to a positive close?

Language and Vocabulary

1. Vocabulary: *digital, simulated, vibrancy, duplication*. Look up the vocabulary words in your dictionary, consider their definitions, and then reread the sentence in which each word appeared. To what extent do they relate back to the editorial title, "The CD and the Damage Done"? How?
2. Develop a paragraph comparing two types (e.g., rock, rap, tejano, country, soul, classical, jazz, blues) of music using the four vocabulary words from Language and Vocabulary Question 1, as well as three other adjectives (words describing nouns) from Young's editorial.

Group Activities

1. Individually, research opinions about analog and digital recordings, past and present. A good place to begin would be to reconsider your Pre-reading Question 2 (your initial thoughts on what you think you hear in a digital recording). By all means, gather information online, in the library and through interviews. Then gather as a group and share your findings, noting where members agree with Young's conclusions as well as why and how they differ.
2. Break the class down into groups of four or six students (an even number) and then pair off into subgroups. Next, have each subgroup select a different genre of music to research in terms of "sound" quality captured by analog or digital recording. For instance, one subgroup might investigate hip-hop while another considers classical music or rock 'n roll. Listen to representative (1) analog and (2) digital recordings of the music under review. When and where were you able to identify differences between the recordings? Discuss

such information in your group as a whole before joining the rest of the class for an open forum on the topic.

Writing Activities

1. Write an essay arguing that Young was or was not prophetic in his claim that "from the early 1980s up till now [1992], and probably for another ten or fifteen years to come—this is the darkest time ever for recorded music." Use a variety of readings, recordings, interviews, and personal experience to prove or disprove his prediction.
2. In July of 2008, Young told the *Financial Times* that the sound quality of digital music "still sucks" and that he had been working on an "alternative digital platform"—one that would offer much higher quality downloads than iTunes. Research the current status of this platform and write an argument of action, explaining why people should disregard or promote such a platform.

Jeanne Wakatsuki Houston

James D. Houston

Arrival at Manzanar

Born in Inglewood, California, Jeanne Wakatsuki Houston has spent most of her life on the Pacific coast. During World War II, her family was moved to the Japanese-American internment camp in Manzanar, California, for four years. Ms. Wakatsuki Houston was only seven years old at the time, and the memories of her years there are recorded in *Farewell to Manzanar* (1973), which she co-wrote with her husband James D. Houston, a well-known novelist. Then in 1988, they collaborated again in *One Can Think about Life after the Fish Is in the Canoe: Beyond Manzanar*. The Houstons also worked on film projects together such as *Barrio* (1978) and *The Melting Pot* (1980). Ms. Wakatsuki Houston's essays, articles, and reviews have appeared in numerous magazines and periodicals such as *Mother Jones, California Living, West Magazine, New England Review,* the *Reader's Digest* (Japanese edition), *Dialogue* (international edition), and the *Los Angeles Times*, as well as several anthologies. Other works include *Don't Cry, It's Only Thunder*, co-authored with Paul Hensler (1984), *Beyond Manzanar: Views of Asian American Womanhood* (1985), and *Legends of Fire Horse Woman* (2004). Among the many awards and accolades that Ms. Wakatsuki Houston has received is the prestigious Wonder Women Award (1984), an award honoring women over age forty who have made outstanding achievements in the pursuit of positive social change.

Pre-reading Questions

1. Answer the following questions in your journal. What do you know about the Japanese-American internment in the United States during World War II? Who was confined in these camps? Why were Japanese Americans confined? What were the results of such internment? What were the conditions of these camps?
2. How would you react if you and your family were suddenly asked to move to an internment camp and to give up your possessions, property, and professions? As you write, think of all your possible actions and the advantages and disadvantages of each one.

---

1 In December of 1941 Papa's disappearance didn't bother me nearly so much as the world I soon found myself in.

2 He had been a jack-of-all-trades. When I was born he was farming near Inglewood. Later, when he started fishing, we moved to Ocean Park, near Santa Monica, and until they picked him up, that's where we lived, in a big frame house with a brick fireplace, a block back from the beach. We were the only Japanese family in the neighborhood. Papa liked it that way. He didn't want to be labeled or grouped by anyone. But with him gone and no way of knowing what to expect, my mother moved all of us down to Terminal Island. Woody already lived there, and one of my older sisters had married a Terminal Island boy. Mama's first concern now was to keep the family together; and once the war began, she felt safer there than isolated racially in Ocean Park. But for me, at age seven, the island was a country as foreign as India or Arabia would have been. It was the first time I had lived among other Japanese, or gone to school with them, and I was terrified all the time.

3 This was partly Papa's fault. One of his threats to keep us younger kids in line was "I'm going to sell you to the Chinaman." When I had entered kindergarten two years earlier, I was the only Oriental in the class. They sat me next to a Caucasian girl who happened to have very slanted eyes. I looked at her and began to scream, certain Papa had sold me out at last. My fear of her ran so deep I could not speak of it, even to Mama, couldn't explain why I was screaming. For two weeks I had nightmares about this girl, until the teachers finally moved me to the other side of the room. And it was still with me, this fear of Oriental faces, when we moved to Terminal Island.

4 In those days it was a company town, a ghetto owned and controlled by the canneries. The men went after fish, and whenever the boats came back—day or night—the women would be called to process the catch while it was fresh. One in the afternoon or four in the morning, it made no difference. My mother had to go to work right after we moved there. I can still hear the whistle—two toots for French's, three for Van Camp's—and she and Chizu would be out of bed in the middle of the night, heading for the cannery.

5 The house we lived in was nothing more than a shack, a barracks with single plank walls and rough wooden floors, like the cheapest kind of migrant workers' housing. The people around us were hardworking, boisterous, a little proud of their nickname, *yo-go-re,* which meant literally *uncouth one,* or roughneck, or dead-end kid. They not only spoke Japanese exclusively, they spoke a dialect peculiar to Kyushu, where their families had come from in Japan, a rough, fisherman's language, full of oaths and insults. Instead of saying *ba-ka-tare,* a common insult meaning *stupid,* Terminal Islanders would say *ba-ka-ya-ro,* a coarser and exclusively masculine use of the word, which implies gross stupidity. They would swagger and pick on outsiders and persecute anyone who didn't speak as they did. That was what made my own time there so hateful. I had never spoken anything but English, and the other kids in the second grade despised me for it. They were tough and mean, like ghetto kids anywhere. Each day after school I dreaded their ambush. My brother Kiyo, three years older, would wait for me at the door, where we would decide whether to run straight home together, or split up, or try a new and unexpected route.

6 None of these kids ever actually attacked. It was the threat that frightened us, their fearful looks, and the noises they would make, like miniature Samurai, in a language we couldn't understand.

7 At the time it seemed we had been living under this reign of fear for years. In fact, we lived there about two months. Late in February the navy decided to clear Terminal Island completely. Even though most of us were American-born, it was dangerous having that many Orientals so close to the Long Beach Naval Station, on the opposite end of the island.

We had known something like this was coming. But, like Papa's arrest, not much could be done ahead of time. There were four of us kids still young enough to be living with Mama, plus Granny, her mother, sixty-five then, speaking no English, and nearly blind. Mama didn't know where else she could get work, and we had nowhere else to move *to.* On February 25 the choice was made for us. We were given forty-eight hours to clear out.

8 The secondhand dealers had been prowling around for weeks, like wolves, offering humiliating prices for goods and furniture they knew many of us would have to sell sooner or later. Mama had left all but her most valuable possessions in Ocean Park, simply because she had nowhere to put them. She had brought along her pottery, her silver, heirlooms like the kimonos Granny had brought from Japan, tea sets, lacquered tables, and one fine old set of china, blue and white porcelain, almost translucent. On the day we were leaving, Woody's car was so crammed with boxes and luggage and kids we had just run out of room. Mama had to sell this china.

9 One of the dealers offered her fifteen dollars for it. She said it was a full setting for twelve and worth at least two hundred. He said fifteen was his top price. Mama started to quiver. Her eyes blazed up at him. She had been packing all night and trying to calm down Granny, who didn't understand why we were moving again and what all the rush was about. Mama's nerves were shot, and now navy jeeps were patrolling the streets. She didn't say another word. She just glared at this man, all the rage and frustration channeled at him through her eyes.

10 He watched her for a moment and said he was sure he couldn't pay more than seventeen fifty for that china. She reached into the red velvet case, took out a dinner plate and hurled it at the floor right in front of his feet.

11 The man leaped back shouting, "Hey! Hey, don't do that! Those are valuable dishes!"

12 Mama took out another dinner plate and hurled it at the floor, then another and another, never moving, never opening her mouth, just quivering and glaring at the retreating dealer, with tears streaming down her cheeks. He finally turned and scuttled out the door, heading for the next house. When he was gone she stood there smashing cups and bowls and platters until the whole set lay in scattered blue and white fragments across the wooden floor.

13 The American Friends Service helped us find a small house in Boyle Heights, another minority ghetto, in downtown Los Angeles, now inhabited briefly by a few hundred Terminal Island refugees. Executive Order 9066 had been signed by President Roosevelt, giving the War Department authority to define military areas in the western states and to exclude from them anyone who might threaten the war effort. There was a

lot of talk about internment, or moving inland, or something like that in store for all Japanese Americans. I remember my brothers sitting around the table talking very intently about what we were going to do, how we would keep the family together. They had seen how quickly Papa was removed, and they knew now that he would not be back for quite a while. Just before leaving Terminal Island Mama had received her first letter, from Bismarck, North Dakota. He had been imprisoned at Fort Lincoln, in an all-male camp for enemy aliens.

14 Papa had been the patriarch. He had always decided everything in the family. With him gone, my brothers, like councilors in the absence of a chief, worried about what should be done. The ironic thing is, there wasn't much left to decide. These were mainly days of quiet, desperate waiting for what seemed at the time to be inevitable. There is a phrase the Japanese use in such situations, when something difficult must be endured. You would hear the older heads, the Issei, telling others very quietly, *"Shikata ga nai"* (It cannot be helped). *"Shikata ga nai"* (It must be done).

15 Mama and Woody went to work packing celery for a Japanese produce dealer. Kiyo and my sister May and I enrolled in the local school, and what sticks in my memory from those few weeks is the teacher—not her looks, her remoteness. In Ocean Park my teacher had been a kind, grandmotherly woman who used to sail with us in Papa's boat from time to time and who wept the day we had to leave. In Boyle Heights the teacher felt cold and distant. I was confused by all the moving and was having trouble with the classwork, but she would never help me out. She would have nothing to do with me.

16 This was the first time I had felt outright hostility from a Caucasian. Looking back, it is easy enough to explain. Public attitudes toward the Japanese in California were shifting rapidly. In the first few months of the Pacific war, America was on the run. Tolerance had turned to distrust and irrational fear. The hundred-year-old tradition of anti-Orientalism on the west coast soon resurfaced, more vicious than ever. Its result became clear about a month later, when we were told to make our third and final move.

17 The name Manzanar meant nothing to us when we left Boyle Heights. We didn't know where it was or what it was. We went because the government ordered us to. And, in the case of my older brothers and sisters, we went with a certain amount of relief. They had all heard stories of Japanese homes being attacked, of beatings in the streets of California towns. They were as frightened of the Caucasians as Caucasians were of us. Moving, under what appeared to be government protection, to an area less directly threatened by the war seemed not such a bad idea at all. For some it actually sounded like a fine adventure.

18 Our pickup point was a Buddhist church in Los Angeles. It was very early, and misty, when we got there with our luggage. Mama had bought heavy coats for all of us. She grew up in eastern Washington and knew that anywhere inland in early April would be cold. I was proud of my new coat, and I remember sitting on a duffel bag trying to be friendly with the Greyhound driver. I smiled at him. He didn't smile back. He was befriending no one. Someone tied a numbered tag to my collar and to the duffel bag (each family was given a number, and that became our official designation until the camps were closed), someone else passed out box lunches for the trip, and we climbed aboard.

19 I had never been outside Los Angeles County, never traveled more than ten miles from the coast, had never even ridden on a bus. I was full of excitement, the way any kid would be, and wanted to look out the window. But for the first few hours the shades were drawn. Around me other people played cards, read magazines, dozed, waiting. I settled back, waiting too, and finally fell asleep. The bus felt very secure to me. Almost half its passengers were immediate relatives. Mama and my older brothers had succeeded in keeping most of us together, on the same bus, headed for the same camp. I didn't realize until much later what a job that was. The strategy had been, first, to have everyone living in the same district when the evacuation began, and then to get all of us included under the same family number, even though names had been changed by marriage. Many families weren't as lucky as ours and suffered months of anguish while trying to arrange transfers from one camp to another.

20 We rode all day. By the time we reached our destination, the shades were up. It was late afternoon. The first thing I saw was a yellow swirl across a blurred, reddish setting sun. The bus was being pelted by what sounded like splattering rain. It wasn't rain. This was my first look at something I would soon know very well, a billowing flurry of dust and sand churned up by the wind through Owens Valley.

21 We drove past a barbed-wire fence, through a gate, and into an open space where trunks and sacks and packages had been dumped from the baggage trucks that drove out ahead of us. I could see a few tents set up, the first rows of black barracks, and beyond them, blurred by sand, rows of barracks that seemed to spread for miles across this plain. People were sitting on cartons or milling around, with their backs to the wind, waiting to see which friends or relatives might be on this bus. As we approached, they turned or stood up, and some moved toward us expectantly. But inside the bus no one stirred. No one waved or spoke. They just stared out the windows, ominously silent. I didn't understand this. Hadn't we finally arrived, our whole family intact? I opened a window, leaned out, and yelled happily. "Hey! This whole bus is full of Wakatsukis!"

22 Outside, the greeters smiled. Inside there was an explosion of laughter, hysterical, tension-breaking laughter that left my brothers choking and whacking each other across the shoulders.

23 We had pulled up just in time for dinner. The mess halls weren't completed yet. An outdoor chow line snaked around a half-finished building that broke a good part of the wind. They issued us army mess kits, the round metal kind that fold over, and plopped in scoops of canned Vienna sausage, canned string beans, steamed rice that had been cooked too long, and on top of the rice a serving of canned apricots. The Caucasian servers were thinking that the fruit poured over rice would make a good dessert. Among the Japanese, of course, rice is never eaten with sweet foods, only with salty or savory foods. Few of us could eat such a mixture. But at this point no one dared protest. It would have been impolite. I was horrified when I saw the apricot syrup seeping through my little mound of rice. I opened my mouth to complain. My mother jabbed me in the back to keep quiet. We moved on through the line and joined the others squatting in the lee of half-raised walls, dabbing courteously at what was, for almost everyone there, an inedible concoction.

24 After dinner we were taken to Block 16, a cluster of fifteen barracks that had just been finished a day or so earlier—although finished was hardly the word for it. The shacks were built of one thickness of pine planking covered with tarpaper. They sat on concrete footings, with about two feet of open space between the floorboards and the ground. Gaps showed between the planks, and as the weeks passed and the green wood dried out, the gaps widened. Knotholes gaped in the uncovered floor.

25 Each barracks was divided into six units, sixteen by twenty feet, about the size of a living room, with one bare bulb hanging from the ceiling and an oil stove for heat. We were assigned two of these for the twelve people in our family group; and our official family "number" was enlarged by three digits—6 plus the number of this barracks. We were issued steel army cots, two brown army blankets each, and some mattress covers, which my brothers stuffed with straw.

26 The first task was to divide up what space we had for sleeping. Bill and Woody contributed a blanket each and partitioned off the first room: one side for Bill and Tomi, one side for Woody and Chizu and their baby girl. Woody also got the stove, for heating formulas.

27 The people who had it hardest during the first few months were young couples like these, many of whom had married just before the evacuation began, in order not to be separated and sent to different camps. Our two rooms were crowded, but at least it was all in the family. My oldest sister and her husband were shoved into one of those sixteen-by-twenty-foot compartments with six people they had never seen before—two other couples, one recently married like themselves, the other with two teenage

boys. Partitioning off a room like that wasn't easy. It was bitter cold when we arrived, and the wind did not abate. All they had to use for room dividers were those army blankets, two of which were barely enough to keep one person warm. They argued over whose blanket should be sacrificed and later argued about noise at night—the parents wanted their boys asleep by 9:00 P.M.—and they continued arguing over matters like that for six months, until my sister and her husband left to harvest sugar beets in Idaho. It was grueling work up there, and wages were pitiful, but when the call came through camp for workers to alleviate the wartime labor shortage, it sounded better than their life at Manzanar. They knew they'd have, if nothing else, a room, perhaps a cabin of their own.

28 That first night in Block 16, the rest of us squeezed into the second room—Granny, Lillian, age fourteen, Ray, thirteen, May, eleven, Kiyo, ten, Mama, and me. I didn't mind this at all at the time. Being youngest meant I got to sleep with Mama. And before we went to bed I had a great time jumping up and down on the mattress. The boys had stuffed so much straw into hers, we had to flatten it some so we wouldn't slide off. I slept with her every night after that until Papa came back.

Post-reading Questions

Content

1. Why does Wakatsuki Houston's mother move her family to Terminal Island? What are some of the results of the move?
2. What does the description of the town suggest about the people and their condition? What specific details give you these impressions?
3. What did the navy decide to do to Terminal Island? How did second-hand dealers take advantage of the situation? Why did the narrator's mother react as she did, smashing her dishes and getting angry?
4. How did the narrator feel about moving to Manzanar? What are some of her initial feelings and reactions upon arriving at the camp? What details and specifics create her first impression of Manzanar?
5. What is the impression you have after reading the description of the camp and its activities? What problems would these Japanese Americans encounter?

Strategies and Structures

1. Wakatsuki Houston's narration explains many causes and effects. What is the cause of her fear of other Asian children? What is the effect of being isolated from other Asians? How does she explain this cause and effect?

2. How does Wakatsuki Houston show the effects of being unable to speak the language of the community? What specifics make this passage so vivid and detailed?
3. Explain the purpose of the episode about the second-hand dealer and the china set. Why is narration an effective means of achieving this purpose?
4. How does Wakatsuki Houston organize her material in order to make this essay easy to follow? What transitional devices and/or linking words does she use to make this organization apparent to the reader?

Language and Vocabulary

1. Often place names are used in narratives to suggest the journey a narrator or character takes; however, if we are unfamiliar with the region, these place names may confuse us. An excellent strategy for getting a sense of place is to consult a map and to try and follow the narrative journey. Wakatsuki Houston uses the following place names in her narrative: *Inglewood, Ocean Park, Santa Monica, Terminal Island, Long Beach, Boyle Heights, Los Angeles, Manzanar, Owens Valley.* Get a map of California and follow Wakatsuki Houston's journey using the above vocabulary words. Consult the essay as needed.
2. Wakatsuki Houston uses several Japanese words in paragraph 5. How does she explain the meaning of these words? Do you find this strategy effective? How might you be able to use such a strategy in your own essays?

Group Activities

1. Due to the fear caused by the ignorance of another culture, many people face hardships throughout their lives. Wakatsuki Houston explains the hardships encountered by Japanese Americans because of the U.S. government's ignorance of Japanese-American culture. As a group, brainstorm and discuss other instances in which whole groups of people faced problems and hardships because of a lack of understanding. What groups have faced problems? What problems have they faced? Why? Whose ignorance has caused these hardships? How have the persecuted people tried to deal with these problems?
2. Wakatsuki Houston explains how she felt about the camp as a child; however, she includes enough details about the reality of the camp to clearly show that it was not a pleasant place. First, freewrite about an experience that you

either enjoyed or found unpleasant as a child but now feel different about. Then share your freewriting with the rest of the group. As you listen to others, note why we change our feelings about an event.

Writing Activities

1. Write about an event in which you faced prejudice and/or hardship because of someone's lack of understanding about you or your culture. What were the causes of your problems and the person's lack of understanding? What were the effects of the person's misunderstanding?
2. Write an essay discussing the initial impression a person(s) had made upon you and how your first impression was subject to change once you got to know that person(s). Make sure you give plenty of examples to illustrate the validity of what you say.

***Internet Connection:* Jeanne Wakatsuki Houston and James D. Houston**

Manzanar and Euphemisms

Who and what are political prisoners as opposed to criminals? Do a bit of online research regarding Manzanar and other relocation camps where the United States interned over 110,000 Japanese Americans during World War II. Take notice of the way the government and many historians used euphemistic terms when they discussed internment (e.g., "evacuation" in reference to the forced removal of the Japanese Americans, and "relocation centers" to refer to what essentially amounted to concentration camps). Next, under "images," Google a wide variety of Manzanar photos. Then put together a PowerPoint presentation wherein you blend text and photos that demonstrate how the euphemistic terms you discovered soften and disguise what people now perceive as a human injustice. How do photographs reveal a reality that no words can obscure or dispute? (You might want to compare and contrast pictures of people sent to Japanese "relocation camps" to photos of prisoners in Nazi "concentration camps.")

Reginald Lockett

How I Started Writing Poetry

A PEN Oakland/Josephine Miles award winning poet, Reginald Lockett's poetry, literary reviews, critiques, and prose have appeared in over forty anthologies and periodicals. His collected works of poetry include *Good Time & No Bread* (1978), verse that prompted poet Al Young to comment that "Like a jubilant Saturday night deejay, Lockett spins out one celebration of life after another in a yea-saying street idiom guaranteed to keep listeners turned to his spot on the dial," and *Where the Birds Sing Bass* (1995), acclaimed by Ishmael Reed as possibly "the best book of poetry in 1995. The voice is hip, urban, observant, and nostalgic. Reginald Lockett brings the world home, and in the process tells us about folks who don't make the news." Most recently, he published *The Party Crashers of Paradise* (2001) and *Random History Lessons* (2007). As Lockett's essay title suggests, his "informational" process essay explains how he began to write poetry.

Pre-reading Questions

1. Cluster the word "poetry." What do you associate with a poem? If someone asked you for a definition of a "poem," what would you say? Do you have any favorite poets?
2. Was there ever a time in your life when you walked, talked, and acted in a particular way just to be "cool" or "fit in"? Freewrite about the experience in your journal. (This assignment encourages greater creativity and imagination than reflection on an actual event.)
3. Experiment. Write a poem that illustrates the theme of innocence in your writing log or journal. Then, project yourself ten years into the future and rewrite the same poem from the point of view of a more experienced person. (This assignment encourages creativity and imagination.)

---

1 At the age of fourteen I was what Richard Pryor over a decade later would call "going for bad" or what my southern-bred folks said was "smellin' your pee." That is, I had cultivated a facade of daring-do, hip,

cool, con man bravado so prevalent among adolescent males in West Oakland. I "talked that talk and walked that walk" most parents found downright despicable. In their minds these were dress rehearsals of fantasies that were Popsicles that would melt and evaporate under the heat of blazing hot realities. And there I was doing the pimp limp and talking about nothing profound or sustaining. All I wanted to do was project that image of being forever cool like Billy Boo, who used to wear three T-shirts, two slipover sweaters and a thick Pendleton shirt tucked neatly in his khaki or black Ben Davidsons to give everybody the impression that he was buffed (muscle bound) and definitely not to be messed with. Cool. Real cool. Standing in front of the liquor store on 35th and San Pablo sipping white port and lemon juice, talking smack by the boatloads until some *real* hoodlum from Campbell Village (or was it Harbor Homes?) with the real biceps, the shonuff triceps and sledgehammer fists beat the shirt, both sweaters, the T-shirts and pants right off of Billy Boo's weak, bony body.

2 Herbert Hoover Junior High, the school I attended, was considered one of the toughest in Oakland at that time. It was a dirty, gray, forbidding-looking place where several fights would break out every day. There was a joke going around that a mother, new to the city, mistook it for the Juvenile Detention Center that was further down in West Oakland on 18th and Poplar, right across the street from DeFremery Park.

3 During my seventh-grade year there were constant referrals to the principal's office for any number of infractions committed either in Miss Okamura's third-period music class or Mrs. George's sixth-period math class in the basement, where those of us with behavioral problems and assumed learning disabilities were sent. It was also around this time that Harvey Hendricks, my main running buddy, took it upon himself to hip me to everything he thought I needed to know about sex while we were doing a week's detention in Mrs. Balasco's art class for capping on "them steamer trunks" or "suitcases" under her eyes. As we sat there, supposedly writing "I will not insult the teacher" one hundred times, Harvey would draw pictures of huge tits and vaginas, while telling me how to rap, kiss, and jump off in some twanks and stroke. Told me that the pimples on my face were "pussy bumps," and that I'd better start getting some trim or end up just like Crater Face Jerome with the big, nasty-looking quarter-size pus bumps all over his face.

4 Though my behavior left a lot to be desired, I managed to earn some fairly decent grades. I loved history, art and English, and somehow managed to work my way up from special education classes to college prep courses by the time I reached ninth grade, my last year at Hoover. But by then I had become a full-fledged little thug, and had been suspended—and damn near expelled—quite a few times for going to knuckle city at the drop of a hat for any real or imagined reason.

And what an efficient thief I'd become. This was something I'd picked up from my cousins, R. C. and Danny, when I started hanging out with them on weekends in San Francisco's Haight-Ashbury. We'd steal clothes, records, liquor, jewelry—anything for the sake of magnifying to the umpteenth degree that image of death-defying manhood and to prove I was indeed a budding Slick Draw McGraw. Luckily, I was never caught, arrested and hauled off to Juvenile Hall or the California Youth Authority like so many of the guys I ran with.

5 Probably through pressure from my parents and encouragement from my teachers and counselors, I forced myself to start thinking about pursuing a career after graduation from high school, which was three years away. Reaching into the grab bag of professional choices, I decided I wanted to become a physician, since doctors were held in such high esteem, particularly in an Afro-American community like West Oakland. I'd gotten it in my head that I wanted to be a plastic surgeon, no less, because I liked working with my hands and found science intriguing. Then something strange happened.

6 Maybe it was the continuous violence, delinquency and early pregnancies that made those Oakland Unified School District administrators (more than likely after some consultation with psychologists) decide to put a little Freudian theory to practical use. Just as I was grooving, really getting into this fantastic project in fourth-period art class, I was called up to the teacher's desk and handed a note and told to report to a classroom downstairs on the first floor. What had I done this time? Was it because I snatched Gregory Jones' milkshake during lunch a couple of days ago and gulped it down, savoring every drop like an old loathsome suck-egg dog, and feeling no pain as the chump, big as he was, stood there and cried? And Mr. Foltz, the principal, was known to hand out mass suspensions. Sometimes fifteen, twenty, twenty-five people at a time. But when I entered the classroom, there sat this tall, gangly, goofy-looking white woman who wore her hair unusually long for that time, had thick glasses and buckteeth like the beaver on the Ipana Toothpaste commercials. Some of the roughest, toughest kids that went to Hoover were in there. Especially big old mean, ugly Martha Dupree who was known to knock out boys, girls, and teachers when she got the urge. If Big Martha asked you for a last-day-of-school kiss, you'd better give it up or make an appointment with your dentist.

7 When Miss Nettelbeck finally got our attention, she announced that this was a creative writing class that would meet twice a week. Creative writing? What the hell is creative writing a couple of us asked. She explained that it was a way to express what was on your mind, and a better way of getting something off of your chest instead of beating up your fellow students. Then she read a few poems to us and passed

out some of that coarse school-issue lined paper and told us to write about something we liked, disliked, or really wanted. What I wanted to know was, did it have to be one of "them pomes." "If that's how you want to express yourself, Reginald," she said. So I started racking my brain, trying to think about what I liked, didn't like and what I really wanted. Well, I liked football, track and Gayle Johnson, who would turn her cute little "high yella" nose up in total disgust every time I tried to say something to her. I couldn't stand the sight—not even the thought—of old monkey-face Martha. And what I really wanted was either a '57 Buick Roadmaster or a '56 Chevy with mag wheels and tuck 'n' roll seats that was dropped in the front like the ones I'd seen older dudes like Mack's brother, Skippy, riding around in. Naw, I told myself, I couldn't get away with writing about things like that. I might get into some more trouble, and Big Martha would give me a thorough ass- kicking for writing something about mashing her face in some dough and baking me some gorilla cookies. Who'd ever heard of a poem about cars? One thing I really liked was the ocean. I guess that was in my blood because my father was then a master chief steward in the navy, and, when I was younger, would take me aboard ships docked at Hunter's Point and Alameda. I loved the sea so much that I would sometimes walk from my house on Market and West MacArthur all the way to the Berkeley Pier or take a bus to Ocean Beach in San Francisco whenever I wasn't up to no good. So I wrote:

I sit on a rock
watching
the evening tide
come in.
The green waves travel
with the wind.
They seem to carry
a message of
warning, of plea
from the dimensions
of time and distance.

8 When I gave it to Miss Nettelbeck, she read it and told me it was good for a first attempt at writing poetry, and since there was still some time left in the period, I should go back to my seat and write something else. Damn! These teachers never gave you any kind of slack, no matter what you did and how well you did it. Now, what else could I think of to write about? How about a tribute to Miss Bobby, the neighborhood drag queen, who'd been found carved up like a Christmas turkey a week ago? Though me, Harvey and Mack used to crack jokes about "her" giving up the boodie, we still liked and respected "her"

because she would give you five or six dollars to run an errand to the cleaners or the store, never tried to hit on you, and would get any of the other "girls" straight real quick if they even said you were cute or something. So I wrote:

Bring on the hustle
In Continental suits
And alligator shoes
Let fat ladies of the night
In short, tight dresses
And spiked heels enter.
We are gathered here
To pay tribute to
The Queen of Drag.

What colorful curtains
And rugs!
Look at the stereo set
And the clothes in the closet.
On the bed, entangled
In a bloody sheet,
Is that elegant one
Of ill repute
But good carriage
Oh yes! There
Was none like her.
The Queen of Drag.

9 When she read that one, I just knew Miss Nettelbeck would immediately write a referral and have me sent back upstairs. But she liked it and said I was precocious for someone at such an innocent age. Innocent! When was I ever innocent? I was guilty of just about everything I was accused of doing. Like, get your eyes checked, baby. And what was precocious? Was it something weird? Did it mean I was queer like Miss Bobby? Was I about to go to snap city like poor Donny Moore had a year ago when he suddenly got up and started jacking off in front of Mr. Lee's history class? What did this woman, who looked and dressed like one of them beatniks I'd seen one night on *East Side, West Side,* mean? My Aunt Audry's boyfriend, Joe, told me beatniks were smart and used a lot of big words like precocious so nobody could understand what they were talking about. Had to be something bad. This would mess with me for the rest of the week if I didn't ask her what she meant. So I did, and she told me it meant that I knew about things somebody my age didn't usually know about. Wow! That could only mean that I was "hip to the lip." But I already knew that.

10 For some reason I wasn't running up and down the streets with the fellas much anymore. Harvey would get bent out of shape every time I'd tell him I had something else to do. I had to, turning punkish or

seeing some broad I was too chinchy to introduce him to. This also bothered my mother because she kept telling me I was going to ruin my eyes if I didn't stop reading so much; and what was that I spent all my spare time writing in a manila notebook? Was I keeping a diary or something? Only girls kept diaries, people may start thinking I was one of "them sissy mens" if I didn't stop. Even getting good grades in citizenship and making the honor roll didn't keep her off my case. But I kept right on reading and writing, looking forward to Miss Nettelbeck's class twice a week. I stopped fighting, too. But I was still roguish as ever. Instead of raiding Roger's Men's Shop, Smith's and Flagg Brothers' Shoes, I was stealing books by just about every poet and writer Miss Nettelbeck read to the class. That's how I started writing poetry.

Post-reading Questions

Content

1. Who got Lockett to consider "pursuing a career after graduation from high school"? What did he plan on becoming and why? What was he referring to when he said, "Then something strange happened" that changed his initial goal and his lifestyle?
2. Which academic courses did the author always "love"? In what way did his academic preparation conflict with his social persona?
3. Who was "Big Martha Dupree"? What sort of reputation did she have? Why?
4. What kind of things did Lockett steal at the start of the essay? What was he stealing at the end of the essay?
5. In your opinion, what audience would this essay appeal to (1) in general, and (2) in particular? Explain how and why you arrived at your conclusions.

Strategies and Structures

1. Why do you imagine the author devotes so much time to providing readers with personal background information before he uses informational process analysis to explain how he became a poet?
2. How does the author's word choice establish and maintain the tone of this essay and reflect his personality?
3. Lockett's essay blends many rhetorical strategies, which lead to the final sentence: "That's how I started writing poetry." Identify some of the rhetorical modes of development at work and comment on their effectiveness.

4. How does Lockett create unity and coherence in this personal essay?
5. Assess how well the inclusion of two poems he wrote for Miss Nettelbeck demonstrates his struggle to find topics and a voice for writing poetry. In what way were the poems different? Which poem was more daring? Why?

Language and Vocabulary

1. Vocabulary: *referrals, infractions, delinquency, precocious.* With the exception of "precocious," the above words all deal with some aspect of human conduct and its consequences. Write a single paragraph about a real or imaginary situation in which you use all the above vocabulary words. You might begin your paragraph with something like: "Precociousness frequently leads to disrespect and trouble .... "
2. The author uses street talk and African-American idioms in this essay to give it a particular flavor. Go through the essay and identify as many of these idioms as you can. Next, write them down and then offer an informal definition for each one. Make a separate list of idioms that you are not familiar with or cannot define. Save both lists for a group activity.

Group Activities

1. Break into groups and exchange your answers to Language and Vocabulary Question 2. Spend the majority of your time discussing unfamiliar idioms and, as a group, attempt to arrive at some tentative translations of them.
2. As a group, examine the difference between justifiable causes for doing something and rationalizing one's behavior *after* doing something. What does Lockett do in his essay?

Writing Activities

1. In a manner similar to Lockett's, write a narrative account of a situation that motivated you to do something or that explains how something was done. Use your local dialect and idioms to give your essay a personal flair—a distinct voice—whenever possible.
2. Cluster the term "self-discovery" and carefully consider the free associations you make and their implications. Then, write an expository essay wherein you relate how you or somebody you know came to a greater understanding of someone or something through personal reflection and self-discovery.

Louise Erdrich

American Horse

Of Chippewa and German-American descent, Louise Erdrich is both a poet and a novelist and frequently writes about the Native-American experience. Erdrich's published works include collections of poetry *Jacklight* (1984), *Baptism of Desire* (1989), and *Original Fire: Selected and New Poems* (2003). Erdrich also has written several novels for adults and children, such as: *Love Medicine* (1984); *The Beet Queen* (1986); *Tracks* (1988); *The Bingo Palace* (1994); *The Blue Jay's Dance: A Birth Year* (1995), a nonfiction work regarding small and large events all parents will relate to *Tales of Burning Love* (1996); *The Antelope Wife* (1998); *The Birchbark House* (1999); *The Last Report on the Miracles at Little No Horse* (2001); *Four Souls: A Novel* (2004); *The Game of Silence* (2005); *The Master Butcher's Singing Club, The Painted Drum* (2006); *The Plague of the Doves* (2008), *The Red Convertible: Collected and New Stories 1978–2008* (2009), and *Shadow Tag* (2010). In 1992, Erdrich published *The Crown of Columbus*, a novel she coauthored with her husband, the late Michael Dorris. The following narrative from *The Bingo Palace* presents a parent/child relationship at odds with a social service agency.

Pre-reading Questions

1. How many times have you—or someone you know—done something because another person said, "It's for your own good"? Describe one of these situations in your journal.
2. What welfare or social agency are you aware of through personal experience, observations, or readings?

---

1 The woman sleeping on the cot in the woodshed was Albertine American Horse. The name was left over from her mother's short marriage. The boy was the son of the man she had loved and let go. Buddy was on the cot too, sitting on the edge because he'd been awake three hours watching out for his mother and besides, she took up the whole cot. Her feet hung over the edge, limp and brown as two trout. Her long arms reached out and slapped at things she saw in her dreams.

2 Buddy had been knocked awake out of hiding in a washing machine while herds of policemen with dogs searched through a large building with many tiny rooms. When the arm came down, Buddy screamed because it had a blue cuff and sharp silver buttons. "Tss," his mother mumbled, half awake, "wasn't nothing." But Buddy sat up after her breathing went deep again, and he watched.

3 There was something coming and he knew it.

4 It was coming from very far off but he had a picture of it in his mind. It was a large thing made of metal with many barbed hooks, points, and drag chains on it, something like a giant potato peeler that rolled out of the sky, scraping clouds down with it and jabbing or crushing everything that lay in its path on the ground.

5 Buddy watched his mother. If he woke her up, she would know what to do about the thing, but he thought he'd wait until he saw it for sure before he shook her. She was pretty, sleeping, and he liked knowing he could look at her as long and close up as he wanted. He took a strand of her hair and held it in his hands as if it was the rein to a delicate beast. She was strong enough and could pull him along like the horse their name was.

6 Buddy had his mother's and his grandmother's name because his father had been a big mistake.

7 "They're all mistakes, even your father. But *you* are the best thing that ever happened to me."

8 That was what she said when he asked. Even Kadie, the boyfriend crippled from being in a car wreck, was not as good a thing that had happened to his mother as Buddy was. "He was a medium-sized mistake," she said. "He's hurt and I shouldn't even say that, but it's the truth." At the moment, Buddy knew that being the best thing in his mother's life, he was also the reason they were hiding from the cops.

9 He wanted to touch the satin roses sewed on her pink tee shirt, but he knew he shouldn't do that even in her sleep. If she woke up and found him touching the roses, she would say, "Quit that, Buddy." Sometimes she told him to stop hugging her like a gorilla. She never said that in the mean voice she used when he oppressed her, but when she said that he loosened up anyway.

10 There were times he felt like hugging her so hard and in such a special way that she would say to him, "Let's get married." There were also times he closed his eyes and wished that she would die, only a few times, but still it haunted him that his wish might come true. He and Uncle Lawrence would be left alone. Buddy wasn't worried, though, about his mother getting married to somebody else. She had said to her friend, Madonna, "All men suck," when she thought Buddy wasn't listening. He had made an uncertain sound, and when they heard him they took him in their arms.

11 "Except for you, Buddy," his mother said. "All except for you and maybe Uncle Lawrence, although he's pushing it."

12 "The cops suck the worst, though," Buddy whispered to his mother's sleeping face, "because they're after us." He felt tired again, slumped down, and put his legs beneath the blanket. He closed his eyes and got the feeling that the cot was lifting up beneath him, that it was arching its canvas back and then traveling, traveling very fast and in the wrong direction for when he looked up he saw the three of them were advancing to meet the great metal thing with hooks and barbs and all sorts of sharp equipment to catch their bodies and draw their blood. He heard its insides as it rushed toward them, purring softly like a powerful motor and then they were right in its shadow. He pulled the reins as hard as he could and the beast reared, lifting him. His mother clapped her hand across his mouth.

13 "Okay," she said. "Lay low. They're outside and they're gonna hunt."

14 She touched his shoulder and Buddy leaned over with her to look through a crack in the boards.

15 They were out there all right, Albertine saw them. Two officers and that social worker woman. Vicki Koob. There had been no whistle, no dream, no voice to warn her that they were coming. There was only the crunching sound of cinders in the yard, the engine purring, the dust sifting off their car in a fine light brownish cloud and settling around them.

16 The three people came to a halt in their husk of metal—the car emblazoned with the North Dakota State Highway Patrol emblem which is the glowing profile of the Sioux policeman, Red Tomahawk, the one who killed Sitting Bill. Albertine gave Buddy the blanket and told him that he might have to wrap it around him and hide underneath the cot.

17 "We're gonna wait and see what they do." She took him in her lap and hunched her arms around him. "Don't you worry," she whispered against his ear. "Lawrence knows how to fool them."

18 Buddy didn't want to look at the car and the people. He felt his mother's heart beating beneath his ear so fast it seemed to push the satin roses in and out. He put his face to them carefully and breathed the deep, soft powdery woman smell of her. That smell was also in her little face cream bottles, in her brushes, and around the washbowl after she used it. The satin felt so unbearably smooth against his cheek that he had to press closer. She didn't push him away, like he expected, but hugged him still tighter until he felt as close as he had ever been to back inside her again where she said he came from. Within the smells of her things, her soft skin, and the satin of her roses, he closed his eyes then, and took his breaths softly and quickly with her heart.

19 They were out there, but they didn't dare get out of the car yet because of Lawrence's big, ragged dogs. Three of these dogs had loped up the dirt driveway with the car. They were rangy, alert, and bounced up and down on their cushioned paws like wolves. They didn't waste their energy barking, but positioned themselves quietly, one at either car door

and the third in front of the bellied-out screen door to Uncle Lawrence's house. It was six in the morning but the wind was up already, blowing dust, ruffling their short moth-eaten coats. The big brown one on Vicki Koob's side had unusual black and white markings, stripes almost, like a hyena and he grinned at her, tongue out and teeth showing.

20 "Shoo!" Miss Koob opened her door with a quick jerk.

21 The brown dog sidestepped the door and jumped before her, tiptoeing. Its dirty white muzzle curled and its eyes crossed suddenly as if it was zeroing its cross-hair sights in on the exact place it would bite her. She ducked back and slammed the door.

22 "It's mean," she told Officer Brackett. He was printing out some type of form. The other officer, Harmony, a slow man, had not yet reacted to the car's halt. He had been sitting quietly in the back seat, but now he rolled down his window and with no change in expression unsnapped his holster and drew his pistol out and pointed it at the dog on his side. The dog smacked down on its belly, wiggled under the car and was out and around the back of the house before Harmony drew his gun back. The other dogs vanished with him. From wherever they had disappeared to they began to yap and howl, and the door to the low shoebox-style house fell open.

23 "Heya, what's going on?"

24 Uncle Lawrence put his head out the door and opened wide the one eye he had in working order. The eye bulged impossibly wider in outrage when he saw the police car. But the eyes of the two officers and Miss Vicki Koob were wide open too because they had never seen Uncle Lawrence in his sleeping getup or, indeed, witnessed anything like it. For his ribs, which were cracked from a bad fall and still mending, Uncle Lawrence wore a thick white corset laced up the front with a striped sneakers' lace. His glass eye and his set of dentures were still out for the night so his face puckered here and there, around its absences and scars, like a damaged but fierce little cake. Although he had a few gray streaks now, Uncle Lawrence's hair was still thick, and because he wore a special contraption of elastic straps around his head every night, two oiled waves always crested on either side of his middle part. All of this would have been sufficient to astonish, even without the most striking part of his outfit—the smoking jacket. It was made of black satin and hung open around his corset, dragging a tasseled belt. Gold thread dragons struggled up the lapels and blasted their furry red breath around his neck. As Lawrence walked down the steps, he put his arms up in surrender and the gold tassels in the inner seams of his sleeves dropped into view.

25 "My heavens, what a sight." Vicki Koob was impressed.

26 "A character," apologized Officer Harmony.

27 As a tribal police officer who could be counted on to help out the State Patrol, Harmony thought he always had to explain about Indians or get twice as tough to show he did not favor them. He was slow-moving and shy but two jumps ahead of other people all the same, and now, as he

watched Uncle Lawrence's splendid approach, he gazed speculatively at the torn and bulging pocket of the smoking jacket. Harmony had been inside Uncle Lawrence's house before and knew that above his draped orange-crate shelf of war medals a blue-black German luger was hung carefully in a net of flat-headed nails and fishing line. Thinking of this deadly exhibition, he got out of the car and shambled toward Lawrence with a dreamy little smile of welcome on his face. But when he searched Lawrence, he found that the bulging pocket held only the lonesome-looking dentures from Lawrence's empty jaw. They were still dripping denture polish.

28 "I had been cleaning them when you arrived," Uncle Lawrence explained with acid dignity.

29 He took the toothbrush from his other pocket and aimed it like a rifle.

30 "Quit that, you old idiot." Harmony tossed the toothbrush away. "For once you ain't done nothing. We came for your nephew."

31 Lawrence looked at Harmony with a faint air of puzzlement.

32 "Ma Frere, listen," threatened Harmony amiably, "those two white people in the car came to get him for the welfare. They got papers on your nephew that give them the right to take him."

33 "Papers?" Uncle Lawrence puffed out his deeply pitted cheeks. "Let me see them papers."

34 The two of them walked over to Vicki's side of the car and she pulled a copy of the court order from her purse. Lawrence put his teeth back in and adjusted them with busy workings of his jaw.

35 "Just a minute," he reached into his breast pocket as he bent close to Miss Vicki Koob. "I can't read these without I have in my eye."

36 He took the eye from his breast pocket delicately, and as he popped it into his face the social worker's mouth fell open in a consternated O.

37 "What is this?" she cried in a little voice.

38 Uncle Lawrence looked at her mildly. The white glass of the eye was cold as lard. The black iris was strangely charged and menacing.

39 "He's nuts," Bracket huffed along the side of Vicki's neck. "Never mind him."

40 Vicki's hair had sweated down her nape in tiny corkscrews and some of the hairs were so long and dangly now that they disappeared into the zippered back of her dress. Brackett noticed this as he spoke into her ear. His face grew red and the backs of his hands prickled. He slid under the steering wheel and got out of the car. He walked around the hood to stand with Leo Harmony.

41 "We could take you in too," said Brackett roughly. Lawrence eyed the officers in what was taken as defiance. "If you don't cooperate, we'll get out the handcuffs," they warned.

42 One of Lawrence's arms was stiff and would not move until he'd rubbed it with witch hazel in the morning. His other arm worked fine though, and he stuck it out in front of Brackett.

43 "Get them handcuffs," he urged them. "Put me in a welfare home."

44 Brackett snapped one side of the handcuffs on Lawrence's good arm and the other to the handle of the police car.

45 "That's to hold you," he said. "We're wasting our time. Harmony, you search that little shed over by the tall grass and Miss Koob and myself will search the house."

46 "My rights is violated!" Lawrence shrieked suddenly. They ignored him. He tugged at the handcuff and thought of the good heavy file he kept in his tool box and the German luger oiled and ready but never loaded, because of Buddy, over his shelf. He should have used it on these bad ones, even Harmony in his big-time white man job. He wouldn't last long in that job anyway before somebody gave him what for.

47 "It's a damn scheme," said Uncle Lawrence, rattling his chains against the car. He looked over at the shed and thought maybe Albertine and Buddy had sneaked away before the car pulled into the yard. But he sagged, seeing Albertine move like a shadow within the boards. "Oh, it's all a damn scheme," he muttered again.

48 "I want to find that boy and salvage him," Vicki Koob explained to Officer Brackett as they walked into the house. "Look at his family life—the old man crazy as a bedbug, the mother intoxicated somewhere."

49 Brackett nodded, energetic, eager. He was a short hopeful redhead who failed consistently to win the hearts of women. Vicki Koob intrigued him. Now, as he watched, she pulled a tiny pen out of an ornamental clip on her blouse. It was attached to a retractable line that would suck the pen back, like a child eating one strand of spaghetti. Something about the pen on its line excited Brackett to the point of discomfort. His hand shook as he opened the screen door and stepped in, beckoning Miss Koob to follow.

50 They could see the house was empty at first glance. It was only one rectangular room with whitewashed walls and a little gas stove in the middle. They had already come through the cooking lean-to with the other stove and washstand and rusty old refrigerator. That refrigerator had nothing in it but some wrinkled potatoes and a package of turkey necks, Vicki Koob noted in her perfect-bound notebook. The beds along the walls of the big room were covered with quilts that Albertine's mother, Sophie, had made from bits of old wool coats and pants that the Sisters sold in bundles at the mission. There was no one hiding beneath the beds. No one was under the little aluminum dinette table covered with a green oil-cloth, or the soft brown wood chairs tucked up to it. One wall of the big room was filled with neatly stacked crates of things—old tools and springs and small half-dismantled appliances. Five or six television sets were stacked against the wall. Their control panels spewed colored wires and at least one was cracked all the way across. Only the topmost set, with coat hanger antenna angled sensitively to catch the bounding signals around Little Shell, looked like it could possibly work.

51 Not one thing escaped Vicki Koob's trained and cataloguing gaze. She made note of the cupboard that held only commodity flour and coffee. The unsanitary tin oil drum beneath the kitchen window, full of empty surplus pork cans and beer bottles, caught her eye as did Uncle Lawrence's physical and mental deteriorations. She quickly described these "benchmarks of alcoholic dependency within the extended family of Woodrow (Buddy) American Horse" as she walked around the room with the little notebook open, pushed against her belly to steady it. Although Vicki had been there before, Albertine's presence had always made it difficult for her to take notes.

52 "Twice the maximum allowable space between door and threshold," she wrote now. "Probably no insulation. Two three-inch cracks in walls inadequately sealed with white-washed mud." She made a mental note but could see no point in describing Lawrence's stuffed reclining chair that only reclined, the shadeless lamp with its plastic orchid in the bubble glass base, or the three-dimensional picture of Jesus that Lawrence had once demonstrated to her. When plugged in, lights rolled behind the water the Lord stood on so that he seemed to be strolling although he never actually went forward, of course, but only pushed the glowing waves behind him forever like a poor tame rat in a treadmill.

53 Brackett cleared his throat with a nervous rasp and touched Vicki's shoulder.

54 "What are you writing?"

55 She moved away and continued to scribble as if thoroughly absorbed in her work. "Officer Brackett displays an undue amount of interest in my person," she wrote. "Perhaps?"

56 He snatched playfully at the book, but she hugged it to her chest and moved off smiling. More curls had fallen, wetted to the base of her neck. Looking out the window, she sighed long and loud.

57 "All night on brush rollers for this. What a joke."

58 Brackett shoved his hands in his pockets. His mouth opened slightly, then shut with a small throttled cluck.

59 When Albertine saw Harmony ambling across the yard with his big brown thumbs in his belt, his placid smile, and his tiny black eyes moving back and forth, she put Buddy under the cot. Harmony stopped at the shed and stood quietly. He spread his arms to show her he hadn't drawn his big police gun.

60 "Ma Cousin," he said in the Michif dialect that people used if they were relatives or sometimes if they needed gas or a couple of dollars, "why don't you come out here and stop this foolishness?"

61 "I ain't your cousin," Albertine said. Anger boiled up in her suddenly. "I ain't related to no pigs."

62 She bit her lip and watched him through the cracks, circling, a big tan punching dummy with his boots full of sand so he never stayed down

once he fell. He was empty inside, all stale air. But he knew how to get to her so much better than a white cop could. And now he was circling because he wasn't sure she didn't have a weapon, maybe a knife or the German luger that was the only thing that her father, Albert American Horse, had left his wife and daughter besides his name. Harmony knew that Albertine was a tall strong woman who took two big men to subdue when she didn't want to go in the drunk tank. She had hard hips, broad shoulders, and stood tall like her Sioux father, the American Horse who was killed threshing in Belle Prairie.

63 "I feel bad to have to do this," Harmony said to Albertine. "But for godsakes, let's nobody get hurt. Come on out with the boy, why don't you? I know you got him in there."

64 Albertine did not give herself away this time. She let him wonder. Slowly and quietly she pulled her belt through its loops and wrapped it around and around her hand until only the big oval buckle with turquoise chunks shaped into a butterfly stuck out over her knuckles. Harmony was talking but she wasn't listening to what he said. She was listening to the pitch of his voice, the tone of it that would tighten or tremble at a certain moment when he decided to rush the shed. He kept talking slowly and reasonably, flexing the dialect from time to time, even mentioning her father.

65 "He was a damn good man. I don't care what they say, Albertine, I knew him."

66 Albertine looked at the stone butterfly that spread its wings across her fist. The wings looked light and cool, not heavy. It almost looked like it was ready to fly. Harmony wanted to get to Albertine through her father but she would not think about American Horse. She concentrated on the sky blue stone.

67 Yet the shape of the stone, the color, betrayed her. She saw her father suddenly, bending at the grille of their old gray car. She was small then. The memory came from so long ago it seemed like a dream—narrowly focused, snapshot-clear. He was bending by the grille in the sun. It was hot summer. Wings of sweat, dark blue, spread across the back of his work shirt. He always wore soft blue shirts, the color of shade cloudier than this stone. His stiff hair had grown out of its short haircut and flopped over his forehead. When he stood up and turned away from the car, Albertine saw that he had a butterfly.

68 "It's dead," he told her. "Broke its wings and died on the grille."

69 She must have been five, maybe six, wearing one of the boy's tee shirts Mama bleached in Hilex-water. American Horse took the butterfly, a black and yellow one, and rubbed it on Albertine's collarbone and chest and arms until the color and the powder of it were blended into her skin.

70 "For grace," he said. And Albertine had felt a strange lightening in her arms, in her chest, when he did this and said, "For grace."

71 The way he said it, grace meant everything the butterfly was. The sharp delicate wings. The way it floated over grass. The way its wings seemed to breathe fanning in the sun. The wisdom of the way it blended into flowers or changed into a leaf. In herself she felt the same kind of possibilities and closed her eyes almost in shock or pain, she felt so light and powerful at that moment.

72 Then her father had caught her and thrown her high into the air. She could not remember landing in his arms or landing at all. She only remembered the sun filling her eyes and the world tipping crazily behind her, out of sight.

73 "He was a damn good man," Harmony said again.

74 Albertine heard his starched uniform gathering before his boots hit the ground. Once, twice, three times. It took him four solid jumps to get right where she wanted him. She kicked the plank door open when he reached for the handle and the corner caught him on the jaw. He faltered, and Albertine hit him flat on the chin with the butterfly. She hit him so hard the shock of it went up her arm like a string pulled taut. Her fist opened, numb, and she let the belt unloop before she closed her hand on the tip end of it and sent the stone butterfly swooping out in a wide circle around her as if it was on the end of a leash. Harmony reeled backward as she walked toward him swinging the belt. She expected him to fall but he just stumbled. And then he took the gun from his hip.

75 Albertine let the belt go limp. She and Harmony stood within feet of each other, breathing. Each heard the human sound of air going in and out of the other person's lungs. Each read the face of the other as if deciphering letters carved into softly eroding veins of stone. Albertine saw the pattern of tiny arteries that age, drink, and hard living had blown to the surface of the man's face. She saw the spoked wheels of his iris and the arteries like tangled threads that sewed him up. She saw the living net of springs and tissue that held him together, and trapped him. She saw the random, intimate plan of his person.

76 She took a quick shallow breath and her face went strange and tight. She saw the black veins in the wings of the butterfly, roads burnt into a map, and then she was located somewhere in the net of veins and sinew that was the tragic complexity of the world so she did not see Officer Brackett and Vicki Koob rushing toward her, but felt them instead like flies caught in the same web, rocking it.

77 "Albertine!" Vicki Koob had stopped in the grass. Her voice was shrill and tight. "It's better this way, Albertine. We're going to help you."

78 Albertine straightened, threw her shoulders back. Her father's hand was on her chest and shoulders lightening her wonderfully. Then on wings of her father's hands, on dead butterfly wings, Albertine lifted into the air and flew toward the others. The light powerful feeling swept her up the way she had floated higher, seeing the grass below. It was her

father throwing her up into the air and out of danger. Her arms opened for bullets but no bullets came. Harmony did not shoot. Instead, he raised his fist and brought it down hard on her head.

79 Albertine did not fall immediately, but stood in his arms a moment. Perhaps she gazed still farther back behind the covering of his face. Perhaps she was completely stunned and did not think as she sagged and fell. Her face rolled forward and hair covered her features, so it was impossible for Harmony to see with just what particular expression she gazed into the head-splitting wheel of light, or blackness, that overcame her.

80 Harmony turned the vehicle onto the gravel road that led back to town. He had convinced the other two that Albertine was more trouble than she was worth, and so they left her behind, and Lawrence too. He stood swearing in his cinder driveway as the car rolled out of sight. Buddy sat between the social worker and Officer Brackett. Vicki tried to hold Buddy fast and keep her arm down at the same time, for the words she'd screamed at Albertine had broken the seal of antiperspirant beneath her arms. She was sweating now as though she'd stored an ocean up inside of her. Sweat rolled down her back in a shallow river and pooled at her waist and between her breasts. A thin sheen of water came out on her forearms, her face. Vicki gave an irritated moan but Brackett seemed not to take notice, or take offense at least. Air-conditioned breezes were sweeping over the seat anyway, and very soon they would be comfortable. She smiled at Brackett over Buddy's head. The man grinned back. Buddy stirred. Vicki remembered the emergency chocolate bar she kept in her purse, fished it out, and offered it to Buddy. He did not react, so she closed his fingers over the package and peeled the paper off one end.

81 The car accelerated. Buddy felt the road and wheels pummeling each other and the rush of the heavy motor purring in high gear. Buddy knew that what he'd seen in his mind that morning, the thing coming out of the sky with barbs and chains, had hooked him. Somehow he was caught and held in the sour tin smell of the pale woman's armpit. Somehow he was pinned between their pounds of breathless flesh. He looked at the chocolate in his hand. He was squeezing the bar so hard that a thin brown trickle had melted down his arm. Automatically he put the bar in his mouth.

82 As he bit down he saw his mother very clearly, just as she had been when she carried him from the shed. She was stretched flat on the ground, on her stomach, and her arms were curled around her head as if in sleep. One leg was drawn up and it looked for all the world like she was running full tilt into the ground, as though she had been trying to pass into the earth, to bury herself, but at the last moment something had stopped her.

83 There was no blood on Albertine, but Buddy tasted blood now at the sight of her, for he bit down hard and cut his own lip. He ate the

chocolate, every bit of it, tasting his mother's blood. And when he had the chocolate down inside him and all licked off his hands, he opened his mouth to say thank you to the woman, as his mother had taught him. But instead of a thank you coming out he was astonished to hear a great rattling scream, and then another, rip out of him like pieces of his own body and whirl onto the sharp things all around him.

Post-reading Questions

Content

1. Identify the subject or theme of Erdrich's narrative. What is the plot? (See the Glossary.)
2. Why did Harmony believe he had "to explain about Indians to others" or treat them tougher than anyone else?
3. Who was Albert American Horse? Explain the significance of his role and the incident with the dead butterfly in the story. Why do you think that Erdrich titles her story "American Horse"?
4. Analyze what happened when *"American Horse took the butterfly, a black and yellow one, and rubbed it on Albertine's collarbone and chest and arms until the color and the powder of it were blended into her skin"*?
5. Why does Buddy start screaming at the end of the story? What does he realize?

Strategies and Structures

1. How might you divide Erdrich's narrative into four distinct parts? How does each division blend into the next?
2. Explain the function of transitions and linking words throughout this narrative story.
3. What strategy does Erdrich use to frame her narrative? Where does her tale begin, how does it conclude, and what—if anything—is resolved?
4. How does Erdrich use her characters' observations of each other as a means of developing individual personalities while advancing the plot?

Language and Vocabulary

1. Vocabulary: *emblazoned, loped, luger, dentures, retractable, deterioration, grille, antiperspirant, pummeling.* Locate the definition of each of the vocabulary words in your dictionary. Then write a descriptive narrative in the manner of Louise Erdrich using at least five of the words.
2. *The American Heritage Dictionary*'s definition of the verb *salvage* is "to save (discarded or damaged material) for further use." With this definition in mind, when Vicki Koob says, *"I want to find that*

boy and salvage him," who and what do you think she is really interested in *saving* or *salvaging?* What is her opinion of herself? Choose some lines from the story to support your position.

Group Activities

1. As a class, weigh the pros and cons of Buddy's staying with his mother Albertine. Then, divide the class in half and debate the rights of a social agency versus the rights of a blood relative regarding the custody of a child.
2. After selecting groups, make plans to visit the child care center at your campus. Plan to take copious notes on what you observe at the center—notes worthy of Vicki Koob's *"trained and cataloguing gaze."* Finally, share your notes with each other at your next class session. What sort of observation was the most common among your peers? What kinds of details were most frequently cited? How did they differ?

Writing Activities

1. Write a narrative wherein you show how a significant incident in your past enables you to act well under pressure in the present.
2. Construct a narrative about a time in your life when you or someone you know hid from an authority figure.

Additional Topics and Issues for Expository Essays

1. Compose and develop an original thesis that says something specific about visual pollution. In doing so, you may want to answer such questions as "What is visual pollution?" "Where is one likely to encounter visual pollution?" and "What can or should be done about it?"
2. Write an expository essay wherein you explain a solution to the overpopulation problem without eliminating any of the people already alive.
3. Explain how economics influences and often dictates our political and social relationships with countries around the world by comparing and contrasting an economic

boom to a recession. If you draw information from outside sources, make sure that you acknowledge them correctly.

4. Explain why it is important to wear all the latest fashions in order to attract a love interest. Begin with a brief discussion of the process of keeping up with the fads. How much money do you have to spend? With whom is it important to be seen? Why? Are there any long-range effects of being a slave to fashion? You will want to conclude your essay with a thoughtful analysis of your topic.
5. Analyze the parking problem at your college. What is the cause of it? How does it affect your daily routine, particularly the time you get up and how much study time you have? Make sure you show your reader what goes on by offering him or her a glimpse into your life.
6. Write an essay wherein you demonstrate how stockpiling or spreading nuclear weapons throughout the world is a deterrent or an invitation to war.
7. After attracting your reader's interest by using a clever anecdote in your thesis, write an essay exposing why and in what ways pets fill an emotional void in many people's daily lives.
8. Much has been written about the effects of television on today's generation. Write an original, insightful essay wherein you explain (1) why you think people spend so many hours in front of their television sets, and (2) the effect of watching too much television.
9. Is beauty really only in the eye of the beholder? Write an essay explaining why you think Americans—or particular cities in the United States—illustrate their preference for ugliness over beauty. Some obvious topics to examine here would be architecture, clothes (patterns, styles), landscaping, and so on. Make sure your reasoning is clear and your examples are representative of your topic. You will want to mention any exceptions to your thesis early in your essay.
10. Write an essay contrasting wanton luxuries versus human necessities. To fully develop your essay, employ additional methods of development, such as illustration and example, division and classification, and description.

CHAPTER 11

Argumentation: The Logical Appeal

Argumentative essays should be based on sound logic. The most elemental forms of reasoning stem from induction and deduction. When preparing to write an argumentative paper, imagine that you are a detective, perhaps Sherlock Holmes, the famous fictional sleuth renowned for the powers of observation that aided his deductive reasoning. Through this deductive reasoning, he was able to solve the most baffling cases. In a similar manner, by carefully observing all aspects of an argument, you may successfully draw conclusions from them, conclusions that are reasonable, logical, and verifiable.

Inductive Logic

Induction moves from the particular to the general. To use induction, you take several representative examples of a person, place, or thing and make a general observation about them. What general observation, for instance, could you make about these three facts?

- 230,000 people lost their lives in the Haiti earthquake in January 2010.
- The northern hemisphere heat wave claimed more than ninety-six lives across twenty-two states in the U.S. during July 2010.
- The Pakistan flood of 2010 destroyed property, caused 2,000 deaths, and produced a significant negative effect on the country's economy.

No doubt you noticed that each fact had two things in common with the others: multiple human deaths and a natural disaster. What can we conclude by considering the three facts? *Natural disasters can be dangerous.*

The greater the number of representative examples (facts) you can offer your reader, the better. Why? Inductive arguments require a *leap in logic*, a leap from specific points to one believable general point, and the more examples you can offer, the smaller the inductive leap. When you check your argumentative essays for weak points, you frequently are searching for places where the connection between your specific points and generalizations requires your reader to place more "faith" in your word than in concrete evidence. Whenever this occurs, your inductive leap—getting from your specific points to a general, logical conclusion—is too broad and therefore unconvincing. Furthermore, since one exception to a claim such as "all men like to play golf on weekends" would disprove your point, you often will want to qualify what you say using words such as "most," "usually," and "often."

Deduction

The opposite of induction, deduction, moves from general points—evidence—to a specific conclusion. A valid deductive conclusion, however, depends on the truth of its evidence. This evidence can be either of major or minor importance. The following logical statement illustrates this point. If I say *All show dogs have pedigrees* (major evidence) and that *My dog Grendel has a pedigree* (minor evidence), I could deduce that *Grendel is a show dog.* What is wrong with my reasoning? We all know that *not* every dog with a pedigree appears in dog shows; therefore, it cannot be concluded that every dog with a pedigree is automatically a show dog. False evidence can lead to untrue conclusions. To ensure that your deduction is logical and valid, qualify your major evidence with a word such as "many": *Many pedigreed dogs are show dogs.* Deductive reasoning, therefore, should be seen as an aid in leading the reader to the conclusion you want him or her to reach. Mark Charles Fissel uses deduction in just such a way in "Online Learning and Student Success" to arrive at the conclusion that many segments of American society can—or in the future, will—benefit from distance learning courses as an alternative method of instruction. However, students must voice their genuine "preferences and needs," rather than allowing cyber marketers to lead the way, and *"ultimately, it is the individual teacher who must take responsibility for the curriculum and how it is taught."*

Types of Argumentation

Are there different types of argumentation? Yes. At times, one will argue for an entire essay that something like censorship is or is not constitutional. Here, an author argues to establish what he or she believes is a convincing fact, a fact that is worthy of a reader's attention. A good example of an argument of fact would be found in "Peyote, Wine and the First Amendment." Therein, Douglas Laycock argues that governmental bodies in the United States—local or federal—should not regulate religious rituals and ceremonies of minor religions, particularly those of Native Americans who use peyote as part of a *"substantial tradition,"* and that their use of peyote is limited to a *"structured worship service."* In arguing his case, Laycock points out that the First Amendment guarantees "the free exercise of religion."

Grace Sumabat Estrada presents another argument of fact, in which she asserts, *"The beguiling presence of animé within North American culture cannot be ignored. We are bombarded by animé merchandise in clothing, electronic, and toy stores."* Throughout her essay, Estrada demonstrates the validity of her argument referring to multiple examples of both animé and Western cartoons. Walt Disney and other animators will continue to thrive; however, *the "animé revolution, without a doubt, is here to stay."*

Anna Quindlen's essay, "Turning the Page: The Future of Reading is Backlit and Bright," argues that books are not dead; technology has not killed them, and e-books, cell phones, and computers have not replaced paper-bound texts. In fact, people on both sides of the issue should take some time and concern themselves with the function of reading rather than the form. Then she goes on to explain how she's cheered by a *"Gallup poll that asks a simple question: Do you happen to be reading any books or novels at present? In 1952, a mere 18 percent of respondents said yes. The last time the survey was done, in 2005, that number was 47 percent. So much for the good old days."* Obviously, the future of reading—regardless of format—looks bright.

At times, however, writing a factual argument is only the starting point of an essay. In such an essay, a problem or issue will be identified and defined in the first few paragraphs. Then an author will propose a logical course of action, convincing the reader of the merit of his or her solution. Arguments containing a *call to action* demand that an author impress his or her readers that a situation exists that needs to be addressed and changed. If your neighbor told you that your best friend is a terrorist and should be turned over to the police or the Federal Bureau of Investigation, what are the chances of your doing so? Without specific evidence, you would be unlikely to embark on any plan of action. Reacting to hearsay and unsubstantiated reason makes an act impulsive, not rational or ethical. In short, provide your reader with sufficient reason to "act."

In "OMG: Tweeting, Trending, and Texting," Mandana Mohsenzadegan provides an argument of fact that leads to an argument of action (moderation in using cell phones) stating, *"We fail to recognize that in its attempt to bring us closer together, telecommunications have only drifted us further apart and placed a superficial veil over our interactions with others, leaving us feeling empty and discontent—despite our having 500+ 'friends' on Facebook."* However, her call to action cautions judicious cell phone use rather than developing a dependence or addiction to them. Mohsenzadegan appeals to her readers ethically (ethos) and logically (logos) because she identifies with them! That is, Mohsenzadegan admits that she owns an iPhone, is a member of a social network, checks her email daily, and cannot imagine living without her computer. Therefore, her proposed plan of action seems more credible than if it came from someone who condemns all forms of telecommunication devices.

Still another form of argumentation is the argument of refutation. In such an essay, an author strives to disprove an opposing viewpoint on a topic. To do so, writers attack generalizations and faulty logic used by their counterparts. In "Soul Food," for instance, Amiri Baraka refutes (argues) that those who claim African Americans lack a distinct cuisine do not know what they are talking about. To tear apart his opposition's argument, he shows through illustration and example that foods such as grits, fried porgie, and black-eyed peas are definite African-American contributions to our country's varied cultural cuisines.

Clearly Stated Thesis

Although the type of argument might be determined by your objective for writing the essay, all types of argument usually have one thing in common: *a strong, clearly stated thesis.* As in most compositions, a specific thesis statement will help you to keep your essay focused as you develop the composition, avoiding digressions and superfluous facts. Such a thesis will unquestionably lead your reader to your opinion and help to frame the supporting points of the argument. An uncertain thesis is bound to result in reader confusion as well as writer confusion.

Avoiding Fallacies

A fallacy is an incorrect or falsely reasoned fact. We could devote an entire course in logic to discussing fallacies, but for our purposes, we will mention only a few fallacies by name—the ones most likely to occur and weaken an argument.

1. *Ad Hominem* ("To the person"): This reasoning twists the focus of an argument by attacking the person who made it rather than arguing the issue at hand. In other words, a person who is guilty of *ad hominem* might spend time attempting to persuade readers that an opponent is disreputable rather than refuting an argument that animals have rights.
2. *Stereotyping:* Since stereotyping inaccurately presents people, places, and things (e.g., all Californians have suntans, only celebrities drive BMW cars, or anyone who lives in Florida is retired), using stereotypes to support an argument will weaken rather than strengthen it.
3. *Faulty Sampling:* When you support an argument with specific examples, you must make certain that your examples are truly representative of your topic. Suppose that you argue that Americans no longer like house pets and say that recently, 90 percent of the Americans surveyed said they do not own or plan to own a pet. If, however, you surveyed only ten people (nine of whom disliked animals), your statement is highly likely to be inaccurate. This points to one of the major problems in using statistics: You can find statistics that say whatever you want.
4. *Sweeping Generalizations:* Often, sweeping generalizations tend to imply that if a group—including people places, and things—has a particular quality, then any member of that group must have the same quality as well. To avoid sweeping generalizations, make use of qualifying words and phrases such as *usually, often, most, some, several,* and avoid the use of absolute phrases such as, "*Everybody* enjoys swimming." One person who dislikes or fears swimming makes your entire statement untrue!

5. *False Dilemma (Either/Or Fallacy):* The false dilemma fallacy oversimplifies issues by assuming that there are only two alternatives in an argument. Thus, instead of exploring possibilities, readers are forced to choose between two extremes when other choices may exist. The sentence, "Christopher must either become a medical doctor or join the United States Marine Corps for life," for instance, inaccurately measures the number and type of career opportunities open to him.
6. *Post Hoc/Ergo Propter Hoc:* The Latin phrase literally translates as: "It happened after this; therefore, it happened because of this." However, the mere fact that one event follows another does not produce a logical, valid cause-and-effect relationship. No true causal relationship is expressed in a sentence like, "Every time I wash my truck it rains." Washing the truck did not cause rainfall to occur. Similarly, a sentence like "Rose Anna gives Wayne a ride home after work every day; therefore, she likes to drive" is equally absurd. Rose Anna does not enjoy driving a car merely because she drops Wayne off at his house after work. Such reasoning will result in faulty cause-and-effect analysis.

Documenting Sources

Referring to authoritative sources can greatly strengthen the credibility of an argument. However, when you quote somebody or paraphrase another person's ideas, it is important to document your reference. Although the *Internet Connection* assignments throughout this text provide ongoing practice documenting sources—something discussed in detail in the Appendix—the first, fifth, and sixth essays in *Chapter 11: Argumentation,* "The Anima of Animé Revisited," "OMG: Tweeting, Trending, and Texting," and "Online Learning and Student Success," respectively, illustrate documentation in action. Additional essays illustrating documentation include "Rediscovering Community" in *Chapter 6: Process Analysis* and "Why We Went to Iraq" in *Chapter 12: Persuasion*. If you have not done so already, you might want to read the Appendix discussion on the MLA format for constructing *parenthetical references* and a list of *works cited* before reading these essays. That way, you will recognize the significance of documentation in context.

Tips on Writing Argumentative Essays

1. Pre-write to generate ideas, to inventory your knowledge about a subject, and to determine what you wish to say about your topic.
2. As mentioned earlier, a very clear thesis is essential, for if you have a fuzzy, unclear thesis, your reader will not know precisely what you are arguing for or against. A seemingly uncertain writer is not too trustworthy or convincing.
3. Do not apologize for your viewpoint; justify it! This is particularly important to remember when you take an unpopular stance on a topic or issue. After all, popular opinion does not depend on ethical or logical reasoning.
4. Be fair. Make sure you can defend what you claim. Have a firm basis for what you are contending. Do not assume that your reader will agree with your social, political, or religious viewpoints. Avoid "leap-of-faith" arguments.
5. Present all sides of your topic or issue; otherwise, your paper is not an argument. If your opponent makes or has a good point, do not ignore it. Place it early in your essay. By acknowledging that no issue is black or white, you will seem ethical and reasonable.
6. Present your material in emphatic order (move from your weakest to your strongest argument). Otherwise, your supporting argument may seem anticlimactic or weak by comparison. Step by step, lead your reader to the conclusion.
7. Use authoritative evidence for technical information whenever you can to make what you claim believable.
8. Provide a thorough argument of fact using plenty of representative—rather than selective—examples before presenting your readers with an argument of action.
9. In arguments of action, show how and why your plan of action is the most logical one to adopt. By taking time to explain who or what will benefit from your proposal, you will appear not only a logical person but also an ethical person.
10. Check your work for faulty logic and generalizations. Do so in all stages of the writing process to avoid building an entire argument on a faulty premise, one that you will only have to rethink and rewrite in order to make rational sense.

Grace Sumabat Estrada

The Anima of Animé Revisited

Grace Sumabat Estrada has worked in the fields of Computer Information Technology and personal finance. Her daily interactions with people from various socioeconomic backgrounds have given her a broad view of life and sensitivity to all aspects of human needs and conveniences. A poet and essayist, her works have been published in everything from *Projections: Brief Readings on American Culture* to *Leaf by Leaf.* Although Estrada cultivates a wide variety of interests, her children, Geoffrey, David, and Ariana, strongly influence her concerns about the world in which they live. Along with her children, Estrada considers her husband, Henry Estrada, his children, Alexander and Katherine, and her family in Canada as being the core of her life and essential in forming the person she is today. Estrada is currently working on her Masters of Arts Degree. In the following essay, Estrada blends comparison and contrast as well as illustration and example techniques to advance her argument about animé in Western society. She attributes the inspiration and development of this revised version of her essay to the animé experts in her blended family.

Pre-reading Questions

1. What criticisms have your heard directed at cartoons during your lifetime? When, where, and how? Why might the very cartoons that some people criticize oftentimes earn praise from other sources?
2. Brainstorm, freewrite, or cluster the words "cartoon" and "anime." What images and qualities do the words bring to mind? How do both words reflect culture values? Explain.

"The blue sky is infinitely high, crystal clear ... that's what the world should be ... a world of infinite possibilities, laid before us, crystal clear"

—*Kintasu* (Samurai X)

1 The beguiling presence of animé within North American culture cannot be ignored. We are inundated by animé merchandise in clothing, electronic, and toy stores. In fact, in the United States, animé has replaced pornography as the leader in the ubiquitous video market (Levine). American artists, realizing the mass animé appeal, have recently incorporated Japanese animé elements into American-made cartoons in the hopes of emulating animé success. One animé series in particular, *Dragonball Z*, is one of the longest-running animated series worldwide. Hundreds of fan clubs exist in Asia, Europe, and North America. It holds a coveted place in the hearts of grade-school children and young adults alike. Very few shows can manage such widespread appeal to such a broad age range. The animé revolution, without a doubt, is here to stay.

2 People use the term animé, in its most basic definition, to describe animated Japanese stories (Lawson). However, the phenomenon of animé has extended far beyond this limited description. It would be grossly inaccurate to make a blanket statement that it is all science fiction, comedy, or children's entertainment. Animé is not a genre—rather, it is a medium of communication, like television, books, or radio (Levine). To pigeonhole animé would be similar to pigeonholing live-action film (Ruth). The world of animé is pervasive, indeed. Animé is available not only on television, but also on VHS and DVD, in the cinema, on console and arcade games, and even on the Internet (Wade). Even Mattel's quintessential all-American female role model, Barbie, has established a line of dolls called *My Scene Barbie* that display very animé-like features. Animé has also transcended the national boundaries of Japan to include other countries such as Korea because the distinctive cartoon style of animé is more defining than its country of origin. If anything, Japan quickly is losing its exclusive ownership of this style of art. North American illustrators are still in the process of examining the underlying factors that have caused animé to be more appealing than their domestic creations. Ironically, Japanese animation can trace its original influences back to America's premier creator of children's entertainment, Walt Disney himself.

3 During the Meiji Restoration era preceding imperialist rule in the late nineteenth century, Japan went through a massive modernization, emulating the West in as many ways as possible. The same mentality was revisited after World War II, and it had its effects even within Japan's failing entertainment industry (Catichi). A few adventuresome Japanese artists decided to mimic Disney's animation style of creating adult characters with adolescent features and exaggerated eyes, and added their own unique Japanese twist. Japan's first animated series was *Tetsuwan Atomu* (aka *Astro Boy*) by Osamu Tezuka, which first aired briefly on American television in 1964 (Wade). No one could predict at that time that it was just the start of a revolutionary artistic phenomenon that would capture global attention.

4 Animé art is vibrant, colorful, and dynamic. Its highly stylized form is easily recognizable, even by those who are only superficially familiar with it. Female characters such as Sailor Moon have extremely large eyes, almost non-existent noses, and petite mouths. Their figures are invariably slim and curvaceous. Faye, from the animé *Cowboy Bebop*, is typical of the female characters in more adult-oriented animé. She is a gun-toting female who wears revealing clothing that seems highly impractical given her line of work. It has been argued, however, that animé artists purposely draw their female protagonists this way in order to show that women can be strong without losing their femininity, since weapons are traditionally male-associated displays of power (Ruth). Interestingly, male protagonists are not as easily stereotyped. Characters like Goku of *Dragonball Z* and Jet of *Cowboy Bebop* often have disproportionately muscular physiques that are impossible to attain. Despite their testosterone-filled exterior, though, there is a surprising naiveté and gentleness in their nature. However, those who aren't portrayed with bulging muscles, such as Kenshin in *Rurouni Kenshin*, Vash from *Trigun*, and *Inuyasha*'s title character, are lanky of build, but are gifted with extraordinary abilities that more than make up for their lack of brute strength.

5 Facial expressions of either sex are often exaggerated to a comical extent—subtlety is not a virtue of animé art. These consistent characteristics of animé serve a dual purpose. First, the features emphasized by animé style are those that address universal standards of sex appeal—the females accentuate their youth and fertility while the males display power through status or genetic superiority. Ergo, consciously or not, viewers inexplicably find animé figures to be aesthetically pleasing. The second reason for portraying characters this way is that it makes it very difficult to determine their ethnic origin. Whereas *Batman* and *Superman* are undoubtedly Caucasian, animé characters tend to display a blend of Asian and European traits. Since both genders often sport unusual hair colors and styles, such as blue bouffants or purple Mohawks, the lines of ethnicity become even further blurred. In *Dragonball Z*, the fighters begin as dark-eyed and dark-haired figures, but become blue-eyed and blond as their power levels jump to a higher level (a Japanese yearning for westernization?). In *Rurouni Kenshin*, the titled protagonist sports a redheaded, bushy pony-tailed look, and in *Witch Hunter Robin*, the six main characters definitely look more Western than Asian. This ethnic ambiguity lends itself beautifully to allowing a wider range of viewers to identify with the characters. Neo-animé, a style in which American artists incorporate animé elements, has started to become more popular, as is evidenced by shows like *Teen Titans, Power Puff Girls,* and *Samurai Jack* (Levine). However, although the physical elements of animé are being incorporated, the emotional and intellectual content of most American animation still tends to be sadly lacking in polish. One would

hope that shows like *South Park* and *Family Guy* don't delineate the sophistication of all Western adult-oriented animation.

6 Although the majority of animé stories take place in outer space or in some other time era, they still have the tendency to portray characters in a more true to life perspective. Naturally, Japanese social customs and culture are somewhat reflected in the shows, but they add an appealing sense of reality and domesticity. It is not unusual to see a hero struggle financially, be told to do homework, eat a meal, or go to the bathroom. In *Cowboy Bebop*, the main protagonists are a group of misfit bounty hunters who are often on the edge of starvation—their usual meal is a cup of instant Ramen. In one amusing scene in a *Dragonball Z* episode, two of its flying child-heroes, Goten and Trunks, decide to play a game of writing their names on a boulder with their urine while they relieve themselves. Imagine Batman and/or Superman engaging in such an activity! North American-made animated shows are often plagued with the handicaps of censors and political correctness. They are sanitized to the point of blandness.

7 The storylines found in animé shows also tend to be more complex than in North American made animation. Typically, Western animators rely on conventional, black and white plots and characters. Superman and his arch-nemesis, Lex Luthor, for instance, are representative of the black and white nature of Western cartoons. Superman, the archetypal *ultimate* Boy Scout, clearly contrasts with Lex Luthor, the supreme manifestation of greed and evil. Even though Batman is generally viewed as a "darker" hero, with more complex psychological issues than Superman, we know he will never kill his enemies. While viewers expect and even relish the conflict between good and bad, they know full well that, in the end, good will prevail—no surprises. Similarly, Disney films are characterized by their handsome/beautiful protagonists, cute animal sidekicks, and sinister-looking villains. Without even knowing the storyline, one could tell who the "bad guy" is within milliseconds of a Disney movie! Unlike animé male protagonists, it is extremely difficult to find a Western male lead who isn't overly muscular and handsome (one notable exception would be the titled hero from the Dreamworks movie *Shrek*). Only in one of its more recent releases, *Lilo and Stitch,* has Disney departed from this predictable formula. In this movie, Stitch, the main character, is actually a genetically engineered alien creature designed to be indestructible but destructive of everything in its way. Stitch's evolution into a socially acceptable citizen of earth and his relationship with Lilo signify Disney's recognition that this new generation of cartoon viewers demands more depth and complexity, even in animated storylines.

8 Animé stories, in contrast to traditional Western storylines, are known for their intricacy. This can partially be attributed to a cultural difference in communication styles. Americans have been considered rude by some

cultures because of the directness with which they speak. Animé follows the traditional Japanese mode of storytelling—they start off gradually and develop characters and the storyline with more deliberation and symbolism than American audiences may be used to enduring (Levine). Characters have multidimensional aspects to their nature, and rather than being black or white, individuals often find themselves in the gray area. Two of the most popular characters of *Dragonball Z* are Vegeta and Piccolo. Both originated as villains but subsequently found themselves fighting alongside the main hero, Goku. Throughout the show, however, it is clear that their combative and contradictory personalities continue to afflict them as a team, bringing forth extremely entertaining interactions. In *Inuyasha*, the titled protagonist is a half-demon who is constantly struggling with his desire to succumb to his demonic impulses to gain more power at any cost. Animé assumes a certain level of maturity and sophistication from its viewers. The most popular animé base their stories on Japanese history (for example, *Rurouni Kenshin*) and the ancient philosophies of Zen and Shinto (Lawson). Major protagonists are often seriously wounded or even killed during battle, making the plots far less predictable than their North American counterparts. For example, we all know that the Joker will never succeed in killing Batman; by contrast, in *Dragonball Z*, the villain Majin Boo killed many of the shows protagonists (in fact, he destroyed the entire Earth). Although the heroes did have a method of returning from the grave (through dragon ball wishes), the intrigue of "when" and "how" still compels viewers and draws them further into the plot. Another example of unpredictability can be found in *Cowboy Bebop*, where the show's main protagonist, Spike, is actually killed in its last episode. In animé, there is no guarantee of immediate gratification or a happy ending.

9 Those new to animé often are concerned by the violence and sexual content of a significant portion of anime movies. However, there is a cultural difference between East and West that must be understood. In America, almost anything cartoon is relegated to the children's section. Due to Disney's popular formula for American-made animated movies, people in this country tend to view all animated films as being family fare. The assumption of sanitized subject matter should not apply for foreign films. In Asia, animé is a genuine form of entertainment for adults. The biggest domestic movie hit of all time in Japan is *Monoke-hime* (Princess Monoke), a non-juvenile animated film by Miyazaki Hayao (Kenji). Animé has overtaken live-action film production in Japan, largely due to the latter's inherent budget and creative limitations (Kenji). Animé offers a relatively inexpensive alternative that can often surpass the visual and intellectual appeal of live-action films. Just as people scrutinize live-action movies for their viewing appropriateness, they should also maintain the same vigilance for animé films.

10 Paradoxically, the world of animé is one that offers a sense of reality coupled with a liberating door to fantasy. Characters perform mundane chores, experience doubt and angst, and have troubled relationships as we do, yet they can also travel to other worlds, interact with aliens, and perform superhuman feats of strength and agility. As with our lives, it is difficult to predict how an anime story will end. The appeal of animé and its growing popularity in mainstream America marks an intellectual and emotional growth in popular consciousness. Perhaps we are ready for a new level of entertainment and creativity; perhaps we no longer need the guarantee of a happy ending.

> *"The blue sky is infinitely high, crystal clear … that's what the world should be … a world of infinite possibilities, laid before us, crystal clear"*
>
> —*Kintasu* (Samurai X)

> *"Always with the end comes hope and rebirth."*
>
> —*Sailor Saturn* (Sailor Moon)

Works Cited

Allison, Brent. "Anime Fan Subculture: A Review of the Literature." Un. of Georgia. 1 July 2005 <www.corneredangel.com/amwess/papers/anime_fan_subculture.html>.

Catinchi, Ruben. "America's Love Affair with Japan." *Professional Writing*. SUNY Cortland, USA. 4 July 2005 <neovox.Cortland.edu/vox/vox_26/vox_26.html>.

Jennings, Michael. "Waiting for Miyazaki, or Thoughts on the State of Animated Movies." *Samizata.Com* 11 October 2003. 19 June 2005. <www.samizdata.net/blog/archives/004736.html>.

Kenyon, Heather. "Editor's Notebook." *Animation World Magazine* 4.8 (November 1999). Online. 1 July 2005 <www.awn.com/mag/issue4.08/4.08pages/4.08editor.php3>.

Lawson, Terry. "What is Anime?" *Detroit Free Press* 31 October 1999. Online. 2 July 2005 <www.freep.com/fun/movies/qanime31.html>.

Levine, Jerry. "Cartoons Are for Kids, and Other Issues: The Japanese Anime Market in the United States." *Patchmonkey*. November 25, 2002. Online. 3 July 2005 <patchmonkey.net/blahlife/animepaper.html>.

Persson, Jonas. "Anime Introduction." *Anime Nation*. 6 July 2005 <www.cabbit.com/anime.html>.

Ruth, Brian. "Liberating Cels: Forms of the Female in Japanese Cyberpunk Animation." *Anime Research*. December 2000. Online. 3 July 2005 <www.animeresearch.com/Articles/LiberatingCels/html>.

Wade, David Allen. "Neo-Tokyo Is About to Explode: The Fine Art of Animé." *Cold Fussion*. December 2002. 2 July 2005 <www.coldfusion.art.msstate.edu/graduate/Dwade/paper_anime.html>.

Post-reading Questions

Content

1. Where does Estrada place the thesis of her essay? Why?
2. List some of animé's dominant characteristics.
3. Identify where the majority of "animé" stories occur?
4. Assess the significant cultural differences in the way people in the East and West perceive the function of cartoons.
5. To what extent do you agree with Estrada's assessment that anime storylines tend to be more complex than in American animation? Why?

Strategies and Structures

1. Why do you imagine Estrada chose to preface her thesis paragraph and follow her concluding paragraph with a quotation by an animé character? What do the quotations add to the essay?
2. Right after her thesis paragraph, Estrada spends time defining anime before returning to argue her thesis. How does this affect the persuasive merit of her argument?
3. Estrada mentions that animé contains several consistent characteristics that serve a dual purpose. Briefly mention some of the consistent characteristics listed in your response to Content Question 2 and then explain their dual purpose in context.
4. Despite their fantastical elements, animé stories often depict an appealing sense of domesticity, according to Estrada, How does she justify this comment? Explain why or why not the same statement could apply to Western cartoons?
5. Explain how Estrada's concluding paragraph pulls together the parts of her essay and refocuses her argument.

Language and Vocabulary

1. Vocabulary: *anima, inundated, beguiling, ubiquitous, coveted, phenomenon, transcended, curvaceous, ergo, domesticity, blandness, arch-nemesis, manifestation, milliseconds, evolution, multidimensional, relegated, inherent, paradoxically, mundane, angst.* After checking the definitions for vocabulary words, consider how

Estrada uses the majority of them to express a quality or modify other words. Then, select at least seven such words, go to a thesaurus, and locate an antonym (word with opposite meaning) and synonym (word with similar meaning) for each.

2. Return to the word "anima" in Estrada's essay title and locate a general dictionary definition of the word, as well as Carl Jung's definition of anima. Which definition do you think Estrada was alluding to, if not both? Explain.
3. Make a list of some specific instances in this essay where Estrada's language indicates or suggests her attitude toward her subject. Then, do the same thing to a recent composition you have written.

Group Activities

1. In her essay, Estrada blends the rhetorical strategies of illustration and example, definition, comparison and contrast to argue "the animé revolution, without a doubt, is here to stay." Gather in groups, pair off, and have each sub-group go back though the essay, identifying instances where she uses specific rhetorical modes of development to develop it. Next, reassemble in your groups, share your insights, and record them on a single sheet of paper. Finally, as a class, compare and contrast group findings.
2. Pair off and explore the world of cartoons in a computer-assisted classroom on your college campus. Have one person jot down the pair's impressions of such popular cartoons in western society as *The Simpson's, King of the Hill, Daffy Duck, Bugs Bunny, Spiderman, Batman, Justice League, South Park, Sponge Bob, The Flintstones, Family Guy*, and so on. Also consider Disney and other animated movies such as *Alpha and Omega, Tangled, Shrek, How to Train Your Dragon, Toy Story, Finding Nemo, Megamind, Ratatouille, Cars.* What are the defining characteristics of the cartoons you looked up (color, style, and so on) on the Internet? Make a copy of your findings for each class member to refer to in a writing activity.

Writing Activities

1. Write an essay where you compare and contrast characters in an animé cartoon and a Western cartoon or movie to argue a specific point. Use parenthetical references, as needed, to cite your sources (see the Appendix).

2. After brainstorming the topics of sex and/or violence in twenty-first century cartoons, write an essay arguing that anime, western cartoons, or both tend to promote violence and exploit sex in North and South America or vice versa. Use sound reasoning, plenty of representative examples, and analysis to prove your argument.

***Internet Connection:* Grace Estrada**

Animé Vs. Cartoon

Research the topic of "animé" on the Internet and then the topic of "Western cartoons." What sorts of articles do you encounter? What claims do they make, and what examples and reasons do they use? Do any of your sources place computer-animated films in their own category? If so, why? Referring to both Estrada's essay and the sources you located online, write an essay arguing that "animé" and "cartoons" do or do not serve a socially constructive role as entertainment in the United States. Be sure to document your sources correctly, using the MLA format. (See the Appendix.)

Amiri Baraka

Soul Food

An essayist, poet, novelist, and playwright, Amiri Baraka was one of the founders of the Black Arts Movement in the 1960s, and his work—especially the early poems—reflects a Black Nationalist's stance. He is well known for his plays such as *The Dutchman, The Slave, The Toilet* (1964), and *Four Black Revolutionary Plays* (1969). Other works include *Preface to a Twenty Volume Suicide Note* (1961), *The System of Dante's Hell* (1965), *Black Magic: Poetry 1961–1967* (1967), *Selected Poetry of Imamu Amiri Baraka/LeRoi Jones* (1979), *Reggae or Not* (1982), *The Music: Reflections on Jazz* (1982), *Wise Why's Y's: The Griots Tale* (1997), *The Fiction of LeRoi Jones/Amiri Baraka* (1999), *Somebody Blew Up America* (2001), and *Tales of the Out & the Gone* (2006). Baraka rejected traditional poetic forms and also the dominant white culture. He denounced his Christian name, LeRoi Jones, and adopted his Muslim name, Imamu Amiri Baraka. Later, with his conversion to Marxism, Baraka dropped "Imamu" from his name as having "bourgeois nationalist" implications. In 2010, Baraka appeared in *Motherland*, an epic documentary about the African continent from Ancient Kemet to the present.

Pre-reading Questions

1. What do you think about when you hear the term "soul" linked with "food" or "music"? Have you any idea where the meaning you associate with such terms originated? Briefly write about your own "word history" for "soul" in your thesis notebook, writing log, or class journal.
2. What does the essay's title suggest to the reader? Have you any idea what soul food is? What is it, or what do you think it might be?

---

1 Recently, a young Negro novelist writing in *Esquire* about the beauties of America mentioned that one of the things wrong with Negroes was that, unlike the Chinese, blacks have neither a language of their own nor a characteristic cuisine. And this to me is the deepest stroke, the unkindest cut of oppression, especially as it has distorted black Americans. America, where the suppliant, far from rebelling or even disagreeing with the forces that have caused him to suffer, readily backs them up and finally tries to become an honorary oppressor himself.

2 No language? No characteristic food? Oh, man, come on.

3 Maws are things ofays seldom get to peck, nor are you likely ever to hear about Charlie eating a chitterling. Sweet potato pies, a good friend of mine asked recently, "Do they taste anything like pumpkin?" Negative. They taste more like memory, if you're not uptown.

4 All those different kinds of greens (now quick frozen for anyone) once were all Sam got to eat. (Plus the potlikker, into which one slipped some throwed away meat.) Collards and turnips and kale and mustards were not fit for anybody but the woogies. So they found a way to make them taste like something somebody would want to freeze and sell to a Negro going to Harvard as exotic European spinach.

5 The watermelon, friend, was imported from Africa (by whom?) where it had been growing many centuries before it was necessary for some people to deny that they had ever tasted one.

6 Did you ever hear of a black-eyed pea? (Whitey used it for forage, but some folks couldn't.) And all those weird parts of the hog? (After the pig was stripped of its choicest parts, the feet, snout, tail, intestines, stomach, etc., were all left for the "members," who treated them mercilessly.) Is it mere myth that shades are death on chickens? (Deep fat frying, the Dutch found out in 17th century New Amsterdam, was an African specialty: and if you can get hold of a fried chicken leg, or a fried porgie, you can find out what happened to that tradition.)

7 I had to go to Rutgers before I found people who thought grits were meant to be eaten with milk and sugar, instead of gravy and pork sausage . . . and that's one of the reasons I left.

8 Away from home, you must make the trip uptown to get really straight as far as a good grease is concerned. People kill chickens all over the world, but chasing them through the dark on somebody else's property would probably insure, once they went in the big bag, that you'd find some really beautiful way to eat them. I mean, after all the risk involved. The fruit of that tradition unfolds everywhere above 100th Street. There are probably more restaurants in Harlem whose staple is fried chicken, or chicken in the basket, than any other place in the world. Ditto, barbecued ribs—also straight out of the South with the West Indians, *i.e.*, Africans from farther south in the West, having developed the best sauce for roasting whole oxen and hogs, spicy and extremely hot.

9 Hoppin' John (black-eyed peas and rice), hushpuppies (crusty cornmeal bread cooked in fish grease and best with fried fish, especially fried salt fish, which ought to soak overnight unless you're over fifty and can take all that salt), hoecake (pan bread), buttermilk biscuits and pancakes, fatback, *i.e.*, streak'alean-streak'afat, dumplings, neck bones, knuckles (both good for seasoning limas or string beans), okra (another African importation, other name gumbo), pork chops—some more staples of the Harlem cuisine. Most of the food came North when the people did.

10 There are hundreds of tiny restaurants, food shops, rib joints, shrimp shacks, chicken shacks, "rotisseries" throughout Harlem that serve "soul food"—say, a breakfast of grits, eggs and sausage, pancakes and Alaga syrup—and even tiny booths where it's at least possible to get a good piece of barbecue, hot enough to make you whistle, or a chicken wing on a piece of greasy bread. You can *always* find a fish sandwich: a fish sandwich is something you walk with, or "Two of those small sweet potato pies to go." The Muslim temple serves bean pies which are really separate. It is never necessary to go to some big expensive place to get a good filling grease. You *can* go to the Red Rooster, or Wells, or Joch's, and get a good meal, but Jennylin's, a little place on 135th near Lenox, is more filling, or some place like the A&A food shop in a basement up in the 140's, and you can really get away. I guess a square is somebody who's in Harlem and eats at Nedicks.

Post-reading Questions

Content

1. What argument of fact does Baraka seek to establish in this essay? Does the author accomplish his purpose? Why or why not?
2. What methods does the author use to illustrate that African Americans, indeed, have a cuisine of their own?
3. What is the author attempting to express by his references to "uptown"? Is this reference meaningful only to African Americans? Provide several examples to illustrate your reasoning.
4. Baraka concludes his essay by saying, "I guess a square is somebody who's in Harlem and eats at Nedicks." (Nedicks is a typical American fast-food restaurant that does not serve soul food.) Why is it appropriate that he end his essay in such a manner? How does his comment reinforce his argument about African Americans?

Strategies and Structures

1. Why does the author first use African-American terms for food and later define these food terms? How does this suggest a two-part argument?
2. What is the value of slang in this composition? Do slang terms serve a strategic purpose in Baraka's argument? Explain.
3. How well does the subject of food work as a unifying device in Baraka's essay? Cite some specific examples that support your claim.

Language and Vocabulary

1. Vocabulary: *chitterling, potlikker, collards, fried porgie, grits.* How many of these words can you find in a dictionary? If you are unable to find all of the words, try using an unabridged dictionary. Next, try to locate recipes for some of these dishes. Choose one recipe that particularly appeals to you and either cook it yourself or go to a *soul food* restaurant and order it. Then write an essay persuading your reader to try the food.
2. Does the use of slang change your conception of *soul food* to the more exotic? Please explain how and why.

Group Activities

1. Get into diverse groups and discuss foods that are typical in each represented culture. Argue for their uniqueness. Are there any slang terms that have developed for the foods that your group considers? If so, are they in common use in America today? What would be lost without the slang terms?

2. Visit a restaurant—other than fast-food restaurants such as McDonalds—that serves a cuisine other than your own. Order a food that you never have tasted, and also sample the foods ordered by other members of your group. Then write an essay in which you defend your own food or promote the new food that you have tried.

Writing Activities

1. Compose an essay based on a cultural issue (food, clothing, habits), arguing for your topic's uniqueness to your culture. Carefully consider any opposing arguments, addressing them as necessary, in order to be convincing.
2. Write an essay arguing how and why America needs to become a multilingual society (one that speaks several languages) in order to preserve cultural differences and enrich society as a whole.

Anna Quindlen

Turning the Page: The Future of Reading is Backlit and Bright

Anna Quindlen, Pulitzer Prize-winning journalist and best-selling author of fiction and nonfiction, has written articles for *Newsweek* and other magazines and newspapers for over thirty years, and her work continues to be among the most popular "nonfiction" anthologized in college textbooks. In addition to her numerous awards and accolades in journalism, she holds honorary doctorates from Dartmouth College, Denison University, Moravian College, Mount Holyoke College, Smith College, and Stevens Institute of Technology. Quindlen's nonfiction books include *Living Out Loud* (1992), *Thinking Out Loud: On the Personal, the Political, the Public, and the Private* (1994), *How Reading Changed My Life* (1994), *Being Perfect* (2005), *Anna Quindlen* (2005), *Untitled on Beau* (2007), and *Naked Babies*, with Nick Keish (2009). Among her best-known novels are: *Object Lessons* (1992), *One True Thing* (1994), *Black and*

Blue (1998), *Blessings: A Novel* (2004), *Rise and Shine* (2007), and *Every Last One: A Novel* (2010). Quindlen's following article, initially printed in *Newsweek,* March 26, 2010, takes an optimistic look at the future of reading in an age of technology.

Pre-reading Questions

1. How many times a day do you read something? What do you read? Where do you read it? For how long do you tend to read in a single sitting?
2. In a few sentences, respond to the statement, "The book is [is not] dead." Offer specific reasons that have shaped your opinions toward books in general and reading in particular.

---

1 The stages of a writer's professional life are marked not by a name on an office door, but by a name in ink. There was the morning when my father came home carrying a stack of Sunday papers because my byline was on page one, and the evening that I persuaded a security guard to hand over an early edition, still warm from the presses, with my first column. But there's nothing to compare to the day when someone—in my case, the FedEx guy—hands over a hardcover book with your name on the cover. And with apologies to all the techies out there, I'm just not sure the moment would have had the same grandeur had my work been downloaded instead into an e-reader.

2 The book is dead, I keep hearing as I sit writing yet another in a room lined with them. Technology has killed it. The libraries of the world are doomed to become museums, storage facilities for a form as antediluvian as cave paintings. Americans, however, tend to bring an either-or mentality to most things, from politics to prose. The invention of television led to predictions about the demise of radio. The making of movies was to be the death knell of live theater; recorded music, the end of concerts. All these forms still exist—sometimes overshadowed by their siblings, but not smothered by them. And despite the direst predictions, reading continues to be part of the life of the mind, even as computers replace pencils, and books fly into handhelds as well as onto store shelves. Anton Chekhov, meet Steve Jobs.

3 There's no question that reading off-paper, as I think of it, will increase in the years to come. The nurse-midwives of literacy, public librarians, are already loaning e-readers; a library that got 10 as gifts reported that within a half hour they had all been checked out. And there's no question that once again we will be treated to lamentations suggesting that true literacy has become a lost art. The difference this time is that we will confront elitism from both sides. Not only do literary purists now

complain of the evanescent nature of letters onscreen, the tech aficionados have become equally disdainful of the old form. "This book stinks," read an online review of the bestseller *Game Change* before the release of the digital version. "The thing reeks of paper and ink."

4 Perhaps those of us who merely want to hunker down and be transported should look past both sides to concern ourselves with function instead of form. I am cheered by the Gallup poll that asks a simple question: Do you happen to be reading any books or novels at present? In 1952 a mere 18 percent of respondents said yes. The last time the survey was done, in 2005, that number was 47 percent. So much for the good old days.

5 But not so fast: The National Endowment for the Arts released a report in 2007 that said reading fiction was declining sharply, especially among younger people. Market research done for booksellers has found that the number of so-called avid readers, those who buy more than 10 books a year, skews older and overwhelmingly female. One of the most surprising studies indicates that the biggest users of e-readers are not the YouTube young but affluent middle-aged men. (Some analysts suggest that this may be about adaptable font size; oh, our failing eyes!) The baby boomers are saving publishing; after them, the deluge?

6 The most provocative account of the effect of technology on literacy is now 16 years old, and while it remains a good read—in ink on paper but not, alas, digitally—the passage of time shows that its dark view of the future is overstated. Sven Birkerts's *The Gutenberg Elegies (http://www.amazon.com/exec/obidos/ASIN/0865479577/?tag=nwswk-20)* notes, correctly, that "our entire collective subjective history—the soul of our societal body—is encoded in print." But the author rejects the notion that words can appear on a computer screen in a satisfactory fashion: "The assumptions that underlie their significance are entirely different depending on whether we are staring at a book or a circuit—generated text," he says.

7 Is that true? Is Jane Austen somehow less perceptive or entertaining when the words "It is a truth universally acknowledged" appear onscreen? It's disconcerting to read that many of the bestselling novels in Japan in recent years have been cell-phone books. But it's also cheering to hear from e-book owners who say they find themselves reading more because the books come to them rather than the other way around. I remember an impassioned eulogy for the typewriter delivered years ago by one of my newspaper colleagues: how, he asked, could we write on a keyboard that *made no sound*? Just fine, it turned out.

8 There is and has always been more than a whiff of snobbery about lamentations that reading is doomed to extinction. That's because they're really judgments on human nature. If you've convinced yourself that America is a deeply anti-intellectual country, it must follow that we

don't read, or we read the wrong things, or we read them in the wrong fashion. And now we have gleeful e-elitism as well, the notion that the conventional product, printed and bound, is a hopeless dinosaur. Tech snobbery is every bit as silly as the literary variety. Both ignore the tremendous power of book love. As Kafka once said, "A book must be the ax for the frozen sea within us."

9 Reading is not simply an intellectual pursuit but an emotional and spiritual one. It lights the candle in the hurricane lamp of self; that's why it survives. There are book clubs and book Web sites and books on tape and books online. There are still millions of people who like the paper version, at least for now. And if that changes—well, what is a book, really? Is it its body, or its soul? Would Dickens have recognized a paperback of *A Christmas Carol (http://www.amazon.com/exec/obidos/ASIN/1449910416/?tag=nwswk-20)*, or, for that matter, a Braille version? Even on a cell-phone screen, Tiny Tim can God-bless us, every one.

Post-reading Questions

Content

1. Identify Quindlen's basic argument about the future of reading in a technology-driven society. To what extent do you agree or disagree with her and why?
2. What does Quindlen mean when she states, "Anton Chekhov, meet Steve Jobs"? How does the comment relate to her thesis in general and her essay in particular?
3. In paragraph 4, why does Quindlen state that "both sides" (traditional, hard-copy readers, and e-readers) need to concern themselves with "function instead of form"? What does she go on to demonstrate by comparing Gallop Poll results in 1953 and 2005?
4. Quindlen argues that "Tech snobbery is every bit as silly as the literary variety." How does she illustrate this point throughout her essay? Locate as many examples of both types of snobbery as you can.
5. Define what Quindlen means by "gleeful e-elitism." Then, offer some examples of "gleeful e-elitism" drawn from your own experiences, observations, and readings.

Strategies and Structures

1. How does Quindlen demonstrate that the growing popularity of e-readers does not necessarily mean the "book is dead" or that "libraries will become museums"?
2. Why does Quindlen reference famous novelists, dramatists, and other writers in her essay? What purpose does this serve? Be specific.

3. In what ways does Quindlen balance her discussion on reading books, past and present? Does she seem like an open-minded, objective author or an opinionated one? How? Why?
4. Explain how Quindlen's concluding paragraph, especially her allusion to Dickens and *A Christmas Carol* in her final two sentences, rounds off her essay. To what extend does it suggest or, as her essay subtitle assures, that *the future of reading is backlit and bright*?
5. How and why does Quindlen's statement that reading "survives" because it "lights the candle in the hurricane lamp of self" reinforce an earlier claim she made about the importance of "function instead of form"?

Language and Vocabulary

1. Vocabulary: *byline, techies, grandeur, ereader, antediluvian, prose, demise, knell, elitism, evanescent, aficionados, direst, hunker, avid, skews, affluent, provocative, disconcerting, impassioned, eulogy, lamentations, pursuit, Braille.* Create a two-column list; place words familiar to you in one list and words you need to check for meaning in another. Then write a brief journal entry or paragraph in a notebook where you compare and contrast two things—one traditional and the other contemporary (e.g., hardcopy newspapers vs. online newspapers, standard movies versus 3D movies, pen-and-pencil tests versus computer exams, and so on). Using at least four vocabulary words from your "unfamiliar word list," revise your paragraph. Keep both versions of your paragraph.
2. As a group, interview other students and family members about their attitude towards reading. Interview people your own age, your parents' age, and your grandparents' age. Be sure to interview at least one male and one female in each age group. Which age group and gender seem to prefer reading books, newspapers, and magazines in hard copy (paper), and which age group and gender appears more inclined to read such materials online? Draw some conclusions about the future of reading and present your findings to the class. Feel free to add an audio/visual element to the presentation.

Group Activities

1. Gather together in small groups and exchange information on your current reading habits (refer back to your Prereading responses). Who reads for enjoyment? What sort of reading do group members prefer? Where do they do most of their reading? Jot down any shared habits and then, time permitting, share your findings with the rest of the class.

2. For a brief collaborative exercise, pair off with another student in class and compare and contrast each other's original paragraph for Language and Vocabulary exercise #1 and the revised version of it. Pay particular attention to how new vocabulary words affected each revision. What conclusions might your draw about the importance of a wide vocabulary for writers?

Writing Activities

1. Write an original essay arguing that viewing and responding to text messages, emails, and tweets is a form of reading and thereby communication. Offer plenty of representative examples to support each part of your argument.
2. Write an essay arguing the superiority of reading paperbound books versus e-books—or vice versa. Be sure to present both sides of the argument using a logical (*logos*) and ethical (*ethos*) appeal to your reader; try to avoid any emotional appeals. Support your claims with plenty of verifiable examples and readings. (See the Appendix on MLA Documentation.)

Douglas Laycock

Peyote, Wine, and the First Amendment

Essayist Douglas Laycock currently serves as the Alice McKean Young Regents Chair in Law at the University of Texas, Austin. His works include *Modern American Remedies* (1985), *The Death of the Irreparable Injury Rule* (1991), and *Collected Works on Religious Liberty, Vol. 1: Overviews and History* (2010). In "Peyote, Wine, and the First Amendment," Laycock examines the privileges enjoyed by major religions, and he argues that the same rights should apply to minor religions. Although his essay first appeared in *The Christian Century* on October 4, 1989, it continues to raise timely issues.

Pre-reading Questions

1. Make a list of freedoms and practices that you believe are guaranteed by the First Amendment. If you are uncertain what the First Amendment is, get a copy of the U.S. Constitution and look it up. Where does freedom of religion fit into our inalienable rights?
2. To your knowledge, is the continuance or growth of non-Christian religions, rituals, and ceremonies (excluding Satanism and death cults) discouraged in America? How many non-Christian religious shows have you seen on television?
3. What is your attitude toward the use of drugs (wine and other alcoholic beverages are drugs) in religious ceremonies? Does it matter that these drugs have been in use for centuries?

---

1 This fall the U.S. Supreme Court will consider arguments in a case that goes to the very heart of the constitutional guarantee of free exercise of religion. The court will decide whether the state can prohibit a religious ritual, and if so, what kinds of dangers justify such an extraordinary prohibition. This litigation involves not a practice of a mainstream faith but the peyote ritual of the Native American Church.

2 Peyote, or mescal, is a small cactus that grows in the southwest U.S. and in northern Mexico. It produces buds or tubers, called buttons, that have hallucinogenic properties. Peyote is an illegal drug, but the federal government and twenty-three states permit its use in at least some religious ceremonies. Federal drug authorities issue licenses to grow and sell peyote to religious users. But the case before the court comes from Oregon, which has no such exemption.

3 If the Supreme Court focuses too narrowly on drugs in this case and misses the larger issue of religious ritual, it could create a devastating precedent for religious liberty. For the Native American use of peyote has substantial parallels to Christian and Jewish uses of wine. If the peyote ritual is allowed only by legislative grace and not by constitutional right, the right to participate in communion, the Passover Seder and Sabbath rituals may rest on no firmer footing.

4 The Oregon case is an odd vehicle for addressing such an issue. It is not a criminal prosecution; questions about criminal prohibitions are involved only because the court reached out for them. Alfred Smith and Galen Black were drug- and alcohol-abuse counselors at a nonprofit agency. When their supervisor learned that they had consumed peyote at a religious service, he discharged them for violating the agency's absolute rule against drug or alcohol use. The supervisor later testified that "we would have taken the same action had the claimant consumed wine at a

Catholic ceremony." But he offered no evidence that anyone had actually been discharged for drinking communion wine, and he did not claim to have inquired about which of the churches his employees attended used wine and which only grape juice.

5 Smith and Black first complained that their employer had discriminated against them based on their religion. Without admitting the charge, the employer changed its absolute rule against religious use of drugs, and it paid Smith and Black some of their lost pay. They agreed not to insist on being reinstated to their jobs.

6 Smith and Black also filed claims for unemployment compensation. A long line of Supreme Court cases holds that states must pay unemployment compensation to employees who lose their jobs because of their religious beliefs. Employees who refuse to work on their Sabbath have been the principal beneficiaries of this rule (in another case a worker lost his job in a brass mill because he refused to help manufacture tank turrets). The Oregon courts followed these cases and awarded unemployment compensation to Smith and Black.

7 The U.S. Supreme Court vacated the judgment, deciding that if Oregon could send Smith and Black to prison for chewing peyote, it could surely refuse to pay them unemployment compensation. Therefore, the court reasoned, the constitutional status of Oregon's criminal prohibition of peyote was logically prior to the unemployment-compensation issue. It sent the case back to the state courts to ask whether Oregon would recognize a religious exception to its criminal laws against possession or consumption of peyote.

8 Oregon's Supreme Court, which had already concluded that this question was irrelevant, dutifully answered that in its judgment criminal prosecution of Smith and Black would violate the federal Constitution. Their consumption of peyote was a constitutionally protected exercise of religion; therefore, Oregon could not send them to prison or refuse to pay them unemployment compensation.

9 The U.S. Supreme Court has agreed to hear the case again. Presumably it intends to decide whether Smith and Black could be sent to prison, even though no one has shown the slightest interest in sending them there. If it has second thoughts about this exercise in judicial activism, it may retreat to the narrower issue and decide only whether Smith and Black are entitled to keep their unemployment compensation.

10 The opinions of the Oregon courts provide few details about exactly what Smith and Black did with peyote. Opinions in other cases provide more information about the peyote ritual, based on the testimony of witnesses and of anthropologists who have studied it. The peyote ritual is no modern innovation designed to evade the drug laws. Native Americans have practiced it at least since 1560, when it was first described in Spanish records. Today the ritual is practiced in substantially similar form from

northern Mexico to Saskatchewan. Believers come from many Native American tribes, although it is not the major religion of any tribe. The faith has absorbed some Christian teachings as well, but peyote remains at the heart of its theology and practice.

11 To the believer, peyote is a sacramental substance, an object of worship and a source of divine protection. Peyote is the focus of the worship service, much as the consecrated bread and wine are the focus of mass and communion. The cases speak of prayers being directed to peyote; I suspect that the believer thinks of himself as praying to the holy spirit who is present in the peyote.

12 The believer may wear peyote on his person for protection; soldiers have worn a large peyote button in a beaded pouch suspended from their necks. While there is no parallel in Christian theology, there is ample parallel in Christian folk-belief—a consecrated communion wafer worn around the neck has been thought to be the best defense against Dracula, and crosses and medals are put to similar use against modern dangers.

13 Finally, and most important for the question before the court, participants in the ritual believe that peyote intoxication enables them to experience God directly. Peyote is consumed for this purpose only at a "meeting," convened and controlled by a leader. It is a sacrilege to use peyote for a non-religious purpose. A meeting is a solemn and somewhat infrequent occasion. Participants wear their finest clothing. They pray, sing and perform ceremonies with drums, fans, eagle bones and other symbolic instruments.

14 The central event is the consumption of peyote in quantities sufficient to produce intoxication. At the appointed time, the leader distributes up to four buttons to each adult participant. There is an opportunity for participants to take additional buttons at a later point in the ceremony. The buttons are extremely bitter, and difficult to chew and swallow. Some groups use a tea brewed from the buttons, but chewing the buttons appears to be the norm.

15 The meeting lasts from sundown Saturday to sunrise Sunday. In the morning, the leader serves breakfast. By then all effects of the peyote have worn off, and the participants leave in a sober state. Smith and Black were fired for participating in a service that, apparently, went according to this generic description.

16 The First Amendment guarantees the free exercise of religion and forbids the governmental establishment of religion. One of the amendment's central purposes is to ensure that religious belief and practice be as free as possible from government regulation. There are limits to this freedom when serious and immediate harm is threatened; hardly anyone believes in a constitutional right to practice human sacrifice. But the Supreme Court has repeatedly said that government can limit religious liberty only for compelling reasons that cannot be served in any other way.

17 Another central function of the First Amendment is to ensure that small, unfamiliar, and unpopular religions get equal treatment with larger, well-known, and politically influential religions. In those compelling cases in which religious liberty must be restricted, the restrictions must be applied neutrally.

18 This principle of neutrality requires us to compare the peyote ritual to the rituals of mainstream faiths. Peyote is not the only mind-altering drug used in a religious ritual. Many Christians drink wine at communion. For Jews, a prayer over wine is part of the Sabbath service, Sabbath meals, all religious holidays and special religious events such as weddings and circumcisions.

19 Wine was once illegal in the U.S., just as peyote is now. But the National Prohibition Act, passed after ratification of the 18th Amendment, exempted wine "for sacramental purposes, or like religious rites." State prohibition laws, some of which survived into the 1960s, either had similar exemptions or at least were not enforced against religious users. (Contemporary local prohibition laws rarely require exemptions; they generally restrict the sale of alcohol, but permit private consumption of alcohol purchased elsewhere.)

20 Why is it that the religious use of wine was exempt everywhere during Prohibition, but the religious use of peyote is exempt in only half the states today? If Oregon may constitutionally punish the religious use of peyote, may it not also punish the religious use of wine? Could Oregon ban communion wine and require that all Christians use grape juice instead? The Supreme Court does not have to answer these questions formally; no case about wine is before it. But it should think hard about these questions, to make sure it is not suppressing a small and unfamiliar religion on the basis of principles it would not apply to a mainstream faith.

21 Oregon may respond that peyote is simply more dangerous than wine. I do not know whether that is true; I am sure that wine is more widely abused. But the court will assume that the legislature had good reason for its ban. It should inquire into dangerousness only in the narrow context of religious use. The judicial question is this: if the Constitution protects the religious use of wine when legislatures believe that wine is so dangerous it has to be banned, does the Constitution also protect religious use of peyote at a time when legislatures believe peyote must be banned? If sacramental uses of wine are protected and sacramental uses of peyote are not, it must be because of some compelling difference between the drugs or the rituals.

22 Each of the Christian and Jewish uses of wine is similar to the peyote ritual in some ways, and quite different in others. Communion resembles the peyote ritual in the liturgical and theological centrality of the wine in the worship service. For many Christians, there are further similarities

in the reverence and even adoration for the consecrated wine and the belief that the deity is present in the wine.

23 However, no one gets intoxicated on communion wine. Well, hardly anyone. In traditions that believe in the real presence of Christ, the priest or pastor may get tipsy from drinking the consecrated wine that is left over at the end of the service, since the blood of Christ cannot just be poured down the drain. This consequence could perhaps be avoided by recruiting enough helpers, but in some denominations only clergy and designated assistants are permitted to help.

24 Not even the matter of intoxication distinguishes Purim, the celebration of the Jews' deliverance from a genocidal plot during the Babylonian captivity. Some Jewish traditions teach a duty to celebrate Purim to the point of drunkenness. Jews drink four cups of wine at the Passover Seder, which commemorates the Exodus from Egypt. Prayer over a single cup of wine is part of the Sabbath service and of Sabbath meals.

25 But one important difference is that an essential part of the peyote ritual is to experience God through the mind-altering effects of the drug; that is not part of the communion service in any Christian tradition, and it is not part of any Jewish celebrations or rituals. Purim, the most intoxicating Jewish celebration, is only a minor festival. Because Purim is far less central theologically, a decision that Oregon could ban the peyote ritual would clearly imply that it could ban the use of intoxicating amounts of wine to celebrate Purim.

26 In an important sense it is a greater violation of religious liberty to ban a ritual that is at the theological heart of a faith than to ban a peripheral celebration. But either act limits religious liberty. We should be uncomfortable with governmental bans on minor religious festivals, or with judges deciding which festivals are important enough to deserve full constitutional protection and which are not. A court that starts down that path might eventually convince itself that wine is not central to the Sabbath or to the celebration of Passover, or that the use of wine is not central to communion. The government could acquire a de facto power to review theology and liturgy.

27 If the court considers communion or the Passover Seder or the Sabbath, its instinct will be to regard these as constitutionally protected. If it considers only peyotism, its instinct may be to consider it a weird and dangerous practice. Comparing familiar and presumptively protected faiths to an unfamiliar one is a way of guarding against unrecognized bias. But this cautionary device will not work if the court jumps at any possible distinction to rationalize its prejudices in favor of the familiar.

28 Thus, the ultimate question is whether Oregon's reasons for prohibiting the peyote ritual are compelling, and, if the peyote ritual is to be distinguished from Christian and Jewish rituals, whether the distinctions are compelling. The only plausible distinction is that Christian

and Jewish uses are generally less intoxicating—but there are important exceptions even to that.

29 The distinction is further blurred by the mystical tradition in every major world religion, including Christianity and Judaism. The mystics often seek to experience God through altered states of consciousness, generally induced by trance or meditation instead of drugs. So neither the use of mind-altering drugs nor the achievement of altered consciousness distinguishes peyotism from mainstream faiths. It is only the combination of these two things that arguably distinguishes peyotism.

30 The most one can say without exceptions is that only in peyotism is drug-induced altered consciousness part of the central religious event. That difference is compelling only if peyote intoxication under the controlled conditions of a meeting poses a serious danger to the participants or others. To say only that Oregon disapproves of peyote intoxication is merely to restate Oregon's disapproval of this mode of worship. Oregon's disapproval does not provide a compelling reason to forbid a religious ritual. . . .

31 It may be that as a practical matter religious use of mind-altering drugs will be limited to groups that can point to some substantial tradition and that limit the use of drugs to structured worship service. Perhaps the practical difficulties of enforcing the drug laws will prevent any broader protection of religious liberty. But both familiar and unfamiliar groups can show a substantial tradition and a structured worship service. At least Christians, Jews, and peyote worshipers fall into this category. Peyote worship should be constitutionally protected, and Smith and Black should be allowed to keep their unemployment compensation.

Post-reading Questions

Content

1. Explain Laycock's concern in this essay. Why does he claim that "peyote worship should be constitutionally protected"?
2. Did Smith and Black's supervisor treat them fairly when he discharged them for using peyote in a religious ceremony? Explain.
3. In what way is the Christian and Jewish use of wine similar to and different from the Native-American use of peyote in religious rituals?
4. Why is it so ironic that alcohol, a drug introduced by Western society into Native-American culture, was "exempt" from Prohibition when used for religious purposes, but the use of peyote, a Native-American drug used by American Indians in religious rituals for centuries, is allowed in "only half the states today"?
5. How does the reader know that Laycock is not advocating peyote use for the sake of *getting high?*

Strategies and Structures

1. How does Laycock use the First Amendment to strengthen his argument in this essay?
2. This essay begins and concludes with references to U.S. governing bodies and laws. Why is the separation of church and state an essential part of his argument?
3. How does Laycock demonstrate that peyote is "a sacramental substance, an object of worship and a source of divine protection"? What makes his argument logical?
4. Why does Laycock point out how Smith and Black have been discriminated against by their employer, the Oregon courts, and the Supreme Court? Why does the employer make them agree not to ask for job reinstatement? Why does the Supreme Court decide to make no judgment? What does Laycock want us to conclude from all these points? Does his strategy work? Why or why not?
5. Why does Laycock want us to feel uncomfortable with the government and judges deciding which religions and religious rituals are important, and which are not? What is his purpose for pointing out what these bans can lead to?
6. After reading this article, what deductions can you make about the legal attitude and treatment of minor religions by the U.S. courts and the government in general? What do you feel is more important to American society: the religious practices of many, the religious practices of a few, or both?

Language and Vocabulary

1. Vocabulary: *litigation, hallucinogenic, sacrilege, sacramental, consecrated, denomination.* Define the above words, then choose one and write an extended definition incorporating your own views and/or observations on the subject.
2. Three of these words—"sacrilege," "sacramental," and "consecrated"—have the same root (*sacr, secr*) which comes from Latin and means "holy" or "sacred." Words with this root deal with religion or ritual. For a journal entry, find at least five more words with the same root and compose two or three paragraphs in which you discuss something that is sacred or holy to you, using each of your chosen words at least two times.

Group Activities

1. Does the U.S. Constitution guarantee the rights of all or just a few? Are some religions better than others? Divide the class into two groups, one assuming the role as spokesperson for a mainstream religion and the other assuming the role as spokesperson for a minority religion, and debate

the issue. Following the debate, each student should write a summary of the opposing group's argument, noting its strengths and weaknesses.

2. When and where does censorship infringe on individual rights? Gather in small groups and discuss how prohibiting traditions and rituals amounts to censorship. (You first will have to have a clear idea of what censorship involves.) What examples of censorship in America today does your group agree with? Why? Now discuss what this censorship might lead to in the future. Finally, write a collaborative essay in which you argue for or against censorship of an ideal, a practice, or a privilege.

Writing Activities

1. Compose an essay arguing that all drug use in religious ceremonies or rituals should be outlawed, including the use of alcohol. Anticipate your reader's reaction to your proposal and defend your thesis with clear reasoning and concrete examples.
2. Write an essay arguing that our freedom of worship in America is in jeopardy if the U.S. government does not stop tampering with the mystical religious traditions and the legality of rituals in practice today.

Internet Connection: Douglas Laycock

Constitutional Rights

Locate a copy of the Constitution of the United States online, and print out the first amendment. Next, insert the key words "Smith and Black" into your research engine and review the number or articles dealing with the religious use of peyote by Native-Americans. You also might reference "Oregon Department of Human Resources vs. Smith" for the U.S. Supreme Court decision on this case. Briefly summarize one of the articles—or the U.S. Supreme Court case—providing readers with specific documentation so that they can find the same articles online. An extension of this assignment would be to write an argumentative essay supporting or refuting the U.S. Supreme Court's ruling on the case. Here, careful reasoning and new information will help to strengthen your claims. (See the Appendix on Documentation.)

Mandana Mohsenzadegan

OMG: Tweeting, Trending, and Texting

Mandana Mohsenzadegan is a 25-year-old Iranian-American woman and often has been put in the category "Generation 1.5." She immigrated to the United States when she was ten years old. Presently, she's an English graduate student at San Jose State, and hopes to obtain her Master's of Arts degree this upcoming May. Mandana also possesses a Bachelor's degree in journalism (with a minor in philosophy) and has published a feature article in *Access Magazine* (2005), and editorials in the *Spartan Daily* and the *Campbell Express* (2008), in addition to an op-ed that appeared in the *Palo Alto Daily* in the summer of 2009. Currently, she is a teacher's assistant in her English department at San Jose State University. A true "people person," Mandana plans to teach at community colleges once she graduates. She also enjoys creative writing and looks forward to publishing more of her creative and critical works in the near future.

Pre-reading Questions

1. Do you or your friends keep track of who's "trending" on the Internet? How often do you "tweet" or "text" others and for what reasons?
2. Freewrite in your journal or notebook on at least two of the following topics: "texting, "tweeting," and/or "trending." What part do they play among your daily activities, if any?

"Simplicity, simplicity, simplicity! I say, let your affairs be as two or three, and not a hundred or a thousand; instead of a million count half a dozen, and keep your accounts on your thumb-nail. In the midst of this chopping sea of civilized life, such are the clouds and storms and quicksands and thousand-and-one items to be allowed for, that a man has to live, if he would not founder and go to the bottom and not make his port at all, by dead reckoning, and he must be a great calculator indeed who succeeds."

—Henry David Thoreau

1 No matter which Bay Area Starbucks we walk into, the familiar text message ringtone of an iPhone (currently, the "glass" sound is the most popular) will be heard intermittently, as we wait in line for our double macchiato or white mocha. Cue the consequent noise of every customer digging into their purses or pockets—(was it mine?)—and we all start tapping away at our touch screens (or keypads, for a Droid or Blackberry loyalist), remembering someone we had forgotten to text or email this morning—a quick response to a friend's joke, a relative's dinner invite, or a boss' inquiry about a project. Eyes remain wholly fixated on these small little devices, as we completely zone out of our physical environment—that is, of course, until a voice asks us what drink we would like to order and if we want a pastry with that. For a few minutes at most, we put away the "phone" (an odd name for a device that also gives us access to the World Wide Web, measures the number of steps we walk in a given day, and allows us to video-chat with someone halfway across the world). The short-lived silence shatters with the sound of glass, bell, or chime, once again notifies us that a highly imperative matter—a Twitter or Facebook update, a funny forward, or a text message—must be immediately answered, placing everything else on hold.

2 People demonstrate an addictive dependence on cell phones in many everyday situations. I once attended a dinner party in which a guest—a young woman around the same age as myself—would repeatedly look down at her phone, chuckling furtively (but perceptively) as she tapped away at the keys, while the host's father—a very kind and respectable gentleman over sixty—attempted to hold a conversation with her on some political matter. The insulted look on his face was hard to miss, and I remember feeling disgusted at the woman's rude behavior. And yet—are we not all guilty of interrupting an in-person conversation every now and then, because of the *clink-clink* of our phone—due to a compulsive need to look down at the received text message? Do we not subconsciously prioritize the world of virtual reality over the concrete world in which we live?

3 Perhaps my generation is too young to have any meaningful recollections of what life was once like when it was free from the mind-numbing dependency of telecommunications—we have no bittersweet nostalgia of a not-so-distant past when "FaceTime" was literal, and the most meaningful relationships arose not from sending four hundred text messages a day to your significant other or family member, but from showing up at their door and actually spending quality time with them.

4 I imagine that in such a time, people reveled in the excitement of long-distance relationships through nightly phone conversations (rather than "textversations"), so that they could hear and feel the emotions of their beloved's voice; then, their attention fixed solely upon the warm,

loving exchange of words, rather than engaging in simultaneous activities or having the "freedom" to take twenty minutes to respond.

5 I imagine a time when our public and private lives did not merge in such a discordant sort of way—that if we were having a bad day or needed a shoulder to cry on, we did not report it to over hundreds of people we barely talk to (via a *Facebook* Status or *Twitter* update), but called up our most trustworthy and loving friend to pour our hearts out in a healthy sort of way.

6 I imagine a time in which there was no "e" in front of mail, and there was actually a thrill of anticipation when the postman arrived at our door; yes, I am referring to the "archaic" practice of good ol' handwritten letter writing—thoughtful missives which were not filled with the "OMG"s, "BTW"s, "LOL"s, and emoticons of our generation, but were creative, articulate, and meaningful expressions of affection (I strongly believe that whoever popularized smiley faces and "<3" signs in written communication was a moron—is it so arduous a task to spell out the four letters of "love"? Must we explain to our recipient that we are flashing our pearly whites, at least a dozen times through the course of five sentences? Ostensibly, expressing our emotions through words seems far too challenging.)

7 Some may consider the letter-writing style of past generations—with the respectful "Dear" and closing salutations of "Affectionately" or "Always"—as dry and formal, but I would argue quite the contrary. The prose styles of traditional letter writing were far more genuine and heartfelt than our short, fragmented sentences and acronyms could ever be: within its supposedly "formal" structure, letter-writing allowed an intimacy and freedom of articulation—the well-written sentences, the organized thoughts, the creative diction, the well thought-out and expressive content—but oh, so much work! Why take the extra time and brain energy to deeply express ourselves to a loved one, when we have "emoticons" to do the job for us?

8 We fail to recognize that in its attempt to bring us closer together, telecommunications have only drifted us further apart and placed a superficial veil over our interactions with others, leaving us feeling empty and discontent—despite our having 500+ "friends" on Facebook.

9 Of course, influential electronic media does not simply affect our personal relationships with others; it has traversed that line and seeped into the very heart of our culture. An unlimited outlet for entertainment and perpetually growing source of information, the Internet controls our daily existence, governs our priorities, and reshapes our thinking. With a seemingly inexhaustible access to worldwide information, our attentions divert from one sound bite to the next. We can log onto Twitter to receive minute-to-minute updates concerning the personal lives of our favorite celebrities or politicians, and we can go on YouTube to watch

TV shows and movies, plug in our earphones and listen to the latest pop songs, with just the click of a button on our handy-dandy little gadgets. Have an obscure question that simply must be answered at this very instant? Have no fear! Google functions like a magic genie. Have a chronic pain but don't feel like going to the doctor? Not to worry, Medline.com allows people to self-diagnose! (And most likely *mis*diagnose.) Feeling too lazy to go the grocery store? Luckily, Safeway offers online shopping so its customers can get those tomatoes and celeries hand-delivered to their door.

10 Often, people feel incomplete without their technological conveniences. For instance, a student of mine wrote that he would never forget the panic that came over him and his father during a camping trip, when they realized they had forgotten their watches (and left their cell phones home due to lack of service). However, he then went on to write that it was the most peaceful, enjoyable trip he had ever had, fishing by the lake with his father, bonding together without any forms of distraction. Time had lost its importance to them, in those three blissful days spent in the woods, and it strengthened their relationship immensely.

11 Nonetheless, who has time for camping trips, when we spend our lives in a constant state of "Go, go, go"? Naturally we would choose to spend our downtime sprawled on the couch watching "reality" television, rather than take a walk in a park, or perhaps pick up a good book and immerse ourselves in rich and meaningful literature to stimulate our brains. Instead we choose to shut them off—let our televisions, Internet, and phones amuse us with endless entertainment—the majority of which is hollow and meaningless at its core.

12 Perhaps one of the greatest 20th century critics of telecommunications was Neil Postman, author of "Amusing Ourselves to Death," a deeply analytic work that expressed his anxiety over the future of technology and what he believed was a subsequent disintegration of meaningful public discourse within communities. The most uncanny thing about his work is, of course, the fact that it was written in 1985—a time which most consider well *before* the boom of electronic media. The main focus of the book rests on television—a powerful medium of entertainment, which permeates, redefines and revalues our culture. Postman writes, "Television is altering the meaning of 'being informed' by creating a species of information that might properly be called disinformation." He goes on to define disinformation not as false information, but as "misplaced, irrelevant, fragmented, or superficial information." Eerily, the premise remains the same for our time, and becomes all the more powerful and relevant for future generations than it was for his. Whether we consider it his prophetic vision or simply a logically deduced prediction of what was sure to follow, the significance of his message remains the same: Take heed.

13 Postman's main arguments were hardly novel—many philosophers and writers before his time have posited similar assertions of resistance to the progression of telecommunications. During the 19th century in his *Walden* essay, "Where I Lived, And What I Lived," Thoreau's wrote an often censured message condemning all aspects of technology that rang loud and poignantly clear: the nation, with all its attempts at self-improvement, had become "an unwieldy and overgrown establishment." Postman himself credits Aldous Huxley for portending the same message back in the 1930s, with the controversial yet widely acclaimed novel *Brave New World*. Having paved the 20th century anxiety toward the advancement of technology, Huxley's message becomes what Postman terms, the "Huxleyan warning."

> In the Huxleyan prophesy, Big Brother does not watch us, by his choice. We watch him, by ours . . . when a population becomes distracted by trivia, when cultural life is redefined as a perpetual round of entertainments, when serious public conversation becomes a form of baby-talk, when in short, people become an audience and their public business a vaudeville act, then a nation finds itself at risk; culture-death is a clear possibility. (Postman 155–156)

14 I would hardly advise people to ditch their cell phones and laptops and run off to live in the woods. Fleeing from civilization, as chaotic as it may be, is never the answer, and would just be plain foolish. In fact, despite all of the grave and serious problems I see with our high-tech society, I am, at the same time, deeply aware and grateful of all the many blessings that it has brought with it. Still, such a long and obvious list hardly needs any extensive enumeration. I will say, however, that the same cell phone which consumes so much of our time also allows us to seek immediate help in natural disasters or accidents. That social networking site which wastes so many of our hours has also enabled the opposition movements of the Middle East and North Africa (Libya, Egypt, and Iran being at the forefront) to organize rallies and send minute-to-minute video footage, photos, and updates, of the brutalities which their ruling tyrants have subjected them to. And the myriad news sites on the World Wide Web, with their appeal to sensationalism and their many periphery headlines about celebrity gossip, offer us a constant sources of knowledge regarding domestic and international affairs—which, considering our current economic troubles, global crises, and involvement in two wars, is of great significance, if not vital importance.

15 Just as a great many things in this world, telecommunications has proven to be neither solely good nor solely bad—but comes as a mixed bag of both. Advocates of technological progress will be quick to point out—and justifiably so—the vast improvements seen in sectors such as medicine, education, and the military. However, critics of technological

progress will also be just as quick to point out the many added problems seen in these sectors. Whichever way the scale may tip makes no matter. Telecommunications are here to stay, for better or for worse. The primary problem with our consumerist-driven society, however, is the constant focus on the former, and disregard of the latter, as it attempts to veil our eyes and hide the serious consequences of our technologically-dependent lifestyles.

16 Like many people, I own an iPhone, am a member of a social network, check my email daily, and cannot imagine living a week without my laptop. Since I grew up in this culture, it would be exceedingly senseless of me to repel it altogether—to metaphorically live under a rock. And yet, I am acutely aware of the significance that comes with *how* I choose to use this double-edged sword. I am daily conscious of the amount of time I spend using my iPhone for entertainment: Rather than spend hours on YouTube or Twitter, I make the choice to pick up a book, or go for a jog and soak up the beautiful California sun. When I am having lunch with a friend or colleague, I choose to show them the dignity and respect of having my full attention, and turn off the sound on my phone. In electronic communication, I take particular delight in adopting the old-fashioned letter-writing style in emails to my nearest and dearest—I take the time to be as expressive with my words as I can be. They have expressed how much they appreciate it, and a few of them also share my preference and do the same in their own correspondences. I also make it known to those important in my life how deeply I prioritize and value face-to-face quality time with them.

17 All of these little daily decisions and countless others determine whether technology controls us, or whether we control it. Looking at younger generations, particularly the children of the 21st century—toddlers already using electronic devices with confidence and ease—I am both in awe and terror at what direction they may take our accelerating advancements in technology: What sorts of lives they will choose to lead? How they will shape the future with the potently powerful tools of our age? It is up to us, the young adults of this generation, to provide them a good example to emulate—to make them deeply conscious and heedful of the moral responsibility and discernment that comes with the uses of our man-made inventions. I know that someday, when I am a mother, I will try to avoid the mistake of past generations in using the television as my children's babysitter (and the computer and Wii, for parents today), and instead, encourage the stimulation of their minds with books, nourish the growth of their little bodies with healthy home-cooked meals, and cultivate their intrinsic human bond with the natural world through constant exposure to the great outdoors. Call me old-fashioned, call me anachronistic, or

hopelessly devoted to post-World War II ideals; perhaps I am a little of all those things, and proud of it.

18 Alas, I have spent too many hours in front of this computer screen, and the softly sprinkling November rain on my windowsill is beckoning me to go out for a pleasant late-morning walk. I cannot help but smile at the prospect of spending a blissful hour away from my phone and computer. This would probably be where I add that smiley at the closing of my last sentence . . . but I have been told that I have a killer smile. An emoticon wouldn't do it justice.

Works Cited

Postman, Neil. *Amusing Ourselves to Death: Public Discourse in the Age of Show Business.* 20th Anniversary Edition. New York: Penguin Group, 2005.

Thoreau. Henry David. "Where I Lived and What I Lived For. In *Walden; Or Life in the Woods*. Annotated Edition. Boston: Houghton Mifflin Harcourt, 1995.

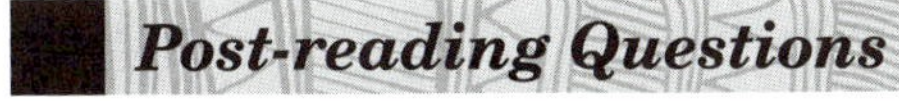

Post-reading Questions

Content

1. Define an "emoticon"? Do you or people you know use "emoticons" when they text, tweet, or email others? Draw some example "emoticons" followed by their meaning.
2. Why does Mohsenzadegan take time to address and validate certain arguments about the benefits of telecommunications if her main objective is to point out its detriments?
3. Paraphrase what Postman refers to as the "Huxleyan warning."
4. Why wouldn't Mohsenzadegan advise others to "ditch their cell phones and laptops" and go live in the wild? How have people benefited from modern technology as a communication tool? List some of her examples.
5. In paragraph 17, what prompts Mohsenzadegan's "awe and terror" as she considers the possible direction children may take our accelerating technological advancements?

Strategies and Structures

1. How and why does Mohsenzadegan establish common ground with her readers in her opening paragraph?
2. Why do you imagine that Mohsenzadegan decided to develop most her essay using a first-person point of view? What does it accomplish?

3. Explain some of the possible reasons why Mohsenzadegan began the first sentence in paragraphs 4, 5, and 6 with the same two words: "I imagine."
4. Mohsenzadegan argues that in its attempt to bring us closer together, technology has drifted us further apart. What kinds of support does she offer for this argument?
5. Where does Mohsenzadegan seem to stand at the end of the essay? Does she appear to favor technology's conveniences over nature's comforts or vice versa? Is there a middle ground between them? What facts and details in her concluding paragraph support your reasoning?

Language and Vocabulary

1. Vocabulary: *intermittently, macchiato, mocha, droid, imperative, subconsciously, prioritize, virtual reality, telecommunication, simultaneous, discordant, archaic, emoticons, missives, ostensibly, recipient, salutations, articulation, traversed, perpetually, inexhaustible, chronic, subsequent, discourse, permeates, poignantly, trivia, vaudeville, myriad, sensationalism, periphery, acutely, prioritize, emulate, discernment, intrinsic, anachronistic.* Circle where the above vocabulary words appear in Mohsenzadegan's essay and attempt to determine meaning by context (sense of the sentence). Then look up the definitions of the words and check your assumptions. Finally, select five sentences where one or more vocabulary words appear, and rewrite each sentence using simple language. How does word choice affect communication?
2. Apart from "emoticons," Mohsenzadegan notes how people today abbreviate information when they communicate by using acronyms (an abbreviation of multiple words in such a way that the abbreviation itself forms a pronounceable word such as ASAP meaning "as soon as possible.") What might be the pros and cons of using acronyms as a communication tool?

Group Activities

1. Take out your cell phones, and then send a text to a family member, friend, or significant other, regarding any recent article or book you have read or movie you have seen which you enjoyed and want to recommend. Use a regular style of texting—not going over a sentence or two. Then, in small groups, share some of the texts members wrote back, writing a few on the board. As a class, examine the style

of writing and devices used—acronyms, fragments, smiley icons, and so forth. Next, rewrite three or four sentences on paper, adopting the more formal letter-writing structure that Mohsenzadegan advocates (e.g., complete sentences, creative word choice, etc). Compare the two styles of writing and discuss the practicality and/or benefits of each in everyday communication.

2. Separate into two groups: One half will be responsible for supporting Mohsenzadegan's position that our society is too dependent on telecommunications. The other half of the class will be responsible for bringing up counterarguments to her position (e.g., why and how the pros of technology outweigh the cons). Both groups will provide evidence gleaned from personal experiences, observations, and readings to justify their claims. Finally, each group will present their case in front of class while three students serve as a "judge panel." The student judges will listen carefully to Group 1 and Group 2, and then award each group a collective score (1-10 scale), objectively explaining their reasons for choosing the winning group. (Groups will be judged on clarity of establishing their position, quality and specificity of examples, and additional tactics for presenting a well thought-out argument.)

Writing Activities

1. In a thoroughly supported essay, argue that the younger generation today does (as Mohsenzadegan claims) or does not have a moral obligation to serve as role models who exhibit responsible use of "man-made inventions."

2. Go for three days without using your computer or cell phone and keep track of how the lack of technological communication opens doors to new or forgotten experiences, creates greater personal inconvenience, as well as promotes self-reliance. Like Mohsenzadegan, use your personal experience and insights as primary evidence to support an essay arguing that in the 21st century, the advantages outweigh the disadvantages of technologically-dependent lifestyles—or vice versa. To add depth to your argument, include additional representative examples based on observations and readings.

Mark Charles Fissel

Online Learning and Student Success

Mark Charles Fissel is a Fellow of the Royal Historical Society in England. He received his Ph.D. from the University of California at Berkeley and has published *The Bishops' Wars: Charles I's Campaigns Against Scotland 1638–1640* (1994), *English Warfare 1511–1642* (2001), *English Amphibious Warfare, 1587–1660: Galleons, Galleys, Longboats, and Cots*, (2005), and articles on educational technologies. A former dean of Harris Manchester College (Oxford) and a Fulbright Senior Lecturer at Bogazici University (Istanbul), Fissel specializes in faculty development. His current essay provides a counterpoint to his previous contribution ("Distance Learning and American Society") to *Visions Across the Americas*, an encomium to distance learning, based on the decade he taught via interactive television (1988–1997).

Pre-reading Questions

1. What images does the word "online" bring to mind?
2. Have you or any of your friends thought about or taken an online college course? Why? When?

---

1 Americans are being told that computerized instruction, drawing from the resources of the World Wide Web, will empower the individual learner much as decades ago televised instruction linked learning communities.

2 Allegedly "knowledge" is expanding, doubling every eighteen months, so that there is more "knowledge" outside of the academy than within its hallowed precincts. Simultaneously, we are becoming "student-centered" educators. Elementary and secondary school students employ multimedia technology in their at least partially "virtual" classrooms. We are, justifiably, concerned with inculcating critical thinking skills in learners, and not so much with memorization (or what we might call "data retrieval"). Never before have we focused so steadily upon the learner,

and provided students with such an array of educational tools. And this optimal environment for study defies space and time. Asynchronous learning and the Internet provide the student with unprecedented opportunities to learn outside the traditional classroom. This halcyon era of public and self-directed Enlightenment surely has produced better students. Legislators, taxpayers, students, and teachers understandably have a right to expect such results. The educational technologists have predicted and promised a brave new world. What are the results?

3 Mean SAT/SAT I scores for college-bound high school seniors have declined since 1972, implying that the age of computers did not accelerate student learning ("Table 1: Mean SAT Scores of Entering College Class, 1967–97"). It may be that learning has become more challenging. Computer technology moves large amounts of data very quickly. The development of critical thinking skills and reflective learning require time and patience, two commodities in rather short supply in the digital culture (Leibowitz A67). While some students have achieved notable success with the new technology, others struggle. When we consider allegations of grade inflation, try to explain the flourishing of home schooling, and the flight to private schools, one must conclude that "computer age" education is still beset with problems.

4 In the meanwhile, many traditional universities have declared their withdrawal from the "remediation business." In other words, students who do not meet some of the academic standards of a given institution find it increasingly difficult to convince universities to admit them with the understanding that they will take non-credit "remedial" classes to make up their deficiencies. Obsessed with quantifiable and measurable "student success," and dependent upon product-minded political institutions for funding, fewer universities feel willing to "take a chance" on a promising but underqualified applicant.

5 Where, then, will these students go, who have been turned away from the gates of the traditional university? Worldwide Web entrepreneurs already offer round-the-clock tutoring (Carr A45). Virtual universities are quick to advertise their own merits as an alternative to the residential or commuter college. Private institutions, such as the University of Phoenix, market "digital degrees," much as a corporation would offer products and service. State-funded virtual institutions, for example the Florida Gulf Coast University, have appeared, offering online students the prestige of being part of a university system electronically.

6 Digital learning in the virtual university is supposed to "make that liberal arts ideal even broader." Not only will the online students have greater flexibility as to *when* they learn, they will also have more courses (and instructors) to choose from. William Draves, president of the Learning Resources Network, claims digital learning will "be more personalized because you as an individual learner will get more feedback on

what you know and how you're proceeding, and you'll have your curriculum tailored toward your learning needs" (Chaudry). Even though "online" learning may involve "megaclasses" of 1,000 or more students taking multiple choice exams, Draves predicts a better education for students that will be more affordable, as automation and high enrollments push down the cost of tuition ("A Distance-Learning Forecast Calls for Megaclasses" A47). "Universities have to be businesses in the Information Age. They have to be cost effective. They have to bring their prices down," insists Draves.

7 But at what cost? Historian David Noble points out that "distance education has always been not so much technology driven as profit driven." While it is indisputable that the Internet has made accessible a greater volume of information, the promotion of virtual universities entails the automation of higher education. Unlike Draves, Noble believes that Web-based instruction necessarily imposes uniformity on curricula, while taking intellectual property from teachers and giving it to institutions. A college education ceases to be an experience and becomes increasingly a commodity in a highly capitalized world. Noble's assertions are buttressed by the evidence of alliances between corporate entrepreneurs and university administrations. UCLA brokered a deal with Onlinelearning.net, Berkeley with AOL, the University of Colorado with Real Education, and numerous university systems with WebCT. Labor union-busting mogul Rupert Murdoch, through his News International conglomerate, forged an alliance among multinational corporations and universities in order to establish a global distance education venture ("5 Corporations Reportedly Bid to Join Universities in Distance Learning" A55). Where Draves applauds colleges' assimilation of capitalist techniques and mentality, Noble sees in it the degradation of students to identityless cogs in a vast machine and the destruction of academic freedom. In an age where information is both wealth and power, the commercialization of colleges and the standardization of a corporately owned curriculum, is a real and present danger (Noble).

8 The justification for the privatization and monopolization of higher education is that online technology helps students learn better. However, the jury is still out on that argument (Merisotis and Phipps 13–17). At a university in Texas, an acclaimed graduate course taught exclusively online garnered complaints by students who protested that they had come to that campus for a classroom experience. The administration felt compelled to offer a "traditional" section of the course, through another instructor.

9 Virtual universities (like home schooling) will flourish under certain conditions. Highly motivated and self-directed students will doubtless bloom in the virtual university. Isolated learners, too, will reap benefits from the ether. But in this bewildering world of exponentially increasing knowledge and techno-solitude, many citizen-students will opt for the safe havens of traditional colleges and universities.

Education, in all millennia, has been a social activity. Building upon the centuries-old traditions of classroom instruction, professors (with student input), can make wise choices of the technologies available to complement, supplement, and expand their learning environment. In the words of the executive director of the American Association for History and Computing, "The most effective use of technology is being made in small classes that also provide face-to-face interaction" (Trinkle A60).

10 What does "online" learning mean to teachers? Academicians are in danger of selling their curricula to the highest bidder, usually a corporate custodian with no pedagogical and ethical commitment to educating society. What about students? Student organizations, especially those with a national membership, should initiate surveys to determine student preferences and needs. We hear a lot from the cyber-marketers, such as WebCT's splashy full-page advertisements in the *Chronicle of Higher Education*. But we've not provided a forum for the average student to express how technology might help that student succeed. And, ultimately, it is the individual teacher who must take responsibility for the curriculum and how it is taught.

Works Cited

"A Distance-Learning Forecast Calls for Megaclasses." *Chronicle of Higher Education*. 10 Dec. 1999: A47. *Chronicle of Higher Education Online*. Online. 11 Dec. 1999.

Carr, Sarah. "Another Web Company Eyes Academe, This One Offering Tutoring Assistance." *Chronicle of Higher Education*. 3 Dec. 1999: A45. *Chronicle of Higher Education Online*. Online. 5 Dec. 1999. Chaudry, Lakshuni.

"Cyber-School's Never Out." An Interview with William Draves. *Wired Digital Inc*. For William Draves' network, see <http://www.lern.org>. He has published *Teaching Online* (Learning Resources Network, 1999).

"5 Corporations Reportedly Bid to Join Universities in Distance Education." *Chronicle of Higher Education*. 3 Dec. 1999: A55. *Chronicle of Higher Education Online*. Online. 5 Dec. 1999.

Leibowitz, Wendy. "Technology Transforms Writing and the Techniques of Writing." *The Chronicle of Higher Education*. 26 Nov. 1999: A67. *Chronicle of Higher Education Online*. Online. 1 Dec. 1999.

Merisotis, J.P. and R.A. Phipps. "What's the Difference? Outcomes of Distance vs. Traditional Classroom-Based

Learning." *Change* 1.3 (May–June 1999): 13–17. Based on a report by the Institute for Higher Education Policy.

Noble, David. *Digital Diploma Mills*. New York: Knopf, 2000. Noble's quotations were drawn from a four part online version of the same work. N. pag. His book, *The Religion of Technology* (Penguin, 1999) is highly recommended to students.

"Table 1: Mean SAT Scores of Entering College Class, 1967–97." *College Board Online*. <http://www.collegeboard.org/index_this/sat/cbsenior/yr1999/NAT/72-99.html>.

Trinkle, Dennis. "Distance Education: A Means to an End, No More, No Less." *Chronicle of Higher Education*. 6 Aug. 1999: A60. *Chronicle of Higher Education Online*. Online. 1 Dec. 1999.

Post-reading Questions

Content

1. What is Fissel's thesis? For what does he argue? To what extent is online learning as relevant to students today as when he wrote this article several years ago?
2. Who will benefit from online learning the most?
3. Does online learning take away from or add to the learning experience? How?
4. Which occupations have the most to gain from online learning? Why?
5. Where will the students who need basic skills instruction turn once four-year colleges turn their backs on remedial education? What is remediation, anyway? Could an emphasis on online education create yet another area of remediation? Why or why not?

Strategies and Structures

1. How does Fissel ethically appeal to his readers? That is, how does he structure his essay and what materials does he present in order to make him trustworthy?
2. In what way does Fissel's diction (word choice) reflect the struggle between virtual learning and the education received in the classroom?
3. How does the use of comparison and contrast help the author to argue his thesis? What conclusion does he reach?
4. How does Fissel actively engage readers to contemplate what it would be like to treat education as a business? Does it make sense that one can buy and sell knowledge? Can an education be packaged as a consumer item? Why or why not?

5. In what way does Fissel strategically use outside sources in his essay? What does the use of outside sources suggest about him? Do you find his use of outside, authoritative sources effective and convincing? Why or why not?

Language and Vocabulary

1. Vocabulary: *virtual, inculcating, asynchronous, halcyon, allegations, quantifiable, entrepreneurs, curriculum, commodity, buttressed, conglomerate, privatization, monopolization, exponentially, techno-solitude, millennia, pedagogical, cyber-marketers, forum.* How many of the preceding words deal with online learning? Can you find all of these words in the dictionary? If you can not, what do you suppose the electronic industry has done to our modern vocabulary and why? Go talk to one of your college computer science or engineering department instructors, or talk with one of the students majoring in these subjects to discover how such industries have added to our vocabulary.
2. Fissel's vocabulary contains many words of more than one syllable. Many of these begin with prefixes (one or more letters attached to a word which change its meaning). Identify five such words and show what the meaning of the root word is and also list how the prefixes have changed that meaning. Find five other words that begin with each of the prefixes and define them.

Group Activities

1. Before gathering as a group, individually locate the distance education or the online courses website at your college—or any other college, for that matter. Then, take the "distance education self-assessment test." How did you do on the test? Bring the results of your experience back to your group and compare and contrast how different members were diagnosed. How helpful did your group members find the self-assessment test in determining if online instruction would or would not be ideally suited to their individual learning styles? Jot down any additional questions that your group believes would benefit students who are unsure if digitized learning is for them.
2. Visit your campus Distance Learning Center for online courses and television instruction, and interview the director or a staff member. What services does the center offer? Which segment of the student population uses these services the most? According to your campus's Distance Learning Center, how might such services promote student success in college courses? What is your opinion on the matter?

Gather together again as a class and have each group share findings from interviews. Finally, use your conclusions as the basis for a student-directed technology forum, a forum that addresses the possible merits and disadvantages of online instruction for the average student.

Writing Activities

1. Write an essay wherein you argue or refute the fact that online college courses offer students a viable alternative to traditional methods of classroom instruction. Consider the five "W" journalistic questions—who, what, when, where, why—while pre-writing on this topic. Then, after drafting your argumentative essay, return to them and question your statements of fact, locating and correcting fallacies in logical reasoning.
2. There are many debates about educational practices besides the current focus on traditional instructional methods and distance education delivery systems: collaborative/interactive activities versus lecture/discussion, heterogeneous versus homogeneous classrooms, home versus public education, and large versus small classrooms, to name a few. Research one of these debates (1) on the Internet, (2) in your library by reading newspapers, magazines, and books, (3) by interviewing your instructors and college administrators, and (4) by soliciting the opinions of your fellow students. Then write an essay in which you argue for one instructional method over another. To what extent might most future instructional methods integrate some aspect of technology or multimedia into them?

***Online Learning and Student Success:* Mark Charles Fissel**

Computers and Education

Using any online database or any search engine you like, type in the title to two of the articles from online journals that Fissel cited to support his argument on the merits of online learning. Read and then write a brief abstract of each article. Then, document each item in an annotated list of works cited (a list of works cited with a brief description of each article). (See the Appendix for more on the MLA format.)

Additional Topics and Issues for Argumentative Essays

1. Write an essay arguing that cell phones are—or are not—an indispensible part of a modern "functional" life. Make sure you provide several representative examples to convince your reader that your insights into cells phones are based on logical and ethical—not emotional—arguments of fact. Feel free to take your argument of fact one step further by designing an argument of action.
2. Argue for one of the following two positions: Money is a basic necessity to happiness, or money creates a feeling of happiness but not true contentment. What observations or experiences lead you to your conclusion?
3. In an argumentative essay, disprove the popular idea that computer games deteriorate reading abilities. In fact, you might want to show that computer games enhance reading abilities.
4. Select a popular television show and argue that it does or does not reflect the values of the average American. Do the characters resemble the sort of people who are your neighbors? Another angle on this topic would be to assess the people who win at all cost on a typical "reality TV" show. Are such individuals really representative of society at large? Use representative examples to prove your thesis.
5. To what extent could your eating habits indicate something about your personality? One variation of this topic might be to argue that being a vegetarian is healthier than being a meat-eater or vice versa.
6. Sexually violent crimes are on the rise. Many lawmakers believe that to reduce such violations, we must extend the death penalty to include rapists, child molesters, and those who are guilty of incest. Take a position on this issue and support it.
7. Recently, an esteemed psychologist declared that automation and technology make people unhappy. Others claim that technology has made Americans lazy. For example, we use calculators to figure out math problems and spell checkers rather than learning to use a dictionary. Argue either in favor of or against the use of this technology and indicate where the line must be drawn between practicality and convenience.

8. Dr. Jack Kevorkian received notoriety for his assistance with numerous suicides. Euthanasia, or mercy killing, usually of the terminally ill or clinically brain-dead (those kept alive by machines), has been a hotly debated issue for the past three decades. In this overcrowded world is it either logical or moral to keep these people alive at a great expense and burden to society? Or should every life be considered sacred and valuable?
9. Select a current issue of social concern for most United States citizens such as a national health plan, affordable housing, school funding and so on. Look carefully at the pros and cons of each side of the topic or issue you choose, eliminating information or supporting arguments which are the result of fallacies in reasoning. Finally, take a position and construct an argumentative essay around it. To establish yourself as an ethical, trustworthy source, make sure you present both sides of the issue. (Ignorance of refutation will undermine your argument.)
10. Is there any such thing as a justifiable war? Who suffer most during armed conflicts? What do battles accomplish? Does a conventional war between countries really offer a lasting solution to terrorists' acts by members of extremist groups? Are soldiers from one country really seen as freedom fighters, opportunists, or heroes in another country? Brainstorm your thoughts on these questions, devise a thesis, and write an argumentative paper justifying your point of view.

CHAPTER

12 Persuasion: The Emotional Appeal

Like formal argumentative essays, persuasive essays attempt to convince readers of a point or issue. However, while authors tend to stick solely to logic and facts (induction and deduction in particular) in formal argumentative essays, they often appeal to a reader's emotions—which frequently are not logical—in persuasive essays. Some common emotional responses would be indignation, joy, fear, love, hatred, compassion, greed, lust, disgust, and jealousy. Understandably, to "play down" the emotions (*pathos*) behind an argument, most persuasive essays make overt appeals to logic (*logos*) and ethics (*ethos*).

How much do our personal values and prejudices toward different words, issues, or situations influence our judgment? Quite a bit! In the past few years, the words "democracy" and "terrorism" have stirred people's emotions, often uniting them in a cause, for they associate democracy with positive issues and inalienable rights, especially equality. Note how often leaders will preface their remarks with something like, "In the spirit of democracy," suggesting a group consensus rather than an individual opinion. Now, take the same phrase and picture a recent U.S. president saying, "In the spirit of communism, I offer you the following resolution . . . ." In America, where communism has been a "dirty" word for decades, the president's resolution—no matter how logical, fair, and humanitarian—would probably not receive any serious consideration because of the negativity associated with communism. Authors use words that elicit emotions in persuasive essays to assist their arguments; authors count on emotional responses to influence readers where logic alone may not impress, motivate, or convince them.

We target different emotional responses for different situations. In "Why We Went to Iraq," for instance, Bruce Henderson seeks to convince prospective readers that the simple, convenient arguments used to justify an immediate invasion of Iraq had been questionable from the start; there must have been other motives behind the so-called "Operation Iraqi Freedom." As Henderson notes, the American public tends to have a relatively short-term memory of things and this creates a serious problem when attempting to contextualize complex events in the Middle East that have deep historical roots." He also observed that even though the "*U. S. has announced the removal of combat troops from Iraq in August 2010, we can expect an ongoing military presence to insure stability of the oil supply from that country. Insurgents must be prevented from attacking pipelines, refining facilities and tanker ports. In the end we are less concerned with who nominally governs Iraq than with this stability so crucial to U.S. interests, which helps assure U.S. international supremacy in the 21st century.*" Here Henderson appeals to his readers' sense of righteous indignation (an emotional appeal), blending *ethos, and logos*, so he can logically and fairly persuade them to at least consider the Iraq invasion in view of all the facts.

Though light-hearted in tone, Phyllis McGinley's essay, "Women Are Better Drivers," engages her readers by addressing *stereotypes* and *sexism.* After making early concessions about things men "can do" or "have done" better than women (e.g., create atomic bombs), she states two things in which women excel: having babies and driving automobiles. The first claim is undeniable; men could not carry a child to term if they wanted to because they are not biologically equipped for it. McGinley's second claim may run into more opposition, so the majority of her examples are geared to persuade the reader that women are better drivers than men because they are more reasonable, more cautious, more practical—especially when it comes to taking advice and jotting down directions—and generally, more skilled (a result of their extensive practice).

Gender equality continues to be a potentially explosive topic in the twenty-first century. However, logic (logos) and ethics (ethos) play a secondary role to emotions (pathos) and humor in Dave Barry's essay, "A GPS Helps a Guy Always Know Where His Couch Is" Therein, he good-naturedly satirizes the male gender and its childlike fascination with technology as compared to practical women. For instance, he claims *"as a guy, I feel I need a new computer every time a new model comes out, which is every 15 minutes. This baffles my wife, who has had the same computer since the Civil War and refuses to get a new one because—get THIS for an excuse—the one she has works fine."* Is he really trying to persuade readers *that "all important inventions were invented by guys"?* Quite the contrary, but the skillful use of humor and does enable him to effectively address a potentially sensitive topic.

Paula Gunn Allen examines gender equity in a more serious vein. Appealing ethically (ethos), emotionally (pathos), and logically (logos) to her reader's sensibilities, Allen persuasively argues that, *"If American society judiciously modeled [and adopted] the traditions of the various Native Nations, the place of women in society would become central, the distribution of goods and power would be egalitarian, the elderly would be respected, honored, and protected as a primary social and cultural resource, the ideals of physical beauty would be considerably enlarged (to include 'fat,' strong-featured women, gray-haired, and wrinkled individuals, and others who in contemporary American culture are viewed as 'ugly')."*

In "Never Too Old," we see yet another example of an emotional appeal—an appeal to fear and apprehension. Tammerlin Drummond shatters illusions about senior citizens as she points out that they are the fastest-growing HIV-infected population in the United States, and that the AIDS virus is not usually contracted through blood transfusions.

Organizing Persuasive Compositions

Persuasive essays are organized like any argument. Initially, you will want to focus in on the topic or issue of discussion, state your thesis, define terms, and present your argument in emphatic order. For instance, in the essay entitled "Drugs," Gore Vidal clearly states his argument on how to stop most American drug addiction in his first paragraph: "Simply make all drugs available and sell them at cost." He then goes on to clarify and define some of the key issues, like *freedom of choice,* and in making parallels with an emotionally charged historical event (Prohibition and its failures), Vidal argues his thesis. Though chances are Vidal has not made us all *believers* of his thesis, he has at least made us consider the merit of his argument by the end of the essay, possibly giving us reason to evaluate and reevaluate our own positions on the issue.

Dealing with emotions can be very tricky. While appealing to a person's feelings may be the most direct way you have of convincing someone of your point of view, uncontrolled emotional appeals can also make you seem like an excitable author, one who is led by the passion of the moment. Just bear in mind that it is difficult for a reader to maintain a high level of emotional intensity in a composition, so you need to keep focused on your argument and limit your emotional appeal only to those responses that further your ultimate objective. For instance, do not be sentimental if you are hoping to enrage your reader.

Tips on Writing Persuasive Essays

1. Target your audience. That is, become acquainted with the values of those whom you address and use your knowledge of their likes, dislikes, fears, and prejudices when selecting words. Your objective here is to get your reader involved emotionally as well as intellectually in your topic.
2. Determine your reason(s) for bringing your readers around to your point of view. Do you want to convince them that a problem exists? Do you want them to support a plan of action that you have devised? Or do you want to disprove something another person has said?
3. Maintain an ethical standpoint; enable your reader to "trust" your material.
4. When you develop the body of your essay, stay focused. Check your thesis occasionally to keep the controlling idea of your composition fresh in your mind. Make sure the facts and details in your body paragraphs have not wandered from your argument.
5. Integrate verifiable facts with information that is geared more to emotional responses than to logical reasoning. Doing so will balance your composition, thus ensuring that it will not be based on illogical conclusions from emotional reactions to your topic.

Phyllis McGinley

Women Are Better Drivers

Phyllis McGinley (March 21, 1905–February 22, 1978) was a prolific essayist and poet. Her works include *On the Contrary* (1934), *One More Manhattan* (1937), *Husbands Are Difficult* (1941), *Stones from Glass Houses* (1946), *Merry Christmas, Happy New Year* (1958), *Times Three: Selected Verse from Three Decades* (1960), *Sugar and Spice* (1960), and *A Wreath of Christmas Legends* (1967). Her numerous other books of poetry and several essay collections include: *The Providence of the Heart* (1959), *Sixpence in Her Shoe* (1964), *Wonderful Time* (1966), and *Saint-Watching* (1969). McGinley first published the following article in The American Weekly in 1959. Of particular interest here is the way in which McGinley approaches her topic by appealing to her reader logically, ethically, and emotionally.

Pre-reading Questions

1. Do you (or someone you know) tend to romanticize your automobile, bicycle, or motorcycle and treat it as something more than it is? Have you named your car? Do you use it to show off? (Respond to these questions in your journal.)
2. What do you think makes any set of standards meaningful and worth aspiring to? In what way does your *value system* help to determine your *standards*? Can one effectively argue that one set of values is better than another? Justify your response.

---

1 That men are wonderful is a proposition I will defend to the death. Honest, brave, talented, strong and handsome, they are my favorite gender. Consider the things men can do better than women—mend the plumbing, cook, invent atom bombs, design the Empire waistline and run the four-minute mile. They can throw a ball overhand. They can grow a beard. In fact, I can think of only two accomplishments at which women excel. Having babies is one.

2 The other is driving an automobile.

3 Don't misunderstand me. Some of my best friends are male drivers. And they seldom go to sleep at the wheel or drive 90 on a 45-mile-an-hour road or commit any other of the sins of which statistics accuse them. But insurance companies have been busy as bees proving that I don't get around among the right people.

4 New York State—where I live—has even made it expensive to have sons. Car insurance costs much more if there are men in the family under 25 driving than if there are only women. Obviously the females of the species make the best chauffeurs.

5 They ought to. They get the most practice. Aside from truck and taxi drivers, it is women who really handle the cars of the nation. For five days of the week they are in command—slipping cleverly through traffic on their thousand errands, parking neatly in front of the chain stores, ferrying their husbands to and from commuting trains, driving the young to schools and dentists and dancing classes and Scout meetings. It is only on Saturdays and Sundays that men get their innings, not to speak of their outings, and it is over weekends when most of the catastrophes occur.

6 Not that men are responsible for *all* the accidents. Some are caused by women—by the little blonde on the sidewalk at whom the driver feels impelled to whistle. Or by the pretty girl sitting in the front seat for whom he wants to show off his skill, his eagle eye, and the way he can pull ahead of the fellow in the red sports car.

7 But it isn't caution and practice alone which make the difference between the sexes. It's chiefly an attitude of mind. Women—in my opinion—are the practical people. To them a car is a means of transportation, a gadget more useful, perhaps, than a dish washer or a can opener, but no more romantic. It is something in which we carry the sheets to the laundry, pick up Johnnie at kindergarten and lug home those rose bushes.

8 Men, the dear, sentimental creatures, feel otherwise. Automobiles are more than property. They are their shining chariots, the objects of their affections. A man loves his car the way the Lone Ranger loves his horse, and he feels for its honor on the road. No one must out-weave or out-race him. No one must get off to a better jack-rabbit start. And no one, but no one, must tell him anything while he's driving. My own husband, ordinarily the most good-tempered of men, becomes a tyrant behind the wheel. "Shouldn't we bear south here?" I inquire meekly on our Saturday trips to the country. Or, "Honey, there's a gray convertible trying to pass."

9 "Who's driving?" he snarls like Simon Legree, veering stubbornly north or avoiding, by a hair, being run into.

10 Women drivers, on the other hand, *take* advice. They are used to taking it, having had it pressed on them all their lives by their mothers, teachers, beaus, husbands, and eventually their children. And when they

don't know their routes exactly, they inquire at service stations, from passers by, from traffic officers. But men hate to ask and, when they are forced to do so, seldom listen.

11 Have you ever overheard a woman taking down directions on the phone? "Yes," she says affably. "I understand. I drive up that pretty road to the Danbury turn-off. Then I bear left at the little antique shoppe that used to be a barn—yellow with blue shutters. Then right at a meadow with two beech trees in it, and a couple of black cows. Up a little lane, just a tiny way beyond a cornfield, and that's your place. Yes. With a Tiffany-glass carriage lamp in front. Fine. I won't have any trouble." Nor does she.

12 A man has too much pride to take such precautions. "O.K." he says impatiently. "Two point seven miles off the Post Road. A left, a rotary, another left. Six point three to—oh, never mind. I'll look it up on the map."

13 When they don't insist on traveling by car, men travel by chart. I've nothing against road maps, really, except the way they clutter up the glove compartment where I like to keep tissues and sun glasses. But men have a furtive passion for them.

14 When my husband and I are planning a trip, he doesn't rush out like me to buy luggage and a new wardrobe. He shops for maps. For days ahead of time he studies them dotingly; then I am forced to study them en route. Many a bitter journey have I taken past the finest scenery in America with my eyes glued to a collection of black and red squiggles on a road map, instead of on the forest and canyons we had come all the way across the country to behold.

15 "Look!" I cry to him as we rush up some burning autumn lane. "Aren't the trees glorious!" "What does the map say?" he mutters. "I've marked a covered bridge about a quarter of a mile along here. That's where we turn." If we should ever approach the Pearly Gates together, I know exactly how the conversation will run. "See all the pretty stars," I'll be murmuring happily. "And, oh, do look over there! Isn't that the City of Gold?"

16 "Never mind your golden cities," he'll warn me sternly, as he nearly collides with a meteor. "Just keep your eye on the map."

Post-reading Questions

Content

1. Where is the controlling idea for the essay located?
2. What are some of the things McGinley concedes that men can do better than women? Are the items on her list all really compliments? Explain.

3. From the author's point of view, what are the major reasons for women being better drivers than men?
4. According to McGinley, in what ways are cars more than simply "property" to men?
5. Who was Simon Legree? How does reference to him firmly characterize the author's portrait of male drivers?
6. From whom have women had advice *"pressed on them all their lives"*? How does the author claim that men usually respond to advice? Do you agree or disagree with her? Explain your reasoning.

Strategies and Structures

1. How does the author's account of a typical trip by automobile illustrate differences in the male/female *mind-set?*
2. In what way does McGinley address "values" in order to argue her thesis? Do you find her argument persuasive?
3. What is the tone of McGinley's essay? How does it assist her in arguing her thesis? Why?
4. How does including dialogue in this essay add to its appeal?
5. The author concludes her essay with a comment on what it would be like to drive through "the Pearly Gates" with her husband. How do these comments thoroughly illustrate the difference in *attitudes* or *mind-sets* between men and women?

Language and Vocabulary

1. Vocabulary: *chauffeurs, routes, Tiffany-glass, furtive, dotingly.* After you locate definitions for these words, return to "furtive" (an adjective) and "dotingly" (an adverb) and write a total of four original sentences using each word as an adjective and an adverb. (Locate the adverbial form of "furtive" and the adjective form of "dotingly" in your dictionary.)
2. What is the author referring to when she mentions "the Pearly Gates" and notices "the City of Gold"? How does an understanding of her allusion enrich a reader's sense of the final two paragraphs?

Group Activities

1. For an entire week, have each member of your group jot down daily observations of (1) how women tend to take advice as opposed to men, and (2) how women take down directions to get somewhere in contrast to men. At the end of a week, get together in your group and share your findings. Then prepare a brief class presentation wherein you refute or add support to McGinley's arguments.

2. Cruise around town, a shopping mall, or your campus with members in your group and note the particular driving habits of men and women. Based on what you witness, what generalizations can your group make about each gender? What stereotypes could you form? Are all stereotypes formed this way? Come to class with your group's stereotypes and conclusions about male and female drivers; be prepared to share your information with the rest of the class.

Writing Activities

1. Construct an essay persuading your readers of the superiority of women or men at performing some activity (e.g., cooking, parenting, or sports). Imitate the author's style by inserting humor into your writing.
2. Write an essay wherein you try to persuade your reader that men and women have fundamentally different conversational styles which bear a direct relationship to their behavior. Use plenty of representative examples drawn from personal experience, readings, and observations to support your argument.

Gore Vidal

Drugs

Born in 1925, Gore Vidal has been a controversial essayist, novelist, and social critic for the past four decades. He has successfully written all major forms of literature and is well known for novels like *City and the Pillar* (1948), *Julian* (1964), *Myra Breckenridge* (1968), *1876* (1976), *Burr* (1981), and *Lincoln* (1984). His plays include *Drawing Room Comedy* (1970), *An Evening with Richard Nixon* (1970), and *On the March to the Sea* (2005). Among his other works are *At Home: Essays 1982–1988* (1988), *Empire* (1988), *Hollywood: A Novel of America in the 1920's* (1990), *Live from*

Golgotha (1992), *The Gospel According to Gore Vidal* (1993), *United States Essays, 1951–1991* (1993), *Palimpsest* (1995), *The Smithsonian Institution* (1998), *Sexually Speaking: Collected Sex Writings* (1999), *The Golden Age* (2000), *The Last Empire: Essays 1992–2000* (2001), *Perpetual War for Perpetual Peace* (2002), *Dreaming War: Blood for Oil and the Cheney-Bush Junta* (2002), *Inventing a Nation* (2003), *Imperial America: Reflections on the United States of Amnesia* (2004), *Point to Point Navigation: A Memoir* (2006), and *The Selected Essays of Gore Vidal* (2008), *Gore Vidal: Snapshots in History's Glare* (2009). The following article, "Drugs," was written in 1970, and yet its content seems as relevant today as when he originally wrote it. People still look for solutions that will curb the tide of drug abuse in the United States against great odds. The recent discovery of alleged Central Intelligence Agency (CIA) involvement in drug trafficking to inner cities to finance covert operations (e.g., the Iran/Contra affair in the 1980s) might suggest the government's lack of commitment to winning a sincere "war on drugs."

Pre-reading Questions

1. Examine your current attitude toward drugs. When you hear the word *drugs*, what is the first thing that pops into your mind?
2. What is the current attitude toward drug use in American society? When and where is drug use socially acceptable?

---

1 It is possible to stop most drug addiction in the United States within a very short time. Simply make all drugs available and sell them at cost. Label each drug with a precise description of what effect—good and bad—the drug will have on the taker. This will require heroic honesty. Don't say that marijuana is addictive or dangerous when it is neither, as millions of people know—unlike "speed," which kills most unpleasantly, or heroin, which is addictive and difficult to kick.

2 For the record, I have tried—once—almost every drug and liked none, disproving the popular Fu Manchu theory that a single sniff of opium will enslave the mind. Nevertheless, many drugs are bad for certain people to take and they should be told why in a sensible way.

3 Along with exhortation and warning, it might be good for our citizens to recall (or learn for the first time) that the United States was the creation of men who believed that each man has the right to do what he wants with his own life as long as he does not interfere with his neighbor's pursuit of happiness (that his neighbor's idea of happiness is persecuting others does confuse matters a bit).

4 This is a startling notion to the current generation of Americans. They reflect a system of public education which has made the Bill of Rights, literally, unacceptable to a majority of high school graduates (see the annual Purdue reports) who now form the "silent majority"—a phrase

which that underestimated wit Richard Nixon took from Homer, who used it to describe the dead.

5 Now one can hear the warning rumble begin: if everyone is allowed to take drugs everyone will and the GNP will decrease, the Commies will stop us from making everyone free, and we shall end up a race of Zombies, passively murmuring "groovy" to one another. Alarming thought. Yet it seems most unlikely that any reasonably sane person will become a drug addict if he knows in advance what addiction is going to be like.

6 Is everyone reasonably sane? No. Some people will always become drug addicts just as some people will always become alcoholics, and it is just too bad. Every man, however, has the power (and should have the legal right) to kill himself if he chooses. But since most men don't, they won't be mainliners either. Nevertheless, forbidding people things they like or think they might enjoy only makes them want those things all the more. This psychological insight is, for some mysterious reason, perennially denied our governors.

7 It is a lucky thing for the American moralist that our country has always existed in a kind of time-vacuum: we have no public memory of anything that happened before last Tuesday. No one in Washington today recalls what happened during the years alcohol was forbidden to the people by a Congress that thought it had a divine mission to stamp out Demon Rum—launching, in the process, the greatest crime wave in the country's history, causing thousands of deaths from bad alcohol, and creating a general (and persisting) contempt among the citizenry for the laws of the United States.

8 The same thing is happening today. But the government has learned nothing from past attempts at prohibition, not to mention repression.

9 Last year when the supply of Mexican marijuana was slightly curtailed by the Feds, the pushers got the kids hooked on heroin and deaths increased dramatically, particularly in New York. Whose fault? Evil men like the Mafiosi? Permissive Dr. Spock? Wild-eyed Dr. Leary? No.

10 The Government of the United States was responsible for those deaths. The bureaucratic machine has a vested interest in playing cops and robbers. Both the Bureau of Narcotics and the Mafia want strong laws against the sale and use of drugs because if drugs are sold at cost there would be no money in it for anyone.

11 If there was no money in it for the Mafia, there would be no friendly playground pushers, and addicts would not commit crimes to pay for the next fix. Finally, if there was no money in it, the Bureau of Narcotics would wither away, something they are not about to do without a struggle.

12 Will anything sensible be done? Of course not. The American people are as devoted to the idea of sin and its punishment as they are to making money—and fighting drugs is nearly as big a business as pushing them. Since the combination of sin and money is irresistible (particularly to the professional politician), the situation will only grow worse.

Post-reading Questions

Content

1. Vidal states that "it is possible to stop most drug addiction in the United States within a very short time." What is the basis of his argument? Do you find it convincing or weak? Support your position.
2. What parallel do you see between Congress's "mission to stamp out Demon Rum" in the early twentieth century and its present mission to punish drug users?
3. How persuasive is Vidal's claim that the American moralist "has always existed in a kind of time-vacuum"?
4. Some readers of Vidal's essay "Drugs" have taken offense at his use of masculine nouns and pronouns in paragraphs 3 and 6. What is your opinion of this? Do his references imply that only men will become drug users? Why or why not?

Strategies and Structures

1. To accomplish his objective, Vidal balances logic and emotion in this essay. Where are some examples of sound reasoning (logic)? How does the author appeal to his reader's emotional prejudices toward drug use and drug users?
2. How well does Vidal address your concerns regarding drug use in American society? Does he seem to consider both sides of the issue carefully? How? What does he omit in his argument?
3. What is the effect of Vidal's final paragraph? How does it relate to his thesis? Why does he conclude a "reasonable" solution to America's drug problem is unrealistic?
4. When, where, and how does Vidal establish himself as an authority on drug use? How would his argument be less persuasive if he had omitted his background on the issue?

Language and Vocabulary

1. How is Vidal's thesis echoed by simple word choice?
2. What words in this essay did you respond to emotionally? Were such words used to support Vidal's position on drugs or to present the opposing point of view?
3. Search online or in your college library for a copy of *Who's Who in America* for background information on Dr. Timothy Leary and Dr. Benjamin Spock. What were they famous for doing? Why do you imagine Vidal refers to them?

Group Activities

1. Have each member of your group collect articles relating to drug use from different newspapers, magazines, and journals for a week. When you meet again with your group,

compare your findings. Were most of the articles you collected extremely biased? How? Were minorities unfairly associated with drug use?

2. Collect articles on alcohol abuse, alcohol consumption, and alcohol-related deaths in America for one week. Based on your findings, develop sound, ethical reasons for reinstituting Prohibition and present your material in a group forum.

Writing Activities

1. Write an essay refuting Vidal's conclusion that a reasonable solution to drug addiction will never be reached because "The American people are as devoted to the idea of sin and its punishment as they are to making money—and fighting drugs is nearly as big a business as pushing them." Appeal to your reader on a logical and emotional level.
2. Develop an argument that persuades your reader that legalizing drugs and drug paraphernalia would decrease crime as well as disease. Consider both sides of the issue and address opposing points of view.

Paula Gunn Allen

Who Is Your Mother? Red Roots of White Feminism

Paula Gunn Allen, a well-known Laguna (Sioux) and Lebanese poet, novelist, and essayist, has written many works touching on themes relevant to the Native-American experience. Her prose works includes *The Woman Who Owned the Shadows* (1983); *The Sacred Hoop: Recovering the Feminine in American Indian Traditions* (1986), the source of the following essay; *Spider Woman's Granddaughters: Traditional Tales and Contemporary Writings by Native American Women* (1989); *Grandmothers of the Light: A Medicine Woman's Source Book* (1992); *As Long as the Rivers Flow: The Stories of Nine Native Americans* (1996); and *Off the Reservation: Reflections on Boundary-Busting, Border-Crossing Loose Canyons* (2002). Allen's considerable poetic works frequently echo themes derived from her Native-American roots, and they include *The Blind Lion* (1974), *Coyote's Daylight Trip* (1981), and *Starchild* (1981), to *Wyrds* (1987), *Skin and Bones* (1988), *The Voice of the Turtle* (1994), *Life Is a Disease: Selected Poems 1964–1994* (1996), and *America The Beautiful* (2008)—a posthumously published volume of poems. Allen retired from her teaching position at UCLA in July 1999, but her accolades never ceased. In 2001, she was awarded a Lifetime Achievement Award by the Native Writer's Circle of the Americas, and in 2004 she received a Pulitzer Prize nomination for her book *Pocahontas: Medicine Woman, Spy, Entrepreneur, Diplomat* (2004).

Pre-reading Questions

1. Most Americans have immigrant origins. An old American saying states, "We all come from somewhere else." What are your family origins? What traditions and customs—holidays, foods, beliefs—does your family still observe?
2. What are some traditions of the Native-American people? Which of these traditions can you speculate have been lost? Which of their lost traditions could enrich American society today?

---

1 At Laguna Pueblo in New Mexico, "Who is your mother?" is an important question. At Laguna, one of several of the ancient Keres gynecocratic societies of the region, your mother's identity is the key to your own identity. Among the Keres, every individual has a place within the universe—human and nonhuman—and that place is defined by clan membership. In turn, clan membership is dependent on matrilineal descent. Of course, your mother is not only that woman whose womb formed and released you—the term refers in every individual case to an entire generation of women whose psychic, and consequently physical, "shape" made the psychic existence of the following generation possible. But naming your own mother (or her equivalent) enables people to place you precisely within the universal web of your life, in each of its dimensions: cultural, spiritual, personal, and historical.

2 Among the Keres, "context" and "matrix" are equivalent terms, and both refer to approximately the same thing as knowing your derivation and place. Failure to know your mother, that is, your position and its attendant traditions, history, and place in the scheme of things, is failure to remember your significance, your reality, your right relationship to earth and society. It is the same as being lost—isolated, abandoned, self-estranged, and alienated from your own life. This importance of

tradition in the life of every member of the community is not confined to Keres Indians; all American Indian Nations place great value on traditionalism.

3 The Native American sense of the importance of continuity with one's cultural origins runs counter to contemporary American ideas: in many instances, the immigrants to America have been eager to cast off cultural ties, often seeing their antecedents as backward, restrictive, even shameful. Rejection of tradition constitutes one of the major features of American life, an attitude that reaches far back into American colonial history and that now is validated by virtually every cultural institution in the country. Feminist practice, at least in the cultural artifacts the community values most, follows this cultural trend as well.

4 The American idea that the best and the brightest should willingly reject and repudiate their origins leads to an allied idea—that history, like everything in the past, is of little value and should be forgotten as quickly as possible. This all too often causes us to reinvent the wheel continually. We find ourselves discovering our collective pasts over and over, having to retake ground already covered by women in the preceding decades and centuries. The Native American view, which highly values maintenance of traditional customs, values, and perspectives, might result in slower societal change and in quite a bit less social upheaval but it has the advantage of providing a solid sense of identity and lowered levels of psychological and interpersonal conflict.

5 Contemporary Indian communities value individual members who are deeply connected to the traditional ways of their people, even after centuries of concerted and brutal effort on the part of the American government, the churches, and the corporate system to break the connections between individuals and their tribal world. In fact, in the view of the traditionals, rejection of one's culture—one's traditions, language, people—is the result of colonial oppression and is hardly to be applauded. They believe that the roots of oppression are to be found in the loss of tradition and memory because that loss is always accompanied by a loss of a positive sense of self. In short, Indians think it is important to remember, while Americans believe it is important to forget.

6 The traditional Indians' view can have a significant impact if it is expanded to mean that the sources of social, political, and philosophical thought in the Americas not only should be recognized and honored by Native Americans but should be embraced by American society. If American society judiciously modeled the traditions of the various Native Nations, the place of women in society would become central, the distribution of goods and power would be egalitarian, the elderly would be respected, honored, and protected as a primary social and cultural resource, the ideals of physical beauty would be considerably

enlarged (to include "fat," strong-featured women, gray-haired, and wrinkled individuals, and others who in contemporary American culture are viewed as "ugly"). Additionally, the destruction of the biota, the life sphere, and the natural resources of the planet would be curtailed, and the spiritual nature of human and nonhuman life would become a primary organizing principle of human society. And if the traditional tribal systems that are emulated included pacifist ones, war would cease to be a major method of human problem solving.

Post-reading Questions

Content

1. In the Laguna tribe, how does one establish his or her identity? What benefits does this form of identity have?
2. Explain the disadvantages of not knowing your mother. What is important to the Native-American way of life?
3. Have contemporary Americans held onto their cultural origins? What forces does Allen suggest have promoted this cultural alienation?
4. What would be the results if contemporary American culture adopted traditional views of Native Americans? Why would American culture change? How would it change?
5. What are the contrasting values of contemporary American and Native-American culture? What results from the contemporary American way of life? What are the results of Native-American cultural values?

Strategies and Structures

1. How does Allen start her essay? Why does she begin her essay this way?
2. Where does Allen present her thesis? How does it help the reader to focus on the controlling idea of her essay?
3. How does Allen use comparison and contrast to support her argument not to reject our traditions? And how does she use this strategy to develop her argument that we should adopt Native-American values?
4. In the final paragraph, Allen suggests the benefits of adopting Native-American values. Why does she present all of the benefits in one paragraph? Discuss the result of structuring the essay in this way?

Language and Vocabulary

1. Vocabulary: *matrilineal, psychic, context, matrix, self-estranged, alienated, antecedents, interpersonal.* Most of these words could cause the reader to lose track of what Allen is trying to say.

Look up the definitions of the words and rewrite the sentences in which they appear, using simple language. Does this in any way change the effect? How? Why?

2. Allen repeats key terms throughout the essay. What are they? How do they help to unify the essay and keep it focused?

Group Activities

1. Form multicultural groups and compare your different beliefs. How have the different cultures retained or rejected their traditions? Who is the traditional head of the household in the different cultures? What are the different relationships between humanity and nature? What are the different religious beliefs? What different political beliefs and institutions exist in the history of each culture? You may want to create a chart in which you list the different cultural beliefs under different headings such as religion, politics, or assimilation.
2. As a group, do a short research project in which you compare three different world cultures and their traditions. What are their political histories? Who have been their leaders? What are their different religious beliefs, and how have they developed over time? What have been their different beliefs about the relationship between humanity and nature? What are the different scientific discoveries that have shaped their cultures?

Writing Activities

1. Do some research on your cultural origins. You may want to interview relatives, do research in the library, and/or watch some films on your culture in the audiovisual center. After researching, write a persuasive paper in which you argue for the inclusion of one of your culture's traditions into mainstream, contemporary American culture.
2. Write a paper in which you argue for or against assimilation or the "melting-pot" theory. Explain the different benefits and disadvantages of assimilation. Explain why immigrants should or should not abandon their cultural traditions in favor of contemporary American culture. Add to the persuasive appeal of your essay by using emotionally charged words.

Dave Barry

A GPS Helps a Guy Always Know Where His Couch Is

Dave Barry was a syndicated humor columnist, and his work appeared in more than 500 newspapers in the United States and abroad. In 1988 he won the Pulitzer Prize for Commentary. He says that many people are still trying to figure out how this happened. Barry also has written a total of 30 books, although he notes that virtually none of them contain useful information. His fiction includes *Big Trouble* (1999), *The Shepherd, the Angel, and Walter the Christmas Miracle Dog* (2006), as well as nonfiction such as, *The Taming of the Screw* (1983), *Babies and Other Hazards of Sex: How to Make a Tiny Person in Only 9 Months With Tools You Probably Have Around the Home* (1984), *Stay Fit and Healthy Until You're Dead* (1985), *Claw Your Way to the Top: How to Become the Head of a Major Corporation in Roughly a Week* (1986), *Dave Barry's Guide to Marriage and/or Sex* (1987), *Homes and Other Black Holes* (1988), *Dave Barry Slept Here: A Sort of History of the United States* (1989), *Dave Barry Turns 40* (1990), *Dave Barry's Only Travel Guide You'll Ever Need* (1991), *Dave Barry's Guide to Life* (1991), *Dave Barry Does Japan* (1992), *Dave Barry's Gift Guide to End All Gift Guides* (1994), *Dave Barry's Complete Guide to Guys* (1996), *Dave Barry in Cyberspace* (1996), *Dave Barry's Book of Bad Songs* (1997), *Dave Barry Turns 50* (1998), *Dave Barry Hits Below the Beltway: A Vicious and Unprovoked Attack on Our Most Cherished Political Institutions* (2001), *"My Teenage Son's Goal in Life is to Make Me Feel 3,500 Years Old" and Other Thoughts On Parenting From Dave Barry* (2001), *"The Greatest Invention In The History Of Mankind Is Beer" And Other Manly Insights From Dave Barry* (2001), *Dave Barry's Money Secrets* (2006), *Dave Barry on Dads* (2007), and *Dave Barry's History of the Millennium (So Far)* (2007), and *I'll Mature When I'm Dead* (2010). Additionally, he published several volumes of collected columns including, *Dave Barry's Bad Habits: A 100% Fact-Free Book* (1987), *Dave Barry's Greatest Hits* (1988), *Dave Barry Talks Back* (1991), *The World According to Dave Barry* (1994), *Dave Barry is NOT Making This Up* (1995), *Dave Barry Is from Mars and Venus* (1997), *Dave Barry Is Not Taking This Sitting Down* (2000), and *Dave*

Barry: Boogers Are My Beat (2003). Barry wryly notes that critics have hailed all his works as "containing a tremendous amount of white space." He plays lead guitar in a literary rock band called the Rock Bottom Remainders whose other members include Stephen King, Amy Tan, Ridley Pearson, and Mitch Albom. They are not musically skilled, but they are extremely loud. Dave has also made many TV appearances, including one on the David Letterman show where he proved that it is possible to set fire to a pair of men's underpants with a Barbie doll. In his spare time, Barry is a candidate for president of the United States. Presently, Barry lives in Miami, Florida with his wife, Michelle, a sportswriter. He has a son, Rob, and a daughter, Sophie—neither of whom thinks he's funny.

Pre-reading Questions

1. Brainstorm the word *technology*. What do you associate with the word in your daily life as well as the lives of others?
2. Who do you think uses technological tools or gadgets most often? Men? Women? Teenagers? Senior citizens? What evidence, whether logical or emotional, informs your answer to this question?

---

1 I'm a big fan of technology. Most guys are. This is why all important inventions were invented by guys.

2 For example, millions of years ago, there was no such thing as the wheel. One day, some primitive guys were watching their wives drag a dead mastodon to the food-preparation area. It was exhausting work; the guys were getting tired just WATCHING. Then they noticed some large, smooth, rounded boulders, and they had an idea: They could sit on the stones and watch! This was the first in a series of breakthroughs that ultimately led to television.

3 So we see that there are vital reasons why guys are interested in technology, and why women should not give them a hard time about always wanting to have the "latest gadget." And when I say "women," I mean "my wife."

4 For example, as a guy, I feel I need a new computer every time a new model comes out, which is every 15 minutes. This baffles my wife, who has had the same computer since the Civil War and refuses to get a new one because—get THIS for an excuse—the one she has works fine. I try to explain that when you get a new computer, you get exciting new features. My new computer has a truly fascinating feature: Whenever I try to turn it off, the following message, which I am not making up, appears on the screen:

5 "An exception 0E has occurred at 0028:F000F841 in VxD—. This was called from 0028:C001D324 in VxD NDIS(01) + 00005AA0. It may be possible to continue normally."

6 Clearly, this message is not of human origin. Clearly, my new computer is receiving this message from space aliens. I don't understand all of it, but apparently there has been some kind of intergalactic problem that the aliens want to warn us about. What concerns me is the last sentence, because if the aliens are telling us that "it may be possible to continue normally," they are clearly implying that it may NOT be possible to continue normally. In other words, the earth may be doomed, and the aliens have chosen ME to receive this message. If I can figure out exactly what they're saying, I might be able to save humanity!

7 Unfortunately, I don't have time, because I'm busy using my new global positioning system (GPS) device. This is an extremely important gadget that every guy in the world needs. It receives signals from orbiting satellites, and somehow—I suspect the "cosine" is involved—it figures out exactly where on the earth you are. Let's say you're in the town of Arcola, Ill., but for some reason you do not realize this. You turn on your GPS, and, after pondering for a few minutes, it informs you that you are in . . . Arcola, Ill.! My wife argues that it's easier to just ASK somebody, but of course you cannot do that, if you truly are a guy.

8 I became aware of how useful a GPS can be when I was on a plane trip with a literary rock band I belong to called the Rock Bottom Remainders, which has been hailed by critics as having one of the world's highest ratios of noise to talent. On this trip were two band members whom I will identify only as "Roger" and "Steve," so that you will not know that they are actually Roger McGuinn, legendary cofounder of the Byrds, and Stephen King, legendary legend.

9 We were flying from Chicago to Boston, and while everybody else was reading or sleeping, "Roger" and "Steve," who are both fully grown men, were staring at their GPS devices and periodically informing each other how far we were from the Boston airport. "Roger" would say, "I'm showing 238 miles," and "Steve" would say, "I'm showing 241 miles." Then "Roger" would say, "Now I'm showing 236 miles," and "Steve" would come back with another figure, and so on. My wife, who was confident that the airplane pilot did not need help locating Boston, thought this was the silliest thing she had ever seen. Whereas I thought: I NEED one of those.

10 So I got a GPS for Christmas, and I spent the entire day sitting on a couch, putting it to good use. Like, I figured out exactly where our house is. My wife told me this was exciting news. I think she was being sarcastic, but I couldn't be sure, because I had to keep watching the GPS screen, in case our house moved. I also used my GPS to figure out exactly how far my couch is from LaGuardia airport (1,103 miles).

There is NO END to the usefulness of this device! If you're a guy, you need to get one NOW, so you can locate yourself on the planet. While we still have one.

Post-reading Questions

Content

1. What is the controlling idea or thesis? Is it an implied or direct statement?
2. Describe the tone of Barry's essay? Does he seem to take his subject matter seriously? Explain your point of view.
3. What sort of evidence does Barry offer readers in hopes of persuading others to adopt his point of view—or at least examine their attitude towards men and technology? What does he actually expose?
4. To what extent do you believe in what Barry claims with regards to men and women? Why personal experience or observations have you made that might add to the persuasive appeal of his argument?
5. Why does Barry identify two band members of the Rock Bottom Remainders simply as "Roger" and "Steve", and then go on to tell you their full names and accomplishments? What are they doing? Explain the irony. In what way does this reflect the spirit of Barry's claims about men and technology?

Strategies and Structures

1. Explain the strategic function of humor in Barry's essay. What would have been lost without it?
2. How does the author develop his controlling idea? What additional ways might he strengthen his claims?
3. Barry spends his second paragraph detailing an absurd history of inventions and gender roles. Why do you imagine he spent so much time on this? What does he try to establish early on in his composition?
4. How might verbal/written irony become a powerful tool in the hands of a skillful writer? How well does Barry make use of irony? When? Where? Why?
5. Throughout his essay, Barry uses a series of rhetorical fragments. Explain the purpose of a rhetorical fragment and why you think Barry intentionally writes them. What purpose do they serve?

Language and Vocabulary

1. Vocabulary: *guys, gadget, GPS, pondering, periodically, sarcastic.* After establishing the definitions of these words, use them in a paragraph written from the point of an irritated, persuasive woman, attempting to convince a man that his fixation with technological gadgets amount to little more than a fixation

with toys—or a self-righteous man who is trying to enlighten a woman about the fascinating mysteries of technology.

2. Barry often uses slang terms and informal language in an attempt to create a clear, down-to-earth tone. List at least four instances of informal language in his essay, and analyze how they reinforce his attitude towards his subject.

Group Activities

1. Personality can be expressed through language (words and phrases), and this exercise demonstrates (1) the power of personality (word choice) in writing, (2) the ways we can use the denotative and connotative meanings of words to achieve a desired tone. In small groups, discuss a potentially divisive issue or subject such as gender roles—real or imagined. Then have each group member write a paragraph attempting to get others to share his or her point of view for ethical (ethos), logical (logos), and emotional (pathos) reasons. Finally, get back into groups and share responses.
2. As a group, identify a current social or academic concern. Brainstorm how this concern could be directly and effectively addressed—a "modest proposal" if you will. Finally, write a persuasive collaborative letter to your college president or a local government official and urge him or her to adopt your group's "modest proposal"—a solution to your group's concern. Feel free to use humor to breakdown barriers and highlight absurdities (e.g., human folly) without making the person you write to defensive.

Writing Activities

1. Pre-write on the topic of gender role and/or gender stereotypes. Once you have inventoried your thoughts, generate a thesis statement that states something about gender role, and support your thesis with a combination of ethical, logical, and emotional appeals to your reader. Be sure to use plenty of concrete references to people, places, and things.
2. Write an essay in which you illustrate the seriousness or silliness of a social issue and convince your readers that action must be taken immediately to address the situation. Attempt to engage the readers' emotions and stir them into action using statistics and specific examples.

Tammerlin Drummond

Never Too Old: Sexually Active Seniors Are One of the Fastest-Growing HIV-Infected Populations in the U.S.

A graduate of Smith College and the Summer Program for Minority Journalists at UC Berkeley, Tammerlin Drummond received her Master of Fine Arts degree from Long Island University. Drummond wrote in the capacity of a featured correspondent for *Time* magazine until 2001, at which time the magazine offered buyouts. She also wrote for *The Day*, the *St. Petersburg Times*, and the *Los Angeles Times*, earning distinction as a member of the paper's Pulitzer Prize winning team who covered the 1992 Los Angeles riots. Currently, Drummond works as an editorial writer and columnist for the *Bay Area News Group* as well as *BANG-EB*; there, she continues to write on issues of immediate social concern as well as teach classes at Laney College in Oakland. Drummond enjoys traveling, cooking, sports, and working as a board member for *Friends of Faith*, a nonprofit organization that gives money to low-income and uninsured women with breast cancer. Additionally, Drummond is finishing a novel based on her experiences in Haiti, where she reported as a Miami correspondent. In the following essay, Drummond examines the little-known fact that as we move further into the new millennium, senior citizens constitute the fastest-growing segment of HIV-infected patients in the United States.

Pre-reading Questions

1. Make a list of qualities and activities you associate with "senior citizens." Upon what did you base your insights? Television? Movies? Parents, grandparents, aunts, uncles?
2. What do you consider "sexually active"? Which age group do you think is the most promiscuous and why?

1 Sue Saunders, a Fort Lauderdale, Fla., grandmother, had the symptoms: rapid weight loss, rashes, fever. But when she went to her local health clinic, a nurse asked incredulously, "What's an old woman like you doing getting an HIV test?"

2 Saunders' positive result came as a shock to the nurse, but it shouldn't have. Seniors are one of the fastest-growing HIV-infected populations in the U.S. Sunny south Florida, a magnet for retirees, has the largest concentration of people 50 or older with HIV. Seniors account for 14% of AIDS cases in Dade, Broward and Palm Beach counties, compared with 10% nationally. "You've got people contracting it later in life," says Drace Langford, a member of the Florida HIV/AIDS and Aging Task Force. But there are also seniors who have been living with HIV for years, thanks to the effectiveness of the new AIDS "cocktails."

3 Before blood screening became mandatory, most older people got HIV from transfusions. But since such transmissions have been all but eliminated, medical workers are being forced to confront the fact that seniors are getting infected primarily during sex. Promiscuity is common in senior centers, where the ratio of women to men averages 7 to 1. Since fear of pregnancy is no longer a concern, many seniors don't use condoms. And Viagra has added more fuel to an already volatile mix. Physically fit single men, dubbed "condominium Casanovas," often flit from one woman to the next, sometimes passing along AIDS. Widowers often hire prostitutes. The manager of a Miami apartment complex once asked former Miami Beach geriatric counselor Vincent Delgado to speak to an 82-year-old woman who brought young men to her apartment for sex whenever she got her Social Security checks. "She said she was going to die anyway," Delgado said, "and to leave her alone and let her enjoy life."

4 Public health officials blithely assumed that seniors weren't at risk because, of course, they didn't have sex. But the increasing numbers are challenging that assumption. The American Association of Retired Persons has produced an AIDS-prevention video called *It Could Happen to Me*, which is distributed to senior citizens nationwide. Meanwhile, public health officials are handing out condoms at senior complexes, offering free HIV tests and training a cadre of the elderly as counselors to help educate their peers about the dangers of unsafe sex.

5 Even so, this demographic group is often difficult to reach. Many elderly people are reluctant to discuss their intimate life with strangers. "A lot of people were taught that you don't air your dirty laundry," says John Gargotta, supervisor for the Senior HIV Intervention Project, an AIDS advocacy group. Most troubling, though, is that doctors often fail to consider HIV as a possible illness among their senior patients. As a result, the elderly are often misdiagnosed. Also, AIDS symptoms like

dementia and weight loss can mimic the ravages of old age. "So there is a higher prevalence of people being diagnosed in the month of death," says Dr. Karl Goodkin, an associate professor at the University of Miami School of Medicine. Goodkin, who is conducting a national study on the rate of cognitive impairment in HIV-infected elderly, says the virus proceeds to full-blown AIDS twice as fast in seniors, making early detection all the more crucial.

6 Early intervention saved Sue Saunders. Her HIV was diagnosed eight years ago, but she is alive today, thanks in part to protease inhibitors. Meanwhile, she has made it her mission to warn others about the dangers of high-risk sex in the golden years. "I'd just like to save one life," she says.

Post-reading Questions

Content

1. Why was Saunders' HIV-positive result a shock to the nurse and to most other people?
2. Before blood-screening for donors became mandatory, how did most seniors become HIV-positive?
3. Describe an AIDS "cocktail." (You may need to research the answer to this question in your library or online.)
4. Drummond contends that "widowers often hire prostitutes" as a partial explanation for how seniors get AIDS. Is she convincing? How might further representative examples strengthen her argument?
5. Why are senior citizens often the most difficult group to reach when teaching about "the dangers of unsafe sex"?

Strategies and Structure

1. How does Drummond use statistics to support her discussion points? Do her statistics seem convincing? Why or why not?
2. Frequently, writers use subtitles that enable readers to predict what will happen in an essay. How well does Drummond's subtitle fulfill this function and why? What would you have predicted about the essay without the subtitle?
3. How does Drummond develop her essay? That is, in what way does she unify her information and establish a clear sense of direction from the beginning to the end of her essay?
4. Explain how the shock value of the author's material establishes a powerful call to action that practicing safe sex has no age barrier?
5. Discuss the tone of Drummond's essay. What does it add to her informative exposition?

Language and Vocabulary

1. Vocabulary: *HIV, incredulously, effectiveness, transfusion, transmission, promiscuity, Viagra, volatile, condominium, Casanova, blithely, cadre, advocacy, dementia, mimic, prevalence, cognitive, impairment, protease inhibitors.* Make a two-part list in which you place all the words above that have to do with medicine in column one and the others in column two. How does the author's diction (word choice) reinforce the seriousness of her topic?
2. Take another look at the list you made in Language and Vocabulary Question 1. Note how many words tend to be argumentative in nature. Write something about how the author's words could be even more persuasive in convincing seniors to be more aware and thus more careful about the dangers of indiscriminate sex.

Group Activities

1. Assemble in small groups and make a list of five to ten questions each member will use to interview seniors in their community. Ask them what they think of this essay. (You probably will have to paraphrase it for them.) When you get back together, share your responses and establish some statistics of your own.
2. Carefully go back through Drummond's essay noting the strengths and weaknesses of her argument. Next divide the class into two parts. The first group will research information on the Internet to back up the author's claim. The second group will seek facts and statistics to disprove what she says. Finally, have the two groups debate the reality and consequences of sexually active seniors.

Writing Activities

1. Compare and contrast the emotional and physical needs of senior citizens as presented in Barrett's essay "Old Before Her Time" in Chapter 3 and Drummond's essay "Never Too Old." Be sure to use plenty of details and examples to support discussion points and to persuade your reader.
2. In what way did Drummond's essay contradict or reinforce your impressions of senior citizens, and how do you feel about them now? Compose a persuasive essay that relates your feelings about this topic—feelings expressed in a clear, concise thesis statement. In what way does innocence affect our perceptions differently than experience? Be specific.

***Internet Connection:* Tammerlin Drummond**

HIV/AIDs

Online, research a number of articles related to AIDs, especially essays identifying AIDs research and the fastest growing AIDs/HIV population in America as of 2008. Use your recent data as evidence, and write an essay supporting or refuting Drummond's claim that "Senior Citizens are one of the fastest growing HIV-infected populations in the U.S." Be sure to document your authoritative sources using parenthetical references, and include a brief list of works cited.

Bruce Henderson

Why We Went to Iraq

Bruce Henderson is Professor of English at Fullerton College. As part of a history minor at Oberlin College he studied history at the University of Wales, Swansea, Great Britain. He has contributed articles to various textbooks and trade books, and has published others in *California English, Teaching English in the Two-Year College, Inside English,* and *Teaching for Success.* He recently studied the history of the Pilgrims and Wampanoag Indians on a grant from the National Endowment for the Humanities. A noted poet and popular speaker, Henderson also has written several novels, published a vegetarian nutrition guide, and currently is working on a critical reasoning textbook. He resides on California's Central Coast, and continues critical research on recent U.S. history. In the following essay, Henderson offers logical, reasonable explanations for the war in Iraq—a counterbalance, if you will, to commercial media that tends to filter what many Americans know about the war.

Pre-reading Questions

1. Before reading this article, reflect on what you know about the War in Iraq. How did the U.S. justify invading the country? Who

or what helped to shape your current attitudes and impressions of the war?

2. Freewrite with focus on the word "terrorism." Who or what causes "terrorism," and what does it take for someone to be labeled a "terrorist"? Why or why not might any person seem like a "terrorist" in the eyes of another individual?

[The U.S. has] about 50% of the world's wealth but only 6.3% of its population. In this situation, we cannot fail to be the object of envy and resentment. Our real task in the coming period is to devise a pattern of relationships which will permit us to maintain this position of disparity without positive detriment to our national security. To do so, we will have to dispense with all sentimentality and day-dreaming; and our attention will have to be concentrated everywhere on our immediate national objectives. We need not deceive ourselves that we can afford today the luxury of altruism and world-benefaction. . . . We should cease to talk about vague and . . . unreal objectives such as human rights, the raising of the living standards, and democratization. The day is not far off when we are going to have to deal in straight power concepts. The less we are then hampered by idealistic slogans, the better.

—Memo by George Kennan, Head of the U.S. State Department Policy Planning Staff. Written February 28, 1948. Declassified June 17, 1974

The people can always be brought to the bidding of the leaders . . . All you have to do is tell them they are being attacked and denounce the peacemakers for . . . exposing the country to danger. It works the same in any country.

—Herman Goering at the Nuremberg Trials

1 At this point in time, eight years after the U.S. invasion of Iraq, what we know for certain is that the original reasons announced for the occupation were wrong. Saddam Hussein did NOT have any weapons of mass destruction (and one has to wonder, if he had any, why he wouldn't have used them when we came after him); he was NOT linked to Al-Queda since his power rested on secular rather than religious government, making them natural enemies; and he was NOT seeking yellow-cake uranium in Niger, a claim based upon documents so obviously forged that some commentators say the real wonder is why our intelligence services couldn't have seen that within even a few minutes of looking them over. On the uranium front, in any case, between obtaining fissionable materials and actually building and deploying a bomb there is of necessity a long stretch of time, yet we were told Hussein constituted an imminent danger to our security.

2 So since none of the original reasons [for the Iraq invasion] proved to be true, and in retrospect we know there was no solid evidence even in 2003 for any of them, then what are the real reasons we invaded Iraq? Put another way, since we did remove Saddam Hussein from power and since he has been executed, what are our continuing objectives in Iraq? Unfortunately, considering the relatively short-term historical memory of most of the American public, answering this crucial question requires context, and most key events in the Middle East have deep historical roots. But our major media cannot spare the time during commercial broadcasts to provide such context, even if they intended to.

3 On top of these shortcomings in understanding why we went to Iraq, some facts that have come to light afterward are not well known because they must be ferreted out of either the alternative press or else by reading long nonfiction accounts or by conducting extensive internet research, none of which most people will take time for. Besides, since volunteers were fighting the conflict in Iraq, after five years, most Americans pressed on with their lives and likely had little motivation for getting to the bottom of things. Conventional wisdom takes the position, "Well, for whatever reasons we're occupying that country, we can't just walk away now and leave a big mess, so our occupation must continue."

4 One significant fact that has come to light goes back to the day of the 9/11 tragedy in 2001. That same afternoon, just hours after the towers fell in New York, Donald Rumsfeld, Secretary of Defense, set in motion plans for the invasion of Iraq, even before Osama bin Laden had been blamed for the attack! Yet this fact would come as no surprise if Americans were familiar with PNAC, the Project for a New American Century. This group, which in the early 1990s drew up plans for the future strategic positioning of the U.S., included quite a collection of notables: Donald Rumsfeld, Dick Cheney, James Woolsey, Paul Wolfowitz, Richard Perle, William Kristol, James Bolton, Zamay Khalilzad, William Bennett, Dan Qualye, Jeb Bush and others. In 1992, Wolfowitz outlined plans for military intervention in Iraq, as an action deemed necessary to assure "access to vital raw material, primarily Persian Gulf oil" (Weiner). This specific goal tied in to their larger vision of maintaining U.S. status as the world's only remaining superpower, in the wake of the ending of the Cold War and the collapse of the former Soviet Union, through economic and political domination of the globe. In essence, their concerns echoed those of George F. Kennan: how can the U.S. maintain its position of global economic and military domination? One crucial consideration is that armies run on oil, so an adequate supply must not only be secured, but also so far as possible denied to any potential rivals.

5 In 2000, after the Supreme Court selected George Bush to be President, these PNAC signers were elevated to key positions in his administration: Cheney as Vice President, Rumsfeld as Defense Secretary, Wolfowitz as Deputy Defense Secretary, John Bolton as Undersecretary

of State and later UN ambassador, Richard Perle as chair for the Defense Policy Advisory Board at the Pentagon, and so on. In short, the PNAC planners gained a lock on military policy in the Bush administration.

6 The PNAC plans could not be pressed into effect during the eight Clinton years. Further, Americans are historically reluctant to undertake war without provocation. We didn't respond militarily in 1933 when Hitler came to power and began rounding up Jews, nor in 1938 when he annexed part of Czechoslovakia, nor in 1939 when he invaded Poland. Not until the end of 1941, with the bombing of Pearl Harbor, were Americans motivated to send troops. The PNAC planners noted this predictable difficulty in changing the reluctance of the American people concerning unprovoked, unilateral projection of U.S. power with the observation that "the process of transformation, even it if brings revolutionary change, is likely to be a long one, absent some catastrophic and catalyzing event—like a new Pearl Harbor" (Bollyn).

7 In a perhaps fortuitous coincidence, a mere eight months following the inauguration of George Bush came the 9/11 attacks. Within hours of those events, Rumsfeld ordered his aides to begin planning to invade Iraq, even though his own intelligence officials told him there was no connection between Iraq and the attacks. In fact, it remains unclear who is responsible for 9/11. The FBI posted on their website that though Osama bin Laden is indeed on their ten most wanted list, he is NOT sought in connection with the events of 9/11, because they have no solid evidence that he had anything to do with those attacks. He is wanted instead for the bombing of the USS Cole in October of 2000 (FBI).

8 As if consolidating the PNAC program, a new National Security Strategy promulgated by the Bush administration in September of 2002 included attacking possible future competitors preemptively, assuming regional hegemony by force of arms, controlling energy resources around the globe, and maintaining a permanent war strategy: an endless "war on terrorism" (White House).

9 Another historic perspective that explains why we are in Iraq involves four oil companies that Saddam Hussein booted out of the country in 1972 when he nationalized the Iraq Petroleum Concession: Exxon, Mobil, Shell, and BP (British). These same companies are now back, 36 years later, having signed on to service Iraq's oil fields under no-bid contracts. Certainly there are many companies who would welcome landing such a contract and would be capable of doing the job. It is therefore all the more telling that these original four have now come full circle.

10 Even so, Hussein was not always our enemy:

> US intelligence helped Saddam's Ba`ath Party seize power for the first time in 1963. Evidence suggests that Saddam was on the CIA payroll as early as 1959, when he participated in a failed

> assassination attempt against Iraqi strongman Abd al-Karim Qassem. In the 1980s, the US and Britain backed Saddam in the war against Iran, giving Iraq arms, money, satellite intelligence, and even chemical & bio-weapon precursors. As many as 90 US military advisors supported Iraqi forces and helped pick targets for Iraqi air and missile attacks. (Everest)

11 Photographs and film easily viewable on the Internet show Donald Rumsfeld, then special U.S. envoy, shaking hands with Saddam Hussein during a visit to Iraq in December 1983.

12 To understand what led up to the Gulf War in 1991 we need only look to the earlier history of Iraq in the 20th century. Modern Iraq was essentially created by Great Britain after WWI to insure British control of its vast oil fields. They set up an arrangement whereby one percent of landowners owned 55% of the land, and the country's oil wealth was handed over to American and British companies for a pittance. To prevent Iraq from becoming a Gulf power, Kuwait was awarded 310 miles of coastline, whereas the much larger Iraq was given a mere 36 swampy miles, setting the stage for many of the tensions which followed.

13 After the first Gulf War which ended Iraq's occupation of Kuwait, during the 1990s Iraq entered into negotiations with French and Chinese oil companies, and for the U.S. and Britain this was the last straw. For example, Hussein signed a deal with Russia's Lukoil in 1997 to develop Iraqi oil fields, along with similar arrangements with the Chinese. France and Russia apparently enjoyed favorable arrangements for a supply of oil during the 1990s while Iraq remained under UN sanctions during the "oil for food" program (Kanter). Certainly our preemptive invasion of Iraq in 2003 repositioned the U.S. as first in line to reap the benefits of pumping Iraqi oil, while simultaneously putting us back in control of the amount, if any, that will be granted to our international competitors.

14 U.S. occupation of Iraq has little to do with spreading democracy, as the patriotic arguments claimed, and much more to do with our strategic energy interests. More specifically, it has to do with returning control of Iraq's oil fields to the four western companies which lost out in 1972. At this point in time it is difficult to distinguish between our national interests and corporate oil interests. Suffice it to say that companies like Exxon Mobil which are amassing historic profits in the early 21st century can afford to lobby politicians to influence legislation toward their own ends.

> One oil analyst, Fadel Gheit of Oppenheimer & Co., told the *Washington Post*, "Exxon Mobil has more seismic data on Iraq than on Houston real estate. If Exxon had security on the ground, the following day it would have crews there. And money would be no object." (Martin)

15 Though the U.S. has announced the removal of combat troops from Iraq in August 2010, we can expect an ongoing military presence to insure stability of the oil supply from that country. Insurgents must be prevented from attacking pipelines, refining facilities and tanker ports. In the end we are less concerned with who nominally governs Iraq than with this stability so crucial to U.S. interests, which helps assure U.S. international supremacy in the 21st century. In turn, stabilization of Iraq becomes part of the larger goal of stabilizing the entire Middle East so that more energy can be extracted and piped from the Caspian Sea region immediately to the north of Iran and Iraq. Already this obvious objective has stirred the ire of Russia, since the Caspian Sea region was formerly under Soviet control. The state of Georgia, for example, under dispute between American and Russian interests, forms part of this region.

Works Cited

Bollyn, Christopher. "America Pearl Harbored." American Free Press. 12 April 2004. Sept. 20, 2008. <www.americanfreepress.net/12_24_02/America_Pearl_Harbored/ America_ pearl_harbored.html>.

Everest, *Larry. Oil, Power & Empire: Iraq and the U.S. Global Agenda.* Common Courage Press 2004. <http://www.truthout.org/docs_2005/WTI062405V.shtml>.

FBI. *FBI. Most Wanted Terrorists*. Sept. 20, 2008. <http://www.fbi.gov/wanted/terrorists/terbinladen.html>.

Kanter, James. "Total Says Executive Questioned Over Iraq Oil Deals." *New York Times*. 21 Oct. 2006. 20 Sept. 2008. <www.nytimes.com/2006/10/21/world/europe/21food.html>.

Kennan, George. "Review of Current Trends, U.S. Foreign Policy, Policy Planning Staff, PPS No. 23. Top Secret." Included in the U.S. Department of State, Foreign Relations of the United States, 1948, volume 1, part 2 (Washington DC Government Printing Office, 1976), 524–525.en.wikisource.org/wiki/Memo_PPS23_by_George_Kennan

Martin, Patrick. "Wall Street Drools over Prospect of Capturing Iraq Oil Wealth." World Socialist Web Site. 6 March 2007. 20 Sept. 2008. www.wsws.org/articles/2007/mar2007/oil-m06.shtml

The New National Security Strategy of the United States. Sept. 2002. 20 Sept. 2008. <www.whitehouse.gov/nsc/nss.pdf>.

Weiner, Bernard. "A PNAC Primer: How We Got into this Mess." Counterpunch. 28 May 28, 2003. 20 Sept. 2008. <http://www.counterpunch.org/weiner05282003.html>.

Post-reading Questions

Content

1. How did former President George W. Bush initially justify a "preemptive strike" on Iraq?
2. What did the U.S. Secretary of Defense set into motion just hours after the tragic fall of the Twin Towers in New York on 9/11/01? How logical, fair, ethical, and humane were his actions? Be specific.
3. Explain the purpose, goals, and objectives of the "Project for a New American Century" (PNAC). Who were some of the notable people involved with the PNAC?
4. What happened when Saddam Hussein "nationalized the Iraq Petroleum Concession" in 1972? Ironically, what occured after the invasion of Iraq and the capture of Saddam Hussein in 2003?
5. Briefly summarize the history of Iraq and Kuwait. Who created the country of Kuwait? When and why was it created? Who benefited from Kuwait's existence and who did not?

Strategies and Structures

1. Assess why Henderson opens his essay with two quotations—one from a declassified "U.S. Policy Planning Staff" file and the other from testimony by Herman Goering (convicted of crimes against humanity) at the Nuremberg Trials? Why do you think that Henderson intentionally referred to sources written before 1950—sixty years ago?
2. How does Henderson demonstrate the fact that, "Americans are historically reluctant to undertake war without provocation"? In what way does this information provide a background for the arguments of fact that follow?
3. Analyze how Henderson's documentation of evidence drawn from a wide variety of verifiable sources helps to strengthen his argument of fact.
4. Why and how do "historical perspectives" on Iraq help readers to better appreciate the complexities of Western powers in the Middle East? In hindsight, what information about Iraq often tends to be overlooked or filtered out of many mainstream (commercial) news magazines and news broadcasts? Why?
5. How does Henderson conclude "Why We Went to Iraq"? In what way do his final sentences open the door for future discussions and debate about the reason the United States continues its presence in Iraq—despite the pull-out of all combat troops in August 2010?

Language and Vocabulary

1. *Vocabulary: disparity, detriment, dispense, altruism, world-benefaction, democratization, hampered, slogans, bidding, denounces, secular, uranium, commentators, fissionable, deploying, constituted, imminent, context, ferreted, conventional, deemed, superpower, domination, adequate, potential, reluctant, provocation, annexed, predictable, unilateral, transformation, catastrophic, catalyzing, fortuitous, coincidence, inauguration, consolidating, promulgated, precursors, pittance, negotiations, sanctions, pre-emptive, repositioned, patriotic, amassing, seismic, insurgents, nominally, stabilization, ire, dispute.* Make a list with the heading, "Words, War, and Iraq." Then, draw three columns—each with a subheading: Words (subheading, column 1), Definitions (subheading, column 2), and Connotations (subheading, column 3). Next, place all vocabulary words in column 1, their dictionary definitions in column 2, their connotations (associated meanings—see the Glossary) in column 3. Look over your list once you have completed all tasks, and write a few sentences explaining how and why Henderson's word choice and use of language serve a strategic purpose in his essay.
2. Rewrite Henderson's following sentence (1) once with words containing positive or neutral connotations, and (2) once with words that carry negative connotations: *"In 2000, after the Supreme Court selected George Bush to be President, these PNAC signers were elevated to key positions in his administration. . . ."*
3. Language can be used to sooth, wrinkle, and excite emotions. However, emotions allow us to dispense with rational thinking and sometimes encourage impulsive, explosive, hostile, or antagonistic behavior and actions. In what way does Henderson use language in general and words in particular to appeal to reason rather than emotions? How does he avoid name-calling and stereotyping? In contrast, how did those who championed the War in Iraq attempt to persuade the masses with word groups, such as: "weapons of mass destruction," "yellow-cake uranium," and "Ba`ath Party"?

Group Activities

1. Gather as a group outside of class and view one or more newscasters as they speak about Iraq. Do they use sweeping generalizations? Do they strive to provide television audiences with "the big picture"? If so, how? If not, why? Ultimately, write a collaborative summary of each newscast you watch—specifically noting what your group did and did not hear about the war in Iraq.
2. Assemble into separate groups of four or five students and research one of the many sources of information in Henderson's essay; however, each group should research

a different source. For example, Group I might research, Larry Everest's *Oil, Power & Empire: Iraq and the U.S. Global Agenda*"; Group II might research George Kennen's "Review of Current Trends, U.S. Foreign Policy, Policy Planning Staff, PPS No. 23. Top Secret"; Group III might research Patrick Martin's "Wall Street Drools over Prospect of Capturing Iraq Oil Wealth"; Group IV might research *The New National Security Strategy of the United States*, September 2002; Group V might research Bernard Weiner's "A PNAC Primer: How We Got into this Mess," and so on. Have each group write a collaborative summary of the article it researched in depth as well as organizing and presenting its findings to the rest of the class. After presentations have been made, discuss the merits of using primary and secondary sources to back up an argument and persuade readers in an essay.

Writing Activities

1. Should blind allegiance to one's country be the only way to demonstrate loyalty or patriotism, or in this highly technical age, do we consider the "one world" concept more important? What is a "patriot" or a "freedom fighter"? What is an "insurgent"? Who tends to categorize people as one or the other and why? Integrating fact with emotion, write a persuasive argument based on this issue.
2. Write an essay in which you prove or disprove that fighting an unjust war in Iraq—a war that already has cost the U.S. more than 3 trillion dollars—was a logical, ethical, and beneficial sacrifice of lives. Back up all of your opinions with verifiable evidence (not merely someone else's opinion) regardless of the position you take on this topic. Avoid using any emotionally charged words aimed at distracting readers from the issue at hand.
3. At a recent Global Leadership Conference in Europe, the United States received harsh criticism for its apparent lack of sensitivity to global issues unless it profits our country. Write an essay arguing that since the United States is the lone remaining superpower on earth, it should or should not have the right to do as it pleases and be accountable or unaccountable to the United Nations and other world organizations. Use specific representative examples follow by analysis to argue and persuade your reader.

Internet Connection: Bruce Henderson
Conspiracy Theories & Media Spin

Once you get access to an online database, research a number of articles related to "conspiracy theories." Begin by inserting the key words "conspiracy theory" or "Cointelpro" (Counter Intelligence Program), the known record of the F.B.I.'s war against domestic dissent in the sixties. What "spin" did the articles take—that is, how did they present information about a controversial subject? Which articles appealed to logic and ethics? Which articles appealed to fear, apprehension, and other emotions? Generate and develop an original thesis on the topic of "conspiracy theories," and write a persuasive paper using *parenthetical references* to document "in text" sources, as well as a brief list of *works cited*. Feel free to move beyond politics to personalities (alleged suicides of entertainers or public figures).

Additional Topics and Issues for Writing Persuasive Essays

1. Write an essay in which you persuade the school to award you a scholarship. You will want to consider why you are a worthy beneficiary and how your scholarship will further your education.
2. Devise an original thesis about the current positions of men, women, children, and/or elderly people in American society. Then write a persuasive essay calling for a change in the way these groups are currently treated.
3. Write an essay in which you persuade your audience that general education courses are useless. How do you expect college to prepare you for your major? In what way do general education courses assist you in achieving your goals? Avoid arguments like "I could get my college degree a lot sooner if I did not have to have a general education."
4. Write an essay persuading your classmates and families to discontinue the use of plastics and/or Styrofoam (petroleum-based products).
5. Persuade your audience in a well-developed essay that all international boundaries should be dissolved and that we

should all become citizens of one world with one governing body, a government that includes the best of all existing political ideologies.

6. Write an essay defending a society that respects an individual's right to an alternative lifestyle.

7. Write a persuasive essay calling for drastic yet fitting punishment for those who sexually, psychologically, and/or physically abuse others.

8. Compose an essay wherein you defend two or three vices you have. Attempt to convince your reader that what society commonly views as a vice (e.g., smoking, drinking, gambling) is—in your case at least—a virtue.

9. Summarize the differences between two opposing points of view (e.g., we should or should not allow people who have tested positive for the AIDS virus to immigrate to America), and then argue for one of the positions.

10. Pick a word such as "prejudice" and write a persuasive essay convincing your reader that the popular definition of the word is misleading and that your definition is more appropriate or useful. Support your claims with a clear definition of terms and examples drawn from authoritative references and personal observations.

Appendix: MLA Documentation

Why should you document sources when you write? Simple. When you draw on a source but do not acknowledge its respective author, you are *plagiarizing* information. In other words, you are claiming another person's words or ideas as your own. Why is that unacceptable in college or in the work world? Plagiarizing material is the same as *stealing.* Paraphrasing information—placing the works of another into your own words—does not eliminate the need to cite your sources either. Furthermore, experts usually write resource materials on specific topics or issues. Thus, proper documentation will usually strengthen the legitimacy of your discussion points. After all, it's important to have an expert on your side when arguing about a controversial issue! For the purpose of assignments in this text, we will focus on the MLA (Modern Language Association) format to document sources.

Typically, instructors and researchers distinguish material as primary and secondary sources. *Primary sources* provide firsthand evidence from people who have witnessed historical events. Although usually in an unpublished form such as a manuscript, a primary source also might be scientific data, transcripts of government proceedings, or statistics. In contrast, *secondary sources* tend to analyze, discuss, interpret, synthesize, or explain primary materials and other secondary sources. Such sources tend to be written by people who did not witness an event themselves or who rely on primary sources for verifiable information. Of course, sometimes, the line between primary and secondary sources becomes rather ambiguous. For instance, a recent article in *Time* magazine might not be considered a primary source, and yet, a *Time* magazine article written in 1968 could serve as a primary source in researching the Vietnam War and American society.

Citing your resource materials is particularly crucial when constructing a research paper; however, documenting sources always is important. While your readers consider the facts, figures, reasoning, synthesis, and conclusions in your paper, they also may want to verify your sources and, perhaps, read more about your paper's topic. The documentation of primary and secondary resource materials consists of two basic components: (1) *parenthetical references* (in-text notes), and (2) a *works cited* list (complete publishing information at the end of the text).

Parenthetical References

A big change occurred in documentation methods in 1984; parenthetical references replaced footnotes that had appeared at the end of an essay or the bottom of a page. Both share a similar purpose—citing sources—however, structurally, parenthetical references differ from footnotes. For one, in a parenthetical reference, the numbering system for footnotes is not used. For another, parenthetical references directly follow quoted or acknowledged sources within the written work while footnotes appear at the bottom of a page. In other words, all the important information a reader needs to locate a source in your list of *works cited* appears in the text—within parentheses—rather than some other location in an essay.

When Should I Use Parenthetical References?

Use parenthetical references:

a) after direct quotations
b) if you refer to another person's ideas or writings
c) when directly referring to part of a source
d) for information that is not common knowledge

What Do My Parenthetical References Tell My readers?

A parenthetical reference informs readers of the author's last name so that they can locate it easily in the alphabetically arranged entries in your *Works Cited* list. Additionally, your parenthetical reference indicates the page number or numbers where readers can locate and verify your sources.

Where Should I Place Parenthetical References?

- Usually, a parenthetical reference will appear at the end of your sentence, directly after quotation marks but before end punctuation such as a period.

Example: "There is something that might be called cinematic beauty. It can be expressed in a film, and it must be present in a film for that film to be a moving work" (Kurosawa 135).

How Should I Structure A Parenthetical Reference?

- Usually, the author's last name and the page number will provide your readers with enough information to locate the piece in your "Works Cited."

  Example: Horse whisperers explain their ability as 'horse language' or 'body language'—or a combination of both (Cossett 1).

- If you have already mentioned the author's name in your text, all you need to do is to place the page number or numbers in parentheses.

  Example: In "Playing God with no Sleep," Anna Quindlen ironically remarks that mothers are "meant to be all things to small people, surrounded by bromides and soppy verse and smiling strangers who talk about how lucky we are" (90).

- When you use two or more works by the same author, include (1) the author's last name, (2) the title of the text, (3) page number or numbers.

  Example: (Erdrich *The Antelope Wife* 52) distinguished from (Erdrich *Baptism of Desire* 52)

- If you have two authors with the same last name, eliminate confusion or ambiguous references by including initials or writing out the entire name for each author.

  Example: (C. Ng 69) or (Christine Ng 69) to distinguish from works by (S. Ng 154) or (Stephen Ng 154)

Again, materials appearing in your "Works Cited" should be arranged <u>alphabetically</u>, and clearly delineated in your parenthetical reference for easy location. The two authors noted above would appear as follows.

Ng, Christine. *Haight Ashury and the Love Generation.* San Francisco: Creative Arts Books, 1999.

Ng, Stephen. "Marbles and Mole Hills." *South Eastern Humanities Quarterly* 7 (2006): 333–367.

Why Is a Complete List of Works Cited Important to the Effective Use of Parenthetical References?

A "works cited" list presents readers with specific information, so they may read more about your subject or validate your source. When books, for instance, are revised and appear in new editions, page numbers often change. Additionally, a complete list of works cited offers readers all the information necessary for them to find the same edition of the text used when citing quotations. Also, acknowledging information, including the author, publisher, and/or publication might strengthen source credibility. For example, if you write a paper arguing that a new species of parrot has been discovered in the Amazon Rain Forest, readers will take you more seriously if you cite sources like *National Geographic* to corroborate your claims rather than sensational magazines like *National Inquirer* or *Star.*

Helpful Tips:

1. *Lead* your reader into a quotation; maintain a clear context for your parenthetical references.
2. *Follow* quotations with a quotation mark, *place* the parenthetical reference in **parentheses**, and then *insert* the end punctuation after the parenthetical references.

Works Cited

At the end of any essay that cites specific sources or at the conclusion of a formal research paper, place a *Works Cited* list. Since a "Bibliography" literally refers to a "list of books," to place resource materials that may include magazine articles, online materials, interviews, television shows, statistics, pamphlets, electronic texts, and newspapers under such a heading would be inappropriate. Granted, the sort of information crucial to completing an entry in your *Works Cited* list will depend on what sort of material you are gathering. Generally speaking, record the following kinds of information that you will need for thorough documentation (or get a computer print-out of it). Then, structure the material in your *Works Cited List* using the appropriate format as illustrated below:

Books:

Author. Title of the book—*italicized* or underlined (be consistent). Edition if applicable. The city of publication: The publisher, the year of publication

Journals and Magazines:

Author. Title of article, short story, or review—in quotation marks. Journal title—*italicized* or underlined. Volume number. Date: pages.

Newspapers:

Author. Article in quotation marks. Newspaper title—*italicized* or underlined, date (day, month, year): Section: page number.

Pamphlets:

Author (if indicated), title of pamphlet—*italicized* or underlined. City of publication, Sponsoring organization, year.

Interviews:

Name of the person interviewed. Topic of discussion—in quotation marks. Interviewer, date of interview. City (location could be important—especially if interviewing a disaster victim).

Films, DVDs, and Videos:

Movie/Video—*italicized* or underlined. Director. Distributor, year.

In contrast to printed sources, *online databases* frequently are updated and corrected. Thus, an article published on August 16, 2008 might contain some significant changes (retractions, corrections, deletions, and additions) by the time someone accesses it on April 19, 2009. In contrast to printed sources, *online databases* are constantly updated and corrected. Therefore, your *works cited* entry for an online source will often contain both dates. Additionally, a citation for an online source should indicate the publication medium and the name of your computer service or network. Conclude your detailed citation with the URL for your online source—but never cite a URL by itself; it tells readers too little about your source. Overall, the additional materials you cite from *online databases* should be structured as follows:

Computer Services:

Author's Name. Article/material accessed (in quotation marks). Other publication information for printed sources (source title or database—underlined). Publication date *(Online)*. Computer service. Access date. URL.

Computer Network:

Author's name. Article or document title (in quotation marks). Journal, magazine, newsletter, or conference—underlined. Identifying numbers (volume, issue). Publication year or date (in parentheses). Number of pages or paragraphs (when provided)) or *n. pag.* for "no pagination." Publication medium *(Online)*. Computer network. Access date. URL.

CD-Rom & Portable Rom or Databases:

Author's name (if provided). Material used (in quotation marks). Product Database title (underlined). Publication medium (diskette, CD-Rom, magnetic tapes). Vendor's or publisher's name (if relevant). Year of publication.

Electronic Text:

Author's name. Text title—*italicized* or underlined. Publication information for printed source (city of publication, publisher, publication date). Publication medium *(Online)*. Repository of the electronic text. Computer network. Access date. URL.

Formatting MLA Entries for a List of Works Cited

Book with One Author

Quindlen, Anna. *Every Last One: A Novel*. New York: Random House, 2010.

Two Books by One Author:

Bolen, Jean Shinoda. *Close to the Bone: Life-Threatening Illness and the Search for Meaning*. New York: Harper, 1998.

___. *Goddesses in Older Women: Archetypes in Women Over Fifty*. New York: Harper, 2010.

Book with Two Authors:

Wolkstein, Diane and Samuel Kramer. *Inanna: Queen of Heaven and Earth*. New York: Harper & Row, 1983.

A Translation:

Alighieri, Dante. *The Inferno*. Trans. Seth Zimmerman. New York: iUniverse, 2003.

A Book That Has Three or More Authors, Has Gone Through Several Editions, and Is One of Several Volumes in a Set:

Abrams, M. H., et al. *Norton Anthology of English Literature*. 7th edition. 2 Vols. New York: W. W. Norton & Company, 1999. Vol. 1.

A Work in More Than One Volume:

Tolkien, J. R. R. *The Lord of the Rings*. 3 Vols. New York: Houghton Mifflin, 2002.

An Essay in an Anthology:

Nhu, T. T. "Becoming an American is a Constant Cultural Collision." In *Thresholds*. Sterling Warner, ed. Fort Worth: Harcourt Brace, 1997. 92–94.

A Poem in an Anthology:

Hughes, Langston. "The Weary Blues." In *Poems, Poets, Poetry: An Introduction and Anthology.* 2nd Edition. Helen Vendler, ed. Boston: St. Martin's, 2002. 504.

A Short Story in an Anthology:

Téllez, Hernando, "Just Lather, That's All." *Contemporary Latin American Authors.* New York: Ballantine, 1974. 209–14.

A Play in an Anthology:

Wang, David Henry. *M Butterfly.* In *The Wadsworth Anthology of Drama.* 4th ed. Boston: Wadsworth, 2004. 1061–1084.

A Forward, Introduction, Preface or Afterward:

King, B. B. Introduction. *Telling Stories, Writing Songs.* Kathleen Hudson. Austin: Texas UP, 2001. xvii–xviii.

An Edition of an Author's Work:

Stoker, Bram. *Dracula.* Hutchinson's Colonial Library. First edition. London: Hutchinson & Co, 1897.

A Magazine Article:

Blake, Sara. "Let's Face It." *YRC* 17 October 2010: 50–51.

A Scholarly Journal:

Bessie, Adam. "Unmasking the Graphic Novel: Learning Summary and Close Reading." *inside english* (2009): 11–17.

A Newspaper Article:

Teves, Oliver. "Philippine Lore Lingers in Jungle Mountains." *San Francisco Chronicle* 1 June 2005: sec. A: 2.

A Lecture:

Andrew Lam. "Vietnamese Diaspora." Evergreen Valley College, San Jose, 12 Oct. 2011.

An Interview:

Devi, Xiormara. "Modern Mass Media, Reality Television, and Murder Trials." Interview. January 8, 2011.

An Encyclopedia:

Cambodian Poetry. Collier's Encyclopedia. 2011 edition.

A Broadcast Interview:

Clinton, Bill. Interview with Larry King. *Larry King Live.* CNN. 24 June 2004.

Computer Network:

Croft, Linda. "What's Thought Got To Do With It?" *Computer Underground* Digest. 2.7 (1991): N. Pag. Online. Internet. 2 June 2010. http://www.soci.niu.edu/~cudigcst/

Electronic Text:

Colleen, Annice,. *Scrapbooks and Memories.* Ed. Scott Rudolph. New York: Penguin, 2006. Online. Evergreen Coll. Lib. Internet. 7 June 2010. <http://www.sjeccd,evc,edu/lib.cat/~scrapmem/>

Computer Service:

Spot, Sylvester. "Phrack Worlds News Special Edition." *Phrack Magazine*. 9 October 2008. *Phrack Magazine Online*. Online. AOL. 1 January 2009.

Computer Software:

hp Office Jet 7100 Series All in One. Hewlett Packard Development Company, 2011.

CD-Rom:

Young, Neil. "The Needle and the Damage Done." *Greatest Hits: Neil Young.* Reprise Records, 2004. CD.

Films:

Pirates of the Caribbean: On Stranger Tides, The. Director: Rob Marshall. Producer: Jerry Bruckheimer. Walt Disney Studios, 2011.

DVDs and Videotapes:

Oh Brother Where Art Thou? Dir. Joel Cohen. With George Clooney, John Turturro, Time Blake Nelson. Walt Disney Video, 2001. 103 minutes. DVD.

Recordings:

Keillor, Garrison. "Pontoon Boat." *More News from Lake Wobegon: Faith.* Audiotape. HighBridge Company HBP 18204, 1989.

Television:

"Elizabeth Taylor: The Beautiful Enigma." *Biography.* OWN Network. 24 March 2011.

Sample List of Works Cited

Bessie, Adam. "Unmasking the Graphic Novel: Learning Summary and Close Reading." *inside english* (2009): 11–17.

Blake, Sara. "Let's Face It." *YRC* 17 October 2010: 50–51.

Colleen, Annice. *Scrapbooks and Memories.* Ed. Scott Rudolph. New York: Penguin, 2010. Online. Evergreen Coll. Lib. Internet. 7 January 2011. <http://www.sjeccd,evc.edu/lib.cat/~scrapmem/>

Bolen, Jean Shinoda. *Goddesses in Older Women: Archetypes in Women over Fifty.* New York: Harper, 2010.

___. *Close to the Bone: Life-Threatening Illness and the Search for Meaning.* New York: Harper, 1998.

Croft, Linda. "What's Thought Got To Do With It?" *Computer Underground Digest.* 2.7 (1991): N. Pag. Online. Internet. 2 April 2011. <http://www.soci.niu.edu/-cudigest/>

Ehrenreich, Barbara. *Dancing in the Streets: A History of Collective Joy.* New York: Metropolitan Books, 2007.

Kenyon, Heather. "Editor's Notebook." *Animation World Magazine* 4.8 (November 1999). Online, 1 July 2005 www.awn.com/mag/issue4.08/4.08pages/4.08cditor.Php3/

Lam, Andrew. *Perfume Dreams: Reflections on the Vietnamese Diaspora.* New York: Heydey Books, 2005.

Loder, Kurt. "The Beatles." *Time* 8 June 1998.

Dark Knight, The. Dir. Christopher Nolan. With Christian Bale, Heath Ledger, and Michael Caine. DVD. Warner Brothers, 2008. 152 minutes.

"Naturopathic Medicine." *Health Response Ability Systems* (1993): 26 pars. Online. Internet. 22 Feb. 2008.

O'Brien, Tim. *The Things They Carried.* New York: Random House, 1988.

Valdez, Alma. "Working at the World Trade Center—Calling in Sick: September 11, 2001." An Interview. October 25, 2001.

Vidal, Gore. *Perpetual War for Perpetual Peace: How We Got to be So Hated.* New York: Nation Books, 2002.

Vonnegut, Kurt. *Slaughterhouse-Five: Or, the Children's Crusade, A Duty-Dance With Death.* New York: Dell Publishing, 1991.

Wang, David Henry. *M Butterfly.* In *The Wadsworth Anthology of Drama.* 4th ed. Boston: Wadsworth, 2004. 1061–1084.

Glossary of Literary and Rhetorical Terms

Acronym A word formed from the first letter or letters of subsequent parts of a compound term. For instance, International Business Machines becomes IBM, the Equal Rights Amendment becomes the ERA, the Central Intelligence Agency becomes the CIA, the Bureau of Indian Affairs becomes the BIA, Also Known As becomes AKA, the Federal Bureau of Investigation becomes the FBI, As Soon As Possible becomes ASAP, Automatic Teller Machine become ATM, Personal Identification Number becomes PIN, and Pretty Hot And Tempting becomes PHAT.

Active Verbs An active verb has the quality or ability of "acting," "causing change," or "expressing motion." To put it another way, action verbs—unlike linking verbs—show rather than just tell your reader what you are talking about. For instance, *Andrea practices medicine* actively expresses the relationship between herself and her profession (e.g., she "practices" medicine). In contrast, a sentence such as *Andrea is a doctor* merely "links" Andrea to an adjective—doctor—that describes her. (See **Voice.**)

Adjectives Words that can indicate the quality of a noun or its equivalent (e.g., the *slippery* pavement, the *rocky* soil, the *blue* sky, the *tangerine* sunset, the *dilapidated* train station). Typically, adjectives answer questions like "which kind?" and "which one?"

Adverbs Words that modify verbs, adjectives, other adverbs, and complete sentences:

Verbs:	Alfredo drove *swiftly.*
Adjectives:	*Extremely* frisky, the cat ran through the house.
Adverbs:	Christina walked *very* slowly.
Sentences:	*Desperately,* Kevin pleaded his case to the jury.

Alliteration The repetition of the same letters or sounds at the beginning of two or more words that are next or close to each other (e.g., "best buy," "my mother makes meatloaf," "Peter Piper picked a peck of pickled peppers").

Allusion A term used when making reference to a famous literary, historical, or social figure or event. For instance, a reference to Watergate refers to (alludes to) political corruption, or more recently, "To Wag the Dog" alludes to a calculated political diversion.

Analogy An extended comparison where an unfamiliar topic is explained by noting its similarity to something familiar.

Anagram A word or phrase created from the letters of another word or phrase (e.g., "acres" is an anagram of "races," "marine" is an anagram of "remain," "flow is an anagram of "wolf," "evil is an anagram of "veil").

Analysis To closely inspect and come to a conclusion on something by separating the topic or issue into parts in order to better understand the whole.

Anecdote A short story that illustrates a point.

Antonym A word that has an opposite meaning to another word (e.g., *accept* is the antonym of *refuse* and *private* is the opposite of *public*).

Argumentation One of the four major forms of essay writing, the others being narration, exposition, and description. In an argument, you prove your point by establishing the truth about a topic or issue. In doing so, revealing the fallacies of another's argument may prove invaluable. For a detailed discussion of argumentation, see *Chapter 11: Argumentation.*

Audience Those you address when you write (e.g., family, friends, professors, public servants). You must consider whether your audience knows nothing or a lot about your topic.

Brainstorming Individually or collectively solving a problem by considering and/or rejecting ideas. A writer brainstorms to generate ideas on a topic and then focuses on a specific controlling idea that will lead to a topic sentence or a thesis statement.

Cause/Effect A rhetorical strategy for essay development that answers the question, *why?* by examining reasons (causes) for something and its corresponding consequences (effects). See *Chapter 9: Cause and Effect.*
Classification A rhetorical strategy for developing essays where a writer divides and classifies information to promote a clear discussion of material. See *Chapter 8: Division and Classification.*
Cliché A trite or worn-out expression that either becomes a stereotype or meaningless in its original context. Example: *I'm as hungry as a horse! It's raining cats and dogs!* (How often have you pictured a hungry horse eating or dogs and cats falling from the sky when someone makes either of those remarks?)
Clustering A type of brainstorming where all the ideas one has about a topic or an issue are written down, circled, and related. Clustering words creates a visual picture of the relationships between ideas which are associated with a topic. For further discussion on this method of "pre-writing," see *Chapter I: Communicating Is Language at Work.*
Coherence A term used to refer to the clear, logical relationship between words, phrases, clauses, and paragraphs. In writing, we use traditional devices and linking words to achieve coherence.
Colloquial Expressions Informal expressions, somewhere between slang and formal language. Colloquialisms are acceptable in speech but not in formal writing.
Comparison/Contrast A rhetorical strategy for developing papers by demonstrating similarities and differences. See *Chapter 7: Comparison and Contrast.*
Concrete/Abstract Concrete words may stand by themselves and be understood because they are perceived through the five senses: touch, taste, sight, smell, and sound. For instance, we can touch, see, and hear a small child; thus the word *child* is concrete. However, the child's anger would be abstract since it is perceived only through its relationship with another word. Abstract words define ideas, concepts, and attitudes (love, hate, ethical, indifference, honesty, pride) and tend to be subjective in their interpretation.
Concrete Nouns (See **Concrete/Abstract.**)
Connotation The meanings or implications associated with a particular word beyond its literal definition. For instance, while a hospital denotes an institution which provides medical care for people, the word also suggests (connotes) fear, pain, misery, and possibly death. (See **Denotation.**)
Context Words that occur before and after a specified word or words and determine its/their meaning.
Controlling Idea The main idea expressed in a paragraph or an essay.
Deduction A form of reasoning that moves from general points to a specific conclusion. See *Chapter 11: Argumentation* for a detailed discussion of deductive logic. (See **Induction.**)
Definition A rhetorical strategy in writing where one develops a topic or issue by applying any single or combination of the following techniques: definition by example, definition by history, definition by comparison or contrast, and definition by negation. See *Chapter 5: Definition.*
Denotation The literal or dictionary definition of a word. (See **Connotation.**)
Description A rhetorical strategy for essay development using details and examples—particularly those that appeal to the senses. See *Chapter 3: Description.*
Dialect A type of informational diction.
Diction An author's word choice. Diction also deals with word usage (e.g., concrete/abstract expressions, denotation/connotation, colloquialisms).
Division A rhetorical strategy for developing essays where a writer divides and classifies information to promote a clear discussion of material. See *Chapter 8: Division and Classification.*
Essay Map An essay map consists of three or more ideas that are attached to your thesis statement, providing you with the controlling ideas for your body paragraphs. In essence, an essay map tells you where to go by providing a specific direction.
Ethos The ethical (what is right or wrong) appeal in an essay. See *Chapter 11: Argumentation.*

Euphemism The substitution of a mild expression for a harsh one. For example, *between jobs* is a euphemism for *unemployed; powder your nose* is a euphemism for a *visit to the bathroom;* and *categorical inaccuracy* is a euphemism for *lie*.

Evidence Facts and examples that prove what you claim.

Exposition A form of writing where the author's main purpose is to explain or expose a topic or an issue.

Fallacy Faulty logic. See *Chapter 11: Argumentation.*

Figures of Speech Terms which are used to add variety to your essay where points are discussed *figuratively* instead of literally. Some of the common forms of figures of speech include metaphor, simile, hyperbole, and personification (listed elsewhere in this *Glossary*).

Freewriting Unstructured, spontaneous writing in which one does not stop to edit material, the objective being merely to generate ideas for one unified paragraph or essay. (See Peter Elbow's essay "Freewriting" in *Chapter 1: Communicating is Language at Work.*)

Generalization A statement made without a foundation in fact or supporting evidence.

Hyperbole A figure of speech wherein one greatly exaggerates to emphasize a point. Example: *Marilyn's so skinny that she must run around in the shower just to get wet.*

Idiom The use of words unique to a particular group or language.

Illustration and Example A rhetorical strategy where a writer uses illustrations and examples as the main tools for essay development. Most essays have some element of illustration and example. See *Chapter 4: Illustration and Example.*

Imagery Concrete expressions that appeal to the senses, often employing the use of figurative language to produce mental pictures.

Induction A form of reasoning which takes several specific points and leads to a generalization about them. See the introduction to *Chapter 11: Argumentation* for a more detailed discussion of inductive logic. (See **Deduction.**)

Inference To draw a reasonable conclusion from presented information or to figure out something by using what you already know.

Introduction In a short essay, the introduction acquaints the reader with the theme or topic which will be explored in depth within the body. Traditionally, one's thesis statement appears in the latter part of an introductory paragraph and provides a focus or direction for developing the remainder of the paper.

Irony Irony is a figure of speech wherein the author states his or her intention in words that carry an opposite meaning. Irony can also be situational.

Jargon Like slang, jargon consists of words or phrases particular to a specific profession or social group. Computer operators, for instance, use terms such as *interfacing* or *networking.* The problem is that many people do not know the definitions of these words, and if you use them in an essay, it will be necessary to define them.

Lexicon A list of words or a wordbook such as a dictionary.

Linking Words Basically, linking words are connectors that refer to transitions and subordinating, coordinating, and adverbial conjunctions.

Logos A principle that originated in Classical Greece, *logos* refers to "universal divine reason." In classical rhetoric, authors used *logos* (the logical appeal in writing) along with *ethos* (the ethical appeal in writing) to argue points and persuade audiences. (See *Chapter 11: Argumentation* and *Chapter 12: Persuasion.*)

Metacognition: Thinking about thinking or having an awareness of one's own learning.

Metaphor A comparison without the use of *like* or *as.* For instance, a simile would state: *My brother is like a prison warden,* a metaphor would simply state: *My brother is a prison warden.*

Mood The mood is the emotional tone of a work (e.g., gloomy, optimistic, pessimistic, cheerful).

Myth A myth is a metaphorical expression of the unknown. Myths include tales and stories about supernatural heroes, heroines, gods, goddesses, and monsters, which originated before written language and were passed on to succeeding generations through the oral tradition of storytelling. The purpose of many primitive myths—and modern myths—is to interpret natural phenomena such as creation and the seasons.

Narration One of the major forms of writing. Narration is used to relate what happened at an event or a number of events. In essence, a narrative tells a story. (See *Chapter 2: Narration* for further discussion.)

Noun A part of speech used to name or identify a person, place, thing, quality, or action. Typically, nouns have both a singular and plural form and are often preceded by a definite or indefinite article. Nouns can function as a subject, direct object, indirect object, object of a preposition, or an appositive.

Noun as Subject:	*Jason* met Medea in Colchis while searching for the Golden Fleece.
Noun as Direct Object:	The police arrested the *CEO* who embezzled money from Cisco.
Noun as Indirect Object:	Phaedra sent her *brother* a text message from a hotel in Maui.
Noun as Object of a Preposition:	After *work*, the construction crew met at McGilly's for a *beer*.
Noun as Appositive:	Cheri, an *author*, continues to work on her great American novel.

Oxymoron A condensed form of paradox in which two contradictory words are used together, as in "definite maybe" or "hell's angels," "deafening silence" (See **Paradox.**)

Paradox A situation or statement which, although it is contradictory to what reason dictates, is nevertheless true. Example: *Japanese citizens patiently waited in orderly lines for food, fuel, and medicine after the 2011 tsunami devastated their homes and buried many loved one's in piles of debris.*

Parallelism Constructing word groups into consistent and balanced patterns using the same grammatical forms. For example, nouns should be combined with similar nouns (*Doctors, lawyers,* and *accountants* were in the room), adjectives with like adjectives (The gardener planted *yellow, white,* and *red* roses), verbs with similar verbs (We *studied, ate,* and then *slept* for ten hours).

Paraphrase To put someone else's ideas or written material into your own words.

Parody A device whereby an author employs humor to make fun of a particular situation or another piece of literature.

Pathos An appeal to the emotions of readers that arouses pity, sympathy, sorrow, and so on. See *Chapter 11: Argumentation.*

Persona A character or voice used as the speaker of an essay or short story. The attitudes of the persona frequently differ from those of the author.

Personification A form of figurative speech, personification is the treatment of animals or inanimate objects as if they were human. Example: *The rose breathed a sigh of relief as the morning sun touched her, bringing warmth and life to her cold petals.*

Persuasion Like argumentation, persuasion is a form of writing where an author attempts to convince his/her reader of something. In contrast to argumentation, however, persuasion includes words that elicit an *emotional* rather than a rational, logical response from a reader to achieve the writer's ultimate objective. That is, the author appeals to one's emotions (pathos) and ethics (ethos) in addition to logic (logos). See *Chapter 12: Persuasion.*

Point of View The perspective from which an essay or story is written. In formal writing, point of view is expressed in first person, wherein the author uses the pronoun "I," and third person, which is a more subjective form of writing, wherein the writer uses "he," "she," or "it" as the narrator. Point of view may also refer to an author's attitude toward his or her subject matter.

Prefix Something added to the beginning of a word to change its meaning or give it a new meaning (e.g., *un* + wanted = unwanted; *re* + united = reunited).

Pre-writing A spontaneous listing of thoughts to aid in the composition of your essay or paragraph. Pre-writing techniques include clustering, freewriting, listing, and mapping.

Purpose The objective or reason for writing.

Rhetoric The study of the elements, such as structure or style, used in writing or speaking.
Rhetorical Question A question which the author offers the reader, with the intention of promoting thought. Often, an author will answer his or her own question within the body of an essay.
Root Word A base word to which prefixes and suffixes are added.
Sarcasm Heavy-handed verbal irony where a person expresses dislike or disapproval in a caustic, demeaning, jeering manner. Sarcasm is intended to ridicule and hurt by taunting an individual in a snide manner.
Satire A form of writing which pokes fun at social conventions or attacks human vice and folly with the hope of getting the reader to reconsider the object of ridicule and thus improve the human condition.
Science Fiction A form of writing in which imagination is the differentiating characteristic of the writer, as well as the reader. It came into being with the new world of invention and technology and is reputed to have begun with Jules Verne—though others credit Mary Shelley, author of *Frankenstein*. It deals with topics that arc not part of our times but usually are set in the future and/or on distant planets.
Simile A comparison with the use of *like* or *as*. Examples: *Cindy's hands were as cold as frost. Marc's pants look like shreds of tissue paper.*
Slang Although often colorful and descriptive, slang is often considered vulgar and/or informal and not recommended for use in a formal essay. Example: Tom, an English Major, considered Queen Elizabeth I *babelicious* (slang). Tom, an English Major, considered Queen Elizabeth I *very sexy and attractive* (standard English).
Strategy The method for approaching, analyzing, and writing about a topic.
Stereotype Giving qualities to a particular person, race of people, or situation which are overly generalized and are not a fair representation of the person, place, or thing to which they refer.
Style How a writer expresses what he or she wants to say. Important factors in style are word use, sentence structure, and voice.
Suffix A syllable(s) added to the end of a word or root word to give the word a new meaning, a different grammatical function, or form a new word (e.g., *wise* + *est* is the superlative form of the adjective *wise*).
Summary Condensing your own or someone else's work into a shorter composition. Summaries are useful for a writer to get a good sense of a larger work, but they are only a starting point for analysis.
Support Facts, details, and examples which illustrate the validity of your points.
Syllogism A three-part form of reasoning consisting of a major premise, a minor premise, and a conclusion. See the introduction to *Chapter 11: Argumentation* for examples.
Symbol Something, which stands for or represents something other than itself (e.g., a flag, just a piece of cloth, can represent a country and thus is a symbol for it).
Synonym Synonyms are words with similar meanings (e.g., skinny/thin, desire/want). Synonyms should be used with care because no two words mean precisely the same thing. (See **Connotation.**)
Syntax Syntax refers to the arrangement of words in a sentence.
Theme Subject or topic on which a person writes or speaks. (*Note:* A theme may also refer to a short essay.)
Thesis The main or controlling idea that a writer seeks to prove in his or her essay.
Tone The expressing of a writer's mood or attitude toward his or her subject through the use of carefully chosen words.
Topic Sentence Much like a thesis, a topic sentence is the controlling idea of a paragraph and is usually stated at the beginning of a paragraph. The sentences that follow must support the topic to provide unity for the paragraph.
Transitions Transitions are words or word groups that aid the writer in moving from one point to the next. Some common transitions include *before, after, thus, therefore, however, moreover, nevertheless.* See *Chapter 1: Communicating Is Language at Work.*

Uncountable Noun Words that cannot be plural because they are considered as a group, i.e., furniture, homework, rice, spaghetti, and so on.

Understatement Intentionally downplaying an important point or a serious situation. Consider the following sentence: *After losing her car, house, and every cent she had to her name, Colleen was a bit annoyed.* To say Colleen was *a bit annoyed* understates the true gravity of the situation. (See **Irony.**)

Unity To provide unity in a composition, the writer must stick to the controlling idea he or she has established without digressing from that major discussion point.

Voice There are two voices—active and passive. In the active voice, the subject *does* the acting (e.g., the hunter *shot* the wolf), and in the passive voice the subject *receives* the action of the verb (e.g., the wolf *was shot by* the hunter).

Credits

This page constitutes the copyright page. We have made every effort to trace the ownership of all copyrighted material and to secure permission from copyright holders. In the event of any question arising as to the use of any material, we will be pleased to make the necessary corrections in future printings. Thanks are due to the following authors, publishers, and agents for permission to use the material indicated.

Photo Credits

p. 4 (Deborah De La Rosa) Photo courtesy of Deborah De La Rosa. **p. 12** (Peter Elbow) Courtesy of Peter Elbow. **p. 26** (Joanne Jaime) Courtesy of Joanne Jaime. **p. 35** (Pat Mora) Courtesy of Pat Mora. **p. 39** (Ray Bradbury) Lennox McLendon/AP Photo. **p. 45** (Amy Tan) Frank Capri/Hulton Archive/Getty Images. **p. 54** (Maxine Hong Kingston) John Nordell/Image Works/Time Life Pictures/Getty Images. **p. 58** (Black Elk) Transcendental Graphics/Getty Images. **p. 62** (Alice Walker) Noah Berger/AP Photo. **p. 68** (Nguyen Ngoc Ngan) Courtesy of Nguyen Ngoc Ngan. **p. 75** (Alma Luz Villanueva) Alma Luz Villanueva. **p. 82** (Arthur C. Clarke) Fiona Hanson/PA Wire/AP Photo. **p. 96** (Langston Hughes) MPI/Getty Images. **p. 101** (Katherine Barrett) Courtesy of Katherine Barrett. **p. 109** (N. Scott Momaday) Christopher Felver/CORBIS. **p. 116** (Barbara Graham) Courtesy of Harper Collins Publishers. **p. 122** (John Steinbeck) AP Photo. **p. 133** (Maya Angelou) **p. 106** Dave Allocca/Getty Images. **p. 144** (Leslie Bow) Atsushi Tajima. Courtesy of Leslie Bow. **p. 149** (Sara Blake) Courtesy of Sara Blake. **p. 154** (Philip K. Chiu) Courtesy of Philip K. Chu. **p. 158** (Ann Scheid) Photo by Robert Hilliard. Courtesy of Anne Scheid. **p. 164** (Stephanie Ericsson) Courtesy of Harper Collins Publishers. **p. 172** (Dan Archer and Olga Trusova) Dan Archer and Olga Trusova sketches by and used courtesy of Dan Archer. **p. 185** (Isaac Asimov) Marty Lederhandler/AP Photo. **p. 188** (Guillermo Gómez-Peña Guillermo Gomez-Pena photographed by Zach Gross, 2007. **p. 191** (Jo Goodwin Parker) Courtesy of Sterling Warner. **p. 197** (Richard Rodriguez) Roger Ressmeyer/CORBIS. **p. 203** (Sravani Banerjee) Courtesy of Sravani Banerjee. **p. 208** (Lee Herrick) Joel Pickford. Courtesy of Lee Herrick. **p. 219** (Kathleen Hudson) Courtesy of Sterling Warner. **p. 226** (Luis M. Valdez) George Rose/Getty Images. **p. 230** (Joyce M. Jarrett) Joyce Jarrett. **p. 234** (Heidi Ramirez) Courtesy of Sterling Warner. **p. 239** (Malcolm X) Eddie Adams/AP Photo. **p. 244** (Christine Ng) Courtesy of Christine Ng. **p. 259** (Barbara Ehrenreich) Kimberly Butler/Time Life Pictures/Getty Images. **p. 263** (Andrew Lam)Andrew Lam. **p. 267** (Carmen Jay) Photo courtesy of Jaime Jay. **p. 273** (E. B. White) Bachrach/Getty Images. **p. 278** (Suzanne Britt) Courtesy of Suzanne Britt. **p. 283** (Cobie Kwasi Harris) Courtesy of Cobie Kwasi Harris. **p. 294** (Roohi Vora) Courtesy of Roohi Vora. **p. 300** (Martin Luther King Jr.) American Stock/ Hulton Archive/Getty Images. **p. 305** (Robertson Davies) Tom Keller/AP Photo. **p. 310** (Constance García-Barrio) John Watson. **p. 315** (Bill Swanson) Courtesy of Sterling Warner. **p. 328** (David Bodanis) Charlie Hopkinson © 2005. **p. 338** (Megan McGuire) Courtesy of Megan McGuire. **p. 342** (Carlos Bulosan) University of Washington Libraries, Special Collections, UW513. **p. 345** (Karen Ray) Photo by Charles Ray. **p. 350** (Phillip Persky) Courtesy of Sterling Warner. **p. 355** (Rose Anna Higashi) Courtesy of Sterling Warner. **p. 359** (Anastasia Toufexis) Photodisc/Getty Images. **p. 370** (Charles Haynes) Courtesy of Charles Haynes and the First Amendment Center. **p. 374** (Cynthia Lopez) Courtesy of Cynthia Lopez. **p. 378** (Neil Young) Jeff Vespa/Getty Images. **p. 382** (Jeanne Wakatsuki Houston and James D. Houston) Courtesy of Jeanne Wakatsuki Houston and James D. Houston. **p. 392** (Reginald Lockett) Photo by Kathy Sloane. Courtesy of Reginal Lockett. **p. 399** (Louise Erdrich) David Ash/CORBIS. **p. 419** (Grace Sumabat Estrada) Courtesy of Grace Sumbat Estrada. **p. 427** (Amiri Baraka) Mike Derer/AP Photo. **p. 431** (Anna Quindlen) Frank Capri/Getty Images. **p. 436** (Douglas Laycock) University of Michigan Law School. **p. 445** (Mandana Mohsenzadegan) Photograph Courtesy of Mandana Mohsenzadegan. **p. 454** (Mark Charles Fissel) Courtesy of Sterling Warner. **p. 467** (Phyllis McGinley) Bettmann/CORBIS. **p. 471** (Gore Vidal) Franco Origlia/Getty Images. **p. 475** (Paula Gunn Allen) Courtesy of Beacon Press. **p. 480** (Dave Barry) Lynne Sladky/AP Photo. **p. 485** (Tammerlin Drummond) Courtesy of Tammerlin Drummond. **p. 489** (Bruce Henderson) Courtesy of Bruce Henderson.

Literary Credits

Chapter 1

p. 4 "Wild Ways with Words." Copyright © 2011 by Deborah De La Rosa. Used by author's permission. **p. 12** "Free Writing" by Peter Elbow, from *WRITING WITHOUT TEACHERS* by Peter Elbow, Copyright © 1973, 1998 by Peter Elbow. Used by permission of Oxford University Press, Inc. **p. 26** "Marriage: The Changing Institution" by Joanne Jaime. Copyright 1993 by Joanne Jaime. **p. 35** "Why I Am a Writer" by Pat Mora From *THE HORN BOOK MAGAZINE* (July/August 1990). **p. 39** "The Joy of Writing" by Ray Bradbury. From *ZEN AND THE ART OF WRITING*. Copyright 1990 by Ray Bradbury Enterprises and Don Congdon Associates. Reprinted by permission of Don Dogdon Association, Inc. **p. 45** "My Mother's English" by Amy Tan. Reprinted by permission of The Sandra Dijkstra Agency and Amy Tan. Copyright © 1990 by Amy Tan.

Chapter 2

p. 54 "Ghosts" by Maxine Hong Kingston, from *THE WOMAN WARRIOR: MEMOIRS OF A GIRLHOOD AMONG GHOSTS* by Maxine Hong Kingston. Copyright 1975, 1976 by Maxine Hong Kingston. Reprinted by permission of Alfred A. Knopf, Inc. **p. 58** Reprinted by permission from *BLACK ELK SPEAKS: BEING THE LIFE STORY OF A HOLY MAN OF THE OGLALA SIOUX*. The Premier Edition by John G. Neihardt. The State University of New York Press © 1932, 1959, 1972 by John G. Neihardt. © 1961 by the John G. Neihardt Trust. Copyright © 2008 by State University of New York. All rights reserved. **p. 62** "Journey to Nine Miles" by Alice Walker. From LIVING BY THE WORD, pp. 114–119 (Harcourt Brace). Copyright © 1986 by Alice Walker. **p. 68** "Saigon, April 1975" by Nguyen Ngoc Ngan, from *THE WILL OF HEAVEN* by Nguyen Ngoc Ngan. Copyright © 1982 by Nguyen Ngoc Ngan & E.E. Richey. Reprinted by permission of the author. **p. 75** "Leaps of Faith" by Alma Luz Villanueva. Copyright © 1999 by Alma Luz Villanueva. Reprinted by permission of the author. **p. 82** "The Star" by Arthur C. Clarke. The Star" initially appeared in *INFINITY SCIENCE FICTION*. Copyright © 1955. Reprinted in a collection of his works, *THE OTHER SIDE OF THE SKY*. Copyright © 1958. Reprinted by permission of the author and the author's agents, Scovil Chichak Galen Literary Agency, Inc.

Chapter 3

p. 96 "Salvation" from THE BIG SEA by Langston Hughes. Copyright © 1940 by Langston Hughes. Copyright renewed 1968 by Arna Bontemps and George Houston Bass. Reprinted by permission of Hill and Wang, a division of Farrar, Straus and Giroux, LLC. **p. 101** "Old Before Her Time" by Katherine Barrett which appeared in the August 1993 issue of *LADIES' HOME JOURNAL* magazine. Copyright 1983 by Meredith Corporation. All rights reserved. Used with the permission of *LADIES HOME JOURNAL*. **p. 109** *THE WAY TO RAINY MOUNTAIN* by N. Scott Momaday, *from THE WAY TO RAINY MOUNTAIN* by N. Scott Momaday. Copyright © 1969 by the University of New Mexico Press. First published in *THE REPORTER* (January 26, 1967). **p. 116** "Confessions of a Quit Addict" by Barbara Graham. Originally appeared in *UTNE READER* (September/October 1996). Copyright © 1996 by *UTNE READER*. Reprinted by permission of Barbara Graham. **p. 122** "The Snake," from THE LONG VALLEY by John Steinbeck. Copyright ©1938; renewed © 1966 by John Steinbeck. Used by permission of Viking Penguin, a division of Penguin Group (USA) Inc. **p. 133** "Champion of the World" by Maya Angelou. From: *I KNOW WHY THE CAGED BIRD SINGS,* Chapter 19. Copyright 1969 by Random House, Inc.

Chapter 4

p. 144 "Camera Ready" by Leslie Bow. Copyright 2008 by Leslie Bow. First published in *MICHIGAN QUARTERLY REVIEW* 47: 2 (Spring 2008), 323–326. Reprinted as, "Now That's Reality TV: An Chinese American Family Dreams of a Family Feud." *UTNE READER* 149 (September/ October 2008), 84–85. **p. 149** "Let's Face It!" Copyright © 2010 by Sara Blake. Used by permission of Sara Blake. **p. 154** From: *THE U.S. NEWS AND WORLD REPORT, V104*, May 18, 1988. Copyright 1988 by *U.S. NEWS & WORLD REPORT.* **p. 158** "21st Century Ragnarok: Is Profit Civilization's Only Motive?" by Ann Scheid. Copyright © 2011. Used by permission of the author. **p. 164** "The Ways We Lie" by Stephanie Ericsson. Copyright 1992 by Stephanie Ericsson. Originally published in the *UTNE READER*. Permission granted by RhodaWeyrAgency. **p. 172** "Lera's Story" by Dan Archer and Olga Trusova. From *Borderland: Seven LivesSeven Stories as Told by Victims of Human Trafficking.* Copyright © 2010 by Dan Archer and Olga Treuscova. Used with authors' permission.

Chapter 5

p. 185 "What Is Intelligence, Anyway?" Copyright © Isaac Asimov. Reprinted by permission of the author. **p. 188** "Documented/Undocumented" by Guillermo Gomez-Peña, from *L.A. WEEKLY.* Translated by Ruben Martinez. Copyright © 1988 by Guillermo Gomez-Peña. **p. 191** "What Is Poverty?" by Jo Goodwin Parker. From: *AMERICA'S OTHER CHILDREN: PUBLIC SCHOOLS OUTSIDE SUBERBIA*. Edited by George Henderson. Copyright © 1971 by The University of Oklahoma Press. **p. 197** "Does America Still Exist?" by Richard Rodriguez. Copyright © 1984 by Richard Rodriguez. Reprinted by permission of Georges Borchardt, Inc. for the author. **p. 203** "Pizza, Pakora and Pancit—The Importance of Global Education." Copyright 2008 by Sravani Banerjee. Used by permission of the author. **p. 208** "What Is This Thing Called Family?" by Lee Herrick. Copyright © 2005. Used by permission of Lee Herrick.

Chapter 6

p. 219 "Why Talk? Interviews Matter!" Copyright © 2011 by Kathleen Hudson. Used by permission of the author. **p. 226** "Perspectives on Borders" by Luis M. Valdez. From a Public Humanities Lecture in 1986 sponsored by California Council for the Humanities. First published in *HUMANITIES NETWORK* (Winter 1987). Reprinted by permission. **p. 230** "Freedom" by Joyce M. Jarrett. From: *AFRICAN AMERICAN READINGS FOR WRITING* (Prentice-Hall) by Joyce M. Jarrett. Used by permission of the author. **p. 234** "Community Re-discovered" by Heidi Ramirez. Copyright © 2008. Used by permission. **p. 239** "A Homemade Education" by Malcolm X. From: *THE AUTOBIOGRAPHY OF MALCOLM X BY MALCOLM X with Alex Haley.* Copyright © 1964 by Alex Haley and Malcolm X. Copyright © 1965 by Alex Haley and Betty Shabazz. Used by permission of Random House, Inc. **p. 244** "Bringing Out the Flirt in You" by Christine Ng. Copyright © 2005, 2008, 2011. Used by permission of the author.

Chapter 7

p. 259 "Liposuction: The Key to Energy Independence" by Barbara Ehrenreich. From: the July 22, 2008 issue of *THE NATION*. Copyright 2008 by *THE NATION*. Reprinted with permission. **p. 263** "They Shut My Grandmother's Room Door" by Andrew Lam. Copyright 1989 by Andrew Lam. Reprinted by permission. **p. 267** "Teaching for Social Justice: Academic Rigor with Love." Copyright © 2010 by Carmen Jay. Used by permission of the author. **p. 273** "Education" by E.B. White. From *ONE MAN'S MEAT*. Copyright © 1939, 1967 by E.B. White. Reprinted by permission of HarperCollins Publishers, Inc. **p. 278** "That Lean and Hungry Look" by Suzanne Britt. Reprinted by permission of Suzanne Britt, the author. **p. 283** "River of Memory: The Ebb and Flow of Black Consciousness Across the Americas" by Cobie Kwasi Harris. Used by permission of Cobie Kwasi Harris.

Chapter 8

p. 294 "Armchair Pharmacologists and the Media." Copyright © 2011 by Roohi Vora. Used by permission of the author. **p. 300** "The Ways of Meeting Oppression." From *STRIDE TOWARDS FREEDOM* by Martin Luther King, Jr. Copyright © 1958 by Martin Luther King, Jr. Renewed Copyright © 1886 by Coretta Scott King, Dexter King, Martin Luther King III, Yolanda King, and Bernice King. **p. 305** "A Few Kind Words for Superstition" by Robertson Davies. From: *ONE HALF OF ROBERTSON DAVIES*. Copyright 1977 by R. Davies. Reprinted by permission of Viking Penguin, a division of Penguin Group (USA) Inc. **p. 310** "Creatures that Haunt the Americas" by Constance García Barrio. As published in *TALK THAT TALK* by Linda Gross & Marion E. Barnes. Copyright © 1989 by the author. **p. 315** "How Films Feed the Mind *or* When I'm Hungry, I Don't Want to Eat Candy." Copyright © by Bill Swanson. Used by permission of the author. **p. 328** "What's in Your Toothpaste" by David Bodanis. From *THE SECRET HOUSE: THE EXTRAORDINARY SCIENCE OF AN ORDINARY DAY* by David Bodanis. Copyright 2003 by David Bodanis. Reprinted by permission of the Carol Mann Agency.

Chapter 9

p. 338 "Growing Up With Two Moms" by Megan McGuire. "Growing Up With Two Moms" by Megan McGuire. From: *NEWSWEEK* (Nov. 4, 1996). Copyright © 1996 by *Newsweek*, Inc. **p. 342** "Labor and Capital: The Coming of Catastrophe" by Carlos Bulosan. From: *IF YOU WANT TO KNOW WHAT WE ARE: A CARLOS BULOSAN READER*. Copyright 1983 by Aurelio Bulosan. Originally appeared: June 15, 1937 in *COMMONWEALTH TIMES*. Copyright by West End Press. **p. 345** "The Naked Face" by Karen Ray. From: *WESTWARD* (June 30, 1985). Copyright © 1985 by Karen Ray. Used by permission of the author. **p. 350** "Guilt" by Phillip Persky. Copyright © 1999 by Phillip Persky. Used by permission of the author. **p. 355** "Eating with Emigrants" by Rose Anna Higashi. Copyright © by Rose Anna Higashi. Used by permission of the author. **p. 359** "The Right Chemistry" by Anastasia Toufexis. From *TIME* (February 15, 1993). Copyright © 1998 Time, Inc. Reprinted by permission.

Chapter 10

p. 370 "Honoring Sgt. Stewart: Wiccans Are Americans Too." Copyright © 2006 by Charles Haynes and the First Amendment Center. Used by author's permission. **p. 374** "Curanderismo: A Healing Art" by Cynthia Lopez. Copyright © 1990 by Cynthia Lopez. From *INTERCAMBIOS* Magazine. Winter 1990 Vol. 5, No. 1. Reprinted by permission *of INTERCAMBIOS*. **p. 378** "The CD and the Damage Done" by Neil Young. From "Digital Is a Huge Rip-off." First printed in *GUITAR PLAYER* magazine (May 1992). Reprinted in *HARPER'S* (July 1992). Copyright © 1992 by Neil Young. **p. 382** "Arrival at Manzanar" by Jeanne Wakatsuki Houston and James D. Houston from *Farewell to Manzanar* by Jeanne Wakatsuki Houston and James D. Houston. Copyright © 1973 by James D. Houston. Reprinted by permission of Houghton Mifflin, Co. **p. 392** "How I Started Writing Poetry" by Reginald Lockett. From: *CALIFORNIA CHILDHOOD*. Copyright 1988 by Creative Arts Books. Reprinted with permission by Creative Arts Books Company, Berkley. **p. 399** "American Horse" by Louise Erdrich. Copyright © 1988 by Louise Erdrich, reprinted by permission of the Wylie Agency. This article first appeared in *EARTH POWER COMING: SHORT FICTION IN NATIVE AMERICAN LITERATURE* in 1988.

Chapter 11

p. 419 "The Anima of Animé Revisited" by Grace Sumabat Estrada. Copyright © 2005 Grace Sumabat Estrada. Used by permission of the author. **p. 427** "SOUL FOOD" from *HOME: SOCIAL ESSAYS BY LEROI JONES*. Copyright © 1963, 1966 by Leroi Jones. Reprinted by permission of HarperCollins Publishers, Inc. **p. 431** "Turning the Page: The Future of Reading is Backlit and Bright" by Anna Quindlen. Originally published in *Newsweek*, March 26, 2010. Copyright 2010 by Anna Quindlen. Reprinted by permission of International Paper Management. **p. 436** "Peyote, Wine, and the First Amendment." Copyright 1989 *CHRISTIAN CENTURY*. Reprinted with permission from the Oct. 4, 1989, issue of the *CHRISTIAN CENTURY*. **p. 445** "OMG: Tweeting, Trending, and Texting." Copyright © 2011 by Mandana Mohsenzadegan. Used by permission of the author. **p. 454** "On-line Learning and Student Success" by Mark Charles Fissel. Copyright © 1999 by Mark Charles Fissel. Used by author's permission.

Chapter 12

p. 467 "Women Are Better Drivers" by Phyllis McGinley. Copyright © 1959 by Hearst Publication Company. Used by permission of King Features

Index